www.wadsworth.com

www.wadsworth.com is the World Wide Web site for
Thomson Wadsworth and is your direct source to
dozens of online resources.

At *www.wadsworth.com* you can find out about
supplements, demonstration software, and student
resources. You can also send email to many of our
authors and preview new publications and exciting
new technologies.

www.wadsworth.com
Changing the way the world learns®

The Role of Work in People's Lives
Applied Career Counseling and Vocational Psychology

SECOND EDITION

NADENE PETERSON

Our Lady of the Lake University

ROBERTO CORTÉZ GONZÁLEZ

The University of Texas at El Paso

Australia ▪ Canada ▪ Mexico ▪ Singapore ▪ Spain
United Kingdom ▪ United States

Dedication

To my husband, Bob.

—Nadene Peterson

To the memory of René A. "Art" Ruiz, Coystal Tabor Stone, and of Jane Becker-Haven, and to seven others who were also instrumental in my own career development (in alphabetical order): Israel A. Cuéllar; Patrick F. Flores, Archbishop of San Antonio; Oscar Guerendiain, *OFM;* John D. Krumboltz; Cathy S. Martin; Amado M. Padilla; and Kathleen A. Staudt.

—Roberto Cortéz González

THOMSON

™

BROOKS/COLE

Executive Editor: *Lisa Gebo*
Acquisitions Editor: *Marquita Flemming*
Assistant Editor: *Shelley Gesicki*
Editorial Assistant: *Amy Lam*
Technology Project Manager: *Barry Connolly*
Marketing Manager: *Caroline Concilla*
Marketing Assistant: *Mary Ho*
Advertising Project Manager: *Tami Strang*
Project Manager, Editorial Production: *Katy German*

Print Buyer: *Lisa Claudeanos*
Permissions Editor: *Kiely Sexton*
Production Service: *Matrix Productions*
Copy Editor: *Ann Whetstone*
Cover Designer: *Denise Davidson*
Cover Image: *Corbis*
Compositor: *Scratchgravel Publishing Services*
Printer: *Quebecor Printing/Kingsport*

Printed in the United States of America

1 2 3 4 5 6 7 08 07 06 05 04

For more information about our products, contact us at:
Thomson Learning Academic Resource Center
1-800-423-0563

For permission to use material from this text or product, submit a request online at
http://www.thomsonrights.com.
Any additional questions about permissions can be submitted by email to
thomsonrights@thomson.com.

Thomson Brooks/Cole
10 Davis Drive
Belmont, CA 94002
USA

Asia
Thomson Learning
5 Shenton Way #01-01
UIC Building
Singapore 068808

Australia/New Zealand
Thomson Learning
102 Dodds Street
Southbank, Victoria 3006
Australia

Canada
Nelson
1120 Birchmount Road
Toronto, Ontario M1K 5G4
Canada

Europe/Middle East/Africa
Thomson Learning
High Holborn House
50/51 Bedford Row
London WC1R 4LR
United Kingdom

Library of Congress Control Number: 2004102633
ISBN 0-534-64183-0

Contents

Preface

First of all, both of us owe a huge debt of gratitude to the assistance and support of Nadene's husband Bob Peterson. We couldn't 'a done it without him.

It is noteworthy for us that when we began working on this book about six years ago, there were many career issues we believed were not being adequately explored in most textbooks. We attempted then to address most of these issues with an emphasis on training practitioners. We started this revision by reviewing the new major texts in the field. To our pleasure, we found other authors who have chosen to include such things as parenting and family influences as a vital part in helping to clear the complex career decision pathway; converging and emerging theories to deepen our understanding of the process; and the willingness to consider the complex issues of those who, because of socioeconomic, minority, or other perceived limitations have less access to the creation of their own successes.

The realities of our fast-changing world have left all of us working to maintain focus and to learn ways of mastering and keeping ahead of change. The speed with which the Internet has grown and information that is available have astounded us. How to sort out what is useful and valuable keeps us returning to trusted colleagues who diligently research pertinent questions, working to validate or improve our ability to serve our clients and students. While this book is a general graduate level textbook for the field, we have attempted to make it applicable to advanced students by directing readers to information for extended pursuit of research or directions to follow narrower interests.

One of our ongoing goals is to apply a basic psychology of work to the task of the career counselor/vocational practitioner. This requires knowledge and understanding both the sociology and the psychology of the role of work in our lives, the effects of the changes in the activities of work, the places of work, and the internationalization of the workforce. This requires a greater depth of understanding and appreciation of cultural, ethnic, and socioeconomic values and practice.

To better accomplish these goals, we have made some extensive changes.

1. We have attempted to stay abreast of the changes in the field of vocational psychology and career counseling by reporting on the latest developments in the field.

2. We have worked diligently to help students understand the rapidly occurring changes in work and work settings and how these new dimensions will affect our clients and us. The new economy, the aging of the baby boomers and its effect on the job market, and the globalization of the workforce are important to our text.

3. We have infused the strong multicultural/diversity focus of the original text into each of the chapters to a greater extent, therefore eliminating a chapter on that issue alone.

4. We have incorporated the information on an Occupational Career and Information Center into two chapters dealing with education: Chapter 9 dealing with grades K–12 and Chapter 10 on postsecondary education and early adult development.

5. We have developed a new chapter to include a comparison of the major theories, emphasis on converging and emerging theories, and explanations of our own theories. We continue to update our thinking, and these models reflect this.

6. We have been greatly encouraged by the renewed vigor of the field of vocational psychology and are hopeful its impact will continue to help those who are on the front line delivering services to clients. We also offer suggestions for areas of further research in vocational psychology.

7. We have included more emphasis on middle school because it is such a crucial time for career information processing. We have added additional programs and resources.

This is more than a new edition, but a rather extensive revision that updates new findings, maintains those ideas that are still relevant, and removes what is already outdated or unconfirmed.

This text is designed for use in graduate level classes. Because we train counselors across disciplines in our programs, the first eight chapters attempt to supply information for all counselors who need to know about careers, career counseling, and vocational psychology. Chapter 9 is designed for those working with students in K–12, Chapter 10 for those working with people in postsecondary education and young adults who are beginning career experience, and Chapter 11 is designed for those counseling with adults, whether in organizations and businesses or in a private practice setting. The Epilogue looks at trends in the world of work, future directions for vocational psychology, research and training, and the expanding role of the career counselor/vocational practitioner. We are continuing to update research findings and will do so until the text goes into production.

We will include instructor's aids, including PowerPoint® presentations of each chapter, interactive exercises, and test items in the previous Instructor's Manual. We continue to recommend the use of our co-edited companion book, *Career Counseling Models for Diverse Populations: Hands-On Applications by Practitioners.*

We are grateful to all the people at Wadsworth, and to Marquita Flemming in particular, for their belief in what we are attempting to do. Their work continues the early support and encouragement of Julie Martinez. We are also deeply indebted to those who have chosen to use our book in their classes and who have used it for their own benefit. One of the greatest sources of pleasure for us is the response from students who find the book interesting, contemporary, and very applicable to their own lives. We are very appreciative of all the encouragement we have received from colleagues as well. We are also grateful to the staff of the Sueltenfuss Library at Our Lady of the Lake University for their help in obtaining information for us.

A belated acknowledgment is due to Pete and Letty Carrasco of Postal Annex®, El Paso, Texas, who went through tremendous confusion when the second author *inadvertently* started using their FedEx number to mail galley proofs of the first edition of this text back to Brooks/Cole from Mexico City. What a mess it was! We can laugh about it now.

Other individuals who have provided important help are Valerie Marie Alcalá, B.A., Tomás García, B.S., Irene Rendon Garza, LMSW–ACP, Anita González, Marjorie Kyle, Psy.D., Ginger Maxwell, M.Ed., and Anita Seamans, M.S.

Nadene Peterson, Ed.D.
Roberto Cortéz González, Ph.D.

The sprawling public laundry works of Mumbai (formerly Bombay), India, are a far cry from the automated washers and dryers in the United States. However, the work gets done. Ordinarily, it is first come, first served, but an unwritten rule allows specific families that have used particular sinks consistently to go ahead of other families waiting in line. Some families hire a tradesman known as a *dhobi* to do their laundry.

Our look at the role of work in people's lives is not limited to paid employment located exclusively in the occupational structure, but includes work done in personal and familial domains (Richardson, 1993), such as laundry. Hence, we will see how even the most mundane work tasks can dramatically differ in form and procedure from country to country.

Photo by Nadene Peterson, January 1997

1

Current Perspectives on Work

What I object to is the "craze" . . . for what they call labour-saving machinery.
[We] go on "saving labour" till thousands are without work and thrown on the
open streets to die of starvation. I want to save time and labour, not for a
fraction of mankind, but for all; I want the concentration of wealth, not in the
hands of a few, but in the hands of all. Today machinery merely helps a few
to ride on the backs of millions. The impetus behind it all is not . . . to save
labour, but greed. It is against this . . . that I am fighting with all my might.

—Mohandas Karamchand *Mahatma* Gandhi
(Cited in Ajgaonkar, n.d., p. 36)

As in Gandhi's time, we are seeing the profound changes in the world of work as a
result of technology and globalization and their effects on individual workers. Gandhi
helped India to move at a deliberate pace toward independence, a modicum of industrial development, and limited occupational disruption for its citizens. Domestic production minimized the amount of corporate colonialism that could have made India
dependent on imports from foreign companies. So, for example, most automobiles,
buses, motorcycles, motorized rickshaws, and bicycles that transport the 1 billion
Indians are manufactured within the country. Many people in India need work; modern tools are, therefore, used judiciously. Road-building equipment in India is mini-
mally used; instead, extended families are hired to manually crush with hammers the
rocks used to pave roads and highways. Genuinely useful communal work that brings

children and adults together also engenders pride and a sense of community from a job well done (Pipher, 1996).

However, the world of work is witnessing unprecedented changes. The twenty-first century provides a unique opportunity to rethink the past and bring the best of the old into the new age. To focus on these concerns, this chapter is divided into five sections: (1) We call for the transformation of vocational psychology and career development to keep up with the profound and sometimes painful shifts in the role work plays in people's lives. In addressing this topic we define our terms (bolded at their first citation and defined in the Glossary) and the way they will be used throughout our text. (2) We place multiculturalism and diversity issues at the forefront of life planning and career development. (3) We discuss the relationship of work to the new economy and its connection to the global economy. (4) We look at the interdependence of social, political, and economic systems. (5) We examine takeovers, mergers, and the corporate climate and future directions.

Throughout this text we present practical applications to help vocational practitioners work on these topics with their clients. We consider how broader external structures impact workers' lives and how the vocational psychology and career development field can adopt a more transdisciplinary approach to vocational practice.

TOWARD A TRANSFORMATION OF VOCATIONAL PSYCHOLOGY AND CAREER DEVELOPMENT

A course in career development and vocational psychology is the last thing many graduate students choose to take. Most do so only because they have to. In our experience, the majority of newly registered students begin the semester with a sense of dread. They expect to be bored to tears by a class that has no relation to what they figure they will be doing upon graduation. Few anticipate that they will become career-counseling specialists. More open-minded students have a wait-and-see attitude, wondering what career development theory has to do with the real world.

All of these students have a point. Vocational psychology and career development are often presented in texts and course work in ways that are far removed from most people's experiences in the **workforce.** The intent of this text is to involve the reader in the process of understanding work and all its ramifications. We reevaluate the role of the clinical practitioner, in general, and the career counselor, in particular, to emphasize how work is integral to one's existence. We explore how different theories can be applied to particular populations, and how such theories still fail to apply to child laborers and others whose work life began in childhood. We use our collective clinical experience to discuss how family and parental influences affect career decision making (see, for example, González & Peterson, 2001). We also consider how work choices and goal setting continue throughout one's life. Because clinical practitioners and counselors will be dealing with these work-related issues across all age groups, there is a need to define or redefine the way we talk about career, job, work, and occupation. The terms used in the past need to be redefined to reflect the unprecedented realities of today's world of work.

Definition of Terms

For purposes of discussion, we have selected Tolbert (1980), who uses the terms **career development, vocational development,** and **occupational development** interchangeably to refer to "the lifelong process of developing work values, crystallizing a vocational identity, learning about opportunities, and trying out plans in part-time, recreational, and full-time work situations. Development involves increasingly effective investigation, choice, and evaluation of occupational possibilities" (p. 31). Career development is a specific aspect of general human development. A **career** is "the sequence of occupations in which one engages" (p. 31). One's career encompasses the school years, work life, as well as retirement. **Occupation** is "a definable work activity that occurs in many different settings" (p. 31). For example, a **dual-career couple** may both be employed but in different occupations. Tolbert acknowledges that for most people the term **work** denotes an activity that is difficult, unpleasant, and done only out of necessity. However, he defines work as "purposeful mental, physical, or combined mental-physical activity that produces something of economic value . . . [and] may produce a service to others as well as a material product" (p. 32). A **position** refers to a "group of activities, tasks, or duties performed by one person" (p. 32), and a **job** is "a group of similar positions in a business, industry, or other place of employment" (p. 31). For example, three positions may be open at a given workplace and someone who has a similar job elsewhere may apply for one of these openings. These descriptions are for the most part still applicable to current work settings.

Traditionally, **vocational psychology** has referred to a social and behavioral science that attempts to explain, predict, and control how people choose their initial occupations and pursue their ongoing careers. Vocational psychology arose in the early-to-mid twentieth century during the United States' great industrial expansion (Osipow & Fitzgerald, 1996). Clearly, vocational psychology is bound historically by its time and culturally by the nation in which it took root and flourished. Issues related to the universal applications of the various theories of occupational development have plagued and continue to confound the vocational psychology field. Explicit in the concept of vocational psychology is the idea of choice and of responding to one's calling (i.e., vocation) in the world of work, rather than merely hunting for a job. Job-hunting as a means of insuring survival characterizes the employment histories of most people. But *which* group of people's behavior is being explained, predicted, and controlled by vocational psychology? Vocational psychology's relevance has been doubtful at best for women, racial and ethnic groups, people with disabilities, gay/lesbian/bisexual people, lower-income groups, the permanent underclass, and international populations (see, also, González, 2002a; N. Peterson & R. Peterson, 2002).

The field is being challenged to dramatically transform itself into a practical source of assistance for people with vast arrays of life situations and work circumstances. The past decade has seen a dramatic broadening of concern for groups that had not been of concern previously. It appears that vocational psychology has quickly come into its own. This can be seen by articles in the *Journal of Vocational Psychology* and many other related journals, which call for the discipline of counseling psychology to restore vocational psychology as part of its study, given that counseling psychology grew out of vocational psychology. Career development encompasses the areas of (1) career guidance, (2) career counseling, (3) career education, (4) career services, and (5) interventions. Career development applies to children, adolescents, and younger adults through older adulthood. The developmental process can be reexamined at various stages in one's career path. Both the *Journal of Career Development* and the *Career Development Quarterly* contribute greatly to research in the field of career development.

As a related term, **career counseling** is used to refer to "planning and making decisions about occupations and education" (Tolbert, 1980, p. 32). The term has evolved into being most applicable to white-collar, college-educated populations and the **professional class.** The word *career* is derived from the Latin *carrus,* meaning, *chariot* (Super & Hall, 1978). Both career and chariot elicit a sense of movement through or progress over time, particularly emphasizing the element of competition, with the goal of placing first. Career also evokes the image of a corporate employee striving along the fast track to the top. Our concern is that career counseling has developed élitist connotations that fail to capture and describe the work experiences of diverse populations. The world of work is changing rapidly, and theories of vocational career development have barely kept pace. Old models of career development no longer apply. This is the major reason we use the term **vocational practitioner** in our text. We believe that it encompasses a broader spectrum of the population who seek job/occupational or career counseling.

From a Psychology of Careers to a Social Analysis of Work

In our first edition, we recognized the value of Richardson's (1993) recommendations for new directions in vocational psychology. These were based on two serious problems with the field. The first problem is the time lapse between advances in developmental psychology and their incorporation into the career development literature. Too few aspects of social psychology and sociological methodology are integrated into vocational psychology, which has its roots in counseling psychology (Dawis, 1992). However, more aspects of political science, international relations, business, economics, women's studies, multicultural studies, and gay/lesbian/bisexual studies must be consolidated into occupational development.

The second problem is that the theoretical and research literature in career development and vocational psychology is oriented toward the White middle class (Richardson, 1993). The **androcentric** foundations of the academic discipline have been attenuated since the 1970s by more focus on women's career development. Yet the almost total absence of literature from low-income and working-class populations of all races and ethnicities (see, for example, Ehrenreich, 2001) neglects a significant segment of the population. This demographic disregard perpetuates the **marginalization** of **oppressed groups** and upholds the implicit **classism, racism,** and **heterosexism** of the external social structure. For instance, consider the issue of **oppression**. Freire (1970/1993) provides a simple definition: "Any situation in which 'A' objectively exploits 'B' or hinders his or her pursuit of self-affirmation as a responsible person is one of oppression" (p. 37). Young (1992) asserts that everyday interactions between human beings are oppressive, yet taken for granted. She provides criteria for oppression with objective social structures and behaviors. **Exploitation** occurs when "the energies of the have-nots are continuously expended to maintain and augment the power, status, and wealth of the haves" (p. 183). **Gender exploitation** occurs when the labor and energy expenditure of women benefits men, be it a homemaker who performs domestic tasks for a husband on whom she's economically dependent or women wage-earners whose energies are expended in the workplace—often unnoticed, unacknowledged, and under compensated—to "enhance the status of, please, or comfort others, usually men" (p. 184). **Racially and ethnically specific exploitation** occurs when "a segmented labor market . . . tends to reserve skilled, high-paying, unionized jobs for whites" (p. 185). **Marginalization** occurs when labor markets systematically cannot or will not employ people, creating a permanent underclass that does not participate in socially productive activity.

Or consider the matter of racism. "Since there are no Asian Americans touched by racism in the United States to use as a control group, the relationship of racism to psychological development becomes a complex issue that cannot easily be resolved" (D. Sue & D. W. Sue, 1993, p. 208). We do think it unfeasible to even attempt to resolve the relationship of racism to occupational development for U.S. workers of Asian ancestry. The undoubted persistence of racism is all the more reason to attend to "the wider social milieu in which behavior and identity originate" (D. W. Sue & D. Sue, 1990, p. 193). Likewise, in choosing a career, African American women may be influenced by perceived racism and sexism in various occupations (Evans & Herr, 1991; Richie, 1992). Perceived opportunity structure can impact aspirations. Anticipation of racial and/or sexual bias can contribute to avoidance by African American women of certain careers. These women seem to aspire to traditionally female-dominated careers with minimal racism and sexism. Richardson (1993) warns that vocational psychology's claim to the scientific validity of its research literature is undermined by the tacit tolerance for all such disenfranchising practices mentioned above.

We are greatly heartened by the renewed interest in vocational psychology by counseling psychologists. A recent president of Division 17 (Counseling Psychology) of the American Psychological Association has written extensively regarding new directions in vocational psychology, and the *Journal of Vocational Behavior* has earned the highest impact rating of any applied psychology journal (Betz, 2001). These publications indicate that the field has taken on a new life.

Richardson's proposals were ahead of their time. We believe they have value now more than ever. These proposals are that counseling psychologists—we would also add other clinical practitioners whose clients present work-related issues—entertain the following three possibilities: (1) focus on work in people's lives rather than on careers, (2) adopt an epistemology of social constructionism regarding work, and (3) view work in people's lives from the perspective of an applied psychology. She further advocates shifting from the study of careers predominantly located in the occupational structure to examining work in people's lives. Work is a central human activity, not exclusively located in the occupational structure. Reasons for this suggested shift are fourfold.

First, career is inherently biased in favor of populations who have access to opportunities to develop occupationally and progress over time; work as a basic human function with multiple meanings would expand the vision of vocational psychology beyond a fixation on careers. Second, career fixation ties itself too closely to the occupational structure, which marginalizes and ignores the work done outside this structure (e.g., the gendered nature of work, work done in personal and familial domains). Third, focusing on work in people's lives emphasizes the multiple contexts of an individual's life, whereas inquiry limited to employment within the occupational structure truncates what is known about people in their multiple and interacting contexts. Holistic practitioners consider clients' work across a full range of life's contexts. Fourth, work has social value and is not done only for individual success and satisfaction, to satisfy achievement needs, to earn a living, and/or to further ambitions. The relation of work to the social order makes explicit that working people exist in a larger community and live for others as well as themselves. Career, on the other hand, has become embedded in an ethos of self-centered individualism and an ethnocentric conception of the self that may actually undermine the fabric of society and culture. Notice how work has taken on a different meaning according to Richardson (1993) in contrast to Tolbert's (1980) traditional and limited rendition.

Richardson's second possibility for new perspectives on work—the adoption of the **epistemology** of **social constructionism**—would turn vocational psychology into more of an interpretive discipline. Knowledge of the world of work would consist of meaning-making through subjective interactions between people (Savickas,

1995). Epistemology addresses the origin, structure, and methods of knowing, and the standards of judging and validating knowledge about the world (Dervin, 1994; Peterson, 1970). The question, "How do we know what we know?" is a question of epistemology. Social constructionism "maintains that individuals' sense of what is real—including their sense of . . . their problems, competencies, and possible solutions—is constructed in interaction with others as they go through life" (De Jong & Berg, 1998, p. 226). Clients' problems become "a function of their current definitions of reality rather than as something that is objectively knowable" (p. 228). Vocational psychology would be based less on scientific objectivity and controlled empirical research, with greater emphasis placed on socially generated narratives. Issues about the adequate training of graduate students and the feasibility of retraining practitioners in qualitative methods arise.

Tinsley (1994) writes that scholars focus on what is of intrinsic interest to them; vocational psychology/career development will become relevant to minorities and working-class people only when a substantial number of people with intrinsic interests and insights into these populations have been trained. However, this overlooks the external barriers that prevent such opportunities from occurring for people with such insights and intrinsic interests (for example, rising educational costs and decreasing financial aid, a lack of abundant numbers of mentors available in the field with similar intrinsic interests, entrenched mind-sets in academia that overtly and covertly seek to prevent a focus on minorities and lower-income people). Recently trained academics often encounter these problems upon their arrival in academic positions where they could make a difference: too many already tenured faculty in higher education with self-seeking political behaviors tend to disregard and/or lack respect for younger faculty from disenfranchised communities and have little tolerance for the missions of their social justice-oriented colleagues.

Savickas (1994) comments on the need to transcend from a *psychology of careers* to a *social analysis of work*. People can no longer build their lives around stable companies to develop their careers. The concept of career is outmoded and should be a subspecialty of the study of work. Others proclaim the traditional career a relic of the past (Hall & Associates, 1997). Savickas also calls for a change in research methodology. He promotes the idea of moving from general abstract principles about individual careers to a socially situated, **localized knowledge** about how the world of work is differentially manifested in various communities. Any theory of occupational development will suffer from what Pipher (1996) calls a **zone of applicability,** limited by the "time, place, occupation, gender and income" (p. 29) of any given practitioner. We see a need for practitioners with varying experiences to update and focus their concerns about work-related issues in clinical practice and research. One of the major areas of concern to be addressed is the understanding of, acceptance of, and attitudes on multicultural perspectives.

Practical Applications

In *Pedagogy of the Oppressed* (1970/ 1993), the late Brazilian educator Paulo Freire [1921–1997] contends that in a racist and class-driven society, those in a dominant position can be oblivious to others' experience and thus to the unexamined effects of the impact of their own race and class privilege. Until the larger external structures of **power,** oppression, hierarchy, and privilege are examined, vocational psychology and career counseling will be remiss in addressing the occupational experiences of diverse groups. As a result, major blind spots will persist in what is known even about the White middle-class experience.

A Freudian legacy to vocational psychology has been to focus on pathologies or problems as residing in the individual and ignoring broader cultural factors, thus making society less accountable to its members (Pipher, 1996). In the twenty-first century, the transformation of career counseling and vocational psychology entails an expanding vision of work and its influence on the quality of life for people of various racial and ethnic groups, nationalities, sexual orientations, and socioeconomic classes. "The greatest strength of vocational psychology is that its core subject matter is of central importance in the lives of individuals in virtually all modern societies and of critical importance to the welfare of families, communities, and nations. No other discipline can make such sweeping claims" (Vondracek, 2001). Practi-

tioners must question how their own race, sexual orientation, educational training, and class privilege contribute to the way they view the role of work in people's lives, and how such views affect their intervention with clients' workplace issues.

Freire (1970/1993) uses the Portuguese word *conscientizaçao,* or **consciousness,** to describe the moment when a person's mind awakens and learns "to perceive social, political, and economic contradictions, and to take action against the oppressive elements of reality" (p. 17). We encourage such consciousness-raising among career counselors and vocational psychologists through socially constructed **discourse**. Discourse is "a system of statements, practices, and institutional structures that share common values" (Hare-Mustin, 1994, p. 19).

Socially agreed upon constructs rely upon **discursive practices** between two or more people in conversation together about a given subject. Discursive practices refer to *"rules by which discourses are formed, rules that govern what can be said and what must remain unsaid, and who can speak with authority and who must listen"* (McLaren, 1994, p. 188, italics in the original). This leads to what Scott (1990) calls **public transcripts** and **hidden transcripts**. Public transcripts refer to subordinate discourse in the presence of the powerful; impression management in power-laden situations is one of the survival skills of subordinate groups. Hidden transcripts "take place 'offstage,' beyond the direct observation of power holders" (p. 4).

There's a scene in a later film version of *A Christmas Carol* (Storke, Kelman, & Donner, 1984) where the character Bob Cratchit is presiding over Christmas dinner with his wife and children. When he proposes a toast to the health of his employer Mr. Scrooge, as the founder (that is, the financier) of their Christmas dinner, Mrs. Cratchit at first refuses to drink a toast to Scrooge's health. She declares that she'd like to tell Mr. Scrooge what she thinks of him, calling him ". . . a stingy, odious, mean, hard, unfeeling man." When her good-natured husband implores her to have some charity because it's Christmas Day, Mrs. Cratchit agrees to drink to Scrooge's health for her beloved husband's sake, and the day's sake, but not for Scrooge's sake. Had Mrs. Cratchit declared her opinion to Mr. Scrooge personally, we would have witnessed ". . . one of those dangerous and rare moments in power relations . . . [w]hen, suddenly, subservience evaporates and is replaced by open defiance . . ." (Scott, 1990, p. 6). The insults and slights to human dignity engendered by the discursive practices of domination and exploitation can only go so far before anger, rage, and violence erupt to reveal the extent of resentment embodied in the hidden transcript of subordinates.

MULTICULTURALISM AND DIVERSITY

The Multicultural Perspective

Throughout this text, we emphasize **multiculturalism** and diversity in work-related issues in clinical practice. Multiculturalism is defined in two ways. Pedersen (1990) believes a **multicultural perspective** in clinical practice includes the following variables: demography (age, gender, place of residence), ethnography (ethnicity, nationality, religion, language usage), status (social, economic, educational factors), and affiliations (formal memberships, informal networks). Admittedly, a clear distinction between culture and ethnicity is lacking in Pedersen's definition. Sexual orientation and members of disabled communities also are not among the variables in his definition.

Here's a good example of why sexual orientation matters in the workplace. Woods (1994) presents the following scenario about what a gay man must deal with as he begins a new job:

Entering the workplace, a gay man faces a host of decisions. The head of personnel wants to know what kind of guy he is: How does he spend his time? What sort of skills and interests will he bring to the company? Will he get along with the others who work there? His officemates will invite him to the local tavern, to the baseball game, or to the Monday morning chat about their weekend conquests. As he climbs the corporate ladder, those above will want to know if he shares their values, if he faces the same demands from home and family, if he can be trusted (p. 25).

The heterosexual mindset most gay men encounter in the workplace mitigates against the creation of a diverse work environment. Nor can he be easily assimilated into the workers' circle if he cannot be who he is. Yet, he can take some heart in knowing that many married men are, to some extent, putting on a façade, even with each other, about the quality of their marriages and family lives, and they cannot be who they are either.

Referring back to multiculturalism, some authors have raised concerns that it confounds race with culture (Helms & T. Q. Richardson, 1997). Nevertheless, when differences exist between a vocational practitioner and a client among these recognized variables, the encounter becomes a multicultural interaction. A client and a practitioner are unlikely to match up exactly along the above parameters.

Pedersen (1990) pointedly differentiates between **multicultural counseling** and the multicultural perspective. The latter term is relatively recent (Baruth & Manning, 1991). Multicultural counseling refers to a specialized aspect or subfield of clinical practice, while the multicultural perspective expands beyond all previously used terms (for example, minority group counseling, pluralistic counseling, and cross-cultural counseling) and is a *philosophical orientation* that encompasses the entire field of clinical practice.

The second definition of multicultural clinical practice is drawn from the **Multicultural Counseling and Therapy (MCT)** of Sue, Ivey, and Pedersen (1996). MCT contains six basic propositions: (1) MCT is a **metatheory,** or "theory of theories" (Sue et al., 1996, p. 12), that forms a means of understanding the numerous helping approaches developed by humankind. Both theories of counseling and therapy developed in the Western world and those helping models of non-Western cultures are judged neither right nor wrong, good or bad. Instead, each theory represents a different worldview. (2) The totality and interrelationships of experiences (individual, group, universal) and contexts (individual, family, cultural milieu) must be the focus of treatment. (3) Development of a cultural identity is a major determinant of clinician and client attitudes toward (a) self, (b) others of the same group, (c) others of a different group, and (d) the dominant group. **Dynamics of dominant-subordinate relationships** among culturally different groups also influence clinician-client attitudes. (4) MCT is most effective when the clinician uses modalities and defines goals consistent with the life experiences and cultural values of the client. (5) MCT theory emphasizes **multiple helping roles**—the one-to-one encounter aimed at remediation in the individual, larger social units, systems intervention, and prevention—developed by many culturally different groups and societies. (6) MCT theory emphasizes the importance of expanding personal, family group, and organizational consciousness into **self-in-relation, family-in-relation,** and **organization-in-**

relation; the resulting clinical work is ultimately contextual in orientation, and allows for the use of traditional methods of healing from many cultures.

As a metatheory, one challenge facing MCT is pragmatic clinical relevance. "Metatheory is far removed from the realities of work with clients" (Berg & De Jong, 1996, p. 388). A second challenge is that MCT is only beginning to be multidisciplinary and has barely incorporated the domains of vocational psychology, marriage and family therapy, group therapy—among other disciplines—into its approach.

With respect to diversity, "for helping activities to be effective with persons from diverse populations, those activities must also be unique. Therefore, to speak of the basic facets, or commonalities, in the professional preparation of persons intending to work with special groups is to raise an inherent contradiction" (Loesch, 1995, p. 340). No unique training methods are needed in working with diverse populations, but rather the unique applications of existing training methods. These unique applications can be developed by a substantial redefinition and innovation of existing training methods, that is, combining old and new helping activities that can be useful for diverse populations in specific contexts (González, 1997, 1998; Hollinger, 1994; Rosenau, 1992). More than ever before, practitioners are being confronted with the necessity of altering clinical approaches to respect a client's culturally influenced family relationships (Schwartzbeck, 1997). Our concern is how such relationships impact the role of work in people's lives.

Multicultural clinical practice tolerates a diverse and complex perspective. Behavior is viewed as meaningful when it is linked to **culturally learned expectations and values.** Furthermore, **within-group differences** are significant for any particular ethnic or nationality group (Pedersen, 1990). Sue (1992) provides further elaboration. The methods, strategies, and goal definitions devised are consistent with the life experiences and cultural values of the client. More than one solution to a problem and more than one way to arrive at a solution are acceptable. No one style of counseling, theory, or school is appropriate for all populations and situations. **Between-group differences** are also honored. Sometimes class differences may be more pronounced than cultural differences (Baruth & Manning, 1991). Our collective experience has taught us that lower-income and working-class people have greater between-group similarities than within-group similarities with higher socioeconomic classes among their own ethnic or racial groups. The multicultural perspective provides the opportunity for two people from different cultural perspectives to disagree without one being right and the other wrong (Pedersen, 1990; Sue, 1992).

Acculturation, Ethnicity, Ethnic Identity Development, and Assimilation

In the United States the social environmental factors of racism and **prejudice,** economic disadvantage, and **acculturation** (Koss-Chioino & Vargas, 1992) cannot be removed from a clinical practice that addresses work-related concerns. Axelson writes, "prejudice is the emotional aspect of racism" (1993, p. 168). Acculturation was first used in the academic discipline of anthropology in the nineteenth century. In the disciplines of counseling and psychology, agreement over the term "acculturation" is ongoing. There has been a host of definitions proffered between various social, behavioral, and health science disciplines (Baruth & Manning, 2003; Boyle, 1999; Gollnick & Chinn, 1998; Landrine & Klonoff, 1996; Lee, 1997; Okun, Fried, & Okun, 1999; Purnell & Paulanka, 1998; Richmond, 1999; Robinson & Howard-Hamilton, 2000; Rotheram & Phinney, 1987; Vontress, Johnson, & Epp, 1999; Wehrly 1995). Mindful of the unsettled state of the definition of acculturation, we define acculturation two ways: (1) as the process of accepting both one's original group values and the values of *at least one* other group (Olmedo, 1979), and (2) as the accumulation and incorporation of the beliefs and customs of at least one alternative culture (Mendoza & Martínez, 1981). What we call **multiculturation,** with the acceptance of both one's own group and the elements of several other groups, is now more common than previous conceptualizations of two-way acculturation.

Practical Applications

In examining the relationship between acculturation and career variables for **Hispanics,** both generational status and acculturation level should be taken into account (Arbona, 1995; Fouad, 1995). With **African Americans,** part of any career intervention should consider acculturation level or identification with an acceptance of the dominant cultural system (Bowman, 1995). Landrine and Klonoff (1996) discuss acculturation as a nonracist framework for examining cultural differences among African Americans. Cultural values may underlie occupational values for some **Asian Americans/Pacific Islanders** (Leong & Gim-Chung, 1995), and therefore acculturation is a useful variable to formally assess. (We write about values in Chapter 2.) **Native Americans** are

more likely to make sound career decisions if values associated with family, tribal traditions, homeland, and community living are explored in a thorough and comprehensive manner (Martin, 1995).

Vocational practitioners can informally and qualitatively assess their clients' level of acculturation through five questions adapted from Marín, Sabogal, Marín, Otero-Sabogal, and Pérez-Stable (1987): (1) In general, what language do you read and speak? (2) What was the language you used as a child? (3) What language do you usually speak at home? (4) In what language do you usually think? (5) What language do you usually speak with your friends? Several acculturation measures are described in Dana (1993) and compiled by Roysircar (2003).

Three constructs related to acculturation are **ethnicity**, **ethnic identity development,** and **assimilation**. Ethnicity is an imprecise concept. It relies on various criteria for definition, including race, language, and region (Peterson, 1980). "Ethnicity patterns our thinking, feeling, and behavior in both obvious and subtle ways. It plays a major role in determining what we eat, how we work, how we relax, how we celebrate holidays and rituals, and how we feel about life, death, and illness" (McGoldrick, 1982, p. 4).

Practical Applications

It is difficult to distinguish how facets of ethnicity explain differences in career choice (Brown, 1995). Ethnic-specific approaches to both outreach and intervention are recommended for diverse populations to increase the perception of relevance and potential helpfulness of career development services offered (Leong & Gim-Chung, 1995).

We suggest that a practitioner can informally and qualitatively assess clients' beliefs about how their ethnicity is relevant at work by asking several questions. Do workers of a given ethnic background believe they need to remain independent or aloof at their employment site because they (1) are the only non-Whites on the job, (2) need to show that they are qualified for the job without performance standards being lowered for them, (3) are vigilant against being coöpted by insecure, threatened White coworkers, (4) have an inbred mistrust of Whites, (5) have, if not mistrust, then a simple (or pronounced) difference in values or motivations for their employment than their White coworkers?

Similar questions can be asked when workers of a given ethnic background believe they must work more closely or become more interdependent with their coworkers. Do they need to (1) show themselves as team players, (2) position themselves politically even if they would personally prefer not to be around certain ethnically different coworkers, (3) receive mentoring, or (4) learn to work like their White coworkers? The list of possible questions is infinite. Career counselors may find that aloofness and closeness as well as independence and interdependence are contextual matters that vary by worker and situation, even by work assignment.

Likewise, *both* individual *and* familial selves (Roland, 1994) are likely to manifest themselves in a client. It can be useful to help clients sort through times when individual and familial ways of doing things are both a help and a hindrance in the workplace (Weinberg & Mauksch, 1991). Inevitably, a practitioner will have clients who demonstrate strong **collectivism** and who appear to put the needs of others first so much that the clients seem to be shortchanging themselves. A vocational practitioner with an orientation of **individualism** may be roused, and an ethical dilemma will ensue, revolving

Continued

Continued

around how directive the practitioner should become, with awareness that the practitioner's own individualistic perspective may be imposed on the client. Bandura (2002) rightly calls this individualist/collectivist issue a "contentious dualism" (p. 269) that fails to take cultural context into consideration and that masks between- and within-group cultural diversity.

In a counseling session, the challenge will be for the vocational practitioner to tell the clients honestly and respectfully that they appear to be getting the short end of the stick, especially in work-related situations where the clients are unassertive and refrain from speaking their minds. Pros and cons of collectivistic-oriented clients becoming individualistic in certain occupational contexts will have to be explored. There are no easy answers for such a clinical occurrence. The practitioner's task will be to explore all possible avenues of conduct for collectivistic-oriented clients being taken advantage of by individualistic workplace politics. Ultimately, the final decision on how to proceed will be up to the clients.

Ethnic identity development refers to "one's sense of belonging to an ethnic group and the part of one's thinking, perceptions, feelings, and behavior that is due to ethnic group membership" (Rotheram & Phinney, 1987, p. 13). Ethnic identity development can be strongly related to how one perceives and effectively responds to racism, prejudice, and so-called acculturative stress in the workplace.

Assimilation refers to "the processes that lead to greater homogeneity in society" (Abramson, 1980, p. 150). Rotheram and Phinney (1987) further define assimilation as "a situation in which a minority ethnic group" gradually loses its distinctiveness and becomes part of the majority group (p. 12). In a landmark work, Robert Park (1950) first articulated the idea of a newer group becoming completely absorbed into a larger, host group. Whenever two ethnic groups come together, assimilation is presumed to occur inevitably.

Milton Gordon (1964) disagrees that assimilation is inevitable. In the case of the United States, Gordon does not see that minority groups have to conform to the White, host group's values and behaviors. We contend that immigrant cohort/generational status can influence the nature of the pressure to assimilate and conform. People who immigrated or who were born in the early 1900s experienced a qualitatively different pressure to assimilate and conform than more recent cohorts/generations. In another, classic work, Gordon (1964) divides assimilation into seven subprocesses, shown in Table 1.1.

In terms of the workplace, acculturation, ethnicity, ethnic identity development, and assimilation all boil down to how *Americanized* a worker is, and how Americanized a worker must become to be successful in a given job. One could argue that affirmative action legislation was intended to help in such Americanization.

TABLE 1.1 Gordon's Seven Subprocesses of Assimilation

1. cultural assimilation	newer/minority group's acceptance of the host/dominant group's language, religion, and customs
2. structural assimilation	newer/minority group's large-scale entry into host/dominant group's cliques, clubs, and institutions
3. marital assimilation	newer/minority group's large-scale intermarriage into host/dominant group
4. identificational assimilation	newer/minority group's development of a sense of peoplehood based exclusively on host/dominant group
5. attitude receptional assimilation	host/dominant group's absence of prejudice towards newer/minority group
6. behavioral receptional assimilation	host/dominant group's absence of discrimination towards newer/minority group
7. civic assimilation	host/dominant group's absence of value and power conflict with newer/minority group

SOURCE: Adapted from Gordon (1954) by Roberto Cortéz González.

Affirmative Action

Similar to acculturation and assimilation, **affirmative action** has hardly been considered in vocational development theories. Over the past several years, the topic of diversity has become increasingly divisive, and the debate over affirmative action has heated up. A *Wall Street Journal*/NBC News survey found that two out of three Americans oppose affirmative action (Roberts et al. 1995). The assault on affirmative action is gathering strength from a slow-growth economy, stagnant middle-class incomes, and corporate downsizing, all of which make the question of who gets hired or fired more volatile.

Recently, the United States Supreme Court ruled on affirmative action programs as part of university admissions decisions.

> In two decisions involving the cases Gratz v. Bollinger and Grutter v. Bollinger, the high court not only upheld racial and ethnic diversity as a compelling state interest at the University of Michigan, but also reaffirmed the importance of giving all colleges and universities leeway in the admissions process. . . . Michigan stressed the educational benefits of a diverse student body and the strong assertion that the federal government has a compelling interest in promoting diversity in education and the workplace . . . (*Higher Education and National Affairs,* 2003, p. 12).

Most relevant for our discussion here are the Civil Rights Acts of 1964 and 1991 (Hagan & Hagan, 1995). The **Civil Rights Act of 1964** was intended to remedy

Practical Applications

Increased attention to the seven subprocesses of assimilation (Gordon, 1964) can add a valuable dimension to the role of work in diverse people's lives. Understanding Gordon's seven subprocesses of assimilation can help racial and ethnic minority clients to decide for themselves where, when, and how much to assimilate. Our combined experience with graduate students and clients indicates that they focus mainly on perceived pressures to culturally assimilate without knowingly considering the other subprocesses.

Assimilation has most often been applied to immigrants to the United States. But there is plenty of potential application to the occupational development of multicultural and diverse clientele. Here are four examples:

1. First-generation college students of any racial or ethnic background face challenges to structurally assimilate into their educational institutions. Structural assimilation can be harder for those whose parents, siblings, or other close friends and relatives have not attended a college or university.

2. Similarly, college and university professors who were themselves first-generation college students also face unique challenges to structurally assimilate into their workplaces (González, 2002b; Nelson, 2002; Welch, 2002; Yanico, 2002). Attitude receptional, behavioral receptional, and civic assimilation may also come into play to varying extents.

3. The Texaco scandal of 1996, in which executives were tape-recorded in the act of ridiculing minorities (Bacon, 1998), remains a blatant example of workplace practices that hinder attitude receptional and behavioral receptional assimilation. A court-created oversight panel reports that Texaco has since made significant gains in diversification of its workforce. Roberts (1998) recounts her experience as an African American employed at Texaco during the scandal.

4. *The Social Register*, a.k.a. the Blue Book, is an almanac that lists the names and addresses of old money families throughout the United States. These are wealthy White families who have been socially, politically, and philanthropically prominent for generations. Although a person in the U.S. frequently can rise from a low-income background to the middle-class, rising from the middle-class to economic parity with old money blue book families is unlikely due to barriers of marital, structural, identificational, attitude receptional, behavioral receptional, and civic assimilation. The *nouveau riche* will never be able to completely buy their way into old money institutions.

discrimination in housing, public accommodation, and education. Title VII of the Civil Rights Act of 1964, as amended in 1972 (Eastland, 1997), prohibits discrimination in employment on the basis of race, color, religion, sex, and national origin. Liability under Title VII can occur for two reasons: disparate treatment and disparate impact.

Disparate treatment refers to instances when an employee is subject to adverse treatment because of the employee's race, color, religion, sex, or national origin.

Employment discrimination must be initially established by a plaintiff/employee through *prima facie* evidence, that is, the employer/defendant must be shown to have discriminated against the plaintiff with four conditions. The plaintiff (1) belongs to a protected class, (2) has applied for and was qualified for a job, (3) has been rejected for a job in spite of being qualified, (4) the job position also has remained open and the employer continues to seek job applicants. If *prima facie* evidence has been established, the employer/defendant must provide a legitimate, nondiscriminatory reason for rejecting the plaintiff. Then the employee must show that the employer/defendant's reason is a pretext for discrimination. "Pretext means that the employer's reason was either insubstantial or not the true reason for treating the employee adversely" (Hagan & Hagan, 1995, p. 4).

In contrast to disparate treatment, **disparate impact** is "discrimination caused by the consequences of a particular practice used by the employer" (Hagan & Hagan, 1995, p. 5). Employment discrimination must be initially established by a plaintiff/employee through *prima facie* evidence with three conditions: (1) The plaintiff applied for a job opening with an employer; (2) the plaintiff was rejected for a job because of an employer's particular practice; (3) the employer's particular practice had a discriminatory effect on the employee/plaintiff's protected class. If *prima facie* evidence has been established, the employer/defendant must show their particular practice is required by business necessity or has a manifest relationship to the business. Then the employee must show that an alternative business practice would be less discriminatory yet serves the employer's business necessity.

Both disparate treatment and disparate impact were altered by the Civil Rights Act of 1991 (Hagan & Hagan, 1995). The employer/defendant now has a greater burden of proof to show why they reject an employee. The employee/plaintiff can also treat an employer's decision-making process as a single, particular practice without the plaintiff having to show which requirement resulted in the discrimination. The 1991 Act also prohibits **race norming** of any employment or aptitude test results. Race norming refers to "adjusting the scores or using different cut-offs based on the race of the person who takes the test" (Hagan & Hagan, 1995, p. 6).

Affirmative action has its adherents and opponents. Among adherents, Bergmann (1996) notes that "private companies with less than fifty employees are exempt from affirmative action regulations. . . . Larger employers are seldom if ever called to account for their staffing patterns by a government agency . . ." (p. 8). Furthermore, "while the government officially promotes affirmative action, it is not an exaggeration to say that its application has been largely voluntary. As a result, desegregation of employment by race and sex has been uneven" (pp. 8–9). G. D. Richardson (1997) writes, "one would have to be either in complete denial or just plain dishonest to dispute . . . [the racial] inequities in most of the lucrative business and career opportunities in America" (p. 15A). She adds, "there is a real hypocrisy in calling for an end to racial preferences without putting the largest and most obvious preference [enjoyed by Whites] on the table for debate" (p. 15A). Tatum (1997) believes affirmative action is necessary to counter past and current systemic exclusion of African Americans.

Among affirmative action's opponents, Eastland (1997) contends that Title VII's intent of nondiscrimination has been distorted by a push for numerical affirmative action that results in quotas and racial preferences, which was never explicitly defined in Title VII, but came about through judicial interpretation of the law. Affirmative action has benefited ethnic and racial minorities from middle-class backgrounds, with lower-income, inner-city minorities hardly affected (S. L. Carter, 1991; Rodriguez, 1982). Steele (1990) observes that affirmative action has served as an excuse for racial minorities to avoid personal responsibility for admitting their fear of all-out competition with Whites. He uses the term **race-holding** to define "any self-description that serves to justify or camouflage a [Person of Color's] fears, weaknesses, and inadequacies" (p. 26). Race is used as an excuse to keep one from seeing something unflattering in oneself, which prevents self-esteem from developing apart from race. McWhorter (2003) opposes affirmative action because it prevents African Americans from truly excelling and enables them and other minorities to be dumbed down.

> [S]tudents who grow up in a system whose message is "You only have to do pretty darned well to get into a top school" will, by and large, only do pretty darned well, with the exception of the occasional uniquely driven shooting star. As such, *to enshrine "diversity" over true excellence* nothing less than condemns black students to mediocrity (p. 155, italics in the original).

He further asserts that ethnic minority students will achieve their highest academic potential only when they are required to do so.

Both of us would like to see Affirmative Action also extended to low-income White people. A friendly, well-meaning reviewer of the first edition of this textbook told us when we met at a professional conference that we're pretty nervy to place multicultural and diversity issues at the heart of our book. Our response was, "How could we not?" Like Sue and Sue (1990) in their work on counseling and psychotherapy, we contend that occupational development does not take place in a vacuum, isolated from the larger sociopolitical influences of our society. Axelson (1993) writes, "Career development in today's society is more appropriately seen as a complex personal process in interaction with cultural, political, and economic forces over a lifetime of experiences" (p. 225). **Historical context** can play a key role in the development of work-related behaviors and trends. We attend to the interaction of all these forces as they pertain to an applied vocational psychology. We also attend to what the general public reads in the popular media about workplace trends. One of these trends is a focus on workplace cultures.

Workplace Culture

Two very current workplace cultures are described and analyzed in the light of what went wrong, what worked, and where do we go from here.

Practical Applications

The U.S. general public is becoming increasingly interested in **workplace culture** in the wake of September 11, 2001, and NASA's Columbia space-shuttle disaster. We think this interest is not something that career counselors and vocational psychologists can casually leave to industrial and organizational psychologists or to other academic disciplines.

In covering the terrorist attacks of September 11, Halberstam (2002) provides a vivid portrait of work life at the Engine 40/Ladder 35 firehouse, located at 66th Street and Amsterdam near Lincoln Center on Manhattan's West Side. Firefighters call it the 40/35. The inside joke at the 40/35 is that "if firefighting was easy, . . . the cops would do it" (p. 12). Firefighters say that their work is done when they extinguish a fire at a burning house or building. In contrast, police officers make an arrest only to have the alleged offender out on bail and back on the streets within a few days.

The firefighters of the 40/35 live together, cook and eat together, sleep in beds next to each other between calls, play sports together, drink in bars together (Brown, 2001; Halberstam, 2002). The environment they create is one of interdependence and cohesiveness. There are few secrets between them, and their unwritten code of conduct is driven by the potentially deadly situations they may face. One retired fireman described his workplace culture as follows:

> [Y]ou lived with other men in genuine camaraderie, and you ended up, almost without realizing it, having the rarest kind of friendships, ones with men who were willing to die for one another. That kind of loyalty was special on this earth. Most important, there was a sense of doing something of value, something that mattered in your community (pp. 66–67).

Firefighters often refer to each other as brother (Halberstam, 2002).

Compassion and generosity of spirit are two innate characteristics of good

Continued

Continued

firemen, something that cannot be taught. These characteristics lend themselves to giving one's life for utter strangers, which firemen are sometimes called upon to do. The loyalty of firemen for one another is absolute and instinctual. Firefighter's lives depend on an unthinking obedience and a stalwart commitment at crucial moments from their coworkers. Because part of their unwritten code is not to worry their spouses unduly, married firefighters don't unburden themselves to their spouses about the hardships of their job.

The Fire Department of New York (F.D.N.Y.) lost 343 men on 9/11 (Halberstam, 2002). "In the 136 years that the [F.D.N.Y.] has existed, 774 men had lost their lives in the line of duty. And then, in two hours, they'd lost half that many" (Friedman, 2001, p. 68). The 40/35 firehouse took one of the biggest hits (Halberstam, 2002). Thirteen firemen left 40/35 for the World Trade Center; after the first plane hit, only one survived.

Langewiesche (2002) fast forwards us to Friday morning, November 2, 2001— seven weeks and three days after the attack. Inconclusive tribal warfare has broken out at the World Trade Center clean-up site. This site is now simply called "the pile." A confrontation arises between the New York Police Department (N.Y.P.D.) and the F.D.N.Y. "[T]he mere act of donning a uniform creates an 'us-versus-them' mentality in which police officers and firefighters are rivals in the search for the bodies at the pile. It is called 'the Battle of the Badges'" (pp. 154–155).

The F.D.N.Y. had been receiving overwhelming public sympathy, enjoying new-found influence, and taking for granted an unlimited access to the pile. The firemen's sense of righteousness and loss had been fed by the attention they'd been receiving in the media and by the public. Eventually, the firemen showed genuine interest only in the recovery of the bodies of their brother firefighters. They cared little, if at all, about recovering the bodies of civilians and uniformed police officers. They had became self-absorbed and isolated from the larger cleanup efforts at the pile.

An unspoken tribal conceit motivated the firemen, ". . . the deaths of their own people were worthier than the deaths of others—and . . . they themselves, through association, were worthier too" (Langewiesche, 2002, p. 156). This grouping and ranking of the dead created tension at the pile, so Mayor Giuliani limited the firemen's access there.

The Battle of the Badges on the morning of November 2, 2001 occurred right outside the confines of the pile (Langewiesche, 2000). From a crowd of more than a thousand people, over five hundred off-duty firemen tried to push through two lines of barricades set up by N.Y.P.D. officers, whose orders from Mayor Giuliani were to guard the pile against any unathorized intruders. The firemen demanded to be allowed to continue their search for their deceased brothers. TV cameras and reporters moved in close, got sound bites from firemen willing to talk to them, and by their mere presence generally reinforced the firemen to strut with bravado while yelling out their demands. At the second barricade line, fistfights broke out between the N.Y.P.D. and the F.D.N.Y. Five policemen were injured. A dozen firemen were arrested. The age-old rivalry between the two had boiled over, out of control, for all the world to see.

In practical terms, the Battle of the Badges began on September 11 when the N.Y.P.D. and the F.D.N.Y. set up separate command posts at Ground Zero after the first plane hit the North Tower. There was no communication between the two command posts. After the collapse of the South Tower (9:59 a.m.), N.Y.P.D. helicopter pilots got a bird's-eye view of the North Tower and advised their command post at Ground Zero to evacuate any police officers inside the remaining tower. Twenty-one minutes before the collapse of the North Tower (10:29 a.m.), the N.Y.P.D. command post radioed their officers and ordered them to evacuate the building immediately. Most of the police officers escaped before the North Tower collapsed.

At this point, differing accounts arise. Langewiesche (2002) writes that the N.Y.P.D. command post at Ground Zero did not communicate their helicopter pilots' evacuation advisory to their F.D.N.Y. command post counterpart. Therefore, the firemen didn't receive an order to evacuate. As a result, more than 120 firemen died in the North Tower's collapse. Court et al. (2001) quote a fireman who says that the F.D.N.Y. command post at the South Tower was wiped out when that building collapsed and so no order to evacuate could have been forthcoming from that quarter. But it's unclear if Court et al. meant the F.D.N.Y. command post at Ground Zero.

Langewiesche (2002) contends that the N.Y.P.D. suffered fewer casualties because they were better disciplined. A lack of discipline is a hallmark of the firemen's work culture, whose views of manliness and bravery are expressed by an eagerness to take on fires. But this worked against firemen on September 11. Sixty off-duty firemen, many of whom had been ordered to stay away, died. Check-in procedures at the F.D.N.Y. command post at Ground Zero were bypassed. There was little coordination among different firehouses and several firemen entered the burning buildings unnecessarily once the F.D.N.Y. command post decided not to fight the fires. More firemen than were actually needed were inside the Twin Towers evacuating office workers. And so when each tower collapsed, a disproportionate number of firemen compared to police officers were killed.

Eventually, there is a fight between the work cultures on the pile. The ensuing Battle of the Badges between the police and the firemen on November 2, 2001, had no apparent winners.

The workplace culture at the National Aeronautics and Space Administration (NASA) came under scrutiny in the wake of the Shuttle Columbia disaster on February 1, 2003, that killed seven astronauts. *The Columbia Accident Investigation Board (CAIB) Report,* issued in August 2003, has numerous findings and recommendations. The following information is relevant for our purposes.

The *CAIB Report* finds that "the intertwined nature" (p. 139) of the space shuttle and international space station programs created a complicated launch schedule with its attendant pressures to perform. At least eight missed opportunities are identified where damage inspections might have revealed the problems caused by foam tiles separating from Shuttle Columbia during liftoff.

Management had a habit of not hearing low-ranking engineers'

Continued

Continued

concerns about safety issues. Safety personnel were also looked down upon and were unable to convey any dissenting views from employees to management, in spite of "the anonymous NASA Safety Reporting System that supposedly encourages the airing of opinions" (p. 183). Managers in charge "resisted new information," (p. 181), and NASA's safety culture was described in the report as "reactive, complacent, and dominated by unjustified optimism" (p. 180). Shuttle program managers based their safety assumptions of Shuttle Columbia's robustness on previous successes, not on "dependable engineering data and rigorous testing" (p. 184). Finances played an influential role in Shuttle safety upgrade programs, which endured repeated cuts in safety personnel and budgets. Success became a matter of "how much costs were reduced and how effectively the [launch] schedule was met" (p. 203). In addition, the CAIB report says, "Managers at many levels in NASA . . . have taken their positions without following a recommended standard of training and education to prepare them for roles of increased responsibility" (p. 223).

At first glance, it may appear that the above assessments of workplace culture mean such endeavors are always negative in nature, that is, a deficit model is required for describing a workplace culture. Perhaps it would be more accurate to say that catastrophic events spurred the above assessments and emphasized what needed to be remedied, not what strengths each culture—the F.D.N.Y. and NASA—possessed.

Identifying positive facets of a given work culture certainly merits consideration. What appears common to the two workplace cultures we address here is that problems—in some instances, fatal problems—occurred because standards were not enforced or were insufficiently articulated for the challenges that arose. Our experience has taught us that a consistent failure to uphold workplace policies, such as ethical and safety codes, and a consistent failure to dole out negative consequences for such infractions, is usually politically based. (Consistency is what we often hear needs to be central to successful parenting.) The question then becomes one of how to address and remedy, without reprisal, what are basically sick workplace policies. In any case, people in the workplace believe that these assessments are an area of consultation that remains to be explored.

Culture assessments still remain largely out of the purview of vocational practitioners, but practitioners working in organizational programs can learn from these examples. The sources cited above (Columbia Accident Investigation Board, 2003; Halberstam, 2002; Langewiesche, 2002) are excellent models for workplace culture assessments.

Diversity of the U.S. Population The current U.S. Census information is a major source of information regarding diversity. An example of this diversity is shown in Table 1.2.

TABLE 1.2   Population by Race and Hispanic Origin for the United States: 2000

RACE AND HISPANIC OR LATINO	NUMBER	PERCENT OF TOTAL POPULATION
RACE		
Total population	*281,421,906*	*100.0*
One race	274,595,678	97.6
White	211,460,626	75.1
Black or African American	34,658,190	12.3
American Indian and Alaska Native	2,475,956	0.9
Asian	10,242,998	3.6
Native Hawaiian and Other Pacific Islander	398,835	0.1
Some other race	15,359,073	5.5
Two or more races	6,826,228	2.4
HISPANIC OR LATINO		
Total population	*281,421,906*	*100.0*
Hispanic or Latino	35,305,818	12.5
Not Hispanic or Latino	246,116,808	87.5

SOURCE: From U. S. Census Bureau, cited in Grieco and Cassidy, (2001), page 3, boldface in the original. Errors in the totals are in the original.

Table 1.2 shows that the White population are three-quarters of the total U.S. population. African Americans and Hispanics are both 12–13 percent of the total population of the United States. Since the 2000 Census, Hispanics have become the largest U.S. ethnic minority group, at 37.4 million, or 13.3 percent of the population (Ramirez & de la Cruz, 2003).

Particularly noteworthy are the "Some other race" and the "Two or more races" categories. These categories were socially constructed in October 1997 by the Office of Budget and Management in response to the changing racial and ethnic composition of the U.S. All racial categories in the census are used for civil rights monitoring and compliance and, with the Hispanic origin category, are defined in Table 1.3.

RELATIONSHIP OF WORK TO
THE GLOBAL ECONOMY

We now turn our attention from the issues of multiculturalism, diversity, and workplace cultures to the issue of work in the present time.

Observations of the past twenty-some years have given Roger Alcaly (2003) perspective on what he calls **The New Economy**. He proposes that the technological revolution that has occurred since the 1980s will continue to impact and focus the

TABLE 1.3 Definitions of Race and Hispanic Origin Used in Census 2000

RACE

White	People with origins in any of the original peoples of Europe, the Middle East, or North Africa. It includes people who indicated their race or races as "White" or wrote in entries such as Irish, German, Italian, Lebanese, Near Easterner, Arab, or Polish.
Black or African American	People with origins in any of the Black racial groups of Africa. It includes people who indicated their race or races as "Black, African Am., or Negro," or wrote in entries such as African American, Afro American, Nigerian, or Haitian.
American Indian and Alaska Native	People with origins in any of the original peoples of North and South America (including Central America), and who maintain tribal affiliation or attachment. It includes people who indicated their race or races by marking this category or writing in their principal or enrolled tribe, such as Rosebud Sioux, Chippewa, or Navajo.
Asian	People with origins in any of the original peoples of the Far East, Southeast Asia, or the Indian subcontinent. It includes people who indicated their race or races as "Asian Indian," "Chinese," "Filipino," "Korean," "Japanese," "Vietnamese," or "Other Asian," or wrote in entries such as Burmese, Hmong, Pakistani, or Thai.
Native Hawaiian and Other Pacific Islander	People with origins in any of the original peoples of Hawaii, Guam, Samoa, or other Pacific Islands. It includes people who indicated their race or races as "Native Hawaiian," "Guamanian or Chamorro," "Samoan," or "Other Pacific Islander," or wrote in entries such as Tahitian, Mariana Islander, or Chuukese.
Some other race	People unable to identify with the five Office of Budget and Management race categories. People who wrote in entries such as Moroccan, South African, Belizean, or a Hispanic origin (for example, Mexican, Puerto Rican, or Cuban) are included in the Some other race category.
Two or more races	
HISPANIC ORIGIN OR LATINO	People with origins in Cuban, Mexican, Puerto Rican, South or Central American, or other Spanish culture or origin regardless of race.

SOURCE: Adapted from U.S. Census Bureau, cited in Grieco and Cassidy (2001), p. 2.

economy for many years to come. "[T]he last few decades of the [twentieth] century marked the beginning of great innovation and revitalization whose impact is likely to be felt for at least another generation . . ." (p. 4). Citing the changes that brought on the Industrial Revolution in the 1800s and the transformation that electric power and mass production produced in the twentieth century, he sees the new economy (based on technology that increases information and potential new ways of working) and the new concept of lean corporations (with mass customizing instead of mass production) as a similar phenomenon. "Moreover, each of these spurts has been accompanied by unrealistic expectations and stock market bubbles—not to mention scandals and shady dealings—whose deflating was painful but never fatal to the bigger changes underway" (p. 4). The only major change that could affect the new economy is the threat of terrorism. Alcaly sees the problem with unemployment spurts, violation of business ethics by corporate executives, and stock market reversals as part of the way the new economy sorts itself out. The cooperation of government regulators, ethical business practices, and investors will keep the economy developing.

Alcaly (2003) emphasizes that workers, while using new technologies, must adapt to change that the new economy brings. "Unlike the rigid contractual arrangements of the post-[World War II] industrial economy, which limited workers' initiative and imaginations, the new setups encourage them to make decisions and support them with more training and with pay tied to their performance . . ." (p. 146). Although this is easy to describe, companies have had difficulty executing this type of working situation and have sometimes left workers behind in the equation. Companies tried downsizing and outsourcing, but found that was not the only answer. The changes necessary for workers to survive and for the new economy to prosper include a systemic change in the way everyone concerned thinks about the management of people and machines. But, as the blackout of August 21, 2003, which hit the northeastern U.S. and southeastern Canada and plunged 50 million people into darkness, showed, any technology that continues to rely on "a woefully fragile electrical system" (Gibbs, 2003, p. 30) could only go so far in producing desired results.

In an interview with Bob Gorman (2002), Roger D'Aprix, author of *Communicating for Productivity* (which contains his Managers Communication Model) and former Xerox leader, was asked to suggest the most significant changes in the world and in the workplace since he formulated his model in 1982. He answered,

1. **The effects of globalization.** More companies today operate beyond their domestic bases, doing business all over the world.

2. **The ridiculous performance expectations increasingly imposed on companies . . . by shareholders and security analysts.** . . .

3. **The end of the Social Contract.** The agreement companies allegedly had (or that employees, at least, believed they had) that worker loyalty would be reciprocated with leadership loyalty has all but disappeared.

4. **The outright devaluing of employees and their contributions to business results.** The leadership of more companies than I can count has declared war on the workforce. In today's global economy, employees often become dispensable.

5. **The explosion of technology over the last twenty years has dramatically changed the way we work.** . . . Anyone without basic technology skills today is virtually unemployable (D'Aprix, as quoted in

Gorman, *Strategic Communications Manager*, 7, No. 1, December/January, 2002, pp.12–15. Boldface in original).

"With cell phones, e-mail and voice mail going 24 hours a day, seven days a week, there's no place to hide. There is a constant pressure of feeling like you're always available. And to some extent, companies do expect employees to be always available" (D'Aprix as quoted in Gorman, 2002, p. 15).

The Global Economy, Global Consequences, and September 11

September 11, 2001, & Terrorism Becker (2003) suggests two economic effects of the events of September 11: (1) the hesitancy of investors to become involved in developing nations; and (2) the unwillingness of wealthy countries to allow "young male students and immigrants to study and work, especially those from Muslim nations or other countries with known hostility and resentment towards the U.S. and other western nations" (p.28). The result is less opportunity for poor nations to develop.

Practical Applications

"The technologies underlying the Internet and telecommunications have increased information flow between countries, speeding globalization. At the same time, the spread of free markets has promoted greater competition worldwide, creating strong incentives for domestic producers to adopt new technologies" (*Occupational Outlook Quarterly,* 2000, p. SS32*).*

A person's success in the emerging global economy will depend on many factors, flexibility being most important. According to Herr, Cramer & Niles (2004), the elements of personal flexibility are **basic academic skills** (for example, the ability to read, follow directions, and use mathematics and computers) and **adaptive skills** (for example, problem recognition and definition, evidence handling, human relations, and the ability to learn, analyze, and implement). They further identify adaptive skills (for example, coping, occupational, employability, and work survival skills) and transfer skills (for example, learning to learn, dealing with changes, self-initiating and self-assessment skills) as essential for today's workforce. Entrepreneurial behavior, which consists of acquiring understanding of systems, risks, and change, is an important ingredient in many aspects of the global economy, as well as in government, service industries, manufacturing, and education. This behavior is critical to many nations in both domestic and international economic development (Herr, Cramer & Niles, 2004, p. 132–134).

Organizations that downsize will find those workers who think like entrepreneurs more valuable, while the world of work will be looking for people who can deal with change and find new solutions to problems. One area of research could be to try to gain more psychological insight into the workings of the entrepreneurial type.

There are many things that money cannot buy, but having enough money is essential. The effects of this growing disparity of wealth is that "in our rush to the future, we have disrupted communities; depleted centuries-old resources; polluted once-pristine air, water, and earth: and littered the world with our castoffs" (Michelozzi, 1996, p. 120). Others (Brown, Flavin, & Postel, 1992) express concern that we are destroying our very life systems.

Today, more people are searching for occupations in business or industry that not only provide an adequate income, but also are committed to the better-ment of the local community. However, with the changes in the economy, the world situation, and their global implications, it is our observation that people, when frightened, tend to look more to government. Concomitant with this are less concern for human rights and more emphasis on conformity.

An estimated 84 percent of world trade wealth flows to the richest fifth of the world's population while less than 1 percent goes to the poorest fifth (Matters of Scale, *WorldWatch,* 1994, cited in Michelozzi, 1996). There is growing concern about the gap widening between those who hold the wealth and those who don't. More people in the Third World are living in deep poverty, which has increased to almost 100 million. This happened while the total world income increased by an average 2.5 percent in the 1990s (Stiglitz, 2003).

INTERDEPENDENCE OF THE SOCIAL, ECONOMIC, AND EDUCATION SYSTEMS

Vocational practitioners today are confronted with assisting clients in making occupational decisions and facing the job market at a most uncertain time. Each practitioner must be aware of the interdependence of social, economic, and education systems, as well as the role politics plays throughout the process. Employment in today's workplace will require specific updated skills, and millions of unemployed workers with obsolete skills may not be able to find employment. "American Management Association studies reveal that over 38% of 1999 job applicants lacked the literacy and numeracy skills required to perform the jobs they applied for, according to the AMA's annual survey on workplace testing" (Herman, Olivo, & Gioia, 2003, p.94). This compares with 23 percent in 1997.

Individuals must become self-reliant and effective in dealing with the changing job market because they may not be able to turn to the government or corporations for help. Even if an employee is well prepared, the problem in certain fields is the rapidly changing and growing knowledge that is required to function effectively.

The International Labour Organization Report of 2000 discusses this issue in terms of lifelong learning, "If knowledge, skills, and learning abilities are not renewed, the capacity of individuals . . . to adopt to a new environment will be considerably reduced, if not cut off entirely. Lifelong learning is a survival issue" (cited in King 2001, p.27).

Social Systems

According to Mark L. Alch (2000), a prolific chronicler of the new generation, the group following the **babybusters,** or **Generation X** (those born between 1965–1976), is being named the **Net** or **echo-boom generation.** As this group (born between 1977–1997) enters the workforce as the largest generation ever at 80 million, they will easily displace the baby boomers (those born between 1946–1964). This group is well versed in computers and new electronic media and exhibits several differences from the previous two generations:

- They appear to be willing to hold part-time jobs in high school and college, suggesting a stronger sense of responsibility.
- They have a greater awareness of the world as a whole entity.
- They readily accept a redefinition of family.
- They view companies as employers whose commitment is to the bottom line rather than employees, and they look more to their abilities, training, and skills as the way to maintain their career development.
- They regard constant and turbulent change as normal, realizing the need to be adjustable and open to change and to have contingency plans as part of their strategies.
- They understand the need for creativity in the use of new technological developments. There is a sense of freedom. They believe in the judicious use of collaboration, interdependence, and networking to achieve their goals. They understand the need for lifelong learning and know they will change careers several times during their lifetime (*USA Today Magazine,* July, 2000).

Human resource leaders and organizational development professionals need to be aware of the needs, motivations, and behaviors of this Net generation. (Changing work values across generations are discussed in Chapter 2.) With the Net generation, the vision of e-learning for America's workforce seems to afford the ongoing professional growth opportunities that this group will require. Because e-learning offers increased opportunities for obtaining and developing the skills necessary for good jobs and economic growth and because its potential for efficiency is strong, building an e-learning future will be a priority in the public and private sectors (Pantazis, 2002).

The Science/Technology Connection The science/technology connection is a critical challenge for nearly everyone faced with making a living (Michelozzi, 1996). Who will benefit from the dramatic science/technology explosion? African Americans, Hispanics, and low-income people may be more spectators than true participants in America's technological renaissance (Hernandez, 1998; Young, 1989). When it comes to computer literacy education in the schools, there may also be a difference between the haves and the have-nots (Poole, 1996), which limits opportunities for children in poorer school districts to learn necessary skills.

Societal Forces Drummond and Ryan (1995) identify societal forces that influence perceptions of what is acceptable in an occupation: (1) *Family socialization* influences work preferences and values of children, as well as educational attainment and occupational achievement. (2) *Socioeconomic level* is also a factor. Higher-income families prepare their children for entering a profession, not unskilled or less prestigious occupations. Such preparation is unavailable for children from low-income families. (3) *Employers* are also influential. They define acceptable work roles for their workers. (4) *Governmental bodies* make laws and regulations that affect individuals (for example, safety standards and minimum wage).

Economic Systems

Inequity and Inequality Two major concerns for most people are making enough money to live on and having a job they can live with (Michelozzi, 1996). But **inequity** and **inequality** continue to be realities. For example, the 1999 median earnings for women aged 15 and older who worked full time, year round was $26,300, compared with $36,500 for their male counterparts (Population Profile of the United States: 2000, U.S. Census). In 2000, the reported medium income of White, non-Hispanic families was $45,856, Hispanic families $33,447, African American families $30,439, Asian and Pacific Islander $55,521 (Population Profile of the United States: 2000, U.S. Census).

In the United States the rise in income inequality remains clear (Boroughs, Guttman, Mallory, McMurray, & Fischer, 1996). Demographics has played a big role in the growth of poor families, particularly in the rise in single-parent families. The proportion of children living in mother-only families has grown from 8 percent in 1960 to 22.4 percent in 2000. Those with a father only equal 4.2 percent, and those with no parent make up 4.1 percent of the population of children. (Population Profile of the United States: 2000, U.S. Census).

The "widening disparity in the fortunes of American workers is becoming an entrenched fixture of the economy" (Holmes, 1996, p. A18). According to Allan (2002), about 90 percent of employers in the United States use temporary workers. In

1999, these workers were usually hired in the manufacturing and services industries, according the Bureau of Labor Statistics. Fewer were hired in wholesale and retail trade. The implications of temporary or contingent working include problems of benefits, such as health and retirement considerations. It also seems likely in the future that employees will determine their own career path. It is common now that a temporary employee is given a 90-day probationary period, which is used by both employer and employee to determine if the job is a match. It is simply another hiring practice.

Wage Stagnation and State Budget Cuts In our first edition, we wrote of wage stagnation as a factor that impacted the economy (Roberts, Friedman, Sieder, Schwartz, & Sapers, 1996). Median household income was flat for twenty years, and workers' real weekly wages had dropped $23, or almost 5 percent. The combination of high profits and low wages fed the perception that working hard and going nowhere threatened the American Dream.

More recently, the National Governors Association has said that states are suffering their worst economic crisis since World War II (Cauchon, 2003). This crisis has less to do with the weak national economy and more to do with the ability of state governors and legislatures to handle money wisely. The states' money mess results from a simple failure to balance expenditures with revenues. States that spent too much or suffered a drop in tax revenues have had to raise taxes, cut spending, or borrow. And the longer a state delayed taking action, the worse the problem got.

A story in *USA Today*, "How the 50 States Rank in Taxing and Spending Wisely" (June 23, 2003), analyzed the financial health of all fifty states to examine how well states managed their finances over the five-year period that the nation's economy went from boom to recession. Results from this analysis are shown in Table 1.4.

States were rated on a scale of 0 to 4 stars (0 = worst, 4 = best) in three categories: (1) spending restraint, (2) bond rating, and (3) tax system.

Spending restraint was calculated from states' Comprehensive Annual Financial Reports and examined how closely each state's spending tracked inflation and population growth over the five years. After subtracting for inflation and population growth, states were awarded stars for the following spending increases: ★★★★ < 1% annually, ★★★ for 1% to 2% annually, ★★ for 2% to 4% annually, and ★ for more than 4% annually.

The bond rating was based on Moody's, Standard & Poor's, and Fitch Rating's assessment of each state's ability to repay debt. These bond-rating agencies use six grades, with AAA as the top rating and A as the lowest. Of the fifty states, thirty-five are rated by all three agencies, eleven by two agencies, and four by one. Agencies' average ratings of long-term general obligation bonds or similar debt were used, along with the state's economy, how well a legislature has managed the state's finances, and the soundness of state pension funds. The top ten states, which have AAA ratings from

TABLE 1.4 How the 50 States Rank in Taxing and Spending Wisely

	SPENDING RESTRAINT	BOND RATING	TAX SYSTEM	TOTAL STARS
Excellent				
Utah	****	****	****	12
Delaware	***	****	****	11
Georgia	****	****	***	11
Michigan	**	****	****	10
Minnesota	**	****	****	10
North Carolina	***	****	***	10
Good				
Florida	**	***	****	9
Hawaii	****	*	****	9
Indiana	**	***	****	9
Iowa	***	***	***	9
Maryland	**	****	***	9
Missouri	*	****	****	9
Washington	***	***	***	9
Arkansas	****	**	**	8
Idaho	***	*	****	8
Kansas	**	***	***	8
Maine	**	***	***	8
Nevada	****	***	*	8
New Mexico	*	***	****	8
Ohio	**	***	***	8
Vermont	*	***	****	8
Fair				
Connecticut	***	**	**	7
New Hampshire	*	***	***	7
Pennsylvania	**	**	***	7
South Carolina	*	****	**	7
Texas	***	***	*	7
Virginia	*	****	**	7
Wisconsin	*	**	****	7
Wyoming	*	**	****	7
Alabama	***	**	*	6
Alaska	**	**	**	6
Kentucky	**	**	**	6
Louisiana	****		**	6
Massachusetts	*	**	***	6
Nebraska	*	**	***	6
New Jersey	*	**	***	6
New York	**	*	***	6
North Dakota	*	*	****	6
Oregon	**	*	***	6
South Dakota	*	*	****	6

Continued

TABLE 1.4 How the 50 States Rank in Taxing and Spending Wisely *(continued)*

	SPENDING RESTRAINT	BOND RATING	TAX SYSTEM	TOTAL STARS
Poor				
Arizona	**	*	**	5
Colorado	***	*	*	5
Illinois	**	**	*	5
Oklahoma	*	**	**	5
Rhode Island	*	**	**	5
Tennessee	**	**	*	5
West Virginia	**	*	**	5
Mississippi	*	**	*	4
Montana	*	*	**	4
California	*		*	2

SOURCE: From *USA Today*, Copyright June 23, 2003. Reprinted with permission.

two or more bond rating agencies, received 4 stars. The next twelve states received 3 stars; sixteen states received 2 stars; and ten states received 1 star. Two states, California and Louisiana, received no stars, because they have ratings two notches below any other state.

Educational Systems

The indisputable gender inequality in the U.S. workplace is evident from kindergarten through twelfth grade (Gaskell & Willinsky, 1995; Gilligan & Noel, 1995; Orenstein, 1994; Pipher, 1994; Sadker & Sadker, 1995; Taylor, Gilligan, & Sullivan, 1995). Girls and boys, as well as adolescent women and men, are differentially reinforced in many school systems. This differential treatment has grave implications for the career development of women in particular.

Educational Opportunities for Diverse Populations More than 80 percent of all college students in the U.S. attend public universities. Research conducted by the Education Trust, a nonprofit research organization, found the gap in educational opportunities between White students and racial/ethnic minority students that narrowed from 1970 to 1990 to be widening again (New York Times News Service, 1997). This trend does not bode well for the long-term occupational development of racial and ethnic minorities. With the observed continued increase in tuition and the scaling back of financial aid, the gap between the haves and have-nots will probably increase.

Budget Cuts and Higher Spending. Higher education is heavily reliant on public colleges and universities.

More than seven million students are enrolled as undergraduates in four year colleges and universities in the United States, and nearly 70% of them attend public institutions, which depend on taxpayer money doled out by legislature for the majority of their funds. The percentages are similar for the 1.8 million graduate students, 60% attend public universities (Uchitelle, 2003, p.43).

The quality of public higher education, however, is being impacted by financial problems.

. . . [T]his cornerstone of the U.S. economy is being threatened by escalating costs, diminishing revenues, and a troubling inability to manage the crisis. College costs are rising faster than any other major sector of the economy except health care. . . . As states continue to scale back support, the burden of getting a degree is pushed increasingly onto students (Symonds, 2003, pp. 74, 75).

Practical Applications

Rodriguez (1994) suggests developing brochures using **racial and ethnic role models** that contain culturally relevant occupational information for minorities. She emphasizes the need to establish a partnership between counseling professionals and sponsors, because minority members of a sponsor group can bring vital firsthand information and experience to the brochure content. Several basic elements are evaluated for inclusion in the brochures: (1) an introductory series of interest-sparking questions to motivate minorities to continue reading the brochure; (2) a question-and-answer format to facilitate reading and defining points for future review; and (3) content written in nontechnical, standard English at the eighth- to tenth-grade reading level. Rodriguez states that role-model life stories provide influential motivational information crucial for career decision making. Few materials currently exist that help racial and ethnic minorities expand their awareness and knowledge of career options. It would be interesting to assess the video and Web sites that are now available for students to preview and see how many minority students are represented in their publicity for the college/university.

While 32.3 percent of Hispanics aged 18–24 are high school dropouts, only 7.6 percent of Whites and 12.5 percent of the total population dropped out. (Population Profile of the United States: 2000, U.S. Census). So what implications do these changing educational opportunities have for minority cultures?

Schools and Technology
McCain and Jukes (2001) write that education has not kept up with, let alone embraced, technology. They suggest it is caught in a paradigm that does not allow for current reality. Their

Continued

Continued

proposals for educational changes include the following:

- Education will not always best be provided in school settings.
- Education will not be offered only at a specific time.
- Education will have many teachers, some not human, suggesting there will be many others employed to coach and mentor.
- Education will emphasize use of technologies for learning rather than paper-based curricula, memorization, and linear learning.
- Education will be for everyone instead of an intellectual elite and will not be concentrated in childhood only. (pp. 78–90).

McCain and Jukes further suggest that students will learn new skills, such as

- problem solving and critical thinking;
- how to use communication to effectively participate in family, community, and work settings;

- adding technical reading and writing to literary reading and writing;
- applied reasoning skills for technology;
- how to handle the overwhelming amount of information available;
- how to make technology a useful tool, not an end in itself;
- time management, self-assessment, and entrepreneurial skills; and
- the ability to think about the future before it happens, and other ways of thinking.

All of this is in the context of a curriculum focused on integration of learning (pp. 91–110).

This educational system, geared to help people deal with the outlook for the realities of work in the near future, is far from current practice. The hope that change will occur soon is not realistic. However, the programs that are currently possible in the education system are discussed at length in Chapter 9.

TAKEOVERS, MERGERS, AND CORPORATE CLIMATE

Many middle-class families experience an "end of optimism" when they are "forced to work two to three jobs to pay the bills" (Tolchin, 1996, p. 51). Seventy-five percent of those polled agree with the statement that "middle-class families can't make ends meet," and 57 percent regard the economy as "stagnating." Two-thirds of those surveyed worried that their children wouldn't live as well as they did, and a majority believed that the American dream was now out of reach for most families. By most indications, the rich are getting richer, the poor are getting poorer, and the middle class seems to be losing ground economically. Even though the middle class has worked hard, studied hard, and tried to do all the right things to climb the traditional career ladder, it is experiencing job loss, falling or stagnating wages, insecure pensions, and reduced home ownership. The middle class realizes it may not be keeping pace financially, and its children will most likely fall even farther behind (Tolchin, 1996).

"[R]ecent polls and studies show that . . . a growing number of Americans are beginning to shift the anger and frustration they once directed at the government to corporate America. This shift is occurring despite . . . the wave of mergers [that are making] big [corporations] get bigger. Profits are up and unemployment is down" (Yates, 1995, p. 6J). Frank and Cook (1995) draw attention to an increasing resentment on the part of the average worker toward executives with huge salaries. Feller (1996) writes that "the pay ratio of chief executives to average workers in big corporations has gone from 41:1 in the mid-1970s to 187:1 in 1995" (p. 145). More recent reports calculate these pay ratios are more separated (Kadlec & Baumohl, 1997; Reingold, 1997). *Business Week* reports that the average CEO pay in 2001 was $11 million; and despite public outrage over Enron, Tyco, Adelphia, WorldCom, and other corporate executive mishandlings, CEO pay will probably remain the same (Wahlgren, 2002).

Other industrialized societies, such as Japan and the reunited Germany, do not tolerate these exorbitant pay ratios (Sanger & Lohr, 1996), while the French have long used "savage capitalism" to describe American economics (Bellah, Madsen, Sullivan, Swidler, & Tipton, 1992, p. 91). Another kind of anger and frustration results from uncertainty about how a merger or takeover will affect the individual. When workers hear of massive layoffs caused by these changes, they become concerned with their own security.

Many of the mergers are promoted in positive terms, but often workers find out later that with little prior notice they may be laid off or forced to retire with the concomitant loss of benefits and health insurance. Over the past thirty years, the accelerating pace of technological change has created new boomtowns and new job opportunities for so-called gold-collar occupations. Improving one's job prospects is contingent upon additional job training. Most workers whose wages have stagnated have had little opportunity to upgrade their skills, either on the job or on their own (Kramer, 1997). The majority of businesses do not invest in upgrading their workers' job skills because then workers are free to take their improved marketability to other employers. At best, upgrading is provided for those workers at the top, with the assumption that the workers they supervise will produce higher returns as a result. Few workers in the lower echelons receive any enhanced training.

> Over the years, executives have complained about the cost of employee training. When hard times hit, the training budget is the first to be cut. Some employers establish policies of hiring only people who are already trained, preferring to pay a little more for the new employee than to put money into upgrading current or future employees (Herman, Olivo, & Gioia, 2003, p. 112).

Two solutions have been proposed to give businesses economic incentives to invest in upgrading their workers' skills: (1) a tax-free compensation program for companies to train all employees or the company loses tax advantages for training only some employees, and (2) contracts for employees receiving training that insure they remain a specified time so that companies could reap the benefit of their investment.

These proposals would be in the economic self-interest of the U.S. government and businesses alike.

Downsizing in the United States

When a large American steel company began closing plants in the early 1980s, it offered to train the displaced steel workers for new jobs. But the training never took; the workers drifted into unemployment and odd jobs instead. Psychologists came in to find out why and found the steelworkers suffering from acute identity crises. "How could I do anything else?" asked one of the workers. "I *am* a lathe operator." (Peter Senge, *The Fifth Discipline,* cited in Bridges, 1994, p. 76).

On Labor Day, 2003, *The New York Times* reported that 2.7 million jobs have been lost in the United States in the past three years. Manufacturing jobs have diminished by 15 percent, apparently due to loss of jobs to countries outside the United States. The article cites Carl Van Horn, director of the Heldrich Center for Workforce Development, who says, "American workers are doing very badly. All the trends are in the negative direction. There's high turnover, high instability, a reduction in benefits and a declining loyalty on the part of employers. At the same time, expectations for productivity and quality are going up." The article goes on to state that the number of Americans unemployed for more than twenty-six weeks has tripled from the level when the recession of 2001 ended. Many have supplanted their lost jobs with new jobs, but the problem is that most of the new jobs pay lower wages and offer far fewer benefits.

Several shifts in the way companies approach the workforce can be seen in the late 1990s. "Unemployment among college graduates has risen faster than for those with high school degrees." (Berner & Zellner, 2003, p. 68). White-collar workers are just as likely to be unemployed as are blue-collar employees (Morris, 2001). Berner and Zellner (2003) also suggest that the people with higher incomes often have less ability to cope with unemployment than do the poor. People who have earned less usually better understand what resources are available when out of work.

A survey of workplace changes found that 25 percent of employees believe their company handled their layoff poorly, and that 24 percent of those who kept their jobs worried they would be next to lose their job or be subject to a cut in pay (Institute of Management & Administration Security Director's Report, 2002). Even though the economy appears to be recovering, the effect of the job market on the average worker is still lagging. At this time, it is uncertain how the apparently recovering economy and the changes in the workforce will interface.

During these upheavals, some dispossessed employees experience a diluted sense of self-worth and shattered confidence (Uchitelle & Kleinfield, 1996) through painful and demeaning job changes. Assurances from employers that a pink slip is "nothing personal" may be pointless for workers whose identities have been based largely on their work life (Bragg, 1996b). But for many it is personal. One worker states, "It's like the company telling you that you're no damn good" (Bragg, 1996a, p. A17).

Families of downsized workers also can experience emotional strain. Deprivations and disappointments can predominate in the home (Bragg, 1996a). The divorce rate is as much as 50 percent higher than the national average in families where one earner, usually the father, has lost a job and cannot quickly find an equivalent one (Uchitelle & Kleinfield, 1996). Some parents angrily regret the late evenings and weekends they gave to their jobs when they realize that company loyalty was all one-sided (Bragg, 1996b). After downsizing has occurred the workplace becomes altered, amid "ghost town" environments, motivation and risk-taking decreases (Kleinfield, 1996). Community and civic life often become fragmented, too. Churches and service organizations lose members (Rimer, 1996; Uchitelle & Kleinfield, 1996). In their civic and work lives, people may seem unwilling to give as much of themselves as they did before. Employees show less desire to be absorbed into their workplace culture, and workers do not give 100 percent anymore (Kleinfield, 1996). One solution is to draw a line beyond which the incursions and compromises of business become too much, and be ready to walk away (Johnson, 1996).

Corporate downsizing replaces team spirit and camaraderie with internal competition. Employees compete for their positions with their own coworkers and with younger prospects. Information sharing between team players becomes information hoarding in an effort to have an edge.

Organizational employees also are competing against themselves. Blinded by the fact that downsizing has often meant adverse working conditions, employees tend to blame themselves when they are unable to meet impossible demands. Thus, they push themselves hard to improve the quantity and quality of the work they produce, leading to longer hours at the workplace. Not surprisingly, employees suffer from tremendous stress and subsequent physical and mental health problems. Bennett (1990) further predicts that the typical employee of the future will have priorities other than settling into an organization for a career life. These people will seek smaller companies in which to work, choose work that is interesting, and expect the corporate environment to be more flexible to individual needs.

Diversity in the Era of Downsizing Daniel Yankelovich, president of the polling firm DYG, Inc., asserts that African Americans, immigrants, and women are among the diverse targets of scapegoating as a consequence of job insecurity in the face of downsizing (Uchitelle & Kleinfield, 1996). Other experts say that part of the growth in membership of so-called hate groups can be traced to disaffected downsized workers. Employer commitment to diversity has eroded in the current environment of uncertainty.

Women and minorities express concern that they are more vulnerable. In some instances, women have been eliminated from jobs disproportionately (Kleinfield,

1996). However, minorities appear to have been most adversely affected. U.S. Department of Labor statistics indicate that employment and earnings of African Americans relative to Whites have unquestionably declined since the 1970s (Uchitelle & Kleinfield, 1996). Diversity becomes a delicate issue in the era of downsizing because the Federal Equal Employment Opportunity Commission sees a red flag whenever the make-up of a downsized workplace deviates more than 3 to 4 percent from the original demographics (Kleinfield, 1996).

Ironically, now that the American White middle class is experiencing what African Americans have dealt with all along—job insecurity and unemployment —the word coined is **downsizing** (Carter, 1996). The term itself has been called a middle-class concept by Lloyd Lewis, Jr., an Ohio state representative (Rimer, 1996). Lewis, an African American, graduated from the University of Dayton with a business degree in 1948. At that time, National Cash Register offered jobs to all his White classmates, but not to him. He notes that job losses and economic uncertainty have now affected the White, middle class, middle management, where no one ever thought it would happen. Lewis also points out that while many African American middle-class workers have also been hurt by downsizing, their sense of betrayal is not as pronounced as that felt by Whites.

Social and behavioral scientists can appear elitist by focusing on the effects of downsizing now that it has hit the White middle and upper classes. For years, blue-collar workers have been laid off when business was bad, with less attention paid to their plight. The difference now is that there are fewer and fewer callbacks; millions of blue-collar workers have been laid off forever (Bragg, 1996b). The reality is that when the White middle class starts feeling anxious and aggrieved, responses are needed from the political system ("Downsizing and its discontents," March 10, 1996), from business, and even from social and behavioral scientists.

Multicultural and diverse clientele who aspire to upward mobility would benefit by understanding that there is something new and disturbing about the current economic woes. The White middle and upper classes—those very groups that have benefited most from the education and training that have for decades provided the main path to upward mobility—are experiencing massive losses of jobs for the first time ("Downsizing and its discontents," March 10, 1996). Practitioners are strongly urged to explore clients' expectations of anticipated economic and material gains to be derived from the world of work.

Clients must realize that the old certainties about work no longer apply (Kleinfield, 1996). A common attitude is that no corporate entity owes anybody a career. Clients entering the job market can learn from more experienced, adaptable workers who are now accepting without sentiment the fact that their company does not owe them as much as people used to expect (Uchitelle & Kleinfield, 1996). These workers figure out the best angles to job security by mastering tasks, developing new skills, and cultivating political ties. Top performers at job sites still have been laid off because they had the weakest political bonds (Uchitelle & Kleinfield, 1996).

Downsizing of the white-collar workforce is a clear indication that a revolution is under way, with the traditionally more secure and best paid jobs in jeopardy. This phenomenon is a first in our society and has garnered much media attention. Yet it happened to blue-collar workers during the 1970s and early 1980s. At that time many towns that relied on steel and iron industries became ghost towns, and few have recovered.

"Work revolutions begin in times of crisis and emerge in the decades following the introduction of new technologies when people finally realize they can no longer resist the inevitable change and must radically re-engineer the workplace," says Dent (1995, p. 22). He further observes that "we are reluctant to accept the inevitable and need to see it as an ally, not a threat. Even though the work revolution appears to be producing a stronger economy, higher personnel keep a job" (Rimer, 1996, p. A18). Once employment has been obtained, upwardly mobile multicultural and diverse clients may need to sharpen skills to enhance their careers. Clients who minimize their expectations about guaranteed, long-term security are less likely to become disillusioned by current trends in the mainstream U.S. workforce.

Linguistic minority clients may need reinforcement about what they can gain by being fluent in their non-English language. Fluency here means basic writing, reading, and conversational skills. Fluency levels required for scholarship or business often can only be achieved through formal training and/or immersion in the second language (Vidueira, 1996). The economic importance of languages other than English remains largely unrecognized in the United States. On the West Coast, for example, several Asian languages, in addition to Spanish, are valuable for conducting business. "[The United States] isn't doing enough to prepare our kids for the emerging global economy," says Elena Izquierdo, Ph.D., Department Chair of Teacher Education at the University of Texas at El Paso. Regarding the economic value of being bilingual, Dr. Izquierdo explains, "Bilingual students enter the job market with a tremendous advantage" (quoted in Vidueira, 1996, p. 16).

Besides linguistic skills, Dent (1995) suggests other skills will be needed: Problem-solving skills [will require that employees] (1) become results-oriented, (2) be proactive, and (3) think creatively. People skills [will challenge workers to] (1) know [themselves], (2) become sensitive to the needs of others, and (3) increase [their] tolerance level. Integrative skills [will emphasize the need for personnel to] (1) expand [their] ability to communicate, (2) sharpen business skills, and (3) get a grasp on information technologies (pp. 191–92).

It is essential that practitioners encourage their clients to develop linguistic skills, problem-solving skills, people skills, and information retrieval skills. These are indispensable to survival in a global economy. Mastery of such skills can reduce gender inequality in the workplace and enhance equal access to occupational opportunities for historically disenfranchised and marginalized people. A transformed vocational psychology will advocate for skill development as never before. The computer, especially, will dictate how we conduct business in the future. But before leaping into the future, it is beneficial to understand the foundations of the current world of work—its ethics and its values and the meaning of work in people's lives. An understanding of these basic ideas will aid the services the vocational practitioner provides. Thus, we examine values, ethics, and meaning in the workplace in Chapter 2.

SUMMARY

With all the changes taking place in the world of work, we have discussed a number of topics to help give us a basic understanding of some of its complexities. Basic terms connected with work, career, and occupations are defined.

Vocational psychology is a vital field that is beginning to expand its reach to diverse populations and those that were traditionally underserved. It is also reconceptualizing work in its psychological, cultural, and social contexts. It is broadening its understanding of careers beyond the past practice of noncontextual considerations to include the current realities for each person, the use of social constructionism to aid in acquiring tools for adapting to the changing world of work, and the recognition of contemporary career theories.

The growth of technology has unified the world in a number of ways, making it necessary to participate with people across cultures. Furthermore, the growing influence of other cultures within the United States and the recognition of diversity as a current reality create a need for understanding the differences in career counseling practice, values, and meaning in our lives. The subtleties of multiculturalism, acculturation, ethnicity, ethnic identity, and assimilation are basic to the ability to provide adequate counseling skills for vocational practitioners. In addition, gender and sexual orientation, socioeconomic status differences, the special needs of those who experience physical, mental, and intellectual limitations, and the culture of workplaces are unavoidable considerations. Understanding and supporting affirmative action and civil rights laws are part of the process in counseling and vocational activities.

The new economy with its emphasis on globalization, downsizing, flexibility, and constant change is a reality that affects the social, economic, and educational systems. Social system change can be seen in generational differences and the altering of family configurations. Economic systems involve ideas of equality and inequity, with the need to balance disparities of income, wage fluctuations, and changing governmental involvement. Educational systems are affected by the need to train students to deal with work and life in the future, which can involve new configurations of programs to allow for differences in training for various career options, with an emphasis on developing the creativity and flexibility that will be needed for the workplace of the future.

2

❖❖❖

Values, Ethics, Meaning,
and Spirituality in the Workplace

You used to be an executive at Enron, didn't you?
(Comment from a Patient while a Physician Was Performing a Colonoscopy on Him)

Work has multiple definitions based on both internal factors (e.g., a person's culture, psychological make-up) and external factors (e.g., the times in which the person lives, the economic situations of that era). In the United States work is central to most people's lives. So in this chapter we discuss several concepts related to work. First, we look at values and ethics in general. Second, we explore work values in particular. Third, we consider work ethics from a historical, cultural, and postmodern perspective. Fourth, we examine the concept of meaning in work/job satisfaction. Fifth, we present the topic of spirituality in the workplace. Finally, we address leisure and avocational activities. Throughout these sections, we incorporate practical applications and examples to be used for further discussion and understanding.

VALUES AND ETHICS

Definition of Terms

Frequently, the terms **values** and **ethics** are used interchangeably, but they are not identical and have distinctions (Corey, Corey, & Callanan, 1993). The word *value* is derived from the Latin *valere*, meaning "strong, brave, courageous" (Raths, Harmin, &

Simon, 1966). As a noun, value means (1) "worth" in terms of usefulness, such as a principle, (2) "that which is of importance to the possessor," such as a standard, and (3) "utility" or "merit," such as a quality. As a verb, value means "to regard highly, to esteem, or to prize." Ethics represent an objective inquiry about behavior. **Behavior** refers to overt actions such as driving a car or playing a guitar (Van Hoose & Paradise, 1979). The goodness or badness of a behavior is the provenance of morality. Pipher (1996) broadly defines morality as choosing wisely and decently how one will be in the universe. **Morality** concerns itself with action that is purposeful and for the good of all.

Ethics address behavior, but not all behavior equally. Ethics deal with **conduct**, or a person's voluntary choice between alternative courses of action that can have negative consequences. Whenever a person asks, "What ought I do?" or "Is it wrong for me to do this?" that person is dealing with matters of ethics (Van Hoose & Paradise, 1979, p. 9). We define **work ethics** as the principles of conduct that govern a person's work-related behaviors. We see clients who seek guidance and meaning when struggling to make well-reasoned and ethical choices about work-related issues, and/or who have questions dealing with the work ethics of their coworkers.

The Nature of Values The nature of values is extremely complex. Considerable argument among philosophers has produced a very broad definition of values (Peterson, 1970; Raths et al., 1966). Given that a simple and generally agreed upon definition of value is difficult to formulate, three common principles help to understand the nature of values. Values (1) are hypothetical constructs, (2) represent what one *ought* to do or what one perceives is the *right* thing to do, and (3) are motivational forces. With respect to the first principle, values must be objectively inferred by the justification of choices made regarding goals or objects; values are subjectively evident by responses involving elements of belief, interests, wants, and desires. Regarding the second principle, values concern themselves with ethics, behavior, conduct, and morality. For the third principle, values influence the role work plays in people's lives.

Constructing a Value In the classic *Values and Teaching: Working with Values in the Classroom,* Raths et al. (1966) proposed seven standards for constructing a value (see Table 2.1).

In Table 2.1, choosing a value relies on a person's cognitive abilities. The person must choose without submitting to externally imposed pressures. Prizing a value emphasizes the emotional level. The key is to refrain from imposing one's declared value upon others. Acting on a value concerns external behavior and moving beyond lip service. A person must be willing to act on the choice in some repeated pattern over time. If all seven standards are unmet, the result is a **value-indicator**, or a value in the process of "becoming."

TABLE 2.1 Seven Standards for Constructing a Value

CHOOSING (1ST PRINCIPLE)	1. freely
	2. from alternatives
	3. after thoughtful consideration of the consequences of each alternative
PRIZING (2ND PRINCIPLE)	4. cherishing, being happy with the choice
	5. willing to affirm the choice publicly
ACTING (3RD PRINCIPLE)	6. doing something with the choice
	7. repeatedly, in some pattern of life

SOURCE: From Raths et al., 1966, p. 30.

Raths et al. (1966) mention several types of values, including:

familial	professional	economic	spiritual
social	cultural	political	individual
artistic	educational	material	institutional

Likewise, there are several types of value-indicators. Positive value-indicators include activities that involve:

goals or purposes	aspirations	feeling
attitudes	interests	beliefs
activities		

Negative value-indicators include:

worries	problems	obstacles

Rokeach (1979) developed self-scoring surveys that contain items related to lifestyle and behavioral values. A list of eighteen terminal and eighteen instrumental values are ranked by highest to lowest value to the individual. Crace and Brown (1996) developed a holistic model of career and life-role choices based on Rokeach's work. Their Life Values Inventory is a measure of values that guide normal behaviors and an intervention to assist clients in prioritizing their values within their life roles. Brown (2002) revised the theory to include differences in cultural values and contextual variables such as socioeconomic status (SES), family or group influences, and discrimination. Properties of Brown's Value Based Theory can be found in his book *Career Information, Career Counseling, and Career Development* (2002).

Cultural Values. We object to the singling out of any cultural value as a primary explanation for behaviors that benefit or impede educational attainment and its related occupational achievement for any multicultural group. Such singling out gave rise to terms like **culturally deprived** and **culturally disadvantaged.** Culturally deprived suggests an absence of culture, and culturally disadvantaged means a person is at a disadvantage because he or she lacks the cultural background of the dominant social and political structure (Atkinson, Morten & Sue, 1993). The implication is that if the cultural heritage one possesses is not the right one, that person is deficient.

The real issue is **ethnocentrism**, where one culture's values matter more than those of another culture (Atkinson et al., 1993). The terms *culturally deprived* and *culturally disadvantaged* ignore society's external structures—political and economic. These external structures strongly contribute to adverse conditions said to reflect cultural values. We see within-group differences, developmental considerations, external structures, and contextual factors (e.g., family background, age at first access to technology) as salient variables for people who enact educational and work-related plans.

Interestingly, Ray and Anderson (2000) recently proposed the existence of a group of people who are quietly changing the world. Calling them the "Cultural Creatives," the authors indicate the major values to which these people ascribe are personal authenticity and a highly developed social conscience. The first is demonstrated by following through on their values and taking personal action. The second includes a belief in altruism, self-actualization, and spirituality. A sense of social action and a belief in social transformation are important to this group of people. The authors emphasize that the cultural creatives have not formed any formal connection and are often unaware that there are many like them. The major factor in identifying this quiet movement is to help build the type of coalition of individuals who will unite to make positive changes in society. That there are people with similar values can encourage a force for change in society.

In addition to Brown and Crace's Life Values Inventory (LUI) mentioned earlier, other work values inventories are available: Minnesota Importance Questionnaire (MIQ), part of the Work Adjustment theory (TWA; see our Chapter 4); Values Scale (VS) and Salience Inventory (SI), both part of Super's Model (see our Chapter 6); and the Work Importance Locator (WIL) and Work Importance Profiles (WIP) to be used in conjunction with the O★Net Occupations Combined list of interests and work values.

Another values instrument Peterson has used for years is the Study of Values, published by Houghton Mifflin. Kopelman, Rovenpor, and Allport (2002) have constructed a 4th edition of this instrument. The six value domains are theoretical, economic, social, political, aesthetic, and religious.

Cultural Values versus Family Values. In *The Shelter of Each Other: Rebuilding Our Families*, Pipher (1996) writes that families are ancient institutions with whom our culture is at war. The entertainment media is an electronic village raising consumers; children are taught drastically different values from those their parents say they value. In his book *High Tech, High Touch*, futurist John Naisbitt (1999) touches upon America's intoxication with technology, and especially the insensitivity toward violence that it breeds in our young people.

Admittedly, the media and the broader culture *are* at fault for conveying flimsy values (Pipher, 1996). The electronic village has created "a home without walls" (Pipher, 1997). Parents must be vigilant about protecting their children from junk values. Children also learn to be consumers from their peers (Pipher, 1996) and by watching their parents' behavior. Many parents unwittingly model consumerist values, and pursuit of material possessions affects parents' work lives. When work becomes the first priority, everything else caters to it. Kids learn that being a successful consumer equals working long hours and living at a hectic pace. Many parents get so busy that they take no time to stop and think about what they are doing.

One's occupation cannot be artificially separated from other parts of one's life (Pipher, 1996, 1997). Families are struggling against external structures that shape the quality of life both at home and at work. The role of work in people's lives needs to include the familial domain (M. S. Richardson, 1993). A transformed vocational psychology will (1) take external structures into greater consideration, (2) search less within families or individuals for the sources of their suffering, and (3) recognize and respect the multiple environments in which families of varying socioeconomic classes currently live.

WORK VALUES

Values are central to an individual's self-definition and motivation (Rokeach, 1973). Values maintain and enhance self-regard by helping a person to adjust to society, defend oneself against threat, and test reality. Although people in all cultures work, people's valuing of and motives for work reflect the nature of a culture at a given time (Axelson, 1993). Biological survival is a primary imperative. Beyond that, the status of work has been based upon (1) social, economic, and religious beliefs; (2) values; and (3) practices in an historical context.

Attitudes toward work have varied over the centuries. Ancient Hebrews viewed work both as painful drudgery, a punishment for moral transgressions, and as self-fulfilling and satisfying, a positive act of redemption that restored one's relationship with God (Axelson, 1993; Borow, 1973). Self-fulfillment through work was a moral obligation firmly rooted in the Judean tradition transmitted to the Christian church in the first centuries C.E. [Common Era, formerly A.D.], and later transformed during the Protestant Reformation in Western Europe in the sixteenth century. This transformation and its enduring legacy are discussed later in this chapter.

Practical Applications

Vocational practice requires assisting clients in identifying their (1) basic survival needs, (2) wants or choices that involve moral reason and judgment, and (3) values (Michelozzi, 1996). Making value decisions is not always easy. They may involve choices between the better of two goods or the lesser of two evils. "But in time a true value will become a comfortable part of your life pattern. Values are what you *do* and not what you *say*" (Michelozzi, p. 16, italics in original).

Becoming aware of one's values is an intrinsic part of each person's life, including occupational choices. Each occupational choice changes a person's lifestyle. The person must learn "new skills, change behaviors to fit [a] new role, make new friends, and learn a new vocabulary" (Michelozzi, 1996, p.17).

Clients may need a friendly reminder from practitioners that they do have choices (Pipher, 1996). They may have internalized values because at a certain time they were the only ones possible. External pressures from parents, economic circumstances, and institutional practices can result in values that are truly not one's own. These would best be described as value-indicators. Externally imposed value-indicators have to be reevaluated. Exploring alternative possibilities about what is good, what one ought to do, and what makes for client happiness offer promising opportunities for both personal and occupational growth.

To aid practitioners, Simon, Howe, and Kirschenbaum (1995) offer literally hundreds of values-clarification ques-

tions. In Chapter 4 we identify several values-clarification surveys useful for clients.

Practitioners who assist clients to sort out their values also help them develop their **character**, strengthen their **will**, and prioritize their **commitments** (Pipher, 1996). Character is that which makes an individual be wise and choose kind (i.e., moral) choices. Will is an individual's ability to act on one's values. Commitment is being available when it is neither convenient nor easy. Character takes a lifetime to develop. Behavior that is in accord with one's value system shows character through **self-regard**, which implies hard won self-knowledge. This should not be confused with **narcissism**, which implies self-absorption and self-preoccupation (Pipher, 1996). In the workplace, a well-developed character is unlikely to adopt the opinions of the last person with whom he has talked. A strong sense of self-regard reduces conduct such as backstabbing, gossiping, spying, discrediting others' efforts, and pettiness toward coworkers.

Practitioners can help clients strengthen their will by encouraging them to consider as victories those times when they have behaved according to what they value the most. Commitment has suffered in many workplaces. Pride in a job done well has been undermined in workplaces hit by downsizing and layoffs (Bragg, 1996a, 1996b), and workers may no longer trust the integrity of their supervisors. Practitioners can help clients to discern what they are willing to be steadfast about when change and crisis occur (Pipher, 1996) and when they need to cut their losses and move on.

Regarding character development and education, Pipher (1996) believes one of the best gifts that parents can pass on to their children is how to work. Several authors have presented a set of ethical values that schools and parents can teach to children. A comparison of some of these sets of ethical values is presented in Table 2.2.

Dosick's (1995) ten ethical values presented in the table are for families, but his book is applicable to adult character development. The Texas Education Agency's (TEA, 1996) curriculum is for elementary schools and has a host of resources listed—activities, films, books. The League of Value Driven Schools bases its values education program on the research of Jack Frymier and colleagues (Frymier et al., 1995, 1996). Character development and values education are crucial components in the preparation of our future workforce and cannot be separated from occupational education activities with children and youth. Of course, the best way for par-

ents, teachers, and other adults to teach children and youth these ethical values is to model them in their conduct both at home and at work.

Work gives structure to people's lives (Pipher, 1996). Independently wealthy people or trust fund babies risk having less reason for getting out of bed in the morning and can experience *ennui*—aimlessness and a lack of purpose. But even with the loss of privilege and position, work can give a person something for which to live. Work in the personal and familial domains (M. S. Richardson, 1993) combine with historical context in the case of Nicholas II [1868–1918], last tsar of Russia. His diary poignantly records the chores he devised for himself and his children in their months of captivity immediately following his abdication in 1917. His captors permitted the family to cultivate a kitchen garden and to gather winter's fuel by chopping down trees and sawing wood (Maylunas & Mironenko, 1997). Growing vegetables and stockpiling firewood gave them dignity and purpose, occupied their days, and gave meaning to their existence during their imprisonment.

TABLE 2.2 A Comparison of Ethical Values That Can Be Taught to Children

DOSICK[1]	TEXAS EDUCATION AGENCY[2]	THE LEAGUE OF VALUE-DRIVEN SCHOOLS[3]
respect	honesty	learning
honesty	responsibility	honesty
fairness	compassion	cooperation
responsibility	perseverance	service
compassion	loyalty	freedom
gratitude	justice	responsibility
friendship	self-reliance	civility
peace	self-discipline	
maturity	integrity	
faith		

[1] W. Dosick, *Golden Rules: The Ten Ethical Values Parents Need to Teach Their Children,* San Francisco: Harper, 1995.

[2] Texas Education Agency. *Building Good Citizens for Texas: Character Education Resource Guide.* Austin, TX: Author, 1996.

[3] Based on J. Frymier et al., *Values on Which We Agree.* Bloomington, IN: Phi Delta Kappa International, 1995.

From the worker's perspective, work today is very different from any time before. In the United States today, mergers and takeovers arise from the value placed on the profit motive or the bottom line. The early American values of self-restraint, self-control, hard work, and frugality created a more desirable moral climate than that we have today (Pipher, 1996). People's desire for work as a social experience has changed very little, but with the emphasis on cutting staff size and outsourcing to small businesses, many people are not finding their need for affiliation met and experience alienation from peers as more are working out of their homes (Licht, 1988). Nearly one-quarter of the workforce already works full time or part time out of their homes. Some positive outcomes from this trend are the higher motivation that occurs from working for oneself and the possibility of having more time to spend with the family. Conversely, family members potentially can be treated more as coworkers.

Work hours per week are increasing. Americans are working an estimated sixty hours a week, fifty weeks a year. Workers dream of owning their own homes and cars, paying college tuition for their children, and having enough leisure time. Unfortunately, to maintain the dream, many homes with dual wage earners have children who are looking after themselves. Family life is thus affected, as workers cannot provide the parenting children need. A recent study conducted by Kids Peace found that 54 percent of working parents had little time to spend with their children and wished for more. Dr. Alvin Poussaint, a Harvard psychiatrist, said approximately 3.5 million households see an hour or less of physical, quality time between parents and children. (Associated Press, 2003). As for the work values traditionally espoused by vocational psychology, Osipow and Fitzgerald (1996) question their relevance to multicultural and diverse populations.

> Possibly the most profound challenge to the generalizability of career development theories is posed by the assertion that many racial/ethnic minority individuals do not share the value systems on which the traditional explanations are based. Virtually every discussion of minority career development contains the assertion that racial/ethnic minority group membership is associated with a more collectivist, group-oriented value system, whereas non-ethnic white Americans are thought to share a highly individual-centered white culture whose values are reflected in the theories used to explain their career behavior. To the degree that such an assertion is correct, it constitutes a profound limitation on the validity of vocational development theories, suggesting that they may not be applicable to many minority individuals (p. 275).

Collectivist societies presumably include most traditional preindustrial societies, the predominantly Catholic countries of Southern Europe and Latin America and most Asian and African cultures (Ross & Nisbett, 1991). In **collectivism**, "in-group norms and role relations provide both the motivating force that drives the individual and the compass from which the individual takes direction" (p. 181). The emphasis is on family and community-based relations and values. Individualistic societies are presumed to include most of the nations in Western Europe—which gave rise to the **Protestant Reformation**—and North America. In **individualism**, the "emphasis [is] on personal goals, interests, and preferences. Social relationships are dictated by commonality of interests and aspirations and are therefore subject to change as those interests and aspirations shift over time" (p. 181). An individual's choices of dress, diet, friends, occupation, or spouse are relatively free of family dictates or from others to whom one might be linked by traditional roles.

Collectivism is most similar to other-oriented values (Raths et al., 1966). Individualism most closely resembles self-oriented values. Current workplace cultures can be a combination of collectivist and individualist values. Mission statements usually provide a value-indicator of workplace aspirations, but a collectivist-sounding mission statement may disguise an individualistic work environment. Familial values are often collectivist in nature and are most likely to collide with professional values that are predominantly individualistic. We discuss this clash of values later in this chapter.

Practical Applications

Individualistic/collectivistic dichotomies across cultures frequently overlook some key points. We offer three cautionary notes to practitioners.

1. Retain sight of within-group differences, including variations within nonethnic White Americans. Even within the same family, a range of orientations from individualistic to collectivistic can occur. Broad statements about any group having an individualist or collectivist value system are dangerous, especially where work-related behavior is concerned. From a multicultural perspective, within-group differences for any particular racial, ethnic, or nationality group are significant (Pedersen, 1990; Sue, 1992), including for the dominant, White majority group. Within-group differences such as "psychological orientation, family structure, socialization, sex, generation, social class, situations,

and technological and economic developments seem to influence the formation and selection of various value preferences or expressions" (Carter, 1991, p. 170). Remaining mindful of such differences minimizes false dichotomies across cultures and enriches vocational psychology interventions for all clients.

The literature on **Black Cultural Learning Styles (BCLS)** (Frisby, 1993; T. Q. Richardson, 1993) is one attempt to use cultural values as a primary explanation for behaviors that benefit or impede educational attainment and occupational development for African Americans. BCLS asserts that African American students' learning styles are fundamentally incompatible with those of European American students. The idea behind BCLS is that **Afrocentrism** (i.e., behaviors based

Continued

Continued

on an African cultural heritage) accounts for behavior differences between Black and White students. African Americans presumably value interconnectedness, cooperative learning situations, and community possessions. BCLS also presumes an African American emphasis on spiritual values and a flexible orientation toward time.

European Americans presumably value separateness, competitive learning situations, and private ownership. BCLS also presumes a European American emphasis on material values and a precise orientation toward time. Frisby notes, however, that BCLS was devised by Western African American scholars who attempted to describe the behaviors of Western African American students, so the European influence on BCLS cannot be discounted. BCLS perpetuates false dichotomies and fails to recognize within-group differences. The *hoop dreams* of literally thousands of young African American males belie an emphasis on cooperative learning situations that BCLS upholds. Hoop dreams are as inherently competitive as any other athletic activity.

Another multicultural example is the attempt to use differences in cognitive styles of Mexican American students to explain behaviors that benefit or impede educational achievement (Buenning & Tollefson, 1987; Saracho, 1989) and occupational development. Presumably, the cognitive styles of Mexican Americans are cooperative and collectivist in learning situations. Again, insufficient attention is given to within-group differences that recognize contextual, as opposed to cultural, aspects of collectivist and individualist orientations.

2. Be alert for when individualistic values and collectivistic values develop in the **worldview** of a single person, dependent on context. A worldview is "the frame of reference through which one experiences life. It is the foundation for values, beliefs, attitudes, [and] relations" (Fouad & Bingham, 1995, p. 335). Failure to understand or accept another worldview can have a detrimental consequence in terms of clinical outcome (Pedersen, 1990; Sue, 1992). While we agree with Ibrahim (1991) that people from different cultural backgrounds perceive the world differently, social psychology persuades us that individualism and collectivism are, more often than not, situational rather than dispositional within a given client. When various work-related issues arise for clients, those with largely collectivistic personal and social histories may begin struggling with individualistic wants and a desire to place their own interests first. Such clients may perceive that in the past, their personal needs and wants have been neglected or set aside in deference to others' interests. Both developmental and contextual factors would form part of such clients' new-found individualistic yearnings.

3. Consider the developmental role of acculturation—indeed, the role of *multiculturation*—in assessing the individualistic/collectivistic role orientation of their clients, especially minority group clients. This can both expand and enhance the validity of vocational development theories and their applicability to many minority individuals. For all clients, an added dimension can be incorporated into occupational counseling when work-related issues are examined in the context of one's own culture, the broader culture, and one's work culture.

To expand on understanding one's worldviews, H. B. Gelatt (2002) suggested in his paper on "The Process of Illumination," ideas on seeing to help examine one's own worldview.

1. What you see is what you look for. It is your subjective view. Being reflective is one of the thinking skills of illumination. Some possible questions career counselors could ask are: Why do you see what you see? Why do you believe what you believe? How could you see things differently? What are the positive and negative consequences of your view (p. 5)?

2. What you don't see is what you don't pay attention to. It is your tunnel vision view (p. 5). Some questions to ask your clients are: Is your mind's eye software up to date? Are you paying attention to what you are paying attention to (p. 6)?

3. What you can't see is what is invisible or hidden. It is your myopic view; it is everyone's visual defect. A possible question to ask your clients is: Do you keep your eye on what you cannot see? Also ask them to imagine what they can't see when considering any career decision they are about to make. What are they overlooking? What parts of the whole system are they failing to notice?

4. What you see that isn't there is called either illusion, an erroneous perception of reality, or creative imagination, a fantasy. Questions to ask clients are: Do you see the glass half full or half empty? Can you dream impossible dreams (p. 8)?

WORK ETHICS

Work ethics are the principles of conduct that govern a person's work-related behaviors. Work ethics form a part of the Judeo-Christian tradition. Included in this tradition are scriptural views of work. For example, the apostle Paul wrote, "Whatever you do, work at it with all your heart, as working for the Lord, not for men, since you know that you will receive an inheritance from the Lord as a reward" (Colossians 3:23–24). The value of working hard, its divine mandate, and its positive consequences are common themes in the Judeo-Christian tradition.

Axelson (1993, pp. 227–28) presents a range of attitudes toward a work ethic:

"Work is the medicine for poverty."
—Yoruba (Afro-Cuban) proverb

"Work with the rising sun, rest with the setting sun."
—Chinese proverb

"Work alone makes life bearable, keeps away boredom, vice, and need."
—François Marie Arouet de Voltaire (1694–1778), French writer and philosopher

"Work consists of whatever a body is *obliged* to do, and play consists of whatever a body is not obliged to do."
—Mark Twain (1835–1910), American writer and humorist

"Life is work."
> —Henry Ford (1863–1947), American automobile manufacturer

"I do the thing which my own nature drives me to do."
> —Albert Einstein (1879–1955), German-born American physicist

The very notion of work ethics took a beating with the financial and accounting scandals that made headlines about the business practices at Enron (Eichenwald, 2002a, 2002b, 2003; Oppel & Glater, 2001), Tyco (Reuters, 2003; Sorkin & Berenson, 2002), WorldCom (Kadlec, 2002; Miller, 2002; Semple, 2003; "The backlash against business," 2002), and other corporations. Enron, the Houston energy company, had "labyrinthine dealings" (Oppel & Glater, 2001, p. 1) with hidden partnerships tied to senior Enron executives whose left hand was investing what the right hand was earning. The culture of "self-dealing and self-enrichment at the expense of the company's shareholders" (Eichenwald, 2002b, p. 1), coupled with a culture of deceit that intentionally manipulated the company's profits by inflating them by almost $1 billion, led to Enron's bankruptcy and took the once prestigious accounting firm of Arthur Andersen down with it ("Accounting in Crisis," 2002; Holstein, 2003; Norris, 2003).

Andersen accountants played both sides of the street by working as both the external and internal auditors for Enron. Tyco, which sells everything from surgical supplies, security alarm services, and plastic hangers to fiber optic cables (Sorkin & Berenson, 2002), had "a corporate culture that openly encouraged managers to push the rules of accounting to mislead investors about the company's [earning] results" (p. 1). Over $2 billion in accounting problems have been unearthed so far (Reuters, 2003). WorldCom, the bankrupt communications giant now known as MCI and the nation's second-largest long-distance company, also gave false information to investors (Semple, 2003) amounting to $3.9 billion in accounting falsifications and problems ("The backlash against business," 2002). "It's getting harder and harder to know what a company actually earns and what its stock is actually worth" (Nussbaum, 2002, p. 1). It's as if the Protestant work ethic has become an obsolete relic of the past, replaced by cleverness and deceit.

The Protestant Work Ethic

Of the many work ethics, the most powerful one in the United States and in the world's predominantly Protestant countries is—or, at least, used to be—the **Protestant work ethic**. Misunderstood by many who tend to view it as a single amorphous entity, in fact, the origins of the Protestant work ethic are more complex than most people realize. No vocational psychology textbook we know of addresses in depth the Protestant work ethic. This omission ignores a major influence on vocational psychology. The Protestant work ethic has both sociological and historical perspectives.

Weber's Sociological Perspective *The Protestant Ethic and the Spirit of Capitalism* (1904/1958) is the most widely known work of sociologist Max Weber (1864–1920). Weber's controversial thesis is that the religious upheavals resulting from the Protestant Reformation, especially Calvinism, produced the psychological conditions that made possible the development of capitalist civilization (Tawney, 1958).

Weber understood Calvin's disciples to believe they could avoid damnation by doing *good works*. "The social activity of the Christian in the world is solely activity in *majorem gloriam Dei*" [Latin for 'to increase the glory of God']" (Weber, 1958, p. 108). Social activity should be understood to mean simply activity within the church, politics, or any other social organization (Weber, 1958). Weber implied that Calvin's perception of divine order entailed participation in a strenuous, exacting enterprise that individuals must choose and pursue with a sense of religious responsibility (Tawney, 1958). The fulfillment of duties in worldly affairs became the highest form of moral activity a person could assume (Weber, 1958).

Weber's thesis was that capitalism became the social counterpart of Calvinist theology: (1) Labor became an economic means to a spiritual end; (2) covetousness was less a danger to one's soul than was sloth; and (3) diligence, thrift, sobriety, and prudence became virtues of both God's *elect* and the commercially prosperous (Tawney, 1958). Western capitalism was conducted by unremittingly devoted businessmen who pursued maximum money profit through nonviolent, legal, and honest means (Lessoff, 1994). Work became an opportunity and a challenge to make use of God-given resources, both in oneself and in the environment (also known as **responsible stewardship**). Each person would be divinely called to use one's talents and abilities for the greater good of all. From this divine calling derives a sense of vocation.

Critique of Weber's Thesis. Quite plausibly, Weber's outlook reflected in part his early years. Weber had a wealthy background; his family enjoyed considerable political and social connections (Miller, 1971). He wrote during Imperial Germany's military and intellectual preeminence (Andreski, 1983). Weber's Germany was characterized by an intense **jingoism**—a pronounced chauvinism and nationalism marked by a belligerent foreign policy, in this case an arms race between the British and German empires. Not blind to his own country's shortcomings, Weber wanted to see Germany achieve full status as a world power. He saw the need for exceptional leaders to rise above tradition and bureaucracy to cope with the dangerous European tensions of the day (Wrong, 1970). In other words, Weber's thesis is bound by his personal upbringing and by the social, cultural, and political milieu of his time. Yet his charisma and moral and intellectual integrity cannot be denied; probably only Marx and Freud are more widely known and respected as social thinkers by the general Western intellectual public (Wrong, 1970). Few historical arguments have produced a greater wealth of intellectually fertile, subtle, and often deeply disturbing responses (Leuthy, 1970). Most relevant here are its impacts on ethics and the world of work.

Weber (1956, 1978) acknowledged that capitalism existed in the ancient civilizations of Greece, Rome, India, and China; in the Islamic empires of the eighth through nineteenth centuries; in fourteenth-century Venice and Florence; and in the Antwerp of the fifteenth century, but argued that the capitalist enterprise had to wait until religious changes had produced a capitalist spirit (Tawney, 1958). Critics charge that instead of Calvinism producing the spirit of capitalism, both with equal likelihood could be regarded as different effects of other large-scale historical changes. For example, the Black Death of the fourteenth century dramatically altered the composition and political influence of Western Europe's workforce; the influx of New World gold and silver into Spain and then Europe generally during the sixteenth century produced skyrocketing inflation. Historically, one tremendous change in societal structures—the broader intellectual movement of the Renaissance of the fourteenth through sixteenth centuries— removed many conventional restraints in Western Europe (Tawney, 1958).

Weber (1976) acknowledged that the political and economic characteristics of ancient societies, not spiritual deficiencies within a group of people, hindered their full-fledged capitalistic development. But Weber ignored the changes that had occurred in the Roman Catholic Church, which by then had incorporated many of Martin Luther's original protests (Severy, 1983) and which no longer served as a barrier to the emergence of capitalism (Miller, 1971). Others contend Weber does not show any logical connection, from a religious point of view, between the work ethic and the profit motive (Lessnoff, 1994). Weber's thesis is also attacked because, while capitalism apparently began as the practical idealism of an aspiring bourgeoisie, it ended up as excessive materialism (Tawney, 1958), originally one of the major complaints of the Protestant reformers about Catholicism (Wrong, 1970). Thus, the impact of drastic transformations in social and economic systems, as opposed to the superior cultural and religious values of one of several multicultural groups, stands as an equally powerful alternative explanation of the rise of capitalism.

Similarly, the present-day global economy is primarily responsible for the abundance or shortage of work opportunities. Infrastructural factors (i.e., social, political, and economic transformations), instead of deficiencies in individuals or cultures, play a more significant role in influencing occupational developments. For example, the Ohio Art Company, makers of Etch A Sketch, the children's drawing toy that has outlasted almost all its competitors, moved the manufacturing of that toy to Shenzhen, China because cost pressures—especially the soaring costs of health benefits—had been dragging down profits for years (Kahn, 2003a). The working conditions at Kin Ki Industrial, the Chinese toy makers of Etch A Sketch, are extremely harsh: 24 cents an hour instead of the legal minimum wage of 33 cents; denial of the legally required nonsalary benefits; 84-hour work weeks, a lot more than the legal maximum and without required overtime pay (Kahn, 2003b). These labor standards were hidden by factory managers from Ohio Art Company executives who visited Kin Ki to inspect working conditions, and Kin Ki's employees—mostly teenage migrants from internal Chinese provinces—were coached on what to say to their American visitors. It was not a failure of individual or cultural values that led to the work being sent to this Chinese factory, but the economic advantages of producing the product there.

Vocational psychology's bias often is on the individual and ignores broader contextual trends. Examining the historical origins of work-related behaviors, such as the Protestant work ethic, helps to clarify how external factors impact individual lives.

Historical Perspectives on the Protestant Work Ethic

The British North American Colonies. The **Puritan work ethic** is a more accurate term for Protestant work ethic in the U.S. An historical and contextual awareness of Puritanism puts into perspective both the Protestant work ethic and vocational psychology. By the late sixteenth century, Puritans had strength and position in English society in far greater proportion to their numbers (Smith, 1971), even before their later dominance in the British North American colonies. The Puritans were radicals. They contended that, as a means of containing corruption, the secular branch of the government should be held accountable to the spiritual branch of the church. For Puritans, the purpose of life was a spiritual one, with the duty of the church to serve God, not the Crown or governmental institutions. In this respect Puritans resembled their contemporary polar opposites, the Jesuits of the Catholic Counter-Reformation (Fuentes, 1992).

British colonial expansion during the seventeenth century occurred largely because of capitalistic and industrial growth. Money was available to finance the pioneering energies of the 1600s, and all English settlements were commercial in their inception, with an understanding that long-term investments and confidence in the future were necessary to realize a return on the original capital. It required all the accoutrements of civilization to initiate and sustain these business ventures. Thus, "Of all the great [European] powers, only England exported her peoples. Spanish imagination was caught by the glitter of gold and the anguish of [Native American] souls crying for salvation [and whose conversion made up for souls lost to Protestantism in Northern Europe]; France sought trade and raw materials" (Smith, 1971, p. 224).

Puritans were one of four waves of Protestant immigrants who colonized British North America (Fischer, 1989). Historically relevant to vocational psychology are two Puritan folkways pertaining to work and time. **Folkways** are "the normative structure of values, customs, and meanings that exist in any culture" (Fischer, 1989). **Work ways** refer to "work ethics and work experiences; attitudes toward work and the nature of work" (Fischer, 1989, p. 9). **Time ways** refer to "attitudes toward the use of time, customary methods of time keeping, and the conventional rhythms of life" (Fischer, 1989, p. 9). Each of the four waves of British North American immigrants had diverse modal characteristics related to work and time. These modal characteristics are presented in Table 2.3.

TABLE 2.3 Four British Migratory Waves to North America: Modal Characteristics Related to Work Ethic and Time Ethic

Region of origin:	East Anglia[1]	South and West[2]	North Midlands[3]	Borderlands[4]
North American destination:	Massachusetts	Virginia	Delaware Valley	Backcountry[5]
Migration Period:	1629–1640	1642–1675	1675–1715	1717–1775
Religion of migrants:	Congregational	Anglican	Friends	Presbyterian and Anglican
Origin of immigrant élites:	Puritan ministers and magistrates	Royalist younger sons of gentry and aristocracy	Quaker traders, artisans, and farmers	Border gentry and statesmen
Work ethic:	Puritan	Leisure	Pietistic	Warrior
Time ethic:	Improving the time	Killing the time	Redeeming the time	Passing the time

[1] East Anglia consisted of the east of England, especially the counties of Norfolk, Suffolk, Essex, Hertfordshire, Cambridgeshire, and Huntingdonshire—plus parts of Bedfordshire and Kent.

[2] The South and West consisted of Cornwall, Devonshire, Somersetshire, Dorsetshire, Wiltshire, Hampshire, West Sussex, Surrey, Berkshire, Oxfordshire, Middlesex, Buckinghamshire, Northamptonshire, Leicestershire, Staffordshire, Warwickshire, and Gloucestershire.

[3] The North Midlands consisted of Yorkshire, Lancashire, Cheshire, Derbyshire, Nottinghamshire, Lincolnshire, Shropshire, Herefordshire, Worcestershire, and the latter four named counties listed under the South and West above.

[4] The Borderlands consisted of the north of Ireland, the lowlands of Scotland, and the northern counties of England—Northumberland, Cumberland, Westmorland, and Durhamshire.

[5] The Backcountry consisted of southwestern Pennsylvania, the western parts of Maryland and Virginia, North and South Carolina, Georgia, Kentucky, and Tennessee.

SOURCE: Adapted from Fischer (1989). Compiled by Roberto Cortéz González.

As Table 2.3 shows, the Puritan migratory wave was the first to occur. They originally came from the east of England between 1629 and 1640 and settled the Massachusetts Bay Colony. Their religious denomination was Congregational.

The Puritan élites consisted of ministers and magistrates. Their work ethic was based on the idea that every Christian had two callings—a general calling and a special calling (Fischer, 1989). The Puritan's general calling was to live a Godly life on earth; their special calling was to vocation. While the Puritans did not believe that success in one's calling insured salvation, they did believe that a sense of vocation was the way to serve God in the world. Work was virtuous. Poverty was the result of one's own lewdness; no virtuous person required charity (Whitmore, 1971).

Puritans invested time with sacred meaning, "God's Time" (Fischer, 1989). An obsession with "improving the time" originally had spiritual connotations that were later transformed into secular and materialist ends. Around 1680, the English Puritan Ralph Thoresby invented the alarm clock to better measure the time.

Other Anglo-American colonists were not occupied with work and time in quite the same way. The colonial Virginians originally came from the south and west of England between 1642 and 1675. Their religious denomination was Anglican. Their elites consisted of Royalist (i.e., supporters of the Crown) younger sons of the gentry and aristocracy whose older brothers had inherited the family property in England. These younger sons made their own way in the New World. In British Colonial North America, they were among the most socially prominent families of their day. In colonial Virginia, most White slave owners worked harder than they cared to admit while attempting to keep up appearances of gentility. "Wealth was regarded not primarily as a form of capital or a factor of production, but as something to be used for display and consumed for pleasure. . . . The economic consequence of this attitude was debt" (Fischer, 1989, p. 367). Time ways were less strict. "The people of Virginia were less obsessed than New Englanders with finding some godly purpose for every passing moment, but their lives were more tightly controlled by the rhythms of a rural life" (Fischer, 1989, p. 369). Tobacco was the main crop. It required unremitting care once planted and consumed the lives of all Virginians, with alternate periods of "killing the time."

The Quakers of the Delaware Valley originally came from the North Midlands between 1675 and 1715. Their religious denomination was the Friends. Their élites consisted of traders, artisans, and farmers. The Quakers encouraged industry and condemned idleness. Their pietistic work ethic reinforced the idea of serving God with one's best talents. Also prominent in the Quaker worldview were discipline, integrity in business dealing, and austerity. Spiritual exercises were prescribed to enhance discipline and to acquire absolute dominion over one's acts. Business integrity was vital; disciplinary hearings for "dishonest dealing" had both economic and moral implications. Austerity meant that money was not to be indulged via conspicuous consumption or vulgar displays of wealth, but rather to be saved, invested, and turned to constructive purposes. Quakers founded that venerable banking institution, Lloyd's of London.

The men and women of the Backcountry originally came from the British Borderlands between 1717 and 1775. Their religious denominations were Presbyterian and Anglican. Their élites consisted of Border gentry and statesmen, and they had their share of social prominence. But the backsettlers had a different lifestyle from the established settlements of the other British colonies. They settled what was then the frontier and initially served as a buffer between the Quakers and the Native Americans. A stereotype arose that their strong warrior ethic made for a weak work ethic (Fischer, 1989). A reliance on farming and herding meant that work was seasonal. Fieldwork was backbreaking: Hoe-husbandry was the main system for crop farming (axe, broad hoe, and narrow hoe); plows were seldom used. The people of the Backcountry perceived the rhythms of life as something that could not be avoided, shaped, or resisted. Hence, the backsettler's belief that they were powerless to change events, as demonstrated in their idea of "passing the time."

The Industrial Revolution to the Early Twentieth Century. The Protestant-based concepts of human nature and work endured until the Industrial Revolution of the late eighteenth century, when the *spiritual man* was replaced by the *economic man* (Herzberg, 1966, p. 53). Hand tools were replaced by machine and power tools, resulting in yet another change in social and economic organization and the development of large-scale industrial production. The PBS Home Video *Mill Times* hosted by David Macaulay (2001) provides an excellent visual understanding of the Industrial Revolution, during which contemplation of the soul was replaced by empirical study of the body (Herzberg, 1966).

The worker was viewed primarily as a creature of physical needs, a creature of comfort. During this time of great industrialization, there was a drive for better production. Out of this pursuit, the principles of scientific management, which led to industrial engineering, were born.

The essence of industrial engineering is individual differences, one of the prime laws of psychology (Dawis, 1992). The emphasis is on eliminating variability in individual differences. This limits the work task so that the one talent held in common will be used, thus minimizing the possibility of error but at the cost of wasted human talent. To justify this denigration of workers, industry developed the myth of the *mechanistic man.* This new myth viewed humans' overriding desire as that of wanting to be used efficiently with a minimum of effort. People were considered to be happiest when they were replaceable parts of replaceable machines that manufactured replaceable parts (Herzberg, 1966). Presumably, people were delighted when they did not have to make decisions.

Upon researching low worker motivation, it was found that an additional myth was needed to keep morale up and production high. The concept created was the *social man.* People were defined essentially as social animals primarily in search of social gratification; their prevailing desire was to be acceptable to fellow workers. Following in the wake of the social man was the idea of the *emotional man,* who was in need of and searching for psychotherapeutic environments (Herzberg, 1966).

Today industry has turned to the *instrumental man.* In the wake of technological development, the level of human activity that serves industry is a person's higher capacities. Workers' intellectual talents must now be organized in the same way that their motor skills were organized for assembly-line operations.

By the 1900s the Protestant work ethic was summarized in a sermon: "Business is religion and religion is business. The man who does not make a business of religion has a business life of no character" (Herzberg, 1966, p. 52). In this context, virtue was defined as economic success, and economic success was defined as virtue. This circular worldview is a legacy of Calvinism's emphasis on the individual's predestined fate: the *elect* are known by their economic success. Hence, the fashion tradition known as *Sunday best* equates Godliness with economic success.

Critique of the Protestant Work Ethic Upholding any type of work ethic in the context of changing cultural values and economic patterns in our society has profound implications. Cultural perspectives arise independently of objective situational forces (Ross & Nisbett, 1991). Values, beliefs, and modes of interpreting events characterizing a given culture or subculture can take on a life apart from the situations that launched them. Cultural artifacts can survive well beyond the demise of those situations. The Protestant work ethic is one cultural artifact, a deliberate contrivance of the cultural élite (Fischer, 1989). It has been severely abused and has endured beyond its usefulness. Too often it has been used to mask greed. Too frequently profit motives are not based on honesty, respect for the law, or worker well-being.

Other weaknesses make the Protestant work ethic outmoded: (1) The ethic is historically based on intentional misrepresentations and calculated exaggerations for political purposes, which has bequeathed an inherently distorted legacy. (2) It has limited multicultural applicability. (3) It is anti-woman and anti-feminist. (4) The Protestant work ethic is a basis for a blame-the-victim belief system. (5) It cannot be readily applied to the working habits of many immigrant populations. Each of these points is explored below.

An Inherently Distorted Legacy. The Protestant work ethic is outmoded because it is the legacy of a religious wing that sought to purify an already reformed church. The Puritans would have done away with all vestiges of Catholic ritual in the Church of England, including wedding rings and ecclesiastical vestments (Ashley, 1980). The severity of such measures is as evident now as it was then. The distortions inherent in such a worldview persist despite the adaptations and secularizations of the work ethic that have occurred through the centuries. A lack of wellness and an unhealthy lifestyle can result when such a distorted worldview goes unexamined.

Limited Multicultural Relevance. A second reason the Protestant work ethic is outmoded is its limited (at best) multicultural relevance. The ethic omits explicit acknowledgment of the debt owed to the Jewish ancestral part of its Judeo-Christian heritage. Jewish peoples' work ethic (Herz & Rosen, 1982) has contributed substantially to the economic, cultural, and social development of the United States (Goren, 1980). The first recorded instance of divine calling appears in Genesis 12, when God called on Abraham in approximately 2000 B.C. to lead his people from ancient lower Babylon to Canaan located several hundred miles west. While the Christian faith views this calling as the defining act of Abraham's life, the Jewish and Islamic faiths join with Christians to view this calling as an internal journey as well, a journey toward understanding how one's own life makes a difference, which certainly has implications today for the role of work in the lives of 12 million Jews, 2 billion Christians, and 1 billion Muslims around the world (Feiler, 2002).

Martin Luther, a precursor of John Calvin, disliked Jewish people's industriousness. In *About the Jews and Their Lies* (1543), he stated, "we do not know to this day which devil has brought [the Jews] here . . . a plague, pestilence, pure misfortune on our country" (quoted in an exhibit panel, "Why the Jews? The Patterns of Persecution," El Paso Holocaust Museum and Study Center, 1997). **Anti-Semitism** was well entrenched by Luther and Calvin's time. The Gospel of John (18:38–40) says that Jesus Christ was crucified by "the Jews," while Matthew (27:24–26) wrote of Jesus as crucified by "the crowd." The El Paso Holocaust Museum and Study Center quotes John Chrysostom of the fourth century condemning the Jews for killing Christ. By refusing to give credit where it is due regarding divine calling, the overt anti-Semitism of the Protestant work ethic reveals its limited multicultural relevance to a historically valuable segment of the workforce in the United States and elsewhere. Religious politics are the worst sort of politics there is; anti-Semitic Christians throughout history would have recognized the Jews as God's instruments of humankind's salvation if it had been expedient for such Christians to do so.

Bowman (1995) notes that the Protestant work ethic teaches that work should be the main focus, if not the defining focus, of one's life, but also presumes that everyone has equal access to occupational opportunities. The ethic appears to ignore the message that African Americans and members of other ethnic minority groups hear on a daily basis; namely, that only certain careers are open to multicultural populations because of their race and/or ethnicity. This message becomes evident when African Americans: (1) seek same-race role models in various careers where there are few, if any, available role models (i.e., engineers, computer scientists, researchers); (2) receive negative feedback about careers because their peers, the elderly, or respected members of other racial groups indicate these are inappropriate career choices; (3) enter a career that has few racial or ethnic minorities and learn that their hiring occurred mainly to fill a quota, implying that the employee was not really qualified; and (4) find themselves in a position that forces them to interact with a system that is often alien, sometimes even hostile, in order to achieve status.

It is hardly surprising, then, that many African Americans tend to select occupations where other members of their community appear to congregate, *protected careers* (e.g., education, social work, and the social sciences) where less racial discrimination is perceived to occur (Murry & Mosidi, 1993). Both current circumstances and historical context demonstrate that external factors are integral in the career development of any client. Thomas Jefferson [1743–1826] recognized in his later years that "the opportunities for the development of [African Americans'] genius were not favorable" (Will, 1997, p. 6A).

Some Asian American students excel academically because they adhere to a **Confucian work ethic**. The Confucian work ethic requires them to do well because they owe it to their parents (Butterfield, 1990). Doing well academically brings honor to the family, although diversity within the Asian American population reflects a range of academic achievement (Hsia & Hirano-Nakanishi, 1989). Confucianism dominated Chinese culture for nearly twenty-five centuries (Yang, 1991). In Confucianism, "patriarchal ideas are embraced and a formal relationship system emphasizes humility, politeness, and respect" (Axelson, 1993, p. 438). Asian Americans are not the *Model Minority* (Suzuki, 1989). This social construction of the model minority has functional value to those who hold power in American society for at least three reasons. First, these stereotypes reassert the erroneous belief that any minority can succeed in a democratic society if the minority-group members work hard enough. Second, the Asian American success story is seen as a divisive concept used by the establishment to pit one minority group against another by holding one group up as an example to others. Third, the success myth has short-changed many Asian American communities from receiving the necessary moral and financial commitment due them as a struggling minority with unique concerns (D. W. Sue & D. Sue, 1990, p. 192). Asian Americans continue to experience inequity in both employment and income (Suzuki, 1989). Furthermore, existing vocational psychology research does not confirm the model minority stereotype (Leong & Serafica, 1995). In our opinion, the Protestant work ethic neither honors nor respects those Asian Americans who adhere to the Confucian work ethic.

An Anti-Woman, Anti-Feminist Ethic. The Protestant work ethic, with its patriarchal posturing, is implicitly anti-woman and anti-feminist. It ignores **gender stratification** in the world of work. Gender stratification refers to "the hierarchical distribution by gender of economic and social resources in a society" (Andersen, 1983, p. 77). The Protestant work ethic ignores women's past and present participation in the labor force; the economic mobility of women workers; how gender issues at work become complicated by race, ethnicity, and social class; and the differential access to social and economic resources (Andersen, 1983). The Protestant work ethic bolsters a sense of male entitlement that has perpetuated an imbalance in the gender division of domestic labor and affects personal relationships as well as domestic and international policies (Baxandall & Gordon, 1995).

A Basis for a "Blame the Victim" Belief System. In his book, *When Work Disappears: The World of the New Urban Poor,* sociologist William Julius Wilson describes the dominant American belief system concerning poverty and welfare; "it is the moral fabric of individuals, not the social and economic structure of society, which is taken to be the root of the problem" (1996, p. 164). The U.S. welfare debate of recent years painted the non-working poor as "immoral freeloaders disdainful of work" (Cose, 1996, p. 47).

Victim-blaming used to be cloaked in kindness and concern, most often obscured by a perfumed haze of humanitarianism (Ryan, 1971). But social policies in the United States have become increasingly punitive (Wilson, 1996). The welfare law passed in 1996 ended unlimited assistance for the poor, set time limits on benefits, and turned public assistance over to the states (Associated Press, 1997). Critics of welfare reform contend that "plunking once-dependent people into jobs won't succeed in the long term if new hires lack education and skills—and the private sector cannot bear the burden of training them alone" (Associated Press, 1997, p. 5A). The persistent and disturbing signs of inequality and the high level of **distress** in the United States are inconsistent with our professed ideals and enormous wealth (Ryan, 1971). These inconsistencies create a state of tension, a dissonance (Festinger, 1957; Festinger, Schacter & Back, 1950) that must be resolved. One contradictory situation or the other must be changed to restore the balance.

An ideal, almost painless evasion, as a means of satisfying one's conscience as well as one's patriotism, is to blame the victim. Given that we cannot comfortably believe that we deliberately contrive and are the cause of that which is socially problematic, we are almost compelled to believe that they—the problematic ones—are the cause, and this immediately prompts us to search for deviance (Ryan, 1971). To blame the victim, identification of the deviance as the cause of the problem has been a simple step that ordinarily did not require the methodical collection of scientific evidence. The pathologizing of women in traditional psychology literature exemplifies how scholarly research has long participated in victim-blaming (Atkinson & Hackett, 1993, chapter 1; Fitzgerald & Nutt, 1986).

In the United States, **belief in a just world** is the tendency to view victims as the cause of their own misfortune. While this belief may maintain a sense of order and reduce fears, the failure to recognize the power of the situation is known in social psychology as the **fundamental attribution error** or bias (Gilbert & Jones, 1986; Jones, 1979; Nisbett & Ross, 1980; Ross & Nisbett, 1991). Indeed, **self-serving bias** often occurs when people invoke situational causes to justify their own conduct, minimizing traits and dispositional causes, especially in circumstances viewed negatively by others. Consequently, people living in poverty or formerly hardworking individuals who have been downsized may have to maintain their dignity just when they are likely to be told that their misfortune is caused by their own character deficits. Of course, since September 11, the just world hypothesis that all hell won't break loose at any given time has been severely rattled, if not shattered completely, for previously naïve Americans. The nearly 3,000 people who died in those terrorist attacks certainly were not the authors of their own misfortune.

In the collectivistic cultures of the East, the presumption is that situational factors play more of a role in determining behavior than in the individualistic cultures of the West (Ross & Nisbett, 1991, Chap. 7). Collectivist people may be less susceptible than individualist people to the fundamental attributional error. Immigrants to the United States from largely collectivist cultures may have a work ethic where they see themselves as less the focal point of attention in their dealings with their peers than their more individualist North American counterparts.

Disrespect for Immigrant Work Habits. A fifth reason the Protestant work ethic is outmoded is its failure to respect immigrant work habits. Politicized during the 1996 U.S.

election year when the anti-immigrant issue raised its ugly head, anti-immigrant sentiments are nothing new. For over a hundred years, U.S. constitutional law has been shaped by anti-immigrant bias rooted in racism, particularly against Asians (Koh, 1994). Sixty percent of American citizens believe that current levels of immigration are too high. The economic impact of immigrants and their effect on American culture are increasingly worrisome for the average worker. Three themes run through the modern U.S. Supreme Court's decisions regarding immigration. First, there is an obsession with sovereignty and governmental power, with the power to exclude aliens, especially those likely to become public charges (Koh, 1994, p. 74). The second theme is an unwillingness to scrutinize the immigration decisions of government officials, with no specified constitutional limitations on the power of Congress to regulate immigration. Third, there is contempt for international law and indifference to the due process and equal protection claims of foreigners seeking entry into the United States, and undocumented workers who have physically entered the country remain legally outside it, denying longtime, but unofficial, residents of the country meaningful constitutional protection.

Lipset (1990) concluded that the Protestant ethic, which has evolved into the work ethic, is not part of the lack of motivation and productivity that is seen now in the workplace. His conclusion opposes that of the American Management Association survey, which stated that the direct cause of the nation's declining productivity is the erosion of the "traditional work ethic." Lipset offers two statistics to validate his opposition: Americans are working more hours now than in the past decade, contradicting predictions of decreased productivity, and they are working out of a desire to work rather than a need (85 to 87 percent of the workforce claims they are satisfied with their jobs).

> Not everyone subscribes to the American Work Ethic. Senator Edward M.
> Kennedy recounts how, during his first campaign for the U.S. Senate, his opponent said scornfully in a debate that this man has never worked a day in his life. Kennedy says that the next morning he was shaking hands at a factory gate when one worker leaned toward him and confided, "You ain't missed a goddamned thing!" (Morrow, 1981, p. 94).

A transformed vocational psychology will allow for multiple work ethics. Socially generated narratives of the role that work takes in people's lives needs to occur. The balance between feeling pressure to work and finding meaning in life is a personal responsibility confronting each individual.

The Myth of Quality Time One way workers with families cope with workplace demands on their lives is to set aside *quality time* to spend with their spouses and children. Quality time is a legacy from the Puritans' preoccupation with improving the use of time. In *The Time Bind: When Work Becomes Home and Home Becomes Work,*

Practical Applications

Even though the Puritan work ethic included a sense of calling or vocation about one's work (Packer, 1990), a major Puritan legacy to vocational psychology and the role of work in people's lives is the secular meaning attached to "improving the time." Alarm clocks and daylight saving time are two cultural artifacts from Puritan folkways. This value placed on improving the time is seen today in attempts to schedule **quality time** into family life. Quality time is a way to compensate for work's encroachment into the familial domain. We shall address whether quality time actually improves the time.

The Virginian gentlemen farmers were the ones who lived beyond their means and who would have maxed-out their credit cards if such things had existed in those days. The need for credit/consumer counseling is hardly new. Like their later counterparts in the Deep South, behind their facade of gentility and manners, the Virginian gentleman farmers also had a vested interest in maintaining slavery, the legacy of which is enduring racism and **discrimination** against African Americans (Hacker, 1992).

We find the Quakers' philosophy to be the most attractive, and would gladly do business with them. Their notion of serving God with one's best talents is especially appealing. Employment, employment opportunities, and all that we consume and use in our everyday lives thereby become God-given gifts for which to be thankful and not taken for granted. The Quakers' integrity also draws us to them. Their scrupulousness exemplifies the kind of coworkers we want for ourselves.

The **myth of rugged individualism** is a legacy of the Backcountry people that still pervades America's work ethic. We propose that this myth be replaced with the **reality of rugged collectivism**. Men hardly settled the Backcountry one by one; they could never have settled there without the help of women. In those rare instances when plows were used in the Backcountry, it was often the wife who pulled the plow if they could not afford oxen. She used what we now call her lower center of gravity to pull the plow; her husband used his upper-body strength to steer the plow. These wives returned to fieldwork as soon as possible after childbirth, sometimes within hours of delivery. Baxandall and Gordon (1995) present an absorbing documentary of the history of working women's contributions to the founding of the United States before 1820. The authors shed light on the collective, community-based values that contributed to the settling of the frontier.

Discarding the myth of rugged individualism and recognizing the reality of rugged collectivism would go a long way toward changing the role of work in people's lives today. Expectations would be more realistic. Work environments would be healthier places. Job satisfaction would rise. Work and leisure would be better balanced. Needless stress would be eliminated. The bottom line could be achieved without downsizing and sacrificing employee wellness.

Being alert to the historical origins of White Protestant work-related behaviors in North America illuminates within-group differences through examining attitudes toward work and the use of time among the Anglo population. These days, the term **Anglo** is a gross misnomer, and its usage perpetuates racism. Less than 20 percent of the U.S. population today has British ancestry (Fischer, 1989); actually, 40 percent of the total U.S. population is of German ancestry. Regardless, the Protestant work ethic has exerted so much influence on our educational, social, political, and economic systems that it is hardly ever thought about, and its values are rarely challenged (Axelson, 1993).

Clients can trace the beginnings of their own work ethic by answering the following questions.

Questions for Examining Clients' Work Ethic

1. Can clients tell a story about the exact origins of their work ways? Of their time ways?
2. Who taught them about work ways? About time ways?
3. What explicit messages have clients received about work ways? About time ways?
4. In what context (e.g., time and place) were these messages imparted to them?
5. Are these messages useful for clients now?
6. Do they wish to retain such practices as part of their behavior?
7. What kinds of coworker conduct do clients deplore and seek to avoid? Admire and seek to emulate?
8. How would clients prefer to use their spare time? What, if anything, prevents them from using their spare time as they would like?
9. Do clients take vacations? If so, how regularly? If not, why not?
10. What are clients' opinions about charity? About welfare?
11. Have they ever received charity? Been on welfare?
12. Under what circumstances would they accept charity? Welfare?

In the interests of self-care, vocational practitioners should periodically ask themselves the questions cited above. The need to enhance one's clinical awareness makes it incumbent upon practitioners to remain alert to how their own work ethic influences their interactions with clients.

sociologist Arlie Russell Hochschild (1997) argues that long-hour work cultures have absorbed increasing amounts of family time. The underlying workplace political issue is whether workers are judged mainly on the excellence of their job performance—their **productivity**—or on their actual amount of time present in the workplace, called **face visibility**. For most employers, face visibility matters more.

Family-friendly policies that would allow for a more healthy balance between work and family by means of flex time, job sharing, unpaid paternity leave, and part-time work do not find widespread acceptance, as appealing as such policies may seem. Hochschild (1997) reviews several possible explanations for why little use is made of

Practical Applications

Former U.S. Secretary of Labor Robert Reich reflects, "Quality time? Forget it. As the father of two teenagers, I've learned that you can't 'pencil in' parenting" (1997, p. 9). His words are uncomfortably true for many. Quality time, with its origins in workplace deadlines, cycles, pauses, and interruptions, is the antithesis of **child time**. Child time is a pace that is flexible and mainly slow, and entails patiently making allowances for "over-see[ing] the laborious task of tying a [child's] shoelace, [tolerating] a [child's] prolonged sit on the potty, [and listening] to the scrambled telling of a tall tale" (Hochschild, 1997, p. 5). Many parents' expectations are thwarted when they schedule quality time, only to find one or more of their offspring peevish, grumpy, sleepy, clingy or aloof, absorbed in a television program or computer game, or preferring the company of a friend to that of their parents. When offspring are not at their best during the precious time set aside for quality relating, frustrations abound for both parent and child. Parents often make quality time mainly to attend their child's performance-based activities. "If you regard your children only as 'pride-producing machines' . . . they will measure their worth by *what they do*, not by *who they are*" (Dosick, 1995, p. 14, italics in original).

Practitioners can help clients sort through their relation to work and personal/family responsibilities. A major issue is the extent to which workers can live the values that they say are important to them as parents. Too often parents are forced by workplace politics to act against their better selves in performing their jobs (Pipher, 1996). Family and work roles are discussed more fully in Chapter 8.

these policies. First, working parents cannot afford shorter hours. Second, workers are afraid of being laid off if they work shorter hours. Third, workers are unaware of the existence of family-friendly work policies, or if they do know of such policies, workers do not know how to get them. During her three years of field research at a Fortune 500 company in the Midwest that she calls Amerco, Hochschild interviewed employees from the executive suite to the factory floor. She learned that for many, life at work was more pleasant and rewarding than life at home. The more that "work in the public realm is valued or honored, . . . the more private life is devalued and its boundaries shrink" (p. 198). Moreover, "some workers may feel more 'at home' at work . . . [because] they feel more appreciated and competent there" (p. 200). Lastly, "the takeover of the home by the workplace is certainly an unacknowledged but fundamental part of our changing cultural landscape" (p. 203).

The ensuing time bind has contributed to the myth of quality time (Hochschild, 1997). Parents who consciously or half-consciously know they are shortchanging their families and home life end up scheduling (for all intents and purposes, into their appointment books) the quality time they spend with their children. In Hochschild's field study, of the 130 Amerco employees she interviewed, one-fifth of the workers openly admitted to a pattern of neglecting family life for their work life, and one-half of the workers voiced a theme that indicated a similar type of neglect. Quality time presumes that the time workers devote to family relationships can be separated from ordinary time, with the hope that scheduling intense periods of family togetherness will compensate for lost hours devoted to work, in the belief that parent-child relationships will suffer no loss of depth. "Instead of nine hours a day with a child, [parents] declare [themselves] capable of getting the 'same result' with one more intensely focused total quality hour" (Hochschild, 1997, p. 50, quotations in original). Thus, unless a child's medical emergency forces parents to take time off from work to tend to them, many parents operationalize quality time, making a point to attend their children's performance-based activities such as sporting events or music/dance recitals. Quality time appears intended to assuage the guilt many parents feel for putting work before family.

A Postmodern Work Ethic for the Twenty-First Century

In Chapter 1 we called for a transformation of vocational psychology. Issues that confront vocational theorists and practitioners include the need to (1) become more interdisciplinary, (2) attend to external structural factors and their impact on the world of work, and (3) expand one's vision on how work affects the quality of life for diverse groups. In this chapter, we have thus far examined how values, work values, and work ethics are influenced by the present-day media, historical context, and other social and cultural trends. Vocational psychology's challenge is to keep pace with the broader cultural shift into the Information Revolution of the post industrial age.

With the unprecedented demands on work and family life, Mark L. Savickas (1993) tentatively proposes a postmodern work ethic for the twenty-first century. He is vocational psychology's leading proponent among a relatively small but growing cadre of postmodern social scientists and clinical practitioners. **Postmodernism** is an intellectual movement with its roots in art and architecture, philosophy, literature, and cultural studies. It questions and rejects the fundamental assumptions of modernism (Burr, 1995). **Modernism** is based on **logical positivism**, a twentieth-century philosophical movement that contends that all genuine knowledge can be discovered through scientific method. Thus, observation and experiment—**empiricism**—are the only valid means of adding to the knowledge base.

The world of work in the modern era was characterized by **industrialism**. Positivistic inquiry guided the rise of industries and manufactured products, particularly by the assembly line method. Job Shock and the Information Revolution, corporate downsizing, multiculturalism in the United States, and the burgeoning global

**TABLE 2.4 The Paradigm Shift from Modern
Objectivity to Postmodern Perspectivity**

MODERN	POSTMODERN
Positivism	Postmodernism
industrial age	information age
printing press	electronic media
Newtonian physics	Quantum physics
demand singular truth	appreciate multiple realities
principles	particulars
empiricism	interpretivism
objectivity	perspectivity
reason	relationships
procedural rationality	interpretive community
concepts	constructs
language reflects reality	language produces reality
definitions describe	definitions inscribe
discover meaning	invent meaning
goal—accurate	goal—useful, interesting
clients receive predefined services	clients agentic in interpreting and shaping their own lives

SOURCE: Savickas (1993), "Career Counseling in the Postmodern Era." *Journal of Cognitive Psychotherapy: An International Quarterly,*
7(3), p. 209. Reprinted by permission of Springer Publishing Company.

economy are creating a paradigmatic shift. A **paradigm** is "a central overall way of regarding phenomena . . . [and] may dictate what kind of explanation will be found acceptable" (Flew, 1984, p. 261). Within the field of vocational psychology, the paradigm shift is from modern objectivity to postmodern perspectivity (Savickas, 1993, 1995b). A proposed list of these shifts is presented in Table 2.4.

"Our society is taking a fundamental step beyond positivism, objectivistic sciences, and industrialism. The question of what we are moving toward, however, remains unanswered" (Savickas, 1993, p. 208). Postmodernism is one possible paradigm shift for vocational psychology. As Table 2.4 shows, postmodernism departs from modernism. Modernism embodies the time from the Industrial Revolution to the early twentieth century. Postmodernism embodies the Information Revolution. The printing press/print media is the major means of mass communication in modern times, the electronic media in postmodern times. Modern Newtonian physics (i.e., natural order or concrete predictability within the universe) is replaced by postmodern quantum physics (i.e., natural chaos or mathematical complexity within the universe).

Modernism demands a singular truth that is scientifically verifiable: universal principles, empiricism, objectivity, reason, and procedural rationality are used to confirm or disconfirm hypotheses. Postmodernism appreciates multiple realities that are subjectively constructed: contextual particulars, interpretivism, perspectivity, relationships, and interpretive communities create **localized knowledge**. Modernism is characterized by concepts presumed to exist independently of the knower. Postmodernism is

TABLE 2.5 Comparisons of Work Ethics

19th CENTURY VOCATIONAL ETHIC	20th CENTURY CAREER ETHIC	21st CENTURY DEVELOPMENT ETHIC
Self-employed farmers	Employed by organizations	Work in teams; craftspeople
Romantic conceptualism (Meaning in the person)	Logical positivism (Meaning in the world)	Postmodern interpretivism (Meaning in the word)
Value feelings	Value facts	Value perspectives
Be creative	Be rational	Actively participate in the community
Success through self-expression & individual effort	Success through moving up someone else's ladder	Success through cooperation & contribution

SOURCE: Savickas (1993), "Career Counseling in the Postmodern Era." *Journal of Cognitive Psychotherapy: An International Quarterly,* 7(3), p. 210. Reprinted by permission of Springer Publishing Company.

characterized by constructs intersubjectively created. Language reflects modernism's independently knowable world, and definitions describe objective reality. Language produces postmodernism's community of understanding, and definitions inscribe subjective reality. With the scientific method as the foundation of modernism, meaning is discovered and the goal is achieving accurate descriptions. With the contextual interpretation that is the hallmark of postmodernism, meaning is invented and the goal is attaining that which is socially useful, relevant, and viable. In modernist approaches to clinical practice, clients receive predefined services. In postmodern approaches to clinical practice, clients are agentic in interpreting and shaping their own lives. Agentic behavior involves action and independence (Barnett & Rivers, 1996). Client expertise plays a greater role in postmodernism than in modernism.

In summary, postmodern contextual interpretation replaces discovering truth in objective reality with understanding truth as a subjectively constructed version of reality. The scientific method sought to objectify and decontextualize phenomena and maximize explained variance by controlling for confounding variables. It is exactly these confounds that postmodern qualitative research and clinical practice seeks to particularize and contextualize. Given the changing role in people's lives, Savickas (1993) presents his twenty-first-century postmodern work ethic by comparing it with the work ethics of the nineteenth and twentieth centuries. These comparisons are presented in Table 2.5.

In Table 2.5, the nineteenth century *vocational ethic* was a secular version of the Puritan work ethic. Independent effort, self-sufficiency, frugality, self-discipline, and humility were valued. Typically, occupational choice followed family traditions like taking over the family business or staying on the family farm. To this day, craftspeople, farmers, and small business operators retain much of this vocational ethic. The vocational ethic fit with Romantic conceptualism that encouraged passion, genius, and

Practical Applications

The postmodern method of inquiry asks, "What perspective is most useful for this particular context?" (Savickas, 1993, pp. 207–208). Instead of one scientific best truth, the postmodern ethic would be based on a dialogic community where language is the primary vehicle for creating meaning in the workplace. Employees would be more proactive in drawing their own vocational path, speaking and acting for themselves, and relating the work role to other parts of their lives—relationships, children, residential environments (M. S. Richardson, 1993; Savickas, 1993). Work would no longer be separated or compartmentalized in people's lives. Subjective perspectives would take on increasing significance, and clinically speaking, one's life story would incorporate work into other facets of one's existence and life theme.

Q. What prevents an open dialogue and an exchange of ideas in the workplace?

A. Coworkers' current jealousy, past dishonesty, reputations for terri-toriality, vindictiveness, and controlling behavior.

A rule of thumb for initiating and maintaining a dialogic community is, "Keep in mind that negative connotation, or the invalidation, of any major participant is destructive to the process of opening space for conversation" (Anderson & Goolishian, 1991, p. 7). Experience has taught both of us that this is much easier said than done. Initial encounters with postmodernism can be jarring for practitioners trained in the modernist tradition. For the moment, we offer no critique of the postmodern paradigm. We first need to acquaint our readers more with postmodernism. Postmodernism is definitely an acquired taste. We explore it further in our discussion of leisure and avocational activities below. Postmodern methods of assessment are briefly considered in Chapter 3. Postmodern approaches to vocational psychology are discussed in Chapter 5. The postmodern family is presented in Chapter 8.

creativity as an outward expression of one's inner being. This idea of an inner being predates the Romantic age of the late eighteenth century and early nineteenth century and originates in ancient Greece. The apostle Paul, who was strongly influenced by Greek culture, uses the term "inmost being" (Ephesians 4:23). Modernism views the self as an autonomous, isolated being; postmodernism views the self as constructed in relationship (Becvar & Becvar, 1996).

As the United States entered the twentieth century, with the emergence of large organizations workers began having careers (Savickas, 1993). Career workers received little reinforcement for self-expression and individual effort. The challenge for working for someone else and moving up their corporate ladder replaced self-employment in small businesses and on farms. Career counseling used the scientific method to determine vocational choice. Interests, values, and abilities became objectively quantifiable entities that existed in the world "out there." A scientifically based psychometric instrument helped to discover the best fit between a person and a work environment. With this matching achieved, the question of career selection was settled. Such career counseling approaches reflected the age in which they were used. These approaches also have ancient roots, which we discuss at the end of Chapter 4. The changing spirit of the current age makes the career ethic less relevant. Given the dramatic transformations in the world of work and in the broader society and culture, vocational psychology's reliance on logical positivism as a foundation for the discipline is engendering increasing ambivalence.

MEANING IN WORK / JOB SATISFACTION

Juliet Schor observes that:

> We've lost a balanced attitude toward time. And the irony of it is that, in the end, many of the people who run around harried and frenzied end up having less time. . . . [Many writers approach this] from a psychological angle—that individuals are working too hard because of a psychological deficit (cited in an interview by Stone and Taylor, 1991, p. 43).

Although some people are unable to balance time issues, Schor notes they are relatively few. A bigger problem exists in "the competitive labor market" where employers demand long hours. People are being overworked, but not by their own choice.

Aside from being overworked by their employers, some workers find comfort in the workplace when there is conflict at home. Work has become comfortable and the worker feels alienated from the family. "Home is where the real stress is" (Barnett & Rivers, 1996, pp. 35–36). People look for happiness at work rather than face the problems waiting outside of work. When work becomes too time consuming, single people may lose personal connections and social support (Schor, cited in Stone & Taylor, 1991). Americans today work one month longer per year than they did in 1970, with more time on the job than any other industrialized country except Japan (Stone & Taylor, 1991). The corporate world believes that to remain competitive with Japan we need to work more hours. But Japan is not the only model for success. Many Western Europeans have managed to maintain their standard of living, keeping wages even and taking six weeks of vacation per year.

While the standard of living increases for those working longer hours, what is the cost? Studies indicate that possession of material things has not engendered any deeper sense of meaning and satisfaction in our lives. Schor suggests that:

if you look at all of the cases of companies that have changed their work week from forty hours to, say, thirty-eight, thirty-seven or thirty-six without reducing pay, workers are happier. They tend to show up for work on time. They don't quit as frequently. They go to the doctor on their own time. They do their work in a shorter amount of time (Stone & Taylor, 1991, p. 102).

And according to O'Toole:

in the 1950s, it was marriage; in the 1960s, it was changing the world; in the 1970s, it was career advancement; in the 1980s, it was money; in the 1990s, it's personal fulfillment—anyway you can get it. Under the new rules for defining success, anything goes, but certain themes recur. A successful life has many parts: it offers opportunities to contribute to colleagues, company and community, it has flexibility, and time for family, friends and personal interests, and it proceeds at a sustainable pace (1993, p. 49). Evidently, ideas of financial success are also shifting. A five-year study conducted at the University of California at Los Angeles Higher Education Research Institute found that the "percentage of U.S. college freshmen who consider it important to be 'very well-off financially' has dropped, while the percentage interested in 'developing a meaningful philosophy of life' has risen" (O'Toole, 1993, p. 52).

Earlier in this chapter, we explored the influence of the Protestant work ethic with one's primary concern being one's work and the view that each job had a calling. Yet the changes occurring in the workforce are causing a reevaluation of the meaning of work in people's lives. For many, the workplace has little sense of community and competition has replaced teamwork, especially in middle and upper management positions. Now that women comprise 47 percent of the workforce, they can address the meaning of work in a different manner. If a shared sense of community is important in all aspects of life, what type of paradigm shift is necessary to reintroduce interpersonal communication at work? Perhaps reframing meaning in work and shifting focus to relational activities, such as family and community involvement, form the basis for such a shift.

Lack of identification with job titles, functions, and one's role in the company mission can reduce meaning in one's work and create job dissatisfaction (Berger, 1990). Work can be satisfying, neutral, or threatening. Most jobs do not allow us to avoid pain or help us grow—two necessities for satisfaction. Employers need to be more honest with prospective workers about dealing with work without meaning, and to emphasize productivity, not face visibility.

Job Satisfaction

People graduating from college in 2001 are projected to hold an average of 11 jobs in their working lifetime (Herman, Olivio, & Gioia, 2003). They may well look at job satisfaction in a different light. Job satisfaction is not a singular term and has been de-

Practical Applications

Most people would choose to work rather than live comfortably for the rest of their lives without working, (Macoby & Terzi, 1981; Vecchio, 1980a). As the rise in the proportion of women and minorities in the workforce indicates, more people are trying to gain access to work, and the demand for paid employment of all types continues to grow.

In most of the work that people do, we find a confrontation of the individual with the organization. The results of this confrontation yield satisfaction or dissatisfaction, feelings of competence or inferiority, and motivation to be productive or work alienation. Corey and Corey (1997) present a self-inventory that practitioners may find useful when clients are dealing with issues related to meaning in work. These items are presented in Exercise 2.1.

The self-inventory in Exercise 2.1 is a useful point of departure for conversations with clients. Specific means by which clients desire to express themselves through work can be explored, expectations and beliefs regarding job longevity can be examined, and particular needs that clients seek to have fulfilled by work can be discussed.

EXERCISE 2.1 Self-inventory on Meaning in Work

Directions: Use the following scale to respond:

4 = this statement is true of me *most* of the time;
3 = this statement is true of me *much* of the time;
2 = this statement is true of me *some* of the time;
1 = this statement is true of me *almost none* of the time.

_____ 1. I wouldn't work if I didn't need the money.

_____ 2. Work is a very important means of expressing myself.

_____ 3. I expect to change jobs several times during my life.

_____ 4. A secure job is more important to me than an exciting one.

_____ 5. If I'm unhappy in my job, it's probably my fault, not the job's.

_____ 6. I expect my work to fulfill many of my needs and to be an important source of meaning in my life.

_____ 7. I want work to allow me the leisure time that I require.

SOURCE: Corey and Corey (1997), p. 139.

---

fined in many ways, with two direct components: (1) *overall satisfaction* with the entire job situation, and (2) *facet satisfaction* with certain aspects of the job. A worker can be dissatisfied with a certain part of one's job (e.g., pay, working conditions, coworkers) but have an overall sense of satisfaction. Equity theory adds other factors relevant to

---

CASE EXAMPLE

Catherine had been working for a small, private organization where decisions were made based on specified criteria, personal fairness, and equity. A change of leadership resulted in a shift in workplace "rules." Decisions at Catherine's workplace were now made based on the new leader's subjective likes and dislikes, with little regard for employees' years of experience or abilities. Sexual favoritism became part of Catherine's workplace politics. Those who did not participate in the after-hours sexual encounters had their own sexuality besmirched by the leader. For Catherine and those of her coworkers who did not take part in such office politics, job satisfaction plummeted, despite having loved their jobs. Salaries and promotions were now based on whatever the new leader deemed "competitive." The men and women who indulged the leader's sexual politics were deemed most competent. Turnover at Catherine's workplace increased as she and her coworkers who had other employment opportunities regretfully departed. Coworkers who benefited from the inequitable arrangement retained their jobs.

---

job satisfaction: personal fairness, justice, and equity (Pritchard, 1969). Equity theory relates to what is obtained versus what is desired in relation to other people. In a survey that polled 5,000 U.S. households, only 51 percent responded as being satisfied with their current jobs. Complaints often focused on low wages, loss of fringe benefits such as vacation time and child day care, and job security (Anderson, 2000).

Factors Related to Job Satisfaction Job satisfaction is directly related to nine factors:

1. prestige of the job;
2. autonomy—control over the conditions of work;
3. cohesiveness of the work group, which facilitates interaction;
4. challenge and variety of job tasks;
5. employer concern and involvement of employees in decision making;
6. wages with respect to both amount and one's perception of adequate wages compared to others performing similar tasks;
7. mobility potential of the job (workers want to feel there is potential for upward movement through the skill hierarchy, the occupational hierarchy, the organizational structure in which the work is performed, or any combination of the three);
8. satisfactory working conditions; and
9. job security (O'Toole, 1993).

People in different cultural settings vary in the way they learn problem solving and in the patterns of skills they acquire. Cultures vary in the salience attached to certain skills, in the combination of basic cognitive processes that are called upon in any given context, or in the order in which specific skills are acquired. Work will have different meanings for diverse populations.

Leisure and Avocational Activities

The cycle of all work and no play can be ameliorated by affordable leisure activities. Factors affecting leisure time include available discretionary income, time, and learning opportunities. Social, physical, intellectual, and creative activities are available that do not require much money. Some of these are joining a community theater group, tutoring or volunteering with children or older adults, enrolling in adult education classes, or organizing a volleyball team. Participating in sports, rather than being a spectator, helps relieve work stress and refocuses our work perspective.

An alternative possibility for satisfying self-expressive needs and meaning in work can occur through leisure and avocational activities. Avocational activities are pursued systematically and consecutively for their own sake; the objective is something other than monetary gain, which may incidentally occur (Super, 1976). Leisure and avocational activities can be especially rewarding when other parts of one's life are not going as smoothly as one would like. People who put all their eggs in one basket, so to speak (whether work, an intimate relationship, or parenthood) risk an imbalance that can adversely affect their well-being as well as that of people around them. Leisure is hardly goofing off. Leisure provides a respite from work responsibilities and pressures.

Practical Applications

Clients may be second-guessed by spouses, family members, and friends about spending money on avocational activities that yield no financial profit. Clients who perceive a lack of support from significant others for avocational activities may benefit from some explicit values clarification for themselves. Practitioners can also help clients to strengthen their **self-regard**—that centered, knowing sense of who one is (Pipher, 1996)—as a means of remedying any self-doubts about the worth of leisure or avocational pursuits. Clients who pursue avocations are likely to value personal growth and development. Practitioners may have to reinforce clients' desires to "explore the choices available to them in significant parts of their lives" (Corey & Corey, 1997, p. vii). They also may have to remind clients that lifelong learning via avocational pursuits is an extremely valuable skill that can be transferred back into the world of work.

Leisure can be consumed unwittingly by two habits: indiscriminant television viewing/channel surfing and regular happy hour participation.

Continued

Continued

Conversely, physical therapists tell of the springtime emergence of **weekend warriors** (usually men more than women), who engage in athletic activities while out of shape, thereby injuring knees or rotator cuffs. These weekend warriors are not using their leisure time efficiently but trying to recapture youthful self-images (whether accurate or not) that they can no longer replicate. This kind of leisure, intended as a relaxation from work, can be no fun at all. Physical limitations due to age, or injuries due to biomechanics or being out of shape, can prevent some athletic activities and require a readjustment of how leisure is spent. Practitioners working with clients' adopting realistic physical expectations may encounter clients' grief and mourning as their leisure is renegotiated. Leisure and avocation may be assessed by the questions in Exercise 2.2.

Some clients may prefer to compartmentalize their lives and keep leisure and avocational activities separate from their jobs. Their paycheck may serve to provide some of life's pleasures away from the job. Leisure and avocational activities—athletic, artistic, musical, creative—can be more enjoyable and rewarding when one has mastered them early in life. We encourage practitioners, teachers, and parents involved with young children to be mindful of the lifelong significance of this foundation setting. The quality of life and work can be enhanced by well-developed (cultivated over a period of time), respectably accomplished (a level of accomplishment that one can respect in oneself) leisure and avocational activities.

EXERCISE 2.2 Personal Reflections on Leisure and Avocation

1. How do you typically spend your leisure time?

_____

_____

2. Are there ways that you'd like to spend your leisure time differently?

_____

_____

3. What nonwork activities have made you feel creative, happy, or energetic?

_____

_____

4. Could you obtain a job that would incorporate some of the activities you've just mentioned? Or does your job already account for them?

_____

_____

5. What do you think would happen if you couldn't work? Write what first comes to mind.

_____

_____

SOURCE: Corey and Corey (1997), pp. 168–169.

CASE EXAMPLE

With support and guidance from Señor Ildefonso Ibarra, a retired gardener, his son Manuel and Roberto Cortéz González cultivate a flower garden dedicated to San Francisco de Asís (1182–1226) at a Franciscan chapel in El Paso, Texas. Daniel Carranco and his little boy Damian attend to the trees at the chapel. And sometimes Damian helps Roberto with the flower gardening. In contrast to Damian, age 5, Roberto did not begin any type of landscaping activities until he was into his 30s. For many centuries now, San Francisco de Asís has inspired many people to approach one's God through His beloved creations (Zeffirelli & Perugia, 1972). Flower gardening, in particular, is a healing activity, an ancient tradition that transcends the practical need for food (Pipher, 1996) and allows for "a powerful and unique expression of human personality" (Strong, 1992, p. 7). As part of the landscaping team, González is able to get out of the office and into the outdoors, and he is enriched on many levels by this leisure activity. Parishioners also derive pleasure from watching the flowers grow from spring through fall. Schultz (2000) writes that, when men garden, "It satisfies the urge to create a world of their own while allowing them to play with toys" (p. 4). One such toy is the hose and spray nozzle. "For lots of psychological reasons, … few gardening chores are as satisfying as … [holding] a hose in your hand, spraying a soft stream of water on your garden. It's like marking your territory" (p. 41).

Roberto Cortéz González

The Chapel of San Francisco de Asís, Montoya, El Paso, TX.

Other Contributing Factors Among the other factors contributing to the meaning of work and leisure are a person's age and socioeconomic class. Postmodernism can also provide a perspective on such meanings.

Age. Sometimes the vocational psychology literature, the popular press, and certain research findings give the impression that processes of self-understanding and finding meaning in achievement or choice are important only during the exploration or anticipation phases of youth. Efforts to help people deal successfully with such needs are most frequently available in schools and colleges, places primarily occupied by youths, rather than in settings primarily occupied by adults (Herr & Cramer, 1996). Adults who have always wanted to try something, but have not had the chance to do so until now, may need to be encouraged by practitioners, family, and friends. Other adults who have substantial work histories may begin to seek meaning in something other than occupational achievement. Values change, and *doing* becomes less important than *being.*

Socioeconomic Class. Class bias is an ever-present threat to the widespread applicability of the meaning of work and leisure. Work and achievement are the main driving forces of most middle class individuals (Payne, 1995). Much of the preceding discussion seems most relevant for such a population. People living in poverty are more apt to be driven by subsistence concerns, survival, relationships, and entertainment as a means of momentary relief from the grind of daily life (Payne, 1995; Zucchino, 1997). The wealthy are more likely to emphasize the maintenance and cultivation of financial, political, and social connections (Payne, 1995). Practitioners are reminded that a client's self-expressive needs and quest for meaning will be influenced by their socioeconomic status.

A transformed vocational psychology includes making it relevant to lower income populations. People living in poverty may espouse concrete values over abstract ones. A present-time orientation may predominate, the future existing only as a word (Payne, 1995). Emotional significance may be used to assign importance to time, not its actual measurement. Work is about making enough money to keep one's head above water. A job is not about a career. A lower-income person's worldview is reflected in the statement, "I was looking for a job when I found this one" (Payne, 1995, p. 109). Practitioners could explore meaning in work with clients for whom a job hunt matters more than career development.

Raw economic necessity may be the predominant theme for people on fixed incomes and those in the lower socioeconomic classes. Meanings of work and leisure may be qualitatively different from those of higher socioeconomic classes. Higher income and independently wealthy people may have existential concerns of another sort. CEOs whose salaries may be 200 times more than their employees (Kadlec & Baumohl, 1997; Reingold, 1997) are likely to experience unique challenges to justify their earnings.

Postmodernism. Meaning in work is imminently suitable for a postmodern vocational psychology. Multiple meanings of work and leisure can be constructed through both personal and social narratives. Narrative approaches focus on the stories clients tell about themselves and others in attempts to make sense out of the world around them (Penn, 1991; Sarbin, 1986). Personal narratives exemplified by constructivism actively construct their personal realities and create their own representational models of the world (Meichenbaum & Fong, 1993).

Social narratives typified by social constructionism view meanings and understandings of the world as developed through social interaction (Gergen, 1985). Both personal and social constructions of reality are subsumed under constructivist epistemologies (Feixas, 1990; Lyddon, 1995; R. A. Neimeyer, 1993b). Constructivist epistemologies conceptualize human beings as "active agents who, individually or collectively, co-constitute the meaning of their experiential world" (R. A. Neimeyer, 1993a, p. 222).

Postmodern meaning-making about work and leisure respects individualism and collectivism. Many possible understandings of behaviors, interactions, or events in a client's workplace would be determined by social, political, and cultural contexts. In postmodern vocational psychology, language used in stories creates meaning, with as many possible stories to tell as there would be clients (Corey, 1996).

Client stories require **narrative viability.** That is, the story has to cohere into the larger system of personally and socially constructed realities into which it is incorporated, and the consequences of the story have to be practical (Granvold, 1996). Whereas a modernist objective reality is observed and systematically known, a postmodernist subjective reality is revealed through language as a function of the situations in which people live and work.

The language process used by practitioner and client to explore meaning in work and leisure is called **discourse.** Discourse is "a system of statements, practices, and institutional structures that share common values" (Hare-Mustin, 1994, p. 19). In personal constructivist discourse, the paramount question would be one of personal consequence. In social constructionist discourse, the paramount question would be one of social consequence. Multiple discourses (i.e., the client's, the practitioner's, the client's employer, any relevant subcultures plus that of the dominant culture's) form the basis for postmodern vocational psychology.

The goal is to allow clients to find new meanings in their work and leisure, and to *restory* these meanings in a way that frees them from the mesmerizing power of the dominant culture (Doherty, 1991). Dominant socially constructed discourses can serve to oppress those not of the majority culture, perpetuate the status quo for those who have political and economic power, and marginalize those who do not share in the co-creation of currently popular and widely accepted stories (Foucault, 1970). For example, women sometimes suspend parts of themselves in the workplace when the socially constructed realities there are at variance with their personal, first-hand experience (McKenna, 1997). Practitioners need to be mindful of not buying into dominant discourses that socially construct workplace realities in a way that negate clients' personal experiences of reality. "Client stories . . . have a vital *intrapersonal* function—namely, to establish continuity of meaning in the client's lived experience" (Neimeyer, 1995a, p. 233, italics in original). The practitioner helps the client to nurture rather than suppress deeply personal narratives. First person narratives are vital to prevent the disenfranchisement of clients who encounter a discrepancy between their personal experience and what is socially constructed by others. This can be done in the form of a work autobiography.

The McDonaldization of Work

Perhaps one of the most insidious contributors to meaninglessness in work is the **McDonaldization** of the workplace. Ritzer (2000) defines McDonaldization as *"the process by which the principles of the fast-food restaurant are coming to dominate more and more sectors of American society as well as the rest of the world"* (p. 1, italics in the original). McDentists and McDoctors, for instance, refer to "drive-in clinics designed to deal quickly and efficiently with minor dental and medical problems" (p. 10). McPaper refers to *USA Today*, with news stories that often start and end on the same or next page, and colorful weather maps and graphics that allow for quick perusal—layout styles that have been adopted by the *New York Times* and the *Washington Post*. "In a world where convenience is king . . . no aspect of people's lives is immune to McDonaldization" (p. 11). The following six paragraphs are based on Ritzer's work.

McDonaldization consists of four dimensions: (1) Efficiency, or economy of motion for getting from one point to another in a predesigned process; (2) Calculability, or quantity over quality; (3) Predictability, or the assurance of a world with few surprises where products and services are the same all the time, everywhere; and (4) Control, or training employees "to do a limited number of things in precisely the way they are told do them" (p. 14).

Throughout society, efficiency is a major attraction—microwavable meals, 10-item limit express lines in supermarkets, cyber shopping, credit cards, publisher-provided test banks for college and university professors, audio books, *Reader's Digest*, salad bars, ticketless air travel, and automated teller machines. Furthermore, efficiency is usually organized for the interests of the companies that institute them, not the consumers who partake of their services and products. In the workplace, efficiency manifests itself in the classic time-and-motion studies that clock the most streamlined way to perform a job task with the most productive results.

Calculability, the second dimension of McDonaldization, helps to measure efficiency and has been greatly enhanced by the modern computer. In one workplace example, profit-making medical corporations pressure physicians to limit time with each patient and to maximize the number of patients seen in a day, thus enabling the corporation to reduce costs and increase profits. Doctors are pressed to view patients as dollar signs, not as individuals. The emphasis is on quantification rather than quality of care. Public school teachers also face pressure to quantify, in this case their students' learning, because standardized assessment of achieve tests loom.

Predictability "emphasizes discipline, order, systematization, formalization, routine, consistency, and methodological operation" (p. 83). In the workplace, predictability most often shows up as "effortless, mindless, repetitive work" (p. 83). Scripted inter-actions with customers are done by fast-food workers and telemarketers. Assembly-line work is also predictable.

McDonaldization's fourth and last dimension is control. In the workplace, control entails employees following prescribed steps to perform their jobs. "[H]uman skills, abilities, and knowledge [are transformed] into a set of nonhuman rules, regulations, and formulas" (p. 110). Minimal intelligence and ability are seen as most desirable for repetitive labor where control is paramount.

There's a downside to McDonaldization for workers. Efficiency robs them of in-centive for taking the initiative and being innovative on the job. Calculability prevents workers from putting that personal touch into their work and from feeling satisfac-tion in a job well done. Predictability can make work become a mind-numbing rou-tine. Control can be dehumanizing and stifle employees' intrinsic motivation. The pervasiveness of McDonaldization may be offset, in part, by a growing interest in spirituality and the stirring of the soul in work.

THE CONNECTION BETWEEN SPIRITUALITY AND WORK

There has been an increasing interest in creating personal and spiritual balance, par-ticularly as it applies to career development. Savickas (cited in Bloch and Richmond, 1997) formulates concepts of **spirit** as "*the activating force or essential principle that helps to give life to physical organisms*" (p. 4; italics in the original). He further suggests that this movement is directional from where a person is to where he/she wants to be. Savickas notes that Miller-Tiedeman calls this movement career. "To have the spiritual courage to move forward . . . defines mental health. . . . In psychodiagnostic terms, stalled or hesitant movement can be called *neurosis*. Moving away from people can be called *psychosis*, and moving against people can be called *psychopathy* [psycho-pathology]" (p. 4-5). He further posits that to practice career counseling in only a rational manner, such as using theory, traits, and interests, is to ignore the spiritual dimension that is more essential to the person's movement toward fulfillment.

Bloch (1997) suggests "a person cannot feel simultaneously with the world and stuck with a meaningless job" (p.187). She further observes that meaningfulness of-ten comes from a sense of harmony with one's self and others with whom one works. Stillness and meditation can be used to focus one's mind on goal setting, work performance, and other aspects of career and life decisions. She describes an exercise in beginning mindfulness (p. 195–196) and one on intentionality (p. 203–204).

"The seat of the soul is there where the inner world and the outer world meet; where they overlap, it is in every point of the overlap" (Cousineau, cited in Briskin [1996], p. 247). Briskin states that "[c]aring for the soul asks us to look below and through the visible world in order to see what truly matters" (p. 265). The challenge of our times is being able to adapt to a world that ignores soul. Each individual soul needs to be nurtured—a world of souls uncared for turns angry. Briskin suggests the question to ask regarding the care of the soul is "Where do I start to heal the wounds that surround me and that are in me?" (p. 268).

Because the workplace is becoming increasingly diverse, it would help if practitioners encouraged students/clients to explore their own work values and work ethic so they can better understand how to deal with coworkers who may not have the same commitment to values and ethics. The next chapter expands on the role of the counselor/vocational practitioner and incorporates ethical considerations.

SUMMARY

Values are defined with ideas on the construction of values. Work values in particular are described, with considerations of individualism versus collectivism. Examples of work ethics that have been problematic in the past decade are discussed. The development of the work ethic in the United States is described with antecedents and outcomes. A postmodern work ethic is proposed.

Meaning at work and job satisfaction are basic considerations for practitioners of vocational counseling. Leisure time and avocational activities are considerations that are addressed. Finally, a perspective on the relationship of spirit and work is proposed.

3

❖❖

Perspectives on the
Career Counselor's Role:
Present and Past

The vocational practitioner/career counselor role frequently has been misunderstood. Graduate students often perceive it as helping a client find a job, a task that seems less important than dealing with emotional and mental health. Allied health professionals sometimes have this same misconception. But, as Krumboltz and Vidalakis (2000) write:

> The counselor's job is not just matching the existing client to an existing job. The counselor's job is to teach clients how to take effective actions to improve their situations. The client's job is to engage in this learning effort. The client-counselor contract can be stated in terms of learning outcomes, not just matching outcomes (p. 317).

Notice how Krumboltz and Vidalakis use the term *counselor,* not *career counselor.* This brings us to the main point we wish to get across here. Vocational psychology is a major specialty within counseling psychology. We believe it's impossible to separate work and vocational concerns from personal identity issues, emotional concerns, family interactions, and social well-being. As such, this chapter is separated into four sections. First, we identify specific roles and competencies for professional practice and career counseling. Second, we provide suggestions for evaluating counselor effectiveness and career programs. Third, we discuss assessment in vocational psychology and career counseling. Fourth and finally, we examine the historical antecedents to vocational psychology.

PROFESSIONAL PRACTICE AND CAREER COUNSELING

Standards and goals for career counseling are found in a publication by the **National Career Development Association (NCDA)**, *The Professional Practice of Career Counseling and Consultation: A Resource Guide,* second edition (1994) edited by Dennis Engels. The following information is reproduced by permission of the NCDA.

Roles of the Career Counselor

Services of career counselors differ depending on the counselor's level of competence, the setting, and the clientele. Professional career counselors, career facilitators, and several other types of clinical practitioners help clients to make and carry out decisions and plans related to both lifestyle and career directions. Practitioner strategies and techniques are tailored to the specific work-related needs of the client. Career counselors do one or more of the following:

1. Conduct individual and group personal counseling sessions to help clarify life/career goals
2. Administer and interpret tests and inventories to assess abilities, interests, and other factors, and to identify career options
3. Encourage exploratory activities through assignments and planning exercises
4. Utilize career planning systems and occupational information systems to help individuals better understand the world of work
5. Provide opportunities for improving decision-making skills
6. Assist in developing individualized career plans
7. Teach job hunting strategies and skills and assist in the development of resumés
8. Help resolve potential personal conflicts on the job through practice in human relations skills
9. Assist in understanding the integration of work and other life roles
10. Provide support for people experiencing job stress, job loss, and career transition (Engels, 1994, p. 21)

These services are available to students from K–12, colleges/universities, and adults in the community. The vocational practitioner/career counselor can also be in private practice.

Ethical Responsibilities

Career development professionals must only perform activities for which they

> possess or have access to the necessary skills and resources for giving the kind of help that is needed. . . . If a professional does not have the appropriate train-

ing or resources for the type of career concern presented, an appropriate referral must be made. No person should attempt to use skills . . . for which he/she has not been trained (Engels, 1994, p. 14).

The National Career Development Association Ethical Standards are presented in Appendix 2.

Career Development Specialties

There are several areas of specialization in career development. These are:

1. *Career counselors* (private and public settings) who possess basic skills in career counseling, consultation, program development, and program evaluation. They may also provide services through the Internet, which may allow for a wider diversity of clients.

2. *Human resource, career development, and employee assistance specialists* (in-house organizational setting or contract services) that participate in individual and group career counseling as well as design and implement programs for employee development and career management.

3. *Career and employment search consultants/outplacement specialists* (private or corporate setting) who offer job search assistance for clients who have been displaced or permanently laid off and need career direction.

4. *Cooperative education instructors* (educational setting) who obtain supervised work experience that is consistent with the curricular activities, needs, and abilities of students.

5. *Career and executive coaching specialists* who can provide services to clients all over the world either by phone or Internet.

6. *Job placement specialists* (public setting) develop effective working relationships with employers, including outplacement services.

7. *School counselors, community college and college counselors, and counselors in postsecondary technical institutes* develop and implement developmental career counseling programs based on models such as the National Career Development Guidelines and **American School Counselor Association (ASCA)** Standards (1997).

Resources for specialty areas include Bench's "Career coaching: The new methodology for maximizing personal fulfillment and human capital" (2001); Boer's *Career Counseling over the Internet: An Emerging Model for Trusting and Responding to Online Clients* (2001); Harris-Bowlsbey and colleagues' *The Internet: A Tool for Career Planning,* 2nd ed. (2002); Montross and colleagues' *Career Coaching for Kids* (1997); Splete and Hopping's "The emergence of career development facilitators" (2000); and Stratford's *Executive Coaching* (2000).

Career Counselor Training and Credentials

Credentials for counselors offered through the National Career Development Association include Master Career Counselor (MCC) and Master Career Development Professional (MCDP). These have been offered since 2001. Minimal credentials include the following:

1. Master Career Counselor (MCC):
   - Two-year membership in NCDA (either professional or regular membership).
   - Master's degree or higher in counseling or closely related field from a college or university that was accredited by one of the regional accrediting bodies recognized by the Council on Post-Secondary Accreditation when the degree was awarded.
   - Three years of post-master's experience in career counseling.
   - Possess and maintain the NCC, state LPCC, RPCC, or licensed psychologist credential.
   - Successfully completed at least three credits of coursework in each of the six NCDA Competency areas (Career Development Theory, Individual/Group Counseling Skills, Individual/Group Assessment, Information/Resources, Diverse Populations, Ethical/Legal Issues).
   - Successfully completed supervised career counseling practicum or two years of supervised career counseling work experience under a certified supervisor or licensed counseling professional.
   - Document that at least half of the current full-time work activities are directly career counseling related.

2. Master Career Development Professional (MCDP):
   - Two-year membership in NCDA (either professional or regular membership).
   - Master's degree or higher in counseling or closely related field.
   - Three years of post-master's career development experience in training, teaching, program development, or materials development.
   - Document that at least half of the current full-time work activities are directly career development related.

The NCDA also offers a credential, the Global Career Development Facilitator (GCDF), for paraprofessionals who work under the supervision of a career counselor. For further information, check the Web site www.ncda.org. Click on link to GCDF or Career Masters Institute for all Career Counselors (www.cminstitute.com). Counselors who meet the following criteria can become GCDF instructors:

1. Earned a graduate degree in counseling or a related professional field from a regionally accredited higher education institution.
2. Completed supervised counseling which included career counseling.

3. Acquired a minimum of three years of full-time career development work experience.

4. Successfully completed the training for GCDF instructor.

Considerations for Practitioner Training

The preparation of professional counselors, counselor educators, and student affairs professionals for the Council for Accreditation of Counseling and Related Educational Programs (CACREP) standards must meet the following criteria. Entry-level degree programs accepted for review will have a minimum of 72 quarter hours or 48 semester hours of graduate studies. Mental health, marital, couple, and family counseling will have a minimum of 90 quarter hours or 60 semester hours of graduate studies. The common core curricular experiences include the following areas:

1. Professional Identity

2. Social and Cultural Diversity

3. Human Growth and Development

4. Career Development

5. Helping Relationships

6. Group Work

7. Assessment

8. Research and Program Evaluation

A working paper entitled "Preparing Counselors for Career Development in the New Millennium," part of the work of a joint commission representing the Association for Counselor Education and Supervision (ACES) and NCDA, states counselor educators need to:

- Understand that career development is a process learned throughout a person's life; that it needs to be taught from a developmental perspective, helping counseling students see that career development is lifelong, starting with life/work duties at home and progressing though the multiple life/work roles encountered and experienced over the life span.

- Assure that the preparation program facilitates the trainees' own career development and understands and appreciates the values, goals, and abilities of their students as they progress through it.

- Help trainees understand the core nature of career issues in people's lives and expose them to both traditional and contemporary theories of career development and models of career decision making.

- Incorporate global career issues into training programs, recognizing that with our mobile, global societies, cross-cultural perspectives need to be integrated (Bemak & Hanna, 1998).

- Make cultural sensitivity and multicultural career counseling integral parts of the curriculum, including diversity of race, ethnicity, gender, socioeconomic class, disability, sexual orientation, age, beliefs, and geographic origin.

- Assist students to understand the contextual (not just intrapsychic) influences in career counseling and the meaning of these for clients (Fassinger, 1998).

- Provide ongoing feedback to students on their career development and career counseling awareness, knowledge, and skills so they may grow and change.

- Use technology in a variety of ways, teaching students how to evaluate and use information systems and the appropriate use of information in career counseling. Also, give appropriate attention to the potential promise and possible ethical issues of the Internet in career counseling and career development, e.g., strategies such as "Career as Story," "Mapping," "Integrative Thinking," "Sophie's Choice: A Values Sorting Activity," and "Career Checkup" (Pope & Minor, 2000).

According to a study that surveyed 290 counseling psychology graduates from twelve counseling psychology training programs (Heppner, O'Brien, Hinkelman, & Flores, 1996), "[r]esults indicate that trainees' most negative experiences were disparaging remarks about career counseling from faculty and supervisors and their formal course work in career development. Conversely, trainees reported that the most positive influences on their attitudes were experiences obtained by working with career clients" (p. 105). Perceived emphasis in counseling training was on "social-emotional counseling," rather than career/vocational counseling.

"The question of how some trainees received degrees from intensive graduate programs in counseling psychology without gaining interest or sufficient skills in career counseling is a critical one" (p. 119). Many students indicated that the quality of the vocational psychology training was a greater problem than the amounts of course work available. Students lacked understanding of how career counseling activities affected their view of the field. The most negative influence came from faculty and supervisors. One student said "her vocational psychology teacher express[ed] her boredom with the topic at each class session, or in more subtle ways, such as being ill-prepared or presenting boring lectures in career development classes" (p. 120). On the other hand, trainees noted their excitement in working with supervisors who had a passion for career/work issues and integrated personal and career counseling in an effective manner. Trainees found positive changes in the lives of their "social-emotional" clients' mental health when occupational concerns were addressed.

Thus the call for more interesting, up-to-date courses in career theories, development, and application. Faculty must clearly model the integration of career and non-career aspects of individual's lives in their career counseling and present information to integrate career and family issues (Swanson, 2002). For example, a career counseling practicum can produce changes in conceptualizing work-related issues in clinical practice. Supervisees can gain understanding about (1) international cultural differences, (2) relating career issues to a counseling theory basis, (3) demystifying career counseling, (4) moving from psychopathology to developmental concerns, (5) working with group process in a classroom or career center, and (6) integration of personal/career information through use of assessments and technology (Warnke et al., 1993). Swanson (2002) further suggests that:

> It is helpful to remember the two directions of integrating these issues. Within supervision of "career" counseling, it is important to keep in mind that clients may raise noncareer issues that are (a) clearly related to their career issues, (b) tangential but relevant to their career issues, or (c) clearly unrelated to their career issues. This perspective is consonant with the new paradigm shift to viewing vocational topics as primary issues as well as contextual factors, depending on the client, the setting, and temporal consideration (p. 828).

A career assessment schema has been developed by Busacca (2002) to assist counselor trainees with a systematic approach to conceptualizing a client's career problem. The assessment encompasses two conceptual domains, which are the interpersonal and the intrapersonal, and three developmental levels. These domains and levels constitute six career service areas: career guidance, career placement, career education, career counseling, career development, and career adjustment. Goals, theories, and outcome measures are described.

Another concept being introduced in the career education literature is that of infusion. Many graduate training programs have infused cultural/diversity/gender issues across the whole curriculum as well as ethics and professional development. We propose the infusion of career/work issues across the curriculum.

Another development is the call for "The Reintegration of Vocational Psychology and Counseling Psychology" by Robitschek and DeBell (2002), who propose that the renewed growth in vocational psychology emphasizes the need for counseling psychology to rediscover a major part of its roots by extending its training to re-include vocational considerations as an integral part of all counseling psychology training programs.

Vocational psychology has been a leader in understanding how work and career are affected by cultural and ethnic values. Our emphasis on the role of work in people's lives is a response to calls for a more complete understanding of what work means in the context of our lives. It constitutes a major portion of our time in adult years and, for many people, is integral to identity development. Consequently, the need for counselors to deal with the whole person has to include the role of work, the relationship of job situations to life stories, personal difficulties, and perspectives on social and emotional well-being.

Career counseling is changing because of the exponential growth of Internet resources. In resources listed earlier were two books on using the Internet as a tool for career planning. Harris-Bowlsbey et al. (2002) provide a very thorough list of Web sites available, a guide to ways to use them, and a thorough discussion of potential problems, ethical issues, integration of standard counseling practices, cybercounseling, and computer-based career planning using the Internet. The fact that these books are available emphasizes the need for computer literacy in career counseling.

COUNSELOR AND PROGRAM EVALUATION

Evaluating career counseling is difficult. An experimental approach is not possible for ethical reasons, and clarity and agreement on the outcomes of the counselor's work are difficult to define (Kellett, 1994). Evaluation is usually overlooked in counselor training, and there is little agreement on the instruments to evaluate outcomes.

> In the absence of some definitive information on the contribution that career and employment counseling can make and [are] making, there is a real danger that counseling, which is not now well integrated with other career and employment programming, will be pushed further to the side, with even less resources given to it (p. 351).

In career and employment counseling circles, program evaluation is an effectiveness and accountability issue. Although counselors frequently lament that they are vulnerable in the face of growing accountability concerns and often approach program evaluation with a negative attitude, they do not view evaluation as a solution. An evaluation course is only an optional part of many training programs. Counselors rarely evaluate their programs and services. They acknowledge that accountability is important, but few models exist for helping them. Most counselors report receiving an annual performance appraisal; however, little firsthand observation of their work with clients is conducted (Conger, Hiebert, & Hong-Farrell, 1993) and rarely are clients asked to give feedback regarding the services.

An evaluation framework is needed that is user-friendly, provides both formative and summative evaluation, and offers counselor feedback regarding their interactions with clients (Hiebert, 1994). **Formative evaluation** refers to program evaluation activities that are conducted during the course of a program. **Summative evaluation** refers to program evaluation activities that are conducted at the end of a program. Both types can be conducted on a given program. Formative evaluation is somewhat more flexible in that adjustments and corrections can be made to evaluation procedures during their ongoing activities.

If a program review is conducted, often clients are not consulted on the process. Counselors report feeling that the attention and administration of time given to program review, evaluation, and improvement is inadequate. But recognition of these concerns does not provide sufficient incentive to change them. A framework is necessary that includes outcome and process as equal partners in the counseling enterprise (Hiebert, 1994). Process without outcome is not counseling any more than is outcome without process. When counseling is successful, counselor and client processes lead to client-learning outcomes. These learning outcomes will impact motivation, self-awareness, capacity for self-direction, personal agency, and other skills necessary for the global changes.

If counseling is to survive reduced resources and increased accountability, a new approach to the role of evaluation needs to be developed. An attempt to evaluate career and employment counseling must begin with the question: What are the legitimate processes and outcomes of counseling? When is career counseling effective, with whom, under what conditions, and on which outcome dimensions?

Another approach to evaluation is a study of cost benefits as an indicator of effectiveness. This requires a different mind-set for most vocational counselors and is complicated to achieve. However, "if the economic benefits to individuals or to society exceed the cost of career guidance or career counseling one can argue that counselors are generators of resources, not simply consumers of them" (Herr & Cramer, 1996, p. 712). Although there is an expectation that counseling should produce results that have a direct socioeconomic impact, often the more legitimate outcomes of counseling are the learning outcomes (Kileen & Kidd, 1991; Kileen, White, & Watts, 1993). For instance, when a client has learned effective coping skills regarding financial challenges, family conflict, and lack of support, counseling should be considered successful, even if the immediate result is not job placement.

In his 1994 article, Flynn discusses approaches to the evaluation of the effectiveness of career counseling. He cites the work of Fretz (1981); Kirschner, Hoffman, and Hill (1994); Nevo (1990); and Spokane (1991), among others, as resources for implementing evaluative processes. Through the interchange with a counselor, a client ideally learns about him/herself, discovers information about jobs and occupations, builds a network of social support, and receives feedback and positive reinforcement. Understanding how personal dynamics can interfere with career decisions is important.

Flynn summarizes Spokane's (1991) hypotheses about the nature of the career counseling process and the reasons why clients appear to benefit in important ways.

1. The career counseling process can be validly represented by a model composed of three states (beginning, activation, and termination) and eight subphases (opening, aspiring, loosening, assessment, inquiry, commitment, execution, and follow-through).

2. Each substage of the process involves a key therapeutic task, a counselor process and technique needed to achieve the task, and an expected client reaction to its successful completion.

3. Before career counseling intervention can begin, clients need to clarify (with the help of the counselor) the nature of the decisions and conflicts they face.

4. Effective career counseling instills a sense of hope in the client that a reasonably congruent career option will be found and implemented (p. 275).

These processes can provide the basis for the development of an evaluation model of career counseling, and the authors cited above give a variety of ideas for developing evaluation procedures.

Individual Career Counselor Evaluation

Loosely based on Appendix L: Descriptors Related to Evaluation Categories in Gysbers & Henderson (2000), we propose that individual counselors be evaluated or evaluate themselves using the following areas.

1. *Careful planning of sessions:* The career counselor has prepared an approach that will be used for individual clients. The plan should have the flexibility to allow for individual differences, needs, situation, and personality considerations. A variety of techniques and potential materials must be at the counselor's disposal.

2. *Presentation of accurate, relevant, unbiased information:* This includes the presentation of information at a level appropriate to the client—vocabulary, amount, and clarity. Important points are clear, and misunderstandings are clarified. The information is selected carefully, with referral to appropriate sources and systems. The counselor is aware of educational and career alternatives and their value.

3. *Appropriate and accurate use of tests, if necessary and helpful:* The appropriateness of the test(s) used, a fair and accurate administration and interpretation of results, and clear guidance on how to use the test results is imperative. This is based on the supposition that the career counselor is aware of the meaning of scores and the limitations of test results and has the ability to present results in a meaningful and helpful manner.

4. *Selection of appropriate tasks for the client that will be helpful in the discovery of career possibilities and how to formulate and achieve goals:* Research that is carefully guided, the use of computer guidance systems, the Internet, and other sources of information are given carefully. Contacts with others that can be helpful and provide information and/or reinforcement are important.

5. *Developing awareness of client's potential and proven strengths as well as areas and issues that can be problematic:* These factors provide important information for a client in the career development process. Building problem-solving skills and using client competencies are part of appropriate counseling techniques.

6. *Use of appropriate consulting and referral skills:* Guiding clients to other people who can potentially help them is important.

7. *Follow-up activities:* The ability to design activities that help the client find success is important for the counselor to achieve.

Developing an evaluation sheet that is part of each client's folder provides an incentive for the career counselor to keep his/her skills current and adaptable.

Approaches to Evaluation Using Existing Models

Evaluation models developed in schools have broad application to vocational counseling. Counselors and counselor educators can use the subject matter (Gysbers, Hughey, Starr, & Lapan, 1992) of comprehensive guidance programs to develop practical means of gathering such needed outcome data. They can also develop evaluation scales that are easy to use and link student-perceived mastery of both career and personal guidance competencies to critical educational outcomes (Multon & Lapan, 1995).

Competencies and Indicators

Competencies and indicators form a Texas model called the *Texas Evaluation Model for Professional School Counselors* (TEMPSC) (1991). TEMPSC evaluates school counselors' performances based on the seven core roles and competencies described in Texas Counseling Association's job description for the professional school counselor: program management, guidance, counseling, consultation, coordination, assessment, and professionalism. Each *role* on the TEMPSC Performance Evaluation Form is described by *competencies,* competencies are described by *indicators,* and indicators are detailed by *descriptors.* The seven roles and role sublevels described in the TEMPSC are not all equally applicable to every counselor.

If a guidance director wanted to develop a program and get specific feedback on the performances of the counselors in a certain role, there are particular subscales that can be used to address that area. Much of the information here can be applied to outcomes for all vocational counselors. Examples of TEMPSC roles for guidance, counseling, and assessment—their competencies, indicators, and descriptors—follow:

ROLE: GUIDANCE

Competency 2.3: Guides individuals and groups of students through the development of educational and career plans

Indicator 2.31: Involves students in personalized educational and career planning.

DESCRIPTORS:
  Helps students establish goals and planning skills
  Assists students in determining their abilities, achievements, interests, and goals
  Makes effective use of consultation skills as needed in the guidance process

Encourages parental input into student planning

Interprets tests results to students in a meaningful manner allowing them to focus on their strengths and improve on their weaknesses

Guides groups of students in the application of their test results to their educational and career plans

Correctly assesses student's educational and career aspirations and information needs

Makes recommendations based on appropriate criteria

Uses appropriately sized groups

Indicator 2.32: Presents relevant information accurately and without bias.

DESCRIPTORS:

Makes no significant errors

Presents information so that students can process/internalize it

Uses vocabulary appropriate to the students

Explains content clearly

Presents appropriate amounts of information

Stresses important points

Clarifies students' misunderstanding

Uses accurate terminology

Makes up-to-date educational and occupational information resources available/ accessible to students

Uses materials effectively

Is knowledgeable about the range of education and career alternatives and the values of each (p. 17)

ROLE: COUNSELING

Competency 3.1: Counsels individual students with presenting needs/concerns

Indicator 3.11: Provides counseling systematically.

DESCRIPTORS:

Responds appropriately to students at their maturity levels in kindergarten through the twelfth grade

Responds to the identified needs of students, such as but not limited to career and educational development issues (p.18)

ROLE: ASSESSMENT

Competency 6.2: Interprets test and other appraisal results appropriately

Indicator 6.23: Interprets tests and other appraisal results to students and their parents.

DESCRIPTORS:

Interprets tests and other appraisal results to students in a meaningful manner, assisting them to focus on their strengths and improve upon their weaknesses

Interprets test and other appraisal results to parents, assisting them to better understand their student's scholastic abilities, achievement, aptitude, interests, and career development (p. 24)

The Missouri Comprehensive Guidance Program (MCGP) is based on three content domains: (1) knowledge of self and others, (2) career planning and exploration, and (3) educational and vocational development. In this program, counselor duties should include:

- implementing curriculum
- counseling individuals and groups with respect to educational and career plans
- consulting with teachers and parents
- referring students to appropriate agencies
- coordinating, conducting, and being involved with activities that improve the operation of the school
- evaluating and revising the guidance program
- continuing professional growth (Gysbers et al., 1992).

A schematic presentation of this evaluation program, which contains both formative and summative evaluation, is presented in Table 3.1.

Focus Groups Bloch (1992) proposes a model for using focus groups to evaluate career development programs. Focus groups provide the opportunity to appraise the knowledge and experiences of a variety of people with a common interest. Through carefully structured questions, materials, and planned interactions within the group, a focused situation is created to yield the desired information in a relatively short period of time. Career Information System of Iowa (CISI) uses focus groups to evaluate the system's effectiveness for the various populations who use it.

Advantages of focus groups include expediency, because within one session opinions can be gathered from a variety of people; cost effectiveness; and group interaction processes (e.g., brainstorming, role-playing, image projection). Focus groups can be used in a variety of settings. They are helpful for program evaluation, modification, planning, and development (Bloch, 1992). However, a focus group cannot replace quantitative studies.

Table 3.1 Personnel Job Description, Supervision, and Evaluation Procedures

PERSONNEL

Job Description	*Performance-Based Evaluation*	
Guidance Curriculum	Formative evaluation	Summative evaluation
Individual Planning	(following observations)	(synthesis of formative
Response Services		evaluation)
Systems Support		
Professional and Interpersonal		
Relationships		
Professional Responsibilities		

Guidance Curriculum

Individual Planning

Response Services

Systems Support

Professional and Interpersonal

Relationships

Professional Responsibilities

SOURCE: Reprinted from Gysbers et al. (1992), p. 568. Copyright 1992 by the American Counseling Association. No further reproduction authorized without written permission of the American Counseling Association.

Performance Assessment Another way to evaluate programs is performance assessment. "In performance assessments, students are active participants, creating answers, products, and performances to demonstrate what they have learned. Performance assessment tasks are often based on real-world problems" (Hutchinson, 1995, p. 3). Techniques include group projects, interviews, demonstrations, role-plays, and portfolios. One constructivist model of performance assessment, Pathways, consists of five modules:

1. "Knowing about Yourself, Knowing about Careers"

2. "Succeeding with the Résumé and the Application"

3. "Succeeding with the Interview"

4. "Solving Problems on the Job"

5. "Anger Management on the Job" (Hutchinson, 1995, p. 4)

The American School Counselors Association portfolio system uses a performance assessment, "Get a Life: Your Personal Planning Profile," and contains sections on self-knowledge, life roles, educational development, and career exploration. In performance assessments, students are motivated; teachers are more accountable to students for teaching concepts and skills that are transferable to the real world; and teachers and counselors gain current information about what students are learning in the classroom. However, performance assessments have never shown that students generalize concepts to more global outcomes.

While many of the evaluation programs cited have come from schools, they provide the seeds that vocational counselors can use in any setting to evaluate their work. More research needs to be done to develop outcome studies and evaluation of the process in which the individual counselor and the client participate.

ASSESSMENT IN CAREER COUNSELING

Assessment has a long-established tradition in career counseling and vocational psychology. Students and practitioners need to be aware of the uses and abuses of assessment, but a complete discussion of assessment procedures is beyond the scope of our text. However, Kaplan and Saccuzzo's *Psychological Testing* (2001) is a well-written, comprehensive source for further discussion of these procedures. Another valuable resource is the **Code of Fair Testing Practices in Education** (1988) (see Appendix 1), written to be understood by the general public, especially test takers and/or their parents or guardians. An overview of the basic principles of assessment is presented, with relevance to multicultural and diverse populations.

Basic Principles

Assessment refers to a procedure used to evaluate an individual in terms of current and future functioning (Kaplan & Saccuzzo, 2001). The general public, as well as graduate students studying to become clinical practitioners, often confuse the terms *assessment* and *testing*. Tests are one of the specific tools of the overall assessment procedure. **Tests** are measurement instruments that quantify behavior, and are sometimes called an **assessment tool.** A **test battery** is a collection of tests whose scores are used together in appraising an individual.

Tests and inventories can serve a number of functions in career counseling. Tests can motivate people by exploring previously unconsidered career options; but tests can limit, as well, by discouraging lower-income minorities from pursuing academic areas that appear out of their reach or by indicating that women are best suited for traditional careers. Interpretation of test results requires that the counselor possess a thorough knowledge of the test, including its psychometric properties, the clinical background to understand the test-taking client, and the ability to communicate test results in a straightforward, understandable fashion.

Assessment instruments are being used to a greater extent, and the number of books published on the role of testing in counseling has also increased. *The Journal of Career Assessment* is devoted solely to the topic. *A Counselor's Guide to Career Assessment Instruments*, Kapes, Mastie, and Whitfield (2002), is in its fourth edition. Each of these books is a valuable resource for career counselors, providing the opportunity to keep abreast of new findings, developments, and instruments. A plethora of instruments are now available, with new ones being developed annually. Not all assessment procedures are tests. Postmodern techniques may use a standard set of questions, but results are not based on any standard scoring procedure, rather on the meaning of the individual's responses. Strictly speaking, an assessment device is a test when its procedures for administration, scoring, and interpretation are standardized.

Test Administration   The act of giving a test (Kaplan & Saccuzzo, 2001) and the procedures surrounding the giving of a test constitute **test administration**. The test administrator is the person who gives the test and must be qualified. A graduate student obtaining supervision at a practicum and/or internship site should have, at the very least, relevant course work and an on-site supervisor qualified to administer any tests that the supervisee is expected to administer. A supervisee, much less a clinical practitioner, has no business administering any test for which they have not received adequate educational training, practice, and supervision. The prioritizing of politics and economics over ethics when it comes to clinical practice and client welfare is simply insupportable. These ethical issues are discussed further in the *Standards for Educational and Psychological Testing* (1985), by the joint committee of the American Education Research Association, the American Psychological Association, and the National Council on Measurement in Education.

Basic to standardized psychological testing is the concept of central tendency. Represented by the bell curve, this theory proposes that the scores of tests will occur most commonly in the middle range. For example, if we were to measure depression across the population of the United States, we would use a **standardization sample** (also known as a **normative sample**) consisting of individuals who have been administered a test under standard conditions as a comparison group. The instructions, format, and general procedures are usually outlined in the test manual so there is **standardized administration** of a test. The sample is theoretically representative of the whole population, allowing us to infer that the test results can be applied to all.

A **norm-referenced test** evaluates each individual relative to a normative group (Kaplan & Saccuzzo, 2001) or standardization sample. **Norms** summarize the performance of a group of individuals on which a test was standardized, and usually include the **mean** and **standard deviation** for a reference group and information on how to translate a raw score into a percentile rank. (A mean is the arithmetic average of a set of scores on a variable. A standard deviation is the square root of the average deviation around the mean and is used as a measure of variability in a distribution of scores.) The standard deviation squared equals the **variance.**

The concept of central tendency allows that the approximate percentage of scores that range from one standard deviation below the mean to one standard deviation above the mean is 68 percent. That group of scores is what we state are *within normal limits,* in a simplistic manner becoming what is described as *the norm.* Not all tests are based on this concept, which is why it is important to know the test, the reason for its use, and the limitations on what a test score indicates. A major potential problem with testing is stretching an interpretation beyond what the instrument is designed to indicate.

Types of Tests An **individual test** can be given to only one person at a time by a test administrator; **group tests** can be given to more than one person at a time (Kaplan & Saccuzzo, 2001). **Percentile ranks** refer to the proportion of scores that meet or fall below a particular score. **Ability tests** "measure skills in terms of speed, accuracy, or both" (p. 11). When taking an ability test, faster or more accurate responses mean a better score on a particular characteristic. For example, on a Scholastic Aptitude Test (SAT) or Graduate Record Examination (GRE), the more mathematics problems one can solve in the amount of time allotted on such subtests, the higher one's score on the ability to solve such problems. However, to suggest that either of these tests is an indication of intelligence or an indication of academic achievement is not supported by research on the test. Both tests are designed for one purpose only—to predict success in college. Any other interpretation, even though it appears to be logically true, is insupportable.

There are three types of ability tests: **achievement tests, aptitude tests,** and **intelligence tests.** Achievement tests measure previous learning. For instance, a test that measures how many words one can correctly spell is a spelling achievement test (Kaplan & Saccuzzo, 2001). Aptitude tests measure the potential for acquiring a specific skill. With a certain amount of training, education, and experience, one's aptitude for a given pursuit can be developed. For example, music aptitude refers in part to how well one might be able to play a musical instrument or how accomplished one might become, given a certain number of lessons. A further example would be cultivating an aptitude for math and science among adolescent females, which is crucial for their current personal and academic well-being (Orenstein, 1994) and for their long-term occupational prospects. Often there is a gap between young people's confidence and their ability and aptitude. Intelligence tests measure the potential to (1) solve problems, (2) adapt to changing circumstances, and (3) profit from experiences (Kaplan & Saccuzzo, 2001).

Achievement, aptitude, and intelligence tests are not always easy to distinguish from one another because they are highly interrelated. Attempts to separate prior learning from the potential for learning have met with little success. Given the considerable overlap among achievement, aptitude, and intelligence tests, all three concepts now are encompassed under the term **human ability tests** (Kaplan & Saccuzzo, 2001).

Personality tests measure overt and covert traits, temperaments, and dispositions (Kaplan & Saccuzzo, 2001). For instance, the tendency to remain aloof from others, while not requiring any special skill or ability, reflects the varying preferences of some people who typically prefer or are disposed to remain isolated.

Structured or objective personality tests are based on self-report statements where the test-taker answers *true* or *false* or *yes* or *no*. Projective personality tests provide ambiguous test stimuli where response requirements are less clear. "Rather than being asked to choose among alternative responses, as in structured personality tests, the individual is asked to provide a spontaneous response" (p. 11). As part of any vocational counseling activity, it is essential to be familiar with different types of tests, what test results can and cannot indicate, and how to incorporate this information into the client's total profile.

Unlike the assessment tools mentioned above, interest inventories and values clarification activities are unique to vocational psychology and career counseling. Interest inventories usually result in a profile in which clients' responses to questions about interests in activities, competencies, and occupations are matched with interests of people already working in various occupations who report that they enjoy their work. Interest inventories do not tell the client what to do for a living, but rather expands their options of occupations to consider.

There are values scales inventories available as well as values clarification activities, usually based on the seven standards for constructing a value (Raths, Harmin, & Simon, 1966) presented in Table 2.1. We include values clarification activities when we teach Master's level courses in life planning and career development. Many of our students who do such an activity for the first time as a class exercise say they wish they had had the chance to do so earlier in their lives. Both interest and value inventories are included in a vocational assessment test battery, as are personality and skills inventories.

Reliability and Validity Two of the most fundamental concepts of standardized assessment are reliability and validity. **Reliability** refers to "the accuracy, dependability, consistency, or repeatability of test results. In more technical terms, reliability refers to the degree to which test scores are free of measurement error" (Kaplan & Saccuzzo, 2001, p.11). Classical test theory assumes that each person has a true score on an ability or characteristic that would be obtained if there were no errors in measurement. Because assessment instruments are imperfect, the observed score that is obtained for each person may differ from the person's true score on an ability or characteristic. The index of the amount of error in a test or measure is known as the **standard error of measurement.**

Classical test theory assumes that errors of measurement are random errors that will be the same for all people. The standard error of measurement tells how much a score varies on the average from a true score. The standard deviation of an observed score and the reliability of the test are used to compute estimates of the standard error of measurement. Types of reliability are presented in Table 3.2.

Betz (2000) makes several points about reliability. No single reliability coefficient describes an assessment tool or test. Coefficient values vary across studies with the same population due to different research methodologies. A test is never reliable. In-

TABLE 3.2 Types of Reliability

Test-retest reliability	A method for estimating how much measurement error is caused by administering the test at two different points in time; test-retest reliability is usually estimated from the correlation between performance on two different administrations of the test.
Alternate forms/Parallel forms reliability	The method of reliability assessment used to evaluate the error associated with the use of a particular set of items; equivalent forms of a test are developed by generating two forms using the same rules; the correlation between the two forms is the estimate of alternate forms' reliability.
Split-half reliability	A method for evaluating reliability in which a test is split into two halves; the correlation between the halves of the test, corrected for the shortened length of the halves, is used as an estimate of reliability.

SOURCE: From Kaplan and Saccuzzo (2001).

stead, an accumulation of evidence supports the reliability of an assessment tool. Reliability coefficients should consistently be above .80. Above .90 is ideal. Any tests with reliability coefficients between .70 and .80 can be used for research purposes. However, assessment tools with reliability coefficients less than .70 require further refinement before use in research and practice. Such instruments don't consistently measure anything. The methods used to establish reliability should be explicitly stated in research articles on the standardization of such assessment tools or in the test manuals that accompany the instruments.

Validity refers to "the meaning and usefulness of test results . . . [and] the degree to which a certain inference or interpretation based on a test is appropriate" (Kaplan & Saccuzzo, 2001, p. 12). **Inferences** are logical deductions made from evidence about something that one cannot observe directly. Given that validity is the evidence for inferences made about a test score, there are three types of evidence, or validity. These three categories of validity are devised by the joint committee of the American Education Research Association, the American Psychological Association, and the National Council on Measurement in Education and appear in *Standards for Education and Psychological Testing* (1985). The three types of validity and their subcategories are presented in Table 3.3.

On the matter of validity, relevant for our purposes here, Betz (2000) writes:

If scores from a test designed to measure career decision-making skills or career maturity actually correlate more highly with verbal ability or socioeconomic status than they do with other career-related variables, we would question the nature of the construct measured by our test (p. 484).

TABLE 3.3 Types of Validity

1. **Content validity**	The extent to which the content of a test represents the conceptual domain it is designed to cover
2. **Criterion validity** (aka **empirical** or **statistical validity**)	The extent to which a test score corresponds to an accurate measure of interest; the measure of interest is called the criterion
	a. **predictive validity**—the extent to which a test forecasts scores on the criterion at some future time
	b. **concurrent validity**—a form of criterion validity in which the test and the criterion are administered at the same time
3. **Construct validity**	A process used to establish the meaning of a test through a series of studies; to evaluate construct validity, a researcher simultaneously defines some constructs and develops the information to measure it; in the studies, observed correlations between the test and other measures come to define the meaning of the test
	a. **convergent validity**—a form of construct validity whereby evidence is obtained to demonstrate that a test measures the same attribute as do other measures that purport to measure the same thing
	b. **discriminant validity**—a form of construct validity whereby evidence is obtained to demonstrate that a test measures something different from what other available tests measure

SOURCE: From Kaplan and Saccuzzo (2001).

Another type of test and two other types of validity deserve mention. A **criterion-referenced test** describes the specific types of skills, tasks, or knowledge of an individual relative to a well-defined mastery criterion (Kaplan and Sacuzzo, 2001). The content of criterion-referenced tests, therefore, is limited to a set of well-defined objectives.

Differential validity is the extent to which a test has different meanings for different groups of people, such as a test that may be a valid predictor of college success for White students but not for Black students (Kaplan & Saccuzzo, 2001).

One can have reliability without validity. But it is logically impossible to demonstrate that an unreliable test is valid. If the test is not reliable, attempts to demonstrate the validity of the test will be futile.

Relevance for Multicultural and Diverse Populations

Stages of the Assessment Process. The practitioner's role is to consider multicultural worldviews (Fouad, 1993). Many trainees, as well as seasoned professionals, can fall into the trap of disrespecting their clientele's lifestyles. Clients' racial and ethnic backgrounds, culture, language usage(s), socioeconomic status, gender, sexual orientation, and religious affiliation can impact self-images and the opportunity structure of the

Practical Applications

The terms we have just defined may be familiar to readers who have taken courses in statistics, measurement and evaluation, or testing and assessment. As faculty members, we have heard graduate students complain about why they have to take such courses, especially because some students do not anticipate that they will be conducting standardized assessments after graduation as part of their future employment. These complaints are short-sighted. The practitioners' role is to retain a solid understanding of the basic principles of assessment, for several reasons. Among the reasons are to be cognizant of the standardized assessments available to clients, to make appropriate referrals if they are not adequately trained to ad-minister such assessment instruments themselves, and to be professionally conversant with their colleagues who do administer and score such tests. Sometimes the practitioner may have to explain to clients in everyday language the reasons for an assessment referral, the purpose of the assessment procedure, and the results of the assessment, particularly if the client has not had the test results clearly explained by the test administrator. "[B]ecause test use occurs with a specific individual in a specific setting for a particular reason, the ultimate basis for judging the utility of a test is the good judgment, sound knowledge, and professional integrity of the counselor" (Betz, 2000, p. 485).

world of work. Consequently, the initial problem clarification stage between practitioner and client (Walsh & Betz, 1990) can result in barriers to effective practitioner-client communication. At this stage, for example, clients' individualistic and collectivist orientations need to be discerned by the practitioner for the assessment procedure to be viable.

During the second stage of the assessment process, information-gathering (Walsh & Betz, 1990) expectations need to be clarified, especially because most clients will be unfamiliar with the need to self-disclose and the limits of confidentiality (Fouad, 1993). Sue and Sue (1990) remind us that various assessment procedures have been used to maintain the status quo and to keep minority individuals in their place. This abuse of power may have been experienced by multicultural clientele in past situations, and so the vocational practitioner needs to be mindful not to stereotype clients.

Understanding the information obtained is the third stage of the assessment process (Walsh & Betz, 1990). Data interpretation and theoretical conceptualization occur at this point. If rapport was not established during the information gathering stage, the information subsequently obtained may be incomplete, marked by careless responses, or marked by socially desirable responses. Current theories of vocational development inadequately consider the impact of race and social class on career development (Fouad, 1993) and are biased toward an individualistic orientation. It is crucial that the counselor be aware of the development of the test, the norm sample, and the allowance for racial and social class differences.

The fourth and final stage of the assessment process is coping with the problem (Walsh & Betz, 1990). Practitioners' ongoing challenge is to allow clients to self-define which solutions are compatible with their world view. Practitioners must avoid imposing their own mind-set on clients who do not share their background.

Understanding Gender Dynamics. More than an awareness of gender differences, the practitioner's role is to understand gender dynamics (Hackett & Lonborg, 1993). For example, a **gender role analysis** assesses the potential costs and benefits for women and men in terms of adopting traditional and nontraditional gender role behavior. These measures are presented in Hackett and Lonborg (pp. 210–211). In addition to understanding basic principles of assessment, practitioners need to (1) be well versed in literature on the career development of women, (2) view assessment as an integral component—not a discrete activity—of career interventions, (3) be aware of possibilities for their own bias, (4) use a gender role analysis as part of assessment, (5) consider qualitative alternatives to standardized testing, and (6) continually examine and work on their own gender-related issues to assure maximum effectiveness and ethical practice in occupational counseling with women.

Background experience plays an important role on girls' and women's test scores on ability and aptitude tests (Betz, 2000). In interest scales, the problem of sex restrictiveness persists; socialized patterns of interest resulting from gender stereotypic background experiences create interest inventory results that perpetuate girls' and women's overrepresentation in traditionally female-dominated occupations and underrepresentation in traditionally male-dominated occupations. Socialization experiences and expectations also affect the results of women's personality tests, so attention to environmental context becomes crucial.

Limited Consideration of Cultural Factors. In her review of the 1991 issues of *The Clinical Practice of Career Assessment* (1991), Bowman (1995) searched the table of contents, the index, and the chapters and examples provided, but found no mention of racial and ethnic issues in assessment. She further warns that unawareness on the practitioner's part of the **potential biases in career assessment instruments** can lead to the dissemination of misleading information to minority clients at best and potentially damaging information at worst. At issue is an etic perspective versus an emic perspective in assessment methods. **Etic** perspectives emphasize universal human behaviors; many cultures are examined and compared, presumably from a position outside those cultures. **Emic** perspectives are culture-specific, examining human behavior from criteria related to the internal characteristics of the culture, presumably from a position within that culture (Dana, 1993).

Another way to look at this issue is through the three types of **test bias** given by Walsh and Betz (1990). **Content bias** occurs when test items are more familiar to one racial or ethnic group than another. Experience has shown that it can include familiarity of objects and terms based upon one's geographical region. Individuals from non-Judeo-Christian, mainstream, American cultures also may encounter content biases. **Internal structure bias** pertains to the relationship among items of a test and the manner in which test takers perceive the items. **Selection bias** occurs when a test's predictive validity is differential across groups.

Similarly, Suzuki and Kugler (1995) summarize concerns about the androcentric tradition in intelligence and personality assessment with multicultural populations. These concerns include (1) inappropriate test content, (2) inappropriate standardization samples, (3) examiner and language bias, (4) inequitable social consequences, (5) measurement of different constructs, (6) differential predictive validity, and (7) differences in test-taking skills.

Values held by multicultural clients can impact vocational test taking and career decision making (Fouad, 1993). Little empirical evidence exists to guide the practitioner's role. Like gender role analysis, measuring acculturation can correct for cultural differences when multicultural clients are not from a White American cultural background (Dana, 1993; Grieger & Ponterotto, 1995; Paniagua, 1994; Suzuki & Kugler, 1995). Acculturation as a moderator variable helps to reliably "estimate . . . the potential contribution of cultural variance to an assessment procedure" (Dana, 1993, p. 113). A host of acculturation indexes are presented in Dana (1993, chapter 7) and in Paniagua (1994, chapter 8).

We believe it should be common practice to administer acculturation indices whenever multicultural populations are participants in career-related research and when vocational assessment instruments are re-normed. This would entail a commitment throughout the academic discipline, from scholars and practitioners of both the dominant cultural background and those of other racial and ethnic origins. Tackling the complexities of occupational references/abilities/aptitudes as moderated by acculturation could transform vocational psychology into an academic discipline that truly mirrors diversity.

The issue of whether acculturation is of intrinsic interest to scholars (Tinsley, 1994) would be transcended. Acculturation has mainly been the interest of racial and ethnic minority scholars and practitioners. If everyone in the field started adding acculturation indices to re-norming activities and other career-related research, this would show the respect due the diversity of the U.S. population.

The results of such a change could show up in the academic discipline within ten to fifteen years. By vocational psychology's 100th anniversary—that is, the year 2009—the field appears to have made broad steps on its way to becoming more relevant to a broader range of people than ever before.

African Americans. The research literature has a long way to go in developing normative samples using African Americans (Bowman, 1995). Normative samples will have to encompass within-group differences for any career assessment instruments to be reliable and valid. With African Americans, if norms on various assessment tools are not available, Bowman contends that it is the practitioner's responsibility to assist in the development of such norms.

Cultural variables that may affect assessment and treatment of African American clients include racial labels, **familism** and **role flexibility,** religious beliefs, **healthy paranoia,** and the language of African American clients (Paniagua, 1994). The following discussion of such variables pertains to vocational and career assessment.

1. *Racial labels.* These have varied historically over time and included *Colored, Negro, Black,* and *African American.* Colored and Negro are now considered derogatory and are inappropriate for practitioner use. Black emphasizes skin color, whereas African American emphasizes cultural heritage. Practitioners are advised to ask clients directly how *they* identify themselves in terms of racial labels.

2. *Familism and role flexibility.* The extent to which nuclear and extended families are an influence in African American clients' lives should be assessed. Familism among African Americans can include both biological and nonbiological members. Collectivism is more likely to be valued than individualism, but this is contextual. A **genogram** is a useful tool for practitioners to compile for illustrating the extended family tree and highlighting the role of work in the familial and personal domains (see González & Peterson, 2001).

Patterns of educational attainment, employment in *protected careers*, and work histories of individual family members can influence African American clients' perceived occupational opportunities. Role flexibility refers to who is the head of the family or a parental figure at any given time, and also to competencies in performing work tasks that have traditionally been part of the gender division of labor. Role flexibility can impact educational attainment and occupational development of individuals and families. Rigidity in terms of gender roles and work tasks can limit individuals and families.

3. *Religious beliefs/church affiliations.* This should not be automatically assumed. Within-group differences will be evident here. If an African American client is an active church member, practitioners should ask if the client has discussed vocational and career concerns with anyone in church. Inclusion of these third parties in occupational exploration activities is a possibility.

4. *Healthy paranoia.* A legacy of past slavery and continued racism, healthy paranoia may be part of some African Americans' social and psychological development. A suspicion of others of different races and values can impact client-practitioner interaction and client occupational development.

Non-African American practitioners should not be surprised if they encounter some healthy paranoia among their African American clients from time to time. Healthy paranoia, not unique to African Americans, can characterize any individual or subgroup that has experienced oppression. A lack of awareness and respect for this phenomenon can make a practitioner appear racist at worst or give the impression of **privileged complacency** at best.

5. *Language.* The Black English and street talk among subgroups of African Americans may not be understood by some practitioners and should be dealt with in a matter-of-fact request for clarification/translation. A very real, if uncomfortable, issue is the extent to which some African American clients can speak Standard American English (SAE). One's mastery of SAE will impact educational attainment and occupational opportunities among African Americans as well as other minorities, as controversies about Black English and bilingual education in recent years have shown (Associated Press, 1996a, 1996b; "'Black English' is stumbling block for black children," December 27, 1996).

Ward and Bingham (2001) address some additional challenges to career assessment with African Americans. The heterogeneity of the African American population means there's no need to continue comparing Black research participants to White ones (a research practice we think is inherently racist because White research participants generally fare better on the measure(s) of interest than do Black participants). A look at within-group differences illustrates such heterogeneity: factors like gender, age, educational attainment, socioeconomic status, parental country of origin (we would add parental educational attainment and parental socioeconomic status of origin), ethnic affiliation, marital status, physical ability, or political affiliation need to be taken into account. This heterogeneity awareness means that a one-size-fits-all approach to career assessment with African Americans would cease. It also means that career counselors would need to acquire more understanding of their African American clients' perspectives and would be less likely to impose their own worldview. The impact of racism and segregation would also need to be considered; our discussion in Chapter 1 about the barriers to assimilation could assist in these matters.

Internal and external barriers to career choice are another challenge to the career assessment of African Americans (Ward & Bingham, 2001). Murry and Mosidi (1993) write that African Americans have largely been confined to

1. blue collar occupations, which are mainly a means of making a living rather than careers.

2. college majors in education, social work, and the social sciences—which have led to **protected careers** where less racial discrimination is thought to occur.

3. positions for African American women where workplace racism and sexism is presumed to be minimized.

The extent to which these barriers exist also need to be examined during the career assessment process with an African American client.

Asian Americans. Leong and Gim-Chung (1995) offer guidelines on conducting and using career assessment with Asian Americans:

1. Use of career assessment instruments needs to be undertaken with caution because of the lack of cultural norms and empirical research demonstrating the cultural validity of such instruments.

2. Probable sources of bias within theories of career choice, such as the North American emphasis on individualism versus the Asian emphasis on collectivism, may turn up as multiple sources of bias in the assessment process.

3. Certain elements in Asian American test-taking attitudes may be important to keep in mind. Asian Americans socialized into an authoritarian family may be less likely to question or challenge the practitioner who is viewed as an authority figure. Thus, when an Asian American client is referred for assessment, the reason and goals for the assessment procedure may need to be carefully explained.

4. The test interpretation/feedback session with Asian Americans is likely to be influenced by cultural factors. Two important interpersonal dimensions are **maintaining face** and preventing **loss of face,** the violations of which can interfere with effective use of the assessment results. There may also be a need for more structured approaches to test interpretations with Asian Americans than would be the case with other clients.

Hispanics. Several concerns on assessing other multicultural populations relate to Hispanics as well. The practitioner's role is to evaluate Hispanic clients' proficiency with English, especially if a Spanish language version of the instrument is available and more appropriate. Appropriate norms are another concern as are whether White norms will be used if Hispanic norms are unavailable (Cervantes & Acosta, 1992; Dana, 1993; Fouad, 1993). The wide range of career assessment instruments may not have the same meaning and interpretation for Hispanics (i.e., differential validity, internal structure bias, selection bias); further research is needed on the affects of acculturation, language proficiency, socioeconomic status, geographic location, and generational status (Fouad, 1995). Recent immigrant status may have a particular impact on psychosocial stressors among Hispanics and can affect assessment results, especially client's reason for immigration (i.e., political refugee versus seeking work), and socioeconomic and educational levels (Cervantes & Acosta, 1992).

Both of us currently work in predominantly Hispanic cities. Many of our counseling graduate students come from a public school teaching background. From what our students, our clinical supervision of counselors within the schools, and our own client caseloads tell us, strict attention to the issues of language proficiency, appropriate norms, and acculturation does not always occur.

Nor is due consideration given to differentiating the effects of income level and ethnicity. Beyond concerns of the content of our Master's students' academic training and the appropriate use of various assessment instruments with Hispanics, we are especially mindful that internal politics within educational institutions continue to impinge upon the educational attainment of many Hispanic children and youth with whom our graduates work. Our impression is that the value of developing occupational awareness among Hispanic children and youth and their families does not appear to be a high priority among educational administrators, teacher educators, and a substantial number of school counselors already in the field.

Native Americans. Martin (1995) discusses five moderating variables relevant to developing an assessment plan with Native Americans:

1. *Language usage.* Use of native language and proficiency in English can have intervening affects on the assessment process. An informal determination of the client's level of English proficiency may be necessary. A native-speaking interpreter may be needed. A developmental history of language usage may be in order. Word recognition, word meanings, spelling, comprehension, narrative analysis, oral language skills, receptive language skills, and those skills that will be most important in the work setting all need to be considered. For those clients who have English usage skills, conventional career assessment instruments are considered appropriate.

2. *Cultural orientation.* It will be useful to determine the extent that home, family, and community figure into the worldview of Native Americans. Varying levels of acculturation also impact how similarly to the American mainstream Native Americans view occupational issues. A case study process is helpful in understanding how culture impacts career decision making. Essential elements to include are (1) family structure, (2) client perceptions of the acculturative process, (3) client involvement in traditional ceremonies, (4) client financial role within the family structure, (5) client short- and long-term goals related to living on one's reservation, and (6) client work-related values (e.g., academic achievement, professional status, income, work independence, and job-related and upward mobility).

3. *Home community.* Environmental context, especially for those living on or near reservations, is vital to enhancing a Native American person's career decision making. The client's history on and off the reservation, work experiences, and vocational training need to be clarified. Family occupational history and that of close friends is useful information to gather. Career developmental tasks and their relation to social networks and traditional value systems also need to be considered.

4. *Family system.* The extent of involvement in nuclear and extended families will vary by individual. A traditional, extended family orientation may mean that individual decision making is subordinated to group decision making because decisions may impact the family, not just the individual. A full exploration of values pertaining to family, homeland, tribal traditions, and community provides a more comprehensive view of the consequences of career decision making. Other factors to consider are: how decisions are made within the family system, who the major decision makers are, client's family roles and responsibilities, family members' expectations for the client's career pursuits, and family willingness to support the client in career planning, vocational training, job searches, placement, and retention.

5. *Communication style.* Maximizing informal interactions during the assessment process with Native American clients can decrease any perceptions of the test administrator as an adversary. The attending, influencing, and focusing microskills of Allen E. Ivey and his colleagues (Ivey & Gluckstern, 1984; Ivey, Gluckstern, & Ivey, 1982) are proposed as minimizing misunderstandings created by differences in language, culture, environment, or lifestyle.

In the psychological evaluation of Native Americans generally (Horan & Cady, 1990) and in vocational assessment particularly, more research, case studies, and the development of practical applications are needed. Conceptual-based articles and chapters risk the appearance of mere academic exercises. A more pressing issue is the kind of research methodology to be used. The limited information on the occupational development of Native Americans is unlikely to be substantially augmented by logical positivism alone.

Gay, Lesbian, and Bisexual People. Basic career assessment procedures need to be modified to take sexual orientation factors into account when the client is gay/lesbian/bisexual (Gelberg & Chojnacki, 1996). Oftentimes, linkages to sexual orientation are not considered in the make-up of various career assessment instruments and the meaning of their results (e.g., differential validity). Sexual orientation does affect career and life planning. Heterosexism and homophobia are rampant in the workplace (Woods, 1994). **Heterosexism** refers to the culturally conditioned bias that heterosexism is intrinsically superior to homosexuality (Rochlin, 1985), whereas **homophobia** refers to an irrational dread and loathing of homosexuality and homosexual people (Weinberg, 1972, cited in Rochlin, 1985).

To counter the shortcomings of heterosexist-based assessment instruments, Gelberg and Chojnacki (1996) suggest a semi-structured interview as a starting point with gay, lesbian, and bisexual people before proceeding on to the conventional vocational assessment route. But two major problems will persist: Current methods of assessment may be biased and/or incomplete in assessing a gay/lesbian/bisexual client's interests, values, experiences, or skills. Career counseling models for gay, lesbian, and bisexual people fail to consider the full repertoire of career developmental tasks and processes.

People with Disabilities. Career development can be curtailed among people with disabilities. They may have had limited opportunities for social and vocational experiences (Curnow, 1989), which can show up on test results. The practitioner's role is to consider the unique problems and needs of people with disabilities that require specialized services.

Regarding secondary special education students, "*Appropriate* assessment relates primarily to asking the 'right' questions (validity), and *competent* assessment pertains primarily to the issues of how well the questions are asked (reliability)" (Clark & Kolstoe, 1995, pp. 104–105, italics in original). The right questions come out of the domains of values, attitudes, habits, human relationships, occupational information, and job and daily living skills. This perspective expands the assessment emphasis beyond academic and cognitive performance or work and vocational outcomes to include other critical concern areas.

Intelligence tests should be used with great caution and only by test administrators who are sensitive to the specific applications of these test results for decisions regarding vocational training or employment (Clark & Kolstoe, 1995). Furthermore, information obtained from intelligence tests should be but one part of the information gathered.

Academic achievement tests are of questionable use with some special needs youth. A functional, life-career development and transition approach may be more relevant. Achievement tests are unlikely to answer questions such as: Can the adolescent read directions, measure flour, make change, or handle his or her own income? These criterion-referenced approaches can provide discrete bits of information that have some predictive utility.

While aptitude tests generally are not used in secondary special education programs, performance aptitude tests that measure manual and finger dexterity, speed, ability to follow directions, and persistence do have some direct applicability.

Interest inventories should be used selectively as gross screening devices and for structuring a process for self-study and guidance activities. Self-study can include formal and informal explorational activities to allow students an opportunity to become acquainted with unfamiliar work activities and environments.

Direct interviews are a useful guidance tool toward the goal of better decision making and goal-setting through self-awareness. Little effort has been expended on administering personality tests to youths with mental and educational handicaps, with more attention given to behavior observations, self-report devices, and interviews.

A comprehensive, ongoing vocational assessment is a necessary and prerequisite condition in creating any vocational education or training program for people with mental retardation (Levinson, Peterson, & Elston, 1994). Typically, this comprehensive assessment entails an evaluation of (1) mental ability, (2) academic achievement, (3) sensory processes and motor skills, (4) vocational aptitudes, (5) adaptive behavior and social skills, and (6) functional living skills and appropriate work habits. Data on each of these areas includes information derived from interviews, paper and pencil tests, performance tests, work samples (i.e., tasks common in a number of jobs within an occupational area that are performed by a client under the supervision of a trained observer), simulated work experiences (i.e., real jobs performed by a client in a highly sheltered, supervised situation), and actual on-the-job work experiences. Naturally, the data-gathering techniques emphasized within an assessment program frequently depend on the philosophical approach taken when conducting vocational assessments. Nevertheless, a comprehensive vocational assessment program makes use of all of the above data-gathering techniques and involves a variety of personnel.

Traditionally, the assessment of individuals with mental retardation has focused on vocational aptitudes and interests, as well as functional living skills and appropriate work habits (Levinson et al., 1994). Results from such assessments have then been used to predict vocational potential. But there are two problems with traditional assessment when used with people with mental retardation. First, there often is a minimal, direct relationship between the behaviors sampled by a test and those behaviors required for successful job performance. Using test behaviors to predict work behaviors is inappropriate. Second, traditional assessment focuses on products of past learning. This approach assumes that an individual's previous experiences have been sufficient for such learning to occur.

Given the limited range of vocational and life experiences of many of these people, this approach is likewise inappropriate. A more useful, contemporary approach to traditional assessment is to focus on actual competencies and skills required for the successful performance of specific jobs. Assessment outcomes directly relate to program planning and include the instructional processes needed to acquire specific competencies and skills.

The assessment of functional living skills represents one contemporary, alternative approach to traditional assessment of people with mental retardation (Levinson et al., 1994). Assessment of functional living skills typically includes:

1. evaluation of self-help skills such as dressing, eating, or toileting

2. consumer skills, including money handling, banking, and purchasing

3. domestic skills, such as household maintenance

4. health care

5. community knowledge, including travel skills and telephone usage

6. job readiness skills, such as interviewing skills and on-the-job information

7. vocational behavior, including job performance and productivity, work habits and attitudes, and work-related skills

8. social behavior on the job, including interactions with co-workers and supervisors. It is precisely the comprehensive and ongoing nature of vocational assessment for people with mental retardation that makes it so challenging.

Recognition of Attention Deficit Disorder (ADD) in adults is recent and not yet widespread. Consequently, little empirical evidence exists to guide practitioners who serve adults newly diagnosed with ADD (Nadeau, 1995). In a comprehensive model for career counseling with adults with ADD, the practitioner's role is to integrate test results from evaluations of ability, achievement, interests, personality traits, and specific problematic learning disorder (LD) and ADD concerns. When administering any test, the individual's attention difficulties should be taken into account. Among these difficulties are impatience, distractibility, motor restlessness, a tendency toward careless errors, and inattention when reading. All of these can affect test reliability and validity. Test administrators can accommodate the strong tendency of adults with ADD to make careless errors by allowing clients to mark their answers next to the questions in question booklets, instead of requiring them to transfer answers onto an answer sheet. The test administrator or a technician/assistant can transfer the answers to any answer sheets at a later time to facilitate computer or template scoring. Paper-and-pencil tests may highlight the reading difficulty of an adult with ADD. Frequent breaks may improve performance for those who have difficulty concentrating.

Clients with an accompanying LD that contributes to reading problems may benefit by having the questions read aloud to them. Breaking a test into one-hour segments may help counteract restlessness, mental fatigue, and distractibility. By all means, testing should take place in a quiet, nondistracting environment.

Assessment Traditions of the Twentieth Century

Several influences contributed by a number of cultures over the centuries have affected the current status of vocational assessment. These include

1. the use of test batteries during Imperial China's Han dynasty (206 B.C.E.–220 C.E.),

2. the work of Sir Francis Galton (1822–1911) and his development of statistical concepts of regression to the mean and correlation, derived from the theory of evolution articulated by his relative Charles Darwin (1809–1882), and

3. the experimental and practical study of individual differences by James McKeen Cattell (1860–1944) at Columbia University (Kaplan & Sacuzzo, 2001; Sattler, 1988).

Most of the major developments in testing occurred in the early twentieth century. Watkins (1992) categorized these developments into four assessment traditions: vocational guidance, psychometric, mental hygiene, and Rogerian.

The Vocational Guidance Tradition Watkins's (1992) first category, the vocational guidance tradition, is traced back to the pioneering efforts of Frank Parsons [1854–1908]. Parsons, a man of unflagging energy, served as a teacher, counselor, lawyer, political activist, reformer, and author (Zytowski, 1985). The impetus for Parsons's contributions and the vocational guidance tradition can be traced to three trends in the beginning of the twentieth century: a wider variety of careers due to increasing industrialization, growth of secondary school enrollment, and difficulties experienced by young men and women in the labor market. These trends combined to create new conditions for educational opportunity and occupational choice. Parsons's views on vocational counseling were published in *Choosing a Vocation* (1909). In conceptualizing the vocational choice process, Parsons said that one must consider three broad factors:

1. a clear understanding of yourself, your aptitudes, abilities, interests, ambitions, resources, limitations, and their causes,

2. a knowledge of the requirements and conditions of success, advantages and disadvantages, compensations, opportunities, and prospects in different lines of work, and

3. true reasoning on the relationship of the first two factors.

To facilitate vocational exploration, he relied on interviewing, assessment procedures, and a diagnostic method.

With some modifications, Parsons's approach to vocational guidance led to the development of the **trait-factor theory** of career counseling. This approach, sometimes referred to as *test 'em and tell 'em* or *three interviews and a cloud of dust,* regards diagnosis, testing, and assessment as central to the counseling process (Crites, 1981). These three activities were aided substantially by the development of interest tests and related measures.

Though the trait-factor approach to counseling is said to be on the decline, the central Parsonian assumption of matching people and jobs continues to underlie the most prominent vocational assessment tools and concepts. This seems to be especially true in regard to the congruence model. This model is very much in evidence today in both career assessment and counseling practice, as reflected in John Holland's work and some of the career inventories, particularly the Strong Interest Inventory and the Career Inventory Assessment (CIA).

The Psychometric Tradition Watkins's (1992) second category is the psychometric tradition. In France, Alfred Binet (1857–1911) and Theodore Simon (1873–1961) developed an intelligence scale to assess a variety of mental functions. One result of their work, the diagnosis of mentally retarded individuals (Sattler, 1988), stimulated the psychometric tradition in the United States. In the 1930s, people involved in the vocational guidance and psychometric traditions combined their efforts and attempted to identify methods by which they could assist the unemployed in finding employment. The Stabilization Research Institute (1931, cited in Watkins, 1992) was pivotal in combining the two traditions. The institute developed psychological tests and methods for the assessment of the abilities and interests of the unemployed, researched the reeducation potential and problems of the unemployed, and demonstrated retraining and reeducation methods. The work at the institute and the contributions of the psychometric tradition provided the vocational guidance tradition with a substantive philosophical and psychological base. The seminal contributions of Strong and Kuder are further examples of the way in which vocational guidance and psychometric traditions were combined.

The psychometric tradition also contributed to the development of personality tests, including the California Psychological Inventory (CPI) (Gough, 1957), the Minnesota Multiphasic Personality Inventory (MMPI) (Hathaway & McGinley, 1943), and the 16 Personality Factor Questionnaire (16PF) (Cattell, 1949). These instruments, among others, show the increasing psychometric sophistication that has been applied to test development over the years.

Each of these instruments has continued to be used, with recent revisions on CPI (Gough, 1990), MMPI-2 (Butcher, Dahlstrom, et al., 1989), and 16PF (Institute for Personality and Ability Testing, 1995). The Adult Personality Inventory (Krug, 1991) and the Millon Clinical Multiaxial Inventory (MCMI) are other examples of the increase in, development of, and use of personality assessments.

In vocational assessment, one can also see this reflected in the Strong Interest Inventory (SII), the Kuder Occupational Interest Survey (KOIS), the Career Assessment Inventory (CAI), and other highly useful and usable career/interest inventories. These are but a few illustrations of the evolution of the psychometric tradition and its continuing effects on the assessment tools that counseling psychologists and other practitioners currently use in their work.

The Mental Hygiene Tradition The mental health tradition is Watkins's (1992) third category of major developments in testing. Mental health and assessment instruments were illustrated in Beers (1908, cited in Watkins, 1992) who focused on two issues: concern over the need to improve the care and treatment of patients hospitalized for serious personality disturbances and concern over how to prevent such disorders. Although Beers's contributions were more indirect in terms of assessment, his humanizing influence may well have spilled over into how mental health professionals think about assessment and its purposes, and how different assessment methods are used.

The Rogerian Tradition Watkins's (1992) fourth category of assessment traditions, the person-centered (Rogerian) tradition, gave us some of our most fundamental ideas about assessment methods and their utilization. This tradition has six guiding ideas:

1. Assessment methods can be used by and for clients.
2. Clients can use their assessment results to their own benefit.
3. Assessment should be a collaborative effort between counselor and client.
4. Clients can benefit most from assessment when they are actively involved in the entire assessment process.
5. Clients can benefit most from assessment information when it is considered in a facilitative, nonthreatening atmosphere.
6. Through providing information that stimulates self-examination, self-exploration, self-understanding, and insight, assessment methods can be facilitative to the client during the counseling process.

The influences that have affected our current use of assessment methods are quite diverse, but are bound by one unifying theme: the desire to assist clients in better helping and understanding themselves (Watkins, 1992). Either directly or indirectly, these traditions in relation to assessment have had humanizing effects upon our views about clients and provided us with means by which client self-exploration, self-understanding, and insight could be facilitated. Some very powerful assessment tools, if used ethically, responsibly, and in an informed manner, can be of considerable value to clients.

Assessment has experienced a renaissance of sorts. It is alive, well, and thriving, and is a diverse and rich area of practice. It is much more important and relevant to the counseling profession than may have been realized during the 1970s and 1980s. Different assessment tools provide objective data to a counseling process that is primarily subjective. The balanced combination of information from both the assessment tools and the person's self-image allows the counselor to help the client integrate these various aspects of the whole person into the career decision-making process.

Postmodern Approaches to Assessment

Traditional twentieth-century vocational assessment was whole-heartedly modernist. Clients without a Eurocentric worldview were pathologized, caricatured, or dehumanized (Dana, 1993). The practitioner's role is not to take for granted the assumption that assessment procedures are universally reliable and valid for all clients—an etic perspective. Without the development of culture specific norms—an emic perspective—an assessment instrument developed on a given standardization sample is of limited use for a nonmember of the cultural group of that normative sample. In the past, lack of culture-specific norms has not prevented the use of a given assessment tool with a client for whom norms do not exist. This type of sloppy scientific method led to postmodern approaches toward assessment.

Other shortcomings of the scientific method have contributed an increased emphasis of postmodernism in vocational psychology and career counseling. Research on job satisfaction and workaholism is incomplete and fragmented, and has not reached the level of empirical refinement that the scientific method demands.

Androcentrism and heterosexism have kept the logical positivist ideals of assessment from being met. Postmodern approaches to vocational assessment therefore merit consideration as a viable alternative to traditional approaches.

New assessment methods and measures for use by vocational practitioners/career counselors give more attention to the client's subjective experience, which is an addition to, not a substitution for, the objective observations yielded by standardized assessment instruments (Savickas, 1992). Contextual interpretation becomes part of a larger, objective test battery. Using a **phenomenological perspective,** counselors "seek to comprehend the meaning of clients' interests and abilities as part of a life pattern" (p. 337). A modern approach to interests and abilities as quantifiable characteristics can unintentionally treat clients as objects. A postmodern approach deals with interests and abilities by helping clients discern what they intend to do with assessment results to fashion a career. Modernism would treat assessment results in terms of predictive accuracy, postmodernism in terms of expressed interests.

Traditionally, objective assessment results have entailed "the delivery of authoritative guidance and concentrate[d] exclusively on the client's role as a worker"

(Savickas, 1992, p. 337). Subjective assessment allows for looking at the role of work in people's lives and removes the artificial distinction between personal and career counseling. Early recollections, occupational daydreams, **life themes,** autobiographies, and the multiple roles and tensions in a client's life become legitimate areas for collaboration between practitioner and client.

Client narratives about their education, employment history, and occupational aspirations can reveal characters, plots, and recurring situations. The practitioner's role is to listen for themes, tensions, and connections in their clients' lives and place the role of work into context with other roles. Practitioners and clients collaborate on the meanings of client life experiences. The practitioner's reading between the lines and making explicit connections between loosely attached ideas takes subjective assessment to another level. An infusion of postmodern contextual interpretation in assessment and occupational development holds some promise to invigorate and transform vocational psychology. As with standards and goals for career counseling, quality assurance issues in program evaluation and vocational assessment will need to be further addressed in the future.

Chartand's and Walsh's (2001) projections for career assessment include several areas that counselors will need to know. "Modern test theory overcomes sample dependency, instead of relying on mathematical model fitting" (p. 242). Item response theory (IRT) allows for the development of instruments that will provide more subtle and discriminant information than possible with classical test theory. Another development is more sophisticated assessments that use new statistical analysis techniques, such as confirmatory factor models, which allow for studying "the equivalence of factor analysis across different groups (e.g., men and women)" (p. 243) and means of "[facilitating] cross cultural applications and multi-instrument assessment" (p. 243). The implications are important for refining the use of assessments to make them of greater value to a wider variety of clients. Two other developments Chartrand and Walsh (2001) note are the growth of computer-assisted test administration and interpretation and the push toward self-directed career planning, both in tests and in Internet services.

HISTORICAL ANTECEDENTS TO VOCATIONAL PSYCHOLOGY

A person's theory and practice of vocational psychology can be truncated by historical ignorance (Dumont & Carson, 1995). Historical "myopia" can contribute to a rigid, "unicultural" perspective (p. 371). The philosophy of vocation did not arise from twentieth-century psychological and sociological theories, but actually predates written history. Only in the mid-1990s did scholars present documentation that revealed the ancient roots of vocational psychology and guidance. Recent scholarship shows that as long as 2,500 years ago, precursors to Parsons's (1909) work and to current theory and practice existed. Predicates of vocational psychology have been unearthed in ancient Egypt, Greece, and China, as well as from the age of classical Islam and the multicultural society of late medieval Spain.

Ancient Egypt and Greece

In the Western world, two of the earliest literate peoples lived in ancient Egypt and Greece, whom Dumont and Carson (1995) refer to collectively as the Eastern Mediterranean civilizations. The following discussion, based on their article, explores Western antecedents to vocational psychology practice.

Ancient Egypt As early as 10,000 B.C.E. (Before Common Era, formerly called *B.C.*, i.e., *Before Christ*), fixed-location agriculture flourished in the Middle East and southeast Africa. Economies in these areas initially were dependent on the seasonal work of planting and harvest. As the population grew, cities formed and governments evolved that eventually led to the development of several Egyptian empires along the banks of the Nile River. The economy gradually branched out to include land and sea-trade routes. A proliferation of occupations arose—architecture, engineering, construction work, seamanship, interior and exterior design—as well as artisans and craftsmen, including what is now called mortuary science. Ancient Egyptian empires, among others, developed what is now called military science. A strong army and navy enabled them to maintain their civilization and expand Egyptian influence throughout the Eastern Mediterranean to encompass Greek and Semitic peoples. Most important for the ancient Egyptians was a writing technology that allowed for record keeping and communications. Predicates of vocational psychology include the division of labor; the use of sociopolitical mechanisms to channel people into appropriate occupational roles; and the allocation of resources for educating, skill training, and socializing people into the workforce.

Ancient Greece From approximately 1000 B.C.E., the ancient Egyptians contributed to later Greek civilizations, especially cultural and religious customs. The ancient Greeks shaped modernist thinking about a wide range of topics, including architecture, drama and athletic competition, politics and ethics, philosophy and psychology, logic and geometry, epic narrative, and mythology.

To support the rich civilization and the complex mercantile economy of the ancient Greeks that superseded that of the ancient Egyptians, sociopolitical mechanisms were necessary to allow young people the opportunity to develop requisite skills. Hesiod, writing toward the end of the eighth century B.C.E., advocated that people engage in occupational activities according to aptitude and emphasized the virtue of earning an honest living. Avocational activities also were encouraged while crops awaited maturation. Thus, amateur seafaring, public debates and oral recitation of epic poetry, boxing competitions, and craft activities filled their leisure time. Later, those who excelled at such avocational activities became professionals at them.

Solon, the great lawgiver of the seventh century B.C.E., recognized aptitudes and interests. In central Greece, Attica developed beyond a land-based agricultural economy to include fishing, the manufacture of weapons and bronze and steel armor, the importation of raw materials and the exportation of finished products, public administration, and education. Citizens of all classes in Attica were accorded the right to progress in their work. Those who became highly accomplished were respected.

The Athens of Pericles in the fifth century B.C.E. also supported an individual's right to achieve what their capabilities allowed without interference from the state. A meritocracy prevailed. The work culture was exclusively male. Captives brought back from foreign wars (mostly women and children; men were usually executed at battle sites) became servants and slaves and were compelled to assimilate into the Athenian underclass, much as immigrants in the West today are pressed to assimilate into their new country's political economies starting from the underclass. Then as now, some members of the underclass became wealthy through commerce and mercantile activities.

The concept of Person by Environment Fit originated in ancient Greece, a legacy of the classical developmentalism of the Greek philosophers. Plato (c. 427 B.C.E.–c. 327 B.C.E.) wrote that the development of vocation begins in childhood. He recognized that a child's education determines success as an adult and proposed an admirably balanced curriculum of aesthetics and athletics, literary and cognitive endeavors. For one to be good at anything, one would have to practice it from their youth onwards. In what sounds like a prescient warning of the evils of television, Plato admonished exposing children to stories that only shaped a lazy or dangerous character. One's competence would determine their status in the republic.

Plato remarked on the desirable qualities for certain occupations. His multimethod screening for police candidates included (1) the extent to which the interests of the republic would rule candidates' lives, (2) tests of judgment from youth onwards, and (3) assessment of candidates' vulnerability to bribery and other corrupting influences. Physicians who had known illness themselves were deemed more able to understand their patients' ailments, but judges need not have committed evil acts to be qualified to condemn those whom they judged.

Marketplace demand was a recognized basis for diversification of vocational opportunities and occupational choices in ancient Greece. The need for specialization, with a natural aptitude for one's work, placed heavy emphasis on training and education. Changing occupations was discouraged by the sociopolitical system. One was expected to spend one's entire life reaching for the highest skills of their occupation.

Ancient China

At the same time that Greece evolved the role of work in people's lives, ancient China transformed from an emphasis on feudalism to a new and efficient centrally administered imperial government. The following discussion is based on Dumont and Carson (1995).

China made the transition from a Bronze Age to an Iron Age in the twelfth century B.C.E., roughly the same time the Eastern Mediterranean civilizations did. By the sixth century B.C.E., the first formulations of Chinese philosophy appeared, resulting in what is traditionally known as the *Hundred Schools*. Taoism and Confucianism are the best known of these schools.

Taoism Taoism purportedly is derived from the writings of a government-employed scribe later referred to as Lao-tzu, "old one." Taoism asserts that one must be true to one's nature in order to live a fulfilled life and follow an occupation consistent with one's true nature. It was believed that propitious events occurred to those pursuing a proper vocation, and one was enabled to pursue a choice of work. Thus, a version of Person by Environment Fit originated in ancient China concurrent with its development in ancient Greece. These events find their present-day counterpart in vocational psychology, when career choice is casually attributed to chance accidents. Taoism conceived of government as a self-perpetuating disorder (Lao-tzu sounds like he was discontented in his work), which placed limits on what we refer to now as personal growth and self-actualization. Government structured and stylized social conditions to meet only its own needs at the expense of the individual. The Taoist notion of excessive government can be generalized to the risks of excessive "rational" and "willful" control over one's occupational decision making. Imposing a rigid, systematic method of occupational decision making on oneself or others risks violating one's true nature and fosters a lack of job satisfaction and productivity.

Confucianism In contrast to Taoism, Confucianism held that a wisely administered government had moral integrity. Confucius was an actual historical person, K'ung Ch'iu, thought to have been an itinerant private tutor and teacher in the China of sixth century B.C.E. He advocated leadership by good example and treating others as one would treat oneself. His faith in the possibilities inherent in wise government predated Plato. Wise government was defined as the orderly concentration of power in the hands of those most capable of administering it. From this basic Confucian philosophy arose the first civil service testing programs. Readers are referred to Roos, Talley, Linden, and Cascio (1996) for more (and digestible) information on Confucius.

Classical Islam

In addition to the precursors of vocational psychology in ancient Egypt, Greece, and China, other historical roots of vocational theory come from classical Islam. Islam was founded in 622 C.E. [*Common Era,* formerly referred to as *A.D., Anno Domini*] in present-day Medina, Saudi Arabia, by the prophet Mohammed (c. 570 C.E.–632 C.E.). He proclaimed himself the latest in a long line of prophets that included Moses, Elijah, and Jesus Christ. In the centuries immediately following Mohammed's death, the Muslim religion spread from North Africa and Spain in the West to Persia (Iran) and India in the East.

The Islamic empire extended further than that of the Greek empire established by Alexander the Great in the third century B.C.E. Classical Islam reached its zenith in the eleventh century with caliphates—great religious capitals and cultural centers—established in Córdoba, Spain, and Damascus, Syria.

Predicates of vocational psychology are mentioned in a tenth-century Iraqi text (Carson & Altai, 1994). The discussion that follows is based on their article. The text, *Rasa'il Ikhwàn al-Safá wa-Khulln al-Wafa* (commonly translated as **Treatises of the Brothers of Purity,** or *TBP*), was written around 955 C.E. by what is believed to be a group of five to ten Muslim reformers from the Basra region of what is now southern Iraq. The group collectively called themselves **Ikhwàn al-Safá** to hide their individual identities for fear of reprisal by Islamic fundamentalists. The initial goal of the authors of the *TBP* was to compile all the known sciences into one work, regardless of the cultural origins of such knowledge. This was a radical concept at the time because only knowledge of Islamic origin was seen as valid and trustworthy. The authors compiled information from Greek, Jewish, Christian, Persian, and Indian sources.

Various sciences were classified as traditional or foreign. Traditional sciences were disciplines based on the Qur'an (the Islamic holy book) and included grammar, poetry, history, theology, and law. Foreign sciences were disciplines based on human intervention and were discovered through the use of reason. Traditional sciences had the weight of divine authority behind them. Foreign sciences did not, so it was more acceptable to criticize and correct them. Islamic fundamentalists were threatened by foreign sciences and tried to suppress them whenever possible.

In the *TBP*, ideas related to vocational psychology fall under the classification of foreign sciences. Three tenets are discussed: (1) information in decision making, (2) congruence, and (3) the components of congruence. These topics are touched upon throughout the *TBP*. As described in the *TBP*, information in decision making was the ruler's prerogative. One usually followed family tradition in terms of work. However, the ruler was expected to be knowledgeable of occupations and to reassign occupational roles when dictated by workforce needs. An appropriate match between people and their jobs was based on the behaviors and mental abilities required to perform job tasks.

Job descriptions mentioned in the *TBP* include musicians, painters, and jugglers. Musicians were expected to be both composers and performers, with emphasis on the nature of the job and the way audiences were affected. Some musicians would only have limited audience appeal, whereas other musicians would enjoy wide popular appeal. Differences in abilities among musicians were acknowledged.

Painters were expected to imitate that which appears in nature, including things, people, and animals. As with musicians, vast differences in acquired skills among painters were acknowledged. Jugglers were expected to possess speed and to make actions appear invisible to the naked eye. Social class differences were noted in response to jugglers' acts—uneducated people laughed, intelligent people were surprised and amazed. Entry into these occupations, the subsequent work path, and aspects of job satisfaction were rarely mentioned by the *Ikhwàn al-Safá*. Ostensibly, many occupations described in the *TBP* were open to both men and women, but one occupation was specifically identified as suitable for women only: weeper at funerals.

Congruence assumes that a person is best capable of one line of work. Long before Parsons (1909), the *Ikhwàn al-Safá* linked presupposed compatibility between a person's individual characteristics to certain occupations. Workers were classified into seven broad groups: (1) artisans and craftsmen, (2) businessmen and traders, (3) construction engineers and workers, (4) kings, rulers, sultans, politicians, and soldiers, (5) employees, servants, and daily workers, (6) the disabled, the unemployed, and the idle, and (7) men of religion and scholars. These broad groups were further subdivided into occupations, with descriptions of the appropriate character, personality type and traits, and relevant goals and prerequisite motivations associated with each occupation. Similar to Holland's (1997) concept of the effects of a vocational environment on an individual's vocational personality, the *TBP* assumed that an occupation would have characteristics that would force workers into certain behaviors while on the job.

The ability of a worker to properly perform a given occupation's responsibilities in the *TBP* was based on four factors: intellective factors and education, temperament and physique, natural environment and chance, and astrological factors.

1. *Intellective factors and education* entailed the content of the domain of knowledge needed for competent performance of the occupation, suitably diverse methods for learning skill acquisition, perceptual ability as grounded in one's sensory organs themselves, and particular features of occupations. The way a person's native intelligence and potential lent themselves to occupational mastery resembles many present-day theories of adult career development.

2. *Temperament and physique* referred to what are known today as a person's intellectual, academic, and occupational interests; innate personality traits; body type; and mental abilities.

3. *Natural environment and chance* could have been chance events of either natural or human origin, and resemble the investigation of the role of chance factors, which are of increasing interest to present-day theorists of occupational development.

4. *Astrological influences* determined personal characteristics. Astrology was not of Islamic origin and therefore considered a foreign science.

Naturally, the foreign science of the role of work in Islamic people's lives was influenced by traditional science divinely inspired by the Koran. Then as now, the example of the Prophet Muhammad's work life was undoubtedly known to all Muslims. "He worked, and joyed in honest labor; /He traded with integrity to himself and to others" (*The Holy Qur'an*, Introductory Commentary, verse 25). Throughout the Koran, conduct is prescribed for work dealings. For instance:

Woe to those/That deal in fraud,
Those who, when they/Have to receive by measure/
From men, exact full measure,
But when they have/To give by measure/Or weight to men,/
Give less than due.
Do they not think/That they will be called/To account?

(*The Holy Qur'an,* Süra [Book] LXXXIII, verses 1–4)

That is, in commercial dealings merchants should not give too little and ask too much. But these verses also pertain to domestic, social, and religious practices as well. Thus we can see in these two brief snippets of the Koran how matters pertaining to work life can hardly be separated from matters relating to one's personal and spiritual lives.

Like Dumont and Carson (1995), Carson and Altai (1994) conclude that gaining an historical perspective on vocational psychology helps to put the academic discipline into context. The historical relevance for multicultural and diverse populations becomes evident in both articles, which helps minimize the apparent twentieth-century androcentric foundations of the field. These androcentric foundations are further eroded when one examines the ideas of occupational choice published in late medieval Spain.

Late Medieval Spain

Medieval Spain was the most multicultural society in Europe. When the rest of the continent was in the so-called Dark Ages that followed the fall of the Roman Empire, in early medieval Islamic Spain the city of Córdoba shone as a brilliant beacon of intellectual and cultural light in an otherwise grim and harsh European civilization (Stewart, 1974/1979). Many historians detest the term *Dark Ages,* but few would argue as to Córdoba's one-time magnificence. Christians, Jews, and Muslims intermingled and frequently intermarried in Córdoba (Ladero Quesada, 2003; Pérez, 2003). Professions such as government administrator, musician, scholar, sailor, merchant, and the medical and apothecary arts were enriched by the integration of practices derived from the multiple coexistent religious groups.

The vibrant Córdovan society produced one of the earliest comprehensive compilations of occupational descriptions, *Speculum Vitae Humana (Mirror of Human Life),* published by Bishop Rodrigo Sánchez de Arévalo in 1468. Sánchez de Arévalo's book is the subject of an article by Chabassus and Zytoski (1987), upon which the following discussion is based. **The Mirror of Human Life** was published when printing with movable type was perfected by Johann Gutenburg (died 1467). Over the next 125 years, the book went through many editions in its original Latin and also in Spanish, French, and German. Based on a public debate Sánchez de Arévalo witnessed in his youth, he subtitled his book *The Advantages and Disadvantages, the Satisfactions and Bitterness, the Consolations and Miseries, the Favorable and Unfavorable Things, the Flattery and Danger of All States of Life.*

Magnificent relic of the past: detail of the exterior of the mosque at Córdoba, Spain.

Book I describes the pros and cons of secular occupations: kings and princes, knights, consorts by marriage (the latter being the only occupational account to mention women), judges and mayors, weavers, blacksmiths, carpenters, hunters, animal caretakers, actors, and physicians ("the most honorable of crafts for it is essential to human life"). One of the drawbacks of being a physician: "They glory in the highly esteemed name of doctor for the sake of profit!" The advantages and disadvantages of the liberal arts as a field of study also are discussed: grammar, logic, rhetoric, sciences, astronomy, music, arithmetic, and geometry.

Book II examines the pros and cons of religious vocations: popes (including the stressors that made so many of them short-lived), cardinals, archbishops, bishops, priests, deacons, cantors (i.e., singers—a Jewish legacy), stewards, schoolmasters, and monks. He does not seem to mention mother abbesses and nuns.

Despite the fact that Sánchez de Arévalo's *Mirror of Human Life* focused only on occupations for men, his work was the most detailed description of available occupations published to date. Like the Islamic *Treatises of the Brothers of Purity,* he lists three fundamental concepts that are especially relevant to present-day applied career counseling and vocational psychology: information in decision making, congruence, and the components of congruence. Regarding information in decision making, Sánchez de Arévalo wrote that occupational choices could not be made without information gathered in advance. A failure to choose well would result from "not sufficiently know[ing] the pleasant and unpleasant . . . , the advantages and disadvantages of various states and ways of life" (cited in Chabassus & Zytowski, 1987, p. 170).

As in the societies of ancient Greece and classical Islam, late medieval Spain recognized that congruence—choosing an occupation compatible with an individual's characteristics—was optimal. "Each has to consider what nature makes him inclined for" (cited in Chabassus & Zytoski, 1987, p. 170), wrote Sánchez de Arévalo. He quoted several ancient Roman philosophers to support his argument, including: "Cicero (106–43 B.C.E.): 'All deliberation needs to encompass one's nature.'" and "Seneca (5 B.C.E.–65 C.E.): 'Forced pursuit is unfruitful, for in opposition to nature, virtue is taken from labor'" (p. 170). Sánchez de Arévalo expounded on Seneca and the ideas that natural aptitude and inclination (e.g., interests, values, and/or personality) are essential components of occupational choice. "Study yourself, measure your forces, consider your fragility, your makeup, your nature, your habits" (cited in Chabassus & Zytoski, 1987, p. 170)—good advice through the centuries, now a guiding influence in modern approaches to vocational psychology.

Fundamental precepts of vocational psychology are usually presumed to have been devised in the twentieth century (Dumont & Carson, 1995). But the above exposition of the historical antecedents to vocational psychology illustrates a venerable ancestry of thousands of years. No student who reads of these earliest ideas could ever again call vocational psychology a dull subject. The history of the academic discipline is lavish in its multicultural and multidimensional contributions to the role of work in people's lives. With this background knowledge, we now can move on to look at some of the basic theories that have shaped the current thinking of vocational psychology.

SUMMARY

In this chapter, we have looked at the roles that counselors assume in the practice of career counseling and vocational psychology, and at an outline of the training requirements for each type of counseling practitioner. The issue of evaluation of programs that are offered and the ways that counselors can be evaluated and can evaluate themselves are presented. The issues surrounding testing and assessment are discussed, along with basic test theory, terms unique to testing, and ethical responsibilities of test administration, scoring, interpretation, and use of assessments. Test issues for multicultural and diverse clients are discussed. The historical traditions of assessments are covered. The chapter then ends with a history of the antecedents of vocational psychology and their meaning for the present.

4

❖

Trait-Factor, Psychodynamic, Existential, and Person-Centered Theories

In this chapter we start our formal discussion of vocational psychology theories. Four approaches rely strongly on the use of assessment instruments: (1) Trait-Factor Theory, (2) Holland's Typology, (3) the Myers-Briggs Type Indicator, and (4) the Theory of Work Adjustment. We also include three of the major theories that have impacted vocational psychology/career counseling—psychodynamic, existential, and person-centered approaches.

TRAIT-FACTOR THEORY

Evolution of Vocational Guidance

Frank Parsons (1854–1908) developed the idea of choosing a vocation rather than hunting for a job. Originally trained as an engineer, he proposed a set of objective standards and assessments to guide a person vocationally. In his landmark, and posthumous, book *Choosing a Vocation* (1909), he proposed three steps to vocational development:

> First, a clear understanding of yourself, your aptitudes, abilities, interests, resources, limitations and other qualities. Second, knowledge of the requirements and conditions of success, advantages and disadvantages, compensation, opportunities, and prospects in different lines of work. Third, true reasoning on the relations of these two groups of facts (p. 5).

Readers will recall that in Chapter 3 we discussed how the Ikhwan al-Safa of tenth century Iraq proposed that there be a similar compatibility between a person's individual characteristics and certain occupations. Williamson (1939) describes a six-step career counseling process: (1) analysis, (2) synthesis, (3) diagnosis, (4) prognosis, (5) counseling, and (6) follow-up. The first three steps involve gathering and synthesizing clinical information to determine client strengths and weaknesses. Conclusions are based on those strengths and weaknesses. These steps help the counselor to identify how well such strengths and weaknesses match client adjustment to available conditions or choices (Chartrand, 1991). At the same time, vocational psychologists at the University of Minnesota developed special aptitude tests, personality inventories, and other devices elaborating and expanding Parsons's three steps, mostly in response to employment problems created by the Great Depression.

All these developments became part of Trait-Factor Theory. **Traits** are learned, which makes them viable for change through lifelong learning. This raises questions about traits' stability and endurance. Traits of greatest interest to vocational practitioners—interests, special aptitudes, and scholastic aptitudes —seem relatively stable (Hogan, DeSoto, & Solana, 1977). When a vocational practitioner administers an interest inventory to a client, he or she is interested in how well the inventory predicts job choice and subsequent satisfaction (**predictive validity**). The practitioner is equally interested in how the same score can help the client identify values, preferences for work activities, decision-making style, and way of being perceived by others (Brown, Brooks, & Associates, 1991).

Reviews of trait-factor research have varied. Klein and Weiner (1977) conclude: (1) Each individual has a unique set of traits that can be measured reliably and validly. (2) Occupations require that workers possess specific traits for success, although a worker with a rather wide range of characteristics still can be successful in a given job. (3) The choice of an occupation is a rather straightforward process, and matching is possible. (4) Brown et al. (2002) emphasized that the closer the match between personal characteristics and job requirements, the greater the likelihood of success—in productivity and satisfaction.

Evaluation of Trait-Factor Theory

Trait-Factor Theory works best with clients who are clear on their **self-concept,** aware of options, and have had various life/work experiences. Assessments used with this theory assume that clients can differentiate between their likes and dislikes, as well as their preferred activities, co-workers, and lifestyle.

For several decades, the trait-factor approach enjoyed considerable success. Until the 1950s it was the major theory used for career counseling. This preeminent position faded as client-centered psychotherapy permeated the counseling field and

Practical Applications

Trait-factor theory views career choice as a straightforward cognitive process (Williamson, 1965). Sharf (2003) summarizes the process as:

Step 1—Gaining Self-Understanding:

1. Aptitudes
2. Achievements
3. Interests
4. Values
5. Personality

Step 2—Obtaining Knowledge about the World of Work:

1. Types of Occupational Information
2. Classification Systems
3. Trait and Factor Requirements

Step 3—Integrating Information about Oneself and the World of Work, including identifying occupational options and developing a plan of action.

Trait-Factor Theory approaches are a useful place to *start* an occupational counseling process.

developmental and social learning approaches to career counseling matured. The current status of Trait-Factor Theory is debatable. Its contribution to vocational psychology continues to be acknowledged, but its viability as a specific counseling approach is sometimes dismissed.

> Both the model and the counseling approach that it spawned have been carefully scrutinized. Some interpretations of the model's underlying assumptions are disputable, but have been widely cited ... [including] the belief that occupational choice is a single event, that a single type of person works in each job, that there is a single right goal for every career decision maker, and that occupational choice is available to everyone (Chartrand, 1991, p. 519).

Counselors who used trait-factor approaches were often criticized for being too directive and forceful in their recommendations. The trait-factor model includes "(a) diagnosis of the client's problem and assignment of multiple tests, (b) interpretation of the test results, and (c) selection of a career alternative based on test results" (Chartrand, 1991, p. 519).

A New Model for Trait-Factor Theory

The trait-factor approach was updated by Chartrand and Bertok (1993), who described a cognitive-interactional view. Their very comprehensive assessment paradigm included attention to a client's cognitions, personality, and interpersonal relations. Including the client's interests, abilities, values, and the characteristic of the client's work environment, the paradigm is meant to apply to a variety of counseling situations, whether one is trying to fit a person to an initial occupational choice or to facilitate adjustment at a later point in career development. A three-dimensional model guides people doing cognitive-interactional assessment: (1) attention to problem type—choice, implementation, performance, adaptation; (2) problem focus—person, environment, or their interaction; (3) timing of the assessment—early, middle, late. Also, a client's perceived level of self-knowledge or knowledge of occupations, perceived work and nonwork stressors, and personality needs to be assessed.

Assessment Instruments Based on Trait-Factor Theory

Trait-factor approaches to test interpretation focus on predicting the likelihood of success based on similarities of responses between the client taking the test and people already in the occupation who report that they enjoy their work. These approaches do not tell clients what job they should have. No attempt is made to predict long-term success.

Clients find occupations that match their current abilities and needs. The practitioner's role is to teach clients how to obtain information from existing sources because few occupational materials contain the full range of information that clients need. Clients determine a tentative occupational choice, then the practitioner directly helps them implement that choice. The practitioner may find a suitable preparation experience, identify employment opportunities, and teach the skills needed to secure the job and hold it. The final step is follow-up. It involves determining whether the course of action established by counseling is correct in the client's view. With satisfactory results, no further steps are necessary. With unsatisfactory results, the process may have to be reinitiated.

Aptitude Tests These aptitude measures were normed on high school and college populations and give some general information regarding aptitude, potential in various learning environments:

- American College Testing (ACT)
- APTICOM (includes interest, assessments of aptitudes, and educational skills development)
- Armed Services Vocational Aptitude Battery (ASVAB)
- College Board Scholastic Aptitude Tests (SAT)
- Differential Aptitude Tests (DAT)
- School and College Ability Tests (SCAT)
- Ball Aptitude Battery (BAB) (Level 1 for ninth and tenth grades, level 2 for eleventh, twelfth, and adult)

Interest Inventories These assessment tools assist in determining a client's range of work interests.

- Campbell Interest and Skills Survey (CISS)
- Career Assessment Inventory (CAI)
- Career Occupation Preference System Interest Inventory (COPS)
- Interests, Determination, Exploration & Assessment System (IDEAS)
- Harrington–O'Shea Career Decision-Making System, Revised (CDM-R)
- Jackson Vocational Interest Survey (JVIS)
- Kuder Occupational Interests Survey (KOIS)
- Self-Directed Search (SDS)
- Strong Interest Inventory (SII)
- Vocational Preference Interests (VPI)
- Wide Range Interest-Opinion Test (WRIOT)
- Reading-Free Vocational Interest Inventory-Revised (RFV-R II)
- O★Net Interest Profiles (O★Net computer database)

Values Inventories These inventories assist clients in clarifying and prioritizing values relevant to career choice and the workplace.

- Minnesota Importance Questionnaire (MIQ)
- Rokeach Values Survey
- Study of Values (SV)
- Values Scale (VS)
- Work mate
- Career Values Card Sort Kit (CVCS)

Personality Inventories Listed here are those that help match personal traits with interests and/or work roles.

- Myers-Briggs Type Indicator (MBTI)
- Salience Inventory/Scale (SS) (SI)
- Sixteen Personality Factor Questionnaire (16PF) (PCD Profile Form)
- Neuroticism, Extraversion, and Openness Personality Inventory, Revised (NEO-PI-R)

Publishers of each test are listed in Appendix 3.

Person by Environment (PxE) Fit

The trait-factor approach has evolved into the **Person by Environment (PxE) Fit,** which is described in Table 4.1. PxE is based on three assumptions. First, people are capable of making rational decisions, which illustrates the appropriateness of cognitive interventions. Second, people and work environments differ across various situations; thus, identifying patterns could be helpful in organizing people and environments. Third, the greater the congruence between personal traits and requirements on the job, the greater the possibility of finding job satisfaction (Chartrand, 1991). In addition, there is a reciprocal process between individuals and the environment (Rounds & Tracey, 1990).

Relevance to Multicultural and Diverse Populations

African Americans. No specific test of the Trait-Factor Theory pertinent to African American populations has been uncovered (Brown, 1995). To understand the diverse life experiences of African Americans, the domain of potential factors salient to the career behavior of these people needs to be adequately defined, operationalized, or investigated. Dismissing Trait-Factor Theory as irrelevant to the career behavior of African Americans may be premature; better-designed research is needed to test its validity here. Since our first edition, such research has not occurred in substantial amounts.

Gay, Lesbian, and Bisexual People. Gelberg and Chojnacki (1996) modify the trait-factor approach to include sexual orientation and level of sexual identity development as personal variables that need to go beyond the traditional consideration of vocational interests, values, and abilities and aptitudes. The degree to which a work environment is either affirmative or hostile to gay, lesbian, and bisexual people needs more attention because incongruence results when a gay, lesbian, or bisexual person is in an overtly or covertly discriminatory work environment.

Hispanics. Available research on the assessment of interests of Hispanics indicates that the interest patterns and structures of interests are not different than for Whites (Fouad, 1995). More study is needed to determine if acculturation, the number of generations in the United States, socioeconomic status, and geographic location modifies the similarity of results across cultures. Again, since our first edition, such studies have not been extensively done.

Asian Americans. Assessment of career interests with Asian Americans using psychometrically valid instruments remains sparse (Leong & Gim-Chung, 1995). This continues to be the case. Representative, normative samples of Asian Americans are needed from across the United States.

TABLE 4.1 Comparisons between the Trait-Factor and PxE Fit

TRAIT-FACTOR	PxE FIT
Theoretical Assumptions	
■ Humans are capable of rational decision-making. ■ Reliable and meaningful individual and environmental differences can be assessed. ■ Matching persons and environments increase the probability of positive outcomes.	■ Humans are capable of rational decision-making. ■ Reliable and meaningful individual and environmental differences can be assessed. ■ Matching persons and environments increase the probability of positive outcomes. ■ Individuals seek out congruent environments. ■ PxE fit is reciprocal and ongoing.
Theoretical Framework	
■ Empirically based formulations that apply matching principle	■ Theoretical formulations that address both structure and process
Counseling Diagnosis	
■ Differential diagnosis of career choice difficulties	■ Differential diagnosis of career choice, planning, and adjustment difficulties
Counseling Process	
■ Williamson's (1939, 1950) six-stage problem-solving sequence	■ Rounds & Tracey's (1990) four-step information processing sequence
Counseling Outcome	
■ Two levels: specific goal attainment and learning decision-making skills	■ Two levels: specific goal attainment and learning decision-making skills
Counselor Style	
■ A supportive teaching style	■ Typically a supportive teaching style ■ Congruence between counselor behavior and client needs
Psychometric Information	
■ Psychometric instruments can be used to predict relevant criteria. ■ Interpretations are made within the broader context of counseling, are based on actuarial and clinical information, and are used to enhance self-understanding.	■ Psychometric instruments can be used to predict relevant criteria. ■ Interpretations are made within the broader context of counseling, are based on actuarial and clinical information, and are used to enhance self-understanding. ■ Client involvement in the assessment process is actively sought.

SOURCE: Chartrand (1991), p. 519. From the *Journal of Counseling and Development*, p. 519, © 1991, by permission of the American Counseling Association.

Native Americans. Of particular concern with Native-American populations is whether people grew up on a rural reservation, in an urban area, or both. PxE Fit becomes especially relevant because it considers an individual's inherent differences and thus allows Native Americans an opportunity to integrate personal, environmental, and cultural characteristics into the career development process (Johnson, Swartz, & Martin, 1995). Awareness of the world of work, characteristic of both trait-factor and PxE approaches, is vital with Native Americans whose knowledge about vocations and careers is limited. Use of local norms for any standardized assessment instruments is strongly recommended. In many reservation communities where job opportunities are limited, an accurate person-job match is facilitated by the trait-factor approach (Johnson et al., 1995; Martin, 1995).

HOLLAND'S THEORY OF VOCATIONAL AND WORK ENVIRONMENT

Before explaining John Holland's topology, it is important to understand his theory on how personally develops. As you can see in Figure 4.1, he incorporates Staats's 1981 theory of social behaviorism as well as Krumboltz's social learning theory.

John Holland's typology has probably driven more empirical research since its initial appearance in the 1950s than any other theory of career behavior. A revision of his theory and its current status reflect a number of significant refinements and improvements (Holland, 1997), and he has become more explicit in explaining the theory in terms of PxE considerations. Four working assumptions comprise the core of his theory: (1) In American culture, most people can be categorized as one of six types: **realistic, investigative, artistic, social, enterprising,** or **conventional.** (2) There are six correspondent model environments. (3) People search for environments that will let them exercise their skills and abilities, express their attitudes and values, and take on agreeable problems and roles. (4) Behavior is determined by interaction between personality and environment.

Five secondary assumptions moderate and explain the differences in the outcomes.

1. Consistency is the degree of relatedness between personality types or between environmental models.
2. Differentiation is the degree to which a person or environment is well defined.
3. Identity estimates the clarity and stability of a person's or environment's identity.
4. Congruence means that different types require different environments.
5. Calculus is the relationship within and between types or environments, and it can be ordered according to the hexagonal model where the difference in the distance between types or environments is inversely proportionate to the theoretical relationship between them (Holland, 1997).

Figure 4.2 shows a hexagonal model for Holland's typology. This is known within the vocational psychology and career counseling field as the *RIASEC Hexagon.*

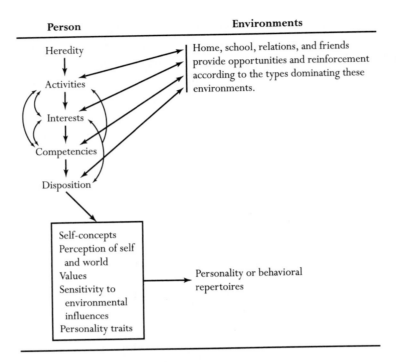

FIGURE 4.1 How Personality Types Develop

SOURCE: Reproduced by special permission of the Publisher, Psychological Asssessment Resources, Inc., 16204 North Florida Avenue, Lutz, FL 33549, from Making Vocational Choices, Third Edition, Copyright 1973, 1985, 1992, 1997 by Psychological Assessment Resources, Inc. All rights reserved.

Personality types and work environments adjacent to each other are presumed to be most similar. Types and environments opposite each other are presumed to be most dissimilar. To further elaborate, a number of principles seem plausible.

The choice of a vocation is an expression of personality.

Interest inventories are personality inventories.

Vocational stereotypes have reliable and important psychological and sociological meanings.

The members of a vocation have similar personalities and similar histories of personal development.

Because people in a vocational group have similar personalities, they will respond to many situations and problems in similar ways, and they will create characteristic interpersonal environments.

Vocational satisfaction, stability, and achievement depend on the congruence between one's personality and the environment in which one works (Holland, 1992, pp. 7–10).

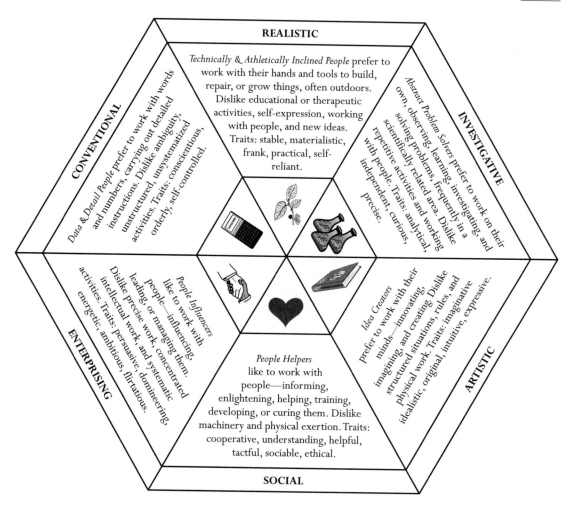

REALISTIC

Technically & Athletically Inclined People prefer to work with their hands and tools to build, repair, or grow things, often outdoors. Dislike educational or therapeutic activities, self-expression, working with people, and new ideas. Traits: stable, materialistic, frank, practical, self-reliant.

CONVENTIONAL

Data & Detail People prefer to work with words and numbers, carrying out detailed instructions. Dislike ambiguity, unstructured, unsystematized activities. Traits: conscientious, orderly, self-controlled.

INVESTIGATIVE

Abstract Problem Solvers prefer to work on their own, observing, learning, investigating, and solving problems, frequently in a scientifically related area. Dislike repetitive activities and working with people. Traits: analytical, independent, curious, precise.

ENTERPRISING

People Influencers like to work with people—influencing, leading, or managing them. Dislike precise work, concentrated intellectual work, and systematic activities. Traits: persuasive, domineering, energetic, ambitious, flirtatious.

ARTISTIC

Idea Creators prefer to work with their minds—innovating, imagining and creating. Dislike structured situations, rules, and physical work. Traits: imaginative, idealistic, original, intuitive, expressive.

People Helpers like to work with people—informing, enlightening, helping, training, developing, or curing them. Dislike machinery and physical exertion. Traits: cooperative, understanding, helpful, tactful, sociable, ethical.

SOCIAL

FIGURE 4.2 A Hexagonal Model for Defining the Psychological Resemblances Among Types and Environments and Their Interactions

SOURCE: *Holland, J. L.*, Making vocational choices: A theory of vocational personalities and work environments *(2nd edition), p. 29. Englewood Cliffs, NJ: Prentice Hall.*

Formulations of the Types

The hexagonal model visually represents the theory, assists one to identify the amount of consistency in one's personality patterns and environments, and enhances awareness of the congruency or incongruency between personal traits and work environments. We use the 3rd edition of *Making Vocational Choices* to describe formulations of the types (Holland, 1997).

The Realistic Type

The development of a Realistic pattern of activities, competencies, and interests creates a person who is predisposed to exhibit the following characteristics:

1. *Vocational and Avocational Preferences*: Prefers Realistic occupations or situations (e.g., electrician or mechanic) in which one can engage in preferred activities and avoid the activities demanded by Social occupations or situations.
2. *Life Goals and Values*: Possesses traditional values. Prefers to work within institutional restraints. Believes in freedom (independence or free choice). Ranks being ambitious and self-controlled as important values and deprecates being forgiving. In general, values concrete things or tangible personal characteristics.
3. *Self-Beliefs*: Perceives self as having mechanical, technical, and athletic abilities. Enjoys working with hands, tools, machines, and electronic equipment. Perceives self as lacking ability in human relations, and believes some social tasks would be frustrating.
4. *Problem-Solving Style*: Uses Realistic beliefs, competencies, and values to solve problems at work and in other settings. Prefers concrete, practical, and structured solutions or strategies as opposed to clerical, scholarly, or imaginative activities.

Because the Realistic person possesses these preferences, beliefs, competencies, self perceptions, and values, he or she is apt to be:

Conforming	Materialistic	Realistic
Dogmatic	Natural	Reserved
Genuine	Normal	Robust
Hardheaded	Persistent	Self-effacing
Inflexible	Practical	Un-insightful

The Investigative Type

The development of an Investigative pattern of activities, competencies, and interests creates a person who is predisposed to exhibit the following characteristics:

1. *Vocational and Avocational Preferences*: Prefers Investigative occupations or situations (e.g., biologist or medical technologist) in which one can engage in preferred activities demanded by enterprising occupations or situations.
2. *Life Goals and Values*: Values scientific or scholarly activities and achievements. Values self-determination (independence) as well as personal traits

such as being intellectual, logical, and ambitious, but holds other life goals or values as less important: family security, being cheerful, having true friendships. Possesses an open system of beliefs.

3. *Self-Beliefs*: Perceives self as having scientific or research ability as well as mathematical talent. Sees self as analytical, curious, scholarly, and having broad interests. Enjoys reading or thinking about solutions to problems. Believes that persuading others about a course of action would be frustrating. Sees self as broadminded and having a wide range of interests. Has moderate to high self-esteem.

4. *Problem-Solving Style*: Uses investigative beliefs, competencies, and values to solve problems at work and in other settings. Seeks challenging problems.

Because the Investigative person possesses these beliefs, preferences, competencies, self-perceptions, and values, he or she is apt to be:

Analytical	Independent	Radical
Cautious	Intellectual	Rational
Complex	Introspective	Reserved
Critical	Pessimistic	Retiring
Curious	Precise	Unassuming

The Artistic Type

The development of an Artistic pattern of activities, competencies, and interests creates a person who is predisposed to exhibit the following characteristics:

1. *Vocational and Avocational Preferences:* Prefers Artistic occupations or situations (e.g., writer or interior decorator) in which one can engage in preferred activities and competencies and avoid the activities demanded by Conventional occupations or situations.

2. *Life Goals and Values:* Values aesthetic experience and achievement. Values self-expression and equality for all as well as personal characteristics such as being imaginative and courageous but not being obedient, logical, or responsible.

3. *Self-Beliefs*: Perceives self as expressive, open, original, intuitive, liberal, nonconforming, introspective, independent, disorderly, having artistic and musical ability, and ability in acting, writing, and speaking.

4. *Problem-Solving Style*: Uses Artistic beliefs, competencies, and values to solve problems at work or in other settings. Perceives problems in artistic context, so artistic talents and personal traits (e.g., intuition, expressiveness, originality) dominate the problem-solving process.

Because the Artistic person possesses these beliefs, preferences, competencies, self-perceptions, and values, he or she is apt to be:

Complicated	Imaginative	Intuitive
Disorderly	Impractical	Nonconforming
Emotional	Impulsive	Open
Expressive	Independent	Original
Idealistic	Introspective	Sensitive

The Social Type

The development of a Social pattern of activities, competencies, and interests creates a person who is predisposed to exhibit the following characteristics:

1. *Vocational and Avocational Preferences*: Prefers Social occupations and situations (e.g., teacher or counselor) in which one can engage in preferred activities and avoid the activities demanded by Realistic occupations and situations. Can also associate with people having similar beliefs and values.

2. *Life Goals and Values*: Values social and ethical activities and problems. Wants to serve others in the context of medical support, institutional service, or reciprocal interactions. Believes in equality for all and the desirability of being helpful and forgiving but deprecates being logical and intellectual or having an exciting life. Values religion.

3. *Self-Beliefs*: Perceives self as liking to help others, understanding of others, having teaching ability, social skills, and lacking mechanical and scientific ability. Most gratified by helping or teaching others.

4. *Problem-Solving Style*: Uses social beliefs, competencies, and values to solve problems at work or in other settings. Perceives problems in a social context so problems are viewed more often in human relations terms; social competencies traits (e.g., seeking mutual interactions and help from others, etc.) can dominate the problem-solving process.

Because the Social person possesses these beliefs, preferences, competencies, self-perceptions, and values, he or she is apt to be:

Agreeable	Helpful	Responsible
Cooperative	Idealistic	Sociable
Empathic	Kind	Tactful
Friendly	Patient	Understanding
Generous	Persuasive	Warm

The Enterprising Type

The development of an Enterprising pattern of activities, competencies, and interests creates a person who is predisposed to exhibit the following characteristics:

1. *Vocational and Avocational Preferences*: Prefers Enterprising occupations or situations (e.g., sales person or manager) in which one can engage in preferred activities and avoid the activities demanded by Investigative occupations and situations.

2. *Life Goals and Values*: Has traditional values (e.g., economic and political achievement). Values controlling others, the opportunity to be free of control, and being ambitious.

3. *Self-Beliefs*: Perceives self as aggressive, popular, self-confident, sociable, possessing leadership and speaking abilities, and lacking scientific ability. Has high self-esteem. Holds traditional values.

4. *Problem-Solving Style*: Uses Enterprising beliefs, competencies, and values to solve problems at work or in other situations. Perceives problems in an enterprising context so problems are often viewed in social influence terms.

Because the Enterprising person possesses these beliefs, preferences, competencies, self-perceptions, and values, he or she is apt to be:

Acquisitive	Energetic	Forceful
Adventurous	Enthusiastic	Optimistic
Ambitious	Excitement-seeking	Resourceful
Assertive	Exhibitionistic	Self-confident
Domineering	Extroverted	Sociable

The Conventional Type

The development of a Conventional pattern of activities, competencies, and interests creates a person who is predisposed to exhibit the following characteristics:

1. *Vocational and Avocational Preferences:* Prefers Conventional occupations or situations (e.g., bookkeeper or banker) in which one can engage in preferred activities and avoid the activities demanded by the Artistic occupations or situations.

2. *Life Goals and Values:* Values business and economic achievement. Believes becoming an expert in finance or commerce, leading a comfortable life,

and doing a lot of work are important goals. Values are characterized by traditional virtues. Has a very closed belief system.

3. *Self-Beliefs*: Perceives self as conforming and orderly, and as having clerical and numerical ability. Sees greatest competencies in business and weakest in the arts.

4. *Problem Solving Style*: Uses conventional beliefs, competencies, and values to solve problems at work and in other situations. Follows established rules, practices, and procedures; looks to authorities for advice and counsel.

Because the Conventional person possesses these beliefs, preferences, competencies, self-perceptions, and values, he or she is apt to be:

Careful	Inflexible	Persistent
Conforming	Inhibited	Practical
Conscientious	Methodical	Thorough
Dogmatic	Obedient	Thrifty
Efficient	Orderly	Unimaginative

Assessment Instruments Used with Holland's Theory

The following assessment instruments are used with Holland's Theory:

1. Self-Directed Search (SDS)
2. My Vocational Situation (MVS)
3. Strong Interest Inventory (SII)
4. The World-of-Work Map (ACT, Inc., 2000)
5. Vocational Preference Inventory (VPI)
6. Career Assessment Inventory (CAI)
7. Harrington/O'Shea Systems—Career Decision-Making, Revised (CDM-R)

Evaluation of Holland's Model

Holland's theory has been extremely well researched, with continual refinements and improvements. Each time revisions are made, nine empirical studies are conducted to further test aspects of his theoretical hypotheses. Throughout the research, most findings corroborate the theory's vitality and validity. The model serves a useful purpose in the field of vocational psychology.

Practical Applications

Various instruments are used to assess Holland's personality types. Most common is the Self-Directed Search (SDS), a self-completed, self-scored look at an individual's occupational daydreams, activities, actual occupations, and self-estimates across several abilities and skills areas. The total score adds up to the relative strength of each area in the RIASEC hexagon. The three highest scores become the three-letter code. This code and others closely related to it become the basis for matching the individual and the occupation. Other instruments used are the Strong Interest Inventory (SII), Career Assessment Inventory (CAI), and the Vocational Preference Inventory (VPI). The Occupations Finder (1997) is an excellent resource that can be used with the SII, CAI, VPI, and SDS results.

A client's hexagon location has many practical applications:

1. Using the three-letter code for occupational groups on the hexagon, clients can find occupations close to their own hexagon locations. For example, clients with an SAI code will see that occupations with ISA, SIA, IAS, and ASI codes also are nearby. Clients may wish to broaden career exploration by looking into those occupations as well.
2. When an interest test is used, such as the SII, determine whether a client's preferred occupation and measured interests have similar (congruent) hexagon locations. To the extent that the locations are similar, the preferred occupation will be supported by measured interests and the client will generally have many occupations available to choose from.
3. Compare the hexagon locations of a client's interests and abilities.

There are several practical implications of the congruence theory, mainly for those who happen to be incongruent in their occupational choice. Some solutions are:

1. Replace their working unit with a more congruent working unit while remaining in the same occupation and specialty.
2. Replace their specialty within their occupation with one that is more congruent for them.
3. Choose an avocational activity that is congruent with their interests (with the option of making it their occupation after a sufficient period of experience and training).
4. Play down the importance of the job and its environment as sources of satisfaction and other measures of well-being, and compensate by enhancing the importance of other kinds of congruence, such as skill congruence, avocational congruence, or congruence with the ideas of the others in one's environment.
5. Change one's occupation and/or environment to a more congruent one (Meir, 1989, p. 229).

Continued

Continued

According to Holland (1997), "maladaptive career development indicates either a failure to develop a clear sense of vocational identity (i.e., a personality pattern that is consistent and differentiated) or a failure to establish a career in a congruent occupation. Maladaptive career development probably occurs in one or more of the seven major ways:" (p. 196)

1. A person has had *insufficient experience* to acquire well-defined interests, competencies, and self-perceptions.
2. A person has had *insufficient experience* to learn about the major kinds of occupational environments.
3. A person has had *ambiguous, conflicting, inaccurate, or negative experience* concerning his or her interests, competencies, or personal characteristics.
4. A person has acquired *ambiguous, conflicting, inaccurate, or negative information* about the major work environments.
5. All four probably contribute to a diffuse sense of identity that makes choosing an occupation or changing jobs much more uncertain.
6. Some people lack the personal, educational, or financial resources to carry out their plans.
7. The availability of different types of work is determined by (a) the sociotechnical nature of the economy, (b) cultural values, (c) stages in the economic cycle, and (d) traditional definitions of sexual or ethnic roles.

In contrast, adaptive vocational behavior is the outcome of the following events:

1. A person has had sufficient experience to acquire well-defined interests and competencies.
2. A person has had sufficient experience to acquire a useful library of occupational stereotypes, especially in his or her area of interest.
3. A person has had sufficient clarifying occupational experience so that his or her library of occupational information and stereotypes (generalizations) has a useful degree of validity and is free of major contradictions.
4. A person has had sufficient self-clarifying experience so that the pictures of his or her interests, competencies, and personal characteristics are accurate.
5. A person has acquired sufficient vocational identity, self-confidence, interpersonal competency, cultural involvement, and other resources to make vocational decisions as the need occurs and to cope with a variety of common job problems.
6. A person possesses the personal, educational, and financial resources to carry out his or her vocational plans.
7. A person's plans are not deflected in any major way by cultural, economic, social, or technological influences.

While this theory attempts to explain considerations of the PxE fit, Schwartz (1992) questions the validity of the concept of congruence. There is no clear evidence that congruence is associated with achievement or stability. Occasionally positive associations between congruence and satisfaction are an artifact of an uninvestigated common association between role-choice clarity and both congruence and satisfaction.

Differences in needs, interests, values, abilities, experiences, and psychological state between those who are most and least satisfied as well as accomplished in their respective occupations could develop PxE fit tests that are more valid than the inventories used today. "Comparatively, little vocational psychology research is devoted to the development of occupation-specific, occupational-specialty specific or occupational-group specific tests. Is Holland's work worthy of so much attention or should vocational psychology move on?" (Schwartz, 1992, pp. 1 85–186). Holland (1996) points to several studies, primarily Helms and Williams (1964) and a reexamination by Helms (1996), that demonstrate strong support for the congruency hypothesis. He cites studies by Carson and Mowsesian (1991) and Gottfredson and Holland (1990) that found a sense of vocational identity more valuable in predicting job satisfaction than congruency of interests and job, and that expectation of job satisfaction was a better predictor of actual job satisfaction than the congruency of interests and job.

The existence of traits and their predictive power merit reexamination. In social psychology, the ongoing debate continues to be whether dispositionism or situationalism explains people's behavior (Ross & Nesbitt, 1991). **Dispositionism** is the layperson's belief "that individual differences or traits can be used to predict how people will behave in new situations" (p. 3). **Situationalism** refers to the belief that the ability to predict how people will react in certain situations is actually quite limited. Quantitative (i.e., modernist-based) research has shown a maximum correlation of .30 between a measure of individual differences on a given trait and subsequent behavior in a new situation where the trait is hypothesized to be strongly predictive. This leaves .70 of the variance unexplained. Many laypeople and researchers fail to realize how the power of situations in general and the power of subtle situational factors in particular determine people's responses to their social environment more than quantifiable measures of traits. This failure to recognize the power of the situation is called a **fundamental attribution error** (Gilbert & Jones, 1986; Jones, 1979; Nisbett & Ross, 1980).

Trait-factor and PxE approaches will only predict so much. Vocational psychologists are advised that these approaches will probably not break the .30 ceiling that social psychologists have encountered when attempting to demonstrate that stable personal attributes can accurately predict the behavior of particular people in particular situations. An unexplained variance of .70 accounts for long-term occupational adjustment, satisfaction, and success. We wonder how vocational psychology and

career counseling would be different if its scholars and researchers had been in dialogue much earlier with the social psychologists. Perhaps postmodern, **contextual
interpretation** would have become a central component much sooner in the vocational guidance and assessment tradition.

Relevance to Multicultural and Diverse Populations

Interest inventories require a client to be introspective, something not encouraged
among subcultures with predominantly collectivist values (Prince, Uemura, Chao, &
Gonzales, 1991). External structural factors also can influence the way multicultural
people view occupations. The RIASEC hexagon's accuracy and meaning across cultures has not been extensively researched. The subtle values with which a practitioner evaluates significant between-group differences on measured interests, especially
when one of those groups is the dominant White population, also should be monitored. Traditional models of assessment may need to be adjusted for multicultural and
diverse populations.

African Americans The historic experience of many African Americans is one of
restricted work options; yet Holland did not address the long-term implications of
this historical reality on the development of work personalities (Brown, 1995). Empirical support does exist for African Americans in different occupations having different patterns of interests. Likewise, empirical support exists for person-environment
fit/congruence, where African Americans of a particular Holland code are found in
occupations with similar classification codes. More research is needed that addresses
the concepts of congruence, consistency, differentiation, and identity for validity with
African Americans.

Hispanics Substantial research attention has been given to career interests with diverse Hispanic subgroups using different RIASEC-based assessment instruments
(Arbona, 1995). Hispanic high school and college students' view of the world of work
is similar to that of the majority White culture. The Holland scales may be considered
appropriate for assessing Hispanic students' interests. However, the general fit between
personality and environment among Hispanic populations remains to be tested empirically.

Asian Americans Marked occupational segregation apparently characterizes the
Asian American population (Leong & Serafica, 1995). **Occupational segregation**
refers to an overrepresentation of specific population groups in some occupations
while being underrepresented in others. Generally speaking, occupational segregation
can be the result of differential access to various occupations, including restricted ac-

cess. Asian Americans are over-represented among physicians, five times more than expected, given their proportion of the U.S. population; three times more than expected among medical scientists, physicists, astronomers, and biological and life scientists; and twice as often among engineers, architects, accountants, and auditors (Hisa, 1988, cited in Leong & Serafica, 1995). Congruence studies are needed to clarify whether occupational segregation reflects vocational choice on the part of Asian Americans—in the sense that Holland conceptualizes choice—or whether segregation results from other factors such as parental pressure, occupational stereotyping, or discrimination.

Native Americans The absence of occupational knowledge or experience can skew the results for respondents of any RIASEC-based instrument. Careful consideration needs to be given to this fact when assessing Native Americans (Johnson et al., 1995).

Gay, Lesbian, and Bisexual People Heterosexual bias is always a risk with any career assessment instrument. Career aspirations of gays/lesbians/bisexuals may differ from heterosexual men and women, and these differences may show up in RIASEC-based instruments (Gelberg & Chojnacki, 1996). Gay men, for example, tend to score higher in the Artistic and Social domains than do heterosexual men. What remains unclear is whether interest inventories are measuring intrinsic differences between gay, lesbian, and bisexual people and heterosexual people, or whether external factors such as social expectations to conform are exerting pressure on response patterns.

People with Disabilities Holland's emphasis on testing and the provision of occupational information to clients is of limited utility for individuals with mental retardation (Levinson, Peterson, & Elston, 1994). Without adequate opportunities for developing the skills upon which vocational potential is measured, testing can become one of the least desirable forms of assessment to use with people with mental retardation. A heavy reliance on self-direction in Holland's approach also restricts its usefulness for such individuals. A clinical modification of this approach can occur, but only in terms of identifying practical occupational options for people with mental retardation.

Women Gender differences in interest inventories have been noted by several scholars (Betz, 1994; Betz & Fitzgerald, 1987; Hackett & Lonborg, 1993; Walsh & Betz, 1990). Sex-restrictiveness in results can occur when uninformed practitioners use interest inventory results to reinforce gender stratification in the world of work. Inventory results that perpetuate occupational stereotypes by gender are still a danger. For women, within-group differences in sex-role socialization can influence the response patterns and reflect differences due to experience, not interests.

THE MYERS-BRIGGS TYPE INDICATOR

The **Myers-Briggs Type Indicator (MBTI)** is not designed as a career development tool but is used in conjunction with other instruments. Research on the MBTI primarily has been done through the Center for the Application of Psychological Type. The MBTI is closely related to Trait-Factor Theory (Sharf, 2002). Based on a theory of personality devised by Swiss psychologist and psychiatrist Carl Gustav Jung (1875–1961), for career counseling purposes the MBTI is used primarily with interests and aptitude assessments. The MBTI and its manual were revised in 1998. The following descriptions of each type were taken from the original source.

> The essence of Jung's comprehensive theory . . . [of] . . . psychological types is . . . that everyone uses four basic mental *functions* or *processes* . . . [:] . . . sensing (S), intuitive (N), thinking (T), and feeling (F). Everyone uses these four essential functions daily . . .
>
> To understand Jung's theory, it is essential to appreciate the uses of the terms *perception* and *judgment*. Perception includes the many ways of becoming aware of things, people, events, or ideas. It includes information gathering, the seeking of sensation or of inspiration, and the selection of the stimulus to be attended to. Judgment includes all the ways of coming to conclusions about what has been perceived. It includes decision-making, evaluation, choice, and the selections of the response after perceiving the stimulus.
>
> Jung divided all perceptive activities into two categories—sensing and intuition. He called these *irrational functions* . . . [in] . . . that these functions are attuned to the flow of events and operate most broadly when not constrained by rational direction . . .
>
> **Sensing (S)** refers to perceptions that are observable by the senses. Sensing establishes what exists. Because the senses can bring to awareness only what is occurring in the present moment, persons oriented toward sensing perception tend to focus on the immediate experience and often develop characteristics associated with this awareness such as enjoying the present moment, realism, acute powers of observation, memory for details, and practicality.
>
> **Intuition (N)** refers to perception of possibilities, meanings, and relationships by way of insight. . . . Intuition permits perception beyond what is visible to the senses, including possible future events. Thus, persons oriented toward intuitive perception may become so intent on pursuing possibilities that they may overlook actualities. They may develop the characteristics than can follow from emphasis on intuition and become imaginative, theoretical, abstract, future oriented, or creative. Jung used the terms *thinking* and *feeling* . . . to refer to the *rational functions* that are directed toward bringing life events into harmony with the laws of reason.

Thinking (T) is the function that links ideas together by making logical connections. Thinking relies on principles of cause and effect and tends to be impersonal. Persons who are primarily oriented to thinking may develop . . . [:] analytical ability, objectivity, concern with principles of justice and fairness, criticality, and an orientation to time that is concerned with connections from the past through the present and toward the future.

Feeling (F) is the function by which one comes to decisions by weighing the relative values and merits of the issues. Feeling relies on an understanding of personal and groups values; thus, it is more subjective than thinking. . . . [P]ersons making judgments with the feeling function are more likely to be attuned to the values of others . . . , [have] a concern with the human as opposed to the technical aspects of problems, a need for affiliation, a capacity for warmth, a desire for harmony, and a time orientation that includes preservation of the values of the past (p. 12, italics in original; boldfaces added).

While the functions or processes are included in the above, Jung was very interested in the complementary attitudes or orientations to life embodied in **extraversion** and **introversion.**

In the extraverted attitude **(E),** attention seems to flow out, or to be drawn out to the objects and people of the environment. . . . [C]haracteristics associated with extraversion [are]: awareness and reliance on the environment for stimulation and guidance; an action-oriented, sometimes impulsive way of meeting life; frankness; ease of communication; or sociability.

In the introverted attitude **(I),** energy is drawn from the environment, and consolidated within one's position. The main interests of the introvert are in the inner world of concepts and ideas. . . . [Introverts have the following] characteristics . . . : interest in the clarity of concepts and ideas; reliance on enduring concepts more than on transitory external events; a thoughtful, contemplative detachment; and enjoyment of solitude and privacy (p. 13).

While Jung did not deal with the importance of judgment and perception directly, Isabel Myers and Katharine Briggs formulated these concepts as a way of describing attitudes and behaviors to the outside world. Furthermore, in relation to the EI attitude, the defining of judgment/perception orientation helps identify which of the two functions, E or I, is the dominant and which is the auxiliary. These help indicate whether thinking-feeling or sensing-intuition are more prominent.

In the **perceptive (P)** attitude, a person is attuned to incoming information. For sensing-perceiving (SP) types the information is more likely to be the immediate realities. For intuitive-perceptive (NP) types the information is more likely to be new possibilities. But for both SP and NP types the perceptive attitude is open, curious, and interested. Persons who characteristically live in the perceptive attitude seem in their outer behavior to be spontaneous, curious, and adaptable, open to new events and changes, and aiming to miss nothing.

In the **judging (J)** attitude, a person is concerned with making decisions, seeking closure, planning operations, or organizing activities. For thinking-judging (TJ) types the decisions and plans are more likely to be based on logical analysis; for *feeling-judging* (FJ) types the decisions and plans are more likely to be based on human factors. But for all persons who characteristically live in the judging (J) attitude, perception tends to be shut off as soon as they have observed enough to make a decision. . . . Persons who prefer J often seem in their outer behavior to be organized, purposeful, and decisive. . . . It is important to make sure it is understood that judgment refers to decision-making, the exercise of judgment, and is a valuable and indispensable tool (p. 14).

Each of these preferences combines to create sixteen different personality type descriptions. These are described in Table 4.2.

Considerable research on the MBTI has been made in conjunction with the Strong Interest Inventory (SII) (Dillon & Weissman, 1987; Levin, 1990; Miller, 1988, 1992). Results of the MBTI and the SII combine to form a career development plan (Hammer & Kummerow, 1993). Figure 4.3 outlines this process.

Evaluation of the Myers-Briggs Typology

The MBTI has been used by many counselors, but has not had universal acceptance. A thorough analysis of many studies involving the MBTI questions the instrument's validity (Pittenger, 1993). It is one of the most researched tests around. However, it is a source of controversy among academics. There are questions about its limitations in counseling, its tendency to make people feel good, and the lack of psychological training of its developers. Yet many counselors believe the information and understanding gained from the instrument have been useful. Our recommendation is that practitioners use it with a full understanding that other instruments may be as effective.

In the revised SII (1994), four Personal Style Scales (PSS)—Work Style, Learning Environment, Leader Style, and Risk Taking/Adventure—have been included. Tuel and Betz (1998) report that a study of the combination of these PSS in the SII, the MBTI, and the Skills Confidence Inventory (SCI) (a measure of self-efficacy expectations) demonstrates an important addition of self-efficacy, to the interest and personality dimensions usually associated with the SII and MBTI. Chapter Six contains a further discussion of self-efficacy.

In other studies, the 16 Personality Factor (16PF) and the Holland scales have been correlated. Pietrzak and Page (2001) found that, while there was some overlap between the personality factors and the Holland types, the congruencies are too small to be very useful.

TABLE 4.2 Effects of the Combinations of All Four Preferences in Young People

CHARACTERISTICS FREQUENTLY ASSOCIATED WITH EACH TYPE

	SENSING TYPES		INTUITIVE TYPES
INTROVERTS	**ISTJ** Serious, quiet, earn success by concentration and thoroughness. Practical, orderly. matter-of-fact, logical, realistic and dependable. See to it that everything is well organized. Take responsibility. Make up their own minds as to what should be accomplished and work toward it steadily, regardless of protests or distractions.	**ISFJ** Quiet, friendly, responsible and conscientious. Work devotedly to meet their obligations. Lend stability to any project or group. Thorough, painstakingly accurate. May need time to master technical subjects, as their interests are usually not technical. Patient with detail and routine. Loyal, considerate, concerned with how other people feel.	**INFJ** Succeed by perseverance, originality and desire to do whatever is needed or wanted. Put their best efforts into their work. Quietly forceful, conscientious, concerned for others. Respected for their firm principles. Likely to be honored and followed for their clear convictions as to how best to serve the common good.	**INTJ** Usually have original minds and great drive for their own ideas and purposes. In fields that appeal to them, they have a fine power to organize a job and carry it through with or without help. Skeptical, critical, independent, determined, often stubborn. Must learn to yield less important points in order to win the most important.
	ISTP Cool onlookers—quiet, reserved, observing and analyzing life with detached curiosity and unexpected flashes of original humor. Usually interested in impersonal principles, cause and effect, how and why mechanical things work. Exert themselves no more than they think necessary, because any waste of energy would be inefficient.	**ISFP** Retiring, quietly friendly, sensitive, kind, modest about their abilities. Shun disagreements, do not force their opinions or values on others. Usually do not care to lead but are often loyal followers. Often relaxed about getting things done, because they enjoy the present moment and do not want to spoil it by undue haste or exertion.	**INFP** Full of enthusiasms and loyalties, but seldom talk of these until they know you well. Care about learning, ideas, language, and independent projects of their own. Tend to undertake too much, then somehow get it done. Friendly, but often too absorbed in what they are doing to be sociable. Little concerned with possessions or physical surroundings.	**INTP** Quiet, reserved, impersonal. Enjoy especially theoretical or scientific subjects. Logical to the point of hair-splitting. Usually interested mainly in ideas, with little liking for parties or small talk. Tend to have sharply defined interests. Need careers where some strong interest can be used and useful.
EXTRAVERTS	**ESTP** Matter-of-fact, do not worry or hurry, enjoy whatever comes along. Tend to like mechanical things and sports, with friends on the side. May be a bit blunt or insensitive. Adaptable, tolerant, generally conservative in values. Dislike long explanations. Are best with real things that can be worked, handled, taken apart or put together.	**ESFP** Outgoing, easygoing, accepting, friendly, enjoy everything and make things more fun for others by their enjoyment. Like sports and making things. Know what's going on and join in eagerly. Find remembering facts easier than mastering theories. Are best in situations that need sound common sense and practical ability with people as well as with things.	**ENFP** Warmly enthusiastic, high-spirited, ingenious, imaginative. Able to do almost anything that interests them. Quick with a solution for any difficulty and ready to help anyone with a problem. Often rely on their ability to improvise instead of preparing in advance. Can usually find compelling reasons for whatever they want.	**ENTP** Quick, ingenious, good at many things. Stimulating company, alert and outspoken. May argue for fun on either side of a question. Resourceful in solving new and challenging problems, but may neglect routine assignments. Apt to turn to one new interest after another. Skillful in finding logical reasons for what they want.
	ESTJ Practical, realistic, matter-of-fact, with a natural head for business or mechanics. Not interested in subjects they see no use for, but can apply themselves when necessary. Like to organize and run activities. May make good administrators, especially if they remember to consider others' feelings and points of view.	**ESFJ** Warm-hearted, talkative, popular, conscientious, born cooperators, active committee members. Need harmony and may be good at creating it. Always doing something nice for someone. Work best with encouragement and praise. Little interest in abstract thinking or technical subjects. Main interest is in things that directly and visibly affect people's lives.	**ENFJ** Responsive and responsible. Generally feel real concern for what others think or want, and try to handle things with due regard for other person's feelings. Can present a proposal or lead a group discussion with ease and tact. Sociable, popular, sympathetic. Responsive to praise and criticism.	**ENTJ** Hearty, frank, decisive, leaders in activities. Usually good in anything that requires reasoning and intelligent talk, such as public speaking. Are usually well-informed and enjoy adding to their fund of knowledge. May sometimes be more positive and confident than their experience in an area warrants.

Left margin: INTROVERTS / EXTRAVERTS. Right margin: INTROVERTS / EXTRAVERTS.

SOURCE: Myers & McCaulley, 1985, pp. 20–21.

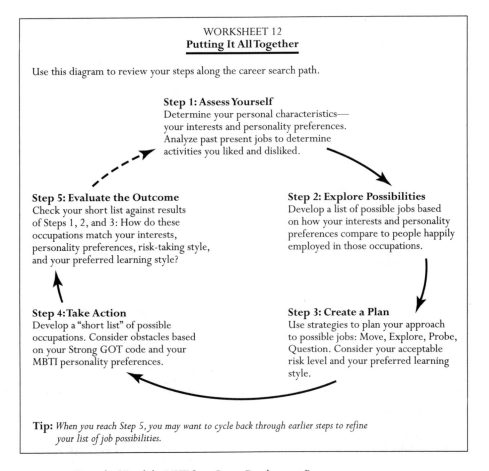

WORKSHEET 12
Putting It All Together

Use this diagram to review your steps along the career search path.

Step 1: Assess Yourself
Determine your personal characteristics—
your interests and personality preferences.
Analyze past present jobs to determine
activities you liked and disliked.

Step 5: Evaluate the Outcome
Check your short list against results
of Steps 1, 2, and 3: How do these
occupations match your interests,
personality preferences, risk-taking style,
and your preferred learning style?

Step 2: Explore Possibilities
Develop a list of possible jobs based
on how your interests and personality
preferences compare to people happily
employed in those occupations.

Step 4: Take Action
Develop a "short list" of possible
occupations. Consider obstacles based
on your Strong GOT code and your
MBTI personality preferences.

Step 3: Create a Plan
Use strategies to plan your approach
to possible jobs: Move, Explore, Probe,
Question. Consider your acceptable
risk level and your preferred learning
style.

Tip: *When you reach Step 5, you may want to cycle back through earlier steps to refine
your list of job possibilities.*

FIGURE 4.3 Using the SII and the MBTI for a Career Development Program

SOURCE: *Hammer and Kummerow,* Strong MBTI career development workbook. *1993. Odessa, FL: Psychological Assessment Resources.*

The NEO Personality Inventory-Revised (NEO PI-R)

An important personality instrument that measures the *big five* personality indicators—neuroticism, extroversion, openness, agreeableness, and conscientiousness—is the NEO PI-R. The instrument was used by Holland and Gottfredson, who developed the Career Attitudes and Strategies Inventory (CASI) (1994) to assess how work and nonwork environments affect career change, work performance, and job satisfaction. The scales include Job Satisfaction, Work Involvement, Skill Development, Dominant Style, Career Worries, Interpersonal Abuse, Family Commitment, Risk-Taking Style, and Geographical Barriers. In comparing Vocational Identity (Holland, Daiger, & Power, 1980) with several scales in the CASI, clearer definitions were found with a high correlation between Vocational Identity and Job Satisfaction and a nega-

---

Practical Applications

When using the combined form Strong Interest Inventory (SII) and Myers Briggs Inventory (MBTI) and the booklet *Introduction to Type and Careers* (Hammer, 1993), the MBTI can foster career development in several ways. Clients can be directed to:

- Use the identified traits and write compositions that describes themselves.
- Describe an ideal work environment based on their traits.
- Divide into subgroups based on type and discuss the similarities and traits.
- Divide into subgroups by diverse types, identify differences, and discuss the implications for a learning environment.

- Choose an occupation, describe the personal traits that would be helpful in that work, and compare their own traits and occupational aspirations.
- Write self-descriptive adjectives.
- Using MBTI and SII results, project their lifestyle five and ten years from now.
- Describe how personal traits influence career development and choices.
- Describe traits and the effect on work environments and interactions at home, if dual-career couples.
- Consider how personal traits contribute to seeking a career change, if they are considering a career change.

---

tive correlation between Vocational Identity and Career Worries or Interpersonal Abuse. When compared with the NEO PI-R, the correlations between Vocational Identity, the scales on the CASI, and the five personality factors of the NEO PI-R indicate much better predictive possibilities for job satisfaction, the ability to change, and possibly even work performance.

THE THEORY OF WORK ADJUSTMENT

As an outgrowth of better rehabilitation services for vocationally disabled clients, René Dawis, Lloyd Lofquist, and their associates at the University of Minnesota developed concepts of Trait–Factor Theory into the **Theory of Work Adjustment (TWA).** Work adjustment is a "continuous and dynamic process by which a worker seeks to achieve and maintain a correspondence with a work environment" (Dawis & Lofquist, 1984, p. 237). Other theories related to career development are primarily concerned with vocational choices. TWA is more associated with the relationship of the person to the job and to the occupational setting. Hershenson's (1993) work adjustment theory is related more to developmental concerns than trait-factor ideas. Although TWA describes factors that influence an individual's adjustment to the work environment, it also works to define a good career choice as one in which individuals are both satisfactory and satisfied (Fouad, 1993).

An important aspect of the work adjustment theory and its related research is the relationship between the individual's needs and the reinforcement systems of those needs that are present in the work setting. Murray (1938) defined needs and Holland (1973) speaks to the tolerability of the work situation and its congruence with the worker's needs. Lofquist and Dawis (1989) listed twenty different reinforcers that can possibly be found in a work setting. These are reduced to six categories: safety, comfort, status, altruism, achievement, and autonomy. Different individuals will have needs that match with the reinforcers of any given occupation or setting. The match between needs and reinforcers will be a likely indicator of job satisfaction and the length of time an individual will work in that particular setting. Job satisfaction and tenure will vary according to closeness of fit or match with needs and reinforcers.

TWA theorizes that each individual seeks to achieve and maintain a sense of **correspondence** with the environment. Correspondence is present when the individual and the environment are attuned and when work meets the needs of the individual and the individual meets the demands of the work environment. Correspondence is a dynamic process because both the needs of the individual and the demands of the job change. However, if the correspondence continues, job tenure is extended.

TWA consists of eighteen propositions and corollaries (Dawis & Lofquist, 1984). Current theory is based on research that modified their earlier work (Dawis, England, & Lofquist, 1964; Dawis, Lofquist, & Weiss, 1968; Lofquist & Dawis, 1969). These can be summarized in four major points.

1. The personality of the worker and the work environment must be in basic agreement.

2. The individual's needs are the primary concern for how he/she will fit into the work environment.

3. To achieve stability and tenure, the individual's needs must correspond to the reinforcer system of the work environment.

4. Job placement works most effectively when the worker's traits match the requirements of the work environment.

Two basic concepts predict work adjustment: *satisfaction* and *satisfactoriness*. Satisfaction is related to the worker and the worker's adjustment to the work environment. Satisfactoriness refers to the employer and whether the needs of the work environment are being met by the worker. TWA concerns itself with (1) turnover, absenteeism, and tardiness; (2) job morale; (3) commitment to the job; and (4) productivity as indicators of work adjustment. TWA differs from Trait-Factor Theory in that it makes use of clearly defined concepts and follows an articulated theoretical model.

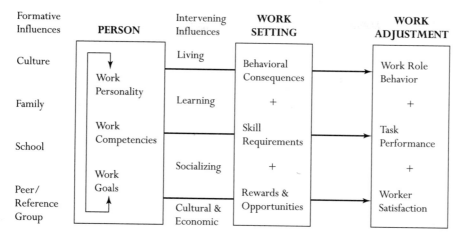

FIGURE 4.4 Hershenson's Model of Work Adjustment

Hershenson's (1996) model of work adjustment contains three interacting subsystems within the person that intervene with the work setting to facilitate work adjustment. His model is presented in Figure 4.4.

Hershenson conceptualizes three interacting personal subsystems: work personality, work competencies, and work goals. Work personality refers to the person's work-related self-concept, motivation, needs, and values and is presumed to begin developing during the preschool years. Work competencies refer to the person's work-related habits and physical, mental, and interpersonal skills that develop during the school years. Work goals refer to the person's development upon leaving school and entering the work world. Formative influences on the person include culture, family (especially on work personality), school, and peer and reference groups (especially on work goals). Intervening influences (e.g., living, learning, socializing, cultural, and economic factors) are carried into the work setting, where behavioral expectations, skill requirements, and rewards and opportunities come into play. These all affect work role behavior, task performance, worker satisfaction, and work adjustment.

Hershensohn's model is contextually based. It allows consideration of many external structural factors. For example, peer and reference groups determine if many high schoolers see themselves as college material and apply for college admission, scholarships, and other financial aid. Family influence can be quite subtle, yet many young people mimic the behaviors and attitudes toward work that they see in the adults around them. Behavioral expectations are another factor: many schools and workplaces have middle-class values that have to be made explicit to individuals from lower-income backgrounds (Payne, 1995).

Hershensohn (1996) further develops his ideas by proposing a Systems Model of Work Adjustment Development (see Figure 4.4) that includes Subsystems of the Person, Elements of the Work Setting, and Components of Work Adjustment. The three subsystems—work personality, work competencies, and work goals—are all influenced by family/living, reference group/socialization, and school/learning. Work personality influences work role behavior, which expresses itself in behavioral expectations in the work setting; work competencies influence task performance, which expresses itself in skill requirements in the work setting; whereas rewards and opportunities in the work setting influence worker satisfaction, which is congruent with work goals in the context of cultural and economic values.

Assessment Instruments Used with Work Adjustment Theory

Abilities Abilities include pervasive attitudes, predicted skills as opposed to acquired skills, and a necessary way to help conceptualize the wide variety of work skills (Dawis & Lofquist, 1984; Sharf, 1996). The General Aptitude Test Battery (GATB) and the Occupational Ability Patterns, both developed by the U.S. Department of Labor, describe the important abilities that are required for a great variety of jobs.

Needs and Values The Minnesota Importance Questionnaire (MIQ) (Rounds et al., 1981) identifies twenty needs:

ability utilization	compensation	security	supervision (technical)
variety	recognition	authority	company polciies/ practices
advancement	moral values	social service	
coworkers	activity	working conditions	supervision-human relations
responsibility	creativity		
achievement	independence	social status	

Job Satisfaction The Minnesota Satisfaction Questionnaire is another part of the system of assessment used in TWA. These instruments are available from Vocational Psychology Research, Department of Psychology, University of Minnesota.

Interests are not part of the usual assessment procedure for TWA because they are defined by abilities and values. TWA uses the Minnesota Occupational Classification System, which has as component parts the Occupational Ability Patterns and the Occupational Reinforcer Patterns to help place clients in appropriate work settings.

Evaluation of Work Adjustment Theory

TWA has been carefully developed with rigorous care to devise appropriate assessment instruments, test hypotheses, and codify a useful tool for fitting people with work environments. Most people work in a situation rather than spend their time making vocational decisions. Practitioners will face many issues related to work situ-

Practical Applications

TWA is useful for conceptualizing the types of problems that an individual may have in adjusting to a particular job. It helps clients with problems with co-workers and supervisors, an inability to meet the demands of a work situation, and pre-retirement/retirement issues. For instance, an individual's skills may not be developed sufficiently to meet the requirements of the job. Furthermore, the job may require skills that the individual is unable to develop due to lack of education or ability. An individual's values and needs are not met by the work environment. Another concern could be that the individual does not understand the reinforcer patterns of the work involved. Sometimes dissatisfaction with the job may be due not to the job itself but to problems outside of work. When a client complains of problems at work, the initial approach is to assess the client's work personality and environment. Assessing the work values and needs of a client can be done by using the MIQ or, if this is not possible, using the conceptual schema of the MIQ along with other measures of adjustment and personality.

ations and person-environment fit. TWA approaches the subject in a systematic manner. More recent findings concerning learning theory need to be incorporated into the research on TWA (Hesketh, 1993). Concerns about the thoroughness of study of gender and ethnic groups have been noted (Tinsley, 1993).

Relevance for Multicultural and Diverse Populations

TWA emphasizes individuals, not groups. Therefore, "gender, ethnicity, national origin, religion, sexual orientation, and disability status are seen as inaccurate and unreliable bases for estimating skills, abilities, needs, values, personality styles, and adjustment style of a particular person . . . [the current functioning of a person is dependent on] opportunity or its absence" (Dawis, 1994, p. 41).

In a comprehensive, well-written article, Degges-White and Shoffner (2002) apply TWA to career counseling with lesbian clients because TWA focuses on the individual's interaction with the work environment. Lesbians have two specific work-related concerns: disclosing sexual orientation to others and experiencing discrimination based on sexual orientation. Workplace discrimination—be it sanctioned or illicit—based on sexual orientation is a very real challenge for lesbians' career development and satisfaction. Such tacit and expressed discrimination can adversely impact person-environment correspondence and foreclose on the possibility of a successful employment relationship. Lesbians who place a high reinforcement value on the need to be open about their sexuality and come out in the workplace risk negative consequences such as diminished compensation and security, isolation from other employees, being left out of informal communication and support networks, and being singled out by sexual majority employees for being different.

> Coming out and being honest about sexual orientation may be valued as the morally correct choice or it may meet a lesbian's need for recognition of her true self on the job. . . . When a lesbian woman is deciding to choose between outness and nondisclosure of sexual identity, she must evaluate potential reinforcement of this choice (p. 90).

Early in the career development process, lesbians may face negation of their abilities and interests through such barriers as stereotyping, gender role expectations, and peer pressure. TWA views ability as a measure of potential, not actual, achievement. Ability is cultivated through skill development and is both an indicator of aptitude and a predictor of future behavior and performance. Lesbians who disclose their sexual orientation may face interference by others that impacts career development, regardless of abilities or interests. From a TWA framework, lesbians' decisions to come out or remain invisible on the job can be linked to the reinforcement value of such a choice.

Several areas of knowledge are incumbent upon the career counselor who works with lesbian clients (Degges-White & Shoffner, 2002). These include:

1. a basic understanding of sexual identity formation and its impact on the client's work, work relationships, reinforcement values, and satisfaction

2. being prepared to assist the client with weighing the values of disclosure versus nondisclosure of sexual orientation

3. assisting the client to manage sexual identity and discrimination within the workplace

4. familiarity with local gay and lesbian news publications, professional and employee organizations, telephone resource centers, and bookstores with adequate selections of lesbian materials

PSYCHODYNAMIC THEORY

The degree to which you can make your work playful,
[is the measure that] you've got it made.
—Edward S. Bordin
(cited in Goodyear, Roffey, & Jack, 1994, p. 571)

The look we have taken at trait factor and the inherent psychological expressions of a person lead us to current theories that look at sources of psychological expression and some of their applications to career development. We focus on psychodynamic

---

Practical Applications

Vocational practitioners will have to decide the extent to which they will become an advocate for lesbians and gays (Hetherington et al., 1989). Gelberg and Chojnacki (1995; 1996) use the term **ally** to refer to heterosexuals who are professionally and personally affirmative to gay, lesbian, and bisexual people. Career counselors with no real understanding of their own homophobia, however well-intentioned they might be, may be offering fear and confusion which masquerades as healing (Markowitz, 1991; Woolley, 1991). Buhrke (1989) provides a useful resource guide for incorporating lesbian and gay issues into both counselor training generally and career counseling particularly. While Buhrke's work may seem dated, it nevertheless provides a good prototype for the kinds of training materials vital for competent practice. Vocational practitioners have a professional responsibility to assist gay/lesbian/bisexual clients in overcoming as much discrimination, prejudice, and oppression as possible. Career counselors also have an ethical and moral obligation to work with such clients in an affirmative manner (Buhrke & Douce, 1991). Gelberg and Chojnacki (1996) provide an excellent appendix of career counseling resources that for gay men includes gay identity development, materials for career centers, organizations and agencies, and more.

---

approaches to work first. Then we discuss the existential and person-centered approaches to vocational counseling.

Before we begin, let us say a few words about the difference between counseling and psychotherapy. Often the terms are used interchangeably because there is no consensus among clinical practitioners about when counseling ends and psychotherapy begins (Sharf, 2002). Without entering this debate, we use the terms interchangeably. Vocational psychology/career development is a useful part of any clinical practitioner's repertoire. The boundaries between vocational psychology/career counseling and personal counseling and psychotherapy are artificial. Many work-related issues concern clients of counselors, social workers, marriage and family therapists, psychologists, psychiatrists, as well as those who seek help from teachers, coaches, and clergy. Frankly, there are not enough specialists in vocational psychology to accommodate all the clients who have work-related concerns.

Traditionally speaking, the term **psychoanalysis** refers to: "(1) a theory of personality and psychopathology, (2) a method of investigating the mind, and (3) a theory of [clinical] treatment" (Wolitzky, 1995, p. 12). The various forms of psychoanalytic theories and therapies trace their origins back to Sigmund Freud (1856–1939), whose original writings comprise twenty-three volumes (Wolitzky, 1995). Most theories of counseling and of marriage and family therapy are reactions against traditional Freudian psychoanalysis. Yet Freud is an intellectual giant of the twentieth century, whose principles have been applied to work, society and the family, music and art, literature and religion (Simpson, 1987).

To discuss traditional psychoanalysis and its variants, often called **psychodynamic approaches,** is beyond the scope of this chapter, and we confine our focus to psychodynamic theory as it pertains to the role of work in people's lives. Beginning with Alfred Adler (whom we discuss in Chapter 7), Carl Gustav Jung, and Karen Horney (also known as neo-Freudians), several of Freud's original disciples broke with him over the issue of libidinal drives in childhood as the primary determiners of mental life and behavior. Libidinal drives are but one example of the **mechanistic model** adopted by Freud and other psychoanalytic and psychodynamic practitioners. Mechanistic models aim to discover scientifically the processes that describe the true mechanisms underlying the explanation of a phenomenon (Flew, 1984). Freud, a quintessential modernist, posited that **unconscious motivation** was the mechanism that determined human behavior. Unconscious motivation occurs out of one's awareness but is revealed clinically through free association and in daily life through slips of the tongue and the jokes one finds amusing.

Edward S. Bordin's psychodynamic approach proposes that play is the basis for the role of personality in work and career. The need for play is fused with the requirements of work to find a satisfying vocation. This approach addresses the decision process made during the quest for an appropriate vocation as well as how individual differences affect "the kinds and styles of satisfactions sought" (Bordin, cited in Brown, Brooks, & Associates, 1990, p. 104).

The spirit of play is caught in the term **spontaneity**, which is used to refer to the elements of self-expression and self-realization in our responses to situations. Spontaneity is a major key to differentiating work from play. What marks the essence of play is its intrinsically satisfying nature. Although we may engage in play for extrinsic reasons—status, achievement, admiration, even money—what distinguishes play from work is the satisfaction gained from simply engaging in the activity (Bordin, cited in Brown et al., 1990, p. 105, italics in original).

Bordin's theory contains seven propositions which appear to be appropriate to our times:

1. All people in all parts of their lives want feelings of completeness and the opportunity to experience profound happiness.

2. Compulsion and effort as part of one's development find expression in combining work and play.

3. One's attempt to find an "ideal fit between self and work" is characterized by "striving for career decisions."

4. "Developmental conceptions" of lifestyles or character expressions provide the basis for finding occupations that satisfy intrinsic motives.

5. Early developmental experiences and feelings provide the basis of the individual's unique career development.

6. "Personal identity" consists of one's unique features, but also incorporates features of each of the parents.

7. When there are unresolved aspects of the self, the effects of doubting and lack of satisfaction will most likely be manifested in difficulty with career decision making (Bordin, cited in Brown et al., 1990).

Bordin wanted "counseling to represent something other than the mechanized testing approach. People have different facets that can be expressed in different ways, in different work roles. . . . [O]ne facet is an emphasis on precision or thorough, systematic thought" (Goodyear et al., 1994, pp. 568–569). Bordin believed his two greatest contributions to the vocational psychology field were his ideas on personality and work, because of their importance to the clinical understanding of a person's potential and their function in "assessing the resources and orientations that a person uses in coping with life's challenges," and his idea of the "working alliance," which can be a potent "means of integrating our various ideas about how to bring about change. . . . [W]ithin that conception is a core for what will amount to the basic science of psychotherapy" (Goodyear et al., p. 570). It should be noted that the match of personality features and work is the guiding influence in most assessments and research in the field of vocational psychology.

If vocational choice is an integral expression of a person's personality, then the same constructs used to understand personality development should be helpful in understanding vocational choice (Segal, 1961). Psychoanalytic concepts such as **identification** (relating to another person or idea by adopting aspects of that person or idea), development of **defense mechanisms** (coping strategies to fend off unpleasant ideations and/or feelings), and **sublimation** (substituting hostile, aggressive, or sexual impulses into a more socially accepted form) can provide insight into personality characteristics of individuals' specific vocational choices.

Matre and Cooper (1984) identify two primary dimensions that impair career decision making: decided–undecided state and decisive–indecisive trait. **Decided–undecided state** is the temporary indecision that accompanies many decision-making tasks. Salamone (1982) believes that indecision is a normal, rational-cognitive issue and can be alleviated through accurate information that helps a person make the decision. **Decisive–indecisive trait** is a more permanent trait that is a part of decision-making tasks. Indecisiveness derives from psychological issues and is associated more with a person experiencing personal problems (Miller, 1993).

Combining the works of Bordin (1946) and Matre and Cooper (1984) results in the following propositions. The **decided-decisive client** could be treated through support because this is not a diagnosable problem. The **undecided-decisive client**

Practical Applications

Applications of the model include: (1) individual vocational counseling, (2) general developmental programs, (3) modification of work to permit more expression of self, and (4) potential application in connection with the closely related concerns of aging and retirement (Bordin, cited in Brown et al., 1990).

Diagnosing career-concerned clients at major decision points in their lives has received limited attention (Miller, 1993). Vocational psychology often is seen as responding solely to career-related problems by applying definite techniques or knowledge to resolve them. Miller combines Bordin's model of diagnostic constructs with an orthogonal model offered by Matre and Cooper (1984) to form the following diagnostic constructs.

Dependence—dependent clients have difficulty solving their problems, are dependent on others to help them, and come to the practitioner for help. It is common for them not to accept responsibility for their own situations.

Lack of information—because they lack the information necessary to make a choice they face, these clients often seek help. As a rule they are responsible for themselves.

Self-conflict—when inner conflicts regarding self-image and behavior are incongruent or even when aspects of self-image are at war, these clients seek help.

Choice anxiety—feelings of being trapped between two less-than-pleasant choices can lead to procrastination, which is anxiety producing in itself, and the inability to organize one's life. Clients with this no-win situation usually experience stress, tension, lack of sleep, and a draining anxiety.

No problem—these clients are in tune with themselves and their environment and check in for a tune-up or a way of finding reinforcement for choices they have made (Miller, 1993, pp. 36–37).

needs more information and would most benefit from assessment and/or career counseling. The **undecided-indecisive client** is experiencing choice anxiety. These clients suffer from anxiety, low self-concept, immaturity, and other negative personality traits that impair career counseling. Personal *and* career counseling are recommended. The **decided-indecisive client** is in self-conflict. They have formed a temporary decision, but are unable to make an actual choice and experience conflict as they want to pursue one career, but have an interest in a dissimilar career (Miller, 1993, pp. 38, 40). An illustration of these theoretical relationships is presented in Figure 4.5.

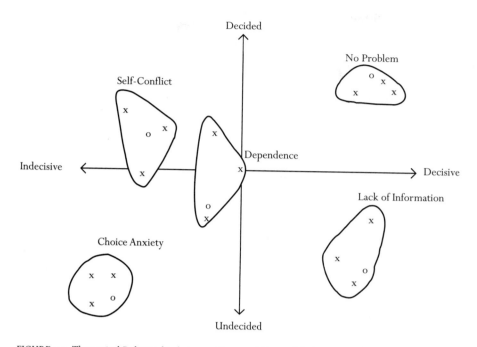

FIGURE 4.5 Theoretical Relationship between Matre and Cooper's Indecision/Indecisive Paradigm and Bordin's Diagnostic Concepts

SOURCE: *Reprinted from Miller, "A Career Counseling Diagnostic Model . . ." Journal of Employment Counseling (30) 35–43, pp. 39. Reprinted with permission. No further reproduction authorized without written permission of the American Counseling Association.*

As shown in Figure 4.5, dependent clients are lodged in the decided-indecisive and the undecided-indecisive quadrants. Lack-of-information clients are lodged in the undecided-decisive quadrant. Self-conflicted clients are firmly lodged in the decided-indecisive quadrant. Choice-anxiety clients are lodged in the undecided-indecisive quadrant, while no-problem clients are lodged in the exact opposite, decided-decisive quadrant.

Practitioners should form a "working alliance" to diagnose the client's conflict before offering a counseling strategy (Meara & Patton, 1994). This alliance uses the theoretical underpinnings of psychoanalytic process. The client must bring to the alliance: (1) a dissatisfaction with where they are emotionally, (2) a recognized need for assistance, (3) the willingness to accept assistance, (4) the ability to create a rational working relationship with the practitioner, (5) an understanding of the difference between observation and experience, and (6) an ability to want to know more about themselves (Greenson, 1967, cited in Meara & Patton, 1994, p. 164). Meara and Patton further discuss client's fears of the counselor, the process, and change, and cite Bordin's model of dealing with the confusions a client may develop, such as goal confusion, task confusion, and bond confusion.

An essential component for counseling success is positive collaboration between practitioner and client (Horvath & Symonds, 1991; Horvath & Greenberg, 1994). Based on Bordin's approach, the Working Alliance Inventory (WAI) was devised to assess the quality of the interaction between practitioner and client (Horvath & Greenberg, 1989). The *WAI* could be a useful quality assurance/program evaluation measure for practitioners, even if they do not use a psychodynamic approach to their vocational counseling.

Evaluation of the Psychodynamic Approach

In vocational psychology, psychoanalytic theory has played a minor role (Osipow, 1983). Psychodynamic theory will probably continue to have limited impact because of the length of time it takes for a client to understand the unconscious motivation that can be a compelling factor in their career selection. Psychopathology may account for many of the vocational problems that individuals have, and difficulty in career decision making may be related to identity problems in youth. A psychoanalytic conceptualization of career choice emphasizes the impulse gratification and anxiety reduction that a particular career offers rather than the interests and abilities that a career may require.

Relevance for Multicultural and Diverse Populations

Renowned psychiatrist Thomas Szasz asserts that one can accept many of the clinical methods and techniques of psychoanalysis without embracing its ideology (Simpson, 1987). In this respect, adaptations of psychodynamic approaches have potential application for multicultural and diverse populations. For example, clients may experience both transference and countertransference reactions to bosses and co-workers. By **transference** we mean that a client may react toward a boss or co-worker in a manner similar to a significant person in the client's past or present. By **countertransference** we mean that a boss or co-worker may react toward a client in a manner similar to a significant person in the boss's or co-worker's past or present. Transference and countertransference reactions are especially likely in an increasingly diverse workforce. The distortions that occur in transference/countertransference reactions can also occur when misunderstandings inevitably arise among diverse co-workers.

Clinically, all psychodynamically-oriented approaches have a built-in, individualistic, Western bias in which the presenting problem is presumed to reside within the client. Clients' social and environmental contexts may come into direct conflict with the presumption that the problem in intrapsychic (Corey, 1996). Oftentimes, systemic approaches that focus on the client's immediate and extended families and network of friends may be more appropriate. A given multicultural client may be both individualistic and collectivistic contingent upon context or issue. To the extent that psychodynamic approaches pathologize populations that have already been oppressed—those who live in poverty, the working poor, people with limited educational and occupational opportunities, people with alternative lifestyles—we do not endorse the application of psychodynamic theory. However, if psychodynamic theory is used to assist the client to better understand the self in the context of social and cultural realities, then it can be an effective tool.

EXISTENTIAL APPROACHES

Pines and Yanai (2001) use a combination of psychodynamic and existential perspectives to formulate a study of career burnout. As noted earlier, psychodynamic theory suggests that "[p]eople choose an occupation that enables them to replicate significant childhood experiences, satisfying needs that were unfulfilled in their childhood and actualize dreams passed on to them by their familial heritage" (p.171). Existential theory is concerned with finding meaning, in this case through work. The authors suggest that a connection exists between burnout and a person's failure to derive existential importance from work. They further propose a three-step plan as a treatment approach:

1. Identifying the conscious and unconscious reasons for the individual's career choice and how the chosen career was expected to provide a sense of existential significance

2. Identifying the reasons for the individual's failure to derive a sense of existential significance from the work and how this sense of failure is related to burnout

3. Identifying changes that will enable the individual to derive a sense of existential significance from work (p.183)

Further questions to ask a client are: Why did you choose this particular career? How did you expect it to provide existential significance? Why did you feel a sense of failure on your existential quest? How is this perceived failure related to your burnout? What changes do you need to take to derive a sense of existential significance from your work?

"The psychoanalytic-existential approach assumes that the root of career burnout lies in the need of human beings to believe that their lives are meaningful, that the thing they so—and consequently they themselves—are important and significant" (p. 170). It is important to listen to the internal worlds of clients. Pines and Yanai quote an unknown Israeli poet. "Under the surface a man is like a river. Under the surface a man knows where he is flowing" (p. 183).

Another application of existential theory proposed by Cohen (2003) applies the theory to career decision making. We discuss decision-making strategies in Chapter 6, but include this now as a model for consideration. Cohen proposes a four-stage model that is sequential and cyclical. The first stage is responsibility and the freedom that goes with it. This stage revolves around the freedom that is limited only by existential situations. This freedom often produces anxiety, but responsibility emphasizes our accountability for ourselves, our future, and the difficulties we face in exercising choices, including career.

The second stage involves evaluating our choices in terms of meaning. Existential theory suggests the search for meaning is basic to our lives and that each individual has to find his or her own meaning. Vocational choice can provide a powerful sense of meaning and purpose in our lives and aid in the search for an authentic self.

The third stage is the action stage, which is the implementation of a vocational preference. Helping clients avoid impulsivity or compulsivity, the practitioner focuses on articulation of career aspirations.

The fourth stage is reëvaluation. When clients fail to find meaning and satisfaction in their choice and experience what Frankl called the "existential vacuum" or when clients have existential guilt or anxiety and regret that a choice is not achieving one's authentic possibilities, a new look at choices is appropriate. This model has some limitations because it is based on an individualistic view of the world and does not allow a collectivistic consideration. There are cases, however, when such a model may be useful.

Evaluation of the Existential Approach

The existential approach to the role of work in people's lives relies on the maturity and age of the client seeking help. It requires a client to be willing to enter into a process to learn about her or his own potential. Time to accomplish the process may be too lengthy and the practitioner may not seem directive enough if there is pressure to obtain work soon.

Relevance for Multicultural and Diverse Populations

Clients from diverse backgrounds can be encouraged to weigh alternatives and explore the consequences of choices they make in their lives (Corey, 1996). While external oppressive forces beyond their control may seriously impinge on clients' quality of life, clients need not allow themselves to be passive victims of circumstances.

Clients can be helped to examine their role in the creation of their problems while at the same time be taught ways to counter their external circumstances. Practitioners can advocate for their clients (Grevious, 1985) without taking over clients' tasks and hindering the development of feelings of competence. But existential approaches may be excessively individualistic and assume that a multicultural client can make all changes internally (Corey, 1996). External realities of power and hierarchy, discrimination and **oppression,** are often dismissed. Clients with a strong sense of collectivism may feel invalidated by having all the responsibility for their condition placed upon themselves.

There is also a likelihood of blaming the victim should a client not exhibit sufficient levels of self-determination. Practitioners with an existential theoretical orientation can come across as too nondirective for those clients desiring answers and concrete solutions to their immediate problems. Structured, problem-oriented approaches to vocational counseling are antithetical to existential approaches.

PERSON-CENTERED APPROACHES

Like psychodynamic approaches, there are a variety of **person–centered approaches** (Bohart, 1995). Also known as humanistic psychology, basic approach was founded by Carl Rogers (1902–1987). We review some of the studies on person-centered approaches to vocational development.

C. H. Patterson (1982) described the core conditions for a therapeutic relationship. First, understand the client; practitioners must empathize to see the world through the client's eyes. Any vocational decision is based on the world as the client sees it, not on the world as somebody else sees it. Second, respect the client, even when the client's behaviors are unlikable. Third, be genuine; whatever the practitioner says to the client is an honest response, not a facade. The practitioner is not playing a role, but is a real person with the client. Finally, be concrete; practitioners need to focus on specific rather then general ideas and behaviors that the client communicates (Freeman, 1990).

In vocational guidance, the practitioner does not relieve the client from responsibility. Nor does the practitioner lead or direct the client to make a choice the practitioner believes is best. The practitioner's role is to aid the client to obtain more information about interests and the world of work. Assessment may be part of that process, but the tests used are based on the client's interest. The practitioner interprets test results to the client and presents test results in a way the client can understand. The client has the freedom to agree or disagree and must be allowed enough time to interact with the results. The client must understand that any vocational choice is not a lifetime decision because most people change jobs an average of seven times over the course of a lifetime. Throughout this process, responsibility and control are left to the client.

Sometimes a client will reveal personal problems that may appear to have little or no relationship to career issues. However, the practitioner needs to be attentive to personal problems because emotions are involved in making occupational choices. The goal, however, is to present occupational choices as logical, cognitive, and rational. "Client-centered counseling is always just that, in career counseling as well as in therapeutic counseling—the client is the center of the process, and the determiner of the

Practical Applications

Our experience shows that understanding the client's needs aids in making a career change. A young woman sought counseling after having several unpleasant job experiences, which contributed to her negative self-concept. She had an accounting degree and was a skilled accountant but disliked her work. Results of an Edwards Personal Preference Schedule (EPPS) demonstrated high needs for affiliation and achievement. She had not experienced much interaction with others in her jobs. Nor did she advance in the field as she had envisioned. Through counseling, she decided to use her skills to further her education, pursue work in the social sciences, and eventually pursue an administrative position.

Another aspect of applying career counseling to the whole person is emphasized in the term *occupational wellness.* Wellness concerns expressed in terms of physical, emotional, and spiritual health need to be translated into the workplace (Dorn, 1992). There is every reason to believe that career concerns affect one emotionally, spiritually, and physically, and the relationship of career and personal identity is a recurring theme in vocational psychology.

Practitioners also need to consider the link between family and work—the role of work in the familial domain (Richardson, 1993). Work is an "extension of family drama . . . [and] . . . interactional problems and interpersonal dynamics are sometimes translated into the work environment" (Chusid & Cochran, 1989, cited in Dorn, 1992, p. 177). The reverse is also true: emotions may advance or hinder career options and impact wellness, just as emotions generated by work affect family and home. Family and work issues are explored further in Chapter 8.

content of the process and its outcome" (Patterson, interviewed in Freeman, 1990, p. 300).

In working with the welfare-to-work clientele, Lent (2001) suggests using a person-centered approach. Individuals in the United States who are seeking employment and look toward assistance from programs in the community often find cross-class challenges. Because of legislative reform, individuals on public assistance are expected to participate in the welfare-to-work employment readiness programs. These programs are primarily created, developed, and implemented by people who are professionals and who have higher socioeconomic class upbringing than those who seek the services. The counselor making a conscious effort to include genuineness and empathy throughout the programs may offset crisscross variables and increase the possibility of achieving the programs goals. The awareness and direction of these programs must begin with the policy makers and extend to those who are frontline employees and to administrators.

This research is founded on the works of others who have researched person-centered counseling theory and career counseling (Boy & Pine, 1990; Bozarth & Fisher, 1990; Raskin & Rogers, 1989; Rogers, 1979). "*Cross-class* here refers to the juxtaposition of experiences, cognitions, and behaviors of persons from different social classes" (Lent, 2001, p. 22). The person-centered theory accentuates the value of using respect, communication, and empathy (a genuine effort to understand the client's point of view) as a means to neutralize the cross-class obstacles. It is important to address and/or assess initially each client's need for a supportive climate; existence of external constraints such as lower socioeconomic class; reading level (some clients may be illiterate); need for support in the area of equipment availability and child care; establishing empathic relationships between staff and clients to gain more accurate understanding of clients' hopes, fears, desires, lifestyles, and self-concepts (pp. 24, 25).

The staff employed to work with these programs must be prepared through training and paradigm shifts to work with this population in a manner which is client-focused rather than task-focused. The leadership style of the administrators and all levels of supervisory staff must be adequately trained in therapy to work with all employees as they work in the program in which they seek to teach those in direct service delivery (Lent, 2001).

Evaluation of the Person-Centered Approach

The supportive tone of the client-centered approach sets an appropriate mood or environment for counseling to occur, but practitioners need more techniques than the client-centered approach alone can provide. These can include work and autobiographical information questionnaires that assist clients in developing a list of traits that describe them, such as the Adjective Checklist (ACL) and the Adjective Self- Description (ASD).

Other theories that are more directly devoted to career development and vocational psychology are covered in the next two chapters. In many cases, the theories involve many of the aspects of trait factor and assessment possibilities, but also include much of the type of thinking that is inherent to psychodynamic and person-centered concepts.

5

❖❖

Developmental Perspectives

Mom and Dad always say, "Edith just be yourself."
Even though they criticize everything about me. And
then when I am being myself, they say, "Stop doing
that." They never seem to get what I was doing was
just being myself. Either they don't know who I really
am or I'm really not who they had in mind.

—Edith Ann
(Wagner, 1994, p. 21)

Edith Ann, a character created by comedienne Lily Tomlin and her partner, writer
Jane Wagner, is a five-year-old girl who expounds on life from the vantage point of
her oversized rocking chair. One can always count on Edith Ann for a perceptive re-
mark on what it is like to be a kid. As the quotation above makes clear, kids receive
all sorts of mixed messages, especially from adults, which can make the choices about
what they want to be when they grow up even more challenging.

In this chapter, we survey different **developmental perspectives** on vocational
psychology. Developmental perspectives presume that one's self-concept—how an
individual sees herself or himself—changes over time as a consequence of age and life
experience. Developmental perspectives also presume that the role of work in people's
lives begins in childhood as a reflection of expectations placed on children by adults
who regularly interact with them. These adults include parents and other relatives,

teachers, coaches, and school counselors, as well as neighbors, family friends, and other caregivers. The media also powerfully impacts the self-concept and related occupational development of children, especially by promoting values claiming that having the money to consume products equals the good life (Pipher, 1996). Because the focus of this chapter is on developmental ages and stages as it relates to career/work decisions, we felt it important to begin with Erikson's theory of development. His stages are used not only to develop school career guidance programs but also to understand young adult and older adult transitions.

ERIKSON: PSYCHOSOCIAL DEVELOPMENT APPROACH

Erik Erikson's (1950) identity theory is well researched. "Although most contributors to the career development literature have acknowledged Erikson as the intellectual father of the construct of identity, none have succeeded in formulating a construct of identity that is more than a caricature of his thinking" (Vondracek, 1992, p.130). Recent theories of identity rest upon Erikson's original theory (1950, 1959, 1963, 1968). In *Identity: Youth and Crisis* (1968), he states:

> The wholeness to be achieved at this stage . . . [is] a sense of inner identity. The younger person, to experience wholeness, must feel a progressive continuity . . . between that which he conceives himself to be, and that which he perceives others to see in him and to expect of him. Individually speaking, identity includes, but is more than, the sum of all the successive identifications of those earlier years when the child wanted to be, and often was forced to become, like the people he depended on. Identity is . . . a crisis to be solved only in new identifications with age mates and with leader figures outside of the family (p. 87).

This idea has some autobiographical basis. Erikson's biological father, whom he never met, was a Danish seaman. He was later adopted by his pediatrician, whom his mother had married. When he immigrated to the U.S. as an adult, he changed his name to Erik *Erikson,* using the Scandinavian tradition of taking a father's first name and adding *son* or *sen* to his for a surname. Because his father was unknown to him, he used his own name to finally give himself some identity.

Embedded within Erikson's (1950) eight stages of life-span growth and development is the stage that mainly occurs during adolescence and post-adolescence, even though each of the stages plays a major part in career development. Erikson focused on the importance of a person's ability to be successful at work within the sociocultural and interpersonal environment. His theory relies primarily on three identity domains—vocation, ideology, and family. Archer and Waterman (1983) expand these domains to include vocational planning, religious beliefs, political ideologies, sex-role

Practical Applications

Identity crisis has become a popular, if negative, term derived from Erikson to describe a disruptive development in an adult's life. We hear the terms *crisis helpline* or *crisis intervention* in reference to dire mental health emergencies. Synonymous with identity crisis are colloquial terms like a person *flipping out*, or *going off the deep end*, or *losing it*. *Midlife crisis* more often than not is used to refer to a man in his forties or fifties who divorces his wife of twenty-plus years, buys a sports car, and takes up with a young woman roughly the same age as his eldest child. Rarely is a midlife crisis seen as something desirable. Yet crises can have positive connotations, too.

A crisis can be reframed to connote growth. Even a living plant that develops a bud that will grow into a new leaf can be said to be in crisis. And the phrase *turning a new leaf* has always referred to a new beginning. This reframing of crisis can be useful to help ease clients' anxiety and tension over unwanted or unexpected changes in their work lives. When an employee is fired or laid off or when the writing on the wall indicates that the employee's days at her or his workplace are numbered and she or he had better find a new job, vocational practitioners can help these employees to realize that growth through crisis can also mean new possibilities and options in one's life.

orientation, values, and family roles (Vondracek, 1992). There has not been much interest in directly applying or expanding Erikson's theory to vocational psychology. However, his ideas continue to influence developmental psychology and life-span thinking in career and vocational counseling.

GINZBERG: A DEVELOPMENTAL APPROACH

Human development has been central to theory and practice in career counseling for the past fifty years. Ginzberg, Ginsburg, Axelrad, and Herma (1951)—an economist, a psychiatrist, a sociologist, and a psychologist, respectively—speculated that career development is a process culminating in occupational choice during one's early twenties. They further assert that: "Occupational choice is a developmental process; it is not a single decision, but a series of decisions made over a period of years. Each step in the process relates to those that precede and follow it" (p. 185).

Four sets of factors influence vocational choice: (1) individual values, (2) emotional factors, (3) amount and type of education, and (4) the effect of reality through environmental pressures (e.g., geographic location, employment opportunities). These

TABLE 5.1 Ginzberg et al.'s Stages of Career Development

PERIOD	AGE	CHARACTERISTICS
Fantasy	Childhood (before age 11)	Purely play orientation in the initial stage; near end of this stage, play becomes work-oriented.
Tentative	Early adolescence (ages 11 to 17)	Transitional process marked by gradual recognition of work requirements; recognition of interests, abilities, work reward, values, and time perspectives.
Realistic	Middle adolescence (ages 17 to young adulthood)	Integration of capacities and interests; further development of values; specification of occupational choice; crystallization of occupational patterns.

SOURCE: Zunker (1994), p. 28.

factors influence the formation of attitudes, which in turn shape occupational choice. Ginzberg et al. view choice as a process motivated by life stages, in which preadolescents and adolescents face certain tasks. As these tasks are confronted, compromises between wishes and possibilities can have an irreversible effect on one's decisions and options (Ginzberg et al., 1951, cited in Herr, Cramer & Niles, 2004). These stages are presented in Table 5.1.

Ginzberg et al. (1951) recognize individual variations in the career development process. There have been at least two basic causes for these individual variations:

1. Developing occupational skills early often leads to earlier than usual career patterns, i.e., teenage world class athletes—professional tennis players, Olympic gymnasts and swimmers—nearly all of whom are *past their prime* by age 30. Some artists and performers also begin their life's work earlier than usual. Then there are those who began working as children and have identified themselves as workers ever since.

2. The timing of the realistic stage may be delayed if factors such as emotional instability, various personal problems, and poverty or financial affluence are present.

Each of these factors can be the *normal* process of developing a career/job skill.

Vocational behavior is rooted in the early life of the child and develops over time (Ginzberg et al., 1951). However, Ginzberg reformulated the theory in 1971 to include three premises:

1. Occupational choice is a process that remains active as long as one is making decisions about work and career.

2. Decisions made during the early period (ages 5–17) will help shape career choices, but changes occurring in a person's own work and life will also influence career choices and patterns.

3. Decisions about jobs and careers are attempts to find a better match between personal needs/desires and work opportunities/constraints.

By 1984 Ginzberg had modified his theory even further, noting that people periodically reassess their satisfactions with work, so that occupational choice becomes a lifelong process. Early decisions restrict later ones when people seek to improve their career goals and fit them into the changing realities of the world of work (Herr, Cramer, &Niles, 2004). Ginzberg and his associates introduced the concept of career development as an active, dynamic process that spans an individual's working life. From this, other developmental career theorists emerged.

Evaluation of Ginzberg's Theory

Seligman (1994) offers two major criticisms of Ginzberg's theory. First, it is a descriptive theory that does not provide much direction to the process of facilitating career development or offer many suggestions for career counseling. Second, the research participants were mostly White males, with questionable generalizability to diverse populations.

SUPER'S LIFE-SPAN, LIFE-SPACE APPROACH

"Few disciplines have the good fortune to have a prodigious scholar at work on its problems for over six decades. Such is vocational psychology's debt to [the late Donald] Super" (Borgen, 1991, p. 276). Super brought comprehensive scholarship to the field of career behavior and development, and in his later years he synthesized much of his theory and research to include stages and substages of career development across the life span. For Super (1980), career is embedded in both the **life-span** and the **life-space**, including life roles and lifestyle. Currently, his work is a loosely unified set of theories dealing with specific aspects of career development, taken from developmental, differential, social, personality, and phenomenological psychology and held together by self-concept or personal construct theory (Super, 1990).

Super's theory is a useful model for several reasons. It covers the entire life span. Inventories were developed to validate the constructs of his theory, giving counselors assessment instruments that cover many aspects of career/job/occupation, including work adjustment, mid-career concerns, and the relationship of job to person. An impressive amount of research has been done in conjunction with the concepts of his developmental theory. And finally, the integration of the self-concept into the decision-making process was proposed.

Super suggested the following fourteen propositions.

1. People differ in their abilities and personalities, needs, values, interests, traits, and self-concepts.

2. People are qualified, by virtue of these characteristics, each for a number of occupations.

3. Each occupation requires a characteristic pattern of abilities and personality traits, with tolerances wide enough to allow both some variety of occupations for each individual and some variety of individuals in each occupation.

4. Vocational preferences and competencies, the situations in which people live and work, and, hence, their self-concepts change with time and experience, although self-concepts, as products of social learning, are increasingly stable from late adolescence until late maturity, providing some continuity in choice and adjustment.

5. The process of change may be summed up in a series of life stages (a "maxicycle") characterized as a sequence of growth, exploration, establishment, maintenance, and decline. . . . A small (mini) cycle takes place in transitions from one state to the next or each time an individual is destabilized by a reduction force, changes in type of manpower needs, illness or injury, or other socioeconomic or personal events. Such unstable or multiple-trial careers involve new growth, reexploration, and reestablishment (recycling).

6. The nature of the career pattern—that is, the occupational level attained and the sequence, frequency, and duration of trial and stable jobs—is determined by the individual's parental socioeconomic level, mental ability, education, skills, personality characteristics . . . , and **career maturity,** and by the opportunities to which he or she is exposed.

7. Success in coping with the demands of the environment and of the organism in that context at any given life-career stage depends on the readiness of the individual to cope with these demands . . . (on his or her career maturity). *Career maturity* is a constellation of physical, psychological, and social characteristics; psychologically, it is both cognitive and affective. It includes the degree of success in coping with the demands of earlier stages and substages of career development, and especially with the most recent.

8. Career maturity is a hypothetical construct. Its operational definition is perhaps as difficult to formulate as that of intelligence, but its history is much briefer and its achievements even less definitive. Contrary to the impressions created by some writers, it does not increase monotonically, and it is not a unitary trait.

9. Development through the life stages can be guided, partly by facilitating the maturating of abilities and interests and partly by aiding in reality testing and in the development of self-concepts.

10. The process of career development is essentially that of developing and implementing occupational self-concepts. It is a synthesizing and compromising process in which the self-concept is a product of the interaction of inherited aptitudes, physical make-up, opportunity to observe and play various roles, and evaluations of the extent to which the results of role playing meet with the approval of superiors and fellow workers (interactive learning).

11. The process of synthesis of or compromise between individual and social factors, between self-concepts and reality, is one of role playing and of learning from feedback, whether the role is played in fantasy in the counseling interview or in such real-life activities as classes, clubs, part-time work, and entry jobs.

12. Work satisfactions and life satisfactions depend on the extent to which the individual finds adequate outlets for abilities, needs, values, interests, personality traits, and self-concepts. They depend on establishment in a type of work, a work situation, and a way of life in which one can play the kind of role that growth and exploratory experiences have led one to consider congenial and appropriate.

13. The degree of satisfaction people attain from work is proportional to the degree to which they have been able to implement self-concepts.

14. Work and occupation provide a focus for personality organization for most men and women, although for some people this focus is peripheral, incidental, or even nonexistent. Then other foci, such as leisure activities and homemaking, may be central. (Social traditions, such as sex-role stereotyping and modeling, racial and ethnic biases, and the opportunity structure, as well as individual differences, are important determinants of preferences for roles such as worker, student, homemaker, and citizen) (Super, 1990, p. 206–208, italics in original).

Super's life-span, life-space approach to career counseling synthesizes theories and models into three graphic representations. The first graphic representation, life stages and substages of developmental tasks, is shown in Figure 5.1.

In Super's Life Career Stages, transitions are mini-stages in which important events take place. If one skips a step in moving from stage to stage, it may cause a negative impact (i.e., if one skips from growth to establishment without exploration, the result could be poor career/job choice and dissatisfaction). While the stages of growth, exploration, establishment, maintenance, and decline apply to the whole life, these same stages are enacted in a mini-version within each age group.

Super's stages provide a framework for vocational behavior and attitudes called **developmental tasks**. A developmental task is a new accomplishment or responsibility to be faced at a certain point in an individual's life, the successful achievement of

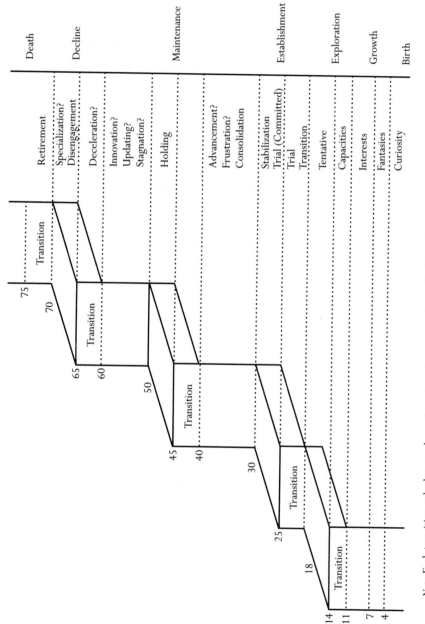

FIGURE 5.1 Life Stages and Substages Based on the Typical Development Tasks, with Focus on the Maxicycle

Note: Each transition, whether psychogenic, sociogenic, econogenic, or all of these, has its own minicycle of growth, exploration, establishment, maintenance, and decline: its recycling.

SOURCE: Brown, Brooks, and Associates (1990). Career Choice and Development, p. 214, Copyright 1990 Jossey-Bass. This material is used by permission of John Wiley and Sons, Inc.

TABLE 5.2 Super's Vocational Development Tasks

VOCATIONAL DEVELOPMENT TASKS	AGES	GENERAL CHARACTERISTICS
1. **Crystallization**	14–18	A cognitive process period of formulating a general vocational goal through awareness of resources, contingencies, interests, values, and planning for the preferred occupation
2. **Specification**	18–21	A period of moving from tentative vocational preferences toward a specific vocational preference
3. **Implementation**	21–24	A period of completing training for vocational preference and entering employment
4. **Stabilization**	24–35	A period of confirming a preferred career by actual work experience and use of talents to demonstrate career choice as an appropriate one
5. **Consolidation**	35 onwards	A period of establishment in a career by advancement, status, and seniority

SOURCE: Zunker (1994), p. 31.

which leads to happiness and success. Five developmental tasks are presented in Table 5.2. In conjunction with the five vocational development tasks are thirteen meta-dimensions of the self-concept (personal construct): (1) self-esteem, (2) stability, (3) clarity, (4) abstraction, (5) refinement, (6) certainty, (7) realism, (8) regnancy, (9) harmony, (10) structure, (11) scope, (12) flexibility, and (13) idiosyncrasy (Zunker, 2002).

Four other concepts help to understand the breadth of Super's theory.

1. Career maturity (see Proposition 8 above) is when one's career is at a peak. There may be several peaks or no peaks.

2. **Salience** is the importance of a role in a person's life.

3. Career determinants in the Archway Model (Figure 5.2) include what we know about person-environment interactions.

4. **Career adaptability** is the ability to cope with career development and adaptation tasks; as one moves through various stages of career development, differing tasks are encountered, as shown in Figure 5.1.

Career adaptability requires that practitioners develop a better understanding of the career transition process and provide adaptability training; adaptability needs to be incorporated into the training with children, adolescents, and adults in the early stages (Goodman, 1994). Savickas (1997) writes that

adaptation seems like a particularly appropriate construct for bridging theory segments because of its great relevance. . . . This shift in attention from the individual to the individual-in-situation coincides with contextual and multicultural perspectives on work. . . . I propose that career adaptability replace

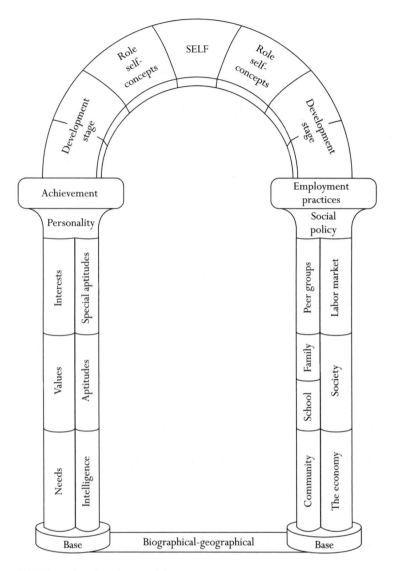

FIGURE 5.2 Super's Archway Model

SOURCE: *Brown, Brooks, and Associates (1990)*, Career Choice and Development, *p. 200. Copyright 1990 Jossey-Bass. This material is used by permission of John Wiley and Sons, Inc.*

career maturity as the central construct in the career development theory segment (pp. 253–254).

Savickas further suggests that adaptability has a continual application throughout the life span. The ease with which an individual moves through these stages and makes adaptations is a result of many factors, as depicted in Super's **Archway Model,** seen in Figure 5.2.

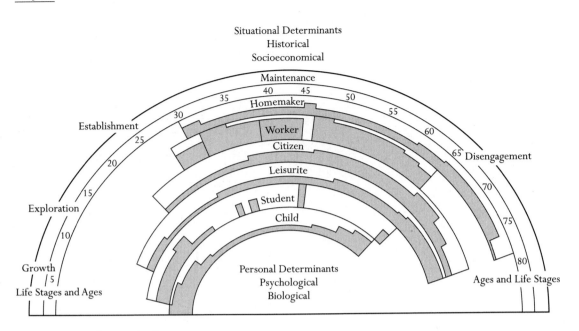

FIGURE 5.3 The Life-Career Rainbow

This model integrates various aspects that contribute to development of the total self-concept (personal construct). The left column represents psychological and personal characteristics and includes needs, intelligence, values, interests, aptitudes, personality, and role self-concepts related to these attributes. The right column represents societal characteristics and includes community, school, family, society, labor market, and role self-concepts related to these aspects of a person's life. While not part of the illustration, the columns interact and are not always separate and independent from each other. The doorstep between the two columns represents the biological-geographical foundations of development. The arch across the top is the career that results from the foundation and the pillars. The keystone of the arch is the person who is the decision maker, in whom all the influences converge from below.

As an individual moves through these stages she or he is also taking on various life roles. The Salience Inventory (SI) was developed to help an individual assess the importance he or she places on each of those roles. These roles are seen in the Life-Career Rainbow in Figure 5.3.

Super's Life-Career Rainbow demonstrates that roles may vary during a lifetime. In adolescence, exploration is paramount, leading to career decisions. In the early adult years, becoming established in a career and finding one's way is major. In the middle adult years, maintenance, job satisfaction, and adjustment to work changes are the focus of attention. In later adult years, slowing down and adjustment to different career concerns occur. As one scans the rainbow for each of the roles, changes in the importance of roles become apparent. Of increasing importance are Super's ideas about life-space. The overarching concern is the changing emphasis in career concerns and relationship of career to roles. Because an individual's work is in the context of a whole life, it is one of many roles across the life span.

> Individuals make decisions about work-role behavior (such as occupational choice and organizational commitment) within the constellation of social positions that give meaning for two individuals who live in different situations. For example, dedication to work may differ between two people in the same job because one is also active as a spouse, parent, and Girl Scout leader while the other is also active as a daughter, sister, and swimmer (D. E. Super, Savickas, & C. N. Super, 1996, p. 128).

Power and Rothausen (2003) developed a work-oriented mid-career development model for middle income workers in the United States as an extension of Super's career maintenance stage. This model was presented to respond to changing employment dynamics by replacing organizationally determined internal labor markets with an individually directed career development structure. This new structure directs workers to define their work, identify its future requirements, and select a developmental direction in an extension of Super's career maintenance stage. It also proposes three levels of mid-career development, including job oriented, work maintenance, and work growth. This model allows mid-career women and men to maintain or grow their employment security, income, and career satisfaction in an environment of increasing mobility and salary compression. Developmental directions, relation to generic roles, types of knowledge and skills most needed, and common career challenges are described in Table 5.3 and the work-oriented mid-career development model is outlined in Figure 5.4.

In a longitudinal study by Jepsen and Dickson (2003), continuity in career development from adolescence to middle adulthood was examined. They tested the proposition that early developmental task-coping activity predicts later task-coping activity. The study included 146 rural high school graduates who reported career exploratory activity in ninth grade and twelfth grade, occupational choice clarity in twelfth grade, and occupational establishment twenty-five years later. The data from this study generally supported the progressive mastery proposition in life-span theory. The developmental concepts of exploration activity and choice clarity are two strong candidates for building school career guidance programs. This suggests that increasing adolescents' exploratory activities and opportunities help them make better choices and decisions.

Madill, Montgomerie, Stewin, et al. (2000) had eleventh graders participate in a longitudinal study of career decision making in which they completed a series of career-related inventories and follow-up interviews. These academically gifted young

TABLE 5.3 Developmental Directions: Relation to Generic Roles, Types of Knowledge and Skills Most Needed, and Common Career Challenges

DEVELOPMENTAL DIRECTION AND GENERIC ROLE CONNECTION	WORK AND LIFESTYLE IMPLICATIONS	KNOWLEDGE AND SKILLS NEEDED	CHALLENGES FACED
Task developmental direction: desire to remain in the current role at current level of performance	Work hours, style, and income vary by the work but stable within a work focus, good for combining with other life roles or interests	Preferred skills and knowledge of multiple employers, recognition of technology or business changes that could change the work	Recognizing the need for development, knowing when current employment is becoming insecure
Specialist developmental direction: desire to develop to fill a role in the technostructure or to add another specialty if already in technostructure	Work often autonomous and flexible, income depends on importance of technology to employer and supply of workers, can be good for combining with other major life roles and interests because of possibilities for autonomy	Specialty and its current evolution, knowledge of a variety of applications, group participation skills	Keeping knowledge cutting edge, recognizing when technology is being phased out or replaced
Vertical developmental direction: desire to fill a role in the strategic apex	Work is generally high pressure with long hours, potential for high income, tournament nature of progression means risk of not advancing, high involvement in more than one life role difficult	Management and leadership, industry and business environment, organizations-specific information	Visibility in the organization and profession, "Plan B" for possible progression plateaus
Niche developmental direction: desire to fill a specialized management role within work organizations	Work similar to vertical but often with less stress, fewer performance pressures, and better defined limits; flexibility and stress levels are dependent on the situation	Understanding the niche and its major players, aspects of specialty knowledge that apply to the niche, management skills	Identifying niches that will remain economically viable and apply across organizations, meeting expectations of vertically focused management

SOURCE: Power and Rothausen, 2003, The work-oriented midcareer development model: An extension of Super's maintenance stage, *The Counseling Psychologist, 31,* 157–197.

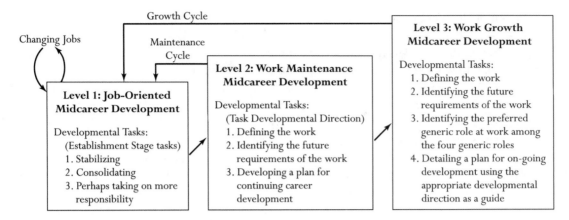

FIGURE 5.4 The Work-Oriented Midcareer Development Model: An Overview

SOURCE: *Power and Rothhausen, 2003, The work-oriented midcareer development model: An extension of Super's maintenance stage,* The Counseling Psychologist, 31, *157–197.*

women were given the Super's Values Scale (VS) and the Salience Inventory (SI) when they were in eleventh grade and again three years later. The study found that values appeared to be quite stable through this time of change for young women, while salience was less stable. Results of this study should encourage counselors to use the VS as a regular part of individual counseling with senior high school students. From Farmer's observations (1997), the SI should be equally valuable in helping young women deal with the early socialization for female nurturing roles. This could be an important time to explore issues surrounding home, family, and career decisions early with both men and women.

Vondracek and Hartung organized a symposium at the APA Conference in 2000 and invited researchers in vocational psychology or related fields to present papers on how developments in life course and life-span theory could add to career development theory, research and practice. The papers are presented in the *Journal of Vocational Behavior,* Vol. 61. Their assessment states that psychology and *sociology* needed to work together to formulate the new vocational science.

> Two orientations share an attribute that must be a signature feature of 21st-century thinking about vocational development, namely an explicit focus on all age groups. In psychology, this orientation is known as a life-span emphasis, while in sociology it is known as a life course framework (p. 375).

To further demonstrate the need for psychology and sociology to work together, Vondracek and Hartung cite Baltes, Lindenberger, and Staudinger (1998), who indicate that life-span psychologists are moving "towards models better able to capture the contextual, adaptive, probabilistic and self-organizational dynamic nature of development" (p. 375). From the sociological standpoint, Han and Moen (1999) propose models to better account for the "multiple, interlocking interfaces between men and women and work and family over time" (p. 376). Savickas (2001b) suggests that "[I]f career development researchers examine how people fit work into their lives rather than how to fit people into occupations, . . . career practitioners will shift their attention from promoting career development to fostering individual development through work and relationship" (p. 375). Finally, Richardson (2002) is recognized for "showing how contemporary changes in the world of work, on the one hand, and the increasing variability in individuals' personal lives, on the other, make contextualism particularly relevant for counselors in general and for career counselors in particular" (p. 377). Developmental contextualism is described in Chapter 9 as it relates to schools.

Super's concept of career maturity has engendered a series of studies. According to his model, individuals are mature or ready to make career choices when their decision-making knowledge is supported by occupational information they have carefully explored. At this point, individuals are ready to discuss the reasons for their choices. Savickas (2001a) suggests counselors "use Super's ideas about career salience, maturity, patterns, and themes to help clients impose meaning into their vocational behaviour" (p. 56).

A study by Savickas, Briddick, and Watkins (2002) investigated the potential link between career maturity as measured on the Career Maturity Inventory (CMI) and personality organization as measured in Gough's California Personality Inventory (CPI). The results indicate that career development in adolescence and young adulthood focuses the *norm-upholding* style of personality organization on fitting work into one's life in a social context. Those with this style were often seen as having a more developed career maturity, and their career patterns were often characterized by congruence, continuity, and early establishment. This, however, does not necessarily mean greater satisfaction or success in their jobs. It refers more to style of making decisions. On the other hand, the CPI *norm-questioning* orientation to forming vocational identity is often viewed as immaturity or pathology. These people reflect a more internal orientation to constructing their identity and are more self-authoring rather than society-minded in their career development. This also offers another way to view career indecisiveness.

Powell and Luzzo (1998) conducted a study of high school students in an ethnically diverse, urban school district to determine career maturity and the attributional style of career decision-making. Using the Career Maturity Inventory – Revised (CMI-R) and the Assessment of Attributions for Career Decision-Making, the results indicated a positive, significant relationship between career maturity and an optimistic attributional style. They found that career maturity differences based on demographic factors such as ethnic background, sex, socioeconomic standing, types of curriculum, or GPA were not significant. However, they did find that young men cited higher levels of control for career decision making than did young women. Luzzo, James, and

Luna (1996) suggest counselors apply attributional retraining strategies to help increase young women's sense of control over decision making, providing program and activity suggestions to accomplish this.

Assessments Used with Super's Theory

Super's measurement instruments are designed to measure an individual's concerns, values, and beliefs instead of measuring personality traits or aptitudes. Thus, his instruments are consistent with his theoretical ideas and include:

1. Adult Career Concerns Inventory (ACCI)
2. Career Development Inventory (CDI)
3. Salience Inventory (SI)
4. Values Scale (VS)
5. Work Values Inventory (WVI)
6. Thematic Extrapolation Method (TEM)
7. Career Maturity Inventory (CMI)
8. Career Adjustment and Development Inventory (CADI)

Practical Applications

Super's developmental model presents some specific guidelines for practitioners to understand and evaluate clients' life stage in order to define relevant counseling goals. Clarifying self-concept and finding appropriate experiences to determine the client's life stage would be essential for a practitioner to accomplish. Super does not talk about specific counseling procedures, but his thinking suggests a non-directive approach to clients. Because the process involves identifying the client's life stage and level of career maturity, an immature client would need to focus on orientation and exploration. Mature clients could concentrate on decision making and understanding the reality of their situations, leading to implementation. Using the tasks listed in Table 5.2, techniques that can be used include problem definition, deciding issues, working toward understanding, using reflection and processing, and using assessments to gain more awareness about work with specific career and occupational information.

Client stages, needs, and level of understanding will differ. For example when working with adolescents, Zunker (1994) cites Super's (1974) outline of six dimensions.

Continued

Continued

Orientation to vocational choice (an attitudinal dimension determining if the individual is concerned with the eventual vocational choice to be made);

Information and planning (a competence dimension concerning specificity of information individuals have concerning future career decisions and past planning accomplished);

Consistence of vocational preferences (individuals' consistencies of preferences);

Crystallization of traits (individual progress toward forming a self-concept);

Vocational independence (independence of work experience); and

Wisdom of vocational preferences—dimension concerned with individual's ability to make realistic preferences consistent with personal tasks. (Zunker, 1994, pp. 33–34)

Of particular interest is Super's Career-Development Assessment and Counseling model (C-DAC) (Osborne, Brown, Niles, & Miner, 1997). The assessment tools in this battery include the Strong Interest Inventory (SII), the Values Scale (VS), the Career Development Inventory (CDI), the Adult Career Concerns Inventory (ACCI), and the Salience Inventory (SI). Two basic sequences of tests follow after a general orientation to the purpose and nature of the battery. Sequence A is: (1) CDI/ACCI, (2) SII, (3) VS, and (4) SI. Sequence B is: (1) SII, (2) VS, (3) CDI/ACCI, and (4) SI. An additional sequence is adapted to special cases and uses other instruments.

The ideas behind the sequences include the following: (1) The CDI is used if the client is a student; the ACCI if the client is an adult. (2) Sequence A is used to look first "at the developmental stage, the tasks, or concerns the individual faces" (Super et al., 1992, p. 77). (3) Sequence B "begins with the client's interests, as some people come to counseling seeking to find or to confirm an occupational choice" (Super et al., p. 77).

No aptitude tests are used because most institutions already screen a person for that. If there has been no screening, then the authors recommended the Differential Aptitude Test (DAT), the Armed Services Vocational Aptitude Battery (ASVAB), or the Miller Analogies Test (MAT), depending on the situation and the age of the client (Super et al., 1992). Niles (2001) suggests the C-DAC be used to identify "the life roles that are important to people, the values sought in each life role, and the individual's readiness for career choice" (p. 138).

Relevance for Multicultural and Diverse Populations

There is limited empirical evidence available about the relevance of Super's developmental theory for multicultural and diverse populations. Examining the extent to which racial and ethnic identity development affects career development could make

Super's theory more relevant to minorities (Fouad & Arbona, 1994). We encourage both logical positivist *and* contextual interpretivist approaches to learn more.

New ground could be broken with the development of multicultural norms on the Career-Development Assessment and Counseling model (C-DAC) to include an appropriate measure of acculturation. This would greatly enhance what is known about the occupational development of multicultural populations.

African Americans The relationship between the self-concept and career behavior has not been systematically investigated with African Americans (Brown, 1995). Nor has the role of socioeconomic status and discrimination on occupational/self-concepts been investigated. Definable stages of career development and variable implementation of the self-concept as a function of the developmental stage have not been validated with African Americans. The concept of career maturity may need revision because it is correlated with socioeconomic status, and most African Americans are lower-income. Differences in the nature of African American self-concepts, and the way in which it is implemented vocationally over time in the way that Super proposed, remain unknown.

Hispanics "Neither theoretical formulations nor empirical research to date have elucidated which specific aspects of SES or ethnicity impact which aspects of career development for specific populations. . . . [T]here is very little empirical information related to the validity of the instruments and the theory among people of low-socio-economic resources (White and non-White) and among ethnic minorities" (Arbona, 1995, pp. 47–48).

Native Americans Johnson, Swartz, and Martin (1995) review three vocational psychology approaches with Native Americans, but Super's developmental approach is not among them. Nor does Martin (1995) specifically mention Super's approach in Native American occupational development. The Archway Model would be relevant for Native Americans, especially given the model's consideration of the economy, community, school, family, peer groups, and social policy that appear on the right column of the arch (see Figure 5.2 above). These factors have not been fully fleshed out for applicability to Native Americans. Economic conditions are especially salient because they are affected by the maintenance of native language and customs (Johnson et al., 1995). The Life-Career Rainbow also has the potential application for widespread application to Native Americans.

Asian Americans "Research on Asian Americans to date lacks a developmental perspective" (Leong & Serafica, 1995, p. 86). We wonder if some of Super's approach is too individualistic for Asian Americans with a strong collectivistic orientation. To the extent that Asian American parents "exert direct influence on the career aspirations and choices of their children" (Leong & Serafica, 1995, p. 71), their youth may have to submit "to the wisdom of the elderly" (p. 71). The Life-Career Rainbow has applicability to Asian Americans (Leong & Serafica, 1995). Asian American college students show less career maturity than their White American counterparts (Leong, 1991), but these results may be considered preliminary at best. Within-group differences (career maturity of college-bound and noncollege-bound Asian Americans) would be more telling.

People with Mental Retardation Little research has been conducted on the application of Super's developmental theory to people with mental retardation (Levinson, Peterson, & Elston, 1994). More broadly, because developmental theories target the nonhandicapped population, the complete application of such theories to individuals with mental retardation seems inappropriate. People with mental retardation generally have been limited in terms of both vocational exploration and range of experiences, so progress through developmental stages may be slowed and nonsystematic, if at all. A modified developmental approach can be adapted for use with individuals with mental retardation, beginning with setting age ranges aside. Degree of retardation and previous range of occupational and life experience will differentially impact the stages that entail (1) increasing self-awareness and occupational awareness, (2) facilitating occupational exploration, (3) implementing an occupational choice, and (4) enhancing adjustment within a given occupation.

Gay, Lesbian, and Bisexual People Modifying traditional developmental theories can contribute to effective career counseling with gay/lesbian/bisexual people (Gelberg & Chojnacki, 1996). The person's level of sexual identity development has to be incorporated into life-span approaches. Cass (1979) presents a six-stage model of sexual identity development that is applicable to gays, lesbians, and bisexuals (see Table 5.4).

The stage of a gay, lesbian, or bisexual person's sexual identity development can influence willingness to enter work environments where homophobia prevails. Self-esteem of gay/lesbian/bisexual people can be affected by the interaction of their sexual identity development and workplace homophobia. Most gay/lesbian/bisexual people live in hiding, also known as living *in the closet* (Mohr, 1988). **Coming out of the closet,** or *coming out*, often becomes a central fixture in the life experiences of gay, lesbian, and bisexual people, and can become intertwined with career decision making. Woods (1994) defines **in the closet** as knowingly misrepresenting one's sexuality to others by encouraging (or at least permitting) others to draw a conclusion one knows is false. He likens closets to dark and cramped spaces in which one can hide but where nobody wants to live. Closets conceal those articles that seem unfit for display in larger, more important rooms. A gay/lesbian/bisexual person who is hiding in a closet is invisible to those outside of it; but working in a closet allows one little room to move about.

TABLE 5.4 Sexual Identity Development Model of Gay/Lesbian/Bisexual People

STAGE 1: IDENTITY CONFUSION

"Who am I?" "My behavior may be called [gay, lesbian, or bisexual]." "Does this mean that I am [gay/lesbian/bisexual]?" With self-labeling of one's own behavior, the realization that feelings, thoughts, or behavior can be defined as gay, lesbian, or bisexual presents an incongruent element into a previously stable situation.

STAGE 2: IDENTITY COMPARISON

"Where do I belong?" "I may be [gay/lesbian/bisexual]." Social alienation, sense of "not belonging" can arise. Loss of self-concept of future heterosexual identity is not yet replaced by another sexual identity. "I do not want to be different."

STAGE 3: IDENTITY TOLERANCE

"I am probably [gay, lesbian, or bisexual]." Any sexual identity turmoil ceases when social, emotional, and sexual needs are acknowledged. Growth occurs when person attempts to resolve inconsistency in view of self, others' view of self.

STAGE 4: IDENTITY ACCEPTANCE

"I am a [gay/lesbian/bisexual] person." Sexual identity validated, normalized. There is acceptance rather than tolerance of sexual self-identity. The nonlegitimizing policy of heterosexuals produces tension.

STAGE 5: IDENTITY PRIDE

"These are my people." Commitment to gay, lesbian, and/or bisexual people is strong. There is awareness of incongruence between self-acceptance and society's rejection. Devaluation of heterosexual others.

STAGE 6: IDENTITY SYNTHESIS

Dichotomy between heterosexual and gay/lesbian/bisexual world decreases. Similarly, dissimilarity between gay/lesbian/bisexual self, and heterosexual others is recognized. Sexual identity honored as one of many aspects of the self.

SOURCE: Adapted from Cass (1979) by Roberto Cortéz González.

Coming out of the closet is an ongoing process that can have enough salience to form a third pillar or column in Super's Archway Model. As part of developmental approaches to occupation, first romantic relationships, leaving home for the first time, and job promotions are also developmental transitions of gay, lesbian, and bisexual people. Recognition that work role and sexual orientation cannot be completely detached from each other—given the social nature of work— makes life-span, life-space approaches to occupations relevant for those in a sexual minority.

Fassinger (1996) summarizes barriers and facilitators to lesbians' career choice, implementation, and adjustment. Barriers to career choice are related to coming out of the closet.

1. Lesbians involved in their sexual identity development may neglect occupational decisions and tasks. This hold-up in vocational development tasks, long after peers have addressed these issues, risks being internalized as individual inadequacy, rather than normalized as a developmental delay.

2. Occupational stereotyping can interact with coming out. Some career options may be eliminated because they are perceived as inhospitable toward lesbians "or, conversely, are associated with lesbians" (p. 163). Christie (1997) profiles lesbians in a variety of jobs that can expand the vision of occupational opportunities.

3. When many lesbians come out of the closet, their families may withdraw financial and psychological support, which can impede vocational planning.

4. Lesbians whose self-esteem and self-confidence decrease during the coming out process can have their career decision making constrained.

5. Bias in vocational assessment can be a barrier.

6. Bias on the part of practitioners is the final barrier related to coming out.

Lesbians' career choices have several facilitators (Fassinger, 1996).

1. In making work-related decisions, lesbians are less likely than heterosexual women to be encumbered by "accommodating men or conforming to traditional gender roles" (p. 164).

2. Lesbians are also less likely than heterosexual women to "anticipate depending on men for financial stability" (p. 165).

3. Financial independence between partners is more likely in a lesbian relationship, partially due to laws and company policies that inhibit legal and economic dependence.

4. Lesbians appear more certain and satisfied with career choices than gay men.

5. A strong focus on career planning and preparation may buffer the coming out process.

In view of the sampling of representative literature on the role of work in lesbians' lives (Fassinger, 1996; Sophie, 1985/86), practitioners can prepare themselves to work with lesbians in several ways (Hetherington & Orzek, 1989).

1. Work to consciously eliminate personal homophobic attitudes.

2. Develop an understanding of the gender issues for women.

3. Learn about lesbian identity development.

4. Help lesbian clients to overcome internalized negative stereotypes.

5. Provide self-exploration assistance in the form of informational interview questions specific to lesbian concerns. Among such questions (Milburn, Eldridge, & Hetherington, 1988, cited in Hetherington & Orzek, 1989):
   a. Is this career available to me as an *out* lesbian?
   b. Have I determined how *out* I want to be before I choose this career?
   c. Are there any work environments in this career that are more open to lesbians?
   d. Is my sexual identity pertinent to this career area?
   e. Will my sexual orientation affect being accepted in graduate school?

6. Develop a list of job search strategies that lesbian clients may use. Among such strategies (Milburn, Eldridge & Hetherington, 1988, cited in Hetherington & Orzek, 1989):
   a. learning which companies have nondiscrimination policies,
   b. learning about the attitudes regarding homosexuality in local communities where a lesbian may consider living,
   c. communicating on one's résumé the lesbian and gay activities in which one has been involved,
   d. handling the situation in which the presence of a spouse is considered beneficial,
   e. handling dual-career issues, and
   f. learning about companies who are sensitive to lesbian concerns.

7. Provide a list of professional associations and resources for lesbian clients.

Because Cass's sexual identity development model for gays, lesbians, and bisexuals was published in 1979, gay and lesbian identities have come under siege by a **poststructuralism** influenced approach called **queer theory**. Similar to postmodernism, poststructuralism rejects the modernist tradition that the real world can be explained by underlying rules and structures (Burr, 1995), and asserts that the self is a fictional interior core (Jagose, 1996). Queer theory contends that the conventional, binary categories of (1) gender identification like male/female and (2) sexual identifications like heterosexual/homosexual, gay/straight, in the closet/out of the closet, are social, cultural, and political constructions that have no basis in nature, but rather are created by discursive practices (Jagose, 1996; Spargo, 1999). Queer theorists refer to these conventional understandings as **heteronormativity**. Heteronormativity presumes that heterosexuality is a normal and natural fact, a simple extension of a biological process, and that other forms of sexual behavior are deviations from this norm. Queer theorists believe that fixed gay and lesbian identities merely serve to perpetuate the heteronormative, hierarchical political power structure.

This power structure is also upheld by liberationist models that seek to free repressed or oppressed natures and by ethnic models that seek to establish lesbians and gays as a legitimate minority group. By kowtowing to the heteronormative power structure, liberation and ethnic models still exclude people who don't fit into their own normative identity categories—including transvestites, transgendered people, drag queens, and bisexuals. Gays and lesbians who espouse either the liberation or ethnic models criticize queer theory for undermining their political and legal gains. Queer theorists contend that by reclaiming the formerly derogatory term *queer* for themselves, they are self-identifying and not being granted begrudging compromises by the so-called *straight* world.

Extensive coverage of arguments for and against queer theory is beyond the scope of our interests here. We acknowledge that in this textbook we use an ethnic model for gays and lesbians. Queer theory's contextualist emphasis may have little to offer parents whose children may be struggling with issues of coming out. It certainly directly challenges the view that homosexuality is itself a natural state (see for example, Rowse, 1977). Yet any future conceptualizations of gays and lesbians in the workplace will have to reckon with queer theory and why it is or isn't a viable way of examining the role of work in people's lives.

Practical Applications

"Lesbians and gay men represent a challenge to some of our most entrenched ideas about the separation of work and sexuality; their mere presence seems to upset our conventional beliefs about privacy, professionalism, and office etiquette" (Woods, 1994, p. 5). For all the eagerness of gay, lesbian, and bisexual employees to detach sexuality from work, the task becomes difficult because work is largely a social activity and personal and professional roles become as firmly intertwined as they do for heterosexual people. As sexual creatures—regardless of one's orientation—humans cannot help that social interactions are colored by sexual possibilities, expectations, and constraints. In dress and in self-presentation, in looks and in flirtations, in jokes and in gossip, in secret affairs and in dalliances, even in the range of coercive

behaviors known as sexual harassment, sexuality is alluded to, both implicitly and explicitly, in the countless interpersonal exchanges that combine to constitute *work*.

Parents and Friends of Lesbians and Gays, Inc. (PFLAG) have a series of supportive, educational, and informational publications that may be especially helpful for practitioners and their clients, particularly when it appears that the exploration of vocational issues might benefit from integration with concerns about sexual orientation. A good place to start is Sauerman (1996). Another PFLAG publication aimed at gay, lesbian, and bisexual youth is *Be Yourself* (1994), with numerous resources provided at the end of the booklet. Two PFLAG publications are aimed at parents: *About Our Children* (1995) includes some sections translated into Chinese, French, Japanese, and Spanish. *Our Daughters and Sons* (1995) is available in English only. Vocational practitioners who do not specialize in gay, lesbian, and bisexual clientele would also find these PFLAG publications useful reading (see also, Thompson, 1994).

A book aimed more toward adults is *A Family and Friend's Guide to Sexual Orientation* (Powers & Ellis, 1996). Especially relevant are stories from the workplace (Powers & Ellis, 1996, pp. 155–89) and the authors' view that a "Don't Ask, Don't Tell" work environment creates "a tremendous and negative impact on the bottom line" (p. 155), with workplace performance deterioration. Managers who send out signals that it is not acceptable to be gay/lesbian/bisexual in the workplace negatively impact performance and force such employees to closet themselves. Excluded sexual minorities are less likely to devote the extra energy needed to make the organization successful. When these issues are ignored in the workplace, productive work relationships can be destroyed and top-notch performance of all workers can be undermined.

Another resource is *Straight Jobs, Gay Lives* (Friskopp & Silverstein, 1995). Using qualitative research, this book examines the role of work in the lives of professional gay men and lesbians who are alumni of the Harvard Business School.

Vocational practitioners also need to be aware of **heterosexual privilege** (Gelberg & Chojnacki, 1996). Heterosexual privilege allows (1) heterosexual partners to publicly display affection without fear of comment or attack by others, (2) inheritance rights, (3) access to a partner in a hospital, (4) the legal right to marry, and (5) the ability to adopt children. Such rights and freedoms are taken for granted by many heterosexuals. Practitioners have to become knowledgeable about the absence of rights for gay, lesbian, and bisexual people because these rights can impact career development and work-related behaviors (Curry, Clifford, & Leonard, 1996).

Evaluation of Super's Career Decision Theory

Super's legacy is designed to be flexible enough to adapt to new conditions. Refinements of Super's theory can evolve as research is conducted to determine how the economic and occupational changes taking place around the world affect and modify the theory and concepts such as the "meaning of work, work identity, and for new or emerging career patterns in many nations" (Herr, 1997, p. 241). Because women "are occupying leadership roles in traditional and nontraditional occupations, greater attention to gender issues in role salience and career decision making needs to be applied to life-space, life-span perspectives" (p. 241). The Work Importance Study in several nations is seminal in its work toward understanding national cultural differences (D. Super, Sverko, & C. Super, 1995). Studies using more than two of Super's constructs—values and work-role salience —are needed (Herr, 1997). There is also a need to focus more directly on the various "obstacles, barriers, reinforcements, received messages, and other variables affecting the career behavior of women, racial and ethnic groups, persons with disabilities, and people of alternative sexual orientations" (p. 243).

OTHER CAREER DEVELOPMENTAL THEORIES

Tiedeman and O'Hara

Tiedeman and O'Hara's approach to career development is basically self-development and includes cognitive development and the subsequent decision-making process of the individual (Tiedeman & O'Hara, 1963). Career development unfolds as one resolves ego-relevant crises, as the evolving ego identity is a crucial part of career development. The evolving self-in-situation develops from the earliest awareness of the self. Evaluating experiences, anticipating and imagining future goals, and storing experiences in memory for future reference are part of the evolving ego identity (Tiedeman & O'Hara, 1963).

Tiedeman and O'Hara's theory is based on Erikson's eight psychosocial crises and from the work of Ginzberg and Super. The theory focuses on ego development, the self-in-situation, and the self-in-world. From this theoretical basis, they proposed a two-stage model of career development with appropriate substages.

1. Anticipation or preoccupation period:
    a. Exploration—awareness of options develops
    b. Crystallization—options are explored, narrowed
    c. Choice—decisions are made
    d. Clarification—plans are implemented
2. Implementation or adjustment period:
    a. Induction—entry into the world of work
    b. Reformation—modification of goals and environment
    c. Integration—becoming an established member of the workforce (Seligman, 1994).

From this model, a person can assess and define vocational/career direction while gaining a better understanding of the basics for the chosen direction. This process forms the basis for career identity. Tiedeman and O'Hara suggested career connections with each of Erikson's eight stages of the life-span.

Gottfredson's Theory of Circumscription and Compromise

In her approach, Gottfredson (1996) combines trait-factor and developmental theories. Major tenets include: (1) self-concept—one's self perception; (2) occupational images—similar to occupational stereotypes but without the negative implications of

Practical Applications

According to Gottfredson, there are five criteria that assess an individual's career success. Failure to meet a criterion indicates a problem(s).

1. Can the client name one or more occupational alternatives? If not, is there a lack of self-knowledge to judge compatibility? Are there internal or external conflicts in the goals?
2. Are the client's interests and abilities a match for the occupation(s) selected? If not, are there external pressures from parents or misperceptions of self?
3. Is the client satisfied with the alternatives identified? If not, was client's choice an unacceptable compromise of interests, sex type, or family concerns?
4. Has the client left any alternatives open? If not, why have alternatives been restricted?
5. Is the client aware of opportunities and realistic about obstacles for implementing the chosen occupation? Is the client failing to overcome obstacles? (Gottfredson, 1996).

Because much of her theory and research concentrated on gender issues, it would seem important to incorporate this in our work with women.

stereotypes; (3) a cognitive map of occupations—based on dimensions such as sex type, occupational prestige level, and field of work; (4) compatibility—assessing different occupations with images of themselves and looking for congruence; (5) social space—range of alternatives in the cognitive map of occupations; (6) circumscription—how individuals narrow the territory or alternatives; and (7) compromise—relinquishing some alternative for the less compatible but more accessible ones.

Gottfredson outlines the following underpinnings for her theory.

1. "Career choice is an attempt to place oneself in the broader social order" (p. 181). "Social" aspects of self (gender, social class, intelligence) are emphasized more than personal ones (values, traits).

2. Cognitions of self and occupations develop early. Career development needs to begin as early as in the preschool years.

3. Vocational choice assists a person in eliminating options and narrowing choices.

4. Individuals compromise their goals as they face the reality of implementing their aspirations.

Blanchard and Lichtenberg (2003) have recently studied Gottfredson's theory of circumscription and compromise. From the 119 university students in the study, it appears that interests play an important role in determining an occupation's acceptability, but the extent of that importance depends on the level of compromise one faces in making a career choice. In other words, "compromise is the process of eliminating preferred alternatives due to obstacles that the individual perceives as insurmountable" (p.251). These obstacles could be due to family obligation, financial stressors, job market predictions, race or sexual discrimination, or lack of opportunities for training.

MULTICULTURAL DEVELOPMENTAL PERSPECTIVES

Vocational psychology can adapt itself to multicultural populations by considering minority identity development (Atkinson, Morten, & Sue, 1989). A model is outlined in Table 5.5. To date, no theory of occupational development accounts for the identity stage of minority development (Osipow & Littlejohn, 1995). This missing information is crucial: an individual's stage of minority development determines conformity to mainstream societal norms. Many people in racial and ethnic minorities face the dual challenge of minority identity development combined with general development. A triple challenge occurs when these people also face questions of gay/lesbian/bisexual identity development and occupational development.

A racial and ethnic minority person in Stage 1 of the model shown in Table 5.5 would have unequivocal Conformity to the dominant group (Atkinson et al., 1989). In a work setting, a Stage 1 individual would feel deficient in perceived desirable characteristics of the dominant culture. These individuals may rely on affirmation from White males (being the dominant group in this country), regardless of how much—or how little—talent or ability the White male may possess. This search for White male affirmation overlaps with **post–colonial theory**.

Post-colonial theory refers to the very first moment of contact between the colonizer and the colonized (Ashcroft, Griffiths, & Tiffin, 1995). *Post-colonial* does *not* mean after-colonial or after independence. Post-colonialism concerns itself with the imperial process of **Eurocentrism**, ". . . the conviction that Europe is an inevitable and necessary global reference point as it is the cultural, political, and economic centre [*sic*] of the world" (Harrison, 2003, p. 107). One finds Eurocentrism in ". . . all societies into which the imperial force of Europe has intruded" (Ashcroft, Griffiths, & Tiffin, 1995, p. 2).

> The term "post-colonial" also refers to an individual identity as much as a group process. Some post-colonized individuals have internalized the image and guidelines of the oppressor (Freire, 1970/1993), which produces **identification with the oppressor**. Such individuals, when they obtain a position of power and authority, become oppressors who do exactly to others what was done to them.

The Dissonance stage, Stage 2 of the Minority Identity Development Model in Table 5.5, will not occur until there is a breakdown in one's denial system. Breakdown of denial can be gradual or abrupt and can occur in many ways. One can have a new

TABLE 5.5 Summary of Minority Identity Development Model

STAGES OF MINORITY DEVELOPMENT MODEL	ATTITUDE TOWARDS SELF	ATTITUDE TOWARDS OTHERS OF THE SAME MINORITY	ATTITUDE TOWARDS OTHERS OF DIFFERENT MINORITY	ATTITUDE TOWARDS DOMINANT GROUP
Stage 1: Conformity	self-depreciating	group-depreciating	discriminatory	group-appreciating
Stage 2: Dissonance	conflict between self-depreciating and appreciating	conflict between group-depreciating and group-appreciating	conflict between dominantly held views of minority hierarchy and feelings of shared experience	conflict between group-appreciating and group-depreciating
Stage 3: Resistance and immersion	self-appreciating	group-appreciating	conflict between feelings of empathy for other minority experiences and feelings of culturo-centrism	group-depreciating
Stage 4: Introspection	concern with basis of self-appreciation	concern with nature of unequivocal appreciation	concern with ethnocentric basis for judging others	concern with the basis of group depreciation
Stage 5: Synergetic articulation and awareness	self-appreciating	group-appreciating	group-appreciating	selective appreciation

co-worker of the same racial or ethnic background but at a different stage in the model, whose worldview makes for a different reading of workplace politics. Blatant racism in the workplace, especially racism that is rewarded or goes unpunished, can jolt somebody out of Stage 1 and into Stage 2.

Growing awareness of inequity and inequality and a realization that not all dominant cultural values serve the best interests of a person from a racial and ethnic minority (Atkinson et al., 1989) can nudge a person on to Stage 3, Resistance and Immersion. Until a person passes beyond at least the Minority Identity Development Model Stage 3, the development of a stable self-concept can be prolonged and the expression of that self through the role of work can be delayed. Issues of oppression in the workplace are also confronted in Stage 3.

Decision-making processes can be most effective with clients in Stage 4, Introspection (Atkinson et al., 1989). Cultural constraints and personal freedom vie with each other at this stage. The racial or ethnic minority person has to resolve these inner tensions. Viewed through the lens of post-colonial theory, post-colonized individuals at Stage 4 of the Minority Identity Development Model would attempt to identify with a native culture that has been destroyed by imperialism and its language. This politics of language is crucial because ". . . a choice of language is a choice of identity" (Freire, 1970/1993, p. 126). And yet, colonization silenced the voices (Parry, 1995) and traditions (Bhabha, 1995) of many indigenous peoples, who became strangers in their own land (Bhabha, 1994). The plight of such indigenous peoples becomes one of **marginality**, life on the periphery of both the native and colonial cultures.

By Stage 5 of the Minority Identity Development Model, the ethnic, racial, or sexual minority person has enough internal skills and knowledge to exercise the desired level of personal freedom (Atkinson et al., 1989). One's sense of minority identity is balanced with an appreciation for other cultures. More psychological resources are present to deal with intractable issues of discrimination and oppression. Post-colonial theory would say that groups or individuals who have been subjected to imperialism will strive to achieve at least a part of their identity uncontaminated by European social constructs (During, 1995).

CASE EXAMPLE

Workplaces can sometimes seem like extremely colonial places to individuals from racial, ethnic, and sexual minorities. The following case example is true. Names and some genders have been changed and/or omitted to protect the guilty from further shame.

Isidro was hired onto the public relations/event production professional staff of a new major league sports stadium in a big U.S. city with a large Hispanic population. As he was also an ardent sports fan, he was thrilled to be using his college degree (journalism major/marketing and advertising minor) in a job in his and his wife Maciel's hometown. They had married out of college, were expecting their first child, and were glad to be back among their family support systems. Isidro believed he had found his dream job, especially because he more or less

knew that the college graduation rate of Hispanics wasn't stellar and few local Hispanics were earning as much as he was. He wrote press releases; supervised the writing, photography, and layout of stadium souvenir programs; conducted press conferences; designed and executed ad campaigns; and sometimes even wined and dined with some of the world's top coaches and professional athletes.

The major league sports stadium also hosted concert venues during the off-season. One day, at a professional staff meeting, Isidro and his colleagues were discussing contractual arrangements for an upcoming concert by a huge Latino recording star. They were reviewing the clause that listed the recording star's requirements for backstage food and drink, which included a specific ethnic dish. When the dish was referred to by its

Spanish name, one of Isidro's White co-workers, Alistair, replied, "Where do we call to find *that* kind of food? 1-800-GUADALOOP?" Isidro's all-White co-workers laughed. He was both startled and stunned by the slur to the Virgin of Guadalupe, an apparition of the Virgin Mary revered by Latino Catholics ever since she appeared to the indigenous Juan Diego (canonized by Pope John Paul II in 2002) atop Tepeyac Hill in 1531 (ten years after the Spanish Conquest of Mexico) in present-day Mexico City.

Right then and there, it was as if Isidro was yanked from Stage 1 to Stage 3 of the Minority Identity Development Model. Although Isidro had been attempting to unequivocally conform to his all-White workplace—he was the token Hispanic on the professional staff—his ethnic pride was wounded by the slur. Alistair's put-down took precedence, from a post-colonial perspective, over Our Lady of Guadalupe's own post-colonial status. Although Isidro deemed it politic to keep quiet in response to Alistair's gross insensitivity, something in him snapped. He stopped trying so hard to fit in with his co-workers, and he realized that not all of them respected his and his wife's cultural background. He certainly wasn't going to tell them that his beloved mother-in-law's name was María Guadalupe.

As he matured personally and professionally, Isidro eventually got to Stage 5, with a selective appreciation of his White co-workers. But Isidro also realized that working on the professional staff at the major league sports stadium had a vastly different meaning for him than for his co-workers, because of his ethnicity and his *home boy* status. He had tolerated being called Izzy by his co-workers; all their names had been shortened. Alistair was Al, Geoffrey was Jeff, Elizabeth was Liz,

Lionel was Lonny, Ruben-James was Rube, and Maximilian was Max. But gradually, as Isidro deliberately began to reclaim his ethnic identity, he began to ask his colleagues to call him Isidro instead of Izzy. Some graciously complied, others did so with bewildered irritation.

And while Isidro learned as many tricks of the trade as he could from his more experienced workers, he never again thought that their ways were always the best ways to do things at work. He came to realize that he had talents and abilities that sometimes superseded theirs, and he developed the self-confidence and self-regard to know that he could interact with the Hispanic community in his hometown on levels that none of his co-workers ever would achieve.

We believe it's important to note that while Isidro had negotiated these stages of the Minority Identity Development Model through high school and college, his new workplace context made it necessary for him to go through these stages anew. This same type of renegotiation of stages may sometimes occur with the Sexual Identity Development Model of Gay/Lesbian/Bisexual People, indeed with any stage model, whenever one starts a new job, moves to a new neighborhood, joins a professional organization, or any type of new situation.

Isidro was fortunate to be able to renegotiate his relevant stage model on his own, but other people may need professional assistance. Vocational practitioners can help clients transition through various stages by extensive familiarity with various stage models—the second co-author of this textbook uses one-page handouts of these models with clients—and by helping clients strategize specific actions and, yes, political maneuvers, to navigate workplace currents.

With affirmative action as a simmering topic in reference to equal access to occupational opportunities, vocational psychology will be remiss until multicultural and diversity issues are solidly at the center—not a subspecialty—of any theory of occupational development.

PEOPLE WITH DISABILITIES

We decided to discuss people with disabilities at length in this chapter because a disability identity has to develop in order for optimal adjustment to occur, whether a person was born with the disability or acquired it at some point in their lives. In the workplace, developmental considerations are pivotal because an employee with disabilities will have uneven development across emotional, intellectual, social, and occupational domains.

> People with disabilities represent a very diverse population. There are many different types of disabilities (e.g., cerebral palsy, multiple sclerosis, low vision, deafness, mental retardation), all of which have substantial variation in possible degrees of severity and functional limitations. Even within specific disabilities, there is great variation in resultant functional limitations. . . .
> [L]ike race and ethnicity, disability is multifaceted, and cannot be examined in isolation in its impact on career development (Szymanski, Hershenson, Enright, & Ettinger, 1996, p. 70).

As of 1997, the latest year for which figures are available, an estimated 52.6 million U.S. citizens—19.7 percent of the population—have some level of disability (McNeil, 2001), which makes them the largest minority group in the United States (Switzer, 2001). Of these, 33 million—12.3 percent of the population—are severely disabled, unable to perform one or more activities and roles. Among those ages 25 to 64 who are severely disabled, 7.9 percent are Asian and Pacific Islander, 11.7 percent are Hispanic, 11.0 percent are White, and 19.3 percent were African American. Percentage rates are not reported for American Indian, Eskimo, and Aleut populations. Disability is associated with lower levels of income and an increased likelihood of living in poverty. Chances for employment are reduced among the disabled. These poverty and unemployment situations are due to inequities in social policy, educational access, opportunities for job training, and society's age-old attitudes toward disability (Bruyere, Erickson, & Ferrentino, 2003).

A major reason for reduced employment opportunities among people with disabilities is an historically negative attitude toward such people. Magiera-Planey (1990) writes:

> Attitudes regarding disabled persons . . . as a group have a long and illustrious history. In the early days of mankind the disabled were often left behind or

eliminated if the group needed to be mobile or if there was a lack of food. In later civilizations many of the disabled and deformed were systematically eliminated as a means of improving the society. These negative attitudes soon included the belief that the disabled individual was being punished for some injustice that he/she had committed (pp. 45–46).

We detect both a "blaming the victim" and "belief in a just world" mentality in the historical view of people with disabilities. In the West, from medieval times through the Industrial Revolution, people with disabilities were consistently devalued (Magiera-Planey, 1990). "Unfortunately disabled persons as a group are still viewed as nonparticipants in society [and in the workforce]" (p. 46). Atkinson and Hackett (1998) present an up-to-date examination of the oppression of people with disabilities.

The Americans with Disabilities Act

Title I of the Americans with Disabilities Act of 1990 (ADA) took effect on July 26, 1992, for employers of twenty-five or more employees (U.S. Equal Employment Opportunity Commission, 1991b, 1992). The ADA took effect for employers with fifteen or more employees exactly two years later. The ADA prohibits private employers, state and local governments, employment agencies, and labor unions from discriminating against *qualified individuals with disabilities* in all employment practices. A person is said to have a "disability" if she or he has "a physical or mental impairment that substantially limits one or more major life activities, has a record of such impairment, or is regarded as having such impairment" (U.S. Equal Employment Opportunity Commission, 1992, p. 1). Prohibited discrimination in employment practices includes the following: (a) job application procedures, (b) hiring, (c) firing, (d) advancement, (e) compensation, (f) job training, (g) and other terms, conditions, and privileges of employment. Employment nondiscrimination requirements also apply to: (h) recruitment, (i) advertising, (j) tenure, (k) layoff, (l) leave, (m) fringe benefits, and (n) all other employment-related activities.

A qualified individual with a disability is a person who meets legitimate skill, experience, education, or other requirements of an employment position that he or she holds or seeks, and who can perform the essential functions of the position with or without **reasonable accommodation** (U.S. Equal Employment Opportunity Commission, 1992).

Reasonable accommodation is any modification or adjustment to a job or the work environment that will enable a qualified applicant or employee with a disability to participate in the application process or perform essential job functions. Reasonable accommodation also includes adjustments to assume that a qualified individual with a disability has rights and privileges in employment equal to those of employees without disabilities (p. 5).

Reasonable accommodation can include, but is not limited to:

1. making existing facilities used by employees readily accessible to and usable by people with disabilities
2. job restructuring, modifying work schedules, reassignment to a vacant position
3. acquiring or modifying equipment or devices; adjusting or modifying examinations, training materials, or policies
4. providing qualified readers or interpreters

Requiring the ability to perform essential functions assures that an individual with a disability will not be considered unqualified simply because of inability to perform marginal or incidental job functions.

If an individual is qualified to perform essential functions except for the limitations created by a disability, then the employer must consider whether the individual could perform these functions with reasonable accommodation. Employers are required to make reasonable accommodation to qualified individuals with disabilities if no **undue hardship** is imposed on the operation of businesses. Undue hardship refers to

> an "action requiring significant difficulty or expense" when considered in light of a number of factors . . . [including] . . . the size, resources, nature, and structure of the employer's operation. Undue hardship is determined on a case-by-case basis (p. 7).

Thus, the ADA pertains to an individual job applicant or employee. However, ". . . even with a disability, the individual must be able to perform the 'essential functions' of the job with or without accommodation" (Baker, 1999, p. 103).

Switzer (2001) writes that ten years after passage of the ADA, ". . . it has not eliminated high unemployment rates for persons with disabilities, nor has it made accessible housing available to every person seeking it" (p. 631). There also remains a need to answer questions related to the costs of implementing the ADA and a need to better understand the implications of ADA for workers' compensation and social security programs. Disability-based harassment in the workplace is also a relatively new issue (Tahvonen, 2003).

Career Counseling for People with Disabilities

Employers are frequently reluctant to hire disabled workers because of unfounded myths and false assumptions regarding (1) nonproductivity, (2) high rates of absenteeism, (3) high risks for accidents, and (4) increased costs through higher insurance rates and special accommodations (Bolles, 1991; Delsen, 1989). Providing career guidance to people with disabilities presents a hurdle (Curnow, 1989), in part because of the limited availability of career development literature as a resource for practitioners. The following is a summary of Curnow's well-referenced article.

Practical Applications

The U.S. Equal Employment Opportunity Commission's pamphlets on the employment rights of an individual with a disability (1991a, 1991d) and on employer responsibilities (1991c, 1991e) are useful for practitioners and clients.

Reasonable accommodation is vitally needed in postemployment services to promote job retention and job satisfaction (Roessler & Rumrill, 1995). Title I of the ADA says it is up to the employee to (1) identify needed barrier reductions, (2) initiate requests for an employer's reasonable accommodation, and (3) implement such accommodations in collaboration with employers. Rehabilitation counselors in the Rehabilitation Services Administration are often pressured by large caseloads and limited resources to close the file of a disabled client who holds a job successfully for 60 days. Yet, for most people with disabilities, interruptions in employment largely occur after the 60-day employment period. Access to postemployment services is clearly needed for a longer period of time.

An ongoing need for postemployment services includes help with (1) the costs of devices that assist, (2) change of jobs in the same company due to disability-related problems, (3) access to fringe benefits on the job, (4) pay and treatment equal to other workers, and (5) long-term services to maintain employment (Roessler & Rumrill, 1995). Career adjustment and advancement become threatened when employees fail to devise integrative responses to on-the-job barriers. Mindful that most postemployment services are needed after 60 days, practitioners can play a crucial role in assisting people with disabilities when such services are needed.

Syzmanski, Hershenson, Ettinger, and Enright (1996) call for a reexamination of rehabilitation agency polices to ensure that people with disabilities receive timely service when they need it and not according to some arbitrary time frame that has no empirical basis. Several types of reasonable accommodation are presented in Brodwin, Parker, and DeLaGarza (1996).

Misleading assumptions toward individuals with disabilities that have restricted the application of vocational development theory include (1) the idea that career options for the disabled are limited, (2) career development is unimportant, arrested, or retarded for individuals with disability, and (3) the career development of people with disabilities are influenced by chance. The rationale for the restricted application of vocational development theories to the disabled is based on the faulty premise that, in comparison with their nondisabled peers, the special needs of people with disabilities preclude the relevance of current theories of vocational development. A contrasting assumption is that current theories may be applicable to individuals with disabilities if practitioners consider their unique problems and needs that require specialized services.

Disabling Conditions and the Curtailment of Career Development Disabling conditions can impede career development because of limitations in early opportunities to engage in vocational exploration, few chances for successful experiences in decision making, and depreciative experiences that may be a common occurrence to individuals with disabilities, which can adversely affect one's self-concept.

Limited Early Opportunities to Engage in Vocational Exploration Individuals with reduced mobility or who require special medical treatment can miss out on opportunities to engage in the vocational exploration that is crucial for later vocational growth and decision making. Childhood experiences are often limited for the individual with a precareer disability and can restrict the range of options perceived by people with disabilities. Insufficient experiences related to the acquisition of interests, competencies, self-perceptions, and knowledge about occupational environments can result in maladaptive development.

Few Chances for Successful Decision-Making Experiences Decision-making ability improves with practice. From a developmental perspective, limitations in early experiences have a later detrimental effect on decision-making ability. Individuals with disabilities who have had few chances for successful experiences in decision making may lack competence in making decisions. This can be manifested by the inadequate acquisition of vocational information, the insufficient use of resources in vocational planning, and a failure to generate enough career options because of personal limitation. Thus, career decision making can be negatively impacted.

Depreciative Experiences and Self-Concept Social attitudes and stereotypes toward disability can be as important as the disability itself. Depreciation from others plays a part in shaping the life role of the individual with disability. Low social status and the prejudicial attitudes of others may be a common occurrence for individuals with disability. Distortions in the client's perception of self or of the occupational world can arise. These individuals are vulnerable to maladaptive career development. Unrealistic vocational aspirations or decisions become vital to assess.

College Students with Disabilities

Overview of Career-Related Issues Disability impacts career development in several ways (Enright, Conyers, & Syzmanski, 1996). Decision-making ability may be hindered by parental overprotectiveness, high personal-dependency needs, and cognitive impairment—which can affect confidence or competence to make career decisions. Self-concept is apt to differ among college students with congenital disabilities or younger age of onset disabilities from students with older age of onset disabilities. Type of disability is another issue for practitioners to consider, especially

---

Practical Applications

Curnow (1989) describes strategies to facilitate the vocational development of the disabled.

1. *Cultivation of a systematic approach.* Career assessment and counseling in a planned, sequential manner are indispensable to the vocational development of individuals with disability. Individualized education plans (IEPs), individual written rehabilitation plans (IWRPs), and individual service plans (ISPs), among others, can include systematic career development components for students with disability.

2. *Early exposure to vocational and social experiences.* To reduce patterns of delayed and impaired vocational development, establish early goals and objectives (i.e., opportunities to explore varied vocational environments; exposure to appropriate role models; development of decision-making skills by increased attention to the knowledge, experiences, competencies, values, and attitudes already acquired in the client's life). Evaluative criteria determine the effectiveness of goals and objectives.

3. *Supportive counseling and developing decision-making skills.* Efforts to assist clients to cope with their feelings and attitudes about their disability can be productive. Exploring client strengths and limitations promotes realistic vocational aspirations or decisions.

Throughout the counseling process, encouraging client involvement and responsibility can (1) enhance social maturity, (2) reduce overprotectiveness and personal dependency, and (3) provide the foundation for clients to learn and practice decision-making skills. Regarding point 2, including family members and other key people can be vital, especially to ensure that counseling interventions are not working at cross-purposes with messages and expectations the client receives from home, school, and workplace.

The feasibility of employing people with disabilities is demonstrated in a video by Attainment Productions, *Every One Can Work* (1995).

---

the disabled student's perception of his or her disability. Likewise, gender issues merit attention because employment rates and income are lower for disabled women than for disabled men.

Disability also impacts participation in postsecondary education (Enright et al., 1996). Transition from high school to college can be fraught with challenges (increased academic demands, decreased contact with instructors, changes in social support, nontraditional status for older disabled students, physical and emotional adjustments for recently disabled students). Adjustment to college life is an integral factor for college students with disabilities. Quality of social interactions with peers and responsiveness of faculty to disabled students' needs are critical. Entry into the world of work is another obstacle to overcome. Selecting careers, obtaining a first job, and later job changes are issues for many college students with disabilities.

Accessibility and accommodation of career services, plus the appropriateness of vocational assessment procedures, are a third set of career concerns for college students with disabilities (Enright et al., 1996). Accessible parking, meeting places, and bathrooms are essential. Vocational assessment procedures may need to be modified to include administration in an oral, large print, or Braille format. Extra time or additional breaks may be necessary during assessment procedures, which may need to be conducted in an individual versus group format.

Responses may need to be recorded through an interpreter, word processor, or nonwritten methods. Adjustable desks that accommodate wheelchairs may be needed. Interpretation of assessment results can be a problem because of test administration modification or a norm-referenced test that lacks people with disabilities in the normative sample.

Overcoming Barriers to Employment Increasing numbers of college students with disabilities are entering the competitive job search. A practical and expedient plan to assist students with disabilities in their transition from college graduate to employment is presented by Thompson and Hutto (1992). This employment counseling model was developed—without funds—by a Master's degree student in rehabilitation counseling to meet an internship requirement. Twelve students, severely disabled with visible disabilities, served by support services at Mississippi State University, took part in this model. The participants required accessible environments, transportation, adaptive equipment, and technology in the pursuit of their professional careers.

Specific Disabilities

People with Mental Retardation The major goal of most services provided to individuals with mental retardation is the acquisition of independent living skills to enable successful community adjustment (Levinson, Peterson, & Elston, 1994). Acquiring and maintaining employment is a vital prerequisite for attaining such a goal. Employment provides individuals with mental retardation with (1) economic self-sufficiency to function independently in the community, and (2) a sense of worth and purpose in life, which is a common fulfillment need for many workers. Historically, vocational counseling has been a main component of programs that provide comprehensive services (assessment, training, and placement) for people with mental retardation.

Practical Applications

No one theory of vocational psychology completely applies to college students with disabilities (Syzmanski et al., 1996). Unique combinations of life experience, interests, resources, and personality traits will mean that no two people will react the same way to the same degree of disability (Bolles, 1991; Brodwin et al., 1996; Magiera-Planey, 1990). "A counselor will need to evaluate what makes sense given a [disabled] student's individual circumstances" (Enright et al., 1996, p. 105). Practitioners can explore several contextual factors with clients: (1) the nature of the student's disability, (2) how it has been incorporated into the student's self-concept, (3) whether the disability is visible, (4) whether the student is informed about the merits and drawbacks of disclosing the disability, and (5) whether the student is informed about the ADA. "The aim in providing guidance should be to assist students in managing their own career development" (Enright et al., 1996, p. 105). Smith (1991), in discussing the feasibility of college for the learning disabled, writes "the learning disabled can achieve almost anything they want, as long as they work harder than other people and use strategies appropriate to their own needs and abilities" (p. 252). She offers eighty-eight strategies for college students with learning disabilities and sixty-six more for dealing with everyday life.

Adults with Attention Deficit Disorder (ADD) The greatest demands placed on an individual for planning, memory, organization, teamwork, and precision occur in the workplace. Consequently, the manifestations of attention deficits in adults often become most apparent in the workplace environment (Nadeau, 1995). Little empirical evidence exists to guide practitioners who serve newly diagnosed adults with attention deficit disorder (ADD). Recognition of ADD in adults is recent and not yet widespread. The population of adults who seek assistance for ADD tends to be skewed toward the high functioning end of the continuum. These people are likely to be relatively well educated, have read articles or viewed television documentaries, and/or attended presentations about ADD in adults. A large percentage of adults with ADD are likely to be found among prison populations, various subgroups of substance abusers, and the unemployed or marginally employed. These people may not be aware of ADD in adults nor have access to treatment.

People with Learning Disabilities Essentially, the central issues that affect the employment success of learning disabled (LD) adults are the very issues associated

Practical Applications

Thompson and Hutto (1992) present several useful counseling strategies.

Students with vocational disabilities are taught ways to reduce the negative impact their disability might have on a potential employer. Students with visual disabilities are made aware of special problems that might limit their effectiveness in an interview situation. Students who use wheelchairs receive advice about the alterations for improved clothing fit while in the seated position. Students are encouraged to seek student work while taking classes. The counselor assists the student in planning alternative strategies in the event that suitable employment is not obtained upon graduation.

The no-cost and minimal-staffing requirements, with an internship level practitioner coordinating the project through her academic department and the student support services office, make this model extremely attractive and feasible. Those who take issue with the directive approaches used are invited to propose viable alternative means of assisting students with disabilities in their transition from college to employment.

with adults with ADD (Nadeau, 1995). Due to the very recent recognition of ADD in adults, the greater emphasis has been placed upon learning disabilities. The attention problems and cluster of problems commonly associated with ADD are presumed to be a subset of the larger group of issues that are typically considered to be features of learning disabilities. Poor academic performance is often the tip of the iceberg, and attention, memory, and social interaction are seen as playing a greater role than previously thought.

Adults with LD are defined as disabled ". . . when the individual's important life actitivities are restricted as to the condition, manner, or duration under which they can be performed in comparison to most people" (Winner, 2000, p. 410). Price and Gerber (2001) report that employers still have little experience or knowledge of how to implement the ADA with people with learning disabilities.

Research on the full range of work patterns of adults with ADD is limited (Nadeau, 1995). Available information indicates that hyperactive and impulsive ADD adults have a work pattern with a wide array of short-lived jobs. Less hyperactive and impulsive adults are likely to present themselves for career-related counseling upon promotion to a position whose demands are beyond their organizational or managerial capacity (Lucius, 1991, cited in Nadeau, 1995). Another work pattern is seen among chronic underachievers, who may possess talent and intelligence, but whose wavering motivation, disorganization, and/or procrastination tendencies permanently relegate them to job tasks below their apparent capability.

Practical Applications

Vocational Training

The vocational practitioner who works with people with mental retardation "should have a commitment to the community integration of [such] persons. . . . This includes a belief that persons with mental retardation, both mild and severely disabled, should have opportunities for interactions with nondisabled persons in integrated settings" (Levinson et al., 1994, p. 277). Ideally, integrated settings will involve activities at home, at work, and in the community, with the ratio of people with and without disabilities mirroring the community as a whole. People with mental retardation benefit by taking as much responsibility as possible in work choices and decision making. Vocational training goals are tailored to clients' individual needs. Treatment success is enhanced with the positive involvement of parents and other family members. Two extremes need to be avoided when assisting a person with mental retardation to process information for decision making and to simplify and clarify options. First, practitioners and family members "may encourage a person with mental retardation to accept options in which the individual is not interested" (p. 277). Second, "individuals may . . . flounder and . . . select options that are clearly unrealistic in light of local resources and opportunities" (p. 277). This is where localized knowledge of the community can benefit the practitioner. Ongoing postemployment services are also required for a person with mental retardation.

Vocational Placement

The ultimate goal of all vocational services for people with mental retardation is job placement (Levinson et al., 1994). Employment options are expanding for people with mental retardation and include competitive employment, supported employment, and sheltered employment.

Competitive employment occurs in regular community jobs without support and—with appropriate selection, training, and opportunities—can include such positions as beauty shop assistant, soda fountain clerk, nursery assistant, mechanic's helper, and fast food worker.

Supported employment is a recent innovation for those with more severe retardation and entails job coaches and ongoing postemployment support services. Several varieties of supported employment exist.

1. *Individual supported jobs* entail intensive one-on-one, on-the-job training by a job coach whose services eventually fade out as on-site job supervisors and co-workers take over the training and supervision. Ongoing postemployment support services are retained, however.

2. *Enclave-in-industry jobs* entail small group placement of people with mental retardation within a regular industry or business with supervision most often provided by rehabilitation or other service agency. When workers meet certain production, quality, and behavioral standards,

Continued

Continued

hiring into a regular work setting is possible.

3. *Work crews* are more mobile than enclaves and move from place to place to perform their job tasks (i.e., lawn maintenance, janitorial work crews). Like enclaves, work crews allow the person with mental retardation to interact with non-disabled workers during work time and break time.

4. *Custered part-time employment* entails negotiating single-skill jobs for a specific individual. Sometimes this work is unpaid or extended training, sometimes unpaid employment. This type of work can provide valuable work experience for people with mental retardation as long as no undue exploitation occurs.

Sheltered employment is a third major option for people with mental retardation and is usually available through human service agencies to employ people with disabilities to perform service or small contract work. See Levinson et al. (1994) for a further discussion of placement of people with mental retardation through job seeking skills training, job matching and referral services, job modification, and community-based training.

People with Autism "Historically, . . . appropriate educational, residential, and vocational services . . . for people with autism have been either nonexistent or inadequate" (Smith, Belcher, & Juhrs, 1995, p. 6). Only gradually are service delivery systems evolving to provide incentives for supported employment of people with autism. A young person with autism loses educational entitlements in public school systems at age 21. There are no stable funding sources that assist in the transition to adult services.

The characteristics of autism impact vocational choice and development in various ways (Smith et al., 1995). For example, an *impairment in verbal and nonverbal communication* calls for a job with limited communication requirements and a job coach to train a person with autism in communication skills. *Deficits in socialization* call for a job with limited social skill requirements and a job coach to train a person with autism in specific social skills (i.e., contact with the general public, nonsolitary job duties). *Abnormal responses to sensory stimulation* (i.e., noise, tactile sensations) call for jobs "that either provide preferred stimulation or avoid nonpreferred stimulation" (p. 9). *Difficulty in handling change* calls for a job with daily stability and predictability and a job coach to teach behavior management skills in dealing with changes, especially unexpected changes. *Enhanced visual-motor skills* call for jobs where such assets are required (e.g., small component manufacturing and printing for someone with fine motor skills, warehouse stock management for someone with gross motor skills). *Mental retardation* in people with autism calls for jobs that mirror one's adaptive and cognitive abilities, with a job coach to provide job skill training as needed. *Behavior problems* call for jobs where such problems pose no danger to co-workers and customers and are not job threatening, with a job coach to initiate a behavior program and to manage difficult behaviors. *Savant and splinter skills* (excellent reading skills despite poor spoken language; ability to match stock numbers to packing lists; good rote memory for visual information; arithmetic skills) are sometimes superior to a person with autism's overall level of functioning, and call for jobs that capitalize on such skills. *Ritualistic and compulsive behavior* call for jobs that are repetitive in nature or that require an attention to detail and exactness that would otherwise bore and demoralize nondisabled counterparts of workers with autism.

Depending on the severity of the characteristics of a person with autism, jobs can be found in manufacturing, retailing, printing and bulk mailing, food service, warehousing, recycling and delivery, and in government (Smith et al., 1995). Funds for training and supporting a job coach are essential for the employment of people with autism to be viable. Many entry-level jobs can be performed by people with autism under the supervision of a job coach.

People with Psychiatric Disabilities Unemployment rates for people with psychiatric disabilities range from 70 to 90 percent (Dalgin & Gilbride, 2003). Implementing the ADA with people with psychiatric disabilities is an ambiguous task because ". . . the components of emotional functioning are the least well defined and least understood compared to physical, cognitive, or even interpersonal functioning" (MacDonald-Wilson, Rogers, & Massaro, 2003). People with schizophrenia and other psychotic illnesses lack skills in emotion recognition, processing, regulation, and expression; they may lack the brain capabilities to do so. Limitations in the emotional domain of functioning are only just beginning to be understood. MacDonald-Wilson et al., (2003) found that cognitive limitations are more common among people with psychiatric disabilities in the workplace than emotional ones. There is also the issue of workers with a psychiatric diagnosis not adopting an identity disability and therefore not disclosing to employers their medical situation (Dalgin & Gilbride, 2003). An additional concern is the Equal Employment Opportunity Commission Guidance on the ADA and people with psychiatric disabilities issued in 1997 ("Guidance") (Starnes, 1999). The Guidance ensures that an employer cannot push a psychiatrically disabled employee out of the workplace, but the employee's behavior cannot be disruptive or endangering to fellow employees, either.

Synopsis

Without ample and continuously available funding, job skills training, job placement, and job retention of people with disabilities is extremely difficult. All the laws passed to assist people with disabilities mean nothing if adequate financial resources are not consistently accessible to back up governmental resolutions. "Empirical research on the impact of disability on careers is at a relatively early stage (Syzmanski, Hershenson, Enright, & Ettinger, 1996, p. 115). Methodological weaknesses in much of the existing research literature (Hagner, Fesko, Cadigan, Kiernan, & Butterworth, 1996) are problematic. A call for qualitative research (Syzmanski et al., 1996) along the lines of contextual interpretivism is a largely unexplored option.

6

❖❖

Social Learning and
Decision-Making Approaches

People make causal contributions to their own psychosocial functioning through mechanisms of personal agency. Among the mechanisms of agency, none is more central or pervasive than beliefs of personal efficacy. Unless people believe they can produce desired effects by their actions, they have little incentive to act. Efficacy belief, therefore, is a major basis of action. People guide their lives by their beliefs of personal efficacy. *Perceived self-efficacy refers to beliefs in one's capabilities to organize and execute the courses of action required to produce given attainment.* The ability to secure desired outcomes and to prevent undesired ones, therefore, provides a powerful incentive for the development and exercise of personal control. The more people bring their influence to bear on events in their lives, the more they can shape them to their liking. By selecting and creating environmental supports for what they want to become, they contribute to the direction their lives take (italics in the original).
(A. Bandura, 1997, pp. 2–3)

Social learning approaches to vocational psychology focus on the genetic and socially inherited attributes that people bring to their work environments. These attributes and environments interact to produce self-views that influence a person's work-related behaviors. Work-related behaviors, in turn, are modified by both natural and programmed reinforcers and punishments. This chapter is divided into three parts. First, we present the concept of **self-efficacy**, which forms the foundation for social learning theory. Second, we examine social learning approaches to the role of work in people's lives. Third, we look at occupational decision-making models, also influenced by self-efficacy and social learning. In Chapter 7, we consider social cognitive career theory, a recent innovation in vocational psychology that is influenced by self-efficacy and social learning.

BANDURA: SELF-EFFICACY THEORY

Social learning theory is based in part on the idea of self-efficacy. Self-efficacy refers to perceived judgments of one's capacity to successfully perform a given task or behavior (Bandura, 1977, 1984, 1986). The basic phenomenon centers on people's sense that they exercise some personal control over events affecting their lives. With self-efficacy, successful performance is the vehicle for change.

Expectations of personal efficacy are derived from four principle sources of information: (1) performance accomplishments, (2) vicarious experience, (3) verbal persuasion, and (4) emotional arousal. Performance accomplishments are based on personal mastery experiences. Mastery expectations are raised depending upon successes and lowered based on failures, particularly early repeated failures. Repeated successes produce strong efficacy expectations and reduce the negative impact of occasional failures. Performance accomplishments are induced by participant modeling, performance desensitization, performance exposure, and self-instructed performance. Vicarious experience relies on inferences from social comparisons (which are a less dependable source of information about one's capabilities than the direct evidence provided by performance accomplishments), and is induced by live and symbolic modeling. Verbal persuasion is induced by suggestion, exhortation, self-instruction, and interpretive treatments. People rely on emotional arousal to judge self-perceived anxiety and vulnerability to stress. High arousal usually debilitates performance. Efficacy expectations increase in the absence of aversive arousal (e.g., tension, visceral agitation). Emotional arousal is reduced by attribution relaxation, biofeedback, symbolic desensitization, and symbolic exposure. Direct mastery experiences and modeling can also reduce arousal.

Cognitive appraisal mediates the impact information has on efficacy expectations. Social, situational, and temporal circumstances enter into such appraisal. Expectation alone does not determine behavior; if competent capabilities are lacking, expectation alone will not produce successful behavior to bring about desired outcomes. The provision of appropriate skills and adequate incentives facilitate efficacy expectations. Bandura's model of perceived self-efficacy is graphically depicted in Figure 6.1.

Figure 6.1 shows the sources of efficacy information on the left: performance accomplishments, vicarious learning, emotional arousal, and verbal persuasion. Qualities of the resulting behavior are shown on the right: the choice to approach or avoid certain situations, competency of performance, and persistence in the face of obstacles.

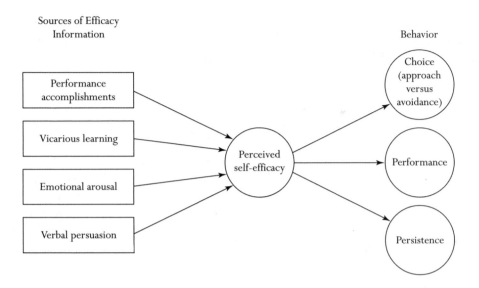

FIGURE 6.1 Bandura's Model of Perceived Self-Efficacy

SOURCE: Betz (1992), p. 23.

A social cognitive perspective for career development has been researched by Mitchell and Krumboltz (1984) and Hackett and Betz (1981). Krumboltz and Mitchell used Bandura's theory as a basis for their own social learning theory of career decision making. Hackett and Betz focused on incorporating career behavior into self-efficacy theory. **Intrinsic interests** show themselves in a person's "enduring interest in activities that engage their feelings of personal efficacy and satisfaction" (Lent, Larkin, & Brown, 1989, p. 280). **Task interest** gives a person more motivation to interact with the task, which in turn offers more of a chance for "personal and vicarious success experiences, and further self-efficacy enhancement" (Lent et al., p. 287). The reciprocal interaction of interests and perceived efficacy greatly affect one's educational/career choice and performance.

Self-efficacy expectations refer to beliefs in one's ability to successfully produce required outcomes. Efficacy expectations affect career decisions and personal achievements. Take, for example, the process of career decision making. Individuals' beliefs about their ability to decide on an appropriate career choice can be summed up in **career decision-making self-efficacy.** As the theory continues to develop, more research is needed on how to treat low career decision-making self-efficacy (Lent & Hackett, 1987; Maddux, Stanley, & Manning, 1987; McAuliffe, 1992).

Several recent studies looking at self-efficacy have implications for career counseling. Smith and Betz (2002) look at self-efficacy, self-esteem, and depression in young adulthood. One of the outcomes was that career indecision appears to be related to depression. Hall (2003) looks at enhancing self-efficacy in a family context using solution-focused and narrative interventions to deal with potential hindrances to self-efficacy. Smith and Betz (2002) isolate social self-efficacy and develop a test for it. In another study, "self-efficacy beliefs were more highly related to vocational interests and perceived career options than were estimates of self-rated abilities" (Brown, Lent, & Gore, 2000, p. 223).

Relevance for Multicultural and Diverse Populations

Gender Differences Self-efficacy theory is relevant to the occupational development of women (Betz, 1992, 1994, 2000; Betz & Fitzgerald, 1987; Betz & Hackett, 1981, 1983). Mathematics self-efficacy, a crucial factor in the selection of a college major, has long-term implications for women's occupation and earning power. In a prime example of how vocational psychology can enrich itself through interface with other academic disciplines, theories of cognitive development and learning teach that:

1. Girls and boys have the same natural ability in math.

2. Girls get better grades than boys in math (Byrnes, 1996). The general public, numerous parents and educators, and many counselors and academic advisors remain largely unaware of these research findings. Too many girls and young women have been told that they naturally have no mathematical ability.

3. Furthermore, "gender differences favoring boys are only likely to emerge if the math test requires problem-solving *and* the students taking the test are either older than 14 or gifted. Gender differences favoring girls are likely to emerge in two situations:
   a. when the math test requires computational skill *and* the students are below the age of 15 or
   b. when the math test contains items that require knowing when you have enough to answer *and* the students are gifted" (Byrnes, 1996, p. 176, italics in original).

Males and females have similar natural ability but different levels of confidence in the fields of education (Sadker & Sadker, 1994), women's studies (Bingham & Stryker, 1995; Orenstein, 1994), and parenting (Elium & Elium, 1994; Marone, 1988). Pipher (1994) thinks teacher education needs to focus on equity training to eradicate even subtle forms of classroom discrimination. She also advocates all-girl math and science classes. We think such all-girl classes should be taught by women. Vocational practitioners, school counselors, allied helping professionals, parents, teachers, and school administrators share an interest in rectifying differences in mathematics self-efficacy.

Beyond the elementary school level, Bingham and Stryker (1995) suggest the following prerequisites for girls to succeed at math. First, girls must see themselves as successful at math. Performance accomplishments matter. Second, support and high expectations need to be conveyed to girls from family, teachers, and peers. Third, girls need to understand what math offers them and why it is important to future success and life satisfaction. The long-term implications for women's occupations and earning power can be affected by many people in a variety of positions and disciplines. Vocational psychologists can help by being aware of the approaches other disciplines take toward mathematics self-efficacy.

African Americans Self-efficacy theory relevance for African Americans remains largely unknown. Brown (1995) states:

> We need to know . . . to what extent do efficacy expectations affect the perceived range of academic and occupational options, the effectiveness of career decision-making, and academic achievement? If self-efficacy is found to play a major role in the career behavior of African Americans, then another set of important questions concerns whether and to what extent the self-efficacy expectations of African Americans are modifiable through career intervention (p. 17).

Occupational self-efficacy has been scarcely researched with African Americans. Betz and Gwilliam's (2002) study of three self-efficacy measures using African American and European American students showed few race differences, but significant gender differences.

Hispanics Few studies have examined occupational and academic self-efficacy with Hispanics (Arbona, 1995). For Hispanic students, occupational and academic self-efficacy are predictive of career choice and academic achievement, respectively. For those seeking to understand the relationship between career-related behaviors of Hispanics and various sociocultural forces (i.e., economic background, minority status, acculturation level), the concept of **collective self-efficacy** holds promise. Collective self-efficacy is predicated on the idea that immigration histories vary for Hispanic ethnic subgroups, with differential socioeconomic and political consequences as well. An Hispanic individual will likely have a sense of both collective and personal self-efficacy, which would be wise to take into account when making occupation-based interventions. Varying rates of academic achievement for Hispanic ethnic subgroups (del Pinal, 1995) make academic self-efficacy relevant to Hispanics (Arbona, 1995).

The College Self-Efficacy Instrument mentioned earlier has been validated successfully on Hispanics (Solberg, O'Brien, Villarreal, Kennel, & Davis, 1993). Two subscales show strong relationships to college adjustment:

1. course efficacy pertains to writing papers, performing well in classes, and time management;

2. roommate efficacy pertains to interpersonal aspects of communal living and managing household management issues.

Self-efficacy expectations as a determinant of college adjustment seems useful to measure at two- and four-year colleges where Hispanics and other minorities form a substantial part of the student body. Self-efficacy's role in persistence and retention of minority college students is another research area that remains largely unexplored.

Asian Americans Collective self-efficacy has potential relevance for Asian Americans when acculturation is assessed as a moderating variable. Asian Americans who are less acculturated to the individualistic American mind-set will probably show more collective self-efficacy than personal self-efficacy. Career decision-making self-efficacy holds promise for Asian Americans (Leong & Serafica, 1995).

Native Americans Occupational self-efficacy can be limited among Native American youth with restricted exposure to the world of work (Martin, 1995). Yet performance accomplishments have a natural relevance for many Native Americans who have learned their traditions and customs through behavioral modeling and experiential-based learning (LaFromboise, Trimble, & Mohatt, 1990).

Gay, Lesbian, and Bisexual People Because of societal **homophobia** and heterosexism, gay/lesbian/bisexual people in the early stages of their sexual identity development may have low occupational self-efficacy and can eliminate occupation options even when their actual abilities in those eliminated occupations are quite high (Gelberg & Chojnacki, 1996). Self-efficacy expectations in job searches as linked to sexual orientation remain unexplored (Gelberg & Chojnacki, 1996).

Practical Applications

Many career decision makers are helped only partially by traditional information-oriented approaches. Practitioners can increase their awareness of the personal-emotional barriers that hinder clients from making and implementing sound occupational plans. Self-efficacy theory can challenge negative expectations (McAuliffe, 1992). Self-efficacy can be valuable in short-term interventions that often happen in occupational guidance situations, ensuring that personal-emotional issues around occupational decisions receive the attention they

deserve. "Assessment of the client's specific career decision-making self-efficacy expectations should precede interventions" (p. 27). Recommended instruments for this approach are the Career Decision-Making Self-Efficacy Scale (CDMSES) (Taylor & Betz, 1983) and the Skills Confidence Inventory (Betz, Harmon, & Borgen 1996).

The latter is designed to measure self-efficacy for the six Holland themes (see RIASEC in Chapter 4). Many studies have shown high validity and reliability for this instrument in predicting similar results for individuals. Moderate to strong correlations were found between interests on several interest instruments and self-efficacy. In a study of the Strong Interest Inventory and the SCI, Chartrand, Borgen, Betz, and Donnay (2002) found that the two constructs help provide a clearer understanding of career behavior and goals. Betz, Borgen, Rottinghaus, Paulsen, Halper , et al. (2002) expanded the number of scales in the SCI by seventeen. This instrument was constructed to relate to the twenty-five basic interests of the Strong Interest Inventory. The correlation remained high. Finally, a meta-analysis of sixty sample groups by Rottinghaus, Larson, and Borgen (2003) indicates a consistently significant relationship between interests and self-efficacy. The integration of theories and test instruments helps to broaden the scope of vocational psychology, providing practitioners with a greater number of options and potential interventions.

After determining where a client demonstrates the least confidence, the practitioner can employ a combination of counseling strategies taken from social-cognitive principles (Bandura, 1977, 1986) and cognitive restructuring techniques (Mitchell & Krumboltz, 1990). Once a client's interests have been determined, various interventions can help develop efficacy expectations.

1. The most powerful intervention would involve the structuring of successful performance accomplishments.
2. The second source of efficacy information—vicarious or observational learning—requires the counselor to find role models of success in the client's feared area.
3. In the area of emotional arousal, techniques of anxiety management may be useful.
4. The counselor can show the client how to become aware of negative self-talk, stop it, and replace it with task-focused cognition—for example, self-statements —focusing on the characteristics of the problem.
5. Verbal persuasion and encouragement are tools that are strengths of the counselor— the counselor can be the reinforcer and can strengthen beliefs of self-efficacy by expressions of belief in the person's potentially underused capabilities (Betz, 1992, p. 25).

The practitioner's support is crucial as clients proceed with steps they hope will advance their careers. Clients' goals may take them into unknown areas, making the practitioner's encouragement valuable.

Another area of practical application is the development of the Career Counseling Self-Efficacy Scale (CCSES) (O'Brien, Heppner, Flores, & Bikos, 1997). The CCSES has been used to train graduate students in vocational counseling and has established reliability and validity. The CCSES can be incorporated into coursework in career counseling and into program evaluation procedures to enhance practitioners' vocational counseling effectiveness and to aid therapeutic outcome. Perrone, Perrone, Chan, and Thomas (2000), using the Career Counseling Self-Efficacy Scale, found that counselors in a Midwestern state rated their lowest competencies in culture, ethnic, and gender issues.

Evaluation of Self-Efficacy Theory

Betz (1992) writes:

> The particular usefulness of Bandura's original self-efficacy model is that the
> elements for treatment were explicitly contained in the theory—because it is a
> social learning model, the causes of the problem, that is, deficits in the informa-
> tion needed to develop strong expectations of personal efficacy, are also the
> means for the cure (p. 24).

This can affect both men and women when their low self-efficacy perceptions limit
their career options, especially if these options are associated with jobs held by the
opposite sex.

Self-efficacy theory has plenty of practical applicability and the potential to be
empirically verifiable for a variety of research participants. However, some discrepan-
cies appear in the theory. First, without any personal mastery experiences, it can be
virtually impossible for both clients and research participants to initially appraise their
self-efficacy with accuracy (González, 1990). Second, self-efficacy theory is inexact.

> For some people, feelings may constitute the dominant basis for making judg-
> ments about self-efficacy. For other people, rational and considered appraisals
> may predominate. Assessing self-precepts of efficacy to perform a given task or
> behavior is highly subjective in nature. Accounting for such subjectivity has not
> been done in research on self-efficacy ... [in] ...various domains (González,
> 1990, p. 217).

Empirical evidence is inconclusive as to whether increases in self-efficacy entirely
reflect behavioral attainment/performance mastery. Ethnographic, qualitative research
could tell what influences self-efficacy estimates, in addition to cognitive appraisal.

Third, it can be difficult to distinguish between efficacy expectations and outcome
expectations (Bandura, 1984; Eastman & Marzillier, 1984; Marzillier & Eastman,
1984). Bandura (1977) originally defined outcome expectations as a person's estimate
that a given behavior will lead to certain outcomes. He defined efficacy expectations
as the conviction that one can successfully execute the behavior required to produce
the outcomes. Ostensibly, a person's efficacy expectations allow for behavior that gives
rise to outcome expectations that produce desired outcomes. But it is not easy to
show that people's estimation that they can perform a given task or behavior is not
influenced by their concern about outcome. Moreover, until a methodological procedure is developed that measures and empirically verifies that efficacy expectations
and outcome expectations do not overlap, particularly with controlling for any external motivators that may influence a ... [person's] efficacy assessment, the validity of
self-efficacy theory remains open to a certain amount of healthy skepticism (González,
1990, p. 238).

For racial and ethnic minorities generally, discrimination and other forms of systematic bias determine outcomes and/or a minority individual's expectations of out-

comes, regardless of the adequacy of that minority individual's behavior (Brown, 1995). As a result, both efficacy and outcome expectations may have both joint and independent effects on career behavior for racial and ethnic minorities, and probably for sexual-orientation minorities as well.

This is a possible refinement of self-efficacy theory. The theory could be expanded if more weight were given to the perceived presence of adequate incentives to facilitate efficacy expectations—broader contextual and external structural factors may provide such adequate incentives. Until then, the question remains unsettled as to whether self-efficacy implies a belief that a particular behavior produces an outcome. A recent study (2001) by Bandura et al. of school children, aged 11–15, confirms gender differences and "parental Influence" affect "perceived occupational efficacy, career choice, and preparatory development." (p. 201). Traditionally, boys have been influenced more toward scientific and technological possibilities and girls more toward social services. Due to demographic changes in college populations, there are increasing numbers of women and ethnic minorities. Our societal response has been to hire foreign nationals rather than encourage and train our youth in science and high-tech occupations, when encouraging women and girls to pursue these interest would create role models (p. 202).

Others have reviewed the limited generalizability of the research on career self-efficacy and occupational considerations (Church, Teresa, Rosebrook, & Szendre, 1992). Gender differences in self-efficacy have relied largely on categorical distinctions between occupations (male-dominated versus female-dominated), whereas more valid research results could occur if gender dominance of an occupation were treated as a continuous variable. Vocational interests, incentives, and aptitudes have had a limited integration into career self-efficacy studies. College students have been most often studied, with little attention given to underachieving and ethnic minority individuals. Reid (1993) refers to college students as **populations of convenience.** Using college students as research participants has always been easy, especially for academic researchers who are pressured to publish, but such populations of convenience make for weak, restricted results and ignore the economic and political realities more representative populations face.

KRUMBOLTZ: SOCIAL LEARNING APPROACH

Krumboltz's (1979) social learning approach to vocational counseling focuses on the self-system and emphasizes behavior and cognitions in making career decisions. Four factors interact to produce movement along one career path or another:

1. **Genetic endowment** and special abilities
2. **Environmental conditions** and events
3. **Learning experiences**
4. **Task approach skills**

Whereas other theories of career development also are concerned with inherited abilities and environmental considerations, social learning focuses particularly on learning experience and task approach skills. Genetic endowment refers to the innate aspects rather than those that are learned. These include (1) physical appearance, (2) race, (3) sex, (4) intelligence, (5) musical ability, (6) artistic ability, (7) muscular coordination, and (8) predisposition to certain physical illnesses.

Environmental conditions refers to (1) the number and nature of job opportunities; (2) the number and nature of training opportunities; (3) social policies and procedures for selecting trainees and workers; (4) rate of return for various occupations; (e) labor laws and union rules; (5) physical events (i.e., earthquakes, droughts, floods, hurricanes); (6) availability of and demand for natural resources; (7) technological developments; (8) changes in social organization; (9) family training, experiences, and resources; (10) educational systems; and (11) neighborhood and community influences; and other social, cultural, political, and economic considerations (Krumboltz, 1979).

Learning experiences are of two basic types. First, **instrumental learning experiences** occur when the individual acts upon the environment in such a way as to produce desirable consequences. There are three components to the instrumental learning experience: antecedents, behavior, and consequences. Second, **associative learning experiences** occur when an individual pairs a situation that has been previously neutral with one that is positive or negative. Two types of associative learning experience are: (1) observation, and (2) classical conditioning (Krumboltz, 1979).

An important part of career decision-making is understanding how an individual approaches a task. Task approach skills include (1) goals setting, (2) values clarification, (3) generating alternatives, and (4) obtaining career information. Interactions among genetic endowment, environmental conditions, and learning experiences lead to skills in doing a variety of tasks (Sharf, 1997).

Social learning theory is grounded in the following constructs: (1) reciprocal determinism, (2) observational learning, (3) extrinsic/intrinsic/vicarious learning, and (4) self-reinforcement. Self-observational generalizations and task approach skills result from the process of reciprocal determinism and learning experiences. An individual can observe his or her performance in relation to the performance of others or his or her past performance and make generalizations about it (Bandura, 1986).

Task approach skills are defined as cognitive, and along with performance abilities and emotional predispositions for coping with the environment, allow for interpreting a task in relation to self-observational generalizations and making covert or overt predictions about future events. Career selection is a natural process influenced not only by decisions made by each individual involved but also social forces that affect occupational availability and requirements. People select, and are selected by, occupations.

Krumboltz's theory has been extended to social learning theory of career decision making (SLTCDM). This theory has two parts: (1) "explain the origins of career choices" and (2) "explain what career counselors can do about many career-related problems" (Mitchell & Krumboltz, 1990, p. 233). Current research is being conducted by Krumboltz et al. regarding the concept of planned happenstance.

Assessments Used with Krumboltz's Model

1. Career Beliefs Inventory (CBI)
2. Values Scale (VS)
3. Strong Interest Inventory (SII)
4. Campbell Interest and Skill Survey (CISS)
5. Self-Directed Search (SDS)
6. DECIDES
7. Myers-Briggs Type Indicator (MBTI)

Practical Applications

Krumboltz's social learning theory pertains to a lifelong process, not a one-time decision. Practitioners help clients learn how to make wise career decisions by using different techniques—including assessment —to integrate genetic factors, learning experiences, and cognitive and emotional responses. After completing the career counseling process, a client should be able to modify current career plans or make entirely new choices depending on their new learning experiences.

DECIDES, a social learning model of career counseling (Krumboltz & Hamel, 1977; Sharf, 1997), is a behavioral approach which provides for reinforcements and consequences. Essentially, it is a problem-solving model of decision making. The seven steps of DECIDES form the acronym that is used: (1) define the problem, (2) establish an action plan,

(3) clarify values, (4) identify alternatives, (5) discover probable outcomes, (6) eliminate alternatives systematically, and (7) start action. Although these steps are presented sequentially, they are flexible in that the individual may backtrack to a previous step and begin the process again.

The first step should be very specific and agreed upon by both practitioner and client. The second step involves putting in written form each action to be taken in each step of the DECIDES process, including written time deadlines. The third step involves identifying and recognizing what the client believes to be important in a career. The client should have an understanding of what is important to him or her based on previous job experiences. At this stage, it is helpful to administer Super's Values

Continued

Continued

Scale (VS). The fourth step involves evaluating the client's beliefs about self-observation and generalizations about their interests or capabilities.

Interest inventories such as the Strong Interest Inventory (SII), Holland's Self-Directed Search (SDS), and the Campbell Interest and Skill Survey (CISS) may be used to illuminate the client's interests and to suggest occupations consistent with those interests. Brainstorming may be used as a client makes a list of occupations which sound interesting.

The fifth step involves discovering probable outcomes of career choices. The client compares the information obtained about the various occupations with his or her identified values, abilities, and interests, and then decides which jobs would bring more satisfaction. Once the client has prepared a comprehensive list of possible occupations to consider, the sixth step is to eliminate the least desirable alternatives. The practitioner should be aware of possible faulty beliefs and/or stereotypes that a client may rely on to eliminate options. The final step in this process is to take action. This is the step in which the client actually engages in job-seeking or school-seeking behavior. This includes making a résumé, getting and filling out applications to schools and for jobs, signing up to take college entrance exams, and going on interviews (Sharf, 1997).

The most important underlying issue in the DECIDES program is whether the client is able to apply wise decision-making skills rather than simply achieve the beginning goal. If this process has been successfully undertaken, it should be applicable to any problems the client encounters, not just career-related ones. The practitioner helps the client learn how to learn.

As a practitioner using the social-learning model, it is very useful to understand client self-observational generalizations and task approach skills used in the past. Consistent with this model, it would be important to teach the client how to evaluate the personal consequences of learning experiences and then arrange an appropriate sequence of career-relevant exploratory learning experiences. The client needs to learn a rational sequence of career decision-making skills.

Krumboltz (1991) published an important assessment tool called the Career Beliefs Inventory (CBI) to help people identify career beliefs that could be hindering them from achieving their career goals. "The fundamental premise upon which the CBI is based is that people make assumptions and generalizations about themselves and the world of work based on their limited experiences" (p. 1). The CBI does not intend to suggest that beliefs are good or bad, but may simply obstruct a client's ability to set or reach goals. The basic areas that the twenty-five scales in the assessment cover are:

1. My Current Career Situation
2. What Seems Necessary for My Happiness
3. Factors that Influence My Decisions
4. Changes I Am Willing to Make
5. Effort I Am Willing to Initiate

This assessment can be used effectively in the DECIDES program.

Relevance for Multicultural and Diverse Populations

Native Americans Given the limited frequency with which Native Americans enter technical or scientific fields (Johnson, Swartz, & Martin, 1995), the availability and accessibility of occupations is an issue. If Native Americans are not seen in certain occupational roles, young people from similar backgrounds may not see such occupations as an option.

Asian Americans "Research is needed as to whether Asian Americans who possess . . . [task approach skills relative to career decision making] . . . to a greater degree than their peers arrive at a career choice more readily and with a higher degree of career certainty" (Leong & Serafica, 1995, p. 97). Further research is needed in the areas of career decision making, career certainty, and maintenance of career choices.

African Americans Research is sparse on the career decision-making processes of African Americans (Brown, 1995). Gender differences and opportunity structure need to be considered for social learning theory's relevance for African Americans (Griffith, 1980). Wilson's (1996) analysis of the disappearance of work opportunities in the inner city poses a formidable challenge for social learning theory and other career counseling approaches to become more tenable for multicultural and diverse populations.

Hispanics Similar to the extremely limited research among Asian Americans and African Americans, the acquisition of occupational knowledge and awareness for Hispanics is an area to which social learning can be applied (Fouad, 1995). Like Native Americans, Hispanics are underrepresented in technical and scientific fields. There is not extensive research literature on programs that promote math and scientific achievement.

Gay, Lesbian, and Bisexual People Social learning theory is relevant for gay/lesbian/bisexual people (Gelberg & Chojnacki, 1996). Occupational stereotyping can impact the degree to which a gay, lesbian, or bisexual person values certain occupations and believes that occupational success is possible. Without sexual orientation minority role models in the workplace, the desirability of those occupations can diminish for gay, lesbian, and bisexual people. Feelings of isolation and negativity can also result for sexual orientation minorities without mentors or role models.

People with Disabilities Social learning theory has its greatest utility in training people with mental retardation to function within a previously identified appropriate job training program (Levinson, Peterson, & Elston, 1994). Behavioral and learning principles can be applied to necessary skill acquisition for completing vocationally appropriate developmental tasks.

Evaluation of Social Learning Theory

The complexity involved in acquiring career preferences, choice, and decision-making skills (Leong & Serafica, 1995) exceeds social learning theory's capacity to explain through empirical, quantitative research methods alone. Ethnographic, qualitative research methods might be more useful for comprehending such complexity (Polkinghorne, 1984, 1991).

We want to see greater emphasis placed on Krumboltz's second factor, environmental conditions and events, which produces movement along one career path or another. Number and nature of both job and training opportunities; social policies and procedures within educational systems; and social, cultural, political, and economic considerations may most heavily impact multicultural and diverse populations. Social learning theory has yet to fully develop its potential along these lines. Ogbu (1992) discusses the nature of the relationship between a given minority culture and the dominant White American culture and the implications on minority education. Differential school success among various minority groups is intimately related to long-term occupational achievement and cannot be artificially separated out from research questions regarding vocational development. Societal and community educational policies and practices have denied multicultural and diverse populations equal access to good education (Kozol, 1991; Sadker & Sadker, 1994). Even in those instances when educational accomplishments have occurred, many minorities have been denied "adequate and/or equal rewards with Whites . . . through a job ceiling or other mechanisms" (Ogbu, 1992, p. 7). Social learning theory needs to exert itself to examine how "the meaning and value students associate with school learning and achievement . . . [determine students'] efforts toward learning and performance" (Ogbu, 1992, p. 7).

Minority groups vary according to cultural differences and social or collective identities (Ogbu, 1992). **Voluntary minorities** immigrate to a country to improve their economic situation (Traindis, 1993) and are inclined to **primary cultural differences.** Primary cultural differences "existed before two groups came in contact, such as before immigrant minorities came to the United States" (Ogbu, 1992, p. 8). **Involuntary minorities** immigrate to a country through forced slavery, political expulsion from their homelands, or other economic or military developments beyond their control (Triandis, 1993) and are inclined to **secondary cultural differences.** Secondary cultural differences "arose after two populations came into contact or after members of a given population began to participate in an institution controlled by the dominant group, such as the schools controlled by the dominant group" (Ogbu, 1992, p. 8) and develop when one cultural group dominates another. The subordinate group copes with its position by reinterpreting its primary cultural differences or showing the emergence of new types of cultural norms or behaviors. Involuntary minorities are more apt to evidence secondary cultural differences via cognitive, communication, interaction, and learning styles, as well as **cultural inversion.** With cultural inversion, involuntary minorities are apt to consider certain behaviors, events, symbols, and meanings as inappropriate for themselves because these characterize White Americans.

Voluntary minorities retain a sense of who they are without developing a non-oppositional social identity in reference to White Americans (Ogbu, 1992). The primary cultural differences of voluntary minorities do not erect insurmountable cultural and language barriers between such minorities and White Americans. Voluntary minorities show an equivalent sense of security and self-worth to White Americans so that such minorities do not perceive a threat to their own culture, language, and identities. Voluntary minorities accommodate, but do not assimilate. They play by the rules of the game for school success because of long-term gains and payoffs and "tend to be enthusiastic about education" (Triandis, 1993, p. 51).

Involuntary minorities develop an oppositional social identity when they are subordinated by White Americans in economic, political, social, psychological, cultural, and language domains (Ogbu, 1992). Secondary cultural differences of involuntary minorities are more likely to erect insurmountable cultural and language barriers between such minorities and White Americans. Involuntary minorities do not show an equivalent sense of security and self-worth and thus perceive a threat to their own culture, language, and identities by White Americans. Involuntary minorities maintain their cultural and language differences as indicators of their collective identities and regard school success as trying to act like the Whites. Involuntary minorities tend to have "anti-establishment attitudes . . . and less interest in education" (Triandis, 1993, p. 51). Both voluntary and involuntary minorities have to adjust to the dominant culture. Yet, whereas voluntary minorities do not equate academic success with adopting the White cultural identity, involuntary minorities do.

Social learning approaches to the role of work in people's lives have the capacity to articulate the environmental conditions and events that characterize the educational and occupational opportunities of both voluntary and involuntary minorities. But social learning theory has yet to do this. Natural and programmed reinforcers and punishments for voluntary and involuntary minorities have not been closely scrutinized as they pertain to occupational development. This closer scrutiny would enrich and elaborate upon learning experiences, task approach skills, and occupationism as they occur among diverse populations. Voluntary minorities are more likely to measure success according to within-group differences. Involuntary minorities are more likely to measure success according to between-group differences. Thus, given two members of the same minority group, the first may assume voluntary status whereas the second may assume involuntary status as a minority.

Krumboltz Extends Social Learning

Krumboltz (1998) recommends that practitioners be open to the possibility of serendipity. A logical extension of his social learning theory, his ideas indicate how unplanned events and situations also influence a client and become part of her or his own reality. Rather than follow the path of "true reasoning," Krumboltz suggests that when clients refuse to predict their own future, practitioners should consider the idea of open-mindedness rather than labeling them as undecided or indecisive. He further recommends teaching that unplanned events are a normal part of the career process, even to the point of encouraging them to understand their part in creating these serendipitous happenstances.

DECISION-MAKING MODELS

Delays have dangerous ends.
—William Shakespeare
(*Henry VI*, Part One, Act III, Scene ii)

Several models for decision making have been proposed. All are designed to aid clients to come to a decision armed with self-understanding and a rational means of choosing vocations and jobs. We have chosen to focus on three specific models with further ideas on types of influences, indecision and indecisiveness.

Gelatt Model

The **Gelatt decision-making model** illustrates the cyclical nature of decision making and the sequence of the decision-making process. This model provides:

1. a framework from which methods and techniques can be derived as guidelines in career-counseling programs.
2. a system to determine values that are a significant part of the decision-making process.
3. a concept of a series of decisions—immediate, intermediate, and future—pointing out that decision making is a process (Gelatt, 1989).

Gelatt's model has five steps to complete the process. The individual:

1. recognizes a need to make a decision and then establishes an objective or purpose.
2. collects data and looks at possible courses of action.
3. uses the data to determine possible courses of action, outcomes, and probability of outcomes.
4. focuses attention on his or her value system.
5. evaluates and makes a decision that can be a terminal decision or investigatory decision (Zunker, 1990).

Gelatt's (1991) later model of career decision making is called **Positive Uncertainty,** a "whole-brained approach to planning your future" (p. vi). "*Uncertainty de-*

scribes the condition of today's river of life. The successful decision-maker navigating the river needs to be understanding, accepting, even *positive* about that uncertainty" (p. 1, italics in original).

The two factors, the unpredictability of the future and the limited rationality of people, make organizational and personal planning unfeasible—-*unless we change how we plan and make decisions*. First, we must accept, even embrace, two facts: the need to change our approach from predicting the future to creating it, recognizing that the future is our present responsibility. Finally, we need to dislodge the superiority of rational over intuitive decision-making because we need both strategies equally to make good decisions (Gelatt, 1991, p. 2, italics in original).

Gelatt (1991) further explains the **two-by-four process,** two attitudes and four factors. The attitudes are: (1) accept the past, present, and future as uncertain; and (2) be positive about uncertainty. The four factors to consider are: (1) what you want, (2) what you know, (3) what you believe, and (4) what you do (p. 6). His theory uses these attitudes and factors to provide flexibility within the model. This model also differs from traditional decision-making models in that he proposes four *paradoxical principles* which are based on creativity: (1) Be focused and flexible. (2) Be aware and wary. (3) Be objective and optimistic. (4) Be practical and magical (p. 6). These variations, from the four factors and two attitudes, are the basic principles of Positive Uncertainty. "Following each principle is an example of a traditional decision maker who needs to become balanced in his or her decision-making approach" (p. 6).

Gelatt (1991) developed the decision tree model, which encourages clients to "think through their uncertainties using both rational and intuitive processes and make their own decisions as to how to decide" (p. 60). This model is presented in Figure 6.2.

It allows the client to use both rational and intuitive methods to make her or his own decisions based on her or his readiness. These steps offer the client the means to develop a whole-brained decision style (Gelatt, 1991). No attempt is made by Gelatt to estimate the combined value of probability and desirability; these will be idiosyncratic to the client. Two questions clients can ask themselves as they use this model are: What else could I do? What else could happen? (Gelatt, 1991, p. 60).

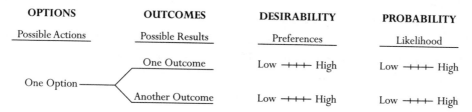

FIGURE 6.2 Gelatt's Decision Tree Imagery

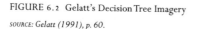

SOURCE: Gelatt (1991), p. 60.

Practical Applications

The practitioner can ask: Is the client aware of the need to make a decision? Does the client possess the resource skills necessary in the decision-making process? Readiness should be considered in the initial exploratory interview conducted by the counselor. A second counseling consideration involves the client's self-knowledge.

Does the person possess sufficient self-knowledge of interests, abilities, values, and relevant past experiences? Does he/she have the skills to apply this knowledge to the consideration of alternatives?

An adequate prediction-system strategy requires both self-knowledge and the ability to apply this knowledge in the choice process. In addition, the practitioner should consider the individual's knowledge of educational training opportunities, as well as occupational environments, requirements, and demands. The more informed individual has a greater probability of a desired outcome. Finally, the client needs to understand the process of decision making, including knowledge of the decision-making steps and of the flexibility required to weigh alternatives (Zunker, 2002).

Gati: The Sequential Elimination Approach

In 1986 Gati advanced a new model for career decision making based on Tversky's (1972) theory of choice. Gati's model used the idea that each occupational alternative has a series of aspects and that at each stage of the selection process, the importance of the aspect becomes the criterion for keeping or eliminating the alternative. He called this the **sequential elimination approach.** It is considered to be a rational manner to approach career decision making, especially when many alternatives are present. The sequential elimination approach identifies various career options that prove compatible to the client's preferences. This goal is achieved by gradually eliminating the options that are not compatible with the individual's preferences.

Gati, Fassa, and Houminer (1996) propose nine steps for sequential elimination.

1. Define and structure the decision problem by clarifying the goal of the decision and determining the alternatives from which to choose.

2. Identify relevant aspects—it is not possible to consider all possibilities. The client will need to choose those on which he/she wants to concentrate. This is important because the outcomes depend on the choices made at this time.

3. Rank aspects by importance—this activity is also crucial because importance is a major criterion for selection.

4. Identify optimal and acceptable levels of compromise one is willing to make.

Practical Applications

The sequential elimination approach can be incorporated into the career counseling process in five sessions (Gati et al., 1996). During the first session, the client's situation can be defined in terms of a decision that needs to be made, with an outline of the alternatives developed. The practitioner explains to the client what will occur in the following sessions.

The focus of the second session helps the client evaluate and compare the different alternatives and includes pointing out aspects the client may have overlooked. After this, the client will be able to assess the importance of each aspect through ranking them. At the end of the session, the client can be told to think about his/her preferences within each of the ranked aspects, realizing the importance of compromising. "The counselor may help the client explicate his/her preferences by suggesting that he/she recall relevant past experiences" (Gati et al., 1996, p. 217).

The sequential elimination process actually begins during the third session. A rank order of importance is assigned to each aspect under consideration, identifying those that meet the optimal level. Then the levels considered acceptable are ordered. The practitioner provides feedback as to the alternatives this order of choices eliminates. The client takes the list of remaining alternatives and compares them with what he/she feels intuitively would be acceptable.

During the fourth session, the practitioner goes over the preceding stages with the client and explains their outcomes. In doing this, the client might identify alternatives that are still worth further consideration. At the end of this session, the client should collect information about the remaining alternatives.

Once the client has comprehensive information, he/she can decide which alternative is the most suitable as well as desirable. During the final session, the considered alternatives can be ranked on the basis of all the available information. The practitioner can help the client outline the steps to be taken to promote the best alternative. "Finally, the nine steps of the process may be reviewed to increase the prospect that the individual will be able to apply them in future career decisions" (Gati et al., 1996, p. 217).

5. Eliminate occupations with incompatible preferences—each aspect is considered as to its importance, with a careful and thoughtfully worked through elimination of options to seven or fewer.

6. Test sensitivity to changes in preferences—after reducing the options to a few, it may be wise to reexamine the earlier stages in order to "reduce the probability of missing a potentially suitable option" (p. 214).

7. Collect additional information—used to compare the alternatives that still remain after the previous steps.

8. Rank alternatives by overall desirability—this involves steps toward deciding which alternative the client will decide to try out first, second, etc. Focusing on the possible advantages and disadvantages will help in this process.

9. Outline steps to actualize the most preferred alternative—the last stage should focus on planning the actions to be taken to act upon the individual's choices. "These may also include actions aimed at increasing the chances of realizing the most desired alternative" (Gati et al., 1996, p. 216).

Sources of Influence

Perrone, Zandardelli, Worthington, and Chartrand (2002) examined role-model influence on the career decidedness of college students, ranging from 18–25 years of age, within the context of the Social Learning Theory of Career Decision-Making (SLTCDM) (Krumboltz, 1981). The participants in the study completed questionnaires that included information on demographics, identification of a role model, role-model supportiveness, role-model relationship quality, and career decidedness. Findings from this study suggest that a supportive, high-quality role-model relationship can benefit both male and female college students as they make career decisions. This study implies that career counselors can be role models with whom college students may develop supportive, high-quality relationships. Secure relationships may decrease career indecision for college students and other career counseling clients.

Paa and McWhirter (2000) presented a study that investigated the perceived influences on high school students' career expectations. Their findings indicate that high school adolescents are aware of the kinds of influences, whether internal or external, that affect their thinking about careers. As might be expected, girls indicate they are more readily influenced by females in their lives than are boys.

Career Indecision

The world is full of uncertainty. One domain where uncertainty plays a significant role is that of career decisions. Feeling positive about uncertainty (Gelatt, 1989) is not enough; individuals have to incorporate uncertainty into their career decisions as they do other relevant information. Disregarding uncertainties may lead to choosing an option that is inferior to others. Sometimes one option is clearly better than or even dominates others. Dominance occurs when one option is better than another in at least one aspect and is at least as good in other relevant aspects (Gati, 1990).

Savickas (1990) concludes that personal counseling may be an option for indecisive clients so that they can deal with the psychological blocks to decision making, reduce their fears, and increase their competence in problem solving. Krumboltz

(1992) suggests that being undecided is not bad, but a welcome challenge to our linear cultural assumptions that one must make a decision and get on with it. Yet, being undecided is bad if it creates psychological distress and nurtures unproductive **irrational beliefs** (Fouad, 1993).

Newman, Fuqua, and Seaworth (1989) address the issue of anxiety in **career indecision.** They define career indecision as a "state of being undecided about a career" and point out that often the practice of career counseling is less than adequate when indecision is involved because it is much more complex than it is usually perceived. Several factors can be part of career indecision: (1) anxiety, (2) external locus of control, (3) problems in self-perception, (4) interpersonal difficulties and dependency, (5) interests, (6) ability levels, and (7) cognitive styles.

Germeijs and Boeck (2003) investigated three factors in high school students' career decision process in choosing further studies. The results indicated that when students make career decisions about future studies, three elements can be differentiated as possible sources of indecision. These sources could be interpreted as information factors, valuation factors, and outcomes uncertainty factors. "The information factor refers to how well students feel informed about the alternatives, the valuation factor refers to valuation problems related to the objectives and the value of the outcomes, and the outcomes factor refers to uncertainty about the outcomes" (p. 23). The study further suggests that a complex issue like career indecision about further studies can be divided into three different components, of which two have an important effect on career indecision in the later stages of the decision process. "Decomposing the problem of career indecision into different components allows for more specific diagnostics and related counseling" (p. 24).

In another study, Jurgens (2000) investigated three parameters: content domain, interpersonal context, and degree of structure. The purpose was to determine the impact of a four-phase combined intervention on outcomes of career certainty, career indecision, and client satisfaction in undecided college students and compare it to a two-phase intervention. "The results of this study indicated that both the four-phase and the two-phase treatment conditions were effective in increasing career certainty participants" (p. 246) and decreasing levels of career indecision. These findings supported previous studies that confirmed that both comprehensive programs and shorter-term interventions can be effective in increasing career certainty and reducing career indecision.

There is a difference between indecision and indecisiveness. Heppner and Heindricks (1995) conducted a process and outcome study of these two factors in career decision making. Undecided clients are more likely to respond quickly to the tasks of vocational search and career decision making. Indecisive clients appear to have issues that override the basic career decision and may often need a more intensively therapeutic intervention. This may involve time to resolve personal issues that may create indecision (such as parental pressures and expectations or fear of failure). This study provides a carefully monitored outcome from which to hypothesize. Too often career indecision is seen as a distinct issue *from,* instead of *in,* career counseling.

Czerlinsky and Chandler (1993) use a structured interview for vocational career decision making. Although this instrument is designed for people with physical disabilities, it applies to several settings, including schools. This type of interview attempts to provide assistance for making a vocational decision and dealing with the implications for training or education needed to implement the decision. One of its strengths is that it faces the problem of career indecision and the obstacles with which individuals are confronted, especially those with physical disabilities. This instrument is called the Vocational Decision-Making Interview Revised (VDMI-R) and can be ordered from Pro Publishing Associates, P.O. Box 35526, Dallas, Texas, 75235-0526.

Assessments for Decision-Making

1. Career Decision Scale
2. Assessment of Career Decision-Making
3. Harrington-O'Shea Career Decision-Making System
4. My Vocational Situation
5. Career Decision Profile
6. Vocational Decision-Making Interview Revised (VDMI-R)

Relevance for Multicultural and Diverse Populations

People with Disabilities The Gelatt model's heavy reliance on self-direction would seem ineffective to use with people with mental retardation (Levinson et al., 1994). However, decision theory can be adapted to apply to mentally retarded individuals. Incorporating a developmental framework, decision theory can be appropriately applied at logical decision points during the vocational counseling of people with mental retardation. These logical points include the time when decisions need to be made about (1) which occupational areas should be explored further, (2) which occupations are realistic options, and (3) which options should be pursued. One clinical modification of this approach would be for the practitioner and the client to collaborate during the decision-making process. Another practical adaptation would be to integrate data derived from any previous trait-factor assessment at the logical decision point when realistic occupational options are being considered.

Gay, Lesbian, and Bisexual People Sexual orientation has been little considered in career decision-making research (Gelberg & Chojnacki, 1996). Among the issues that can arise for gay/lesbian/bisexual people in career decision making is how to handle (1) workplace discrimination, (2) work relationship issues, (3) gender role issues when making career decisions, (4) coming out of the closet in a particular work environment, and (5) the level of gay, lesbian, and bisexual affirmation in a given city or geographical region. A client's stage of sexual identity development will influence the way these issues are handled.

Other Multicultural Populations Harrington (1991) writes about the cross-cultural application of the Harrington-O'Shea Career Decision-Making System (CDM). For cross-cultural adaptation within the same country, the CDM was translated for usage among the U.S. Spanish-speaking population. In an example of the kind of multidisciplinary efforts we would like to see in vocational psychology, personnel at the National Assessment and Dissemination Center for Bilingual Education assisted in producing the Spanish version of the CDM. The CDM has been translated for usage among the Canadienne Quebeçois French-speaking population, with assistance from the Ontario Institute for Studies in Education. English language versions of the CDM also have been produced for use in Canada and Australia. In each instance, construct and concurrent validity of the CDM has remained intact.

The regular use of My Vocational Situation with college students who have not selected a college major has been reported by the Career Center (CPPC) at the University of Missouri-Columbia (Candrl & Heinzen, 1994; McDaniels, Carter, Heinzen, Candrl & Weinberg, 1994). CPPC staff purposely avoid using the term *undecided,* which has negative connotations and implies that something is wrong with a student undecided about a college major. Instead, they use the term *deciding* to normalize the process, especially for freshmen and sophomores, and to emphasize that deciding students are not alone and have plenty of company in terms of focusing on a career path.

Evaluation of Decision-Making Models

Most career decision making has focused on high school and college populations. An inherent weakness in the career decision-making research is an excessive reliance on **populations of convenience,** largely college students (1) from introductory psychology classes (Cohen, Chartrand, & Jowdy, 1995; Solberg, Good, Fischer, Brown, & Nord, 1995; Temple & Osipow, 1994), (2) from other courses (Solberg et al., 1995), or (3) recruited from flyers posted on bulletin boards (Blustein & Phillips, 1990). Career decision-making research can be immeasurably strengthened by more sophisticated sampling techniques that tap more representative populations whose occupational struggles are of a qualitatively different nature from that of undergraduates. Career decision-making research suffers from incipient **classism.** We encourage more occupational decision-making research to be done on

1. noncollege bound populations.
2. students in poor junior high and high schools who already are underserved by school counselors and who would benefit by research and intervention on occupational decision making.

3. welfare recipients who are mandated by reform measures to get a job and achieve a long-term livelihood.

4. displaced blue collar workers.

5. reentry women and immigrants with high school educations or less.

Social learning theory and the related emphasis on career decision making has added perspective of the role of the counselor. Krumboltz and his associates have attempted to put more emphasis on the activities of the counselor in working with clients. To help determine actions to be taken in the context of the client and his/her strengths and weaknesses that go beyond genetic endowments, the practitioner can offer services that encourage effective and efficient decision making. The issues of indecision and indecisiveness are often indicative of life themes that encompass more than career concerns.

These problems can relate to family situations and influences, which we explore in depth in Chapter 8. While the foremost counseling, developmental, and social learning and career decision theories have influenced vocational psychology practice, less attention has been given to family and parental influences. We will attempt to discover the effects family has on career paths and choices.

7

❖

Focus on Current Theories
and Practices

One of the most interesting developments in the past decade has been the convergence of theories regarding career development and the practice of career counseling/vocational psychology. We have looked at theories based on trait factors, psychodynamics, developmental considerations, social influences, and career decision. Now we turn to another aspect of vocational psychology—the integration of ideas, sometimes into new theories, sometimes into new practice approaches. Another major influence on contemporary career counseling is the ability to use technology to access information, disseminate test results, and provide new interactions that allow a change in the delivery of career counseling and career development services. With all the information now available and the uniqueness of each theory, it is important that we as practitioners be able to synthesize in an intelligent and congruent manner the values contained in the work that precedes us. To this end, we approach this chapter.

It is important that we understand the value of knowing a particular theory well in order to move to integration. The realities of practice require us to remain open to the possibilities in the individual differences of our clients. Knowing other points of view, understanding other perspectives, and being sensitive to other realities are necessary for our effectiveness.

We take a wide-ranging view of the theoretical underpinnings of current practices, including our own, in this chapter. We look at a rethinking of Adlerian ideas on work, their implications for practice, and Savickas' application of these ideas. We consider the understanding that cognitive behavior therapists have provided and how the

Cognitive Information Processing model combines cognitive processing, decision making, and other facets of human existence into a workable model that builds on the possibilities that technology provides. We look at the combination of Social Learning and Cognitive Processes within the Social Cognitive Career Theory and its many extensions that use self-efficacy, cognitive structures, outside influences, and contextual concerns that affect our career choices. We consider L. Sunny Hansen's Integrative Life Planning theory with its emphasis on critical tasks and changing life patterns. It uses the metaphor of a quilt and the various patterns and materials woven into it that create a life in the context of a changing world. We also give an overview of Positive Psychology as applied to careers by Savickas. We look thoroughly at postmodern, social constructivist thinking and the ways it influences career and life planning.

Finally, in order to give real depth to the issue of integrating theory and practice, we each provide a detailed description of the individual working models that we use in our own practices. Over time, we have both developed practices that support our belief systems, that allow us to work effectively with our clients. All of this, we hope, provides a way for students and practitioners to continue their own growth.

ADLER: LIFE TASKS OF VOCATION

Adler contends that there are five major life tasks that humans must meet:

1. vocation—giving by working
2. society—interpersonal and intra-societal relationships
3. love—intimacy and family
4. spirituality—relating to Higher Beings and/or the universe
5. self—dealing with the personal self

Adlerian-oriented vocational research typically has revolved around **birth order, lifestyle, early recollections,** and **social interests** (Watts & Engels, 1995). Birth order is thought to affect the child's place in his or her family, and on a larger scale, the child's future place in society.

> Different ordinal positions (e.g., first-born, only child, among others) each entail a distinctive, developmental experience in relation to various family members. From this experience, the child learns diverse coping patterns and behaviors . . . and . . . a means of establishing a place in the family system. Such learnings are believed to crystallize into a coherent, consistent and unitary perceptual adaptational set: the lifestyle. Once developed, the lifestyle serves as a stable frame of reference for the individual, providing a method for both organizing and interpreting internal and external events (Watkins, 1984, p. 29).

Lifestyle, although self-sustaining, is supported by a person's early recollections.

Based on Adler's theory that birth order has a strong psychological component in development, Leong, Hartung, Goh, and Gaylor (2001) found in two studies that support was present to "support the conceptual and empirical works asserting the merit of assessing birth order and examining with clients the extent to which interests and values develop from their experiences in their families of origin" (p.36). Vocational practitioners can make good use of this information in their counseling work.

Assessment Used with Adlerian Vocational Counseling

BASIS: An Inventory (Basic Adlerian Scales for Interpersonal Success—Adult)

Multicultural Applications of Adlerian Concepts to Vocational Counseling

In a symposium on multicultural career counseling, Hartung (1992) presented a case study. One of the responses was Adlerian, provided by Powers and Griffith (1993), and began with a brief description of the three life tasks that Adler felt confront all human beings and define the requirements for successful adaptation:

1. the social task of friendship—making one's place in the community

2. the task of love and sexuality

3. the task of work

In career counseling, Adlerians address all three.

There are several strengths of the Adlerian approach that are particularly applicable to multicultural populations. Parents not of the U.S. mainstream can be helped to understand how they influence the directional striving of their children. Parents who reinforce cooperative behaviors among their children ("be good in school") send a different message than parents who reinforce competitive behaviors among their children ("do well in school"). These messages also relate to a second consideration, perceptions of child and adolescent striving. When families have the worldview of involuntary minorities, a child who is an outstanding student can get criticized within the family for "thinking they are better" or "trying to be like the Whites" (Ogbu, 1992).

The successes of a child from a multicultural family are more likely to be celebrated when families are voluntary minorities (Ogbu, 1992). Culturally learned expectations and values are useful for an Adlerian-oriented vocational practitioner to assess. It is crucial not to confound socioeconomic class with race/ethnicity. Adlerians will be pressed to determine the appropriateness of their counseling style for a diverse clientele. Such determination is vital when labeling "errors" in life scripts or when considering how multicultural clients evaluate openings for advancement. One other limitation is Adler's concept of the task of love and attachment to the opposite sex. The presumption of heterosexuality may be misplaced and can perpetuate heterosexism in the workplace.

Savickas Rethinks Adler

Savickas (1989) adapts generic Adlerian counseling into occupational guidance. Adlerian counseling can enhance the matching of people to environments by including considerations of belongingness and ability to contribute and cooperate. Such enhancement adds to the dimension of making social contributions rather than simply earning personal success and satisfaction. Another addition of Adlerian techniques is an emphasis on the uniqueness of the individual: "Clients' goals and means reveal their uniqueness more than do interest inventory profiles" (p. 294).

Instead of focusing on interests, the life goals of a person determine interests (Savickas, 1989). Therefore, the career path is important to understand because the career decision-making process is more important to the Adlerian practitioner than the specific occupation chosen. Clients have evolved a private logic to deal with life, and the practitioner must be attuned to that logic.

Rather than the usual test batteries, Adlerian practitioners use another set of interests to begin the counseling process. The career-style interview consists of eight stimulus questions geared to elicit life goal and lifestyle information (Savickas, 1989):

1. role models—concentrating on what the client admires
2. favorite books
3. magazines the client reads
4. leisure activities
5. how the client did in various school subjects—to obtain a type of work environment to which the client responds
6. mottoes and sayings the client uses and likes
7. ambitions parents had for the client and which the client has
8. decisions as examples of strategies used

This information gives the practitioner the basis of assessment.

The seven assessment steps are:

1. Review the responses to the role model question, assessing problems and interests that will help resolve the problem.
2. Review the leisure question to determine actual interests and the types of "roles, functions and rewards that intrinsically attract the client" (Savickas, 1989, p. 306).
3. Magazine questions help identify the types of people, things, and ideas that the client values.

4. School questions help identify a client's response to work environments and demonstrate reasons for success and failure he/she has experienced.

5. Occupational fantasies, parental expectations, and the client's own ambitions describe self-images.

6. By now, the practitioner may have some clear ideas about a client's career style. This step can begin the process of identifying occupational possibilities.

7. It is now time to begin a more formal procedure that may involve the use of Holland's occupational codes and other tools. The process moves on to counseling with a focus on career style and path, decision-making obstacles, interests, occupational prospects, and choice barriers (Savickas, 1989).

COGNITIVE INFORMATION PROCESSING (CIP)

Peterson, Sampson, and Reardon (1991) use a **Cognitive Information Processing** (CIP) perspective to describe the career development of individuals. Taking ideas from cognitive behavior interventions, decision-making strategies, and other sources, they combined them with available technology. While not totally new, the research and expansion of theory and practice produced by this group centered at Florida State University helped build a valuable working approach.

In CIP, a pyramid divided into four sections on three levels visually represents important domains. The base of the pyramid is divided into two kinds of knowledge. The first domain, **self-knowledge** (knowing myself), includes values, interests, and skills. The second domain, **occupational knowledge** (knowing options), forms the other half of the base and includes information about individual occupations and a schema for organizing occupations. The third domain, **decision-making skills** (knowing how I make decisions), is in the center section of the pyramid and entails understanding and mastering the decision-making process. The fourth domain, **metacognitions** (thinking about my decision making), forms the top of the pyramid and involves the executive processing domain of self-talk, self-awareness, and the monitoring of cognitions. See Figure 7.1 for the Pyramid.

There are specific terms used by CIP; particularly important are *problem, problem-solving,* and *decision making.*

- *Problem*—concerns a *gap* between what currently is and what is the ideal. Gaps can consist of knowing one needs to make a choice and knowing one made a good choice. Other gaps that are part of career problem-solving may involve occupational choice, training choice, and job choice.

- *Problem-solving*—involves thought processes to arrive at a course of action to close a gap. Becoming aware of a gap, finding its causes, formulating alternative possibilities, and the selection of one are involved in the process.

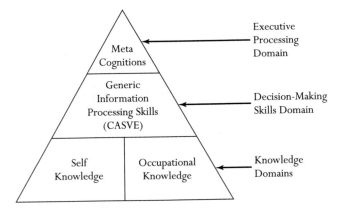

FIGURE 7.1   Pyramid of Information Processing Domains
in Career Decision Making

SOURCE: *G.W. Peterson, J. P. Sampson, and R. C. Reardon,* Career Development and Services:
A Cognitive Approach. *Copyright © 1991 Brooks/Cole Publishing Company, Pacific Grove,
CA, 93950, a division of Thomson Publishing, Inc. Used with permission.*

- *Decision making*—extends the problem-solving process as well as the cognitive, affective, and other processes that result in turning a selection into action. These include making a plan or strategy to accomplish the action, the ability to be involved in risk-taking, and a commitment to complete the plan.

CIP encompasses a cycle of generic career problem-solving and decision-making skills. This cycle is called the **CASVE Cycle** (Figure 7.2).

1. *Communication*—understanding the gaps that exist for each of us that signal the need to begin problem-solving. These gaps may be external demands such as poor work behaviors, self-destructive behaviors, or physical deterrences or complaints, or internal states such as depression, anxiety, or other emotional feelings that suggest unease. The communication takes form in two basic questions: What am I thinking and feeling about my career choice at this moment? What do I hope to attain as a result of career counseling? (Peterson, Sampson, Reardon, & Lenz, 1996, p. 436)

2. *Analysis*—clarifying or obtaining knowledge about self, occupations, decision making, or metacognitions. This involves steps needed to acquire the knowledge we need.

3. *Synthesis*—elaborating and synthesizing alternatives. Elaborating involves looking at possibilities to find as many solutions to problems as possible. The synthesizing or crystallizing stage works toward closing in on those solutions that are consistent with the knowledge of oneself.

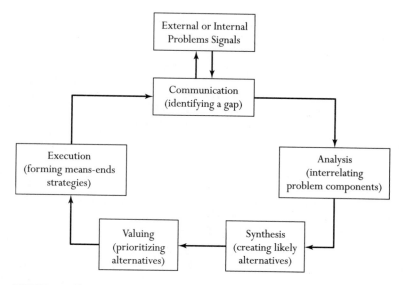

FIGURE 7.2   The CASVE Cycle

source: by G.W. Peterson, J. P. Sampson, and R. C. Reardon, Career Development and Services: A Cognitive Approach. *Copyright © 1991 Brooks/Cole Publishing Company, Pacific Grove, CA, 93950, a division of Thomson Publishing, Inc. Used with permission.*

4. *Valuing*—prioritizing alternatives and making tentative choices. This involves choosing the best possibility after studying how the alternatives best fit oneself, the environment, and the people who are most involved in their lives.

5. *Execution*—formulating a plan for implementing a tentative choice that includes a preparation program, reality testing, and employment seeking.

"The cycle is a **recursive process:** individuals move backward and forward through the cycle in response to their emerging decision needs and the availability of information resources" (Sampson et al., 1992 p. 68). The assumptions that underlie CIP appear in Table 7.1.

TABLE 7.1 Assumptions Underlying the Cognitive Information Processing (CIP) Perspective of Career Development

ASSUMPTION	EXPLANATION
1. Career choice results from an interaction of cognitive and affective processes.	CIP emphasizes the cognitive interaction of an interaction domain in career decision-making, but it also acknowledges the presence of an effective source of information in the process (Heppner & Krauskopf, 1987, Zajonc, 1980). Ultimately, commitment to a career goal involves an interaction between affective and cognitive processes.

Continued

TABLE 7.1 Assumptions Underlying the Cognitive Information Processing (CIP) Perspective of Career Development *(continued)*

ASSUMPTION	EXPLANATION
2. Making career choices is a problem-solving activity.	Individuals can learn to solve career problems (that is, to choose careers) just as they can learn to solve math, physics, or chemistry problems. The major differences between career problems and math or science problems lie in the complexity and ambiguity of the stimulus and the greater uncertainty as to the correctness of the solution.
3. The capabilities of career problem solvers depend on the availability of cognitive operations as well as knowledge.	One's capability as a career problem solver depends on one's self-knowledge and on one's knowledge of occupations. It also depends on the cognitive operations one can draw on to derive relationships between these two domains.
4. Career problem solving is a high-memory-load task.	The realm of self-knowledge is complex; so is the world of work. The drawing of relationships between these two domains entails attending to both domains simultaneously. Such a task may easily overload the working memory store.
5. Motivation	The motivation to become a better career problem solver stems from the desire to make satisfying career choices through a better understanding of oneself and the occupational world.
6. Career development involves growth and change in knowledge structures.	Self-knowledge and occupational continual knowledge consist of sets of organized memory structures called *schemata* that evolve over the person's life-span. Both the occupational world and we ourselves are ever-changing. Thus, the need to develop and integrate these domains never ceases.
7. Career identity depends on self-knowledge.	In CIP terms, career identity is defined as the level of development of self-knowledge memory structures. Career identity is a function of the complexity, integration, and stability of the schemata comprising the self-knowledge domain.
8. Career maturity depends on one's ability to solve career problems.	From a CIP perspective, career maturity is defined as the ability to make independent and responsible career decisions based on the thoughtful integration of the best information available about oneself and the occupational world.
9. The ultimate goal of career counseling is achieved by facilitating the growth of information-processing skills.	From a CIP perspective, the goal of career counseling is therefore to provide the conditions of learning that facilitate the growth of memory structures and cognitive skills so as to improve the client's capacity for processing information.
10. The ultimate aim of career counseling is to enhance the client's capabilities as a career problem solver and a decision maker.	From a CIP perspective, the aim of career counseling is to enhance the client's career decision-making capabilities through the development of information-processing skills.

SOURCE: W. Peterson, P. Sampson, and C. Reardon, *Career Development and Services: A Cognitive Approach*. Copyright 1991 by Brooks/Cole Publishing Company, Pacific Grove, CA 93950, a division of Thomson Publishing, Inc. Used by permission.

Decision-Making Readiness

Sampson, Reardon, Peterson, and Lenz (2004) say there are two aspects that help determine the readiness of a client for decision making. Capability is the internal mechanisms such as self-knowledge, motivation to learn about the larger world of work, and willingness to be involved in career problem solving and decision making to arrive at a decision point. It involves an individual's metacognitions—self-talk, self-awareness, and monitoring of cognitions—for making a career choice. Complexity involves external factors such as family, social, economic, and organizational factors in career development.

They have a sequence for career counseling and guidance services:

1. Initial interview

2. Preliminary assessment

3. Define problem and analyze causes

4. Formulate goals

5. Develop individual learning plan (ILP)

6. Execute individual learning plan

7. Summative review and generalization (Sampson, Peterson, Reardon, & Lenz, 2003).

To promote cost-effectiveness, there are three levels of career services in CIP:

1. Self-help services. These are generally for those who have a high readiness for career decision making and often involve use of self-guided assessment and information.

2. Brief staff-assisted services. These are for those who have moderate readiness and can use self-directed career decision making with larger groups, career courses, short-term group counseling, and workshops.

3. Individual case-managed services. These are generally used for those who have low readiness and may involve individual counseling, career courses with smaller groups, and long-term group counseling (Peterson, Sampson, Reardon, & Lenz, 2003).

Assessments used with CIP

1. Career Decision Scale (Osipow, Carney, Wine, Yanico, & Koschir, 1976)

2. My Vocational Situation (Holland, Daiger, & Power, 1980)

3. Career Decision Profile (Jones, 1988)

4. Career Factors Inventory (Chartrand, Robins, Morrill, & Boggs, 1990)

5. Career Beliefs Inventory (Krumboltz, 1991)

6. Career Attitudes and Strategies Inventory (Holland & Gottfredson, 1993)

7. Career Maturity Inventory-Revised (Crites & Savickas, 1995)

8. Career Thoughts Inventory (Sampson, Peterson, Lenz, Reardon, & Saunders, 1996; 1998) (Peterson et al. 2003).

Evaluation of CIP

The development of this theory and its practice in a university setting has allowed for a great deal of research to be undertaken that adds value to the underlying tenets of the conceptualization offered in CIP. By including ideas from cognitive psychology and applying cognitive and affective domains to the process of career development, the CIP theorists have been able to formulate in a very clear manner a series of applications in various settings. The extension of the concept of the executive processing domain (metacognitions) and its application to career development has been a valuable addition to understanding the process of decision making. By determining the level of individual readiness, it can provide cost-effective delivery of services. The types of settings where it has been effective, such as one-stop career centers, higher education, community services, secondary schools, correctional institutions, and adults in general, demonstrate the applicability of the theory to a broad spectrum of career services. It has a large number of resources, including a readiness assessment instrument (the Cognitive Thoughts Inventory), a workbook (CTI Workbook; Sampson, Peterson, Lenz, Reardon, & Saunders, 1996), a career assessment card sort, instruction for a credit course, and counseling handouts and exercises, which provide help for the counselor. Because it has been developed extensively in both theory and process, CIP looks to be one of the important forces in the field of vocational psychology for the future.

SOCIAL COGNITIVE CAREER THEORY

Lent, Brown, and Hackett (1996) propose a new approach, called Social Cognitive Career Theory, that combines the ideas of Bandura and Krumboltz with those of Hackett and Betz (1981). Social Cognitive Career Theory (SCCT) makes four basic assumptions:

1. Interests are strongly related to one's self-efficacy and outcome expectations.

2. Performance accomplishments in a specific endeavor will lead to interests in that endeavor to the extent that they foster a growing sense of self-efficacy.

3. Self-efficacy and outcome expectations affect career-related choices largely (though not completely) through their influence on interests.

4. Past performance affects future performance partly through people's task mastery abilities and partly through the self-efficacy percepts they develop, which presumably help them to organize their skills and persist despite setbacks (p. 400).

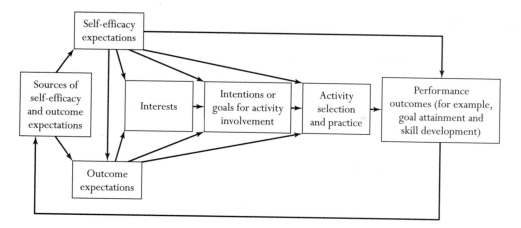

FIGURE 7.3   Basic Model of How Career Interests Develop over Time
SOURCE: *From R.W. Lent, S. D. Brown, and G. Hackett,* Social Cognitive Career Theory, *as cited in Brown & Associates (Eds.),* Career Choice and Development *(4th ed.), 2002, p. 266. Used with permission.*

SCCT can expand the interests of clients and help facilitate their choices, aid in dealing with barriers to decision making and success, and improve their perspective regarding their own self-efficacy (Lent et al., 1996). Self-efficacy, outcome expectations, and personal goals are not purely objective constructs, but are interpreted in a contextual framework. SCCT uses the client's own experiences as well as other variables, such as "gender, race/ethnicity, physical health/ability, genetic endowment, and socioeconomic status" (Lent et. al, 1996, p. 386) as a means of identifying the interplay between the concepts. SCCT adopts ideas from various career theories, including self-efficacy, social learning, and cognitive processing, and can include assessments used in trait-factor approaches. The contextual emphasis allows for cultural and gender differences by emphasizing individual experiences as a basis for career development.

SCCT proposes three interlocking models regarding interest, choice, and performance. These models can apply to a cross-section of people because they allow for individual contextualizing. The first model is seen in Figure 7.3. It suggests how basic career interests develop over time.

The choice model can be seen in Figure 7.4. This uses the interest model but adds to it the diverse person, contextual, and learning influences on choice.

[T]he choice process can be divided into three parts:

1. The expression of a primary choice (or goal)

2. Actions, such as enrolling in a particular training program, that are designed to implement one's choice

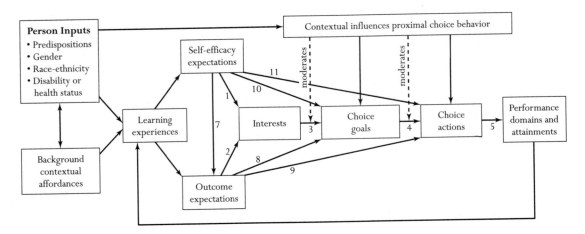

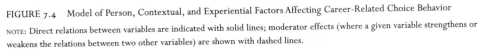

FIGURE 7.4   Model of Person, Contextual, and Experiential Factors Affecting Career-Related Choice Behavior

NOTE: Direct relations between variables are indicated with solid lines; moderator effects (where a given variable strengthens or weakens the relations between two other variables) are shown with dashed lines.

SOURCE: From R.W. Lent, S. D. Brown, and G. Hackett, Social Cognitive Career Theory, as cited in Brown & Associates (Eds.), Career Choice and Development (4th ed.) 2002, p. 269. Used with permission.

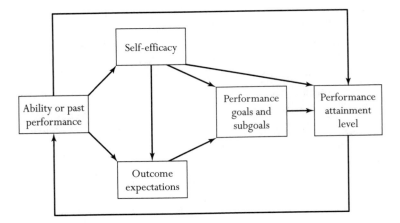

FIGURE 7.5   Model of Task Performance

SOURCE: From R.W. Lent, S. D. Brown, and G. Hackett, Social Cognitive Career Theory, as cited in Brown & Associates (Eds.), Career Choice and Development (4th ed.) 2002, p. 277. Used with permission.

3. Subsequent performance attainments (successes, failures) that form a feedback loop, affecting the shape of future career behavior (Lent, Brown, & Hackett, 2002, in Brown & Associates (eds.), pp. 272–273)

   The performance model has to do with the level of accomplishment and the ability of the person to maintain that level. It is seen in Figure 7.5

Several studies have supported the overall model. Fouad, Smith, and Zao (2002), using the model in Figure 7.6, found consistent results in predicting vocational choices based on self-efficacy, interests, goals, outcome expectations, gender, high school GPA, subject GPA, and parental education. SCCT is a recent development in the ever-growing convergence of ideas from various theories into practical applications.

Evaluation of SCCT

The value of this theory is that it puts together in a logical manner concepts of self-efficacy and outcome expectations, social influences, cognitive structures, and contextual information. This allows for applications across diverse concerns, such as race, ethnicity, gender, sexual orientation, and economic status. It is extensive in that it looks at the above ideas but also adds performance standards, working toward a congruent view of person and environment.

INTEGRATIVE LIFE PLANNING

Using a different convergence of ideas and theories, The Integrative Life Planning (ILP) model developed by L. Sunny Hansen (2001) suggests a way to move from the traditional *trait and factor* career planning approach to one that matches people and jobs in planning life courses in a holistic manner. Basic to her ideas are those of Donald Super (see Chapter 5) who suggested that a career is "the development and implementation of a self-concept with satisfaction to self and benefit to society and as a sequence of roles a person holds in a lifetime, of which occupation is only one" (p. xii). She supports the view of Mark Savickas, who

> suggested that Frank Parsons's logical rational model was a solution for vocational guidance at the beginning of the century and that Donald Super's career development theory was a solution for the second half of the century but that new solutions are now needed that are appropriate to the context of people's lives and to career counseling as we end this century and move into the new (p. xiii).

The Integrative Life Planning model has six basic principles in its structure.

1. "[I]t is a way of seeing self and the world that takes into account both personal development and the contexts in which we live; local, national, and global change; work, family, and education and leisure changes; cultural changes and changing roles of women and men; the relative importance of various life roles (that is learning, loving, working, and relaxing); the need for reflection on one's own developmental priorities for mind, body, and spirit; and the importance of change itself, both personal and social.

2. Rather than focusing only on work, the model incorporates a greater totality, including career and where we work, "gender roles, multiculturalism and diversity, and social and personal change."

3. "[T]he integrative model involves examination of the society; the organization (especially the work organization), the family, and the individual, and it considers relationship goals in human development as well as achievement goals and community goals. It presents a context of societal changes that makes new approaches necessary, and it provides an expanded framework for career development, career planning, and human resource development.

4. The model considers the various formations of the family that now exist in society and creates a means for making "connections and links" within various family structures.

5. ILP emphasizes the role of "spirituality, meaning, and purpose" in life planning and career development, as a counterbalance to the solely rational manner of making career decisions.

6. ILP is designed to help "people manage change and understand their life choices, decisions, and transitions in a social context." The changes we make affect our own lives, the lives of others, and society at-large, both local and global. This requires influences from literature and "diverse fields of knowledge" (pp. 17–18).

The Integrative Life Planning model is organized into six critical tasks that Hansen views as necessary to career development and career decision making.

Critical Task 1: *Finding Work That Needs Doing in Changing Global Contexts:* She immediately places the context of work to something "that needs doing" and moves away from total individualism to a sense of community, all within a full global perspective.

Critical Task 2: *Weaving Our Lives into a Meaningful Whole:* Using the idea of BORN FREE, she asks for an expansion of life career possibilities for both men and women.

Critical Task 3: *Connecting Family and Work:* She calls for much more new thinking about family, work, roles, partnership, and care giving.

Critical Task 4: *Valuing Pluralism and Inclusivity:* She requests a new look at the value of pluralism and the incorporation of global village thinking into our work and our social lives.

Critical Task 5: *Exploring Spirituality and Life Purpose:* She recommends a new emphasis on exploring meaning, self-actualization, purpose, personal values, wholeness, community, and a sense of a higher power.

Critical Task 6: *Managing Personal Transitions and Organizational Change:* She proposes exploring themes such as new relationships between decision making and transition making as it relates to the totality of one's life, positive uncertainty as a way of coping in a changing world, and helping people becoming agents of change (pp.19–21).

Hansen says that her approach is all-encompassing. In connecting life and society instead of compartmentalizing them, the model works in a systemic manner. "*Identity* (ethnicity, race, gender, class, age, ability, beliefs, and sexual orientation)" is fully explored; "*human development* (social, intellectual, physical, spiritual, emotional, career)" is accomplished with awareness; "*roles* (love, labor, learning, and leisure)" are fully understood; and, "*context* (society, organization, family, and individual)" is fully integrated (p. 22).

Hansen's call is for a collectivistic orientation toward life planning that places less emphasis on the individualistic outlook. Whereas as trait and factor rational applications to matching people with jobs was dominant, she suggests that in the context of the changes which have taken place in the world, including globalization of work and communication, the evolution of family configurations, a deepened concern for the well-being of others as well as the environment, it is necessary to broaden the scope of career development to allow for the world in which we find ourselves. Multiple possibilities for the individual now exist and may be required by the modifications of the social context of the world. The path to meaning is involved in individual wholeness that benefits self and community.

Hansen's ideas generally suggest a very different approach to the concepts involved in the theories and process discussed earlier. The reality that technology and new communication have made possible reduces the world to a much more explosive or cohesive reality. Her ideas are a proposal and a plea for a new paradigm that will aid in facing the reality of intense differences.

POSITIVE PSYCHOLOGY

This is a movement that may have a direct impact on how we think about career development. Rather than concentrate on problems and defining them, there may be value in using some of the tenets of positive psychology in career counseling. Three general topics have been the subject of research:

1. Experiences that people value subjectively, such as hope, optimism and happiness

2. Positive individual traits, such as the capacity for love, work, creativity and interpersonal skills

3. Positive group and civic values, such as responsibility, nurturance, civility, and tolerance (Santrock 2003, p. 18)

What are the implications of these concepts for career development? Instead of looking at career indecision, lack of career identity, career unhappiness, or job dissatisfaction as problems to be solved, consider them to be a lack of expression of positive characteristics described above.

Savickas (2003) proposes that counseling has usually taken a more positive approach to possibilities. In this context, he defines career counseling as "developmental interventions that build the human strengths and practice the coping response that individuals need to choose an occupation and secure a place in it" (p. 230). He rejects the idea of occupational fit as a means of vocational guidance. He suggests "career-development models are taxonomies of psychosocial strengths and may be more useful in considering how to build the human strengths and civic virtues" (p. 231) that are listed in Santrock above.

Savickas (2003) goes on to discuss how career counseling builds human strengths. The first of these is *Hoping: Developing Career Concern*. A sense of future is important in Western civilization, and the development of hope by a career counselor is vital.

The second human strength is *Willing: Developing Career Control*. In Western terms, having personal control over one's future is primary. Savickas suggests that career counseling "interventions induce or increase a sense of responsibility, ability to delay gratification, knowledge of the principles of decision making and practice in their application, and decisiveness" (p. 236).

Purposing: Developing Career Convictions is the third strength. "In the end, career counseling helps the client identify and articulate a purpose in life, one that synthesizes selfish goals and selfless outcomes" (p. 238).

Endeavoring: Developing Career Competence is next. Feeling self-confident is one of the basic components of competence. Equality with others and a sense of one's own ability is basic to happiness.

Committing: Developing Career Choices is the fifth human strength. He cites Erikson (1963), who stated that society helps define identity with "'the tangible promise of a career'" (pp. 261–262 in Erikson). Career identity is helped by becoming aware of "dependable strengths and enduring motive" (p. 240). This is the result of the ability to commit to a career choice, a vocational identity.

Relating: Developing Partnerships is the finding of community, company, and coworkers that enables one to feel a sense of connectedness and belonging. Aspects of this are "improving coworker relationships by communicating appropriately, supporting colleagues, encouraging peers, demonstrating goodwill to supervisors, tolerating differences and tolerating diversity" (p. 242).

The values of positive psychology and its effect on clients are difficult to underestimate. While the positive psychologists have questioned the apparent emphasis on problems, Savickas demonstrates that career counseling does work toward positive outcomes and promotes healthy development.

POSTMODERN APPROACHES

[Work] is about a search . . . for daily meaning as well as daily bread.
—STUDS TERKEL, *WORKING* (1974, P. XIII)

In Chapter 2, we introduced postmodernism in regard to a work ethic for the twenty-first century. Postmodernism questions and rejects logical positivism (belief that the scientific method is the only basis for genuine knowledge) and asserts that there are valid alternatives to empiricism (observation and experiment) as a means of adding to the realm of knowledge. Modernism and the idea of an autonomous, isolated self date back to ancient Greece. In contrast, many postmodern approaches view the self as constructed in relationship (Becvar & Becvar, 1996).

O'Hara and Anderson (1991) write in "Welcome to the Postmodern World":

Without quite noticing it, we have moved into a new world, one created by the cumulative effect of pluralism, democracy, religious freedom, consumerism, mobility and increasing access to news and entertainment. This is the world described as "postmodern" to denote its difference from the modern world most of us were born into. A new social consciousness is emerging in this new world and touching the lives of all kinds of people who are not the least bit interested in having a new kind of social consciousness. We are all being forced to see that there are many beliefs, multiple realities, an exhilarating but daunting profusion of world-views to suit every taste. We can choose among these, but we cannot choose not to make choices (p. 20).

Gergen (1991b) contends that the technological advances of the late twentieth century—computers, electronic mail, satellites, faxes—mark an accelerating social connectedness leading to a state of multiphrenia, where the individual is split into a multiplicity of self-investments. This **social saturation** of the self changes the coherent and unified sense of self, inherent in modernist conceptualizations, into a multiphrenic, postmodern condition where an individual swims in a sea of drowning demands. Rather than an objectively detected modernist reality, the subjectively created postmodernist reality is part of what is clinically known as the constructivist epistemologies. Constructivist epistemologies view human beings as active in the individual and collective co-creation of their experiential world (Neimeyer, 1993). The emergence of constructivism represents one of the most profound developments within cognitivism (Granvold, 1996). The practical contrasts between traditional cognitive and emergent constructivist approaches to therapy are presented in Table 7.2.

As shown in Table 7.2, cognitive approaches attend to specific disorders. Automatic thoughts or irrational beliefs are isolated to correct present dysfunctions (Neimeyer, 1993). Constructivist approaches attend to more comprehensive belief systems or

TABLE 7.2 Practical Contrasts Between Traditional Cognitive and Constructivist Approaches to Psychotherapy

FEATURE	TRADITIONAL COGNITIVE THERAPIES	CONSTRUCTIVIST THERAPIES
Diagnostic emphasis	Disorder-specific	Comprehensive, general
Target of intervention and assessment	Isolated automatic thoughts or irrational beliefs	Construct systems, personal narratives
Temporal focus	Present	Present, but more developmental emphasis
Goal of treatment	Corrective; eliminate dysfunction	Creative; facilitate development
Style of therapy	Highly directive and directional	Less structured and more exploratory
Context of therapy	Individualistic	Individualistic to systemic
Therapist role	Persuasive, analytical, technically instructive	Reflective, elaborative, intensely personal
Tests for adequacy of client beliefs	Logic, objective validity	Internal consistency, consensus, personal viability
Interpretation of client's meanings	Literal, universal	Metaphoric, idiosyncratic
Interpretation of emotions	Negative emotion results from distorted thinking, represents problem to be controlled	Negative emotion as informative signal of challenge to existing constructions, to be respected
Understanding of client "resistance"	Lack of motivation, dysfunctional pattern	Attempt to protect core ordering processes

SOURCE: R. A. Neimeyer (1993), p. 225. © 1993 by the American Psychological Association. Reprinted by permission.

personal accounts that have developed over time to form present fundamental assumptions about one's self and one's world. Thus, styles of therapy differ.

Cognitive approaches are highly directive to promote a systematic revision of one's beliefs (Neimeyer, 1993). The individual is the sole focus of cognitive treatment. Client verbalizations are subject to tests of empirical validity. To paraphrase Aaron T. Beck, a cognitive practitioner may ask a client, "What evidence do you have for that belief?" Constructivist approaches are less structured and more exploratory. Both the individual and broader systems (family, workplace) are the focus of treatment, with the practitioner as co-author of the client's newly emergent narrative. The new story has to have narrative viability. To paraphrase Mark Savickas, a constructivist practitioner may ask a client, "How is your belief useful or meaningful for this particular circumstance/context?" Cognitive interpretations of client meanings are presumed to be literal and universal in nature; constructivist interpretations metaphorical and idiosyncratic to that client (Neimeyer, 1993). Cognitive approaches view client negative emotion as a distorted appraisal of situations. Distortions need to be controlled or eliminated. Constructivist approaches view client negative emotion as a warning sign, a challenge to a client's attempts to make personal meaning of current experiences. Client "resistance" is seen by cognitivists as a lack of motivation or a dysfunctional pattern that the practitioner actively disputes, and by constructivists as self-protection of core ordering processes with which clients make sense of their world.

"The boundaries distinguishing traditional cognitive approaches from constructivist approaches are not well defined" (Granvold, 1996, p. 347). The picture is complicated by constructivist approaches that look at personal versus social constructions of reality. **Social constructionism** views meanings and understandings of the world as the result of interactions with others (Berger & Luckmann, 1966; Gergen, 1985), with several possible understandings of behaviors, interactions, or events determined by the cultural and social contexts in which a person is interacting. Language is the primary vehicle for the transmission of meanings and understandings (Anderson & Goolishian, 1988). Historical context can play a key role in how one constructs an interactional experience (Osbeck, 1991). Social constructionist practitioners explore the client's perceptions and understandings about clinical issues, including lifestyle and work. Practitioners do not have preconceived notions about the universal nature of psychological problems, diagnoses, or change.

Social Constructionism

Taylor Rockwell's Approach In an early example of the social construction of careers, Rockwell (1987) considers influences that significant others have on one's thoughts and feelings about the career options one is considering. Development of work roles is influenced by parents, teachers, peers, siblings, coaches, and neighbors. "A person's self-perceived profile of talents, skills, and competencies" (p. 97) are socially constructed as a consequence of the way a person is steered and rewarded by important people in their life. Approval expectancy for a given occupational choice is constructed by those with whom a person has significant emotional ties. Using the scientific method to provide empirical evidence of socially constructed realities, Rockwell shows that the career decision maker's expectation of approval from significant others strongly influences certain occupational choices.

The Rockwell Occupational Approval Grid (ROAG), developed by Rockwell (1986), with an accompanying manual for counselors, is an assessment instrument to be used with this approach. At the time of this writing, they are available from Taylor Rockwell, Brownlee Dolan Stein Associates, Inc., 90 John Street, New York, NY 10038.

Mark L. Savickas's Approach "Vocational psychology is a product of modernity" (Savickas, 1995b, p. 17). The scientific method was and is the primary basis for explaining career choice. Scientifically based assessment instruments predominate as a way to discover the best fit between a person's traits and a work environment. Career counseling approaches have always reflected the historical context of the age in which they appeared. Dramatic transformations are happening in the world of work because of changing economic patterns and cultural values across the globe. This means that sole reliance on logical positivism as a foundation for vocational psychology is the discipline's Achilles heel. Incorporating additional ways of knowing has become more urgent than ever. Working one's way up the career ladder was a common metaphor used throughout most of the twentieth century to describe mainstream careers. But large organizations that support long-term employment are rapidly disappearing, and the concept of career—and certainly, career ladder—is relevant for fewer people. In this sense, Richardson (1993) advocates that career counseling becomes a specialty within vocational psychology and that the role of work in people's lives is more representative with the advent of the twenty-first century. Career counseling needs to keep up with society's progression into the postmodern era; postmodernism has propagated, if not converged with, six innovations that have emerged in career counseling (Savickas, 1993).

"No more experts" (p. 210). Savickas sees a second-order change in the way career counselors practice. Rather than being expert interpreters of interest inventories and possessing privileged information about occupations, vocational practitioners are validating clients' efforts to actively and independently shape their own lives. Career counselors are moving (sometimes unwittingly) from acting as agents of the dominant culture to opening a space for conversations that have a range of occupational possibilities.

"Enable rather than fit" (p. 211). Postmodern approaches to career foster **deconstruction** of the Person by Environment Fit (PxE) paradigm. Multicultural and diverse discourse is moving from marginal status to center stage. An enablement paradigm is replacing PxE and encourages clients to express and devise their own life plans.

"Rewrite the grand narrative" (p. 211). The **Grand Narrative** of the twentieth century emphasizes new advances in human productive capacities founded upon reason and freedom. The role of work in people's lives provides a key link to the reality of the Grand Narrative and one's social identity within that Narrative. Yet, multiculturalism and diversity undermine the coherence of and conformity to the Grand Narrative. A legacy of the Puritan work ethic, one's work role and career is central to the Grand Narrative. The multiple perspectives of postmodernism make work one of many roles in a person's life, but not always the central role. Life design will become the overarching construct of career coun-

seling in the postmodern era, with occupational choice as but one aspect of such a design.

"Career is personal" (p. 212). Part of this refers to the artificial concept that places career counseling as separate from personal counseling. The subjective and personal meanings that clients construct to make sense of life and work have often been ignored up to now. Intersubjective concerns will become an added part of objective methods of vocational assessment and career guidance.

"Career development theory is not counseling theory" (p. 212). Over-reliance on objective assessment put the original focus on how clients choose occupations and develop careers. Vocational guidance has been the focus more than the career counseling process. In this sense, career development theory has never been counseling theory. Postmodern approaches to career become activities where the practitioner and client co-construct or socially construct the meaning of the client's direction in life. This quest for sense is one of invention, not discovery. *Hermeneutical activity,* with its emphasis on the methodological principles for interpreting the meaning of a literary passage in a text, becomes central. The literary qualities of a client's story become primary.

"Stories rather than scores" (p. 213). The singular focus on objective career with its concepts like PxE Fit is a legacy of modernism, with remote ancestry in ancient Greece and ancient China. Postmodernism views clients as concerned with life purpose, not job positions; with subjective meanings to solutions in growing up, not the meanings of interest inventory scores that tell clients their stronger than average preferences for an occupation when compared to a normative group. Objective developmental tasks become subjective social expectations or existential themes. Objective identity becomes subjective striving for establishing inner continuity of lived experiences (Neimeyer, 1995b). Values become the expression of a central life theme (Savickas, 1993).

In the postmodern approach to career counseling described by Savickas (1993), the influence of social constructionism is apparent. Enablement gives clients the chance to deconstruct by freeing themselves from the mesmerizing discourse of the dominant culture (Doherty, 1991) and allows them to define for themselves the meaning of success, the role of work in their lives, and what else matters as much as, if not more than, work. The same can be said for practitioners who help clients rewrite their part in the Grand Narrative of their century. Many workers who uncritically bought in to the Grand Narrative found themselves in an unrewarding Rat Race (see Hochschild, 1997; McKenna, 1997; Pipher, 1996). Several scholars and practitioners, whether or not self-identified postmodernists, have not felt comfortable with the artificial, arbitrary distinction between career counseling and personal counseling. Savickas's notion of the career as personal is similar to feminism in career counseling and the idea of the personal as political (Brooks & Forrest, 1994). The practitioner and client's co-construction of the meaning of the client's direction in life is fine as long as narrative viability is maintained. It is no use encouraging a client to believe that he will be a member of the U. S. polo team in the next Olympics if that client has no horsemanship skills, cannot swing a mallet, and does not have the financial means to train for the Olympic team. Hermeneutic activity will come most easily to practitioners with extensive backgrounds in English or other literature, Bible studies, or narrative histories.

The emphasis on stories over scores is paramount. Both of us have long been appalled by unskilled career counselors who simply give a student computer-scored results and computer-generated reports of vocational assessment instruments without really taking the time to listen whether a computer-generated profile coheres with the meaning making of the student or how it matches what one knows about oneself. Savickas (1992) writes that the boredom many career counselors feel when doing the same old thing can be alleviated by adopting more intersubjective approaches that actively engage the client in a quest for meaning. This different way of doing things is one of the most refreshing aspects of a postmodern approach to occupational development. Clients can benefit enormously by a practitioner's infusion of some of these approaches into clinical work.

Career has been deconstructed by postmodern discourse (Savickas, 1995b). Burr (1995) defines discourse as "a systematic, coherent set of images, metaphors and so on, that construct an object in a particular way" (p. 184). Furthermore,

> discourses offer a framework to people against which they may understand their own experience and behavior and that of others, and can be seen to be tied to social structures and practices in a way which masks power relations operating in society (Burr, 1995, pp. 71–72).

Historically, career has mainly meant work in the occupational structure by degreed professionals. Work performed at home and in the community has been marginalized (Richardson, 1993), and people who performed such work have been disempowered. Dominant discourses often mask inequitable social arrangements that support the interests of relatively powerful groups in society (e.g., males, the upper class). In vocational psychology, the focus on women and work-family issues confronts the privileged position of many males in the workplace.

From a postmodern perspective, work is more than an occupational role. It is but one of many contexts in people's lives. The fracture of the modern career ethic (Savickas, 1993, 1995b) potentially could be

> replaced by a postmodern work ethic rooted in a new perspective on the occupational role, one that emphasizes connectedness and social contribution. Correspondingly, vocational psychologists are being challenged to revise their core philosophy of science and to reform their field into an interpretive discipline (Savickas, 1995b, p. 18).

TABLE 7.3 The Debate over Which Philosophy of Science Vocational Psychology Should Use: Logical Positivism versus Contextual Interpretivism

LOGICAL POSITIVISM	CONTEXTUAL INTERPRETIVISM

1. Epistemic Individualism
     individual as principal agent of knowledge production; knowledge already exists separately from the individual in an objectively knowable world
	Epistemic Collectivism
	     communities as primary agents of knowledge production; knowledge is mediated through discourse, socially constructed subjectivity

2. Objectivity
     scientific method is universal method because it controls biases and leads to knowledge, prediction, and control
	Perspectivity
	     scientific method is only one method, not "the" method; behind the facade of value-free objectivity is a commitment to technical rationality; multiple perspectives produce richer, deeper, more complex knowledge

3. Universality
     generality of testing principles; theoretical; design experiments
	Particularity
	     examine locally situated practices that seem useful in specific circumstances; seek stories of individual's experiences and problem descriptions

4. Validation
     knowledge validated in reference to theory; seek universal properties that govern human conduct (e.g., singular truths)
	Legitimation
	     knowledge legitimated by its usefulness when implemented; seek diverse interpretive communities that share a local perspective (e.g., multiple realities)

5. Essence
     essentialized selves; context, culture is a variable; vocational behavior is a pure category
	Context
	     social context and unique circumstances; culture as the context of meaning; vocational behavior is part of a complex of coherent interrelationships within which it is embedded

6. Concepts
     concept as something already existing in nature that was discovered and named; directly reflect reality through the filters of self-chosen vocabulary
	Constructs
	     constructs as personal and cultural component of meaning making; linguistically invent reality through lived experience

SOURCES: Best and Kellner (1991), Harding (1993), Savickas (1993, 1995b).

Six issues debated between logical positivists and contextual interpretivists over which philosophy of science vocational psychology should use are presented in Table 7.3.

The debate summarized in Table 7.3 is unlikely to be resolved anytime soon. We hope to see a middle road evolve where instead of either/or, both logical positivism *and* contextual interpretivism are used in vocational psychology without any contradiction in the duality of such an existence. This would really honor and respect multiple perspectives. Epistemic collectivism means that a person's thoughts and beliefs as expressed through epistemic individualism become situated knowledge when communities socially legitimate those thoughts and beliefs. However, a counterpoint is provided by the late Russian constructivist Lev Vygotsky (1896–1934), who noted that a child's cognitive development occurs on the social level first—i.e., inter-psychologically, between people—and on the personal level second—i.e., inter-psychologically, within the child (1978). In other words, the individual still constructs a personal meaning even after a community socially legitimates situated knowledge. This is a recursive process where a personal construction of reality (epistemic individualism) is legitimated through a social construction of reality (epistemic collectivism) and then idiographically understood as yet another personal construction of reality (a second draft, if you will, of epistemic individualism). Both epistemic individualism *and* epistemic collectivism go through endless multiple drafts of reality construction.

Both universality *and* particularity can have practical applications to the role of work in people's lives. Beginning with universality, a practitioner could say to a client, "When a lot of people feel job stress, [and then utter the results of generalizable research findings, such as symptoms]." To tailor for particularity, the practitioner can then ask, "Do any of these [generalizable objective research findings] seem like they fit for you?" The same principle applies to the issue of validation versus legitimation. Beginning with validation, the practitioner could say, "When a lot of people are burned out from work, [then impart singular truths validated in reference to theory]." To make it legitimate for the client, the practitioner can then ask, "Does any of this sound like something you are going through?" Many practitioners probably particularize and legitimate without using these terms.

Essence is losing ground to context because of broad external factors beyond the control of logical positivists and contextual interpretivists. Yet, concepts continue to be a fact of daily life for most people. O'Hara and Anderson (1991) and Savickas (1993, 1995b) temper their enthusiasm by acknowledging that modernism and its counterpart, the scientific method, are alive and well.

Constructivism

Personal Construct Psychology Personal construct psychology (PCP) offers a philosophical rationale that has a well-articulated foundation and a methodology that was developed during years of study (Kelly, 1955). PCP is one form of constructivism. Evolutions of PCP are discussed in Feixas (1990, 1995). Various forms of constructivism are examined in Lyddon (1995).

PCP makes the case for having the career explorer determine the dimensions used to foster self-understanding. The methodology is based on the Role Construct Repertory Tests (Reptest), a structured exercise developed by Kelly (1955) and subse-

Practical Applications

The Goals Review and Organizing Workbook (Forster, 1986) has been used in a variety of settings, including high schools and college counseling centers. Client evaluations indicate it is useful for clarifying and organizing personal goals. GROW gives four guidelines for facilitating the articulation of personal goals:

First, participants begin this sequential process by remembering and designating several personal events that are meaningful and easily differentiated from other past events.

Second, participants use those events to elicit personal constructs that allow them to differentiate these events from other events. Third, when differentiating among events, the nature of the elicited personal constructs is framed by the potential use that is specified. Fourth, after a variety of constructs have been elicited and used to describe aspects of the self, they are prioritized and then tested for usability.

GROW has five steps that facilitate the participant's articulation of several goal statements.

1. Take an inventory of your Daily Activities and Identify Constructs.

This step is initiated when participants complete the One-Week Activity Inventory, which can be recalled from the previous week or completed as a record of the current week.

2. Recall Special Events and Identify Possible Reasons. Participants identify seventeen additional events.

3. Write Goal Statements Using Personal Constructs or Reasons. The main activity is to use ideas or constructs elicited in the previous steps to make goal statements.

4. Prioritize Your Goal Statements. Participants are asked to list their goals statements by choosing between two goals at a time, and continuing this paired-comparison process until choices have been made for all possible combinations.

5. Use Your Top Goals To Rate Representative Activities from Your Past Week. Participants try out their prioritized goal statements by using them to evaluate representative activities randomly selected from their One-Week Activity Inventory (Forster, 1992).

quently modified by many PCP practitioners to address various domains of study. *The Goals Review and Organizing Workbook* (GROW) (Forster, 1992) is a structured exercise designed to facilitate career-related self-understanding using a PCP rationale. GROW is based on the premise that career explorers benefit from articulating their own dimensions when they see increased understanding of themselves. In PCP terms, the dimensions are called constructs. A person's goals are equivalent to desired anticipations. The personal construct can be used as the primary conceptual unit for investigating the elicitation and articulation of a person's goals (Forster, 1992).

Assessments Used with Personal Construct Psychology. In addition to GROW, two other PCP-based instruments have been designed to facilitate self-understanding. The Job Attribute Clarifier (JAC) (Forster, 1982) elicits personal constructs used by participants when they differentiate among jobs that they know about. Prioritized job attributes can be used to write an ideal job description. The Dependable Strengths Articulation Process Short Form (DSAP-S) (Haldane & Forster, 1988) guides participants through a sequence of exercises that lead to the articulation of personal strengths considered by the participant to be dependable and valuable. DAP-S is based on practices developed by Haldane (1988). A description of an intervention using the DSAP-S and its effects on self-esteem has been reported by Forster (1991).

Constructivism and Career Indecision Most vocational psychologists and career counselors have relied on logical positivism as a basis for studying and treating **career indecision** (Savickas, 1995a). Frank Parsons scientized vocational guidance and made it an objective enterprise by concentrating on *true reasoning* as a way of making it a legitimate science for the twentieth century. Career counselors "abstracted career indecision from its context and objectified it with reliable and valid measurement procedures" (p. 364). Subsequently, career indecision as an objective phenomenon evolved over three phases.

1. Indecision as a dichotomy categorized career clients as decided or undecided, and implied that indecision was symptomatic of a personality problem or defect. The decided/undecided dichotomy prevailed from the 1930s until the late 1980s. The Parsonian concept of well-developed aptitudes and interests as a personal perquisite for a reasonable vocational choice implied that indecision was symptomatic of immaturity or psychopathology. Practitioners tried to cure underlying causes (i.e., defects in one's inner being) of indecision. "Intrapersonal anxiety, interpersonal conflict, cultural differences, lack of skill, [and] limited self-knowledge" (Savickas, 1995a, p. 364) were presumed to be defects of self that could be objectively detected and treated.

2. Indecision as a universal continuum replaced the decided/undecided dichotomy and was popularized by John L. Holland and Samuel H. Osipow. During the 1970s, each developed scales to assess a client's position on the indecision continuum.

3. Indecision as a multidimensional concept recognizes the heterogeneity of undecided people. In the late 1980s and early 1990s, several scales were developed to assess the multidimensionality of indecision.

From a constructivist perspective, the subjective experience of indecision has not been fully explored (Savickas, 1995a). Because of the overwhelming objectification and decontextualization that has occurred from the positivist perspective, indecision has largely been operationally defined from objective test scores.

The constructivist approach switches this definition to "subjective stories told by a client" (p. 365). Indecision for a constructivist is normal, not pathological. Indecision is a transformation in progress that occurs when a person appears to be on the verge of losing their place in the world (or at work) and is confronted with resolving a **wavering** doubt (Cochran, 1991). Unsettled wavering is movement toward meaning and a life-shaping decision that can alter the course of a person's life. "We think and represent life in story" (Cochran, 1991, p. 20). Thus, narrative becomes an inherent part of the experience of indecision. Decision making is a settling of one's orientation to life, the narrative one strives to realize. The narrative a person attempts to clarify and refine is called a **life theme.**

Csikszentmihalyi and Beattie (1979) define life theme as "an affective and cognitive representation of existential problems which a person wishes to resolve. It becomes the basis for an individual's fundamental interpretation of reality and a way of coping with that reality" (p. 45). Indecision occurs because a person has not recognized his or her life theme (Savickas, 1995a). One cannot voice one's own life project when one has not yet thought it through. A constructivist practitioner concentrates on how a client's indecision is embedded within an ongoing pattern of meanings being lived by the client.

Thorngren and Feit (2001) propose another career intervention, the Career-O-Gram, which may be useful in determining the influences with which a client must deal in obtaining and retaining employment. This method uses the same principles as the genogram developed by Bowen (1978) for use in family therapy. Verbal and pictorial means are used to examine the influences that impact career history, which is the focus of this intervention. The benefits of this tool include simplicity, flexibility, and the ability to study the complex nature of career seeking. The Career-O-Gram has the potential for assisting a counselor in gathering information about the client's skills, abilities, value and belief systems, interests, and relevant influences. This is an intervention that provides the client and counselor with insight and direction.

Constructive Developmental Theory and Career Transition McAuliffe (1993) explores **constructive developmental theory,** or an individual's meaning-making framework, for career transitions. "In psychological terms, career can be an act of meaning construction" (p. 23). Most adults' meaning making can be characterized by three balances.

1. *The Interpersonal Balance.* "I am my relationships" rather than "I have relationships" (McAuliffe, 1993, p. 24, quotations in original). This person
   a. is entirely embedded in relationships.
   b. has no center to author a story of "how things should be" (p. 24, quotations in original).
   c. cannot generate a perspective separate from the relationships in which they live.
   d. has insufficiently individuated and does not have a coherent identity.

Practical Applications

Savickas (1989, 1995a) presents a five-step model of constructivist counseling for career indecision.

1. Practitioner collects client stories that reveal a client's life theme. Literary criticism is relied upon for what makes a good story. "A life theme is like a plot in literature" (Savickas, 1995a, p. 367). The client's plan of action is composed of various plots. Meaning is inscribed into events that form part of an integrated whole. The interaction between life events and the plan of action form the life themes. Two kinds of stories—those that focus on the client's central life concern and those that focus on the career indecision—are useful for the practitioner to elicit. The practitioner's attention is given to troubles, imbalances, or deviations that client stories accentuate. A good place for practitioners to start is to ask about stories regarding the client's family. We think it is telling whenever clients' faces light up as they tell their story, and we attend to moments when clients beam with delight as well.

2. As a reality check, the practitioner narrates the theme back to the client, who then has a chance to edit the practitioner's feedback narrative. In addition to family stories, stories about client identity will help to reveal the narrative goal by addressing the "gap between what is and what ought to be" (Cochran, 1991, p. 12). Any heroes or heroines the client had growing up and the ways the client puts meaning to his or her experiences, recalls events that led to the crystallization of the client's self, and rehearses ways to cope with life will also provide the practitioner with identity stories (Savickas, 1995a).

3. The meaning of the client's current indecision is discussed with the counselor in relation to the life theme. Several questions can be asked here:
   a. Under what circumstances did you recognize your indecision?
   b. What does it feel like to be undecided?
   c. Does this feeling remind you of anything else from your life?
   d. Tell me another story about a time when you had this same feeling.
   e. Is there anything that haunts you?
   f. From what you have told me about your life, what part of the story is most related to your indecision? (Savickas, 1995a).

4. Practitioner and client jointly extend the life theme into the future. Interests and occupations are named that clients might have hesitated about before. Client interests are used by the practitioner to guide story construction and become "future solutions to old problems" (Savickas, 1995a, p. 372). Occupational choices can help clients deal with unfinished business, settle old scores, or compensate for something missing from childhood.

5. Practitioner and client use behavioral counseling methods to specifically identify and put into place the plan to achieve a particular occupational choice. The intersubjective reality of the client is quite evident in Savickas's (1995a) constructivist counseling for career indecision. McAuliffe (1993) adds a developmental component when constructivism is used to address career transition.

This person's occupational choices—if choices they be called—are often based on unquestioned assumptions or uncritical acceptance of the line of work appropriate for someone of his or her reference group (i.e., family, peers, ethnicity, socioeconomic class, religion). Blind adherence to the Interpersonal Balance can stifle one's own voice and lead one to miss one's calling. The limits of the Interpersonal Balance are reached when the environment challenges the individual to generate his or her own point of view.

2. *The Institutional Balance.* "I am my occupation" rather than "I have an occupation" (McAuliffe, 1993, p. 24, quotations in original). This person becomes thoroughly identified with a particular life role (a sole job title or position) and cannot self-correct to connect to the larger purposes (a workplace mission statement) of which he or she is merely a current expression. Such rigidity or single-mindedness can blind one to one's larger occupational potentials. Meaning making becomes enhanced when one can reflect on a broader, future perspective and can see possible occupational roles into which one can evolve. The limits of the Institutional Balance are reached when one recognizes that he or she has been conserving a product (a job title or position) rather than cultivating a process (potentially multiple positions or occupations).

4. *The Inter-individual Balance.* "Who am I becoming and how shall I express this emerging self?" rather than "What does my community, my family, my ethnic or religious group expect of me?" [Interpersonal Balance] or "How do I maintain the current form I am in?" [Institutional Balance] (McAuliffe, 1993, p. 25, quotations in original). This person is open to new information that may challenge the occupational choice made, is able to hear dissonant and even contradictory voices, and is not preoccupied with "preserving its own coherence at all cost" (p. 24). These people have developed flexibility to negotiate life choices and transitions and have maximized their options to respond to both their internal needs and the external environment. The Inter-individual Balance accepts incompleteness, and thus is most desirable for managing career transition.

Constructive developmental theory posits that most people's meaning making will be characterized by two of the above balances, with one of the balances predominating. Within each balance is the maintenance of an equilibrium between the poles.

Practical Applications

The developmental level of the client's meaning-making system is assessed to clarify whether surface adjustments or cognitive transformations occur. Surface adjustments are similar to first-order change. **First-order change** is "any change in a system that does not produce a change in the structure of the system" (Lyddon, 1990, p. 122). Cognitive transformations are similar to second-order change. **Second-order change** is "a type of change whose occurrence alters the fundamental structure of a system" (p. 122). Surface adjustments, or first-order changes, would be like a lateral move that a worker makes between similar positions within the same occupational field. Cognitive transformations, or second-order changes, would be like a revision that a worker makes by leaving one occupational field for another. First-order change in the world of work would include a student transferring from one school to another, a worker relocating across town or leaving one corporation for another, or a person in a religious vocation going from one assignment to another within the religious order. Second-order change in the world of work includes the transition from school to work, becoming a new parent and hunting for child care, relocating to a different town, a downshift from the corporate world, and the departure from the secular world to enter a religious vocation.

Practitioners can elicit cognitive developmental information by questioning clients about the costs of changing fields and they know when a decision is correct for them. Clients' responses will reveal their primary emphasis on Interpersonal or Institutional Balances as the meaning making that currently predominates.

Sometimes first-order change is all that is needed, especially if the client's meaning making appears adequately calibrated within a given Balance. The practitioner uses "reflective clarification, information giving, encouragement, and . . . *rational* decision making" (McAuliffe, 1993, p. 25, italics added). At other times, second-order change is needed, especially if the client's meaning making in response to environmental demands is inadequately calibrated within a given Balance. Second-order change is called for when there is a challenge to the major assumptions of a client's self-definition or what he or she knows about the world of work. The way one defines self and occupation is transformed. The practitioner helps the client obtain more information about the self and the world of work. Further practical applications of constructive developmental theory are found in McAuliffe (1993). For more in-depth understanding of second-order change, we recommend the classic Watzlawick, Weakland, and Fisch (1974).

There is a presumed developmental progression from Interpersonal to Institutional to Inter-individual Balance. An authentic occupational/vocational quest is most likely to occur when the Inter-individual Balance predominates.

Evaluation of Postmodern Approaches

Postmodern approaches in vocational psychology are in the nascent stage. They are very much works in progress. The literary quality of clients' clinical statements is emphasized over scientific properties. Practitioners who can see all sides of a story will find postmodern approaches congenial; others may have a harder time letting go of their modernist training.

Social Constructionism Similar to Thomas Szasz's assertion that one can accept many psychodynamic clinical methods without adopting the ideology (Simpson, 1987), a vocational practitioner can use social constructionism without abandoning modernism completely. Vocational practitioners may want to take advantage of what social constructionism has to offer without becoming casualties of its excesses (Rosenau, 1992).

Constructivism "Constructivism is more highly developed philosophically than methodologically" (Granvold, 1996, p. 349). The efficacy of constructivist approaches has not been fully established (Gonçalves, 1995; Guidano, 1995; Neimeyer, 1995a). Internal tensions exist within the constructivist movement between proponents of the individualistic perspective and proponents of the communally defined language perspective (Neimeyer, 1995b). Lyddon's (1995) attempt to incorporate social constructionism into the larger constructionist taxonomy are likely to be resisted by those who prefer to keep social constructionism separate from constructivism. Constructivist clinical practitioners acknowledge arbitrary boundaries between psychotherapy and counseling and between separate therapy traditions. Critical scholarship is a provisional solution to the challenge of internal tensions within the constructivist movement (see Neimeyer, 1995b).

Critics of the constructivist epistemologies include Held (1990), who writes, "the view that we cannot, under any circumstances, know an independent reality is itself, paradoxically, a reality claim" (p. 181). Coale (1992) writes, "The emphasis on language as *the* mechanism for changing meaning is a contradiction of the constructivist position that all reality is non-objective and, therefore, that there is room for many ways of understanding and doing anything" (p. 23, italics in original). Rosenau (1992) and Burr (1995) are two good books for readers to learn for themselves about postmodernism and social constructionism, respectively.

Postmodern interventions hold the most promise with clients whose occupational life has been disrupted to such an extent that their core assumptions about reality, self, and the role of work are no longer functional (Lyddon, 1990; Richardson, 1993). When a client has been downsized, laid off, fired, or passed over for promotion or has reached a saturation point that looks like overwork and exhaustion, we see the value of attending to both personal and social constructions of reality. We also remain vigilant about postmodern conversational artistry degenerating into plain old con artistry (Efran & Fauber, 1995); at present there is no system of checks and balances that prevents postmodern approaches from being used in an unscrupulous manner and as a cover for deceit and dishonesty. "Constructivism allows for a retention of personal responsibility that can balance social constructionism from deteriorating into political manipulation and/or oppressive conspiracies of silence" (González, 1997, p. 379).

In the workplace, a profound difference between what is said and what seems to be can contribute to employee disengagement, stress, and wavering. An overemphasis on the social construction of reality can eclipse individual employee rights and fail to acknowledge the existence of work that takes place outside the formal occupational structure (Fisher, 1995; Richardson, 1993).

Relevance for Multicultural and Diverse Populations

Not everyone lives in a postmodern world. "Pockets of postmodernism exist, as do pockets of appalling premodern poverty" (González, 1997, p. 378). Practitioners need to stay mindful of how their own class privilege (Freire, 1993) and education levels can sway them into uncritical acceptance of the idea that we have uniformly entered a postmodern age. Proclamations that the modern world is rapidly waning (Srivastva, Fry, & Cooperrider, 1990) or dead (Hoffmann, 1991) are premature at best, elitist at worst. At first glance, the pluralism espoused by multiculturalism and the multiple perspectives espoused by postmodernism appear to be compatible, but closer inspection reveals issues of classism, sexism, and elitism that simply will not go away. The modern world that postmodernism reacts against was not the world of multicultural peoples (Johnson, 1991). Feminism and postmodernism are not necessarily conceptual and political allies (Benhabib, 1992). Nor is postmodern discourse frequently heard among construction laborers or public housing residents (Russell & Gaubatz, 1995).

Objectively detectable social and political realities of oppression DO exist outside the realities created—or glossed over—by language. Socially constructed, dominant discourses can serve as smokescreens to disguise inequality (Hare-Mustin, 1994). At other times, indirect talk—coded, politically laden, and sarcastic language—is a socially constructed reality that aims to silence others (Capper, 1995). González (1998) is concerned about postmodernism being foisted on multicultural and diverse clients without their informed consent. Many of these clients will not match their practitioners' familiarity with the postmodern literature, which makes consensual cocreations of reality quite unlikely. González is concerned about postmodernism as part of a hidden agenda, to be insinuated into clinical dialogues with unsuspecting and unaware clients. It is not the practitioner's place to disabuse any lower-income or immigrant client from pursuing a part in the Grand Narrative of the twentieth century. For many racial and ethnic minority people, fine words from people of the dominant culture can quickly lose their credibility unless supported by actions (Sue & Sue, 1990).

Confrontations between cultures have brought home the fact that people see the world differently (Smith, 1989). But the pendulum has swung too far in the direction of multiplicity. "Multiple views, yes; multiple realities, no. . . . Even if reality were no more than the sum of all . . . multiple realities . . . , that sum would stand as the inclusive reality which would not itself be multiple" (pp. 234–235). Moreover, "it is impossible that any one system has all the truth" (p. 240).

Postmodern strands represent the most recent perspectives, but all of these important movements have broadened our understanding of mental health interventions. While none of them was designed to specifically address the issues involved in career counseling, we have attempted to clarify the ideas and techniques that can be useful to career counselors. Individuals cited in the chapter, such as Bordin and others, Koehn, Sampson, and Savickas, have developed workable applications of these major theories for use by vocational practitioners.

Another strong sphere of influence of career counseling comes from those theories that see career choice as an integral part of one's development across the life span. Chapter 5 is devoted to the major ideas of developmental theorists.

NADENE PETERSON'S MODEL

"Know Thyself"

Development of the Model

This model was developed primarily during my doctoral studies and later became the basis for my dissertation. Results showed a profound difference between subjects that had been involved in group counseling and those in the control group, and the model became the core of my working plan as a vocational practitioner. It was based on a combination of assessment instruments and Herbert Shepard's (1975) Life Planning Model, which include written exercises such as:

1. Drawing a Life Line
2. Identity Search
3. Writing One's Obituary
4. Fantasy Day
5. A Way of Life

6. A Review of Highs

7. Purpose and Themes

8. What Should I Start Doing Now?

9. What Should I Stop Doing Now?

In addition, I have found narrative stories, intersubjective interaction, and embedded work values help clients to make appropriate work decisions. Various writing exercises—autobiographical, guided imagery, and the use of metaphors—are techniques clients have used successfully to formulate occupational decisions.

While this model is useful to me, each practitioner needs to find an approach that is useful and meaningful. I do not use each part of the model in every case, but adapt it to the client and the circumstances. From my experience, this model works best with adults of all ages with a variety of occupational backgrounds and situations. It has proven effective with individuals, groups, and organizations and can be adapted to high school/college age populations.

Assumptions

I have been a career/vocational practitioner for thirty years. Certain underlying assumptions influence my clinical practice and teaching. Tolbert (1980) has been a major influence. From this I developed seventeen working assumptions:

1. A person's career/vocational choices or happenings are among the most important decisions and occurrences in his or her lifetime and are a reflection of his or her total life story.

2. Vocational/career awareness and development should be integrated and emphasized in the school curriculum from K–12.

3. By the end of high school, a student should have taken a variety of assessments (whether objective- or perspective-oriented) and received consultations, including interpretation and recommendations, from a counselor in order to assist the student in making appropriate decisions for vocational/technical school, college, apprenticeship training, or school-to-work transition.

4. Gender and culture biases need to be addressed in occupational materials and assessment instruments so that stereotyping is minimized and special allowances and understanding for each individual's realities are integrated into the process.

5. Most students from minority populations will have been channeled into occupations in vocational tracks without ample consideration to vocational decision-making opportunities in the world of work and without due consideration for their abilities, aptitudes, and life experiences. Those practices must not continue.

6. The family is a significant influence on career decision making. Therefore, parents should be informed and trained as to their role in their children's awareness and decision making regarding education, training, jobs, and careers.

7. A person needs to know who she or he is, and what she or he likes in order to make an appropriate match between person and environment.

8. If a person makes an appropriate/well-matched career decision, it will influence his or her choices in work and social relationships, and consequently provide more work/life satisfaction.

9. Awareness of developmental stages and assistance in accomplishing these career development tasks for each state is an essential skill for a career practitioner.

10. Career planning is a lifelong process. Practitioners need to teach *process* rather than impart information.

11. To continue to be effective, a career counselor/practitioner needs to have a current awareness of (a) the *global economy*, (b) changes within the *workforce* (retooling, retraining), and (c) future trends and job requirements.

12. Adaptability of job skills is important in an ever-changing work environment; and continued career development is essential in order to maintain job security, flexibility, and employability.

13. Exploring self-efficacy, *values*, mission, and goals is integral to the career counseling process. When necessary, personal counseling issues need to be addressed.

14. Incorporating a process for decision making in career planning is essential.

15. All roles a person takes on interact, but the career role exerts a major influence on all other roles.

16. Lifestyle is a major source of satisfaction and meaning, and one's occupation determines, to a great extent, one's *lifestyle*. If one is happy in one's work, it is likely to bring satisfaction and meaning to that person's life.

17. Continued learning and leisure activities also are important in maintaining balance in lifestyle.

Philosophical and Theoretical Underpinnings

I agree with Imbimbo (1994) who states, "career counseling has often been viewed as separate and distinct from personal counseling, ignoring a long tradition in the career development field that has consistently recognized the importance of personality factors in the presence of choosing and maintaining a career" (p. 50). In order to attend to

> both the personality and career development theories[,] [t]he counselor is required to be able to move back and forth between the active and directive role of the career counselor and the facilitative and exploratory of the personal counselor. . . . To suggest that career and personal counseling should be mutually exclusive or that individuals can separate their personal issues from what happens in their career lives is simplistic (Imbimbo, 1994, p. 50).

Practitioners must (1) have a theoretical base well established, (2) draw from other personality and career theories and techniques in order to be effective in assisting clients in making occupational/vocational choices, and (3) provide information regarding the current world of work. "Eclectic career counseling is a complex process that demands broad-based information and the ability to comfortably switch counseling styles as needed" (Imbimbo, 1994 p. 52).

Personal and career counseling no longer need sharp distinctions, because people who come for career counseling often require both, and the reverse is often true. Counselors and psychologists need to be trained in career development so they know when career-counseling interventions are appropriate. For both Master's- and doctoral-level students in counseling psychology, more training in personality theories and techniques and their application to vocational psychology would be useful. The challenge for career practitioners is to be able to provide a comprehensive service to clients who have comprehensive needs (Imbimbo, 1994). Richardson (1993) suggests that rather than conceptualizing career counseling as a separate entity from personal counseling, practitioners might best consider it as a type of brief *focused counseling*. A deeper understanding is needed as to when counselors should give information as opposed to when they should probe for understanding and insight into dynamics that may block realization of career goals. It has been my experience that most people who experience difficulty making vocational decisions often have questions about other aspects of their lives. A good area for future research is the interface of career and personal counseling.

Another element I incorporate into the vocational counseling process is creativity. "The capacity for fantasy and daydreams may be our most important human quality. It may also be evolution's greatest gift to us" (Singer & Switzer, 1980, p. 5). Many different paradigms accomplish a deeper understanding of the person other than assessments alone. These involve the practitioner's *and* the client's own creative processes. Creative thoughts and behaviors exist in many different ways in the counseling process (Heppner, Fitzgerald, & James, 1989). Counseling creativity "involves the combination of information, often in unique and novel ways, that is ultimately used to elucidate or solve a client's problem by extending the client's experiential world in some way" (p. 272). Practitioners are urged "to shift the career counseling paradigm from assessment, match and terminate sessions to dynamic, creative and challenging interchanges" (Heppner, O'Brien, Hinkelman, & Humphrey, 1994, p. 77).

Several activities can assist the practitioner in the creative process (Heppner et al., (1994).

- *Guided imagery* is a structured activity that provides guidelines in order to stimulate the imagination of the client. "Internal images can be a motivational and inspiring way to capture occupational daydreams that the clients may frequently experience" (p. 79). I integrate this into the counseling process by asking the client to describe a day or week in a job they would "love to do," including people, place, duties, and how the time is spent.

- *Idea journals* are a client's record of vocational daydreams/ideas that occur on a daily basis. I ask a client to keep a diary/journal over time regarding feelings and thoughts about work, such as what gives her or him a sense of satis-faction/fulfillment, and when she or he feels bored or unhappy with the job.

- *One minute free writes* are a client's opportunity to record for one minute any words or phrases that are associated with a particular career daydream.

- *Career genograms* enable a client's identification of occupations in the family across generations to observe patterns of career choices.

- *Metaphors* generated from a client's internal world can develop a story.

- *Use of early recollection* allows a client to select two or three early memories and describe them in as much detail as possible in order to identify themes. I have asked clients to describe the first five years of life and those experiences that they recall vividly.

- *Career bingo* is a technique developed to facilitate interaction among group members and assists the participants in thinking about different careers and what qualities/values are required (Bikos & O'Brien, 1993, cited in Heppner et al., 1994).

- *Collage and other art media* provide a client the opportunity to produce a collage of all the things that come to mind when he/she thinks about a ca-reer/occupational choice.

- *Analysis of hero and heroines* is a client's opportunity to write or talk about someone they admire and the characteristics he or she possesses. I often ask clients to make a list of people who have been influential in their lives and in what way they were impacted by them.

- *Time line analysis* is a client's opportunity to recall and explore the signifi-cance of important life events. This can be depicted visually by drawing peaks and valleys in one's life. Another technique is to draw a time line for future goals. I use Shepard's Draw Your Life Line exercise to identify signifi-cant events.

- *Life mapping* involves the client listing important people or events on small slips of paper and then arranging these papers in a meaningful way on a larger sheet of paper.

Krumboltz, Blando, Kim, and Reikowski (1994) suggest " [e]mbedding work val-ues in realistic occupational narratives may provide a more meaningful way of stimu-lating clients to explore the impact of alternative occupations on their future lives" (p. 57). In their study, work values were explored by embedding them in realistic descrip-tions of a day in the life of various people employed in different occupations.

Heppner, O'Brien, Hinkelman, and Humphrey (1994) give a clear summation of our discussion of creativity in vocational counseling.

As surveys of counselors as well as clients continue to show a dissatisfaction with career counseling, it seems imperative that one investigates dynamic new ways of helping clients think about their life/career planning. As we model

creativity in our own lives and practice, clients will vicariously experience
people who are truly excited about their occupational employment. This alone
may assist career clients in achieving their dreams and maximizing their creative
potentials (p. 85).

Assessments that incorporate the use of fantasy/daydreams/guided imagery include:

1. The Self-Directed Search (SDS) (Holland, 1985) begins with occupational day-
    dreams; a first activity is titled *Occupational Daydreams* and the instructions ask the
    reader to list the careers about which he or she has daydreamed.
2. Figler (1975) has a career workbook called PATH. The user of the workbook is
    asked to think about and write past, present, and future fantasies.
3. Skovholt (1981) developed a Career Imagery Card Sort, which helps sort out
    occupations that are part of daydreams, using guided fantasy to help activate the
    daydreams.

Process

When working with an individual in occupational and career counseling, I use the
following process.

In the initial interview, it is important to explain to the client the breadth of the
counseling process. Many clients want a quick answer, a test-and-tell experience,
without giving the necessary understanding of themselves that helps determine a successful intervention. Initial assessment becomes the basis for understanding what is
happening in the client's external and internal life (Imbimbo, 1994). Use of the life
story (autobiographical data), including significant events, people, and influences from
the past, is important for a client to understand her or his own reality. During assessment, I gather information regarding the client's family and her or his work patterns,
educational and work history, and physical and health status. If appropriate, various
assessments are administered.

By the second session, results are briefly explained, with the assignment being to
read all the materials before the next session, identify information that seems accurate,
and make a list of questions to be discussed in session three. All the data is analyzed
and interpreted through patterns and themes from both the standardized and informal assessments. The client is then asked to make a list of interests, personal traits,
skills, and values taken from the assessments he or she has just completed. During any
of these sessions, if concerns regarding work performance, relationship issues, or financial security arise, these are dealt with in the context of helping the client resolve
conflicts so he or she can be free to make the best decision possible. The occupational
counseling process not only focuses on the external factors of world of work, but on
the integration of these factors with the client's internal, intrapsychic world.

The fourth session is a culmination of all the information gained, and goals and
time lines are developed for the next month, six months, and year. The client will

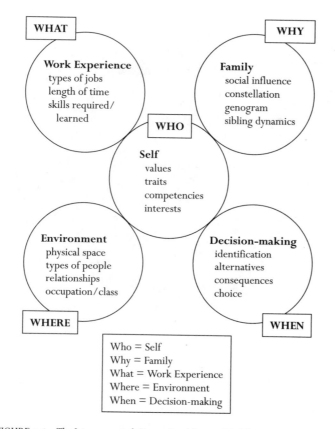

FIGURE 7.6   The Interconnected Occupational Process Model

choose three occupations he or she wants to learn more about and will be given the assignment to search out information. I keep a list of people who are willing to be mentors/advisors and who are available to meet or talk with clients. Also, I keep a list of various computer-assisted programs and other resource materials available in the area.

Career/occupational counseling requires that the counselor be trained and familiar with many vocational theories and techniques, as well as having a wealth of information about the job market, training requirements, availability of programs, and contacts within the business community.

The Interconnected Occupational Process Model is a visual representation of the process I use (See Figure 7.6). In the center is the Who. This involves defining self-information. The first step is to identify basic *needs* (Maslow, 1954). Needs are basic for survival at the physical, emotional, intellectual, and social levels. *Wants* go beyond needs and represent quality of life choices (i.e., type of surroundings we live in, environmental concerns, cultural and educational activities, travel). Knowing a client's needs and wants helps identify values, which, as described in Chapter Two,

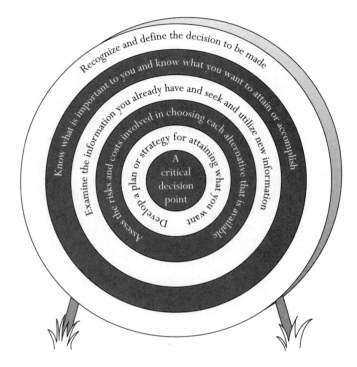

FIGURE 7.7   Decision-Making Process

SOURCE: Gelatt, Varenhorst, Carey, & Miller (1973), p. 7.

reflect our beliefs and lifestyles. Our actions are based on values, which can lead to meaning and mission. Finding an ultimate goal/purpose for life is aided by discovering meaning and mission. A sense of vocation and calling helps in job/occupation/career choice. Having answered such questions as what and why leaves a client open to work on the questions of how, where, and when. The model is designed to help a client explore needs, wants, and values in order to determine mission/calling/vocation. This can lead to decision and action.

Gelatt, Varenhorst, Carey, and Miller (1973) developed a circular model for decision making. Decisions are based on what you know and what you want. See Figure 7.7. The decision-making process involves using what you know (or can learn) to get what you want. **Decision-Making: The Process** [Gelatt, Varenhorst, Carey, & Miller (1973), p. 7.] demonstrates what is involved in making a well-considered decision.

This model also can be used with **dual career couples**. Each partner completes all the assessments. When the results come in, both have a chance to see the other's results and discuss what this means in terms of making a decision regarding each one's career. The values survey and the life goals inventory are helpful for dual career couples to get a clear picture of high priorities for each of them. Do results complement each other, or is there conflict? This process is crucial for couples struggling with dual career and lifestyle concerns. Marriages have a better chance of surviving if these decisions can be made with shared concerns and understandings.

The case examples presented here demonstrate how I work, and the types of issues that can confront clients and vocational practitioners. Several of the examples show successes, but as any experienced practitioner knows, there are clients who will not respond to any intervention. Case 4 demonstrates this.

Case Examples

Case 1 Brian, 42, reported that the bank where he worked was downsizing. Several colleagues in other banks had already lost their jobs, and he was concerned he might have to change careers. He did not want to relocate because his family had always lived in the town where he worked.

Married with children, he wanted a steady income. In addition to the exercises by Shepard mentioned above, he completed the Motivated Skills Chart by Bernard Haldane in which he identified his ten greatest achievements, then marked on the chart what skills he had to have to accomplish those achievements. Brian completed these on his own time and was also administered a **test battery** including the SII, MBTI, 16PF Career-Personal Development Profile (CPDP), EPPS, and Rokeach's Values Survey.

Several patterns emerged from the integrated results. Brian demonstrated a marked interest in the Enterprising and Social areas on the SII. His personality traits indicated that management and supervisory responsibilities would be a good match for him (CPDP). In the other forms, Brian indicated he had always harbored an interest in caring for children and identified in his Review of Highs that he had often thought about managing a child-care center. He expressed an interest in social work, but did not prefer the one-to-one work with clients. Using his skills and interest in business, he conducted a needs assessment for day-care facilities in the city where he lived, as well as other feasibility studies (i.e., costs, space, state regulations, staff needs). He established a center within six months. Six years later, his day-care center still is operating very sucessfully. Using his creativity, interests, and business acumen, Brian made a positive job transition.

Case 2 Helena, 23, whose mother was a physician, began college majoring in pre-medicine, but realized she did not want to go to medical school. She took some classes in theology to explore church ministry or religious education, but completed her bachelor's degree in biology. Graduate study in psychology or theology became options. After completing the vocational assessment battery, social work became the area that most clearly met all the ideas, dreams, and aspirations Helena had been able to delineate in the exercises. She identified a specific area of the country where she wanted to live and determined she wanted to study in a small private university. Using the computer-assisted Guidance Information System (GIS), she located a small university in her chosen state with a degree program in social work. She enrolled, completed her degree, and has been working in her chosen field. After four years, she is very satisfied in her work, but realizes that in the next two years she may be ready to transition into another career, one that may include more of her spiritual and religious interests.

Case 3 Thom, 20, had just finished probation for a drug-related offense. He was a high school dropout, but finished his GED. He enrolled in a community college for one year, did poorly, and had no motivation to return. Thom's father was a successful businessman. The family had always lived well. Thom wanted the lifestyle he had known, but his values and lifestyle were in direct conflict with his parents'. He had moved away from home and found a job, but wanted to decide what occupation he should pursue. From his counseling sessions and assessment information, he decided to enroll in an electronics program in a community college. He continued monthly visits as part of his support system. He achieved excellent grades and regained his self-confidence. He obtained a job using his new skills and has said he plans to complete a bachelor's degree in electrical engineering.

Case 4 Gloria, 38, came for counseling after leaving her tenth job, stating, "I could not work for these people any longer." She had recently moved to a new city to "start all over." She had a bachelor's degree, but had rarely used it in her primarily clerical jobs. She fantasized that if she had a Master's degree in a specific field, she would have more skills and could obtain a better job. The SII, the 16PF CPDP, the MBTI, and various Shepard instruments were administered to understand her continued job dissatisfaction. The patterns indicated she wanted a job that would allow her to work alone, rather than with a team or a group, and that occupational and physical therapy showed a correlation with her interests and personality. Gloria stated she was intrigued and wanted more information. While I was meeting with her to interpret the tests and develop a plan of action, I observed several indications of depression, including difficulty getting up in the morning, little or no joy in her life, loneliness, and isolation. I reported my observations to her and asked if she felt personal counseling would be helpful and offered the names of other therapists if she wanted to pursue that. I also recommended she pursue more information about occupational and physical therapy and return in two weeks. She never returned for follow-up visits. She responded to requests for payment by reporting she had moved to another city and did not feel obligated to pay the bill because she felt that my intervention had not been helpful to her.

I would not usually be so direct about personal counseling, but it seemed so clear to me that much of her unhappiness in her vocation was directly tied to her unhappiness in her personal life. I took the risk and gave her feedback on my observations, and she chose to terminate therapy. My prognosis is that unless she has dealt with her own intrapsychic processes, she is still changing jobs frequently and remains dissatisfied in her work settings.

THE LOCATION OF STUDY
OF ROBERTO CORTÉZ GONZÁLEZ

The purpose of life is not to be happy but to matter:
to be productive, to be useful, to have it make
a difference that you lived at all.
— Lesman
(*Heart Warmers,* 1991)

During the past eighteen years, I have completed my graduate training and have held positions as a university faculty member and clinical supervisor of graduate students in counseling education, in counseling psychology, and in marriage and family therapy. I am committed to providing clinical services to lower-income, disenfranchised, and Spanish-speaking populations. *Work-related issues in clinical practice* have always influenced my classroom teaching, clinical supervision, and clinical practice. I never have understood why the distinction between personal and career counseling even exists.

I focus my energies on more substantial concerns than artificial dichotomies regarding personal/career counseling. Most recently, I have been influenced by the late Michel Foucault [1926–1984] and the late Paulo Freire [1921–1997]. My primary concerns are first, the ethical issues linked to the epistemological claims (Rabinow, 1984) of vocational psychology which are based on research conducted largely on *populations of convenience;* second, the economic structures and political climates of society that dictate what gets research in the first place (Ginsburg, 1997; Knijnik, 1997); and third, the *dynamics of dominant-subordinate relationships* that characterize our race- and class-driven society (Freire, 1997), which have an incalculable impact on *educational attainment* and its related occupational development. Leong's (1995) edited text shows how little vocational psychology and career counseling has attended to these issues with multicultural and diverse populations.

In this section, I first define what I mean by location of study. Second, I briefly discuss the integration of multiple paradigms into my clinical work. Third, I tell how my comparative perspective influences my worldview. Fourth, I offer some observations on diversity in the workplace. Fifth and finally, I present a case study that demonstrates how I work. Influenced by systemic approaches, the circular and reflexive questions for use with work-related issues in clinical practice appear in Appendix 5.

Definition of Location of Study

By **location of study** (Richardson, 1993), or **situated knowledge**, I mean "a point of view, a perspective of the knower in relation to what is known" (p. 427). I work from a location of study as opposed to a framework, which connotes "a kind of scaffold or structure for organizing knowledge, questions, and so forth. . . .[A framework] is useful for organizing 'knowledge out there' and implies an independence or disconnection between the knower and the known" (p. 427).

I locate myself as a moderate postmodernist. **Moderate postmodernism** encourages substantive redefinition and innovation in the social and behavioral sciences (Rosenau, 1992). In contrast, **extreme postmodernism** "is revolutionary; it goes to the very core of what constitutes social science and radically dismisses it" (Rosenau, 1992, p. 4). I agree with Hollinger (1994) who states: "Coming to terms with postmodernism does not mean throwing out everything in the classic body of writings, but finding new ways to make old and new ideas work together in specific contexts" (p. 186). The disparate, multicultural clientele I work with requires the flexible stance of moderate postmodernism because these clients have assorted—and often incompatible—ways of knowing and existing.

An Integration of Multiple Paradigms

In my current location of study, or working model for work-related issues in clinical practice, it is clinically pragmatic to blend paradigms. *Paradigm* refers to "a central overall way of regarding phenomena . . . [and] may dictate what type of explanation will be found acceptable" (Flew, 1984, p. 261). With multicultural clientele, I am finding it increasingly functional to work with their multiple explanations for construing both their intrapersonal and interactional processes. This integration of paradigms strives to honor and respect my multicultural clients' multiple perspectives—regardless of whether these perspectives resemble the romantic, modernist, or postmodernist intellectual traditions (González, 1998).

The main priorities here are human beings and the work-related concerns they present in clinical situations, not the intellectual traditions that often are far removed from the life struggles of my clients. The value being upheld here is that of aspiring to alleviate client issues that make the integrating of paradigms desirable, sacrificing generic purity. It has become increasingly difficult for me to accept that one paradigm is any more infallible or effective than any other. I have a genuine and growing conviction that, when a client talks in romantic or modernist terms, these paradigms may be of greater relevance for clients in the particular contexts where these ways of regarding phenomena may arise. This is consistent with the multicultural perspective's recognition of the importance of client values and goals (Pedersen, 1990; Sue, 1992).

For my location of study, romantic conceptualizations of human functioning place primary emphasis on the soul, with meaning residing in the person (Gergen, 1991b, 1994b; Savickas, 1993). Modernist conceptualizations of human functioning place primary emphasis on objective knowledge and stable predispositions revealed by the scientific method, with meaning residing in the world (Gergen, 1991b; Savickas, 1993). Postmodernist conceptualizations of human functioning place primary emphasis on subjective knowledge and contextual ways of being, with the self split into multiphrenic investments, and with meaning residing in words used to interpret and inscribe various situations (Burr, 1995; Gergen, 1991a, 1991b; O'Hara & Anderson, 1991; Savickas, 1993).

Ultimately, clients have the final say in determining what works best for them. Of course, those clients who come into a first session at their wits' end will hardly be in the mood to hear that they will know what is best for themselves. From my situated knowledge, the effective ingredients of clinical practice will be driven in part by clients' aims of their stories.

In an adaptation of Lyddon (1990), romantic-based interventions are appropriate for issues about morality, the existence of the soul, the self-identification of deep internal feelings that are coming to the surface, and spiritual issues related to the world of work—such as working for an unjust employer, which we discuss in the section below on spirituality. Modernist-based interventions will be most useful for clients who require immediate symptom relief and/or prompt reestablishment of emotional equilibrium, and whose core assumptions about reality, self, and world require only peripheral adjustments in their system. Postmodernist-based interventions will be helpful with clients whose developmental life challenges are such that their core assumptions about reality, self, and world are no longer functional (Lyddon, 1990).

Mindful that postmodernism cannot replace modernism, experience and local knowledge can enrich and make unique contributions to theory and universal principles (Savickas, 1994). Given that in multicultural clinical practice, the emphasis is placed equally on the impressions that are found in both the *personal* and *social* experiences of both clinician and client (Axelson, 1993. p. 3, italics in the original), the potential, multiple dimensions of multicultural interactions in therapy are endowed with moderate, postmodern *discourse.* Some clients have an **individualistic orientation,** other clients will have a **collectivistic orientation,** and yet another subgroup of clients will have a given orientation based on context. Context may also influence the exhibit of a client's incompatible ways of knowing and existing. For example, a person may be a rational objectivist when it comes to finances, more of a postmodern perspectivist when it comes to their wide range of friends, and of staunch faith when it comes to God. Multicultural clinical relevance entails, at the very least, a tolerance for these inherently contradictory—yet human—ways of being in the world.

Moderate postmodernism allows for a retention of romantic and modernist paradigms, as well as non-Western modes of consciousness. Moderate postmodernism also concurs with Bauman (1993), who acknowledges that, "A sufficient residue of modern sentiments has been imparted to all of us by training" (pp. 33–34) and remains with us in our everyday life (O'Hara & Anderson, 1991). The multicultural perspective's emphasis on recognizing that the differences within a racial or ethnic group are often greater than differences between groups (Pedersen, 1990; Sue, 1992) also coincides with a moderate postmodern location. This location also enables a recognition that modernist variables such as race, culture, ethnicity, gender, demographics, and socioeconomic status are irreducible categories of human existence that more extreme formulations of postmodernism attempt to deconstruct. Objective social and political structures of oppression *do* exist outside the realities created—or glossed over—by language.

Sometimes, these realities are perpetuated by socially constructed, dominate discourses that serve as smoke screens to disguise **inequity** (Hare-Mustin, 1994) or by indirect talk—coded, politically laden, and sarcastic language—that aims to silence others (Capper, 1995). I strive to incorporate these considerations into multiculturally relevant clinical practice (González, 1997, 1998).

A Comparative Perspective

My location of study is powerfully influenced by the geographic area where I live. El Paso, Texas, U.S.A., and its *un*identical twin city, Juárez, Chihuahua, México, comprise "the most heavily populated metropolitan area on any international border *in the entire world*" (Draper, 1995, p. 121, italics in the original). There is no place else in the world like the El Paso/Juárez metropolitan area.

Living and working in El Paso has convinced me of the merits of situated knowledge. El Paso differs from my native San Antonio, where I grew up, attended public schools, and worked for seven years during and after my graduate work. Both cities, predominantly Hispanic and originating from the founding of Spanish Colonial missions, differ significantly, including (1) Spanish colloquial phrases and idioms, (2) climate and geography, (3) developmental histories, (4) preferences in types of Mexican music and traditional songs, (5) cooking styles, (6) names for exactly the same Mexican pastries, (7) number of institutions of higher learning, (8) average educational attainment levels, and (9) job opportunities

El Paso County has an estimated 72,750 people residing in *colonias* that lack clean drinking water and adequate sewage systems (Self, 1995), while the City of El Paso contains the third most poverty-stricken census tract in the U.S.A. (Leticia Paéz, M.A., M.P.A., personal communication, November 1, 1995). The North American Free Trade Agreement (NAFTA, effective January 1, 1994) and the devaluation of the Mexican *peso* (December 1994) have injured El Paso's economy. An estimated 8,000 El Paso workers have lost their jobs since NAFTA began, the most of any U.S. city (Flynn, 1997). Traditional job retraining programs for displaced workers often require literacy training and a high school diploma (Baake, 1997), which creates bureaucratic hurdles for some displaced workers. As I drive to work on U.S. Interstate Highway 10, I have daily views of the impoverished outskirts of Juárez, clearly evident across the Rio Grande (known as the *Río Bravo* to the *Méxicanos*). The overwhelming majority of Juárez public schools are not equipped with the educational technologies of social saturation of which Gergen (1991b, 1994b) writes. In co-authoring this book, I have increasingly wondered how traditional theories of vocational development pertain to the community where I reside. **Localized knowledge**, a moderate postmodern adaptation of traditional modernist theories, has become more a part of how I work because of what I have read and where I live.

For the past three years, in the name of the University of Texas at El Paso, I have conducted personal supervision of Master's interns and provided clinical services for so-called nontraditional populations at no charge in a field-based educational setting. A strictly enforced attendance and appointment cancellation policy minimizes the problem of no-shows, premature terminations, and keeps the waiting list to less than three months. More than half of the clients are low-income and Spanish-speaking. Socioeconomic levels range from public-assisted fixed-income to professional class. Some of these clients live in *colonias*. All clinical forms are in Spanish and English; intake forms do not ask for place of birth or citizenship status.

I am licensed in Texas as a psychologist. In my clinical work, I see all kinds of clients except substance abusers and those with eating disorders. My caseload has ranged in age from four to eighty-two. Currently, I see individuals, couples, and families, and have extensive group experience. The role of work in my client's lives is a regular theme. Personal and social constructions of reality form a basis for my clinical work, which is influenced by cognitive-behavioral, social learning, systemic, and constructivist approaches. But, I have learned from lower-income clients who talk in a **casual register** that their stories do not always match the three prototypical narrative forms identified by Gergen and Gergen (1984):

1. **Progressive narratives** enhance progress toward a clinical goal.
2. **Regressive narratives** impede progress toward a clinical goal.
3. **Stability narratives** produce no change and neither enhance nor impede progress toward a clinical goal.

There is not always a sense of connectedness or coherence to my low-income clients' stories, and I must intervene to keep them on track. Sometimes, my clients talk in what I call **diversionary narratives**, which enable them to remain comfortable when the going gets rough as we progress toward a clinical goal. Other times, clients talk in what I call **incidental narratives**, which inadvertently reveal crucial pieces of information ("Oh, by the way" bombs) as we progress toward a clinical goal. At the same time, when my clients talk in a casual register and I respond in the same, or when I can engage them directly in their preferred Spanish, I have entered more deeply into their world than someone who talks like an academician (**formal register**) or who cannot speak Spanish.

Case Example

Cristina, 35, was a bilingual Mexican American, married for eighteen years with three teen-aged children. She had worked full-time for many years as a seamstress in her younger sister Carlota's bridal shop. Of all their brothers and sisters, Carlota was always "the go-getter" in the family; Cristina "the responsible one."

Originally, Cristina came to therapy grieving the death of her mother. I used a romantic paradigm as we discussed her mother's soul being at rest and everlasting life. As Cristina's grief receded, work-related issued came to the fore.

On one hand, Cristina described her job in Carlota's shop as better than working for the garment industry. At least Cristina was not stuck at the same sewing machine all day long, and she had never been laid off by Carlota. Cristina sewed several wedding gowns and bridesmaids' dresses from patterns, hand-stitched lace and appliqués onto wedding veils, and was present for brides' final fittings. She was often invited to the weddings themselves, and attended as many as she could with her husband and family. She especially liked seeing the results of her work. She was very skilled at what she did.

On the other hand, Cristina was tired of working for her sister. Carlota was charming and outgoing to her customers, but impatient and demanding with her employees. Cristina described it as working for Dr. Jekyll and Mr. Hyde. I asked her what she did when Carlota got impatient and demanding [reflexive, observer-perspective question/to explore interpersonal reaction]. Usually, Cristina became quiet, kept a low profile, and just tried to ignore her sister.

Whenever Cristina asked for time off to take one of her children to the doctor or to attend one of their school-related activities, Carlota would sigh dramatically. As Cristina put it, Carlota did not actually say no, but her sighs showed her disapproval. Yet, Carlota dropped everything when her only child was ill or had a school-related activity. I asked Cristina what it meant when Carlota dropped everything for her only child [circular, categorized context questions/examining relationship between meaning and action]. Cristina admitted to perceiving Carlota as a self-centered person who just used people.

More broadly, Cristina voiced discontent with always doing so much for other people. Being "the responsible one" was weighing her down. She was becoming emotionally exhausted and feeling taken for granted. Cristina revealed that, as a full-time employee, she did not even have medical insurance through her job. To save Carlota money, Cristina was covered by her husband's workplace medical plan. When I asked where the belief came from that she should always do so much for others, Cristina replied that her religion taught her this was the right thing to do. I have seen many clients with the same belief. If they are Bible readers, I refer them to 2 Corinthians 8: 13-14, "I do not mean that others should be eased and you burdened, but that as a matter of equality your abundance at the present time should supply their want, so that their abundance may supply your want, that there may be equality." Sometimes, clients who give so much of themselves find they are in chronically unequal relationships. I encourage clients to decide these matters for themselves.

Cristina was toying with the idea of "doing something different" with her life. She mused about getting her GED, and then maybe going to community college "before it was too late." I asked Cristina to describe what she would do if Carlota became upset about her plans [reflexive, future-oriented question/potential catastrophic expectations]. Cristina was more concerned about her husband's and children's reaction than with Carlota's. I asked Cristina who in her immediate family would think getting her GED was a good idea? Who would think this second most strongly? [circular, categorical differences question between beliefs]. Cristina responded anxiously to these questions, unsure how her immediate family would react.

Cristina's husband, Gabe, and their three children came to a session for what I informally called a "one-shot consultation." I asked them for their understandings about why Cristina was coming to therapy, and for their opinions about her job at Carlota's. Gabe and the children all understood that Cristina was coming to therapy because she was grieving her mother, and they had noticed that Cristina seemed to be doing better in this respect. They were mildly surprised when Cristina told them she had also been discussing work at Carlota's, but they were unanimous that Cristina should leave the shop if she wanted. They were glad Carlota—nosy and bossy—knew nothing about Cristina coming to therapy. Gabe had been employed for many years at a dairy and was used to his wife's working outside the home. He was more supportive about Cristina getting her GED than she thought he would be, but he did have some reservations about her getting another job where there were other men around (there were no male employees in Carlota's bridal shop). Cristinas's eldest daughter, a forthright young woman, thought it would be terrific if she and her mother got their high school diplomas at the same time.

While Gabe and the children were present, I casually handed Cristina a Self-Directed Search (Holland, 1985) with an Occupation Finder. I had allies in Gabe and the children. I invited Cristina to take the SDS home and fill it out when she had the chance. She had a busy life between work and family, and I did not want to rush her. It turns out I did not have to.

Soon after, Cristina informed Carlota that she would be cutting back at work to serve only the close family members of previous clients. Carlota sighed dramatically, but Cristina held her ground. As a compromise, Carlota requested that Cristina be available full-time during the months of May and June, their busiest time of the year. To keep the peace in the extended family, Cristina agreed to Carlota's request. Cristina began her GED classes at her daughter's high school as soon as they became available.

Meanwhile, we discussed the results of her SDS. I like to give my clients a chance for narrative responses to any assessment results (Jones & Thorne, 1987). I asked

Cristina, "What was it like to answer this questionnaire? How correct do you think these results are? Do the results describe the way you see yourself? Which occupations sound like something you would like to do? Which occupational suggestions are a surprise for you?" Using the RIASEC hexagon and the DOT, we discussed in detail the qualities of and qualifications for several occupations. Contextualing the results to Cristina's geographic region, we looked at course offerings at the local community college and explored the local job market for various occupations.

Cristina's work-related clinical issues consisted of many facets, including family issues—with both individualism and collectivism as considerations. From an individualistic orientation, Cristina had a lot of things going for her: naturally bright, bi-lingual, motivated, with an accomplished work record of which she could feel proud. When Cristina had to, she could stand up to Carlota. From a collectivist orientation, to keep peace in the extended family, Cristina agreed to be available full-time in Carlota's shop during May and June. Gabe and the children were supportive of her—sometimes loved ones are not—although Gabe did have some reservations about where she would work next. As he told Cristina, he did not mistrust her, but other men in the world of work. I told Gabe I could educate Cristina about **sexual harassment** and how to deal with it, and invited him to come back with her for that session. The chance for Cristina to respond narratively to the SDS results—a solid, modernist-based assessment instrument—and the contextualizing of her next move according to her own time availability and local offerings, show moderate postmodernist clinical interventions.

Diversity in the Workplace

I was struck by some remarks about workplace diversity made by actor Eriq LaSalle, who plays Dr. Benton on NBC's *ER*. He says women and minority members have to hold themselves to a higher standard in the workplace (Zaslow, 1995). LaSalle, an African American, recounts a dinner he had a few years ago with a movie studio executive, a White man. The executive confessed to being an underachiever, skipping classes in college, and failing courses. Still, because he was gregarious around other White men, "out of college [the executive] was given one major position after another. I don't see women or minorities in situations like that." LaSalle says, "You've got to work, work, work to show you can do the job" (p. 14). My own professional experience has taught me that members of the dominant culture with mediocre ability often land major positions. As a feminist woman friend and colleague tells me, "White men don't have to be bright to get ahead." If only more bright women and minorities knew this, especially those from the lower-income classes, then perhaps their perceived *academic* and *occupational self-efficacy* would increase.

The quality of K–12 education has future ramifications for diversity in the workplace. Ginsburg (1997) captures some of what I have seen clinically with children from lower-income families:

Johnny fails in school not solely or primarily because he is dumb, but because of the motivation linked to his implicit beliefs concerning his place in the class and caste system, because of the way in which he is treated by teachers whose choice of profession is itself influenced by the class system and by social expectations concerning sex roles, and because of political-economic factors beyond his control that place him in a jobless family with few material resources. Education is a socio-political phenomenon as much as a psychological issue. The espousal of a narrowly psychological perspective is naïve (p. 149).

I would like to see vocational psychology articulate a more explicit socio-political perspective. Until then, it is way too soon to talk about convergence of vocational theories (Savickas & Lent, 1994). I would also like to see all teacher education and educational administration majors be required to take a course in occupational development from a socio-political perspective. From what I have seen during the school visits I make to my supervisees and on behalf of my child clients, the achievement expectations that teachers and administrators convey to students have a more powerful impact than many school personnel realize. A school counseling intern of mine taught art at a middle school. One day after school, her principal stopped by her classroom, examined the students' artwork exhibited on the classroom walls, then told her that the art students showed great promise as future jailhouse artists! Such unprofessional and disrespectful attitudes among school personnel are more prevalent than most people care to admit.

Similar attitudes about workplace diversity pertain to that messy issue of *affirmative action*. Vocational practitioners need to acquaint themselves with both sides of the debate (Bergmann, 1996; Carter, 1991; Curry, 1996; Eastland, 1997). In the discourse of the affirmation action debate, I never hear mentioned how talented *women* and *people of color* who work hard to show they are qualified to do the job simultaneously arouse the envy and jealousy of less gifted members of the dominant culture. Dedicated, talented women and people of color are often a threat in the workplace. A sense of mission is even more threatening to those who have coasted along in *privileged complacency*. This can make for a hostile work environment, with those least confident in their *occupational self-efficacy* doing the most political maneuvering. Cherniss (1995) writes that human service training programs need to do more to prepare their students for these types of workplace political realities to enhance *professional self-efficacy* and prevent *burnout*. Based on my years of teaching, supervising, clinical work, and constant reading, I strive to raise issues about these political realities in the classroom.

To complete our discussion of theories, Table 7.4 is a comparison of the theories presented which allows for a quick contrast of them.

While the trait and factor, foremost counseling, developmental, and social learning and career decision theories have influenced vocational psychology practice, less attention has been given to family and parental influences. We will attempt to discover the effects family has on career paths and choices in Chapter 8.

TABLE 7.4 Comparison of Major Career Theories

CAREER THEORY AND THEORIST(S)	KEY CONCEPTS	COUNSELING GOALS	TECHNIQUES	ASSESSMENT INSTRUMENTS
Trait and Factor	Personal characteristics and job characteristics can be assessed and matched to help in job/career selection	Understand relationship of personal and occupational factors and how these affect occupational decision-making; in groups, brainstorming can be used to identify more options	Complete battery of tests, interpret results, and develop profile	KOIS CSII SII Values Scale VS CPI 16PF MBTI GATB ASVAB DAT
Holland Typology	Develop congruency in one's view of self and occupational preference	Advise and direct goal setting strategies to assist people to develop self-knowledge, occupational information; and make a match between personal traits and job requirements	Learn to use resource center, including DOT, COH, Dictionary of Holland Occupational Codes, Occupations Finder	SDS VPI SII MBTI Strong/MBTI workbook, computerized versions
Theory of Work Adjustment Dawis Lofquist	Identifying traits and factors of an individual and matching with job requirements and reinforcers; contains 18 theoretical propositions	Assist the individual in career selection based on work needs; can also be applied to work adjustment and retirement issues; matching abilities, values, and reinforcers	Complete assessment instruments, including abilities, values, interests, and personality style	GATB MIQ MJDQ MOCS

Developmental Life-Span Ginsberg Super	Occupational choice is a developmental process that is finalized in stages over one's life span	Understand the stage development of the client as well as career maturity; determine appropriate interventions based on the stage; determine an occupational plan based on this information. Groups emphasize various roles, levels of involvement, self-concept, and occupational choices.	Assist in a client's mastery of tasks for current developmental stage, i.e. self-concept, development of interests, competencies, balancing of various roles, identifying values	Values Scale Salience Inventory CDI ACCI CSII
Tiedeman O'Hara	Career development is a continuous process of evaluation of ego identity, completing developmental tasks, and decision making	Assist in self-awareness as part of decision-making process, including ego differentiation and integration; moving on to occupational awareness; and then to implementation and adjustment	Evaluate processes involved in decision-making exercises	
Miller-Tiedeman Tiedeman	Constructive-development, life is a learning process, client constructs own reality. Life career theory comes from internal frame of reference, predominantly existential.	Understand process as developmental and decision-making strategy; realize internal frame of reference	Narrative and interactional approaches; help client search within to find career direction	

Continued

TABLE 7.4 Comparison of Major Career Theories (*continued*)

CAREER THEORY AND THEORIST(S)	KEY CONCEPTS	COUNSELING GOALS	TECHNIQUES	ASSESSMENT INSTRUMENTS
Circumscription and Compromise Gottfredson	Occupational preferences emerge from physical and mental growth; socioeconomic background and intellectual level strongly influence self concept, narrowing of alternatives, predicts gender influences on occupational preferences, hypothesizes circumscription and compromise as necessary because of accessibility of occupations	Process includes self-concept, occupational imaging, cognitive maps of occupations, compatibility of occupations, space-range of alternatives, narrowing choices, and compromise	Use imaging and cognitive procedures	
Self-Efficacy Bandura Best	Perceived judgments of one's capacity to successfully perform a given task or behavior	Learn areas of strength and belief in ability to accomplish tasks or behavior	Use self-efficacy measurements	Career Decision-Making Self-Efficacy Scale (CDMSES)
Social Learning Krumboltz Mitchell Gelatt	Career decisions are significantly influenced by life events, including genetic endowments, special abilities, environmental conditions and events, learning experiences, and task approach skills	Explore life events and the impact on decision-making, use specific models to improve skill building. Can use small group learning experiences in helping individuals make career decisions.	Use role models, shadowing, mentoring, work cooperatives, practicum/internships	DECIDES Career Beliefs Inventory CDM Self-Efficacy Scales

Decision-Making Model Gelatt	Decision-making model that provides a framework that can be used as guideline in career counseling programs and a system to determine values; series of decisions include immediate, intermediate, and future.	Complete five-step process so client can make a decision	Decision & Outcomes (workbook for high school students); Positive Uncertainty (workbook for both high school students and adults)
Sequential Elimination Approach Gali	Purpose is to identify a set of career options that are compatible with the individual's preferences	To use a step-by-step procedure to eliminate those options that are not compatible with the preferences and follow nine steps outlined; guide and teach an individual career decision making	Use clearly defined steps
Cognitive Information Processing Sampson Peterson Reardon Lenz	Concerned with thought and memory process for solving career problems and making career decisions. Success more likely when client acknowledges, defines, solves, and acts. Domains include knowledge, decision-making skills, and executive functioning.	Develop self and occupational knowledge; develop decision-making skills through use of CASVE; identify dysfunctional metacognitions; define problems; formulate goals; develop individual learning plan. Can be used with computers, with graduate level course, or with a group.	Initial interview; preliminary assessment; identify interests, skills; write an autobiography; list likes, dislikes; look for themes; storytelling; gathering information; teach CASVE paradigm; use computer guidance system; confront dysfunctional beliefs; use relaxation, guided imagery	Career Thoughts Inventory with workbook CAI SII KOIS SDS

Continued

TABLE 7.4 Comparison of Major Career Theories (*continued*)

CAREER THEORY AND THEORIST(S)	KEY CONCEPTS	COUNSELING GOALS	TECHNIQUES	ASSESSMENT INSTRUMENTS
Social Cognitive Career Theory Lent Brown Hackett	Emphasizes cognitive processes and individual belief systems that affect behavior. Building blocks are self-efficacy, outcome expectations, and personal goals.	Encourage involvement in activities, learning new skills, setting goals, and developing plan of action; can be used as group model	Similar to social learning, but emphasis on broadening awareness of opportunities for women and ethnic minorities	May use interest inventories, other assessment tools as needed
Integrative Life Planning Hansen	A way of seeing self and the world. Incorporates totality of life. Examine society in its forms. Redefine family. Understand choices and decisions in a social context.	Find work that needs doing in a changing global context. Weave life into a meaningful whole. Connect family and work. Value pluralism and diversity. Explore spirituality and purpose. Manage transitions and change.	Develop collectivistic orientation. Develope a worldview. Consider well-being of others. Find the path to meaning.	
Family/Parental Influence Roe	System based on the parental style of child rearing and its influence on occupational choices, uses Maslow's needs, genetic endowment, and biological factors	Goal is to help set patterns that are helpful to developmental life goals; Understand parental influence on career decision-making	Dramatize family roles, formulate family constellation genogram, life review exercises, structured interviews, autobiographies	World of Work (ACT) Interest Inventory, Interest and Values Inventories The Parent Child Relations Questionnaire II

8

❖

Family and Systemic Influences
on Occupational Choice

Just think: Your family are the people
most likely to give you the flu.

—Edith Ann
(Wagner, 1994, p. 126)

In Chapter 5, we met Edith Ann, the little girl who dispenses pearls of wisdom from her oversized rocking chair like a guru perched on a mountaintop. Edith Ann is an astute observer of family life. Families can give you more than just the flu. Sometimes, families inspire us to go into a particular line of work. Family influences on occupational choice are receiving greater attention in vocational psychology, although the notion that the role work plays in people's lives is affected by their family-of-origin is hardly new.

We begin this chapter with traditional family systems approaches to occupations. Then we look at work-family conflict, dual-career families, and single-parent families. Next, we examine the recent phenomenon known as the postmodern family as it applies to the workplace. Finally, we offer some observations on incorporating a systemic approach into vocational psychology.

We'd like readers to understand that in instances where we've retained references from the 1980s and 1990s, we believe those original citations are still useful for the points we wish to convey. We saw little need to cite later references that rehash points that were effectively presented in the first place. Some things haven't changed much.

We'd also like to recommend to our readers the 2001 special issue of the *Career Planning and Adult Development Journal* (Gelardin) on family influences on career choice and success.

The nuclear family was once the predominant type in the United States. Today, the breadwinner father and stay-at-home mother comprise less than 3 percent of American families; 60 percent of families have dual earners (Barnett & Rivers, 1996). The U.S. Department of Education, National Center for Education Statistics (no date, cited in *Single Parent Central*, 2004a), indicates that 88 percent of children whose mothers have full-time work receive child care or early education from a nonparent. Given these changes in our families and in the role of work, this chapter is designed to help practitioners realize the influence families have in occupational development.

Family and culture determine career selection or, even more basic, whether one intentionally chooses a career. Incorporating the individual's operational definition of family (sometimes extended family) is an important point to consider in examining the family life cycle in relation to career issues. Incorporating cultural sensitivity in the relationship with a client increases the possibility that an effective, individually tailored strategy will be developed. If a counselor lacks knowledge founded in the client's worldview and if there is not a culturally appropriate approach, counseling efforts can easily be ineffective. Multicultural families and their relationship to career development are affected by several factors, including socioeconomic status, language barriers, generational conflicts, and perception of employment discrimination. White families have determined the characteristics currently dominant in society —task, success, and future orientation. Other characteristics include rugged individualism, hard work, and stoicism (Evans, Rotter, & Gold, 2002).

TRADITIONAL FAMILY SYSTEMS APPROACHES TO OCCUPATIONAL DEVELOPMENT

Numerous laypeople seem to know intuitively that their decisions, conflicts, priorities, and outlooks have been heavily influenced by their families-of-origin. Practitioners are well aware of family influences on self-esteem, maturity, motivation, and resources. For many of us, whether layperson or practitioner, our most significant others are our families. What is the best way to address family influence in vocational psychology?

Family systems approaches are fundamentally different from traditional vocational psychology approaches. Systemic approaches to clinical practice focus on interactions *between* individuals. Traditional vocational psychology approaches focus on interactions *within* an individual. A full discussion of theories of marriage and family therapy is beyond the scope of this chapter. A vocational practitioner may want to further explore systems theory by reviewing the classic work of von Bertalanffy (1968). The list of primary references in Becvar and Becvar (1996) is another useful resource. In this section, we explore several categories of family systems: family-of-origin, family configurations, socioeconomic effects on family functioning, genograms, dual-career and single-parent families, and postmodern families.

Family-of-Origin

Family-of-origin is used by psychodynamic family theorists and therapists to examine interactions between couples; however, it has been rarely applied to relationships in the workplace (Weinberg & Mauksch, 1991). Family-of-origin can have a very strong influence on all aspects of life. The rules that govern what behaviors are appropriate in a given setting are learned at a young age and can partly be determined by socioeconomic status, sex-role socialization, and ethnicity. In terms of occupational development, culturally learned expectations and values and family-of-origin influences can be great or small. Workers can play roles in their job sites that they played in their families while growing up. The concept of **organizational transference** whereby a boss or co-worker represents an important family member to an employee is especially intriguing (Weinberg & Mauksch, 1991). The employee can project unresolved issues with a family member onto the boss or co-worker.

Cultural influences (which may be traditional, modern, or postmodern) on the family-of-origin determine the method used to deal with issues. Throughout life, traditional family lifestyles emphasize close ties to family and community. Modern family lifestyles emphasize individual competition and assign great importance to science in explaining the mysteries of life. Postmodern family lifestyles emphasize that each member may be in a different groove, lacking the sense, therefore, that the family is moving in a common direction (discussed at the end of this chapter).

Family-of-origin and expectations are closely related. A young person beginning to think in terms of life planning is affected by modeling and expectations from the family, the parents' educational levels, and the importance of a career/vocation versus a job. Parents who are interested and involved in their child's life naturally have a different kind of influence than parents who are uninterested and uninvolved. By demonstrating interest in their own career and life planning, parents are influencing their children to place importance on these issues as well. Parental and peer influences are powerful and are instrumental in shaping ambitions more directly and with greater impact than are scholastic aptitude, previous academic achievement, or social origin. These influences continue to be relevant today.

Although peer pressure is one of the most influential factors in a child's life, researchers have found that the family has an even greater impact. Parents have more influence on their child's occupational and educational aspirations than do their friends. Significant others' aspirations also directly influence a child's own aspiration. Children who perceive that their parents have high aspirations for them will be more successful than those whose parents have low aspirations for their children. This is especially applicable for adolescents who use their parents' perception of them as the framework for the development of self-perception.

Family background is a factor in a person's lack of vocational aspiration and inability to make a decision. When faced with this situation, career development specialists need to assess the sources that impede motivation, for example, family atmosphere and relationships. A person's relationship with parents and/or siblings can have a negative impact on vocational aspirations. A vocational practitioner (with client's authorization) may choose to corroborate a client's report on family situations by consulting with at least one of the client's family members.

Although she doesn't use the term *family-of-origin,* Jacobsen (1999) uses the term **hand-me-down dreams** to refer to

1. the goals, interests, and behaviors that families both encouraged and discouraged, ignored, and punished.
2. the values about work, money, success, and happiness that families conveyed.
3. the roles and rules applied to different family members.

Not all of these were necessarily made explicit. Jacobsen believes that families are often a hidden source of career-related problems. Among the manifestations of these problems are:

- Feeling stuck in a disliked job
- Stagnating career
- Experiencing chronic conflict with bosses, peers, and supervisees
- Feeling confused or hopeless about finding the *right* career
- Feeling unmotivated or fearful of change, even when one knows what career one wants to pursue
- Feeling confused about one's goals despite having consulted career books, vocational practitioners, career counselors, and interest inventories
- Feeling taken advantage of by bosses or colleagues and wanting to learn why and what to do
- Feeling as if one hasn't had a career, just a series of jobs
- Believing that one is working at less than one's full potential
- Feeling trapped by one's responsibilities and resigned to not really *living* until one retires
- Feeling afraid of repeating one's parents' lives without intending or wanting to
- Taking care of people at work just like one does at home
- Ensuring that one's child follows his or her own career path, rather than echoing a parent's

The next three paragraphs refer to these ideas from Jacobsen's book, *Hand-Me-Down Dreams,* unless otherwise indicated.

Messages that children receive from parents about duty, genes, and destiny are what starts the cycle of hand-me-down dreams. Duty refers to an obligation toward others' expectations for a particular action or achievement. It is a moral imperative not to be confused with or distorted into the parents' need to choose college majors or occupations for their children. Adults resist connecting childhood duties with their career choices because as adults they (1) want to see themselves as self-reliant, (2) don't want to show disrespect toward parents by exposing parents' emotional needs beneath parents' definition of duty, and (3) may have already obtained good jobs, earned money, and made their parents proud—they don't want to cause trouble for their aging parents. Career counselors may need to help clients discover what the client wants, not what others expect from the them, and help clients define duty in their own ways in order to make career decisions and plans accordingly.

Genes are used by some parents to suggest that children are genetically predisposed to select certain occupations. These suggestions of predictable and repetitive roles give a family a sense of distinctive, inherited identity and coherence. These suggestions also become emotional expectations and prescriptions for how one should behave and how one will be perceived within the family. Consequently, adults may grow up not being seen as themselves and often choose a career based on the need for family continuity. Jacobsen provided exercises to help clients discover their own uniqueness.

Destiny can be an overwhelming force when families believe that God, good or bad luck, the stars, social and economic oppressions, or any combination thereof, make a child's career choice unnecessary or irrelevant. Here the family's emotional need is disguised as prophecy. Adult clients will be faced with the challenge of redefining their destiny, choosing their own work, and learning what one feels *called* to do from within to express one's own talents and fulfill one's own purposes. Jacobsen has an exercise to help one discern his or her own calling—vocation. She goes on to discuss

1. how indirect and unspoken requests are communicated by parents to children, even when parents don't want that to happen.

2. how parents can continue to be demanding even when their children fulfill parental expectations.

3. family systems and how they can convey misguided assumptions about family love and loyalty.

4. why rebellion against parents doesn't work.

5. birth order and gender considerations.

6. multicultural applications.

7. how unresolved issues from one's family-of-origin manifest themselves in the workplace.

Both of us highly recommend Jacobsen's book to vocational practitioners and readers who want to learn more about unwanted family influence on career paths.

Intact or Nuclear Families

Pipher (1996) captures the essence of the traditional, intact nuclear family with the Irish proverb, "It is in the shelter of each other that people live." Couples in nuclear families will ultimately address work responsibilities in the occupational domains and the division of labor in the familial/personal domains (Richardson, 1993). As the nature of work changes, recent research has focused on **work-family conflict** and the negative effects on an individual's health. There are three forms of work-family conflict:

1. **time-based conflict**—time can only be spent on one role, which neglects the other roles
2. **strain-based conflict**—stress from one role effects all areas of performance
3. **behavior-based conflict**— behavioral styles are not compatible throughout all roles (Greenhaus & Beutell, 1985).

Most of the past research focused on women, because they were considered the primary caretakers of a family. However, as men become more involved in the family, more study is needed on how work-family conflict affects men (Barnett & Rivers, 1996). Conflicts arise when a person's values are in direct opposition to one another. For example, women's dilemma is often that they want to work in order to help support the family, but not at the cost of caring for and nurturing the children. Men's dilemma is often that they realize the importance of their family, but they also have to deal with the values of success associated with the male identity (Voydanoff, 1988). In studies related to marital and job satisfaction, flexibility, skills in negotiation/ compromise, a couple's joint self-esteem, and ability to assess problems were all important variables (Derr, 1986; Meeks, Arnkoff, & Glass, 1986; Rachlin & Hansen, 1985). Consider the pressures to separate work and family life.

When Michigan State University researchers surveyed 95 supervisors and 300 employees at two big multinational corporations, they found that 85 percent were doing some work at home—often without their supervisor's knowledge. The least stressed: workers who established clear boundaries between the office and family life. The most stressed: multi-taskers who tried to integrate job and personal life. 'Work is a powerful force that can take over our personal lives, pulling us in many directions at once,' says study author Ellen Kossek, Ph.D., a labor and industrial relations expert (Harrar & Dollemore, 2003, p. 46).

Families with young children will have to arrange for child care when both parents work full time. Most marital conflict at this stage revolves around child care for dual-earner couples (Carter & McGoldrick, 1989). The Children's Defense Fund (no date, cited in Single Parent Central, 2004a, p. 1) says the cost of full-time day care is prohibitive, potentially costing as much as college tuition at a public university. One of three families with young children has income totaling less than $25,000 per year. According to the National Center for Community Education (no date, cited in Single Parent Central, 2004a), 78 percent of mothers with 6–13 year olds work full time. Approximately 15 million children are left unsupervised from 3:00 P.M. to 8:00 P.M., during which time juvenile crime triples. More often than not, responsibility for arranging for child care falls upon the wife. Couples who jointly undertake this responsibility are in the distinct minority. Child care arrangements for dual-earner marriages are most often seen as a women's issue. Child care arrangements will continue to be a women's issue unless fathers realize their own emotional health suffers when they fail to see child care as a men's issue as much as a family issue. Fathers need to begin voicing requests in the workplace for satisfactory provision of family needs (Barnett & Rivers, 1996).

It is little wonder that the highest rate of divorce occurs at this point in a nuclear family's life (Carter & McGoldrick, 1989). The U.S. Census Bureau (no date, cited in Single Parent Central, 2004c) indicates that 2.5 million people divorce each year. In these divorces, in nineteen states reporting custody, 72 percent of cases had child custody awarded to the mother, and 12 percent to the father. In 16 percent, joint custody was awarded. The Census Bureau and the Department of Human Services (April 1999, cited in Single Parent Central, 2004b) state that the 7 million noncustodial parents who owed child support in 1995 had a greater tendency to make payments if they had been awarded joint custody or visitation rights.

The transformation of the family system during adolescence may make the occupational self-concept vulnerable to negative feedback and needless neglect, especially for teenage females (Gilligan & Noel, 1995; Orenstein, 1994; Pipher, 1994; Sadker & Sadker, 1994; Taylor, Gilligan, & Sullivan, 1995). Common adolescent symptoms (drug and alcohol abuse, teenage pregnancy, delinquency/gang membership) also need to be assessed and addressed (Carter & McGoldrick, 1989). These symptoms cannot be artificially separated out from occupational development. Midlife career changes due to forced layoffs and downsizing can be extremely stressful to parents with adolescent children (Bragg, 1996b).

The *empty nest* is the most problematic because it is the newest and longest phase (Carter & McGoldrick, 1989). The *empty nest syndrome* can leave one or both parents at a loss for what to do with their time. Mothers who have focused most of their energies on their children may have to change their lifestyle but feel unprepared to face the world of work. Fathers who have focused most of their energies on work may regret not spending enough time with their now departing children. At least twenty years of work life may still be available for both parents. The potential exists for disruption and disintegration of the parental couple or for moving into uncharted possibilities—new careers, continued education, hobbies, travel, and a more balanced lifestyle.

Families in later life may have to deal with adjustments to retirement (Carter & McGoldrick, 1989). This can create a vacuum for the retired worker and can strain previously existing balances in marriages. Financial insecurity and dependence are another set of issues to be dealt with, and can be particularly difficult for those who have been long accustomed to self-reliance during their working years. In family-owned businesses, elderly parents may sometimes be reluctant to hand over the reigns of power. At the other extreme, some formerly industrious parents may become completely dependent on their grown children. Status changes as a result of aging can affect men and women differently and should be closely monitored.

Vocational psychology can transform itself in part by giving increased consideration to a family life cycle perspective. In many current articles, there is recognition of the importance of families. The extent to which companies and their CEOs will advocate for work-family issues remains unascertained.

> Although still uncommon, more companies are developing work-life and after-school programs that focus on the needs of parents with older children, including "tweens" ages 10 to 13 and teenagers. Companies are stepping up to fill the gap by providing flexible work hours, funding for community after-school programs, and in rare cases, creating options for older kids in on-site day-care centers.
>
> Because job demands make it impossible for parents to beat the kids home from school, for many parents after-school arrangements are essential. But quality programs—those with an educational as well as a recreational component—are harder to find than day-care options for younger children (Taylor, 2003, no page number given).

Phyllis Moen of Cornell University's Employment and Family Careers Institute (cited in Keller, 2000) found that employees who described their jobs as demanding or who reported job insecurity were less able to achieve a work/family balance, whereas those with job autonomy and a supportive supervisor fared better.

NONTRADITIONAL FAMILIES

Divorced Families

Census Bureau and Department of Human Services statistics (April 1999, cited in *Single Parent Central*, 2004b) indicate that 32 percent of parents who went without receipt of child support payments (awarded to them in 1995) were poor. In 1995, it is estimated that 5.9 million custodial parents made 13 million contacts with a child support enforcement office or other governmental agency for one or more services related to child support issues.

A major dislocation in family life can occur with divorce (Carter & McGoldrick, 1989). Work performance can suffer for both men and women during the divorce and its aftermath. Homemakers who are compelled to re-enter the workforce for financial reasons may have issues related to low self-confidence, rusty job-related skills, lack of knowledge of job search and decision-making skills, and reactions of family and friends (Betz, 1994). Our clinical experience has shown that a woman re-entering the workforce is more vulnerable to sexual harassment, especially if it is known that she is recently separated or divorced. Child support and custody issues can take a heavy emotional and financial toll, and the latter can distort the role of work in one's life. Because the man's potential earning power is often greater than the woman's, states with no-fault divorce contribute to the so-called feminization of poverty.

Step Families

Divorce is not the only instance when family life requires restabilization to proceed developmentally. Remarriage and the blending of families have their own prerequisite attitudes and developmental issues. Remarried families can take either a step up or a step down in socioeconomic level. When both parents remarry, children have to learn two sets of rules and navigate two sets of lifestyles as they travel back and forth between mom's house and dad's house. Refusal to cooperate on financial arrangements can have an adverse impact on children caught in the middle. Our clinical experience has taught us that when academic and behavioral problems develop out of children's response to divorce and remarriage, these problems should be attended to immediately because they can have long-term implications for educational attainment and occupational development.

Low-Income Families

Proctor and Dalaker (2003) report that in 2002, 10 percent of all White people in the United States lived below the poverty level, as did 10 percent of all Asian people, 22 percent of all Hispanic people, and 24 percent of all Black people. The official poverty rate rose from 11.7 percent in 2001 to 12.1 percent in 2002 or from 32.9 million people to 34.6 million people. This increase occurred despite welfare reform, which we address in Chapter 10.

When a first pregnancy occurs to an adolescent daughter from a low-income family, her educational attainment and occupational development can be adversely affected (Fulmer, 1989). A second teenage pregnancy further impedes upward mobility. A daughter from a professional family who concentrates on pregnancy prevention is free to focus on earning an undergraduate and graduate degree, while continually gaining more independence from her parents and developing a professional identity of her own. The teenage mother from a low-income family is more likely to (1) acquire adult status at an earlier age, (2) marry and divorce, (3) maintain connections with her kinship network, and (4) become a grandmother at an earlier age than her female counterpart from a professional family. She is also likely to experience ongoing financial stress.

Helping young people and adults from low-income families to maximize their occupational achievement remains a largely unmet challenge for vocational psychology. Ironically, low-income families could benefit most from occupational guidance and information. Such attention would both refine and revise traditional theories of vocational *choice* for applicability to a broader population. And yet in many inner city schools, relatively few resources are available for students to learn about occupations through modeling, mentoring, computer-based information, or life experiences.

Hidden rules and **unspoken cues** characterize different socioeconomic classes (Payne, 1995). Patterns of thought, social interaction, and cognitive strategies are part of hidden rules. Given that schools and businesses operate from middle-class norms, students from poverty must be explicitly taught those middle-class habits to help them succeed in school and in the world of work. **Generational poverty** refers to families that have lived in poverty for two or more generations. Situational poverty refers to families that have lived in poverty for a shorter time due to circumstances such as death, illness, or divorce. Major differences, based on more than money, exist between those in generational poverty and the middle class. Payne defines poverty as "the extent to which an individual does without resources" (p. 15), and identifies these resources as financial, emotional, mental, spiritual, physical, support systems, role models, and knowledge of hidden rules.

Financial resources, having money and purchasing power, when taken alone fail to explain why some individuals leave or remain in poverty. **Emotional resources**—the ability to exercise self-control and the possession of the stamina to weather negative situations and feelings—are the most necessary to move up from one class to the other. **Mental resources**, having the abilities and skills (e.g., reading, writing, computing) to process information and use it to negotiate daily life, lead to self-sufficiency. **Spiritual resources,** believing in a higher power that provides guidance and an understanding for life's purpose, helps one seeing oneself not as hopeless but rather as capable, worthy, and valuable. **Physical resources,** being able-bodied and mobile, lead to self-sufficiency. Another resource, **support systems,** having friends and family who have valuable knowledge to share and will back up a person in times of need, is external in nature. **Role models,** knowing and having access to adults who are nurturing and appropriate in their behavior toward children and who do not demonstrate habitually self-destructive behavior, are particularly helpful in teaching one how to live one's life emotionally.

Knowledge of hidden rules, having an awareness of the unspoken understandings and cues that allow a person to fit into a certain group, is essential if one wishes to survive in a particular socioeconomic class. The major hidden rules among the classes of generational poverty, the middle class, and the wealthy are presented in Table 8.1.

In this table, hidden rules about money, personality, social emphasis, time, education, destiny, language, and driving force are most relevant to the world of work. The

TABLE 8.1 Major Hidden Rules Among the Classes of Poverty, Middle Class, and Wealth

	POVERTY	MIDDLE CLASS	WEALTH
POSSESSIONS	People	Things	One-of-a-kind objects, legacies, pedigrees
MONEY	to be used, spent	to be managed	to be conserved, invested
PERSONALITY	is for entertainment. A sense of humor is highly valued.	is for acquisition and stability. Achievement is highly valued.	is for connections. Financial, political, social connections are highly valued.
SOCIAL EMPHASIS	Social inclusion of people they like.	Emphasis is on self-governance and self-sufficiency.	Emphasis is on social exclusion.
FOOD	Key question: Did you eat enough? Quantity important.	Key question: Did you like it? Quality important.	Key question: Was it presented well? Presentation important.
CLOTHING	Clothing valued for the individual style and expression of personality.	Clothing valued for its quality and acceptance into the norm of middle class. Label important.	Clothing valued for its artistic sense and expression. Designer important.
TIME	Present most important Decisions made for the moment based on feelings or survival.	Future most important. Decisions made against future ramifications.	Traditions and past history most important. Decisions partially made on basis of tradition/decorum.
EDUCATION	Valued and revered as an abstract but not as a reality.	Crucial for climbing success ladder and making money.	Necessary tradition for making and maintaining connections.
DESTINY	Believe in fate. Cannot do much to mitigate chance.	Believe in choice. Can change the future with good choices now.	Noblesse oblige (an obligation to display charitable conduct)
FAMILY STRUCTURE	Tends to be matriarchal.	Tends to be patriarchal.	Depends on who has the money.
WORLDVIEW	Sees the world in terms of local setting.	Sees the world in terms of national setting.	Sees the world in terms of international view.
LOVE	Love and acceptance unconditional, based upon whether or not an individual is liked.	Loved and acceptance conditional and based largely on achievement.	Love and acceptance conditional and related to social standing and connections.
LANGUAGE	Casual register Language is about survival.	Formal register Language is about negotiation.	Formal register. Language is about connections.
DRIVING FORCE	Survival, relationships, and entertainment	Work and achievement	Financial, political, and social connections.

SOURCE: Payne (1995), pp. 91–92. © 1995 RFT Publishing Co. Reprinted by permission of Ruby K. Payne, Ph.D.

following discussion is based on Payne (1995). In the interest of brevity, we do not focus on the wealthy.

Among the hidden rules of the middle class, money management is vital. A stable, achievement-oriented personality is desirable. Self-governance and self-sufficiency in social interactions is attractive. A future time-orientation with decisions made against future ramifications is preferred. Education for climbing the ladder of success is crucial. Good choices made now to impact future destiny are considered wise. The language of negotiation is valued. Work and achievement are the driving forces that characterize the middle-class lifestyle. Notice the legacy from the Protestant work ethic in these hidden rules (e.g., self-discipline, self-regulation of one's conduct), which make for good business sense and for reliable employees.

In contrast, the hidden rules of those who live in poverty do not seem to emphasize self-discipline and self-regulation. Money is to be spent, but then, an insufficient amount to meet expenses makes money management difficult. A personality that focuses on entertainment and humor, which helps to deal with the frustrations, restrictions, and deprivations of poverty, is highly prized. The social inclusion of people they like creates two difficulties. First, kids from poverty who do not like their teachers are less likely to do their homework. Second, adult employees from poverty are more prone to quit their jobs if they do not like their bosses. A present-time orientation, with decisions based on feelings or survival, can appear as a lack of foresight to the middle class and the wealthy. But in the context of poverty, a present-time orientation often makes sense. Parents who live in poverty often value education. Naturally, many of these parents want a better life than they had for their children. But because many of these parents do not know how to guide their children through the school years, education is valued in abstract, not concrete, terms. The belief in fate and that one cannot do much to mitigate chance can appear as passive submission to destiny. This worldview is hardly conducive to instilling progress. The language of survival is also not predictive of success. Survival, relationships, and entertainment are the driving forces that characterize a lifestyle of poverty and a collectivist orientation where reliance on interconnectedness with others is paramount.

The casual register of the language of poverty and the formal register of the language of the middle class need further explanation here. Joos (1967, cited in Payne, 1995) describes **casual register** as that language which (1) friends use, (2) with a general, nonspecific word choice; (3) is dependent upon nonverbals for assistance in conveying meaning, and (4) with often incomplete sentence syntax. **Formal register** is language that (1) is used in work and school, (2) with a specific word choice, and (3) with complete sentences and standard syntax. Students from low-income and racial and ethnic minority backgrounds often have no access to formal register in the home. These students are at a severe disadvantage in the world of school and work, where "ability to use formal register is a hidden rule of [the] middle-class" (Payne, 1995, p. 63). An ability to use the formal register enables one to perform well academically, score high on standardized tests, and make a good impression in job interviews.

Mead (1992) provides a highly readable analysis of the nonworking poor in America before the welfare reform of 1996. His book is also useful as historical context. When it comes to discussing poverty in America, both conservative and liberal political thinking take a view of human nature, which Mead calls *the competence assumption*. The **competence assumption** takes for granted, "that the individual is willing and able to advance his or her own economic interests. . . . Americans are in motion toward *economic* goals" (p. 19, italics in original). He explains, "competence here means all the qualities that allow a person to get ahead in economic terms—not only intelligence, but foresight, energy, discipline, and the ability to sacrifice for the future" (p. 19).

The competence assumption places work as the central role in people's lives. Work in the occupational domain is given precedence over work in the familial and personal domains (Richardson, 1993). The competence assumption's emphasis on foresight, discipline, and delayed gratification resemble the hidden rules of the middle class (Payne, 1995). Welfare recipients have been judged by standards that do not characterize their lifestyles, and they have not been consulted as to whether or not such standards are even relevant. The competence assumption also echoes the limitations of the Protestant work ethic and the historic work ways of the British American colonists (Fischer, 1989). In addition, the competence assumption ignores the growing trend among parents in the middle and professional classes, who are now more "willing to sacrifice on-the-job advancement for time with their children" (Barnett & Rivers, 1996, p. 84). Thus, the underlying premise of the competence assumption is flawed in many ways. But, that's politics.

Practical Applications

Students from poverty need to be taught the hidden rules of the middle class without having their own lifestyles denigrated (Payne, 1995). This leaves students the choice to use middle-class rules if they desire. But middle-class solutions should not be imposed on students and adults from poverty when alternative, feasible solutions can be found. Practitioners can learn to become aware of the hidden rules of poverty and lessen the anger and frustration educators feel at times when working with students and adults from poverty, as well as reduce the classism that pervades much of vocational psychology. A common attitude of those living in generational poverty is that society owes them a living. Those living in situational poverty tend to have pride and a disdain for accepting charity. Clients in situational poverty usually have more resources, including knowledge of the formal register, than clients in generational poverty.

With a tendency to focus on current feelings instead of long-term outcomes, students and adults from poverty who get angry are apt to quit if they do not like the teacher or boss. These same students and adults will work hard if they

Continued

Continued

like the teacher or boss. Conflict resolution skills may need to be taught as part of the hidden rules of the middle class, which values negotiation. Students and adults from poverty have learned to distrust organizations as basically dishonest and require a demonstration of integrity from the teacher, the boss, or the management. Physically hard work is more the norm among men from generational poverty. This differs from the male provider role of the middle class.

Payne (1995) summarizes that, at school, students from poverty are more apt to

- be disorganized— lose papers, lack required parental signatures.
- do homework less often, even when they are capable of doing well in school.
- use physical aggression to settle conflicts.
- focus on part of an assignment or part of what is on the written page.
- not start a task or monitor their own behavior.
- laugh inappropriately when disciplined.
- use the casual register.
- be unaccustomed to or not know how to use middle-class courtesies.

Without intervention by a school counselor or other practitioner, these behaviors do not bode well for the development of desirable work habits on the job.

Adults from poverty who have managed to work their way into the middle class are nevertheless likely to retain vestiges of their earlier background. Sometimes the term for reverting to these vestiges is called **gettin' ghetto,** which can remain useful in specific times and places. But then, the point is not to eliminate behaviors that characterize

living in poverty, but to augment behaviors that characterize living in the middle class. People who get out and stay out of generational poverty most often do so through education. Four motivators help people leave poverty behind:

1. A goal, vision, or something they want to be, have, or accomplish
2. A painful situation where anything would be better
3. An educator, spouse, mentor, or role model who *sponsors* them, shows them a way, or convinces them that a different lifestyle is feasible
4. A specific talent or ability that provides a way out of poverty (Payne, 1995).

Practitioners teach more about hidden rules and provide resources through program development, program evaluation, clinical intervention, and research. More cohesive research is needed on mentoring students and adults from poverty. Kuehr's (1997) review of the literature reveals a lack of uniformity in research regarding mentoring at-risk youth to reduce school dropout rates. Most of the studies she reviews come from the field of educational leadership, school counseling, and child and family studies. Clinical intervention and research with low-income populations is a far cry from the populations of convenience obtained by using college students from introductory psychology courses as research participants. Vocational psychology/career development could be transformed if it were more available and amenable to populations that definitively need occupational information and related interventions. This means going into the community colleges and inner city schools to do research and provide appropriate services for this population.

Genograms

A useful means of analyzing the family's influence on occupational development is to devise a **genogram** of the client's family. A genogram is a family assessment process that clients seem to enjoy and rarely find threatening. McGoldrick and Gerson (1985) write:

> A genogram is a format for drawing a family tree that records information about family members and their relationships over at least three generations . . . [and] display family information graphically in a way that provides a quick gestalt of complex family patterns and a rich source of hypotheses about how a clinical problem may be connected to the family context and the evolution of both problem and context over time (p.1).

To obtain data on the occupational patterns of a client's family, the practitioner begins by simply asking the client to name family members and to identify each family member's occupation. The practitioner usually starts with the family-of-origin and proceeds back through the grandparents, aunts, uncles, and cousins. The client is asked to tell what they know about the occupational development process of various relatives (e.g., level of education, employment history, reasons for any job changes, current occupational status, and work ethic). Graphic depictions form the backbone of any genogram (McGoldrick & Gerson, 1985). Each graphic depiction or symbol denotes the biological and legal relationships among family members from one generation to the next.

Genogram symbols help practitioners grasp client occupational development issues from the purview of family structure dynamics (McDaniels & Gysbers, 1992) (see Figure 8.1). Genograms in occupational counseling can help clients understand work-family roles and responsibilities. The genogram is an effective tool for recording information as the client and practitioner make written notes about people in the client's family-of-origin and respective types of occupations. The client's uniqueness is emphasized when seen in the context of the family. Mitchell and Krumboltz (1984) suggest four major assessment areas to be examined when a client's career decision-making problem is believed to be related to inaccurate or dysfunctional self-observation and/or worldview generalizations:

1. The content of the client's self-observation and worldview generalizations
2. The processes by which they arose
3. Whether these beliefs and generalizations truly create problems
4. Whether stated beliefs disguise more fundamental and as yet unarticulated beliefs.

Okiishi (1987) integrates these four assessments into areas of discussion to include client perceptions of

1. the family member's success as a spouse, parent, employee, friend, and relative.
2. the increased or decreased geographic mobility associated with the family member.

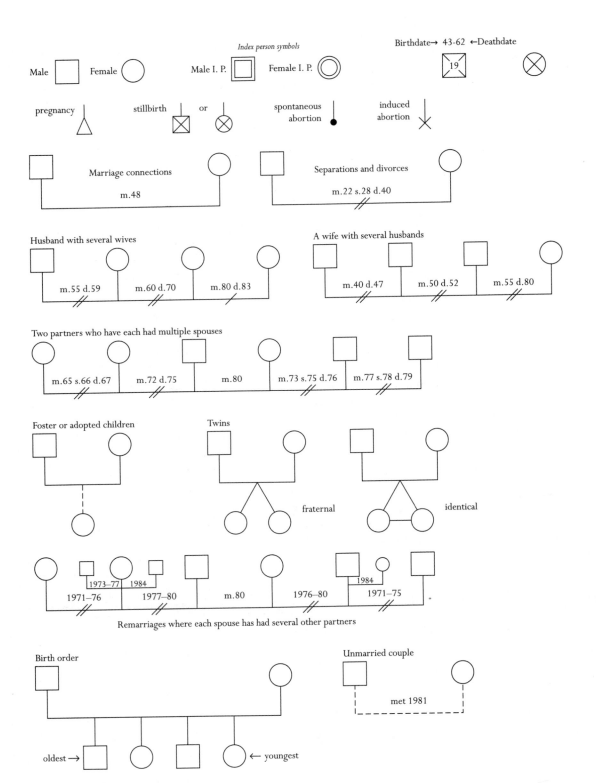

FIGURE 8.1 Genogram Symbols and Procedures

SOURCE: *McGoldrick and Gerson (1985),* Genograms in Family Assessment, *pp. 10–14. New York: W. W. Norton.*

Practical Applications

Genogram use in occupational counseling involves at least three steps:

1. At the client's direction, the practitioner constructs the genogram.
2. The practitioner documents with the client the occupations of relatives mentioned on the genogram.
3. The practitioner explores with the client the relatives mentioned on the genogram, noting especially the role modeling as the client perceives it and the reinforcement provided to the role model (Okiishi, 1987).

Some possible areas to investigate with the client are:

- Multigenerational themes concerning education, careers, work values, work ethics, and gender roles
- Multigenerational family decision-making patterns
- Family rules about the *acceptable* range of employment possibilities, and locations
- Changing career patterns across several generations of the family
- The influence of larger social changes or historical events on the family members' career choices

- The career patterns of various family members—Who did what when? How do family members play out their leisure role? What is their citizen role? What number of roles are family members expected to carry?
- The emotional charge around career issues in the family—loyalty issues, aborted dreams, achievement expectations (Moon, Coleman, McCollum, Nelson, & Jensen-Scott, 1993).

Family influence on occupational development is usually not confined to one generation. This influence is substantial across three generations (McGoldrick & Gerson, 1985). One way to examine this is to construct a work-related genogram of at least three generations that depicts the occupations of as many family members as possible. This genogram is useful in generating ideas and understanding of family influence, and one's view of the world of work.

---

3. how time, space, money, and relationships were managed in and outside of the family.

4. each person's integration of various life roles, including work.

A genogram can help practitioner and client determine the individuals in the client's family who may have been significant in the formation of the client's career expectations. Practitioners gain a better understanding of the client's view of the world of work. The client can identify possible barriers posed by significant others and perceived restrictions. Sex role stereotypes could be pinpointed. Questions asked may include: "At what age did each relative begin working? How often were jobs changed? What kind of emotional or financial assistance was offered and accepted? What kinds of satisfaction did the client perceive as gaining from various work experiences? What are the disadvantages in the relatives' work experiences?" (Okiishi, 1987, p. 139).

CASE EXAMPLE

The Most Hated Women in America

Figure 8.2 presents a work-related genogram of five living generations of the Boone and Williams family, featured in Pulitzer Prize winning journalist David Zucchino's book, *Myth of the Welfare Queen* (1997). Between July 4, 1995, and January 1, 1996, Zucchino followed the lives of several unmarried welfare mothers residing in a ghetto in North Philadelphia (Philadelphia, Pennsylvania). He quotes community activist Cheri Honkala that welfare mothers are "the most hated women in America" (p. 62). Unwed mothers are stereotyped as the primary drain on the U.S. welfare system. In fact, before the welfare reform measures of 1996–1997, one-third of all welfare mothers were women in their thirties, not the unwed teen mother of popular stereotype. The Boone and Williams genogram portrays the family in 1995, before welfare reform took place. We use a *work-related genogram* to describe this family, because *career genogram* would hardly be appropriate.

The **index person** in Figure 8.2 is 56-year-old Odessa Boone, shown as a circle (for her female gender) with the lines doubled (for her status as index person). Her late father is Shellmon Boone, shown as a box (for his male gender) with an X inside (for his deceased status).

Her mother is Bertha Hill, age 81.

Shellmon Boone sharecropped in Georgia's red dirt country. He labored at one farm until there was no more work and then moved on to the next farm where work was available. His wife Bertha and their three children accompanied him on his job moves, "always hungry, always on the bottom edge of poverty" (Zucchino, 1997, p. 32).

Bertha Hill grew up in a sharecropper's shack. Both her parents worked the fields. From the time Bertha could walk she also worked the fields, earning up to $1.25 per day chopping cotton and pulling green beans.

Odessa Boone began working the fields at age 5, adding to the family income. Shellmon and Bertha separated in 1950 (as indicated by the double slash / /) after his drunken rages and physical abuse became intolerable. She and the children moved to North Philadelphia to live with her sister and brother-in-law. Bertha found work as a farmworker in southern New Jersey and occasionally earned extra money as a seamstress and housekeeper. Odessa, age 11 when the move occurred, spent her summers as a farmworker alongside her mother. Odessa spent the school year living with relatives in Georgia, where she had contact with her father. Bertha's two severely handicapped sons, Junior and Charles, lived year-round with Bertha's sister.

Bertha went on welfare in 1967, at age 53. After nearly fifty years of farm work, and nearly twenty-five years of lifting and bathing her two handicapped sons by herself, Bertha's health began to fail. She had never seen herself as dependent on anyone else. She had always shunned any sort of charity. Bertha Hill was a worker. She went on welfare as a last resort because it was available and after so many years of backbreaking work, she felt entitled to government benefits. In 1967, those benefits were $90 every two weeks.

Odessa began taking care of herself at age 13. That year, a racial incident happened at school in Georgia: Odessa refused to call a White girl the same age "ma'am." The fathers of both girls agreed the White girl was old enough to be shown this kind of respect, due a White woman in the South. Odessa's refusal earned her a death threat from the White girl's father. Odessa's school days ended. For safety's sake, her father sent her to live with relatives in the Georgia countryside, where she worked the fields for $3 a day. Here she met sharecropper Willie Williams. They married on August 20, 1955 (as shown above the solid line that connects them in the genogram), when Odessa was eight days past her fifteenth birthday.

Willie and Odessa moved to North Philadelphia in 1956 to be near her mother. Willie found work as a mechanic and later as a burner of scrap metal with an acetylene torch. Odessa Boone considered herself a worker. She completed an eighteen-month mechanics course and then worked two-and-a-half years repairing cars at a garage in North Phila-

delphia before being laid off and then worked various jobs.

Five critical incidents in the life of our index person deserve mention:

1. Odessa accidentally sliced open her ankle as a young woman. Without access to proper medical care, the wound never healed properly. Sometimes the ankle collapses. She taught herself to move slowly and to balance herself on her good ankle to keep from toppling over.
2. In 1957, 1962, and 1967, Odessa had nervous breakdowns. She is currently on Valium.
3. In 1968, Odessa broke her pelvis in a car accident, but the fracture went undiagnosed until she had an x-ray in 1991. She has lived in chronic pain all these years.
4. In 1986, she suffered a mild stroke.
5. Currently, Odessa weighs 240 pounds. She is asthmatic and always carries an inhaler. At home, she has a nebulizer. She has high blood pressure.

Odessa went on welfare in 1967 out of desperation. Willie had grown increasingly jealous and physically abusive. She was unable to find work, and by then she had eight children to feed. As with most women in abusive situations, the violence increased when she actually tried to leave. Willie threatened to kill her. She managed to get out alive, but she suffered her third and most severe nervous breakdown in the process. Welfare was the only option available to her at the time.

Her mother taught Odessa "you make do with what you have" (Zucchino, 1997, p. 17). Odessa "makes do" by trash picking. She calls it her "trash therapy"

Continued

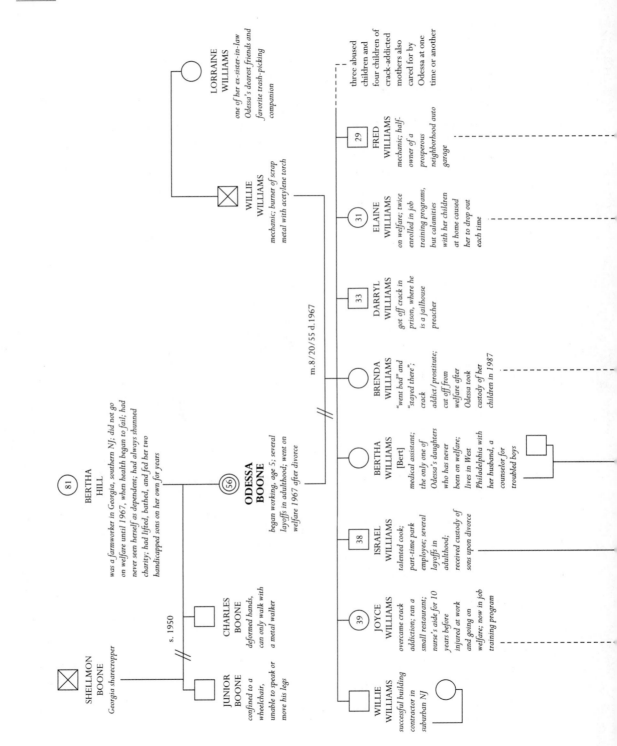

SHELLMON BOONE
Georgia sharecropper

BERTHA HILL
was a farmworker in Georgia, southern NJ; did not go on welfare until 1967, when health began to fail; had never seen herself as dependent; had always shunned charity; had lifted, bathed, and fed her two handicapped sons on her own for years

s. 1950

JUNIOR BOONE
confined to a wheelchair, unable to speak or move his legs

CHARLES BOONE
deformed hands, can only walk with a metal walker

LORRAINE WILLIAMS
one of her ex-sister-in-law Odessa's dearest friends and favorite trash-picking companion

WILLIE WILLIAMS
mechanic; burner of scrap metal with acetylene torch

ODESSA BOONE (56)
began working, age 5; several layoffs in adulthood; went on welfare 1967 after divorce

m. 8/20/55 d. 1967

three abused children and four children of crack-addicted mothers also cared for by Odessa at one time or another

WILLIE WILLIAMS
successful building contractor in suburban NJ

JOYCE WILLIAMS (39)
overcame crack addiction; ran a small restaurant; nurse's aide for 10 years before injured at work and going on welfare; now in job training program

ISRAEL WILLIAMS (38)
talented cook; part-time park employee; several layoffs in adulthood; received custody of sons upon divorce

BERTHA WILLIAMS [Bert]
medical assistant; the only one of Odessa's daughters who has never been on welfare; lives in West Philadelphia with her husband, a counselor for troubled boys

BRENDA WILLIAMS
"went bad" and "stayed there"; crack addict/prostitute; cut off from welfare after Odessa took custody of her children in 1987

DARRYL WILLIAMS (33)
got off crack in prison, where he is a jailhouse preacher

ELAINE WILLIAMS (31)
on welfare; twice enrolled in job training programs, but calamities with her children at home caused her to drop out each time

FRED WILLIAMS (29)
mechanic; half-owner of a prosperous neighborhood auto garage

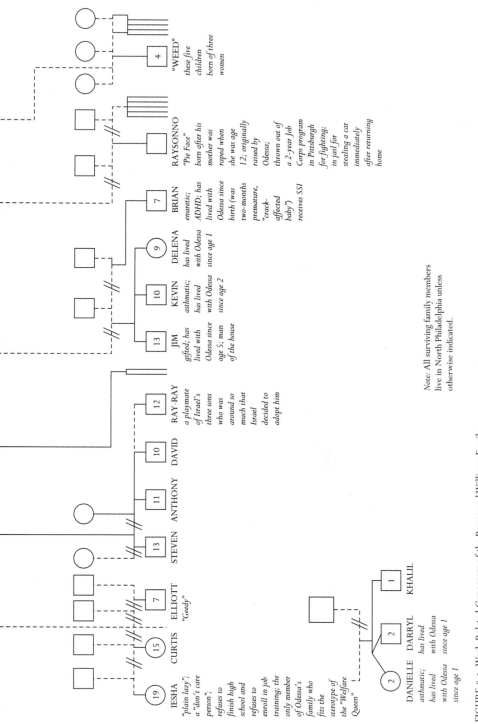

IESHA
"plain lazy";
a "don't care
person";
refuses to
finish high
school and
refuses to
enroll in job
training; the
only member
of Odessa's
family who
fits the
stereotype of
the "Welfare
Queen"

CURTIS

ELLIOTT
"Geedy"

STEVEN

ANTHONY

DAVID

RAY-RAY
a playmate
of Israel's
three sons
who was
around so
much that
Israel
decided to
adopt him

JIM
gifted; has
lived with
Odessa since
age 5; man
of the house

KEVIN
asthmatic;
has lived
with Odessa
since age 2

DELENA
has lived
with Odessa
since age 1

BRIAN
enuretic;
ADHD; has
lived with
Odessa since
birth (was
two-months
premature,
"crack-
affected
baby")
receives SSI

RAYSONNO
"Pre Face"
born after his
mother was
raped when
she was age
12; originally
raised by
Odessa;
thrown out of
a 2-year Job
Corps program
in Pittsburgh
for fighting;
in jail for
stealing a car
immediately
after returning
home

"WEED"
these five
children
born of three
women

DANIELLE
asthmatic;
has lived
with Odessa
since age 1

DARRYL
has lived
with Odessa
since age 1

KHALIL

Note: All surviving family members
live in North Philadelphia unless
otherwise indicated.

FIGURE 8.2 Work-Related Genogram of the Boone and Williams Family, 1995

source: Adapted from Zucchino, 1997, by Roberto Cortéz González.

Continued

(p. 18). To Odessa, receiving welfare benefits does not mean she is helpless or dependent. Trash picking is not stealing —that would be against Odessa's sense of decency: she allows no cursing in her home and reads half a chapter of the Bible every night at bedtime. Besides, people foolishly throw away a lot of good things.

Among Odessa's trash picking finds are an entire china set, unopened and still in its original packing box. Some newlyweds probably received the china as a wedding gift, disliked the pattern shown on the box, and threw it away intact. Another one of Odessa's prized trash picks is a nearly new king-size mattress and box spring. She has trash-picked perfectly usable appliances. Trash-picked luggage, curtains, and adults' and children's clothes—including a child's snowsuit— have all contributed to making Odessa's house a home. When Odessa finds something she already has, she trash picks it anyway to sell later. Each trash-picked item sold is not income for which welfare would penalize her. As she puts it, "I'm not ashamed to go after what I need" (Zucchino, 1997, p. 41).

By 1995, Odessa's eight children are grown and have extremely divergent occupational paths.

The eldest son, also named Willie Williams (age not mentioned), is a successful home building contractor in southern New Jersey. He often helps his mother and grown sisters with repairs at their homes. He also repairs and maintains Odessa's trash-picked appliances.

The second child and eldest daughter, Joyce Williams, 39, started well. A serious, determined person with an entrepreneurial spirit, she decided to become a successful career woman while still in high school. She ran a small restaurant in North Philadelphia before becoming a casualty of the crack epidemic that hit her neighborhood in the mid-1980s. The readily available money in her restaurant cash register facilitated her drug use. Joyce overcame a crack addiction through her own willpower. She then worked for ten years as a nurse's aide before injuring her back trying to lift a heavy patient. The injury left Joyce unable to perform her job's physical demands and she had to quit. By then she had four children to feed, including Iesha, Curtis, and Elliott—nicknamed "Geedy" for his greedy appetite (as shown in the genogram by the dashed line leading vertically down from Joyce; one child's name, gender and age not mentioned).

Currently, Joyce receives AFDC, food stamps, and cash assistance for her three youngest children. Joyce's children were born of four different fathers (as shown in the genogram by the four boxes and dashed lines that appear below Joyce); none has ever provided child support. Joyce is on welfare reluctantly. She is unaccustomed to depending on others and is humiliated that she can no longer rely on herself. Her welfare caseworker helped Joyce enroll in a JOBS program, a business administration course in northeast Philadelphia where Joyce is learning all the latest computer programs. Joyce hates being on welfare; to her it's like taking charity. Of her self-image, she says, "I'm a person who *needs* to work" (Zucchino, 1997, p. 26, italics in original).

Israel Williams, 38, is a divorced father with custody of his four sons: Steven, Anthony, David, and Ray-Ray, who is adopted (as shown in the genogram by the horizontal dashed line leading to the right from David). In Odessa's family, the men are not expected to marry the mothers of their children; however, it is important for men to economically support those children. Israel is an outstanding example of an honorable man who provides for his children. A talented cook, he helps his mother prepare huge family dinners at Thanksgiving and Christmas. He has held several jobs as a cook, being laid off each time. His later employment has included furnace repair, occasional auto mechanic work, temporary jobs at a computer chip factory and the post office, and part-time work as a scrap metal burner. At times, Israel relies on Emergency Assistance for food stamps to feed his four sons.

Bertha Williams (age not mentioned), nicknamed Bert by Odessa, is a high school graduate and has worked her entire adult life. Bert is the only one of Odessa's daughters married to the father of her children (number, names, genders, and ages not mentioned) and the only daughter never on welfare. Bert works as a medical assistant and her husband (unnamed in the book) is a counselor for troubled boys. They live in a fine house in West Philadelphia. Odessa's 1984 Chevrolet Caprice Classic was a gift from Bertand, Bert's husband. The Caprice is Odessa's only transportation because she is too heavy to comfortably navigate the public bus system. In addition, because of her bad ankle, Odessa risks toppling over and being prey to crack addicts who would willingly rob her. Odessa earns extra cash by driving grocery shoppers home from the store. She can judge who is safe and trustworthy and has made many acquaintances among the shoppers. They are always glad to pay for a ride home to avoid being vulnerable on the bus, their arms full of grocery bags.

Brenda Williams (age not mentioned), in Odessa's words, "went bad" and "stayed there" (Zucchino, 1997, p. 27). Brenda was a sweet and respectful little girl. At age 13, her behavior changed, and she began talking back and staying out late at night. She became addicted to crack and turned to prostitution to support her habit. She had a series of drug-addicted boyfriends, one of whom fathered her three eldest children, Jim, Kevin, and Delena; another man fathered Brenda's fourth child, Brian (as shown in the genogram by the dashed line leading vertically down from Brenda and by the two boxes and dashed lines that appear below Brenda). Brenda lost custody of her children to Odessa in 1987, who ended up on welfare a second time to care for them. Odessa receives AFDC, food stamps, and cash assistance for Brenda's four children. Odessa also receives Supplemental Security Income (SSI) for Brian, a crack-affected baby. Currently, Brenda is a prostitute who lives in crack houses and turns up at Odessa's from time to time. Crack is easy to find. From her front porch, Odessa can see crack dealers plying their trade on the street corners at both ends of the block.

Darryl Williams, 33, is currently in the State Correctional Institution at Graterford, PA, fifty minutes away from Odessa. A crack addict, he figured that "prison would be the best place to clean himself up" (Zucchino, 1997, p. 15), so he deliberately broke his probation on charges of drug possession and of breaking and entering. He has found Jesus and is a jailhouse preacher. Two part-time jobs await him upon parole: one with eldest brother Willie's home building business and the other with youngest brother Fred's auto garage.

Continued

Continued

Elaine Williams, 30, Odessa's youngest daughter, lives in a row house at the opposite end of the block from her mother. Elaine is a good-natured woman who takes life as it comes. She had six children (as shown by the dashed line leading vertically down from Elaine; names, genders, and ages not mentioned in the book). As with Joyce and Brenda, Elaine receives no child support from the biological fathers of her children, but receives AFDC, food stamps, and cash assistance for her five youngest children. Elaine enrolled twice in JOBS training programs, and each time had to leave the program due to a calamity at home with her children. During those times of crisis, Elaine's children were her foremost priority. Strict attendance policies at the JOBS programs exclude any leave of absence, and she chose to stop attending the program. Although welfare pays for child care, Elaine feels her children are not properly taken care of and wishes she could be at home with them. Elaine believes that children need their mother at home. With her case manager's help, she is scheduled to enroll in a third JOBS program (enrollment in two JOBS programs is usually the maximum number allowed) at a trade school in northeast Philadelphia, studying hotel management and food services. Given Joyce's progress in her business administration and computer JOBS program, Elaine is feeling family pressure to start and finally complete this third JOBS program.

Fred Williams, 29, Odessa's fourth son and youngest child, is a mechanic and half-owner of a prosperous auto garage in the neighborhood. He has five children by three women (as shown in the genogram by the dashed line leading vertically down from Fred and by the three circles and dashed lines that appear below Fred; names, genders, and ages of four of the children not mentioned in the book). At one point, the three women and their children all lived under one roof! Like Israel, Fred does the honorable thing: he provides for his children, and that is what counts.

In addition to rearing her own eight children and Elaine's eldest son Raysonno, Odessa took in seven other children at one time or another as a certified foster parent for the Department of Human Services (three abused children and four children of crack-addicted mothers, as shown on the genogram by the dashed line leading horizontally to the right from Fred). Including the six children who currently live with Odessa—daughter Brenda's four children and granddaughter Iesha's twins, Danielle and Darryl—Odessa has reared twenty-two children at one time or another from three different generations. With spiritual resources and an extended family support system (Payne, 1995), Odessa makes do.

Iesha, 19, Odessa's granddaughter, is the only member of the extended family who comes anywhere close to fitting the stereotype of the Welfare Queen. A social construction of politicians, their speechwriters, and the media, the stereotypical Welfare Queen is an African American, unwed teenage mother living in the inner city. She is a product of generational poverty. The Welfare Queen uses multiple aliases, social security cards, and addresses to cheat the welfare system out of thousands of dollars. With Medicaid providing health benefits, on her tax-free income the Welfare Queen is a Cadillac owner and lives a lavish, big-spending lifestyle (Zucchino, 1997).

The Population Reference Bureau reports that most welfare recipients are actually White, reside in the suburbs or rural areas (Associated Press, 1996a), and live in situational poverty with nearly one-third lifting themselves out of it within a year (Associated Press, 1998). Of the 38 million poor people in the United States, 40 percent are children not of legal age to work and 10 percent are 65 or older. Less than half of the nation's poor received any cash assistance from the government. In 1996, the government's definition of poverty was a household income of $16,036 or below for a family of four (Jones & Belton, 1997).

Iesha is described by her mother Joyce as "just plain lazy" (Zucchino, 1997, p. 26) and by Odessa as a "don't care person" (p. 340). Iesha has no interest in finishing high school or enrolling in any job-training program. She lives with her aunt Elaine and the latter's children. Welfare is a way of life for Iesha, who collects $248 in cash every two weeks and $288 in food stamps once a month. Some of this cash and food stamps she must give to Odessa, who houses Iesha's two-year-old twins. Iesha simply refuses to take care of her babies. As with Joyce, Brenda, and Elaine, Iesha receives no child support from her children's biological father. Rumor has it that he became a crack addict and is serving prison time for armed robbery.

Among Odessa's other grandchildren is Brenda's son Jim, 13, a gifted and talented youth who has lived with Odessa since age 5. Up to now, Jim's being the man of the house has not weighed too heavily upon him. Our concern about Jim's future is whether the environment will wear down his stamina and defeat his ambitions (Kozol, 1991). Jim is the age his mother was when her behavior changed irreparably for the worse.

Jim's half-brother Brian, 7, born a crack-affected baby, may have the duration of his SSI benefits limited by stricter standards for disability mandated by Congress. Any termination of SSI benefits may be accompanied by a lack of readily available information on the right to appeal the cutoff of funds (Los Angeles Times, 1997). Families like Odessa's often do not understand that they must act quickly—request a continuance within ten days to continue receiving benefits during the first level of appeal and appeal the termination within sixty days. Information on appeals is often buried deep within termination letters and is not clearly understandable to many recipients.

Elaine's son, Raysonno, likewise has an uncertain future. Expelled from a two-year Job Corps program in Pittsburgh for fighting, he ended up in jail for stealing a car immediately after returning home. Raysonno typifies the person from generational poverty whose conflict-resolution skills and emotional resources are inappropriate to middle-class expectations for conduct on the job (Payne, 1995).

For Odessa and many of her family, welfare reform will have changed their lifestyles in ways that cannot even be calculated. The varied employment routes taken by Odessa's children are especially remarkable. Why did the eldest child (Willie), the fourth child (Bert), and the eighth child (Fred) become middle class when their five siblings did not? Perhaps Willie, Bert, and Fred mastered the hidden rules of the middle class (Payne, 1995). By the third generation of the above genogram, generational poverty does not persist in all branches of the family. The range of oc-

Continued

Continued

cupational achievement among Odessa's eight children points to within-group differences.

In one family, whatever the cultural/racial background or socioeconomic origins, individual needs and talents combined with parental dispositions (Clark, 1983), life experiences, and opportunities will influence educational attainment and occupational development. Odessa's parental disposition and interpersonal relationships probably differed with each child in her household. She never dreamed that Brenda, her sweet and respectful little girl, would grow up to become a drug addict and a prostitute. Odessa did not come from this kind of family. From a dislocation of family life perspective (Carter & McGoldrick, 1989), as a postdivorce family, Odessa did not receive coparenting support in rearing Brenda from her ex-husband, the noncustodial parent. Nor did Willie maintain financial responsibilities to his ex-wife and children.

Even the effects of the crack epidemic on the Williams family show within-group differences. Joyce overcame her addiction through her own determination. Darryl detoxed in prison. Brenda is still an addict and is all but homeless. The crack invasion in North Philadelphia and elsewhere in the late 1980s is a practical and unpleasant, if lucrative, example of the global economy in action—through drug smuggling into the country and drug dealing within it.

Similar to systems approaches, family-of-origin, and various models of the family life cycle, genograms offer a rationale and an intervention useful to the practitioner whose major goal is to help clients make decisions with full awareness of all important factors of self, family influences, and family work patterns.

DUAL-CAREER AND SINGLE-PARENT FAMILIES

With the increasing numbers of single parent employees
and dual-career couples, and the rising expectations
regarding both quality work and family involvements,
it becomes crucial to assist individuals in achieving
balance in their work and family demands.
(Loerch, Russell, and Rush, 1989, p. 307)

In this section, we examine in more depth dual-career families, single-parent families, couples living together, and singles. The term *typical family* has multiple meanings in today's society. In the United States, and increasingly elsewhere, most people will experience many types of family systems throughout their lives.

Dual-Career Families

Marin E. Clarkberg of Cornell University (cited in Keller, 2000) estimated that as of 1998, there were more than 30 million dual-earner households in the United States. Fields (2003) reports that in 2002, 62 percent of all children (31 million) in the

United States lived in families with both parents in the labor force. However it's looked at, the increase in numbers of **dual-career families** suggest an even greater need for systemic attention and focus on the part of vocational practitioners. Working couples today have to develop new ways of living and relating to each other and to the world. One of their greatest challenges is finding adequate child care. The increase in the number of women working outside the home, particularly mothers with children still at home, is one of the most dramatic social changes in American history. Organizations have been slow to respond to the needs of dual-career families. Dual careerism will continue to be a major factor affecting the family for years to come.

How do couples engage in dual careers and integrate parenting and child care? Richter, Morrison, and Salinas (1991) make some observations about the ways couples deal with this issue. If a couple puts **career first, then family**, the issues they will experience are:

1. The woman's biological time clock
2. The man's physical degeneration and lowering of stamina
3. Age differences between parents and children
4. Ambivalence about having children

If a couple puts **family first, then career**, the issue becomes

1. Less affluence, money, and options for having material things
2. Shorter or lessened career opportunities
3. Less guilt feelings for neglect of family-oriented value
4. More marital satisfaction
5. One stays at home for a few years while the other works, then they trade off.

If a couple **shares career and family together**, each can (1) share the problem of task overload and emotional overload, and (2) have the best of both worlds. If a couple considers **child care options**, the possibilities become

1. Staggered parental care
2. Care by extended family member
3. Family day care
4. Group day care
5. Full-time babysitter/housekeeper/nanny
6. Both parents dovetailing their work schedules
7. Taking a child to work
8. A parent cooperative
9. Children in charge of themselves
10. Drop-in centers
11. Working from home
12. A combination of the above

If a couple concerns itself with **parenting issues**, they will need to decide

1. how it will be done.
2. who will do it.
3. who will be responsible for discipline.
4. what will be the shared responsibilities—quality time with children, physical needs, security, recreation/leisure time, autonomy for children, delegation of household chores.

Another concern is that of equity, the sense of fairness that exists in the dual-career couple's relationship. Because there are household and family responsibilities to share, considerations of each other's career and the decisions as to time commitment and job requirements must be balanced. Rachlin and Hansen (1985) found that women tend to take more responsibility because they have been socialized to do so, and it is very likely that the scenario has not changed drastically since that time. Moen (2000, cited in Keller, 2000) states: "It's hard to pursue two full-time careers and have a family. It's just about impossible unless you can afford to hire a full-time nanny" (no page given).

The dual-career couple is also faced with the demands of their respective careers. Conflict between work and family demands often appears to force choices as to which is the most important. While values may play an important part in the day-to-day decisions, the overall concern is the marriage relationship itself. Balancing career, home, family, and relationship is a daily task. **Negotiation** is an important *art* in the dual-career marriage. Couples that know how to negotiate see conflict in a different way. The focus is on resolving an issue in the most mutually satisfactory manner possible, rather than on changing the other spouse's point of view (Hall, 1989).

As a society, people have been focusing on changing organizations so that women can have a career and a family, but recent research on dual-career couples shows that men share the same problems. "We do know that some men make career accommodations for the sake of a career, wife, or the family, but the question is, how many men make career accommodations, and how much accommodating do they do?" (Hall, 1989, p. 7).

Hall (1989) uses the term **invisible daddy track** to refer to men who are not vocal about child care concerns, so the public is unaware of the strain on fathers. Oftentimes, men who use paternity leave or flexible work schedules are viewed as not being serious about their careers, which leads them to stay silent about child-related concerns. Many men sacrifice aspects of their career for their family, but do it quietly.

There are at least five ways to approach the problem of work/family balance for men (and women).

1. Restructure work arrangements for more flexibility.
2. Women who regularly note their career accommodations can keep them private the way some men do.

3. Women who want flexibility can consider part-time work or other ways to find time away from work.

4. Consider home-centered work for one spouse or both.

5. Consider any work/family choices as a one-time career decision (Hall, 1989).

Unfortunately, many corporations do not allow the type of flexibility needed to promote work/family balance. As the threat of downsizing and restructuring increases, employees are being pushed to produce more, work harder, stay longer, and work on weekends to keep their jobs. This leads to an inevitable paradox: employees are placing more importance on their families at the same time the unstable job market is causing them to spend more time on their jobs. As the number of dual-career couples increases, practitioners will need to help women and men explore how work and family issues influence their career choices. Lesbian dual-career couples receive even less external support than their gay or heterosexual counterparts (Fassinger, 1996).

Single-Parent Families

The single-parent family is a growing phenomenon, often subject to extreme economic problems. Day (1996) offers projected changes in the number of households and families in the United States from 1995 to 2010. Households headed by single mothers are projected to change from 11.4 million families—6.6 percent of all families—in 1995 to 13.9 million (6.3 percent) in 2010. Single father headed households are projected to remain steady at 1.6 percent of all families, 3.5 million families in 1995 to 4.6 million in 2010. Other reports seem to place single mothers at 12 percent of the population, single fathers at 4 percent (Fields & Casper, 2001). However such variables are measured, most single parents experience difficulties with role identity, social stigma, providing financially for the family, and balancing work/family responsibilities. A lack of formal education and job skills limit access to occupations that provide income for an acceptable standard of living. Households headed by working single mothers form 29 percent of all families that live in poverty (Proctor & Dalaker, 2003), as compared with households headed by working single fathers, at 13 percent. Projections for the years 2005 to 2010 are that roughly 35 percent of African American families will be headed by a single parent (Day, 1996), as compared to 12 percent for White families, 15 percent for Asian and Pacific Islanders, 24 percent for Hispanic families, and 25 percent for American Indian, Eskimo, and Aleuts.

Poverty is a major issue for single-parent households, especially those led by women. Inability to find appropriate child care at a reasonable cost affects a single parent's employability. Sometimes it is cheaper for mothers not to work than to work and pay the exorbitant cost of child care. Often these single mothers are uneducated and from cultural minorities—many displaced homemakers and teenage mothers (Burges, 1987). Single motherhood can cause decline in psychological well-being due to the stressors of living in near poverty. If these women have never been a part of the workforce, they are especially prone to depression. Single fathers also find it difficult to be a competent wage earner and parent. Single parent pressures make it difficult to make time for personal development. "As a result overload and interference with necessary tasks often occur. Single-parent families lack the personnel to fill all the roles expected of a family in our social structure" (*ERIC Digest,* No. 75, 1988).

Given the link between poverty and unemployment, occupational planning is imperative. For the single parent, the benefits of receiving vocational counseling and learning a skill are twofold—increased job opportunities and income, and a greater sense of self-esteem. For women, the economic security of a job often will motivate them to leave abusive situations.

To achieve effective job training and placement, the following factors need to be considered: emotional support, job-seeking skills, basic skills instruction (especially literacy skills), outreach and recruitment, child care, gender role analysis, self-concept building, skills assessment, challenges of combining work and family responsibilities, nontraditional job skills, and parenting education.

Multicultural Implications of Dual-Career Families and Single-Parent Families

Multicultural dual-career couples may be vulnerable to acculturative stress from the lifestyle they lead and the struggle to retain their original group values while attempting to incorporate the mainstream values of their work cultures. Politically induced workaholism perpetuated by their jobsites may be especially difficult to manage. Like many workers, multicultural dual-career couples may believe they are putting in too many hours on the job because they have to. Values clarification and assessment of leisure activities may be useful. Working twice as hard to appear at least as competent as co-workers from the dominant culture is a struggle faced by many multicultural dual-career couples. For clients originally from the lower socioeconomic classes, the meanings they attach to work may require exploration. Vocational practitioners can help clients assess the question, "Is this your idea of upward mobility?"

African Americans It is crucial to develop programs for African American adolescents to inform, educate, and train them so they can be financially better prepared to deal with the stressors of this lifestyle. From the single parent's perspective, children need to find role models and mentors to assist them in the occupational process. What are the values, work attitudes, and goals in these families, and how does the socioeconomic system affect their decisions? (Clark, 1983). What support systems are available from, say, extended family, community, or church? (Gilbert & Bingham, 2001; Brown & Pinterits, 2001).

To what extent do African American and Hispanic single parents have the same needs as Whites? Are the structures we have in place meeting the needs of these cultural groups? If not, what needs to be developed? How much flexibility is there in tailoring programs and models to suit the needs of individuals within families?

In *Children of the Dream: The Psychology of Black Success,* Edwards and Polite (1992) describe African Americans who do not allow race to be an obstacle to their occupational success. A common feature of successful African Americans is a strong patriarch and, in the absence of that, a loving and supporting family where a sense of responsibility predominates (Edwards & Polite, 1992). A second feature is a strong sense of race and an affirming sense of power, defined here as "the ability to provide for and get things done" (p. 187). A third feature is knowledge of how to interact with Whites—and the ability to distinguish which Whites are willing to be open (also known, bluntly, as **White people skills**). Successful African Americans have discerned the hidden rules of the White middle class (Payne, 1995) and, in some cases, the wealthy class. Another key ingredient to success is risk-taking, a perception many White men have not had of African Americans in the world of work (Edwards & Polite, 1992).

Occupational success for African Americans has several drawbacks.

1. "Even as blacks integrate into mainstream occupations and professions historically denied them, real corporate power remains elusive" (Edwards & Polite, 1992, p. 58).

2. The very sense of community that originally set the foundation for success so many years ago and that bolstered the self-confidence of these African Americans and their willingness to persist in their struggles appears to be mostly absent nowadays.

3. Salary discrimination remains.

4. Then there is the matter of being qualified. Unlike Whites, for whom success is frequently a matter of contacts, connections, family combinations, and in the end simply the circumstance of being born White, Black success seems always to carry certain prerequisites, chief among them the requirement that a Black first prove he or she is *qualified* for achievement.

The very notion of becoming qualified, of course, assumes an element of deficiency, a lacking of the skills, training, values, talent, or intellect that ordinarily renders one fit for accomplishment. . . .

The idea of becoming qualified is a psychological assault on African American occupational aspirations and is used by opponents of affirmative action to discount equal opportunity. Each generation of African Americans has faced the struggle of proving themselves, of being counted as qualified. As an unnamed, African American Harvard law professor tells Edwards and Polite (1992), the struggle to be counted as worthy for holding his job position is **"a presumption against my competence"** (p. 200). When an African American man experiences "a presumption against my competence," White men in the world of work question his ability to perform well in something other than athletics or the entertainment field (Edwards & Polite, 1992). African American males between the ages 15 to 24 are the most vulnerable. This age group is most at risk for dropping out of school, fathering an out-of-wedlock child, enduring unemployment, running into trouble with the law, or becoming a victim of homicide (see also Muwakkil, 1988; Parham & McDavis 1987).

Historically, the African American male in the United States has been denied power. **Power** is "the capacity to influence for one's own benefit the forces that affect one's life space and/or as the capacity to produce desired effects on others" (Pinderhughes, 1995, p. 133). Yet, the African American male is confronted with the task all men in the United States face in terms of exercising their power: working, earning money, taking care of the women and children in their lives, leading their communities, and determining their own destinies (Edwards & Polite, 1992). Successful African American males know that gaining power threatens White men, who fear that what will be done to them is what they have done to African American men. Successful African American men are not threatened by the power of successful African American women. An instinctive understanding of the nature of power characterizes many successful African American men. They know power can be denied. It can also be assumed and seized. Power is not finite or ordained. It can be elusive and fleeting, resulting from an act of courage as much as from exercising will. For the African American male to be a success, he must balance **self-regard**—that hard-won self-knowledge and centered sense of knowing who one is (Pipher, 1996)—with an awareness of the impression he makes on others. And he must realize that natural power can neither be masked nor denied.

The narratives in Edwards and Polite (1992) closely resemble the kind of ethnographic, qualitative research sorely needed in vocational psychology. These first-person accounts of successful African American women and men are a valuable source of information for any person striving to overcome seemingly insurmountable odds.

Career counseling practitioners also need to be mindful of within-group differences among African Americans, especially gender distinctions (Bingham & Ward, 2001). African American males, in particular, may not seek assistance from vocational practitioners, and so innovative outreach attempts are needed. Dual-career couples are a long-established norm among African Americans (Gilbert & Bingham, 2001), and it is an historical expectation that African American women will work. Racism is a constant in the career lives of African Americans, and culturally appropriate intervention strategies and assessment are essential.

Hispanics Among Hispanics, it is useful to surmise how many extended family members take responsibility for child rearing and providing financial assistance. However, not all Hispanics have extended family nearby to lend a hand, and even for Hispanics with extended family members nearby, social support may not be available for a variety of reasons. It is dangerous to stereotype that, among Hispanics, extended family are willing and able to help. More broadly, lack of education and skills predominates among the U.S. Hispanic population. Jamieson, Curry, and Martinez (1999) report that Hispanics have an annual high school drop out rate of 7 percent, although other reports place it at 21 percent (Dell'Angela, 2004). Many Hispanic parents want their children to obtain a higher education but don't know how to go about helping them do so. Other Hispanic families pressure their children to stay nearby and contribute to the family income, thus discouraging matriculation at colleges far away. For Hispanics, little has been done "to empirically measure *perceived occupational opportunity* or *perceived barriers to occupational attainment*" (Arbona, 1990, p. 316, italics in original). Broader social and economic contexts need further exploration with regard to occupational aspirations (Arbona & Novy, 1991).

Acculturation may be related to on-the-job behaviors and career progression for Hispanic white collar workers (Arbona, 1990). Similar to the psychology of Black success (Edwards & Polite, 1992), practitioners can assess Hispanic professionals' knowledge of the hidden rules (Payne, 1995) of the White middle class. The paucity of research on job satisfaction and on occupational values (Arbona, 1990) prohibits a summary of these topics. In addition to socioeconomic status, acculturation may be another moderator variable in research on Hispanic vocational interests. Arbona (1990) calls for additional research on (1) "the predictive validity of . . . Spanish and English versions of career interest inventories," (p. 306), (2) gender differences, and (3) applying the RIASEC model to Hispanics in specific occupations—the last of which would diminish reliance on populations of convenience.

A major determinant of Hispanics' disadvantaged position in the labor market is their low educational attainment (Arbona, 1990). **Discrimination** in the schools (i.e., grade delay, minimal basic resources such as library holdings and teaching staff, tracking into dead-end general or vocational programs as opposed to college prep or honors programs) is the experience of many Mexican American and Puerto Rican students. Widespread poverty in Hispanic households negatively impacts academic performance. Small sample sizes in research on Hispanic women's educational attainment impede generalizations about barriers and facilitators of educational and occupational progress. Information on Hispanics' career decision making is sparse.

Practical Applications

A huge gap in the career counseling literature is the role of family influence on Hispanics' occupational development. An organized body of knowledge remains to be produced on this topic. On a related subject, Sosa (1998) writes of the

"Latino disconnect," a lack of awareness of one's roots and history—which is a result of post-colonialism—that impedes Latino success in business and in life in the United States. He suggests that

Continued

Continued

the values taught by a Latino's family and church need to be more closely scrutinized because they can hold back educational attainment and occupational achievement.

Another largely unexamined area is the role of work in the lives of Hispanic immigrants. The immigration issue raised its ugly head during the 1996 U.S. presidential campaign. Politics being what it is, false and exaggerated accusations were made about immigrants coming to the United States to freeload off of welfare and Medicaid (Marquez, 1996). Expediency often dictates ignoring the positive impact immigrant workers have had on their host societies (see, for example Sowell, 1994, chapter 2). Many U.S. high technology companies—which are among "the most powerful and fastest growing companies in the country" (Associated Press, 1996a, p. A2)—voiced concern that hostility toward immigration would bring fewer graduate students from abroad. Immigration reform threatened to prevent the hiring of such foreign-born, U.S.-educated science and engineering talent. The *better sort* of immigrant is always welcome, however, especially to that U.S. presidential candidate who vowed to build a security fence across all 2,000 miles of the United States-Mexico border, "and we'll say, 'Listen, José, you're not coming in!'" (New York Times News Service, 1996, p. A1).

Several big U.S. industries—including construction companies, nurseries, and fruit growers—rely on low-wage labor from Mexico and Central America and often knowingly hire these undocumented workers/illegal immigrants (Hedges, Hawkins, & Loeb, 1996). We wonder how José will be kept out of the United States when meatpacking plants in the Midwest aggressively recruit thousands of Mexicans and Central Americans to perform their dirty, dangerous jobs (Hedges et al., 1996). Some meatpacking companies advertise for prospective employees on Spanish-language radio stations along the Texas-Mexico border. "Meatpacking has the highest injury rate of all U.S. industries; 36 percent of employees are seriously injured each year" (Hawkins, 1996, p. 40). Needless to say, health insurance and other benefits are sometimes lacking for these workers. Little vocational psychology research exists on immigrants to the United States, be they Hispanic or otherwise. Valuable information awaits in the stories to be told about the role of work in undocumented Latino workers' lives (see, for example, Langewiesche, 1998; Urrea, 2004).

CASE EXAMPLE

Jesús Ruíz

"Five million people live illegally in the United States. Two million live in California alone. More than half of those are Mexican, and by the standards they left behind almost all are doing well" (Langewiesche, 1998, p. 138).

Langewiesche goes on to tell the story of Jesús Ruíz. Jesús Ruíz is a 22-year-old Zapotec Indian from the mountain village of Santa Ana Yareni in the Mexican state of Oaxaca [pronounced: whoh-háh-cah]. His primary language is Zapateco. Like many of the Indians in southern Mexico, Jesús has not culturally assimilated into that society. He speaks very little Spanish and no English.

It is the winter of 1997–98. Jesús is living in a makeshift shack in a ravine located in the craggy mountains above Escondido (San Diego County), California. The undocumented workers living in the brushy, trash-strewn ravine have named it *Los Olvidados*— the forgotten ones—because its hundred or so residents live there like unseen ghosts. Jesús's shack is made

> of plywood and corrugated plastic, patched with black plastic sheeting, and held together with nails, branches, and the frame of a wheelbarrow, which had been wedged into the dirt. . . . The center of the shack [is] a roofed but open-sided living area, which [looks] out over the ravine below; it [is] joined at one end to a three-walled kitchen, with rough shelving and a gas burner on a plywood table, and at the other end to a windowless sleeping room about the size of a big mattress. The sleeping room [has] a door that [can] be locked with a bicycle cable.
> (p. 138)

Like the others living in *Los Olvidados*, Jesús is a day laborer. He finds jobs by knocking on doors or standing on the streets. Usually he works as a gardener.

Jesús first came to *el norte* in 1991. He has gone home to Oaxaca four times, preferring the five-hour plane flight from Tijuana to the eight-day bus ride.

Like any other working person, Jesús's time is worth money. He sees no point in a prolonged, roundtrip bus journey.

Jesús's home village of Santa Ana Yareni first became connected to the U.S. labor market in 1984, when a California flower grower recruited workers for his farm an hour north of Los Angeles. The Zapotec men from Jesús's village who ventured north were taken by train to Tijuana, smuggled across the border, and then were virtually enslaved when they arrived at the flower grower's. The Zapotecs were forced to work sixteen-hour days and threatened with being turned in to the Border Patrol if they did not cooperate. In 1990, some of the Zapotecs sought legal recourse. The flower grower was indicted by a federal grand jury in Los Angeles on charges of slavery, but he plea bargained and was charged instead with corporate racketeering and labor and immigrant violations. The Zapotecs managed to make their way to *Los Olvidados,* where a small group from Santa Ana Yareni had established themselves. The day-to-day job opportunities that presented themselves to the Zapotecs of *Los Ovidados* were preferable to the enforced servitude of the flower grower's farm. Jesús had not yet come north at the time of the flower grower's incident, but he still felt its impact. He remains in *Los Olvidados* because of the horror stories he has heard about life outside the ravine.

On one of his trips home, Jesús married Juana. They are now the parents of three young children, the latter two born in the United States. Juana worked part time cleaning houses while other women in *Los Olvidados* watched her babies. Then the Border Patrol raided *Los Olvidados* in November 1997. Juana and a visiting cousin shut themselves in the

Continued

Continued

shack, but the crying babies led them to be found by Border Patrol agents. When the agents heard that the babies were U.S. citizens, the family was left in peace.

El Niño was ultimately responsible for driving the family apart. Unusually heavy rains made life in *Los Olvidados* too hard for Juana and the babies. Jesús bought his wife and children one-way plane tickets to Mexico City, where they went to live with a relative. There is nothing for them back at Santa Ana Yareni. Jesús abandoned his extended family obligations back home, and he is no longer welcomed there.

Jesús dreams of one day buying a piece of land on the outskirts of Mexico City and building a one-room house with money saved from his work in the United States. In addition to gardening, Jesús and the other Zapotec men of *Los Olvidados* take jobs house painting, cement laying, house moving, and fence building. The Zapotecs have learned to claim expertise in any job a customer needs, to negotiate the wage in advance, and to get paid in cash if possible. The contrast between Jesús's lifestyle and the wealthy people he works for does not escape him. He attributes a higher-income lifestyle to the fact that both husband and wife work.

Jesús and his fellow Zapotecs are slowly becoming Americanized. They have learned enough English phrases to negotiate jobs and wages. Some of the men have learned the public transit routes. Others among the men have joined church parishes. Two of the younger Zapotec men have even taken up surfing.

Jesús's primary concern is his wife and children in Mexico City. He quietly admits that a difficult future in the United States is less daunting than his impossible dream of life in Mexico. He has no time to worry about projected increases in Border Patrol budgets to add more agents that will make it harder to cross into the United States. While Jesús is unlikely to ever gain U.S. citizenship status, he has no retreat. He lives a marginalized existence as he looks forward to the day when he can bring his wife and children back to the United States.

Asian Americans Confucianism, Buddhism, and Taoism have all affected Asian cultural values (Axelson, 1993), with Confucianism the dominant influence in Chinese culture for nearly twenty-five centuries (Yang, 1991), as it is today despite Communism's tenure in mainland China. In **Confucianism**, "patriarchal ideas are embraced and a formal relationship system emphasizes humility, politeness, and respect" (Axelson, 1993, p. 438). In **Buddhism**, "self-improvement can be found through doing good work and study and through the control of undesirable emotions; optimism, calmness, and harmony are valued" (p. 438). In **Taoism**, "ancestor worship provides guidance and advice for present living. . . . Traditionally, followers of Taoism are attached to burial sites (location) of ancestors, where they can go to pray, meditate, and pay respects before the graves of the ancestors" (p. 438). Many refugees who were

Practical Applications

More consideration needs to be given to broader, external structural factors—such as institutional racism and cultural racism—that influence the occupational development of U.S. workers of Asian ancestry. **Institutional racism** refers to "social policies, laws, and regulations whose purpose it is to maintain the economic and social advantage of the racial/ethnic group in power" (J. Jones, 1972, cited in Atkinson, Morten, & Sue, 1993, p. 11). **Cultural racism** refers to societal "beliefs and customs that promote the assumption that the products of the dominant culture (e.g., language, traditions, appearance) are superior to other cultures" (J. Jones, 1972, cited in Atkinson et al., 1993, p.11). An unwillingness to address issues of racism, among other forms of oppres-

sion, can look like privileged complacency on the part of vocational practitioners. Career counselors' receptivity to exploring the unique cultural history of their clients of Asian ancestry means reducing their reliance on articles that have failed to capture the within-group differences of the group that scholars have broadly labeled Asian Americans. Anti-immigration political sentiments—of which racism is admittedly part—also need incorporation into the occupational development of some Asian subgroups. These Asian immigrant subgroups probably need occupational guidance more desperately than many Asian American college students who, in spite of barriers they may encounter to their occupational development, are already well on their way

accustomed to visiting their ancestors' graves are apt to feel lonely in the United States and unable to make decisions without the advice of their forebearers.

Hsia and Hirano-Nakanishi (1989) write:

> With the exception of scholars, bureaucrats, and political activists, Americans of Asian ancestry rarely think of themselves first and foremost as "Asian American." Most ethnic Asians, particularly newcomers, are more likely to identify with their specific national or regional identities: Vietnamese, Korean, Hmong, Punjabi Sikh, Cantonese or Taiwanese, Visayan or Ilocano (p. 24).

In addition, Asian Americans come from countries as disparate as Bhutan and Burma, Laos and Malaysia (Barnes & Bennett, 2002). In countries like India and China, ethnic and regional differences are extensive. Thus, in the same way that social constructions of the model minority are inaccurate, use of the term *Asian American* by vocational practitioners may not be helpful either.

Career counselors will hardly get an accurate sense of whom their clients are if they already have a preconceived notion of how clients identify themselves. Within-

Practical Applications

Discussion of ethnic identity among Asians in the United States is found in Sodowsky, Kwan, and Pannu (1995). We suggest that career counselors assess the extent to which traditional Asian cultural values are present in their clients' lives, without automatically assuming that such values are uniformly present for clients (see, for example, Mizokawa and Ryckman, 1990). Very likely, the presence of traditional Asian cultural values is going to be contextual in nature, contingent upon such things as ethnic subgroup and birth order. A second- or third-born son may feel less family pressure and perceive greater occupational pos-

sibilities than a first-born son. For others, partial cultural assimilation may occur, with native language (Chen & Leong, 1997), religion, and customs predominating at home, but English predominating at school and in the workplace. Structural assimilation may be difficult in cases where large numbers of Asian students in a university's freshman class (Butterfield, 1990) result in college admission quotas (Chen & Leong, 1997). Marital assimilation may occur among more educated, higher-income Asian Americans (Chen & Leong, 1997), but not for those who are less educated, lower income.

group differences among U.S. workers of Asian ancestry are vast, even more so than among Hispanics. It may not be useful to persist in using the term *Asian American,* especially if the people to whom it refers do not embrace it. Given that vocational psychology lacks a cohesive framework for working with U.S. workers of Asian ancestry, continued use of an irrelevant term will only muddy the waters even more.

Literature on counseling those of Asian ancestry states that an active, directive practitioner style is most effective (Exum & Lau, 1988, cited in Baruth & Manning, 1991; D. W. Sue & D. Sue, 1990; Yagi & Oh, 1995). Ivey (1988) notes that giving advice, providing information, and focusing on a specific problem are frequently used in vocational planning. Ostensibly, then, some U.S. workers of Asian ancestry should be highly amenable to occupational guidance interventions. But the available empirical evidence is disjointed (Leong & Gim-Chung, 1995; Leong & Serafica, 1995). While case studies can be immensely useful (Chen & Leong, 1997; Cook, 1997; Fouad & Tang, 1997; Shanasarian, 1997), "educators, counselors, and pupil personnel workers often do not have enough knowledge of the Asian-American experience to make enlightened decisions" (D. W. Sue & D. Sue, 1990, p. 202). This knowledge base could be expanded by increasing the use of contextual interpretivism as a research methodology.

Acculturation will moderate family influence on occupational development of U.S. workers of Asian ancestry (Leong, 1993; Leong & Tata, 1990; Yang, 1991). Strength of **filial piety**—that is, the child's sense of allegiance and obligation to parents (D. Sue & D. W. Sue, 1993)—also will vary by acculturation. So will the interdependence of family members, the restraint of potentially disruptive emotions, the tradition of patriarchy, and the inculcation of guilt and shame.

Native Americans Several areas await further research and practical applications for vocational psychology and career counseling among Native Americans. To the extent that collectivism rather than individualism "forms the normative base of Native American [individual's] culture" (Pedigo, 1983, p. 274), then client occupational concerns will need to be considered "within the context of a larger family and community social system" (LaFromboise, Trimble, & Mohatt, 1990, p. 642). "Many Indian people view family, home, and community as the center of their existence rather than a job or career" (Martin, 1991, p. 275).

Contextual interpretivism merits closer scrutiny to move forward the knowledge about Native American work lives, including the persistence of **career myths.** Herring (1990) defines career myths as "irrational attitudes about the career development process. These irrational attitudes most often are generated from historical, familial patterns of career ignorance and negative career-development experiences" (p. 13). Native American youth particularly are vulnerable to career myths.

Three common influences on career myths have been identified (Herring, 1990). First, research on Native American occupational development emphasizes populations on Western reservations. Historical and sociological perspectives predominate, and most research has been conducted by non-Native Americans, which can "lack both cultural and ethnic perspectives" (p. 15). Second, continued negative stereotyping by the media and by "school materials (e.g., textbooks) need to be purged of any inadvertent illustrations, photographs, and references that inaccurately depict Native Americans" (p. 15). Practitioners can help clients determine how negative stereotyping overlapped into myths about occupational development. Third, a lack of career information and related training requirements can impede occupational development of Native American youth. These misconceptions can adversely affect aspirations, decision making, and job satisfaction.

Herring (1990) concludes:

> To attain the desired goal of the elimination of barriers to the successful career development and the subsequent restoration of rational career thinking will require a multifaceted intervention, which will entail improving counseling techniques (individual and family) and improving the current, unequal career opportunity structure and poor educational systems that created the disparity in achievement and the low expectation levels of Native American students (p. 17).

Once again, we can only note how occupational development cannot be artificially separated from external structural factors that impinge upon the role of work in people's lives.

THE POSTMODERN FAMILY
AND VOCATIONAL PSYCHOLOGY

With increased attention on dual-career and single parent families, vocational psychology has yet to attend to the postmodern family. Gergen (1991) describes a scene from the postmodern family's daily life:

> Tommy needs to eat at 6:00 because of a school function at 7:00. His sister, Martha, must be picked up from her field hockey game at 7:15. Both children are upset because their mother, Sarah, has an office function and can't get home until after 8:00—thus, no dinner and no transportation. Sarah asks her husband, Rick, to come to the rescue, but he has to work late to prepare for a flight to Dallas the next morning. It is also Sarah's mother's birthday the next day, but Sarah is not prepared. Urgent messages await on the answering machine, one from a longtime friend of Rick's, in town for a day and wanting to drop by, and another from a close friend of Sarah's in tears because of her floundering marriage (p. 29).

Rick and Sarah experience more dread, guilt, and anxiety that they should be spending the evening helping their children with their homework, planning for their family vacation, paying long-neglected bills, or spending quality time together.

The postmodern family is likely to feel scattered by the intensifying busyness of their lives. Social saturation has shrunk the family's physical world while their cultural and social worlds have expanded and grown more complex. In addition, rising divorce rates and remarriages, as well as other variations in living arrangements (homosexual couples, housemates), have muddled the definition of family. This blurring of boundaries has given rise to what is now called the *floating family*.

The Floating Family

The **floating family** transcends the boundaries of traditional family units related by blood, common residence, and shared surnames (Gergen, 1991), and consists of relationships that can be in a more continuous state of flux than with one's family of origin. Floating-family networks are based on affectional ties of choice rather than blood ties of chance, and often occur when traditional family members withdraw from the family's orbit through connections established by the technologies of social saturation. An individual's most important relationship may be with an unrelated person who lives far away; the connection largely maintained by electronic mail and/or long-distance telephone calls, with only occasional visits. The floating-family network fluctuates and shifts with circumstances and time.

The Formed Family

What Gergen (1991) calls the floating family, Pipher (1996) calls the **formed family,** although she does not use the term *postmodern*. Similar to the floating family, the

Practical Applications

Several issues acknowledged by Gergen (1991) can guide practitioners working with clients from saturated and floating families. Some clients may initially feel disconcerted when they begin to notice extensions of familylike relationships with co-workers on the job. It is not unusual for some clients to feel more at home during a Monday lunch with a longtime working comrade than the traditional family members with whom the client shared a Sunday dinner the night before. Are practitioners willing to normalize their clients' co-worker floating-family connections? The practitioner can help clients determine whether such connections are mutual; one-sided floating-family feelings toward co-workers can set the client up for disappointment.

When floating-family feelings among co-workers are mutual, some clients may feel guilty or confused about the connections, believing that such primary relationships should only be reserved for spouses, romantic partners, and/or traditional family members. At such times, the practitioner can explore with the client whether nostalgia and sentimentality are present or whether

upon closer inspection the idealized safe, secure, nurturing, stable, traditional family was not also oppressive, sexist, inflexible, and emotionally stultifying. Another issue related to the real losses involved in the client's traditional family transformation is what ideals co-workers as floating family can offer as compensation. Practitioners can listen for the value clients place on having a broader understanding of the world provided by co-workers as floating family. Practitioners can collaborate with clients in weighing whether traditional family relationships are being taken for granted.

With clients who see themselves in a saturated world, practitioners have to decide whether to knowingly adopt a moderate postmodern stance and support the idea that there are many aspects to the self—if not actually many selves—and whether emotional sustenance for the client can be derived from various co-worker, floating-family members. Another possibility is for practitioners to actually give clients O'Hara and Anderson (1991) and Gergen (1991) to read as a bibliotherapy intervention for further discussion.

formed family evolves for those people who do not have access to a supportive biological family or for those who prefer a community of friends to the families into which they were born. The staying power of a formed family is contingent upon whether its members stay together despite disagreements, lend each other money when one member loses a job, or visit one another in a convalescent center after one has been paralyzed in a car crash. Pipher also notes that some immigrants become formed family members to help each other in a new country. Formed families also

---

Practical Applications

To help clients discern the reliable members of their biological or formed families, practitioners can ask questions like (Pipher, 1996): If you lose your job, who will lend you money to pay the rent? Our concern is whether it is wise to establish a formed family with co-workers. What are the political risks of establishing such relationships at work? Will certain information be used against you (e.g., fighting with your mate, going through a period of depression) when it comes time for job-performance evaluations, pay raises, or promotions? Clients may need to think through the pros and cons of making co-workers part of their formed families.

---

occur when biological families do not stick together during a crisis. Requisite social skills are needed to be in a formed family: dull, abrasive, and shy people can be left out of formed families.

The Myth of Workplace as Family

Floating-family networks are based on affectional ties of mutual choice rather than blood ties of chance. This can mean that, given the number of hours co-workers can spend in each other's company at the workplace, it would hardly be surprising for some employees to have a family-like feeling with co-workers on the job (Gergen, 1991). In fact, some workplaces may encourage employees to feel as if they are part of "one big happy family." This is a myth that can lull one into a false sense of security. Unstated assumptions go along with the myth of workplace as family.

Thomas (1990) writes that viewing the workplace as family "suggests not only that father knows best; it also suggests that sons will inherit the business, that daughters should stick to doing the company dishes, and that if Uncle Deadwood doesn't perform, we'll put him in the chimney corner and feed him for another 30 years regardless" (p. 115). Such unstated assumptions have their constituencies and defenders. If Uncle Deadwood was told he did good work for ten years, but the last twelve years or so were unproductive and it was time to help him find another chimney, then shockwaves would travel through the workplace. Every family-oriented employee would draw their swords in defense of the sanctity of guaranteed jobs.

Another outgrowth of the myth of workplace as family is unchallenged paternalism (Thomas, 1990). If father knows best, then managers will seek employees who will follow their lead and do as they do. If the managers cannot find employees who are exactly like themselves, then they will seek people who aspire to be exactly like themselves. Employees become extensions of managers' hands and minds, responsive to every unspoken cue and compliant. But what happens to the workplace as family when there is a shake-up in management?

Relevance for Multicultural and Diverse Populations Workplace as family is dishonest mythology (Thomas, 1990). Father does not always know best; in fact, sometimes he is completely out of touch. Managers cannot buy into the "father knows best" concept, seek employees exactly like themselves, and create a workplace that is truly hospitable to multicultural and diverse populations. These populations can learn from the experiences of members of the dominant culture who have been burned by their workplaces that posed as families.

INCORPORATING A SYSTEMIC APPROACH INTO VOCATIONAL PSYCHOLOGY

For vocational psychology to incorporate a more systemic approach, closer attention will have to be given to family practice in the twenty-first century. Three major movements represent an overall epistemological shift in the marriage and family therapy fields: feminism, social constructionism, and multiculturalism (Hardy, 1993). These three movements are also shaping the vocational psychology field. Both fields could gain immeasurably by entering into a dialogue on how these three movements affect issues of mutual interest, especially as the full impact of these movements has not been realized in either field.

Practitioners will need knowledge of "how the dynamics of power affect all levels of human functioning, particularly with regard to differences related to race, ethnicity, gender, and class" (Pinderhughes, 1995, p. 139). Dynamics of power clarify the value society assigns to a multicultural group's status and how such status influences between-group differences. To avoid an abuse of power and exploitation of clients, practitioners need to be aware of their own "internalized responses to power in relation to racial, ethnic, gender, and class differences" (p. 138).

9

❖

Career Counseling in the Schools

Here is something adults always say that I do not like:
"Edith, what do you want to be when you grow up?"
As if what I am right now is not enough.

—Edith Ann
(Wagner, 1994, p. 20)

Many of us can remember being asked, "What are you going to be when you grow up?" We probably felt proud when we had a ready answer to give, or confused or worried when we could not give a definite response. As Edith Ann so aptly puts it, the question can make a child feel inadequate, as if enjoying childhood were not enough. In this chapter, we begin by examining the *National Career Development Guidelines*. We also consider the school counselor's role in career development using American School Counselor Association guidelines. Then we present programs, techniques, assessments, and resources for career counseling for students K–12. Finally, we address an often-overlooked aspect of occupational guidance programs—the involvement of parents.

THE NATIONAL CAREER
DEVELOPMENT GUIDELINES

Before discussing the application of career counseling to various age groups and populations, we want to mention a major resource that details the national standards for career development, starting with kindergarten and carrying through until adulthood.

In 1996 the National Occupational Information Coordinating Committee (NOICC) published the *National Career Development Guidelines,* a handbook of information for anyone responsible for career development in any setting for any age group.

The purpose of the handbook is "to strengthen and improve comprehensive, competency-based career counseling, guidance and education programs" (p. i). It explains its standards, including national, state, and local roles, discussing organizational commitments, structure, and support; presents a proven implementation process to establish new programs or enhance existing ones; discusses marketing the program and the competencies and indicators for elementary, middle, and high schools; provides information for getting started, with examples of lesson plans and activities; and presents the competencies and indicators, as well as information on building career development programs for adults in various settings. Information about the *National Career Development Guidelines* and other publications can be found on the NCDA Web site (http://www.ncda.org).

SCHOOL GUIDELINES

The NOICC (1996) defines the National Career Development Guidelines Competencies and Indicators for elementary, middle, and high schools. Factors pertaining to self-knowledge, educational and occupational exploration, and career planning are presented in Tables 9.1, 9.2, and 9.3.

In 1997 the American School Counselor Association (ASCA) changed its national standards for school counseling programs to include three broad areas: academic development, career development, and personal/social development. Following are the nine national standards:

Academic Development

Standard A: Students will acquire the attitudes, knowledge and skills contributing to effective learning in school and across the life span.

Standard B: Students will complete school with the academic preparation essential to choose from a wide range of substantial postsecondary options, including college.

Standard C: Students will understand the relationship of academics to the world of work and to life at home and in the community.

Career Development

Standard A: Students will acquire the skills to investigate the world of work in relation to knowledge of self and to make an informed career decision.

Standard B: Students will employ strategies to achieve future career success and satisfaction.

Standard C: Students will understand the relationship between personal qualities, education and training, and the world of work.

TABLE 9.1 Self-knowledge

ELEMENTARY	MIDDLE SCHOOL	HIGH SCHOOL
Knowledge of the importance of a positive self-concept	Knowledge of the influence of a positive self-concept	Understanding the influence of a positive self-concept
Skills to interact positively with others	Skills to interact positively with others	Skills to interact positively with others
Awareness of the importance of growth and change	Knowledge of the importance of growth and change	Understanding the impact of growth and development

SOURCE: NOICC (1996), pp. 1–8.

TABLE 9.2 Educational and Occupational Exploration

ELEMENTARY	MIDDLE SCHOOL	HIGH SCHOOL
Awareness of the benefits of educational achievement	Knowledge of the benefits of educational achievement to career opportunities	Understanding the relationship between educational achievement and career planning
Awareness of the relationship between work and learning	Understanding the relationship between work and learning	Understanding the need for positive attitudes towards work and learning
Skills to understand and use career information	Skills to locate, understand, and use career information	Skills to locate, evaluate, and interpret career information
Awareness of the importance of personal responsibility and good work habits	Knowledge of skills necessary to seek and obtain jobs	Skills to prepare to seek, obtain, maintain, and change jobs
Awareness of how work relates to the needs and functions of society	Understanding how work relates to the needs and functions of the economy and society	Understanding how societal needs and functions influence the nature and structure of work

SOURCE: NOICC (1996), pp. 1–8.

TABLE 9.3 Career Planning

ELEMENTARY	MIDDLE SCHOOL	HIGH SCHOOL
Understanding how to make decisions	Skills to make decisions	Skills to make decisions
Awareness of the interrelationship of life roles	Knowledge of the interrelationship of life roles	Understanding the interrelationship of life roles
Awareness of different occupations and changing male/female roles	Knowledge of different occupations and changing male/female roles	Understanding the continuous changes in male/female roles
Awareness of the career planning process	Understanding the process of career planning	Skills in career planning

SOURCE: NOICC (1996), pp. 1–8.

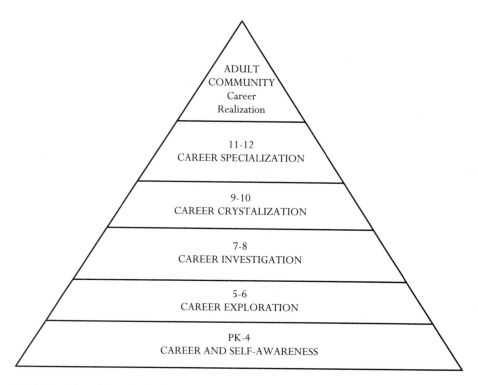

FIGURE 9.1 Career Education Design

Personal/Social Development

Standard A: Students will acquire the attitudes, knowledge and interpersonal skills to help them understand and respect self and others.

Standard B: Students will make decisions, set goals and take necessary action to achieve goals.

Standard C: Students will understand safety and survival skills.

In career development, students learn to "employ strategies to achieve future career success and satisfaction . . .[and] understand the relationship between personal qualities, education and training, and the world of work (Campbell & Dahir, 1997, pp. 17, 19). Table 9.5 provides an example of delivery-system activities in a program that represents compliance with a state comprehensive guidance program and gives the counselor's role in each activity defined.

Figure 9.1, the Career Education Design, gives an example of a career and technology department program that implements the career education process for a school district. The program was developed and implemented by Linda Catherine in the East Central Independent School District (ECISD) in San Antonio, Texas, and is still being utilized effectively.

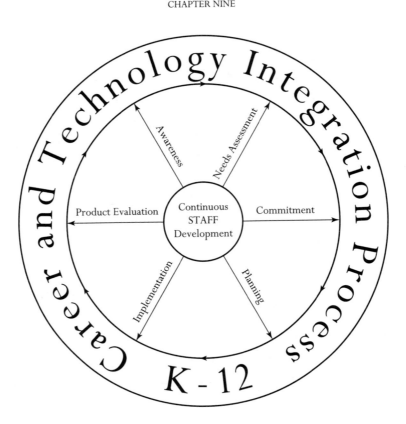

FIGURE 9.2 Career and Technology Integration Process

At East Central ISD, all education is viewed as career education. The classroom becomes the workplace, the student's first job. From K–12, experiences and activities at each level provide readiness for the next level. Although the means and methods of instructional emphasis may shift, learners will encounter career education from pre-kindergarten through grade twelve. Academics and work ethics combine to teach life-long skills such as teamwork, attendance, problem solving, technology, and product excellence. East Central gives each student the opportunity to achieve his or her highest potential. Table 9.4 outlines the specific components of each of the steps in the Career Education Design.

Figure 9.2 is a graphic representation of the Wheel-Hub Model of the Career and Technology Integration Process. The two considerations of the model in Figure 9.2 are that career and technology integration in K–12 be a comprehensive systematic and developmental process involving all ECISD staff and students and that through the career and technology integration process, students will develop the (Labor) Secretary's Commission on Achieving Necessary Skills (SCANS) skills (described in more detail in the high school section) and competencies necessary to be successfully

TABLE 9.4 East Central Independent School District Career Education Design

Level / Stage		(CAT LAB)
ADULT COMMUNITY Career Realization and Employment 11–12+ Career Specialization	(CAT LAB) Assessment Instruments Database Colleges and Careers Business Partnerships 1–1 Career Counseling Portfolio/Career Pathways update (Grades 8–14) Employment Information Resource and Referral Center Financial Aid SAT/ACT/TASP Information College Representatives and Recruiters Scholarships, Grants	(CAT LAB) Shadowing/Mentorships Business Panel Discussion and Speakers Mock Interviews Teacher/Counselor Inservice Vocational Student Organizations Coops School To Work Articulation Tech Prep College/Career Day, College Visits Internships
9–10 Career Crystalization	Career Pathways Update (Grades 8–14) Career Search and Research Career Instruction Portfolio/Resume Assessment Instruments and Inventories Database College and Careers Teacher/Counselor Inservices	
7–8 Career Investigation 5–6 Career Exploration	Database College and Careers Career Pathways (8th) Interest Inventory (8th) Career Pathways Brochure (Doors) Career Resource Libraries Career Days Career Instruction 6th and 8th Grades Presentations	Vocational Biographies Business & College Field Trips Second Step 6 & 6 Social Skills Career Investigation Course for All 8th Graders
PK–4 Career and Self-Awareness	Career Resource Libraries Career Instruction 1st and 4th Grade Presentations Hands-on Career Activities Guest Speakers Field Trips Career Integrated Curriculum and Resources (CASA) Career Guidance in the Classroom Career Fairs/Career Pathways	Second Step (Social Skills) Career Interviews

employed in the global workforce of the new millennium. The pervasive integration of career thinking and relevance throughout the school program can prepare students for the lifelong task of finding suitable and satisfying work.

THE SCHOOL COUNSELOR'S ROLE IN CAREER DEVELOPMENT

An essential role of the school counselor is to facilitate students' career development from pre-K through grade twelve using a comprehensive guidance program, such as one described in Gysbers and Henderson (2000). The authors present their updated guidance program as an example of a current and widely used student-centered program in the schools that is specifically designed to facilitate students' personal, career, and academic development with strong support from and in collaboration with parents, teachers, administrators, and community members, including personnel in the business and labor communities. One of the focuses of the model is Life Career Development: Student Competencies by Domains and Goals.

In an evaluation of the comprehensive guidance program in Salt Lake City public schools, "Nelson and Gardner (1998) found that students in schools with more fully implemented guidance programs rated their overall education as better, took more advanced mathematics and science courses, and had higher scores on every area of the ACT" (cited in Gysbers, 2002, p. 152).

It is Gybers and Henderson's belief that the same organizational structure for guidance that works today will work in 2021. Some of the guidance activities, procedures, and professional time allocations will probably change, but the basic organizational structure for guidance will remain. An example of how Henderson has incorporated career education from pre-K through grade twelve using the total comprehensive guidance program, is illustrated in Table 9.5.

Until we begin to view students and teachers as workers and the classroom as a workplace, career education can never become a top priority for education reform. "Work is clearly the bedrock of career education. Unless and until we define work and understand it, there is no easy way of defining and describing career education" (Hoyt, 2001, p. 2). He further discusses the need for career education to be tied to education reform. In order for the reform of K–12 education, he suggests several changes that must:

- Involve activities that most teachers are capable of performing and that both teachers and their pupils find interesting and enjoy doing
- Be inexpensive to carry out
- Provide teachers with a sense of ownership of the project
- Yield increases in student development

TABLE 9.5 Facilitating Students' Career Development Through Comprehensive Guidance Programs: Delivery System Activities

GUIDANCE CURRICULUM	INDIVIDUAL PLANNING SYSTEM	RESPONSIVE SERVICES	SYSTEM SUPPORT
Provides guidance content in a systematic way to all students Pre-K–12	Assists students in planning, monitoring, & managing their personal & career development	Addresses the immediate concerns of students	Includes program staff, and school support activities and services
Self-Understanding Educational & Work World Information Decision-making skills Goal-setting skills Planning skills	Educational Planning & Decision-Making Career Planning & Decision-Making Assessment for Self-understanding Information Resources for Exploring & Planning the Work World Student Advisory Program Parent Involvement	Small Group Counseling Parent Consultation Individual guidance Individual counseling	Advisor Consultation Administrator/Consultation
Counselor Role: Group Guidance Consultation	Counselor Role: Assessment Guidance Consultation Coordination	Counselor Role: Counseling Consultation Coordination	Counselor Role: Professionalism Program Management Consultation

SOURCE: Patricia Henderson, Ed.D., Northside Independent School District, San Antonio, TX.

- Involve communities, including parents
- Result in some kind of credit or award for the teachers who participate in the project (Hoyt, 2001, p. 5)

Career education needs to be tied to education reform. "In career education, the word 'work' is defined as intentional effort, other than that whose primary purpose is either coping or relaxation, aimed at producing benefits for oneself or for oneself and others" (Hoyt, 2001, p. 2). If all educators were to consider seriously the application of the word *work* to what they are doing, they could make substantial progress toward real reform of education.

Part of education reform involves career educators becoming proactive in the use of computer assisted programs in their work with students and teachers. This involves incorporating technology in all career classes, teacher in-services, and parent programs. We must recognize that there is a growing gap between the skills, knowledge, attitudes, attributes, and behaviors that most students leave our schools with now and what is needed in the workplace. Career educators can assist in students' learning what they need to survive and thrive in the culture of the twenty-first century.

Gysbers' vision for guidance and counseling in the twenty-first century is that guidance and counseling program be fully implemented in every school district in the United States, serving all students and their parents, and staffed by active, involved school counselors.

> When guidance and counseling is conceptualized, organized and implemented as a program, it places school counselors conceptually and structurally in the center of education and makes it possible for them to be active and involved. As a result, guidance and counseling becomes an integral and transformative program, not a marginal and supplemental activity. It provides school counselors with the structure, time and resources to fully use their expertise (Gysbers, 2001, p. 103).

If the career counselor's role in educational reform as we have highlighted is to be effective, administrative support is needed.

Career Assessment in the Schools

If one wishes to gauge the extent of career assessment in school counseling practices, Freeman's 1996 study of high school counselors' use of standardized paper-and-pencil and computer assisted tools is enlightening. Sixty-nine percent of those who use career assessment tools use more than one, and forty-four percent use both computer and paper-and-pencil tools, indicating there is no clear preference of any one tool. Thirty percent of high school counselors never use any career assessment tool, and nearly half do not use a computer in assessment. This may indicate a low priority given to career-planning activities, even at a time when the world of work is so rapidly changing. Perhaps greater priorities within some schools revolve around (1) scheduling, (2) increasing standardized achievement test scores, (3) gang/drug/ alcohol-related issues, (4) crisis management, (5) academic failure, and (6) remedial problems. The emphasis on career development goals in the American School Counselor Association guidelines coupled with the results of surveys by the National Career Development Association (Brown, Minor, & Jepsen, 1992), which reported that the public highly supports career development in the schools, show a need for more career development activities in the schools.

Given the increased pressure for career guidance in the schools on one hand and the apparent failure to use assessment tools on the other, the disparity between goals and practice needs to be addressed. Freeman (1996) asks several pertinent questions:

> Are the roles of school counselors too fragmented to allow for systematic career development activities? Do counselors prefer not to use assessment tools? Do schools perceive career assessment activities to be a lower priority than working with at-risk students? Are the tools inappropriate for the school setting? Have school counselors been trained to use career counseling computer assisted and paper-and-pencil systems? (p. 194).

In a review of twenty-nine national reports on educational reform, increased attention to career guidance with education as preparation for the world of work was identified as the most important function of school counselors (Hoyt, 1989). The school counselor's role in educational reform highlights the need to understand the counselor's role, with administrative support vital in countering negative stereotypes and facilitating shared decision making and multidisciplinary efforts (Allen, 1994).

Administrative Support

School counselors often find their roles to be more like administrative assistants than counselors. This raises the issue of administrative support for school counselors. Are principals and administrators aware of the ASCA guidelines for school counselors? Do school counselors get placed in the roles of paper pushers or disciplinarians? Do principals give career and occupational development high priority? Lack of support from their administration leaves school counselors in the dilemma of wanting to provide counseling and guidance but having their time delegated to mundane tasks, with little time or energy for guidance. Nonetheless, school counselors must take responsibility for informing administrators of the scope and value of their services and skills.

Much research has been done on the ambiguity of a counselor's role and job tasks. School counselors appear to underutilize career assessment tools. Some school counselors may see career counseling as a lower priority than other roles, whereas others may see career guidance as a higher priority, but lack time, support, or knowledge of the area.

Some school counselors do place a higher importance on counseling for personal development and negate the importance of career counseling. But by practicing career counseling, a school counselor may help a student find his or her own niche in the world of work, which positively affects a student's personal development.

We're suggesting that a career education course be required for all teacher education and education administration majors. A current challenge to vocational psychology is for practitioners to increase their dialogue with school administrators at all levels regarding the importance of continuous, ongoing education of students about the world of work. Even schools in the same district vary dramatically in the time and attention administrators allow school counselors to devote to career and work-related educational activities. A once-a-year *career day* is not enough, particularly if school counselors get so busy booking speakers and coordinating exhibits that students in personal crisis are ignored (we have seen this happen repeatedly). And while career-related information may be included in curricula pertaining to math, science, social studies, and languages, teachers may have to receive constant reminders about opportunities that exist in the world of work that are relevant to the subjects they teach.

Teachers who have never worked in any other profession may especially benefit from in-services on educating their students about the work world, expanding beyond the vocational education tracks available in many school district programs. Optimally, a required course in career development for all teacher education majors would transform how opportunities in the world of work are taught in the schools. It could change the way teachers think about their subject matter's relevance and help school counselors whose hands are often tied by administrative responsibilities.

In addition, a required career education course for all educational administration majors, including those on the graduate level who plan to become principals and superintendents, would reinforce the importance of career education in the schools. If educational administrators took such a course, they would be more aware, supportive, and respectful of school counselors' and teachers' efforts to inculcate their students with knowledge of the work world.

Administrators, teachers, and school counselors all need to be informed about ways to incorporate occupations/careers into the learning process. Dialogue between their respective state and national professional organizations would be useful in coordinating career education efforts among all school personnel. Most states have an education agency that sets parameters and guidelines for career education programs in the curriculum. Oftentimes there are separate state agencies: one for career education and one for vocational education, including career technology and school-to-work. These agencies determine the types of information and competencies that are required for each age group. In many places, sad to say, these mandates are not followed, or they are merely recommendations that are not enforced. Whether mandated or recommended, these guidelines can help obtain funds for implementing various special programs through Work Force Development, School-to-Work, and Tech Prep allocations.

PROGRAMS, TECHNIQUES, ASSESSMENTS, AND RESOURCES FOR CAREER COUNSELING K–12

Elementary Schools

The American School Counseling Association (ASCA) realizes the importance of career guidance in the schools for students from pre-K through grade twelve. A comprehensive developmental guidance program is encouraged because children and adolescents pass through various developmental stages as they mature. Using this type of program addresses the personal/social, educational, and career development needs of all students. By understanding what happens at each developmental stage, the counselor can be more effective in working with students' attitudes toward learning, attainment of their career goals, and awareness of their responsibility for self, society, family, and career. Career guidance programs should help students become lifelong learners who can access and understand information about themselves and the world of work to help them make wise and timely decisions (Ettinger 2001).

Exploring the world of work in elementary school helps students begin to focus on self-understanding and to have an awareness of where they can fit into the world of work. They should begin recognizing a variety of work settings and careers, including work roles and responsibilities, each occupation's contribution to the quality of life in a community, and technology's role in the workforce. Elementary years are also a time to begin developing important interpersonal skills such as listening, communicating personal needs, and managing conflict (Ettinger 2001).

The following program idea is an Experiential Model for Career Guidance for Early Childhood. The goal is to create learner-centered, experiential hands-on activities that facilitate career awareness. Schools with grades K–2 involved in this model need to have school stores. The children earn play money by coming to school, by earning good grades, and by performing activities and behaving in an outstanding manner. Once a month, the children are allowed to buy things from the store with money they have earned. The stores have penny items, books, toys, and games that may relate to the theme or unit they are exploring in the classroom. There also may be career-oriented dramatic play kits, books, videos, tapes, records, games, and toys. Another activity in this model is a field trip to a children's museum as part of a unit or theme, especially when there are career-oriented activities (Kyle & Hennis in Peterson & González, 2000, Chapter 1).

A program for grades 3–5 is Finding Out the Child's Underlying Self: A Career Awareness Model for Children (FOCUS). The model includes a basic four-step assessment:

1. Self-report of the child about his or her interests
2. Assessment of the child's indicated interests
3. Assessment of the child's basic personality through another measure
4. Observation of the child in a natural setting

This basic FOCUS model can be applied in a variety of ways. See Figure 9.3.

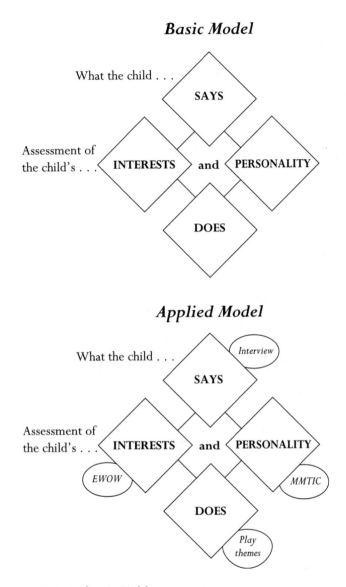

FIGURE 9.3 The *Focus* Model

SOURCE: Smith et al., in Peterson and González, Chapter 2, p. 11.

Assessments of Elementary School Students' Career Interests and Preferences

1. Information interviews of teacher to assess interests
2. Exploring the World of Work (E-WOW)
3. Job-OE
4. Career Trek

Practical Applications

A series of books for elementary school girls encourages them to consider non-traditional occupations. Astronomer (Ghez & Cohen, 1995) and cardiologist (Redborg & Cohen, 1996) are explored in English language books. Architect (Siegel & Cohen, 1992a, 1992b), engineer (Cohen, 1992, 1995), marine biologist (1992a, 1992b), paleontologist (Gabriel & Cohen, 1993a, 1993b), and zoologist (Thompson & Cohen, 1992, 1993) are explored in both English- and Spanish-language books. These innovative books raise occupational possibilities for little girls before they reach an age where they are told they can't do something. The Berenstain Bears (Berenstain & Berenstain, 1974) also convey a can-do attitude that encourages girls to remain confident in their capabilities to accomplish various tasks.

As we will discuss, the confidence gap that widens between adolescent females and males in middle and high school can be minimized by a solid foundation set for girls during their elementary school years. "By sixth grade . . . both girls and boys have learned to equate maleness with opportunity and femininity with constraint" (Orenstein, 1994, p. xiv). Canfield and Wells (1994) provide teachers with 100 ways to enhance children's self-concept, which can only maximize occupational potential for all students.

---

5. Dream Catchers

6. Elementary Careers

7. Children's Dictionary of Occupations

8. The Murphy-Meisgeier Type Indicator for Children (MMTIC)

9. Early School Personality Questionnaire (ESPQ)

10. Personality Inventory for Children (PIC)

(See Appendix 3 for publisher and test detail information.)

Resources for Elementary Career Education Activities

1. American School Counselor Association. (1997). *The National Standards for School Counseling Programs.* Alexandria, VA: Author.

2. *Career Immersion: Silver Spring Elementary School, Wisconsin.* (Online.) Retrieved June 17, 2003, from http://ici.umn.edu/schooltowork/immersion.html.

3. Catlett, J. L. (1992). The dignity of work: School children look at employment. *Elementary School Guidance & Counseling, 27,* 150–155.

4. *Elementary Career Awareness Guide: A Resource for Elementary School Counselors and Teachers.* (Available online at http://icdl.uncg.edu/ft/060200-01.html)

5. Experiential Activities for Teaching Career Counseling Classes and for Facilitat-
    ing. *Career Groups*, Volume 1—National Career Development Association, 10820
    E. 45 Street, Suite 210, Tulsa, OK 74146.

6. *Lessons for Life*—The Center for Applied Research in Education, West Nyack,
    NY 10994.

7. Peterson, N., & González, R. (2000). *Career Counseling Models for Diverse Popula-
    tions: Hands-On Applications by Practitioners.* Belmont, CA: Wadsworth/Brooks
    Cole/Thomson Learning.

8. *Ready for School—Ready for Work: School to Careers Classroom Manual.* (1996). New
    Orleans, LA: National Telelearning Network, Inc./Syndistar, Inc.

9. Wahl, K. H., & Blackhurst, A. (2000). Factors affecting the occupational and
    educational aspirations of children and adolescents. [Electronic Version]. *Profes-
    sional School Counseling, 3*, 367–374.

10. Williams, J. (1999). *Elementary career awareness guide: A resource for elementary school
    counselors and teachers.* (Online). Retrieved June 17, 2003, from http://
    icdl.uncg.edu/ft/060200-01.html

Middle School

The middle school exploratory phase of career development helps students to determine who they are and where they fit into the world of work. This involves exploring the wide variety of careers and opportunities available. Activities to promote
self-knowledge and understanding the world of work will help prepare middle school
students for the educational and career-related decisions that they need to make
(Ettinger 2001). Their primary focus is on self-definition, finding out who they are
and what they like and dislike. During this stage, students are only beginning to develop more mature social relationships, strive for independence, and create their own
sets of values. For a career guidance program to effectively target this age group, it
must take into account developmental needs of early adolescence and provide assistance in the transition from elementary school to high school.

Counseling should focus on helping these students develop a clear understanding
of their competencies, identities, and relationships with others, and provide opportunities for career exploration. Impressionable adolescents often experience defining
moments in their middle school years that can have lifelong implications. The career
exploration process is one defining moment. Belvis, Rodriguez, and Fellan (1996)
present the following career counseling program by grade level.

Sixth Grade Most sixth-grade students are usually between the ages of eleven and
twelve. Because these students' exposure to the work world comes only from observing family members or their teachers, coaches, and clergy, the counselor's task is to

widen their knowledge base by acquainting them with many different occupations, not to direct them toward any particular career. The following six-week curriculum module presents an example of a program that can be integrated into the last six weeks of school, allowing students to continue researching various occupations during the summer break.

Week One focuses mainly on widening the student's knowledge of work and job opportunities through two assignments that involve making a list of all the occupations the student has ever heard of or dreamed about. Through group discussion, students exchange various ideas and add more occupations to their list. Students can make a poster or collage by drawing or cutting out pictures from magazines of people doing jobs that appeal to them, offering an artistic outlet while doing the research. In Week Two, students narrow their lists to four or five occupations that seem especially appealing. This should be completed individually so students do not collaborate and end up with identical lists. Students learn how to gather information about a wide range of careers and understand the dignity of each worker, regardless of the prestige connected with the job. The teacher is integral at this stage, making sure that there are no duplications.

During Week Three, the students research the jobs they chose to find the requirements for each. Included in this research should be such areas as educational requirements, salary, job duties, responsibilities, uniforms (if needed), working conditions, and job outlook for the twenty-first century. This information can be obtained from the library, interviews with people who currently work in the desired positions, and in-class research. In Week Four, students write a brief description of their jobs, including a paragraph on the reason why they chose to study each one and a discussion of both positive and negative aspects of each. The teacher must remain impartial to all descriptions, regardless of status. During Weeks Five and Six, students share their job descriptions with other class members. Each student chooses one occupation on which to make a short oral presentation. In this way the class learns of about twenty different occupations.

The goals of this project are to enable students to broaden their perceptions of occupations as well as to learn about diverse job opportunities. The interaction of teacher/counselor and peers is crucial to this knowledge. Though the students will not be expected to focus on a particular future job, their ability to make appropriate career decisions will be greatly increased through this practice.

Seventh Grade Seventh-grade students, who are usually between the ages of twelve and thirteen, are experiencing emotional and physical changes. Peers are becoming more important in their lives. Therefore, a seventh grade career counseling program needs to increase a student's self-awareness and confidence through learning and experiencing both personal and group success, and offer hands-on experience by observing and/or shadowing different people at work. By the seventh grade, a student should have a basic knowledge of the world of work and build on that knowledge to make academic choices.

Two types of hands-on experiences involve trips to various occupational settings and opportunities for people from different occupations to come into the classroom to explain what they do and how they do it. These experiences give students the chance to question workers about their jobs and or careers.

Interaction and participation of the students is vital to this process. The counselor can also develop a plan for students to visit different work environments so they can observe people working. Using groups of four or five students effectively provides more opportunities for experiences to be shared with the entire class. Group discussions, led by the teacher or counselor, can provide important opportunities for the students to consolidate their thinking and begin the task of incorporating their individual interests and abilities into their awareness.

Another activity to promote career awareness in the seventh grade is for students to develop their own career center. The career center can grow as the students' knowledge grows. Included in this center are the students' job descriptions, reports from their respective field studies, and information gathered from teachers and counselors. Each student should contribute an entire file with at least five job descriptions to the center. Parents and community can also be asked to contribute books and any information that they have about occupations and the world of work. By the end of the year, the career center will be started, offering incoming students the opportunity to contribute to and learn from the work of the previous students. At the seventh grade level, the primary objective of career exploration is to acquaint the student with the world of work and learn more about various occupations that interest them, rather than decide on a particular occupation. Broader knowledge will be valuable as the students grow and change as individuals.

A six-week curriculum for seventh grade could include the following. In Week One, students review the twenty or so occupations they learned about in sixth grade and select six of them to pursue further. Two occupations should have a field trip involved to allow the students to see firsthand what is involved. The other four occupations could be explored by having workers in those occupations come speak to the class. During Week Two, speakers continue to come to class and students write one-page summaries of what they learn. By Week Three, the two field trips have been completed. Students again write a one-page summary of what they have learned. Beginning in Week Four, students start to organize all the information into a career center. By Week Five, each student contributes four new job descriptions to the career center files (different occupations will be assigned to each student). In Week Six, students bring in books, pamphlets, and any other information they have collected for the career center. If a computer is available, all the information can be entered for ready access. The goal for the year is to continue to gather information about as many occupations as possible and to organize it into a career center.

Eighth Grade Eighth-grade students are usually between the ages of thirteen and fourteen. They need a basic knowledge of the world of work and various occupations. The eighth-grade curriculum should build on the knowledge acquired in sixth and seventh grades. The goal of this curriculum is to give the students information that will become a basis for decision-making during high school and beyond. Eighth-grade students have reached a higher level of maturity and self-understanding and are ready to explore occupations in greater depth. Their abilities to think in abstract terms and to introspect help them be aware of and realize their capabilities and explore their interests.

In the eighth grade, the career program needs to include biweekly classroom visits by people from different occupations who discuss their career and its educational requirements, training, and apprenticeships. These speakers should represent a variety of occupations and levels from the surrounding community, allowing students to see the skills required for many kinds of jobs and to understand that dignity and pride can come from any line of work. Presenters need to be males and females from diverse ethnic backgrounds. It is imperative that students see that they have the capabilities to achieve goals regardless of gender or ethnicity. This in-depth interchange with workers provides students a clearer understanding of different occupations and allows them to interact with the presenters.

By the end of the first semester, all eighth grade students should have taken an interest and personality assessment. At least two job site visits should be arranged so students can observe workers in their environment. In doing so, the students are able to evaluate the situation, answering questions such as, "Is this really the kind of work that interests me?" and "Does the work environment match my personality?" Asking questions of various people in the workplace and even being allowed to use equipment involved helps students see whether their career dreams are appropriate and if they should pursue their goal further or reprioritize their list of options.

Counselors can provide classroom presentations and role-play situations. Students can be put in small groups so they can develop skills working within a group or team. One goal for eighth graders is that they obtain enough information regarding self and occupations to assist in course selection in high school, particularly when choosing electives and the classes they need to pursue their occupational dreams.

Grant (1997) identifies goals counselors must consider when dealing with middle school students:

1. Reinforce each student's resiliency strengths and relate them to the world of work.

2. Get students involved in extracurricular activities.

3. Develop and identify a student's relationship with a significant adult in his or her life or community.

4. Be aware of drastic developmental differences, which run the gamut between concrete and abstract reasoning.

Grant designed an activity to convey the idea that school is work for middle school classes. It is particularly effective with at-risk students. See Report Card Paycheck activity in Box 9.1.

Data from Pyne, Bernes, Magnusson, and Poulsen's (2002) study suggests that youth are actively thinking about their future, that they have discussed their plans with others, and that they think about their future in terms of what job they would eventually like to have. Seventh grade students tended to define both occupation and career as a job or a way to earn a living to receive extrinsic rewards. Possible reasons for this include the students' limited exposure to the workforce, lack of practical experience needed to differentiate between these terms, or lower vocabulary skills. Eighth grade students introduced the concept of responsibility when defining occupation. This could be due to associating occupation with earning money in order to pay bills. These older students connected jobs not only with extrinsic rewards, but also with the desire for security (Pyne et al., 2002).

Middle school students need to develop skills for evaluating, locating, and interpreting information about career opportunities. This can be accomplished by using career development models that include guidelines for self-knowledge, educational and occupational exploration, and career planning. A comprehensive program for middle level students developed by Saskatchewan Education (1995), *The Middle Level Guidance Curriculum* program, includes the four areas mentioned and takes the students' developmental level into consideration. (More information can be obtained from the Web site: http://www.sasked.gov.sk.ca/docs/midcareer/usi.html)

The Teen Exploratory Career System (TECS) is designed to process adolescent female students through the growth and explorative developmental career level (Craig, Contreras, & Peterson in Peterson & González, 2000, Chapter 3). Various areas were selected as integral to the process. The chosen areas are (1) societal roles, (2) sexual identity, (3) interpersonal skills, (4) aptitude skills, (5) family influences, (6) personal traits and strengths, (7) goal setting, and (8) decision making. The TECS model is general in nature so that every racial or ethnic group can be processed through the system without losing any of its integrity.

Another program idea is Career Quest 2001, A Discovery Camp, Independent School District, Galveston, TX. This is a mentoring experience for eighth graders the summer before entering ninth grade. It includes group dynamics, academic skill builders, career investigation in the computer lab, and tours of work sites. Journal writing helps the students link school activities and electives with careers. For more information, see the PowerPoint® presentation on the web. (Go to http://www.gisd.org/ball/roy, and click on Career Quest 2003 Slide Show.)

BOX 9.1

Report Card Paycheck

Guidance/Small-Group Lesson Plan
Report Card Paycheck
Objective(s):
- identify needed qualities for a good report card
- identify needed qualities for a good paycheck
- relate report card to paycheck
- identify connection between learning now and career opportunities in the future
- apply report card paycheck to a monthly personal budget
- adjust budget to fit paycheck
- identify ways to improve either budget or paycheck by adjusting budget or report card
- name ways to improve report card

Materials:
Copies of report cards
Report Card Paycheck Worksheet—½ sheet
Report Card Paycheck conversion sheet
Computer
TV/VCR or large-screen projector
T-view

Lesson Sequence:
Stage 1: (one class period)
1. Ask students:
   - Why do people work? Write answers on board.
   - What do employers look for in an employee? List on the board.
   - Identify those traits that are also helpful in school and have students state the area of the report card that reflects that trait.
2. Ask students: What is your job now as a _____ grader? Make list.
   What is your "pay" for doing job now? (How do you know how you're doing?)
   How is your report card like a paycheck?
3. Use the Career Pyramid illustration for discussion of how their years of education build the foundation for their career.

Continued

Continued

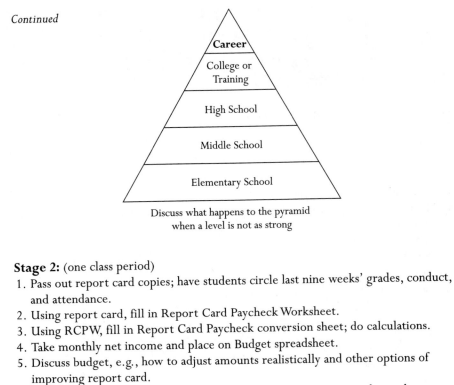

Discuss what happens to the pyramid
when a level is not as strong

Stage 2: (one class period)
1. Pass out report card copies; have students circle last nine weeks' grades, conduct, and attendance.
2. Using report card, fill in Report Card Paycheck Worksheet.
3. Using RCPW, fill in Report Card Paycheck conversion sheet; do calculations.
4. Take monthly net income and place on Budget spreadsheet.
5. Discuss budget, e.g., how to adjust amounts realistically and other options of improving report card.
6. Goal Setting: Take students through the goal-setting process to achieve the needed changes discussed in #6 on their report card.

Name: _____

Report Card Paycheck Worksheet
Number of :
(Grades)   (Conduct)   (2nd Period Absences)

_____A's   _____E's   _____

_____B's   _____S's   _____

_____C's   _____N's   _____

_____D's   _____U's   _____

_____F's

SOURCE: Grant (1997). For more information regarding this project, contact Grant directly at dcgrant@stic.net. (Chapter 3 in Peterson and González's *Career Counseling Models for Diverse Populations* is a program for middle school.)

Name: _____

Report Card Paycheck Worksheet

(Grades)	(Conduct)	(2nd Period Absences)
_____ A's	_____ E's	_____
_____ B's	_____ S's	_____
_____ C's	_____ N's	_____
_____ D's	_____ U's	_____
_____ F's		

Report Card Paycheck

Number of:

Grades

_____	A's	×	$250	=	_____	
_____	B's	×	$175	=	_____	
_____	C's	×	$125	=	_____	
_____	D's	×	$75	=	_____	
_____	F's	×	−$100	=	_____	**Total Grades:** $_____
		Total:	$ _____			

Conduct

_____	E's	×	$50	=		
_____	S's	×	$25	=		
_____	N's	×	−$25	=		
_____	U's	×	−$50	=	_____	**Total Conduct:** $_____
		Total:	$ _____			

Second period absences (place a "1" in the appropriate blank)

_____	0–2	$300		
_____	3–6	$150		
_____	7–more	−$100	_____	**Total Absences:** $_____
	Total:	$ _____		

Total Monthly Paycheck: $_____

Yearly Salary: (Total Monthly × 12) $_____

Continued

BUDGET

	PROJECTION	AUG.	SEPT.	OCT.	NOV.	DEC.	JAN.	FEB.	MARCH	APRIL	MAY
Income:											
Net Income											
Expenses:											
House:											
mortgage/rent/taxes	$450.00										
electric/gas/water	$80.00										
phone	$25.00										
long distance	$25.00										
Total	$580.00										
Laundry/Dry cleaning	$50.00										
Food	$250.00										
Entertainment	$100.00										
Gas	$100.00										
Vacation	$75.00										
Storage	$25.00										
Christmas	$80.00										
Auto Insur./Deductible	$175.00										
Auto Repair	$40.00										
Medical/Dental insurance & bills	$75.00										
Clothing	$40.00										
Gifts	$17.00										
Total	$1,027.00										
Loan payments	$200.00										
Total	$200.00										
Totals	$1,227.00										
Surplus/Deficit											

Assessments for Middle School

1. Interest, Determination, Exploration, and Assessment System (IDEAS)
2. Career Assessment Inventory (CAI)
3. EXPLORE
4. Myers Briggs Type Inventory (MBTI) for adolescents. This information is used to assist in scheduling classes for high school.
5. Harrington-O'Shea Career Decision Making System (CDMS)
6. Kuder Occupational Interest Survey (KOIS)
7. Differential Aptitude Tests—5th edition
8. OASIS-2: Aptitude and Interest
9. Rokeach Values Survey
10. Work Values Inventory
11. Informal Values Interviews
12. CareerKey (measures skills, abilities, values, interests, and personality)

Middle School Resources

1. http://www.theeducationconnextion.com (Web site that compiles lists of reference materials for elementary, middle, and high school)
2. http://www.cdsways.com/Products/CareerWAYS.htm (Web site for CareerWAYS, an electronic portfolio and career planning system and career vision information system)
3. http://www.careerkey.com (online networking resource to increase awareness of the career marketplace)
4. http://www.academicinnovations.com (Web site for *Instructor's and Counselor's Guide for Career Choices* 2000–2002)

At-Risk Students Because there are increasing numbers of students who are at-risk of dropping out of school, the particular situations of these students deserve attention. Basic to the success of any program for at-risk students is addressing students' basic needs (see Maslow) to get them motivated and interested in career development activities. For a variety of reasons, some students do not finish high school; earlier intervention may encourage the completion of high school requirements. Common factors for at-risk students are low self-esteem, substance abuse, underachievement (may be learning or emotionally disabled), teen pregnancy, and violence and crime.

An eight-week program by Kuczynski (1997) for at-risk students in the eighth grade includes a workbook and other materials. It is outlined briefly here. Beginning in Week One, complete demographic information about the students, including information about living situations and educational level of parents, grandparents, or guardians. Read and discuss *Dropping Out of School*. Complete IDEAS Survey. In Week Two, go over test results of IDEAS. Research five occupations in which they have interests in the *Occupational Outlook Handbook* (hard copy or disk). Start exercises in the workbook *What Do You Want to do When You Grow Up?* Complete Interest Inventory Checklist. In Week Three, go to a Career Resource Center to examine college catalogues, including vo-tech schools, community colleges, colleges and universities, financial aid programs, entrance requirements. Complete information sheet on the above data. Plan a visit to one of the institutions. In Week Four, emphasize motivational considerations. Several possibilities, such as a video like, "You Deserve It" and others, show role models for various populations. Discuss motivation, training, education, work ethics, and goals. In Week Five, read a two-page summary of the film or other resource used in the previous week and complete the questionnaire "What Can You Do Now to Get Where You Want to Be?" In Week Six, complete parts two and three of the workbook. Complete the interview sheet for the next week. In Week Seven, discuss the information from the interviews. Complete the Happy/Success exercise. In Week Eight, schedule a field trip to a state prison for a program called Project Reality, a look at the consequences of dropping out of school and engaging in a life of crime.

Another program described by Marcos (2003) has been implemented in Glasgow Middle School in Fairfax County, Virginia. Glasgow has a large population of at-risk students—70 percent of students receive free or reduced lunch. The program used GEAR-UP (Gaining Early Awareness and Readiness for Undergraduate Programs) to develop a career education model for its school. Students in this program have responded enthusiastically to the initiatives undertaken by completing career inventory programs; learning about careers in subject areas; attending career days and assemblies; using job shadowing; visiting colleges; and using career resources at the school Web site. The program also reaches out to parents who are such a critical part of its mission.

The U. S. Department of Labor's Secretary's Commission of Achieving Necessary Skills 1992 report on earning a living suggests that the importance of the work ethic be emphasized with at-risk youth. For economic, social, cultural, or academic reasons, these students do not have access to educational or occupational opportunities or have experienced a cycle of failure and poverty. At school they often have attendance problems or discipline problems, or are in trouble with the law. These behaviors jeopardize students from gaining or retaining employment. The related characteristics of a work ethic are individual responsibility, self-esteem, sociability, self management, and integrity.

Hill and Rojewsky (1999) used the Occupational Work Ethic Inventory (OWEI) and the Social Cognitive Career Theory (SCCT) to assist counselors in working with at-risk students. The OWEI examines key work ethic constructs of interpersonal skills, initiative, and dependability. The SCCT approach emphasizes the development of self-efficacy, outcome expectations, and personal goals. In addition to using these tools, counselors who work with at-risk students need to include work ethic, work attitudes, dependability, and conscientiousness in their work with this population.

Career Counseling for the Gifted: From At-Risk to "At-Promise" It has long been recognized that there are special issues and needs in academic and work-related counseling for the student who is functioning one to two standard deviations *below* the norm. However, those students whose intellectual functioning falls within the gifted ranges (i.e., two or more standard deviations *above* the norm) also have critically different needs from the more typical student being served through the regular education program (see Figure 9.4). Under IDEA, public schools are legally required to meet the special learning needs of each student who is identified as functioning below a designated level by developing an individualized education program (IEP) (Hourcade, 2002). There is nothing comparable for the identified gifted student within most public school systems in the United States, despite the fact that the intellectual differences at both ends of the continuum are equally significant when compared to the norm.

In this chapter we focus primarily on these significant differences and the needs of the early elementary-age gifted student through graduation from high school. Chapter 10 continues the discussion as applied to post-secondary and adult clients. To be most effective, we must "begin with the end in mind" (Covey, 1990). It is suggested that the school counselor working with a gifted student of *any* age become very familiar with what the future holds for the adult gifted in terms of their significant differences from the majority of the population. It cannot be overemphasized that the counselor must have a clear understanding of the unique personality and decision-making characteristics that are present in the gifted student beginning in the preschool years. Without a solid grounding in the nature and needs of the gifted, interventions and career guidance will be of limited use to this client group.

It is an all too frequent belief that because of their ability, the gifted do not need special consideration or assistance in career planning. There is mounting evidence that it cannot be assumed that high achievement in one or multiple areas of academic study will, by default, point the way toward a fulfilling career. Studies conducted with

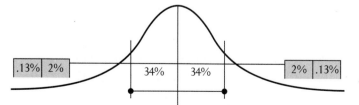

FIGURE 9.4 Theoretical Curve of Distribution of Intelligence in the General Population

SOURCE: Peterson and González (2000).

such groups as Presidential Scholars and National Merit Scholars, as well as students who have been identified and served through programs for the gifted, indicate that these young adults often had a complicated and difficult passage into the world of work (Kerr, 1990; Colangelo, 2002; NAGC, 2003). " 'Being gifted' does not relieve one of making the same choices or feeling the same pressures. Indeed, special labels, even those with [initially] positive connotations, bring additional special problems" (Bireley & Genshaft, 1991, p. 1). Special problems not usually encountered with non-gifted students include "personality issues such as students who are used to knowing all the answers and who are very fragile in the face of challenges; students who are realistically anxious about the outcome of high-stakes testing; perfectionistic or meticulous students" (Robinson, 2003).

In the main, career education programs have provided well for the needs of the general secondary school student. However, it must also be recognized that "in the same way that the students at each end of the general population spectrum—those in intellectually disabled student programs and those in gifted and talented student programs—need special support to achieve at their full potential in their schooling experiences, the same students also require career education programs oriented to meet their special needs" (Boyd et al., 2003).

A number of well-documented personality and learning style factors characteristic of this population may result in intense job dissatisfaction, ruptured professional and personal relationships, as well as depression and isolation if not addressed through counseling and career guidance. The emotional, social, aesthetic, and intellectual inner life of the gifted individual is *substantially* and *qualitatively much different* from his/her more average peers. Many express a feeling of being "out of sync" with the rest of the world, and there are valid reasons to support that conclusion. Some of the attributes common to this group that are significantly outside the norm are *asynchronous development* (Silverman, 1991); *multipotentiality* (Kerr, 1990); *introversion* (Laney, 2002; Silverman, 1991); *sensory, imaginational, emotional and psychomotor intensity* (Dabrowsky, 1993); *cultural stereotyping* (Hollinger, 1991), *intense perfectionism and relentless self-criticism* (Adderholdt-Elliott, 1987; Silverman, 1991); and a *feeling of alienation* by the larger society. Each of these characteristics is further complicated by any socioeconomic, gender, and ethnic/racial differences. Consideration must also be given to the fact that these differences are present beginning in early childhood and will continue to have an impact throughout the life span. It will therefore be necessary to revisit each of these problematic areas as the individual works through each of Erickson's psychosocial stages of development.

These fundamental differences greatly impact career choice and preparation, and ultimately the level of satisfaction found in the choice(s) made. Because these hallmarks of giftedness are routinely ignored, criticized, ridiculed, and/or pathologized in our culture and most educational settings, many of the gifted are often unaware that they are, in fact, well within the norm *for their intellectual group*. Counseling and career guidance intervention should ideally begin in kindergarten and continue throughout the academic career and into adulthood. However, unless the counselor is also aware of and sensitive to the differing needs and values of this population, *and makes the necessary adjustments to their services*, interventions will have limited success. The goal of counseling should be to normalize and validate the gifted experience for these clients and assist them in developing coping and decision-making skills. The higher the IQ score, the more obvious and intense these differences appear to others and the more critical this counseling becomes. Gifted students will have a lifetime of dealing with the demands and pressures to conform to society's norms and the expectations and stereotyping of others within and without the workplace. They will need assistance to develop coping skills, a positive self-identity, and an effective and satisfying life plan.

Gifted and At-Risk. Without direct intervention, gifted students are at-risk for serious academic difficulties, dropping out of school, developing emotional problems, and struggling with a poor work history or career development path. Studies with school age children (Kerr, 1991; Betts and Neihart, 1988, cited Bireley 1991; Reis, 1998), suggest that gifted students can be conceptualized as belonging to particular subcategories organized around a cluster of behavioral characteristics. Betts and Neihart (1988, cited Bireley, 1991, p.5) have categorized the gifted child as falling into one of six different subgroups:

1. *Successful gifted:* conforming, achieving at a high level, extrinsically motivated, and perfectionistic. *Often refuse to take intellectual or academic risks, unassertive and extrinsically motivated people-pleasers.*

2. *Challenging gifted:* creative, bored, frustrated, rebellious, inclined to engage in power struggles and unable to consistently and successfully work cooperatively with others. *Need support for their creativity; develop self-control and awareness; develop a sense of group belonging and increased flexibility.*

3. *Underground gifted:* insecure, quiet/shy, poor self-concept, compliant, and often unidentified as gifted. *Need to develop a functional gifted identity, self-awareness, and acceptance, encouragement to take risks and make choices, increased interactions with other gifted students.*

4. *Gifted dropouts:* angry, explosive loners who are burned out. *Need their affective and educational needs met; development of self-acceptance, self-control and a positive gifted identity.*

5. *Double-labeled gifted:* learning disabled, physically handicapped, or with emotional problems; often frustrated and angry with low self-esteem; are often seen as being of only average ability or as defined only by their handicapping condition. *Need accurate assessment and services.*

6. *Autonomous gifted:* good sense of self, enthusiastic, self-aware, intrinsically motivated, and psychologically healthy. (Betts & Neihart [1988], cited Bireley [1991], p. 5.)

Without intervention, five of the six categories will experience substantial difficulties in making major life decisions. These subgroups often emerge in the late elementary and early middle school years, thus making it of special concern to the school counselor. Super (1963, cited in Bireley, 1991) conceptualized career choice as a reflection of one's self-concept that clearly speaks to the need for early assessment and, if indicated, intensive intervention for the gifted at-risk student.

While students at any level may or may not be correctly or formally identified as gifted, they are often quite aware of those areas of study at which they are capable of excelling. Career counseling issues for this group may be less about ability and aptitude assessments and more about those characteristic clusters of personality factors that can short-circuit a successful and satisfying personal and professional life for the gifted individual.

Additional/Alternative Assessment Instruments. The procedures used with the more average student in career development (i.e., selection and administration of interest, ability, personality, and values assessments) are certainly relevant and necessary with the gifted population. However, it is in the counseling process that notable differences should occur. Suggestions for alternate or additional assessments that may be relevant with individual students will be followed by recommendations and models that address the need for adjustment of the counseling process.

WISC-III and Stanford-Binet Form L-M. There is as much qualitative difference between the highly gifted and profoundly gifted individual as there is between the average student and the gifted. In a discussion of the need to differentiate children in the profoundly gifted range from their more moderately gifted peers, Silverman recommends use of the SBL-M (Riverside Publishing) in addition to testing on the WISC-III. A newer version, the Stanford-Binet Intelligence Scale, Fifth Edition (SB-5), generates IQ scores up to 160 with instructions specifying how scores can be calculated as high as 200+. Of the two tests, the SBL-M is stronger at measuring verbal abstract reasoning abilities, has a higher ceiling, and generates scores as high as 262+.

The SBL-M is recommended as a **supplemental** above-level test when a child achieves two or more scores at the 99th percentile on a more recently normed IQ test. These scores indicate that the child has reached the ceiling of the test and that the IQ score may be an underestimate of the child's abilities as the newer tests have lower ceilings and may actually disguise the profoundly gifted as highly gifted. Just semantics? "We have seen dramatic differences in the thought processes, need for advanced work, social concerns, and emotional development of children beyond 160 IQ, compared with children who scored within the norms of current IQ tests" (Silverman, 2003).

The Myers-Briggs Type Indicator (MBTI) and Murphy-Meisgeier Type Indicator for Children (MMTIC). In addition to the information presented in other chapters of this text, both the MBTI and MMTIC are critical components in career and personal planning with the gifted student. The concepts and language of the MBTI limit its use below seventh grade with gifted students, so the school counselor will need to assess younger children using the MMTIC. An advantage to using the Murphy-Meisgeier is its use of the same scales as the MBTI (i.e., introversion/extroversion; sensing/intuition; thinking/feeling; judging /perceiving). According to Jungian theory (on which the MBTI is based), personality preferences as measured on each of these scales is present from birth. Increasing use of the MBTI with the gifted population indicates that the most typical gifted type is INFP/INTP. The frequency of the introversion preference is higher than 80 percent in the gifted population and less than 25 percent in the general population. There is a correspondingly high number of the gifted indicating type-preference of intuition (80 percent) in comparison to less than 25 percent in the general population.

The use of the MMTIC and later the MBTI with gifted students is critical in assisting and supporting a group that is so different from the general population in terms of personality and ways of perceiving and thinking about the world around them (Bireley, 1991). Information from these instruments will be useful for students of all ages in developing a gifted self-identity and coping skills, and making informed career decisions with or against type. The gifted individual may well experience high levels of frustration, resistance, lower achievement, and significant emotional distress if forced into an against-type career path or preparatory classes. Further use of the MBTI with gifted adults will be discussed in Chapter 10.

Gifted Identity Formation Model. The Gifted Identity Formation Model (Mahoney, 1998) addresses the need for an effective counseling model to assist in the formation of a gifted person's identity. A large body of literature exists that indicates that career education for gifted students should be designed to accommodate and support the special needs of this population. In particular, it should emphasize

- decision-making skills within the context of the child's multipotentiality.
- where to focus student effort.
- the involvement of students in their program construction.
- support to reduce career stereotyping, particularly gender-based.
- development of aspiration enhancement, especially for students from low socioeconomic backgrounds.
- finding personal meaning and reflecting one's own values through career choices (Boyd, 2003).

Kerr (1990) provides the school counselor with an outline of career development components addressing the problematic issues of multipotentiality or early emergence

Practical Applications

Gender Differences

Academic performance cannot be artificially separated from future occupational considerations for adolescents, especially for young women. Research in cognitive development and learning shows that as early as the first grade, females perform better than males on reading comprehension and writing tests; by adolescence, males perform better on math, science, and most social studies tests (Byrnes, 1996).

Even when ability in math and science is the same for adolescent females and males, confidence levels are often higher for males than for females (American Association of University Women [AAUW], 1991; Orenstein, 1994). This confidence gap also is apparent in higher career aspirations expressed by adolescent males than females:

> There is a circular relationship between liking math and science, self-esteem, and career interests. . . . Because of the differences in the ways adolescent women and men think about math and science, the influence of teachers on young women and their self-esteem and careers is particularly strong (AAUW, 1991, p. 15).

The AAUW's observation regarding teacher influence on young women's career aspirations reinforces our opinion that *all* teacher education majors should take a required course in career development. Boys' dominance in the classroom can create a kind of passivity on the part of girls' class participation, especially in the middle school years, so that young women become passive observers to the learning process rather than competent participants (Orenstein, 1994). An increased awareness on the part of teachers, especially math and science instructors, about how young men are reinforced more than young women to participate in class, even disruptively, could have a dramatic impact on how our youth are educated and their related occupational paths, because many adolescent young women do not pursue occupations that require math and/or science.

Parents will find practical assistance about how to enhance their daughters' confidence and self-steem in Bingham and Stryker (1995), Elium and Elium (1994), and Marone (1988). Brzowksy (1998) provides information on how parents can prevent their daughters from being shortchanged when it comes to computers and technology, which are nontraditional occupations for women.

Ethnic Differences

Academic performance also impacts the occupational achievement of multicultural populations. Research on cognitive development and learning shows that across all subject areas—reading, writing, math, science, and social studies—"White students perform substantially better than both African-American and Hispanic students, and Hispanics perform slightly better than African-American students" (Byrnes, 1996, p. 266). Among adolescent females, African Americans show more pessimism "about both their teachers and their schoolwork than . . . [White or Hispanic] girls" (Orenstein, 1994, p. xvii).

of career aspirations that arise in work with this kind of student. **The Career Awareness Model for Girls** (Tobin & Fox, 1980, cited in Bireley, 1991, p. 210), **Project CHOICE** (Fleming & Hollinger, 1979, cited in Bireley, 1991, p. 210), and **Project REACH** (Bell, 1989, cited in Bireley, 1991, p. 210) are all programs designed to combat stereotyping in career development for girls. Project CHOICE focuses not only on career development, self-exploration, skills development, role models, and mentors, but also includes the critical component of psychological education.

Special Issues. There are a number of special issues that begin impacting gifted students, male and female, from early childhood. A more detailed discussion of these issues is presented in Chapter 10, but it must be noted that intervention at the college or adult stage of development may be a case of too little, too late. The school counselor is in a unique position to intervene systemically and directly with individual students to change institutionalized cultural stereotypes of all kinds. School counselors must be aware of the nuances and effects of each of the following in the cluster of characteristics that identify the gifted student:

- Introversion
- Stereotyping
- Dabrowsky's framework of "over-excitabilities" in the gifted
- Multicultural issues in developing a gifted identity

For more background and suggestions in addressing these issues and how they impact career choice and satisfaction, see Burruss and Kaenzig (2003), Bireley (1991), and Laney (2002) for discussions on the impact of introversion; Hollinger (1991), Kerr (1985), Keown (2003), and Reis (1998) for information on the effects of gender stereotyping; and Dabrowsky (1993), Lovecky (1986), and Silverman (1993) for discussions on the impact of intellectual, physical, and emotional sensitivity in the gifted. There is an increasing interest in the literature on gifted minority issues, and more information may be found in Bireley's discussion of various representative cultures in *Understanding the Gifted Adolescent: Educational, Developmental, and Multicultural Issues* (1991).

Rural Students To offer descriptive data on the differences in career interests between adolescents at the beginning and end of the fourth stage of vocational development (e.g., knowledge of skills necessary to seek and obtain jobs [see Table 9.2]), Hall, Kelly, and Van Buren (1995) studied eighth grade students, primarily from rural settings. Research participants consisted of 986 students (508 female, 478 male; 592 rural, 394 urban).

Results suggest concern for the future personal and economic well-being of rural students. These students exhibit relatively low interest in investigative and social occupations, areas of significant job growth in the next decade. The relatively high interest of rural students in realistic occupations is a sector of the labor market in which no job growth is expected (Berman & Cosca, 1992). Given this combination of individual interests and labor market growth, rural students are most likely to find future employment opportunities in enterprising and conventional occupations in the service sector, where the greatest number of jobs will be created. Most of these jobs, with the exception of managerial positions, do not pay as much as those that will be created in the investigative and social interest areas. Rural students will be economically disadvantaged in tomorrow's job market relative to students from urban areas. There needs to be further study on the fourth stage of vocational development. Particularly intriguing are questions of when compromise begins and how economic and labor market realities are reflected in personal interests (Hall et al., 1995).

Post, Williams, and Brubaker (1996) conducted a study in which gender differences in rural eighth grade student's curricular, career, and lifestyle expectations were examined. Boys and girls both have equal interest in careers, plan to work, expect success, and take science courses with about the same regularity. A larger number of girls, however, plan to go to college, want to work with people instead of things, expect to make allowances in their work life in order to have children, are more likely to consider nontraditional occupations, and are more strongly influenced by their mother's work life.

Marshall, Shepard, and Batten (2002) found that when youth aged sixteen to nineteen from three small coastal and rural communities in British Columbia were interviewed, three consistently recurring themes were identified:

1. Staying in the community versus leaving it
2. The implementation of possible selves
3. The development of self awareness

Because connection and attachment is important to youth in small communities, counselors should pay particular attention to developing relationships that help students feel secure and willing to engage in exploration of life-career plans. Helping young people consider multiple options both within and outside their community is critical. This is particularly important because these students may experience a narrow range of work and relationship options related to traditional gender and cultural expectations (p. 6).

Programs designed to provide rural students the opportunity to investigate and obtain career information on a wide variety of career choices are needed to provide a positive impact on the future of the rural students. An example of such a program is Career Expo 2003 held in San Antonio. Area high school students were invited to a San Antonio convention center to have the opportunity to meet and talk with business leaders about career opportunities with their respective companies. Seminars on transition from high school to the workplace, Internet applications, interview preparations and behavior, and resumé writing were available for the students to attend.

High School

High school career development programs continue the work begun at the elementary and middle levels. It is important that students become aware of whom they are and build confidence in their abilities. The program should help students see the wide variety of options available to them and help them develop and implement a career plan. High school students also need guidance in developing their study habits, human relationship skills, job search techniques, and interviewing skills (Ettinger 2001).

The U.S. Department of Labor's Secretary's Commission on Achieving Necessary Skills (SCANS) (1992) lists the competencies necessary to prepare students with the skills for transitioning into the world of work after high school or college. The goal of SCANS is for teachers and counselors to incorporate these skills into the curriculum so that students will learn to reason and think on their own.

The skills identified by the SCANS report cover five competencies and a three-part foundation of skills and personal qualities needed for solid job performance. The five competencies include:

1. *Workers' productive use of resources*—that is, allocating time, money, materials, space, and staff

2. *Interpersonal skills*—working on teams, teaching others, serving customers, leading, negotiating and working well with people from culturally diverse backgrounds

3. *Information*—acquiring and evaluating data, organizing and maintaining files, interpreting and communicating, and using computers to process information

4. *Systems*—understanding social, organizational and technological systems, monitoring and correcting performance, and designing or improving systems

5. *Technology*—selecting equipment and tools, applying technology to specific tasks, and maintaining and troubleshooting technologies (United States Department of Labor, Special Commission on Achieving Necessary Skills, 1991, Appendix B)

The three-part foundational skills and personal qualities include:

1. *Basic skills*—reading, writing, arithmetic, and mathematics; speaking and listening

2. *Thinking skills*—thinking creatively, making decisions, solving problems, seeing things in the mind's eye, knowing how to learn, and reasoning

3. *Personal qualities*—individual responsibility, self-esteem, sociability, self-management, and integrity (U.S. Department of Labor, Special Commission on Achieving Necessary Skills, 1991, Appendix C)

While much of the research and many of the programs developed for high school have focused on college-bound students, recent emphasis has included students who do not go on to college. We have three major concerns. The first is that occupational and career planning become an integral part of the curriculum in schools. The second is that curricula have the flexibility to allow students to follow most closely matched career goals and opt for the training that meets those goals, including postsecondary education of all types, if applicable. The third is that an occupational/career center primarily for students going from school to work be established to aid in the planning and transition involved in this process.

Basic Occupational/Career Counseling Tasks in High School Each academic year should include specific units that prepare high school students for occupational goals. Wood (1990) describes a four-day career preparation unit for ninth graders that involves completing a self-scoring interest survey and interpretation of the results, choosing careers to research further, and planning a tentative schedule of classes for the next three years. The advantages of this program are that it acquaints counselors and students with available resources and helps students and teachers clarify goals and determine how to meet them in the classroom.

Tenth grade provides the opportunity for students to broaden their understanding of a life plan. The PLAN program from ACT, Inc., is one of the computerized programs that systematically guides the student through curriculum and training. Family influences, parental involvement, and timelines are helpful to high school sophomores. Eleventh grade is typically when students take precollege tests such as the ACT or SAT to determine further educational goals. Additional help can come from personality and values assessments. Volunteering, firsthand observations, shadowing, and part-time jobs are possible learning tools for this age group. Seniors are at the decision-making point, whether it be college, vo-tech training, on-the-job training, or work.

Guidance in decision making is an integral part of the counselor's role, and skills to implement plans need to be emphasized. Information from knowledge and understanding gained each year should be organized so students can develop a beginning profile that includes abilities, interests, values, and personality factors.

The portfolio is a means by which students can collect, organize, and use this information to provide a focused and structured approach to career planning and decision making. A portfolio typically includes the following: self-assessments, work preference, evidence of community service and work experience, academic assessments, career plans, and a resumé. Samples of projects, papers, or other works completed by the student may be included in the portfolio. Two examples of portfolios are *Get a Life: Your Personal Planning Portfolio,* published by the American School Counselor Association, and *Career Options Planner and Career Options Portfolio*, available from the Center on Education and Work Publications Unit (1025 W. Johnson Street, Madison, WI 53706). The use of these portfolios are discussed at length in Examples of Portfolios and Career-Planning Tools, available at the Georgia Learning Connections of the University of Georgia Department of Education. The Web address is http:// www.glc.k12.ga.us/.

Willars (2003) suggests that counselors who work in religious settings must consider the unique sense of vocation or calling that is part of a strong religious belief, in addition to the more standard counseling and career development.

Gaining Early Awareness and Readiness for Undergraduate Program (GEAR UP) is a national initiative that began in 1999 to encourage young people to stay in school, study hard, and take college prep courses. The national goal is that every college should partner with at least one middle school in a low-income community to help raise expectations and insure that students are well prepared for college. It is administered by the U.S. Department of Education and involves students, parents, and the community as multiple resources to promote early career awareness and academic achievement for all students (Schmidli 2001).

Work-Based Learning Hoyt and Wickwire (2001) discuss the emergence of information technology and the need for

an increasingly close relationships between education and work. If these relationships are to be effective, four growing needs of all school leavers must be recognized. These include the need to

1. Plan for postsecondary career-oriented education
2. Acquire general employability, adaptability, and promotability skills to enable occupational changes during adulthood
3. Emphasize the importance of work values
4. Plan ways of engaging in both paid and unpaid work as part of total career development (Hoyt & Wickwire, 2001, p. 243)

Today's school counselors can make important contributions toward meeting these needs if they attempt to do so in the context of career education. Work-based learning gives students an opportunity to see how their education is important in the world of work and assists them in making decisions about what careers they want to explore.

According to Stasz and Stern (1998), work-based learning can:

1. enhance students' motivation and academic development.
2. increase personal and social competence related to work in general.
3. broaden students' understanding of an occupation or industry.
4. provide career exploration and planning.
5. help students acquire knowledge or skill related to employment in particular occupations, or help them practice more generic work competencies (Ettinger, 2001, p. 220).

The following structures can help educators deliver work-based experiences:

- *Youth Apprenticeship* Students participate in school-based and work-based learning.

- *Cooperative Education Programs* Students engage in a coordinated program of school-based learning and career-related work experiences during the later year(s) of high school.

- *Service Learning* Students participate in unpaid volunteer experiences outside the classroom within the service sector.

- *School-Based Enterprises* Students work part-time in a school-owned business and take elective classes that teach occupational and entrepreneurial skills.

- *Job Shadowing* These work experiences options allow students to learn about a job by walking through the work day as a *shadow* to a qualified worker.

- *Internships* Students learn while they carry out productive responsibilities in a work setting outside school.

- *Clinical Training* Students undertake a course of study and hold a series of worksite training positions. The course of study, work experience, and adequate scores on an external exam are required for licensure.

- *Career Academies* These are smaller, more personal "schools within a school" in high schools. Groups of students attend a career-oriented academy focused on one cluster of occupations (Ettinger, 2001, p. 220–221).

The William T. Grant Foundation's Commission on Youth and America's Future makes policy recommendations from existing research regarding the problems students are currently facing. The commission has found that students planning to enter the workforce with a high school diploma and no specific training or skills have fewer economic opportunities available to them.

Herr (1995) specifically suggests approaches and activities that counselors can use with "employment bound" youth. He expresses concerns that most systems (parents, schools, peers, and media) tend to work more with college-bound students at the expense of students who will need or want to find employment upon completion of high school. These latter students particularly need to learn the basic skills described in the SCANS report. Gray and Herr (2000) observe the "mismatch between projected demand and supply of credentialed college graduates when one looks at data from selected occupations" (p. 72). See Table 9.6.

Table 9.6 shows more future openings in fields other than professional. To facilitate planning for the school-to-work student, we have included current thinking regarding possibilities, an example of programs, and considerations for special groups.

James Rosenbaum suggests in *Beyond College for All* (2001) that high schools can prepare students for the workplace by emphasizing different skills and expanding goal choices (cited in Coles, 2003). The labor market requires higher skills than in the past. Many good jobs do not require college skills, but math, reading, and writing skills at the ninth- to tenth-grade level are essential. Employers also view *soft skills*—

TABLE 9.6 Projected Average Annual Job Openings: 1990–2005

	OPENINGS	NUMBERS OF CREDENTIALS AWARDED	NET OPENINGS
Professional Managerial			
Executive, Administration	436,000	506,830	−70,830
Construction Managers	7,000	825	+6,175
Marketing, Advertising, and Public Relations Managers	23,000	66,416	−43,416
Professional Specialty	*623,000*	*1,120,063*	*−497,063*
Physical Scientists	8,000	35,163	−27,163
Lawyers	52,000	85,611	−16,308
Technical			
Technicians	183,000	212,767	−29,767
Health	79,000	71,804	+7,196
Engineering	52,000	85,611	−33,611
Blue-Collar, Technical			
Craft, Precision Metal, and Specialized Repair	455,000	133,057	+321,943
Mechanics, Installers, Repairers	160,000	91,758	+68,242
Service Occupation	*882,000*	*237,062*	*+644,938*
Operators, Laborers	*447,000*	*41,504*	*+435,496*
Farming, Forestry, Fishing	*90, 000*	*14,547*	*+75,453*

SOURCE: Gray & Herr (1995), p. 75.

noncognitive skills such as attitude, personal interaction, communication, and problem solving—as their greatest need.

Rosenbaum recommends the following actions for policy makers to help high school students not on the college track succeed in the workplace:

Develop evaluations to tell students what actions to take in high school for future career success.

Improve vocational programs to be relevant and to be perceived as valuable.

Use vocational courses to teach soft skills.

Use vocational teachers as a valuable resource for networking

Reward teachers for placing students in good jobs (p.8).

In support of work-based learning, Flouri and Buchanan (2000) show that having a role model and having work-related skills were strongly related to career maturity in adolescents aged 14–18 years. The findings also show that having basic work-related skills and an absence of career pressure were strongly associated with career maturity. This study shows that basic work-related skills are positively related to career maturity in adolescents and that providing adolescents with basic work-related skills can make an important contribution to both their subjective and their economic well-being.

Johnson (2000) finds that students' awareness of the relevance of school to career indicated little understanding of how school relates to the real world. They also had limited awareness of the skills and knowledge needed for success in the future. A good percentage of them recognized the value of extracurricular activities in relation to their future, but few of them understood the relevance of general academic studies. These students were not aware of the connections between school and work and simply did not see how school applied to the outside world. In summary, schools need to do more to build overall learning pathways for students both inside and outside the classroom. Students need to know how academics and their application to the work environment are linked.

Two recent programs that can be used for in-service training and for classroom materials are Achieving Success Identity Pathways (ASIP) and Tools for Tomorrow. These were designed to promote School-to-Work-Life (STWL) for low-income and diverse urban youth. The curricula are described in Solberg, Howard, Blustein, and Close (2002).

The Kmart Employment for Youth (KEY) program was evaluated to ascertain if the curriculum developed proved to be helpful in the confidence level of the participants, especially as it related to job skill competencies. "The curriculum consists of the following components: (1) attaining a job, (2) dressing for success, (3) job-interviewing skills, (4) job-retention skills, (5) assertiveness training, (6) career planning, (7) team building, (8) conflict management skills, (9) merchandise strategies, and (10) store operational procedures" (Lingg, 1996, pp. 264–65). The purpose of the program was to teach skills to chronically unemployed minority teenagers. Results demonstrated that the students who completed the ten-week course were more confident about planning and developing their careers to find a job than students who did not complete the course. Although this involved minority youth, it also has implications for the type of training that is needed by any teenager who is chronically unemployed and can be targeted as an at-risk student in high school.

Another program, Counseling for High Skills: Vo-Tech Career Options, funded by the DeWitt Wallace Readers Digest Fund, is administered by Kansas State University.

> The overriding basic goal of this project is to increase significantly the percentage of high school students not bound for four-year colleges who (a) enroll in some kind of postsecondary vo-tech educational program, and (b) secure employment in the primary labor market in jobs related to the educational programs they pursued (Hoyt, Hughey, & Hughey, 1995, p. 11).

Practical Applications

Vocational practitioners need to assist youth to participate in mentoring and apprenticeship programs, thereby encouraging younger adolescents (tenth graders) to be aware of career options. Dialogue with business and community leaders could lead to developing cooperatives to make job apprenticeships available upon high school graduation. Practitioners should realize that students are more likely to make decisions based on what mentors say than what counselors advise (Hoyt, 1994). Regardless of community participation, educators must focus on students' acquisition of several kinds of skills including "(a) . . . adaptive skills that will enable them to change with change, . . .

(b) work skills identified in the SCANS Report (1991), and . . . (c) . . . work values . . . " (Hoyt, p. 222).

High school counselors should organize career counseling activities that assist students in moving from an explicit setting of values to an implicit use of those values in evaluating alternatives. Career activities also need to stimulate thoughts about the person's own particular decision-making style. One practical way of accomplishing this task would be to provide feedback to students on how they make decisions, with the understanding that families remain a powerful influence on career decisions.

The success of this program will depend on helping high school counselors use the data and their assisting high school students in making decisions to attend postsecondary vo-tech educational programs.

The Oklahoma Consortium to Restructure Education through Academic and Technological Excellence (CREATE) is composed of five school districts in a suburban area of northwestern Oklahoma City with the purpose of changing the direction of school guidance programs toward more of a career development focus. The consortium is made up of career cluster teams that include counselors, teachers, administrators, and parents. The counseling effort is assisted by representatives from the school districts, vocational center, district office, state agency, and community college, which has raised the credibility and importance of this strategy for students and parents.

The state of Oklahoma developed a statewide School-to-Work model upon which the dual foundations of academic achievement and career development are based. See Figure 9.5. (For a complete description of the model see Chapter 5 in Peterson and González [2000].) The Oklahoma model advocates that career awareness be integrated with academic education each year from kindergarten through sixth grade. Career awareness establishes an understanding of the role of work in society.

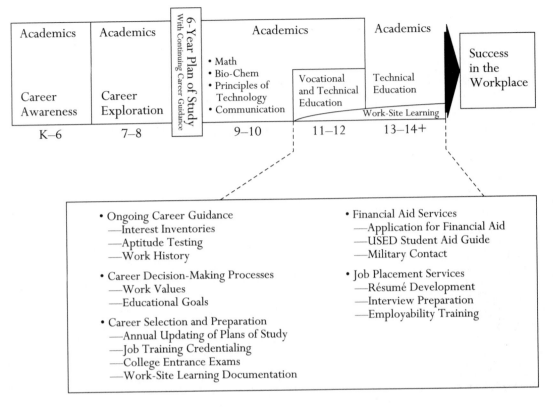

FIGURE 9.5 Guidance Model School-to-Work Program

SOURCE: *Peterson and González,* Career Counseling Models for Diverse Populations, *2000, p. 55.*

Jobs in the twenty-first century will require high academic and high-tech skills. With this in mind, students clearly need to pursue more rigorous courses of study that will provide them with opportunities in the world of work. According to Gray & Herr (2000), data indicate that only 43 percent of students have completed a college prep program of study and only 11 percent of students completed a vocational education program. "*Thus, the largest group of students in high school are really in the general curriculum, meaning that they graduate neither prepared for college nor for full-time employment*" (Gray & Herr, 2000 p. 48, italics in original).

High school should meet both the students' academic and career goals while providing purpose and reason for attending and remaining in school. The Oklahoma School-to-Work model is a six-year plan that provides a blueprint for schools and creates an awareness of the need for guidance of a different type (Peterson & González, 2000 p. 52–60).

In order to effectively implement and facilitate career development in the high school, specific assignments need to be made in the curriculum. The model in Table 9.7 is one example.

TABLE 9.7   Model for Integrating Career Development into the High School Curriculum

ACTIVITY	PERSON RESPONSIBLE	GRADE LEVEL
Assessment & Interpretation (Interest, Personality, Aptitude)	Counselors	8th (EXPLORE, IDEAS) 10th (PLAN, Kuder) 11th (Strong/MBTI, ASVAB)
Career Exploration	English Teachers CDF (in Career Center)	9th (Research paper on career area from 8th grade assessment)
Internet Career/College Search	Computer Teacher Librarian CDF (in Career Center)	10th (use as topic for teaching Internet searching)
College Essay/Application Letter (Use common application for examples of essay topics)	English Teachers Computer Teachers CDF (in Career Center)	11th (write college essays & application letters to have at beginning of senior year)
Resumé and Letters of Recommendation	Teachers Computer Teachers CDF (in Career Center)	11th & 12th (complete resume & get letters of recommendations from teachers)
College & Scholarship Search	Computer Teachers Librarian CDF (in Career Center)	11th & 12th (identify up to three colleges to send applications to & search for scholarships)
FAFSA (Free Application for Federal Student Aide)	Counselors	12th (form available after Jan. 1)

SOURCE: Maxwell, 2003.

Assessments for High Schools

Interests

1. Career Strong Interest Inventory (SII)
2. Kuder Occupational Interest Survey (DD)
3. California Occupational Preference Survey (COPS)
4. California Aptitude Preference Survey (CAPS)

Personality and Values

1. Myers-Briggs Type Indicator (MBTI)
2. 16 Personality Factor (16PF Adolescent)
3. Values Clarification
4. Work Values Inventory

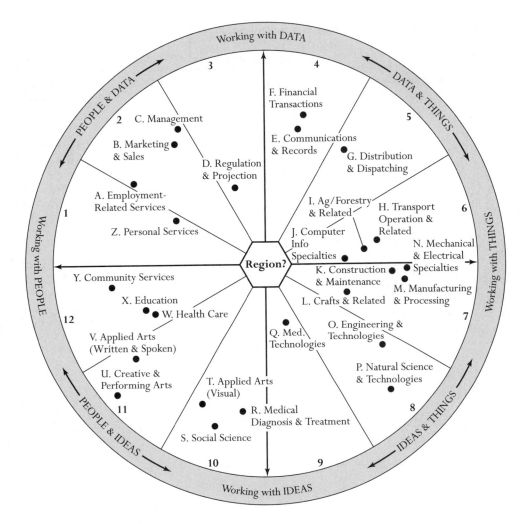

FIGURE 9.6 World-of-Work Map

SOURCE: *From ACT, Inc., Copyright © 2003. Available on www.act.org/wwm/index.html. Used with permission.*

Computer Assisted Programs

1. DISCOVER – The source for the World-of-Work Map (See Figure 9.6.)
2. SIGI

High School Occupational Counseling and Information Center (OCIC) We have discussed various high school career programs and some useful assessments. Now we discuss the Occupational Counseling and Information Center (OCIC), a model for developing a comprehensive career center in the high school. The focus of these centers is on life after high school, which for some includes college and for the majority involves vocational/technical school, apprenticeship programs, or working. The OCIC offers students a place to locate the information needed to prepare for life after graduation. The center should be located in a place that is accessible to all students. An orientation for incoming high school freshmen should be required because exposure to the center early in their high school experience can alleviate the concern for or fear of exploration.

It is the school counselor's responsibility to inform students and faculty about the center's resources. It is the responsibility of the OCIC director to coordinate with teachers times when each student can visit the center every year of high school to complete a specific assignment. Ideally, each student will have visited the center a minimum of four times during high school.

Although most high school OCICs focus on students who plan to enter college, the reality is that on the average, only 40 percent attend college and only 25 percent earn a bachelor's degree (Gray & Herr, 1995). Therefore, high school OCICs need to focus on serving those students who are not going to college, whatever the reason. In order to make the center user-friendly for everyone, procedures must be available to help every person feel comfortable and hopeful by using the services provided. Any career center also needs to have access to the resources on the Internet. An excellent listing of resources, as well as how to use them, is in *The Internet: A Tool for Career Planning* by Harris-Bowlsbey, Dikel, and Sampson (2002). A more complete listing of Web sites can be found in Chapter 10.

We propose that a high school OCIC have two tracks from which students can choose. One is the School-to-Work Track, which will prepare students to enter the job market upon graduation. The second track is the School-to-School Track, which is adapted to students who plan to further their education upon graduation. While some of the services overlap, a particular emphasis needs to be developed for each track. The School-to-Work Track services will include resources for:

- Identifying interests, aptitudes, abilities, and achievement levels
- Identifying occupational awareness and possibilities based on interests, etc.
- Building decision-making skills
- Locating information about jobs, and how to apply
- Providing opportunities for shadowing, firsthand observations
- Teaching basic job-seeking skills, including appearance and attitude, practice interviewing, things to avoid, socially acceptable and expected behaviors
- Teaching work behavior skills, including punctuality, attitude, attempting to ascertain expectations on the job, dealing with hierarchy, and accountability
- Teaching social skills in the work setting, including understanding boundary issues, employer and supervisor relations, peer relations, and the interaction of personal responsibility and self-protection

- Developing résumé and portfolio organization
- Networking and correct uses of it

The School-to-School Track services will include resources for:

- Identifying interests, aptitudes, abilities, and achievement levels
- Identifying occupational awareness and possibilities, based on interests, etc.
- Building decision-making skills
- Identifying college/voc tech/community college interests
- Surveying possible schools and programs
- Learning application process to various colleges and universities
- Providing financial aid availability and application process assistance

An adaptation of these tracks needs to be made for special needs students as well. Other information may need to be sought, with special assessments of aptitudes, abilities, and job possibilities, as part of the OCIC services.

Springfield High School in Vermont (2003) has an exemplary career resource center that can be accessed through the Internet. The school begins the career counseling process with the incoming freshman and concludes it with the graduating seniors. The center's resources encompass more than providing information; there are also counselors who are available to the students to answer questions and aid in the career/job/college search. Aside from the materials that need to be a part of every career resource center, the setup of the center is of equal importance. Springfield High School's resource center is organized in such a way that many students can access different parts of the center at the same time. Obviously, in order for a high school to offer even the minimum career guidance services, there needs to be a strong commitment from the school board and administration to hire trained staff and provide the necessary space and equipment. Ideally, it needs to be a district-wide commitment so all high schools have comparable resources.

Other resources current at the time of writing are:

- http://www.mapping-your-future.org begins with educating middle school students on career planning and proceeds through graduate and adult students. It is also an excellent resource for middle/high school counselors.
- http://www.thehighschoolgraduate.com and http://www.makingitcount.org are other sites that specifically target high school students.
- http://www.essayedge.com is a site that provides useful help in writing the college essay.

Excellent sites for high school guidance and career center are:

1. Guidance Department at Marblehead (MA) High School (http://www.marblehead.com/guidance/)

2. Valencia (CA) High School (http://www.hart.k12.ca.us/calencia/guidance/career.htm)

3. Nathan Hale High School (WA) (http://hale.ssd.k12.wa.us/c-ctr/career-center.htm)

4. Woodinville (WA) High School (http://whsweb.norshore.wednet.edu/counseling_career_ctr_index.html)

The above sites could serve as examples of how to set up a high school career program.

Relevance for Multicultural and Diverse Populations

Women. **Sexism** in the schools remains a formidable barrier to occupational development. Sadker and Sadker (1994) pinpoint the dilemma faced by young women in high school.

> Many . . . [young women] think that being bright is in conflict with being popular. To go to the prom with the right date, to be a cheerleader, to be chosen as most popular, to be elected class officer—such is the stuff of high school dreams. High academic success is not always congruent with these new priorities (p. 101).

At this age, a young woman's intellectual achievement may intimidate her peers, particularly young men. No one wants to be perceived as uncool, and such pressure to be popular pushes too many young women out of advanced math and science courses. Curricular choices made at this stage may prevent later access to further training in science and technology, or as Sadker and Sadker note, "[Young women in] high school . . . who avoid these courses are making their first career move, and most of them don't even know it" (p. 101).

Ethnic Differences. Mau (1995) studies minority students' ideas about educational planning, aspirations, and achievements. Regarding educational planning, he finds African American students generally are more active than White students in using counselors to plan for careers. It is unclear if this is counselor-initiated or student-initiated. More significantly, the study finds that students are much more likely to go to peers for career planning and information than to counselors or teachers. The need for counselors to include peers in the counseling process becomes obvious.

In the area of educational aspirations, Mau (1995) finds that Hispanic and Native American students generally have lower aspirations. Students who have better academic achievement, regardless of race or ethnicity, also have higher aspirations.

The importance of recognizing within-group differences—whether ethnic, gender, or achievement levels—is emphasized as well. Understanding external barriers of bias, stereotyping, and discrimination, and internal barriers of aspirations, motivation, and self-esteem will add to the effectiveness of counselors (Mau, 1995).

Practical Applications

The Understanding Adolescence Study (Taylor, Gilligan, & Sullivan, 1995) of multicultural young women at risk for early motherhood and school dropout has practical applications for the occupational development of such populations. Broadly speaking, the researchers' goal was to bring young women "into psychology as first-person narrators so that women's and girls' voices can directly inform theories of human development" (p. 6). More specifically, the researchers found that, across different racial and ethnic groups, when the young women imagine their future, "they describe job or career goals first and mention marriage, family, or other significant relationships second, or not at all" (p. 177). Obstacles to future career plans were said by many young women to take the form of relationships.

> The specific relationships they refer to are those with a spouse or male partner and with children. While a few . . . [young women] cite "money" or "grades" as potential problems, the most common answers to the question of what might get in the way [of future plans] are "kids," "a boy," "getting married too soon," or simply "getting married." Obstacles to future career plans include not only the obvious one of pregnancy but also relationships formed too soon after high school, before careers and jobs are well under way (p. 177, quotations in original).

Aspirations are more likely to part company with expectations for poor and working-class young women than for middle-class and affluent young women. Poor and working-class young women are more likely to see a di-

chotomy between "relationships or 'being single with a job'" (p. 186, quotations in original).

Taylor et al. (1995) note that to listen to young women requires adults learning how to do so and recognizing resistance to do so. The learning part entails adults overcoming limited understandings of the meanings of cultural and class experiences as they impact a young woman's family life, relationships, education, and future opportunities. The recognizing resistance part entails adults' willingness to deal with a young woman's questions and statements that adults would prefer not to hear. Young women who are "socially marginalized because of their class, race, ethnic background, or sexual orientation" (p. 193) are most apt to have their voices stifled or negated by adults who would rather not deal with painful realities. We wonder if this is why vocational psychology has not launched a strong and authoritative response that addresses the occupational development of adolescent females, especially poor and working-class young women.

Women often lack job skills and occupational information (Rea-Poteat & Martin, 1991). A ten-day summer career exploration program, "Taking your place: Exploring technology and tomorrow," emphasizes career possibilities and self-image for adolescent girls. Using visits to women at work in a nontraditional setting, hands-on opportunities, and counseling, the program has been effective in opening these young women's minds to occupational possibilities. A workbook titled *CHOICES: A Teen Woman's Journal for Self-Awareness and Personal Planning* (Bingham, Edmonson, & Stryker, 1994) was used in the program.

Youth with Disabilities. Those with disabilities typically have difficulty gaining early work experience, which can adversely affect later work opportunities. Students who need to work during high school years often experience difficulties with combining the two activities. Lichtenstein (1998) writes about high school work experience and later success in the workforce or in college, a popular topic for debate in the popular press, at school board meetings, and even in the academic literature. The debate centers on the time constraints that are imposed on students who combine school and work. The concern is that jobs held by youth and young adults result in less time devoted to studying and homework, and thus lower academic performance and postsecondary education aspirations (p. 15). Work during high school most often becomes a problem when a young person is employed more than twenty hours a week.

For youth with disabilities, excessive hours are not a problem because obtaining employment opportunities during high school—and even after—is difficult. The greatest obstacles await young women with disabilities. The greatest obstacles await young women with disabilities. Compared to young men with disabilities, young women are less likely to finish high school, less likely to find jobs if they do finish school, and more likely to have jobs in low-wage service occupations. Furthermore, the wage gap between disabled young women and disabled young men is greater than their nondisabled counterparts.

Syzmanski (1998) proposes an ecological approach to assist youth with disabilities from diverse backgrounds in the transition from school to work.

> According to the ecological model, career development is determined by the dynamic interaction of individual, contextual, mediating, environmental, and outcome constructs with congruence, decision-making, developmental, socialization, allocation, and chance processes (p. 127).

Among the ecological considerations for transitioning, *individual constructs* include aptitudes, abilities, and interests. *Contextual influences* on occupational development include family background, socioeconomic status—especially poverty and poor schools—limited work opportunities, and war. Individual and social *mediating constructs* include work personality, self-efficacy, outcome expectations, acculturation, and racial identity. *Environmental constructs* refer to work environment (e.g., skill requirements and reinforcers, employee's work interests, occupational structure, workplace organizational structure, the labor market), and the physical nature of the workplace (e.g., architectural design, job accommodation). *Outcome constructs* include **job satisfaction, work adjustment, job stress,** discrimination, and prejudice. The process of *congruence* refers to the Person by Environment Fit (PxE). *Career decision-making* especially needs to be nurtured during the school-to-work transition for youth with disabilities. *Developmental process* refers to career maturity. The *socialization process* is "important to examine [so as to assess] the extent to which [disabled] students have been socialized to expect or pursue less than their potential" (p. 135). *Allocation* refers to the gatekeeping process/role

---

Practical Applications

Rusch and Millar (1998) offer the following critique of transitioning practices. "Complete consensus has not been achieved within our society on what constitutes desirable postschool outcomes for all youth as a result of an effective education" (p. 42). The authors add "Although numerous . . . [vocational education programs for youth with disabilities] have been attempted, few have been rigorously evaluated or researched to determine effective practices or their impact on student postschool outcomes" (p. 52). The School to Work Opportunities Act of 1994, which was intended to aid transitioning, is reviewed by Cobb and Neubert (1998). The act's implementation is further discussed by Seigel (1998). Comprehensive transition assessment and evaluation of students with disabilities is examined by Thurlow and Elliott (1998).

---

played by parents, teachers, counselors, and personnel directors. *Chance processes* include unforeseen events and the importance of planning skills for disabled students to capitalize on chance.

Hanley-Maxwell, Pogoloff, and Whitney-Thomas (1998) consider families to be at the heart of the school-to-work transition process for youth with disabilities. Several barriers to family involvement exist.

1. There can be a family lack of knowledge, personal resources, authority and power, and communication.
2. Practitioners' perceptions of appropriate family involvement can be limiting.
3. It can be useful to determine the extent to which the family has been discouraged in the past regarding involvement in educational decisions.
4. Confused expectations can complicate matters.
5. Other demands and commitments can limit a family's opportunity to participate.
6. Usual family stresses can impede involvement in a disabled student's transition.

Family involvement in transition can be supported through relationship building (including the highlighting of family expertise), getting to know the family (including characteristics, lifecycle stage), restructuring role (including parents and families as collaborators, assessors, and policy makers), and through exchanging information (including information resources).

PARENTING PROGRAMS FOR CAREER AWARENESS

Surveys show that parents are the strongest influence on the education and career choices of students. It is important that parents be able to provide up-to-date information to help students explore career choices in today's workforce. Parents can assist their children in developing awareness of themselves and careers, and their educational and career plans. Ettinger (2001) suggests that in order for parents to assist in this process, they need to help their children answer the following career related questions: Who am I? Where am I going? How do I get there? Because activities and experiences need to be age appropriate, parents need to understand the stages of career development. Table 9.8 illustrates the developmental traits, career needs, and parent involvement for pre-K through grade twelve.

Parent involvement is essential to successful efforts to get students to be receptive to alternatives other than four-year colleges. Gray and Herr (2000) recommend the following four-step program beginning at the eighth grade:

Step 1: Have an Eighth-Grade Parent Meeting Involving parents in their child's education plans when they are getting ready for high school provides the best opportunity to get their attention and involvement. This parental involvement program is much more extensive than the one-shot orientation most schools have.

Step 2: Involve Parents in the Career Plan The Individual Career Plan (ICP) for the student should represent a joint effort by each student and his or her parents in determining the student's career interests and postsecondary education plans. At the least, the parents should approve the plan.

Step 3: Provide Objective Feedback at Strategic Times Data such as test scores and course grades should be provided at key points during the student's high school career. This gives parents and students the opportunity to test the reality of the IPC and alter is as necessary.

Step 4: Provide Opportunities for Individual Assistance Parents should be provided with the opportunity for individual advising from guidance staff or teachers at the end of every parent meeting.

Parents need to be aware of the following points before encouraging their children to pursue a four-year college degree:

1. The school's role is to help you make the best decision for your child, not to make the decision for you.

2. Focus on postsecondary success, not on college admissions.

3. Know the odds and know the costs.

4. If the goal is a better job, then do not confuse education with occupational skills.

5. Consider all the postsecondary alternatives (Gray & Herr, 2000, pp. 125–131).

TABLE 9.8   Child's Career Development and Parent's Involvement

DEVELOPMENT TRAITS	CAREER NEEDS	PARENT INVOLVEMENT
Pre-kindergarten–3rd Grade		
Needs and seeks attention	Distinguish between work and play	Listen and encourage
Has boundless energy	Identify different types of work	Encourage involvement in various sports/hobbies
Considers fantasy as reality	Learn how play relates to work	Positively reinforce completion of chores
Needs confidence-building experiences	Identify personal feelings	Praise work effort as well as accomplishments
Shows a variety of tension-releasing behaviors	Incorporate career work ideas into curriculum with play activities that demonstrate jobs	Show interest and stress importance of school
		Give toys that promote role playing and learning
		Help teach decision-making process
4th Grade–6th Grade		
Is moving toward independence	Recognize personal interests, abilities, strengths, weaknesses	Encourage good work habits at home, add responsibilities
Feels that belonging to a group and friends are important	Describe how work at home relates to jobs in the community	Avoid assigning jobs by sex role stereotyping
Can assume more responsibility	Describe how work is important and attainable to all	Visit different places of employment to see what workers do
Has a surprising scope of interests	Describe how beliefs and values affect decision making	Encourage child to think on his/her own
Can think on own, but is influenced by others	Know the skills needed to obtain work/jobs	Participate in the school's career education program
		Listen as child makes decisions
7th Grade–8th Grade		
Undergoing dynamic physical and hormonal changes	Demonstrate effective skills in working with others	Discuss child's skills, interests, abilities, and goals to help plan for the future
Is sensitive and has need for approval, especially from peers	Show appreciation for similarities and differences among cultures and genders	Encourage participation in service-oriented activities
Tries to build a unique personality apart from parent's influence	Describe individual skills as needed to fulfull life roles	Help child meet workers, using observations, field trips, and personal interviews
Wants more independence	Identify strategies for managing personal finances	Use guided money management and allow child to make economic choices

TABLE 9.8   Child's Career Development and Parent's Involvement *(continued)*

DEVELOPMENT TRAITS	CAREER NEEDS	PARENT INVOLVEMENT
7th Grade–8th Grade (continued)		
Is curious but not ready for planning	Describe skills needed to obtain a variety of occupations and training	
Expresses feelings more openly	Demonstrate skills needed to obtain and keep a job	
	Complete interest assessment and make an academic plan for high school	
High School		
Develops a sense of self-identity	Understand how individual personality, abilities, and interests relate to career goals	Help child make independent decisions
Begins a more realistic work/career search	Understand how education relates to college majors, further training, and/or entry into the job market	Encourage exploration of all kinds of postsecondary education opportunities
Develops a concern about social issues	Provide mentoring, shadowing, and cooperative experiences	Be involved in child's future planning
Matures sexually with physical and emotional changes	Demonstrate transferable skills that can apply to a variety of occupations and changing work requirements	Give certain economic responsibilities
		Keep informed
Increases independence	Be able to use a wide variety of career information resources	Encourage job awareness
Peer approval and acceptance are very important	Show responsible decision making regarding academic choice and plans for the future	Be flexible as the decision-making process evolves
	Gather information from computer assisted career guidance systems	Encourage some part-time work experience or volunteering in interest areas

Turner and Lapan (2002) examined the relationships among perceived parent support, career self-efficacy, career planning/exploration efficacy, gender, and the career interests of middle school students. The results suggest that there is a stronger association between young adolescents' perceptions of parental support for pursuing particular types of careers and the confidence young adolescents have for performing tasks related to those careers than is true of older adolescents. With young adolescents, parental support accounted for as much as one-third to one-half of their children's career task-related confidence. It may seem then that early adolescence is a critical time for parental involvement in the career development of their children (Turner & Lapan, 2002).

In the Parent Involved Career Exploration (PICE) program, Amundson and Penner (1998) place parents in the role of observer in the career counseling process. Children are given the opportunity to complete activities with a minimum of interference from parents. Parents listen to what is being said but also have designated periods for responding. The following specific steps characterize this one-session intervention:

1. Introduction
2. Pattern identification exercise
3. School preferences and performance
4. Perspectives on education and labor market opportunities
5. Setting the next step (action planning) (Amundson & Penner, 1998)

Kush and Cochran (1993) tested the effectiveness of a Partners Project for parents to help their adolescent children develop increasing responsibility regarding a career. By providing a situation that is accepting and encouraging, parents can help (1) adolescents understand motives; (2) develop goals based on that understanding; (3) formulate plans based on the goals; (4) work to accomplish them over time; and (5) keep a sense of responsibility, "taking ownership for motives, goals, plans, actions, and consequences" (p. 435). They applied this to a standard career counseling strategy, emphasizing self-responsibility in an encouraging environment. In comparison with a control group, students who completed the Partners Project showed "an enhanced sense of agency regarding career. More certainty in career direction and less indecision indicate greater confidence. More career salience and crystallization of ego identity indicate more meaningful motivation, a basis for self determination in career" (p. 437).

An impressive amount of career growth and maturity is possible when parents work together with their adolescent children, with the added values of the parents clarifying their own career concerns and improving family communication. The focus is on maximum involvement by parents in their children's career exploration. Family interactions are strengthened when parents understand from the beginning that the emphasis will be on parental expectations and behaviors. When parents identify their own interests and then indicate what are their children's interests, it is a worthwhile exercise for increasing the parent's insight about themselves and their children. From a **family systems** orientation, exploration of family values can lead to an analysis of roles, boundaries, values, traditions, and messages that have a bearing on their children's abilities to look at career options. A caution for parents is that even though they want to be sure their child selects the correct career, their emphasis should be on supporting the gathering of information, allowing the child autonomy in taking responsibility for the search. It is easier to encourage parents to become involved in family counseling when the concerns are centered on their involvement in their child's career concerns. An interesting side benefit is that some parents have been able to clarify their own career concerns in the process.

Lapan, Osana, Tucker, and Kosciulek (2002) suggest developing community career partnerships to promote career development for students K–16. The authors recommend school-based learning, work-based learning, parental involvement, business/ trade union involvement, and counselor and administrator involvement. Community career partnerships represent a collaborative, sustainable means of providing such needed career services.

SUMMARY

In this chapter, a complete overview of the standards for school interventions put forth by various organizations involved in career development concerns have been discussed. In looking at the role of the school counselor, we have attempted to present a thorough discussion of the issues involved in school settings, including the need for administrative support. We have looked at approaches and programs that can be effective in creating an effective awareness of the relation of career to life in all levels of the school system—elementary, middle, and high. We have also looked at programs for various types of students—at-risk, gifted and talented, and multicultural backgrounds.

Work-based learning programs are increasingly used in the schools, and we attempt to present the most current ideas in this area, especially for students who are not necessarily college-bound. We also give extensive coverage on the possible involvement of parents in the development of students' career and life planning.

The next chapter focuses on many of these same career challenges for students in postsecondary education, whether in job training, community colleges, or four-year colleges and universities.

10

❖

Career Counseling for Adults, Part I—Postsecondary Education and Training

I won't do work that hurts children.

A PLEDGE FOR YOUNG PEOPLE TO CONSIDER WHEN THEY GRADUATE FROM
HIGH SCHOOL OR COLLEGE, AS SUGGESTED BY MARY PIPHER (1996, P. 266).

Chapters 10 and 11 deal with various stages in adulthood. This chapter addresses people who are postsecondary to mid-thirties and choose to continue their education, and Chapter 11 deals with adult career decisions, changing careers, job displacement, retirement, and other considerations that occur throughout middle and older adulthood. This chapter is divided into seven sections: (1) vocational/technical schools, (2) community colleges, including welfare reform programs, (3) colleges and universities, (4) career counseling at the postsecondary level, (5) models for career decision-making courses at both the freshmen and senior college student level, (6) technology in career development and counseling, and (7) an Occupational Counseling and Information Center (OCIC). Each setting requires a different emphasis or methodology of vocational career counseling.

While reading, keep in mind the overarching concerns facing adults discussed in earlier chapters. These include changes of relationship to work settings and company loyalty; changes in the workforce, lifestyles, family structure, and function; in technology and its influence on work; and the globalization of the workforce. In order to set the parameters for our considerations, we cite the National Career Development Competencies for Adults in Table 10.1.

TABLE 10.1 National Career Development Competencies for Adults

SELF-KNOWLEDGE

1. Skills to maintain a positive self-concept.
2. Skills to maintain effective behaviors.
3. Understanding developmental changes and transitions.

EDUCATIONAL AND OCCUPATIONAL EXPLORATION

4. Skills to enter and participate in education and training.
5. Skills to participate in work and lifelong learning.
6. Skills to locate, evaluate, and interpret career information.
7. Skills to prepare to seek, obtain, maintain, and change jobs.
8. Understanding how the needs and functions of society influence the nature and structure of work.

CAREER PLANNING

9. Skills to make decisions.
10. Understanding the impact of work on individual and family life.
11. Understanding the continuing changes in male/female roles.
12. Skills to make career transitions.

SOURCE: NOICC (1996), pp. 1–8.

Facing adult responsibilities for the first time can be challenging. Young people must make decisions that will affect the rest of their lives. They may obtain jobs that provide focus for future career decisions, allow time to decide career/family options, and/or enable a journey of self-discovery. Many post-high school adolescents are leaving home for the first time to be on their own. For some, the major issue becomes survival. For others, this may be a time for idealism to pervade their worldview before the pragmatism of family and daily responsibility modify their perceptions.

The diverse needs of students enrolled in postsecondary education require flexibility on the part of the career counselor. Many students are anxious about selecting a major yet confused about the whole process of career exploration. Other students may already have selected a major, yet have no idea how to translate their major into a career. Still other students may need to engage in self-assessment to discover their strengths and weaknesses.

Most students lack access to current career and labor market information. As graduation approaches, they are faced with a great deal of uncertainty. There are also many subpopulations in postsecondary institutions that have specific needs—returning adult students, students from minority cultures, economically disadvantaged students, and students with disabilities (Ettinger 2001, p.133). Each needs career services designed specifically for its unique requirements.

VOCATIONAL/TECHNICAL SCHOOLS

The mention of vocational education sometimes triggers strong responses. Arguments for vocational education are based on the premise that "all persons are created equal," but in terms of actual abilities that is not reality. Some students have severe reading and writing difficulties that are often physical or chemical in nature, but they may possess exceptional visio-spatial coordination abilities. Ideally, all citizens would learn to read, but the truth is that some will never read well enough to attain standard educational requirements. Yet these people may excel in mechanical skills that require strong hand–eye coordination such as electronics or computer repair. Major criticisms of vocational education generally center on *dumbing down* requirements and abuses in government-supported programs that yield less than effective results.

Different types of vocational education include:

- High school vocational/technical education
- Privately funded postsecondary vocational training
- Special education aimed at vocational rehabilitation
- Publicly funded vocational education (which prepares people to acquire additional skills within their present job setting and/or community)
- Other types of vocational education that vary depending on particular needs.

Most practitioners do not hesitate to recommend training or education to prepare individuals for their respective roles in the workplace, but many are uncertain which type of vocational education is most appropriate.

ITT Technical Institute, National Institute of Technology, and Hallmark Institute of Technology are examples of private technical schools. There are also numerous programs available locally. Job Corps (a federally funded program) provides a range of services for young adults ages 16–24. Check in local phone directories (Yellow Pages) under listings for schools (industrial, technical, and trade) to find local technical schools. It is important to check out the credibility, longevity, and percentage of students placed in jobs after receiving the training in these private technical schools. Hall, Hayes, Morris, Rendón, and Zepda (1993) suggest a list of questions that a person should ask when considering enrollment in a voc-tech school:

- What are the programs offered (e.g., length, certificate or degree, options)?
- Is it accredited (e.g., agency, date, current standing, including temporary or provisional)?
- How much does it cost (e.g., differences for each program, available financial assistance)?
- What is the default rate, and how is it calculated?
- Who are on the faculty, and what are their credentials?

CASE EXAMPLE

Let the Buyer Beware

A young woman attended a court reporting school for two years but had not graduated because she had not yet attained the speed required for a certificate. She continued attending class several hours each week and was steadily improving her speed. One day she went to the school to find all the doors were locked and a sign reading, "School is Closed." There was no indication of whom to call or what to do. The school never reopened, and the other court reporting school in the city would not accept any of the credits she had earned. She lost two years of her life and was $10,000 in debt. Fortunately she had kept her job as an office administrator, so she at least could keep paying her bills.

- What is the placement profile (e.g., specific companies who have hired graduates [ask for a list]; which programs place best, worst; how placement rates are calculated)?

- Are career development, résumé preparation, and interview skills training offered?

- Are tours of the school offered when students are present (e.g., apparent satisfaction of the students, conversations with students)? Ideally, information from students before seeing the campus may give more ideas of questions to ask.

- What is the interview procedure (e.g., what is promised, how much time is allowed for decision making, professionalism of the personnel)?

- What other type of information is available (e.g., brochures or literature, commission or salary for the admissions people, appearance of facilities and size of classrooms, retention programs in existence, if equipment is current and in sufficient numbers, and enrollment fluctuation)?

The usual academic requirements of a vocational instructor include a bachelor's degree. Professional experience and/or certifications may be considered in lieu of this requirement. The instructor must relate well with students and other faculty, maintain poise and a professional perspective when classroom discipline needs to be imposed, have a professional attitude at all times in the classroom, and adhere to the school's policies and procedures. Because many of the vocational training schools are privately owned and often are relatively new in the community, it is a buyer-beware situation.

Private technical schools usually do not offer academic credit that can be applied toward four-year degree programs. However, additional technical training can be obtained through associate degree programs in local community colleges. These programs also allow you to articulate into a four-year degree program, that is, there is an agreement with colleges to accept credit for specific high school courses. (More of this on p. 393.)

COMMUNITY COLLEGES

In addition to vocational programs, many community colleges have certification or two-year associate degree programs to train people for specific occupations. The American Association of Community Colleges (AACC, 1996) reports that "community colleges have emerged as vanguard institutions in preparing workers and their companies for the challenges ahead" (p. 1). To remain competitive in the global economy, "frontline workers will be expected to have essentially the same broad set of skills previously required only of supervisors and managers" (p. 1). All levels of workers will require advanced skills, and community colleges offer programs and certificate to gain these skills.

Three AACC Councils—COMBASE, the National Council for Continuing Education and Training, and the National Council for Occupational Education—have completed the National Workforce Development Study of employers/consumers and community college providers of workforce development programs. This study includes the following findings:

1. Businesses of all types and sizes are served by community colleges in the United States, with concentrations in industry/manufacturing, government/public services, and health services.

2. Technological changes have increased the need for workforce development, especially computer skills.

3. Employers also desire "basic communication and computational skills, . . . , enterprise-specific skills, the ability to work with others in solving problems, and strong work ethics" (AACC, 1996, pp. 2–3).

4. Employers value community colleges for cost-effective, customized, and convenient training programs.

5. Most employers—95 percent—would recommend community colleges.

Crosby (2003) uses current population statistics to illustrate the value of an Associate degree. She says that some of the fastest growing jobs in the United States are in areas where an Associate degree is not required, but is sufficient. Associate degrees have the advantage of flexibility, allowing more choice of a major and a variety of opportunities from job placement to further education. Furthermore, many programs

Practical Applications

Career counseling is a major role of community college counselors. Nyre and Reilly (1987) conducted a study of career counseling programs at several different community colleges in California and found that most students consider career counseling a valuable asset of the college. Unfortunately, the results of the study also showed that many students are not properly informed about what is available to them in terms of career counseling, or their expectations differ from what the actual career counseling programs have to offer. Another service of community college counseling centers is career courses, which include specific information for displaced workers, undecided majors, job search skills, students with special abilities, returning students, those who plan to go on to a college/university, and those who are seeking to go directly into jobs (Robinson, 1996).

Community colleges often have a vocational/technical component along with a college transfer program. In many states the college transfer program allows students to transfer to four-year institutions without losing credits. Students select community colleges for a variety of reasons, including (a) financial concerns, (b) remedial study, (c) the desire to determine whether post-high school study is for them, and (d) because they can earn a degree in two years. Students who have academic difficulty may also regain their eligibility to reenroll in four-year institutions by demonstrating their competencies in community college. A remarkable aspect of community colleges is their open-door admissions policy, which enables students to begin at their academic competency level and advance their education. However, this open-door policy does not extend to all programs offered in these institutions. Vocational-technical programs and nursing, accounting, and other programs have established admission standards (Isaacson & Brown, 1993).

Some major state universities have reached their capacity in the number of students they can serve and need to limit the number they admit. Some are requesting potential students to attend a community college for two years prior to transferring into the university. As a rule, if students are able to maintain a "B" average, they will be admitted to the four-year school.

Career development programs in community colleges can assist in student retention, especially those with low career maturity (Smith, 1987). Academic advisors in each department or division can identify incoming students in need of special career planning services and refer those students to the career center.

Men usually hold higher status jobs than women while in community college, and the more challenging students' college work experience is the more it affects their grades (Healy & Mourton, 1987). Higher level jobs during community college can complement course work in developing career skills and in networking. Gender differences in attempts to find jobs indicate that women might not recognize as well as men how jobs held during college relate to career development. If paid employment during college studies is important to career progress, women need to consider placing more emphasis on finding paid work while in college.

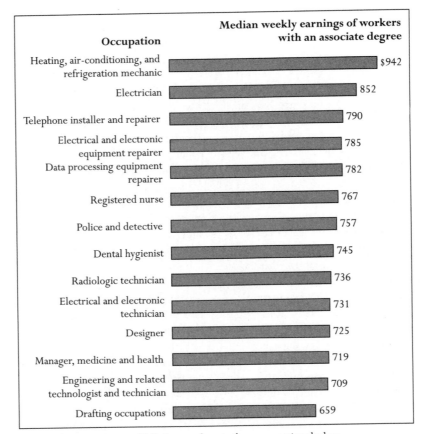

Occupation	Median weekly earnings of workers with an associate degree
Heating, air-conditioning, and refrigeration mechanic	$942
Electrician	852
Telephone installer and repairer	790
Electrical and electronic equipment repairer	785
Data processing equipment repairer	782
Registered nurse	767
Police and detective	757
Dental hygienist	745
Radiologic technician	736
Electrical and electronic technician	731
Designer	725
Manager, medicine and health	719
Engineering and related technologist and technician	709
Drafting occupations	659

Note: At least 15 percent of full-time workers in these occupations had an associate degree in 2001.

FIGURE 10.1   Highest Earning Occupations Commonly Held by Workers with an Associate Degree

SOURCE: Occupational Outlook Quarterly, *Winter 2002/03, p. 7.*

in community colleges are geared toward the needs of local businesses. Figure 10.1 and Figure 10.2 show the current salary level and the future outlook for jobs for those with an Associate degree.

Welfare Reform

Since so many welfare recipients are already attending job training programs in our postsecondary institutions, it seems necessary for career counselors to understand the U.S. welfare reform act of 1996. Welfare reform actually refers to **House Rule (HR) 3734, the Personal Responsibility and Work Opportunity Reconciliation Act**

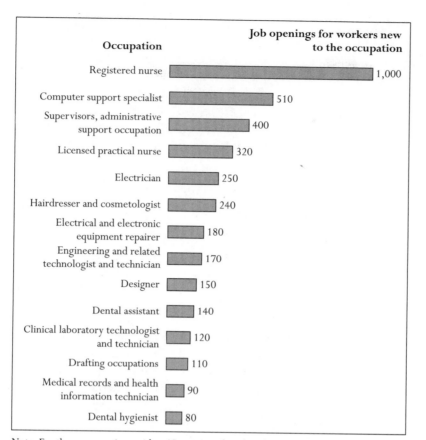

Note: For these occupations, either 15 percent of workers have an associate degree or BLS analysts consider an associate degree to be the most significant source of job training. Analyst discretion applies for occupations for which reliable educational attainment data are not available.

FIGURE 10.2   Job Openings in Occupations Commonly Held by Workers with an Associate Degree

SOURCE: Occupational Outlook Quarterly, Winter 2002/03, p. 9.

(PRWORA), passed by both houses of Congress in August 1996. Notice the Protestant work ethic's influence via the *personal responsibility* part of the PRWORA. PRWORA replaced:

- **AFDC—Aid to Families with Dependent Children,** which expired in October 1996
- **JOBS—the Job Opportunities and Basic Skills** training program
- Emergency Assistance programs
- Entitlements to cash assistance (Hard & Schoenmakers, 1997)

State welfare reforms have also had an impact. Texas nondrug users are more likely to be employed in welfare to work programs than drug users (Montoya, D. C., Bell, Atkinson, Nagy, & Whitsett, 2002). In 2003, Texas state budget cuts did away with Medicaid reimbursements for mental health services for those over age 21, meaning that drug users on welfare won't have mental health and drug treatment available.

TANF—Temporary Assistance for Needy Families was created in October 1996 and replaced the AFDC and JOBS programs. Block grants are provided to each state in the form of cash assistance and employment services for TANF recipients. TANF aims to

1. provide in-home care for children of needy families.
2. end dependency on the government by promoting job preparation, work, and marriage.
3. prevent out-of-wedlock pregnancies.
4. encourage two-parent families (Hard & Schoenmakers, 1997).

Time limits for TANF recipients depend on client's education and/or work experience. These time-limited benefits are a labyrinth of requirements that are going to entail the guidance of well-informed vocational practitioners. Vocational psychologists—the majority of whom were conspicuously silent during the public debates on welfare reform—can transform their academic discipline by contributing to the job preparation and work-related aspects of TANF through program development, program evaluation, clinical intervention, and research. TANF recipients will have a five-year maximum eligibility. Job training is a vital part of the welfare to work transition (The Center for Public Policy Priorities, 1997).

These welfare reforms helped move 4.7 million Americans from welfare rolls to self-sufficiency within three years of enactment (Agency Group 09, 2003). Welfare rolls have also declined 54 percent since 1996. In January 2003, President George W. Bush proposed a welfare reform agenda that includes a requirement that welfare recipients work 40 hours per week either on a job or in a job skills training program, that families would receive $16,000 per family in federal and state welfare, child care, and job training resources. He also proposed that welfare programs (i.e., food stamps, housing, workforce programs, and adult education) be consolidated.

Results of welfare reform show that, on the average, single mothers formerly on welfare were financially better off working or combining work and welfare than were nonworking welfare recipients (Danziger, Heflin, Corcoran, Oltmans, & Wang, 2002). Nationally, while there has been a sustained decline in African American child poverty (Agency Group 09, 2003), almost half of those former welfare recipients were still below the poverty level in 1998 (Danziger et al., 2002). The Bush administration also committed federal funds to continue the TANF and food stamp programs (Agency Group 09, 2002a, 2002b). But job training programs typically don't have sufficient resources to meet the needs of all those welfare recipients who apply for such assistance, and job training programs have a tendency to cream applicants, that is, select those with the greatest probability of success (Bell & Orr, 2002). Two important sources of information regarding workforce development is the John J. Heldrich Center at Rutgers University (http://www.heldrich.rutgers.edu/workingahead) and Workforce Innovations, which focuses on workforce investment (http://www.workforceinnovations.org). There is also useful information in Harris (2002), who reports on a welfare-to-work program by Ford Motor Company to train unemployed inner city Detroit residents as technicians at Ford dealerships, with most of the tuition paid for by the government (Harris, 2002).

Because the change in welfare policy requires recipients to find employment and job training, it is essential for workforce development centers and community colleges to work together to help train and prepare these people for the job market. Because many welfare recipients have low job skill levels, vocational practitioners who work with them will have to be able to match work and job skills. Career counselors will also have to be aware of the environmental and personal factors that impinge on welfare recipients' ability to "leave the system" (McDonald, 2002). These clients will need to find work close to public transportation and locate adequate child care. If one of these support systems is not available, it will be difficult to maintain worthwhile employment.

Mary Contreras, a counselor in a community college, has developed a program for transitioning the nonworking poor into the working poor. The complete model is described in Chapter 7 in *Career Counseling Models for Diverse Populations* (Peterson & González, 2000). Another program that provides a continuous education from one level to another is the Tech/Prep-Community College partnership. The TechPrep program starts in high school, where students are able to enroll in classes that are part of the articulation agreement with community colleges, and then they continue their education/training at the community college. The students can earn a certificate, an Associate of Arts degree, or continue on to work on a Bachelor's degree. Most of these programs are coordinated with the high school career and technology department, whose teachers are often aware of the training programs available at the community college involved. To locate further information regarding a Tech/Prep program in your areas, go to http://www.techprep@(yourstate).org.

Community colleges often have a vocational/technical component along with a college transfer program. In many states, the college transfer program allows students to transfer to four-year institutions without losing credits. Students select community colleges for a variety of reasons, including financial concerns, remedial study, the desire to determine whether post-high school study is for them, and the ability to earn a degree in two years. Students who have academic difficulty may also regain their eligibility to reenroll in four-year institutions by demonstrating their competencies in community college. One remarkable aspect of community colleges is their open-door admissions policy, which enables students to begin at their academic competency level and advance their education. However, this open-door policy does not extend to all programs offered in these institutions, especially those in the medical field.

Often when major state universities reach their capacity in the number of students they can serve and need to limit the number they admit, they suggest a community college to some students for two years before transferring into the university. As a rule, if students are able to maintain a B average at the two-year college, they will be admitted to a four-year school.

COLLEGES AND UNIVERSITIES

Colleges and universities tend to be more selective in the students they admit. While career counseling practices are similar in all educational settings, the differences in the services offered have more to do with the types of students in the institution and the differences in occupational goals that individuals possess.

Nationally, an estimated 75 percent of all freshmen and sophomores are in the process of declaring an academic major. These students need particular help to decide major fields of study. Students graduating with bachelor's degrees may need special services to determine job placement, interviewing skills, portfolio development, and other job-seeking skills. Decisions regarding graduate schools may also be involved.

Elwood (1992) proposes a pyramid model as a tool in career counseling with university students. See Figure 10.3. To understand this figure, view the pyramid from above and look down on it. The base of the pyramid is a triangle with the three sides representing interests, abilities, and personality traits. The three ridges or edges of the pyramid that lead to the center (the self) are emotionality, intellectuality, and sexuality. Elwood suggests that the intellectual ridge represents the activities of the brain—inventing, thinking, verifying. Feeling is represented by the emotionality line. Sexuality is the holistic part of the figure with motivation that involves the whole body. Influences are pictured on all sides. The strength of the model is that all parts support the sense of self. This seems to be an effective, relevant model for college-age students.

CAREER COUNSELING AT
THE POSTSECONDARY LEVEL

While the needs of students may vary in each educational setting, vocational practitioners will need to fulfill certain duties and responsibilities in order to provide services to benefit students. Olson and Matkin (1992) provide a comprehensive list of activities which career counselors in postsecondary education and training institutions should provide. This list reflects the current job descriptions of career counselors:

Assessment

1. Administers and interprets interest, personality, skills and values assessments.

2. Provides values clarification exercises.

3. Interprets achievement and ability assessments to individuals.

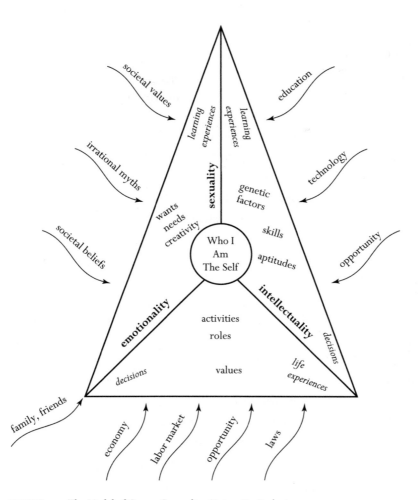

FIGURE 10.3 The Model of Career Counseling University Students
SOURCE: Elwood, 1992, p. 52.

Counseling

1. Counsels individuals about their personal problems.
2. Explains the roles that lifestyle and leisure play in career development,
3. Assists individuals in exploration of their occupations of interest.
4. Helps individuals understand the world of work.
5. Assists students in using computerized guidance programs.
6. Broadens awareness of nontraditional career opportunities.
7. Assists special populations (women, minorities, handicapped, disadvantaged, etc.) in their unique career development needs.
8. Provides for job adjustment counseling.

9. Provides academic advising and resources.

10. Conducts group counseling.

Teaching

1. Teaches skills necessary to understand the interrelatedness of their career decisions and life roles.

2. Teaches decision-making skills and goal-setting.

3. Teaches skills necessary for acquiring employment.

4. Demonstrates job interviewing skills.

5. Teaches career awareness and exploration classes.

6. Provides workshops on study skills and time management.

Coordination

1. Keeps occupational and labor market information current and is aware of future trends in the job market.

2. Coordinates career fairs.

3. Coordinates current employment information.

4. Provides information on educational trends as well as state and federal legislation that influences career counseling.

Program Direction and Evaluation

1. Establishes goals and objectives for the center.

2. Evaluates the effectiveness of specific career services.

3. Serves as liaison between educational and community resources.

4. Conducts in-service career workshops for staff, administrators, and teachers.

While all these activities may be related to various aspects of career counseling, not all are applicable in every setting. However, this long list helps to develop a perspective about the range of responsibilities entailed in the job, as well as the training needed to assume such a position.

SELECTED STUDIES AND APPLICATIONS FOR CAREER COUNSELORS IN POSTSECONDARY EDUCATIONAL INSTITUTIONS

Groups and Career Counseling

Groups have long been used to promote career development. Group approaches range from providing information (group guidance) to counseling (group counseling). Career development groups can be organized according to the degree that the approach is directive (information/didactic-oriented) or nondirective (feeling/affective-oriented). Career counseling involves both areas. Individuals need to get in touch with feelings and issues of identity while gaining information that will be of value in choosing a career or occupation. Group career counseling has two major tasks—dealing with feelings and dealing with information. Pyle presents a person-centered approach to career group counseling in Chapter 11 in Peterson & González, 2000.

Halasz and Kempton (2000) note that in a 1997 survey from the National Association of Colleges and Employers four out of five career centers provided group-oriented career counseling interventions. This trend is expected to continue as colleges and universities work toward a more comprehensive preparation of student to work in a global workforce. In group interventions, students can explore career options, provide motivation for each other, practice job interviewing skills, and share personal concerns and obstacles. If career courses are limited in size, they can also serve as a group intervention model.

A course entitled Exploring Careers met for two hours a week for fourteen weeks. Goals for the course included helping students gain a greater understanding of their interests, skills, and values and how this information related to academic majors and careers. Decision-making skills and job search strategies were also included. The results indicate that the students who completed the courses were more comfortable with their career decision-making processes and more certain of their career choices and academic major choices than those students in the control groups.

Zagora and Cramer (1994) conducted a study of client/treatment interaction in a group career-counseling situation with community college students. The authors found that when groups were homogeneous (for instance, all undecided), the learning for the participants was somewhat more effective than when participants were involved in a group with mixed levels of vocational identity. In other words, it is incumbent upon the counselor to be aware of the within-group differences between students and their particular needs to best serve them.

Programs for Career Counseling

The University of Cincinnati's Career Center developed and implemented the Career Navigator Series (2002) program to assist undecided/undeclared students with their career decision making and to increase retention. The Career Navigator Series consists of six stages:

1. Information/Assessment
2. Decision-Making Workshop
3. DISCOVER Computer Assisted Guidance System
4. Individual Counseling
5. Professional Forum
6. Follow-Up Individual Counseling Session.

This program has been shown to have several student benefits. Students significantly increase career certainty; significantly decrease career indecision; and increase self-esteem and self-efficacy in decision making. The benefits to the university are an increase in retention among first-year students and the forming and maintaining of collaborative relationships with employers and various colleges and departments within the university community. The benefits to the employers/community are that students are more goal directed and had more realistic expectations for initial employment, which translates into better retention rates for them as employees, and employers have a means of *connecting* to campus, thus giving them the opportunity to network with other employers, students, and university personnel. The two limitations of the Career Navigator Series are time and cost (Jurgens, 2002).

A series of career/life planning modules developed at the University of Calgary facilitate students' concept of themselves as **active agents** in the career planning process. One of the modules, "Translating a degree into an occupation," helps graduating students identify the unique skills and personal attributes they bring as potential employees. Liberal arts students have participated extensively in this workshop. The following principles provide the basis for the workshop:

1. Career planning is a developmental process that will occur throughout the lifetime of an individual. . . .

2. Students will understand that career development occurs during their postsecondary program as they face three major career decisions over that time, namely: choosing a program of studies, choosing occupational fields, and choosing a job. . . .

3. Career planning skills are necessary life skills because career development is ongoing throughout the individual's lifetime. . . .

4. Career planning is lifestyle planning. . . .

5. Clients are viewed as and assisted to become "active agents" in the process of career planning (Crozier, 1991, pp. 100–101, quotations in original).

These modules are designed to be taken sequentially during a student's four-year university program. Although this is not a requirement, students may, with the assistance of a counselor, choose to do later modules without having completed the earlier workshops. The module format offers the presentation of separate units of content that are designed to meet students' needs and time requirements. An overview of the modules is shown in Figure 10.4.

The University of Calgary has also begun a mentorship program that is useful to liberal arts students. Students identify occupational areas to do an information interview. The student is then paired with an alumnus who has previously agreed to the interview. The university also has a volunteer center to place students in experiences that will suit their interests and offer them opportunities to develop skills (Crozier, 1991).

Career/Life Planning Model for University Liberal Arts Students

Module 1: A Beginning

1st & 2nd year Undergraduates	3rd & 4th year Undergraduates & Graduate Students	3rd & 4th year Undergraduates & Graduate Students
Choosing an Educational Program	Choosing Occupational Fields	Choosing a Job

| Module 2: Exploring Yourself | Module 4: Translating a Degree into an Occupation | Module 5: Résumé Writing |
| Module 3: Career Research & Decision-Making | | Module 6: Interview Skills/Job Search Techniques |

FIGURE 10.4 An Overview of Crozier's Modules and Their Sequencing

SOURCE: Crozier, S. D. (1991). *Empowering the Liberal Arts Students with Personal Flexibility for the World of Work.* Canadian Journal of Counselling, 25, *(2), p. 102. Reprinted with permission.*

Bradley and Mims (1992) blend family systems and birth order dynamics to develop a college course for career planning entitled "Decision-making for Career Development." A brief summary of the exercises follows:

1. A lecture on family structure with questions such as "Whom do you turn to when faced with making an important decision?" and "How has your family influenced your career/occupational choice?" Assignment: construct a genogram of your family; identify messages, boundaries, roles, myths, rules, and relationships; share your genogram in a small group.

2. A lecture on birth order and the Adlerian concept of striving for significance. Assignment: list siblings by sex from oldest to youngest, noting age spacing between each; identify what each sibling did best in the family. If an only child, discuss how the lack of siblings affected you. (For information on the genogram, Chapter 8 in this text and Chapter 12 in Peterson and González [2000] may be of help.)

Luzzo's (1996) study examines "the relationship between perceived occupational barriers and the Career Decision Making (CDM) attitudes, knowledge of CDM principles, and CDM Self-Efficacy of college students." He uses his study as a way of building on previous research in order to clarify "the role that perceived barriers play in the CDM process" (p. 240). Results of his study show that college students who

Practical Applications

By asking clients to indicate the specific barriers they believe they have successfully overcome, practitioners might emphasize such accomplishments to help clients recognize that many perceived occupational barriers are surmountable. Increased awareness might help clients develop higher levels of self-efficacy for overcoming similar occupational barriers. Practitioners might also help clients identify potential barriers to future occupational goals. Practitioners can raise student awareness regarding the difference between real and perceived barriers in the workplace.

think they will have to overcome many obstacles in the future have more problems in the CDM process because they have less confidence in their ability to make effective decisions than do students who do not see as many barriers. Interestingly, those who "perceive they have overcome family-related barriers in the past have developed more mature CDM attitudes and . . . [have gained more] confidence in their ability to make effective career decisions" (p. 246). Luzzo suggests that discussing ways to overcome occupational barriers may be helpful to students, and refers to two "psychometrically sound instruments for measuring perceived barriers[:] . . . the Perceived Barriers Scale (McWhirter, 1994) and Swanson and Tokar's (1991) Career Barriers Inventory . . . " (p. 247).

Relevance for Multicultural and Diverse Populations

Most existing assessment tools reflect the dominant culture of American society (Heppner & Johnston, 1993). When used with ethnic or cultural minority groups, such assessment may produce false or misleading results. Bingham and Ward (1994) report that African American women tended to have Social as their highest Holland code through paper-and-pencil assessment, but this may simply reflect the structure of occupational opportunity rather than the types of occupations most suitable for them. The need for instruments that are free of cultural biases and stereotypical presentations is obvious and has long been recognized. Card sort techniques allow the counselor to observe the process of the client responding to the assessment (Heppner & Johnston, 1993). Focusing on the process gives the counselor more opportunity to intervene during the actual assessment (Heppner & Duan, 1995). Career counseling professionals need to become advocates for individuals and groups who face possible bias and discrimination in their pursuit of careers (Sue & Sue, 1990).

Postsecondary Career Counseling for the Gifted

Common sense may dictate that effective career guidance for the gifted college student should result in course selection, academic programming, and specialized training, resulting in the high-prestige/high-income careers that may not be open to less creative and capable students. However, several salient characteristics of the gifted adult often make this option not only undesirable but also unattractive.

Characteristics of gifted adults impacting the work experience are:

- As independent thinkers, they do not unquestioningly accept decisions by their supervisors and often have difficulties with authority figures.

- Their high need for independence in thought and actions may be threatening to people in authority.

- They frequently find themselves in a position of knowing more than their supervisor.

- They may often be impatient with others who do not see/think as they do.

- They tend to be holistic, global thinkers in a largely linear, sequential work world.

- They are frequently overwhelmed by the large number of areas in which they are interested and in which they know they could excel.

- They often are unable to prioritize or select one field of study.

- They often have enormous difficulties with career decision making.

- It is common they are not necessarily popular or understood; they are often introverted and nonconforming.

- They often have a very strong and personal moral code that may result in decisions that appear to be unrealistic or impractical.

- They may be judged only in terms of their behavior, which is much different from their extroverted counterparts.

- They often have poor communication skills that can create the appearance of arrogance and superiority.

- The inward focus of the introvert may lead to the appearance of narrow-mindedness or argumentativeness with co-workers.

- They appear to have an inherently strong need for accuracy and thoroughness.

- They often exhibit chronic perfectionistic behavior in terms of meeting their own standards and expectations and not necessarily those of the outside world.

- They may be unable to excel in any one area because of the inability to limit their focus to a single area; persistence and perfectionism may lead to appearance of rigidity.

- They will persist with inner standards even when others do not see the need to do so.

- Many cannot tolerate any violation of their personal sense of ethical or moral standards by self or others and may appear inflexible.

- They often retain childlike approach to tasks, are often easily frustrated with repetition and tasks that appear pointless, and may need to be coached in how to play the school game.

- They often are unwilling to take intellectual risks.

- Usually, they have a high need for novelty and intellectual challenge.

- They are more likely to follow their own inner agenda, which is overwhelmingly one of deep commitment to mankind's survival and global betterment, with a strong sense of identification and personal/spiritual connection to global societies, events, and issues.

This last characteristic is one of the hallmarks of the gifted. With startling consistency, the gifted display an early and ferocious awareness of moral issues and an intense need to "make a difference" in the quality of the lives and the world around them. This is often in conflict with the career expectations of others (most often parents) and may not correspond with the demands and outcomes of a high-powered career path. Whereas most highly successful people may quite possibly be gifted as well, it is also true that most gifted people do not want, seek, or achieve fame. Not surprisingly, many of the gifted gravitate toward careers in the helping professions. See Tye and Bireley (1991) for a discussion on the moral and spiritual development of the gifted and how this trait may impact career choice.

Due to their multipotentiality, the gifted are often unable to make a choice because selecting one out of many options translates into abandoning the others. Knowledge of type will assist not only in selecting which area of interest and ability on which to focus time, energy, and money, but will also provide important information on the related work environments of each option being considered. Because so many of the gifted are introverts and most work places are filled with extraverts, work environment is an important consideration. Knowledge of type will enable an informed decision regarding working with or against type and the personal adjustments that may need to be made. Gifted young adults should be guided to consider pertinent goals within the context of their individual value and belief systems when engaged in life planning. Such general goals should be assigned a level of value (high, medium, or low), with consideration given to the cross-impact of stressing one goal over another and with career being only one element of importance in the development of a *life* plan (Bireley, 1991).

Pertinent Goals and Needs When doing life planning with the gifted, the individual's goals and needs must be considered. The relative need for and the degree of availability of each item provided in various career choices must be considered:

- Intellectual stimulation and challenge
- Status and respect
- Personal interest or professional necessity for continued education
- Community service/philanthropic work
- Spiritual growth
- Independent or group work responsibilities
- Degree of autonomy
- Monetary and other material rewards
- Leisure time
- Family commitments and responsibilities
- Personal growth
- Career satisfaction
- Role that will be assigned to other areas of high ability
- Degree of routine/repetition

It is during this stage of life planning that a clear distinction be made and articulated between *personal* needs and goals and the expectations and possible pressures exerted by important others. Because of their high level of ability, many of the gifted are implicitly expected to desire and reach a level of unusual success *as defined by the dominant culture*. Many often experience intense pressure to do so both culturally and within the family system.

Components of a successful career counseling program at the postsecondary level should introduce students to various fields of study, including those outside the traditional sex-role for their gender, mentoring by successful gifted adults who have made a range of career and lifestyle choices, internships in fields of interest, and biographical research that can enable identification with those who have made great contributions while overcoming adversities (Boyd, Hemmings, & Braggett, 2003).

Because 75 percent of the general population are extroverts, it becomes immediately apparent that gifted students and adults will come into intimate daily contact at home and/or school with an overwhelming majority who differ *substantially* from them in some very fundamental ways. "Introversion is not a pathological condition; it is not an abnormal response to the world. It is simply a personality trait found in a small percentage of the total population" (Burruss & Kaenzig, 2003).

There are certain qualities of the gifted experience that transcend age, nationality, ethnicity, gender, socio-economic status, occupation, interests or talent domain: good problem solving, abstract reasoning, thriving on challenge, *curiosity, vivid imagination, intensity, sensitivity, complexity, perfectionism, introversion.* Gifted people not only think differently, *they feel differently.* Giftedness is a different way of being, and these differences affect one *throughout the lifespan* (italics added, Silverman, 2003).

These differences, along with the supportive data of IQ testing, help distinguish the high-achiever from the gifted student. It is also these differences that impact the gifted individual's workplace experience and level of satisfaction with his/her life plan. In decision-making activities, gifted students need to be aware of what an introvert is and how they differ from the extraverted world.

Multipotentiality Multipotentiality is defined as "the ability to select and develop any number of career options because of a wide variety of interests, aptitudes, and abilities. The broad range of opportunities available tends to increase the complexity of decision making and goal setting, and it may actually delay career selection" (Kerr, 1990). This is usually an issue that only the moderately gifted, academically talented, or those who have two or more outstanding but very different areas of ability will have to struggle with. At the college age, multipotential students often graduate with multiple academic majors. Numerous changes in the declared major in the early stages of the college career is not unusual and indicates a certain level of difficulty in committing to long-term goals. These students may be very successful academically in the university setting with notable involvement in extracurricular activities but unable to select one area of study on which to focus. They may also "make hasty, arbitrary, or 'going-along-with-the-crowd' career decisions and frequently suffer from the pain of having to lose opportunities in one area of interest in favor of another" (Kerr, 1991). The emotional dilemma and distress in taking care of this issue of multiple, equally viable, interests and choices are very real for these students and should not be taken lightly.

Students functioning in the highly and profoundly gifted categories are much more likely than the moderately gifted (IQs of 125-140) to have a very focused career interest at an early age. Others do not become focused until late high school or the start of college. Whatever the eventual decision may be, career counseling should emphasize rigorous academic preparation and high aspirations because this will keep the number of options open for these students and prevent premature closure of other possible choices (Colangelo, 2002). Kerr (1991) cites research that indicates that, although equally multipotential, females and minorities of high ability often do not have correspondingly high aspirations or career goals that are certainly warranted based on their past academic or creative abilities.

Minority and Gifted It has long been recognized that minority populations (with the exception of Asian Americans) are substantially under identified and underrepresented in public school programs for the gifted. By the time the highly able minority student (who has been neither identified nor academically challenged) reaches the postsecondary level, a number of opportunities and experiences have already been irretrievably lost along the way. The middle and high school years are not only extremely critical in the development of a positive gifted identity, but also equally formative in the emerging sense of efficacy, resilience, and confidence necessary for such work traits as willingness to engage in challenge-seeking behavior, to do hard work, take risks, and accurately self-evaluate work performance. The teenage years are the most difficult socially for any child but most especially the gifted. To be both gifted and a minority creates additional social difficulties for these students. If gender stereotyping by both the dominant and the minority culture is factored in, then it may also be true that gifted female minority students have the most difficulty establishing a positive gifted identity and place in the work world. Although it begins in the preteen years, social discomfort and avoidance will often extend into the postsecondary years and will need to be addressed.

Research indicates that African Americans, Latinos, and Native Americans are well aware of their presence and/or absence from gifted education, high-prestige university programs and career opportunities and that they are also very conflicted about participating in such programs. Most unfortunately, minority students often report that academic excellence and/or gifted identification is associated in their cultures with *acting White*. Until this perception by both the dominant and minority cultures is identified, acknowledged, and really addressed, we will continue to miss highly capable gifted minority students because of their conflict about wanting to be found or identified. The impact of this cultural perception cannot be underestimated in academic and career planning.

The Gifted Female "In our society, it is not smart to be smart" (Colangelo, 2002). It might fairly be added "especially if you're a woman"! Despite improvement in pay and career options available to women, gifted females still face daunting challenges. Stereotyping based on gender (as well as giftedness) significantly deters gifted women from meeting the promise of their full potential. Most tragically, it is not only stereotyping from significant others and the general culture that does much damage, but also the internalization of the stereotypes into the self-image.

Gifted females discover quickly the choice they are given in our culture: being smart carries a very high price, so choose well. Gifted women are especially vulnerable to a preoccupation with the expectations and opinions of others and still come under enormous pressure to conform in comparison to their male counterparts.

MODELS FOR COURSES

Another service of community college counseling centers is career courses, which include specific information for displaced workers, undecided majors, job search skills, students with special abilities, returning students, those who plan to go on to a college/university, and those who seek to go directly into jobs (Robinson, 1996).

Drawing on her experience in both community college and university settings, Nadene Peterson (2000) designed a two-phase model for a course in a community college setting. While designed for a particular situation, it can provide the basis for a class in any postsecondary education and training institution.

Career/Occupational Exploration

Peterson begins career exploration using the concepts of WHO, WHY, WHAT, WHERE, and WHEN. Each step in this first phase is then followed by suggested assessments and tasks.

WHO involves self-exploration

1. Interests—The Strong Interest Inventory, Self-Directed Search, Kuder DD, or Career Assessment Inventory, depending on the age or experience of the students.
2. Values—The Life Values Inventory, Rokeach Values Survey, or Values Scale.
3. Skills—Haldane's Motivated Skills Chart, *The Quick Job Hunting Map* (Bolles), Campbell Interest and Skills Survey (CISS).
4. Personal Traits—Myers-Briggs Type Inventory combined with SII, DISCOVER (computer assisted), Sixteen Personality Factor (16PF), Personal Career Development Profile (PCDP), Adjective Checklist, Adjective Self-Description.
5. Life Goals—Life Goals Inventory (three different forms).

WHY involves exploring family and social influences

1. Family influences—fill out a genogram; study family relationships, such as parents, siblings, blended families.
2. Social influences—use the Career Beliefs Inventory discussed in Chapter 7.

WHAT involves occupational exploration

1. Nature of work—taken from RIASEC and types of jobs, computer assisted programs, *Dictionary of Occupational Titles* (O*NET)
2. Requirements:
   a. Training
   b. Education
   c. Skills
3. Potential for Advancement
4. Employment Outlook
5. Salary and Benefits

WHERE involves the following:

1. Region (State, Country); Metropolitan, Suburbs, or Rural
2. Cultural, ethnic, gender, sexual orientation , disability considerations

WHEN involves decision making

1. Using Gelatt's Decision Making model in Chapter Seven:
   a. identify alternatives.
   b. list consequences for each alternative.
   c. make choice that best matches your person and environment.
2. Develop a plan of action with timelines and specific goals to be met.

Up to this point we have discussed exploration of careers, which is Phase I. Phase II involves entering the field, that is, learning how to get a job. This involves five steps:

1. Writing a résumé/developing a portfolio
2. Interviewing skills
3. Researching the organization (including identifying key personnel, learning philosophy and mission of the organization)
4. Making initial contacts/using networking
5. Communicating clearly how your traits and skills match with the organization's needs and mission.

Michelle Casto (2002) proposes a course, Senior Year Experience, using the text: *Get Smart! About Modern Career Development: A Personal Guide to Creating Your Own Life's Work* by Casto (2002). The course outline is:

Student Academic Outcomes

1. Learn how to access and use ten or more assessment-based career resources
2. Synthesize and understand his/her own individual career development process
3. Observe and participate in a career resource center
4. Complete a comprehensive career portfolio

Course Requirements:

Career Research Paper Students will write a 5–6 page paper (double-spaced) on their desired career. The paper will explain and provide evidence of labor market information and future forecasting of the viability of the career, necessary credentials, and similar information. Students should conduct an informational interview with at least two people doing the job. Students will discuss their readiness level to enter into the chosen career field. Students should also be prepared to present their research to the class.

Employability Skills This includes positive attitude, punctuality, attendance, teamwork, high work ethic, completing homework assignments, interviewing skills, visiting a career resource center(s), and overall class involvement. Students should volunteer 5–10 hours in a related work environment.

Personal Journal Students will keep a personal journal during the course of the class. They will turn in five typed journals for review by the instructor (may be emailed). Journal topics can be found in the textbook, and students may choose any that appeal to them.

The Career Preparation Portfolio includes two versions of their résumé (a chronological, functional, or computer version), a sample cover letter (to a specific person at a company of interest), references sheet, and three media resources.

This course can be offered as a semester class worth three hours credit and can be administered by a qualified professor in departments or schools. More information about the program can be found at http://www.getsmartseries.com.

Working with students who are applying for jobs requires that the practitioner as well as the client understand the parameters of this search. Locating a job may be the result of the above process, but it is also important to prepare for the role of happenstance, networking, and sheer luck. Realizing that career shifts are part of life is basic to keeping the flexibility that makes changes possible.

As we will see in the continuation of our look at the types of changes for which adults need to be prepared, the perspective given during the first real job seeking experience can prepare the young adult for the realities of the future workforce.

TECHNOLOGY IN CAREER DEVELOPMENT AND COUNSELING

The use of computers with various systems and approaches to career guidance is a rapidly developing area counselors have available for their practices. There are various technological options for providing career counseling services—in free-standing computer-based programs, in Internet programs, and in distance learning. We shall also attempt to sort through the nearly overwhelming number of sources and amount of information available to those with Internet access. We will then look briefly at standard sources of information. One of our tasks as counselors is to help clients access information on the Internet and other computer assisted programs in an efficient and helpful manner, but still allow for interpersonal interaction, which will always be an integral part of vocational counseling.

Computer Assisted Career Guidance Systems (CACGS)

The benefits computers provide include:

- A more efficient use of time for practitioners
- Immediate access to assessments results
- Accuracy of administration and scoring
- Efficient sequential steps that can be guided by the client

- Adaptation to specific vocational theories
- Opportunities for research
- Popularity with students/clients

Potential problem areas include:

- Loss of client/counselor interaction
- Assumption of a certain level of cognitive functioning
- Potential loss of privacy
- Difficulty in allowing for client idiosyncrasies

Self-motivated individuals may be better candidates for using computer assisted career guidance systems (CACG) (Kivlighan, Johnston, Hogan, & Mauer, 1994).

The three major CACG systems are **DISCOVER, SIGI PLUS,** and CHOICES. These widely used systems have been upgraded and expanded, but there are others available as well.

DISCOVER, under lead developer Jo Ann Harris-Bowlsbey, released a multimedia version in 1997, which is available in English and French and adapted for use in Canada and Australia using occupational information relevant to those countries. It is also available on the Internet. DISCOVER has several versions representing various ages and groups. The system is designed to be interactive, so users are given exercises that help them gain self-knowledge, identify their interests and abilities, prioritize their values, and inventory life work experiences. Within the DISCOVER system, the user can access the results of each inventory/assessment immediately and be provided with a list of occupations to explore, based on the information the personal profile contains. These results are then placed in the context of the World-of-Work Map, which organizes occupations into clusters, regions, and families. See Figure 10.5. For a model using DISCOVER for college students and adults, see Chapter 8 in Peterson & González, 2000. DISCOVER is available from ACT.

The System of Interactive and Guidance Information (SIGI PLUS), developed by Martin Katz, was designed to help college students clarify values, identify occupational options, and develop rational career decision making (CDM) skills. Katz (1993) explains that the basis for SIGI systems include the domain of self-understanding, which includes needs, values, interests, temperaments, and aptitude. Needs may be considered as basic motivating forces for which satisfaction is sought. "To the extent that needs reside below the level of consciousness, they are best handled in guidance through their outer manifestations and expressions, as values" (p. 105). Values order, arrange, and unify the interactions of psychological and social forces in the process of career decision making, as well as allow for the expression of culturally influenced needs. Interests relate to the means by which a goal that represents values may be met. Temperaments define and can be subsumed in values and interests. Aptitude "appears to mean whatever a given developer decides it is to mean" (p. 144).

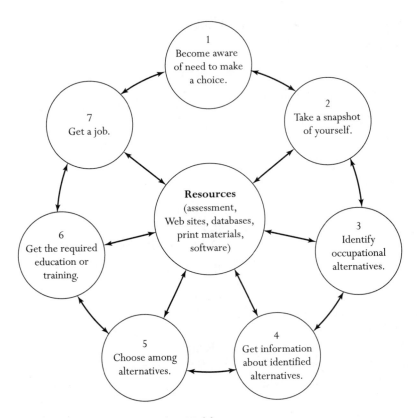

FIGURE 10.5 Planful Decision-Making Model

SOURCE: The Internet: A tool for career planning *by Joann Harris-Bowlsbey, Margaret Riley Dikel, and James J. Sampson, Jr. (2nd ed.), p. 1. Copyright 2002 by The National Career Development Association. Reprinted with permission.*

Skills are further elaborated in SIGI PLUS. Occupational information, strategies for decision making, and turning decisions into actions are expanded by separating out the preparing component. This element uses what is typically required for entry into an occupation by defining steps and listing resources, such as time, money, the ability to cope with difficulties, and motivation. Coping is designed to deal with the special needs of adults in transition, whether going into a new occupation, reentering the labor force after a period of unemployment, or changing occupations. For more information about these systems and their development, Katz (1993) is a good resource. Information about SIGI Plus is available from ETS.

CHOICES is designed to help high school students make informed and educated decisions about their future, whether it be to attend a university or begin a career. CHOICES offers information about everything from vocational technical schools to financial aid, and its services include:

1. A career interest checklist that helps students relate their interests to occupations
2. A college letter writer that writes letters for catalogues or more information from selected colleges
3. A financial aid letter writer that generates letters to sources of financial aid for more information

Information is also available regarding occupations, state and local information, education and training, and financial aid.

Selecting and Using Computer Assisted Career Guidance Systems

A benefit of CACG systems is their flexibility and accessibility across programs. Most systems offer

- occupational information.
- armed services information.
- information about postsecondary institutions.
- information on technical/specialized schools.
- financial aid information.
- interest inventories.
- decision-making skills.

Other common components include

- local job information files.
- ability measures.
- value inventories.
- predictions of success in college.
- job-search strategies.
- how to prepare a resumé.
- information on job interviewing.
- components for adults (Zunker, 1994, pp. 126–127).

Practitioners should take these steps when using CACG systems:

1. Assessment of needs—understand each individual's needs in order to determine which parts of the program should be used.
2. Orientation—explain the purpose and goals of the program and give a clear explanation of the mechanics of the system.
3. Individualized programs—assist when needs are determined.

4. Practitioner intervention—assist when necessary to help the user work toward occupational choice.

5. Online assistance—assist when different stages are explored during the process.

6. Follow-up—encourage, motivate, set goals, and interpret outcomes before he/she leaves (Zunker, 1994, pp. 133–34).

When selecting a CACG system, it is important to obtain information from colleagues, see a demonstration of the system and evaluate its products, understand the cost to install and to run, and survey equipment needs to determine what can best meet the needs given the available budget. It is important to know what system will be used before selecting hardware to assure a good and adequate fit. Sampson (1994) also emphasizes

1. integrating the CACG system into the career services center.

2. using hands-on training for the staff to ensure (a) acceptance and involvement with the CACG, (b) ability to operate the system with ease, and (c) a clear understanding of the role of the system in the context of the counseling process.

3. building in evaluative processes to monitor the effectiveness of the CACG system continually.

Technical Concerns

Aside from the advantages and disadvantages of computers versus paper-and-pencil tests, there are technical concerns that are entirely unique to computer systems. Certain expectations must be met when choosing a computerized system, including flexibility, accuracy, usability, and readability. Flexibility is important because the user must be allowed to change his/her answers after they have been entered into the system. Without this, mistakes cannot be rectified. Aside from flexibility, the information must be accurate, easy to understand, and comparable to standard career guides now on the O★NET.

Gati (1994) sees four problems with CACG systems: the database, the decision-making process, the interactive dialogue, and the context on which the system is built. With occupational information, Gati suggests there is an "image of accuracy" in computerized information, even though human judgment plays a critical role in the information and is subject to unintentional biases. Another concern with the database is how to present "within occupational variance" without being overwhelmed. Regarding the decision-making process, Gati suggests five problematic subareas: eliciting aspirations while encouraging compromise, increasing the number of considered alternatives, the validity of the idea that some alternatives are better or as good as others, whether to rank alternatives in some descending order, and dealing with uncertainty. Effective interactive dialogue needs to provide relevant information, be sophisticated rather than simplistic, be flexible instead of constrained, and be attractive. It is essential that practitioners familiarize themselves with CACG systems to use them effectively and adapt useful features into the occupational counseling process (Gati, 1994).

Ethical Issues

One possibility facing vocational counseling is the issue of stand-alone CACG systems. There are serious concerns about the ability of these systems to provide satisfactory service. However, their cost effectiveness makes them attractive, and the sophistication of their development may overcome many of the objections to their use. According to Sampson (1997), the issue of making a stand-alone CACG system available and the decision about the type and amount of staff assistance to provide clients is important when picking and integrating a CACG system. "The need for counselor intervention is ultimately a function of two factors, the characteristics of the CACG system and the characteristics of the user" (p. 5).

Some CACG systems are not meant to be stand-alone systems and should be accompanied by the proper support of a counselor. Then, an ethical dilemma arises over how much time a staff member should provide to a client using a CACG system. Both over-helping and under-helping a client is detrimental to the client's career decision-making process, and a counselor must be able to differentiate between the client who is able to use a CACG appropriately and requires little help and the client who is struggling with the system. The information provided by a CACG does not always mean that the client is getting the needed services. It is important to ascertain if the client and the CACG are compatible, providing orientation as may be necessary and follow-up to determine the effectiveness of the intervention.

Another ethical dilemma arises from the expectations of a client using a CACG system. Sampson (1997) says "inappropriate expectations about using a computer assisted career guidance system may limit critical thinking and exploratory behaviors necessary for effective career decision-making" (p. 3). Herr (1997) notes that "the *ethical obligations* of counselors to clients (e.g. respect, dignity, confidentiality, disclosure, prevent harm, do not harm) change very little . . . but the *roles* of counselors change as new technologies and scientific knowledge bases expand to modify what counselors do" (p. 2). He recommends that to work within ethical guidelines, practitioners see CACG systems as part of the process for all clients, and must "work to demysticize technology" (p. 4). For a comparison of three sets of ethical guidelines for use of the Internet, see Appendix 2.

For more information about CACG systems, how to install and operate them, and how to be aware of current practices, the Center for the Study of Technology in Counseling and Career Development at Florida State University is an excellent source (http://www.career.fsu.edu/techcenter).

Practical Applications

With the increasing use of technology in vocational psychology, it is essential that practitioners be trained to access the systems and sort through the plethora of information available. The amount of data can be overwhelming, and users will need assistance to prioritize and take action. K. Richard Pyle, who worked with the DISCOVER program, discussed the need for in-service training of counselors to assist them in learning the elements of occupational/career groups as an adjunct to CACG systems with Nadene Peterson (Conversation, 2002).

From these groups, the students can

1. determine which occupations they want to pursue and the educational/training requirements involved.
2. identify traits, interests, and values.
3. respond to subjective aspects of that information and obtain feedback from peers.
4. explore the *fit* of occupational information with personal traits.
5. suggest opportunities for shadowing, mentors, advisors, work experience, and volunteer activities.

This information is an update of his earlier article (Pyle, 1985; see also Peterson and González, 2000, Chapter 11). The advantages of group counseling are that more students can be serviced at one time and students have an excellent opportunity to learn from each other. It encourages commitment to plans by requiring them to report each week what they have learned and accomplished. If completing a CACG program is a requirement for high school students, it can provide services to a wider variety of students, not just those who are college-bound.

TABLE 10.2 Computer Assisted Career Guidance System Developers

Bridges.com
Career Development Systems
Chronicle Guidance Publications
COIN Educational Products
American College Testing (DISCOVER)
InfoCareers
JIST Publishing
Peterson's
Riverside Publishing
Educational Testing Service (SIGI PLUS)
Sigma Assessment Systems

SOURCE: http://www.acinet.org/

Online Services

The explosion of information available through online systems and the Internet have made it nearly impossible to keep pace with developments. Herr (1997) sees several concerns with this expansion of information:

1. The accuracy, relevance, and timeliness of information
2. Adequate preparation for the user to know how to process the information
3. Opportunity for follow-up to correct or confirm the information
4. Confidentiality and privacy
5. The potential for violation of copyright law
6. Ethical exchange of information between sites and users
7. Lack of training with the technology for counselors
8. Conduct of research, with concomitant issues such as informed consent, trust, and protection the identity of participants

We want to emphasize the concerns about practitioner preparation. Most practitioners probably have not had much opportunity to keep up with the new types of information, let alone current information. Because technology changes and develops rapidly, it is imperative for practitioners to keep abreast of Web sites for career and vocational information and to check the accuracy and credentials of the sources of information.

Internet Counseling The use of the Internet for career counseling is growing. McCarthy, Moller, and Beard (2003) cite Koonce (1997) regarding the proliferation of career-related Web sites and Sampson, Kolodinsky, and Greeno (1997) concerning the lack of study on the usefulness of the new developments. McCarthy et al. propose that before a person approaches any career-related Web site, he or she seek help from a career practitioner regarding relevant sites and ways to use them. The study provided training for a group of graduate students in using Gysbers's and Moore's (1987) Life Career Assessment structured interview, which is based on Adler's Individual Psychology and works to assess the interviewee's functioning in particular life roles. The students also became familiar with Gilster's (1997) book, *The Web Navigator*. With this and other information, the structured interview proved to be very helpful to those clients who used Internet resources for career planning (McCarthy et al. 2003).

Another use of the Internet is in distance training methodologies in career development. Malone (2002) offers proactive suggestions and cautions regarding developing such a program. These go beyond computer assisted guidance systems or computer information dissemination systems. Malone focuses on the "establishment of a working alliance or counseling relationship through the use of technology-assisted methodologies such a synchronous/asynchronous e-mail, telecounseling, and videoconferencing" (p. 1). He goes on to recommend specific distance career counseling practices:

- A clear and comprehensive Web site
- Comprehensive, technology-assisted, precounseling in-take registration and protocol
- Personalized selection and assignment of a well-matched counselor
- Technology-assisted strategies
- Structured distance career counseling interventions
- Maintaining counselor-client contact between sessions
- Providing clients with thoughtful, written feedback from their counseling sessions
- Evaluating distance career counseling practices

For more information on this topic, an excellent resources is *Cybercounseling and Cyberlearning: Encore* by J. W. Bloom and G. R. Walz (Eds.) 2002.

Sources of Information: The Internet and Print The fastest-growing source of information about careers, jobs, and related areas is on the Internet. Because a comprehensive listing is beyond the scope of this book and e-mail addresses are subject to change, we have chosen to focus on areas of interest and some major sources. As a source of information, Internet sites suffer from possible lack of reliability, changeability of Internet addresses, and short lifespans. A helpful resource in career planning that uses the Internet is the National Career Development Association's *The Internet: A Tool for Career Planning: A Guide to Using the Internet in Career Planning* by Harris-Bowlsbey, Dikel, and Sampson (2002). The list of resources is exhaustive, but the problems listed above require constant updating of information. It is a challenge for practitioners to keep abreast of all the information available as well as the changing emphases in the field of vocational psychology. Terms to look under in search engines include: careers, jobs, job search, career development, career guidance, career information, and career counseling.

Some major sources include the following sites. Many other universities in addition to those listed below maintain helpful Web sites.

- Department of Labor (http://www.dol.gov/)
- Career Counseling Resources (http://www.hawk.igs.net/employmentplanning)
- Career Counselors Consortium (http://www.careercc.org/)
- School-to-Career and Career Resources for Counselors (http://www.azstartnet.com/~rjm/index)
- National School to Work Learning Center (http://stw.edu.gov/)

- ADA Information Center (http://www.jan.wvu.edu/links/adalinkhtm)
- Distance Learning Technology Programs (http://www.dce.ttu.edu/)
- Career Development Systems CareerWAYS (http://www.cdsways.com)
- Career Key (http://www.careerkey.com)
- America's Career Infonet (http://www.acinet.org/acinet/)
- O★NET Online (http://online.onetcenter.org)
- National Career Development Association (http://www.ncda.org)
- Academic Innovations (http://www.academicinnovations.com)
- The Center for Education and Work, University of Wisconsin (http://www.cew.wisc.edu/)
- The Center for Technology in Counseling and Career Development, Florida State University (http://www.career.fsu.edu)
- The University of Missouri-Columbia (http://www.missouri.edu/~cppc)

There are also many useful books in this area. Some of these guides are available on the Internet as well.

- *Occupational Outlook Handbook*
- Dictionary of Occupational Titles
- Enhanced Guide for Occupational Exploration
- Dictionary of Holland's Occupational Codes
- Peterson's Guides and Directories
- Careers in the Non-Profit Sector
- The Complete Guide to Public Employment
- National Trade and Professional Associations
- Global Employment Guide
- Directory of Special Programs for Minority Group Members
- Directory of Special Opportunities for Women

Some useful periodicals are the *Occupational Outlook Quarterly, Career Opportunities News,* and *Federal Jobs Digest.*

DEVELOPING AN OCCUPATIONAL COUNSELING
AND INFORMATION CENTER

Although the top ten reasons to visit an OCIC are a humorous take on these resources, there is a ring of truth in each statement. Unfortunately, many students pass through high school and college without ever being aware of or properly trained to

---

BOX 10.1

The Top Ten Reasons to Visit Your Career Center

1. Your friends are sick of hearing that you don't know what to do with the rest of your life.
2. You can have something to tell your parents when they ask you (again) what you're doing about finding a job.
3. Career counselors get lonely when you don't visit them.
4. Once school is finished, you will never be able to get unlimited, free, professional career advice again.
5. Some career centers will videotape you in a practice interview. You can take the tape home and watch it over and over again.

6. Find out who's recruiting on campus before all the interview slots are filled.
7. Get your resumé reviewed by an expert so you don't look like an amateur.
8. You'll feel better when you see how many other people don't know what they want to do with their lives.
9. You've already seen the cafeteria, registrar's office, admissions hall, and other campus highlights.
10. Hey, it's something everyone has to do before they graduate.

—Village, Inc.

---

use these centers. The OCIC is an invaluable tool and, if set up correctly, should provide a vast array of knowledge of the world of work— whether one is graduating from high school or college or is an alumnus/alumna making a job transition.

Rationale and Services

Several areas must be considered before attempting to design an OCIC. These are primary to a successful and effective delivery of services that will be both attractive to users and thorough in its perspective. An OCIC can be organized around four major factors:

1. Philosophy of purpose, including major client base
2. Theoretical basis
3. Design of service delivery
4. Evaluation of outcomes

The rationale for a center is to provide occupational and career-design services for clients using all the information available. Defining the major client base is basic to any design that may be instituted. The level and needs of the students/clients, the complexity of the interventions that will typically need to be made, and the competencies needed by staff to properly meet the needs are important considerations.

The theoretical foundation is important because many of the programs, computer-assisted guidance systems, and assessment instruments should be chosen with a predominant theory in mind. It is probably wise to be somewhat eclectic theoretically because many of the tools can be used with more than one theory. However, when initiating a center, it is advisable to begin with a consistent approach to the intervention.

College/University At the college and university level, OCICs should be an integral part of a student's education. More often than not, these centers are underfunded, understaffed, and given little prominence on the campus. A college career center should focus both on a freshman career orientation course as well as a senior course, as discussed earlier in this chapter. Life after graduation is central. The special services for this OCIC should include both a school-to-work track and school-to-school track. School-to-work track services to provide are:

All services listed as general to all OCICs

Special emphasis on using alumni to mentor/advise

Extensive use of networking with alumni

On-campus recruiting services

Information on jobs and study abroad

School-to-school track services to provide include:

A complete listing of catalogues with graduate programs

Preparation materials for the GRE, MAT, MCAT, LCAT, and other entrance examinations

Application information and assistance to various universities

Financial aid, internship, fellowship, and other types of aid

Advice on networking through departments and faculty

Information on study abroad

Another function these OCICs can provide is that of operating work-study programs on campus and training work-study students (Routh, Chretien, & Rakes, 1995). The center can provide the necessary occupational decision-making skills to help place students in appropriate work-study positions, some of whom can be trained to work in the OCIC (Pharr & Glover, 1995).

Adults OCICs for adults have a different focus. These deal primarily with people who are in career transition, are undergoing job changes or job/career loss, or are

Practical Applications

There are a number of similarities that exist when establishing an OCIC in a variety of settings and also when meeting specific developmental needs of users in terms of age, ethnicity, religion, education, gender, and special needs. Many of these ideas are derived from Nadene Peterson's experience in establishing two career resource centers.

A center can be housed in a high school, community college, college or university, or community center such as an occupations/employment one-stop center or a workforce development center. Space requirements, furniture, hardware, software, online capabilities, media equipment, and library resources (e.g., standard reference books, periodicals, job-related books, interviewing, resumé writing) and personnel are similar, regardless of location.

Space requirements include modules for each of the activities available, office space for individual counseling, library resources, study and work areas, assessment and testing areas, group and small classes area, and storage area. Basic equipment needs are computer hardware, VCRs, videotaping materials for practice interviews, word processors, and study and work stations with appropriate furniture.

Software needs include computer assisted career guidance systems (CACGs), online access to databases, and resumé writing and interviewing techniques. Testing and assessment materials can be on software or completed as paper-and-pencil tasks. Staffing needs are similar for all centers, regardless of size. The management and staff of the center should be thoroughly trained as career/vocational counselors. Master Career Counselors (MCC) who specialize in career counseling are highly recommended for the director position. Global Career Development Facilitators (GCDF) are paraprofessionals who have specific training in career counseling. They are hired to work in college and university career centers to provide advising and assistance to students seeking career information.

Each staff member needs to be thoroughly familiar with the systems, equipment, location of information, and resources contained in the center. Training and effectiveness of the staff is crucial to the success of the center. This is an ongoing process, as new information, sources, and programs are acquired. Staff must be aware of new resources and how to access them, as well as be able to teach classes in vocational decision making, resumé writing, interviewing techniques, job-seeking skills, networking strategies, and orientation to the center.

Marketing the OCIC is a staff responsibility that includes coordinating career fairs, finding alumni to serve as mentors/advisors, organizing internships, scheduling visits by new students on campus, making presentations to community groups, meeting with academic counselors on campus, and building career services into the curricula. All of these tasks need to be managed and accomplished. Services that can be provided are assessment and testing, counseling, resumé writing and interviewing skills, job shadowing, mentoring/advising, internship placement services, contacts with businesses, and information via software programs and the Internet as well as via hard copy reading materials.

affected by changes in health or abilities. While many of the same programs apply, there is a different emphasis. Oftentimes this will have to do more with immediate job placement.

For this center, the job listings on the SOICC and other job data banks will be primary. Careful determination of the reason for the change is part of an interview process. If the change is due to factors outside the individual's control, then job placement may be the major consideration. See Appendix 4 for a more complete listing of resources.

OCICs within Industries Yet another type of OCICs are those within industries. These centers usually have two emphases in their services. One is the workforce development emphasis, which deals with employees who are not functioning at a satisfactory level, need additional training and skills in order to stay on the job, or need to be assessed for a possible lateral move within the organization. The goal is to upgrade skills, abilities, and competencies to avoid a downward move or dismissal. The other emphasis is to provide services for those looking to advance or move to a different type of job, including management and supervision within the organization. Oftentimes, personality inventories, interest inventories, and aptitude measures will be most helpful in these settings, and person/environment fit considerations become especially important. There are many books that deal with how the business environment is changing: business skills, job exploration and management, management development, and personal growth and development that should be part of the OCIC.

In this chapter we discussed career development programs for adults ages 18–35 and described a career center with resources and Web sites for this population. In the next chapter, we will be looking at career development programs, transitions, and employment concerns for adults ages 35 through older adulthood.

❖❖❖

Career Counseling for Adults, Part II—Career Transitions

No sooner had I learned to tell time,
than I began to arrive late everywhere.

—Edith Ann
(Wagner, 1994, p. 11)

Most of us constantly try to fit more time-based projects and activities into our lives than there is time for. Often, the result is being slaves to deadlines and not being proactive in planning for the future. Faced with quick changes and unexpected transitions, people lack the time and energy to effectively adapt to situations. Many times, people are unaware of the problems, issues, and factors that affect the decisions they are or will be making.

In this chapter, we first look at workplace issues, including gender, sexual harassment, ageism, and other concerns relevant to most job sites, regardless of the type of work performed. Second, we highlight values differences between workers entering the job market now and those of earlier generations. Third, we explore adult transitions and career development programs in organizations. Fourth, we address stress at work and career burnout, which can occur when a person's work ethic creates an unexpected imbalance between work and leisure. Fifth, as the number of people to fill jobs diminishes with the smaller, upcoming generation, ideas about retirement, older workers, and government support for aging people will become part of a national dialogue. Our hope is to further the discussion of these changes facing adults.

Consider population facts. Seventy-six million babies were born in the United States between 1946 and 1964; in the next twenty years (Schatz, 1997) 59 million babies will be born. Because it takes approximately 3.2 workers to support each retired person, simple math indicates that retirement as the older generation knows it will have to be rethought.

Another issue is having an adequate number of people to maintain the workforce. **Baby boomers,** those born between 1946 and 1964, will still need services for many years. Although technology has taken over many jobs once performed by people, the number of job openings will still be greater than the next generation can fill. The Bureau of Labor Statistics is projecting that "our economy will support 167,754,000 jobs by the end of the decade. That's great news for prosperity, until you learn we'll only have 157,721,000 people in the workforce to fill those jobs" (Herman, Olivo, & Gioia, 2003, p. 49). That's a shortage of 10 million workers in 2010. "Worse, many of the people who are available are not qualified to perform the duties required by those jobs now, let alone what those jobs will become in the future" (p. 49).

Who will do these jobs? Many baby boomers will probably be asked to continue working, and they will provide a major resource for employers. How will this work out? What will happen to the retirement age? When the retirement age was set at age 65 in the 1930s, the average life span was 61.7 years; now the average person lives to be an octogenarian.

An additional issue is the difference in values between older adults and the so-called *nexter* generation. As a rule, the new workers are not as willing to commit themselves to companies as their parents were. The baby boomer generation has had an incredible impact on society. How this group will affect the picture of retirement remains to be seen. Responsible occupational practitioners need to be aware of the changes and the concomitant needs of the people involved in these developments.

WORKPLACE ENVIRONMENT

Common workplace issues that affect workers' ability to operate efficiently include gender differences, sexual harassment, career plateauing and resiliency, career development, and ageism. Practitioners must have awareness of how these issues impact the workplace, regardless of the particular role they have—outside-the-work-environment as therapist, employee assistance program team member, career development specialist within industry, or career coach.

Gender Differences

During middle childhood, when considerable portions of social play time are spent in segregated groups of one's own sex, the distinctive interaction styles of all-boy and all-girl groups have implications for same-sex and cross-sex relationships that people form as they enter adolescence and adulthood (Maccoby, 1990). Different interactive styles develop in same-sex groups. Girls tend to be more concerned with issues of cooperation to maintain group functioning, so verbal exchanges serve largely to establish linkages and sustain social bonds. Boys tend to be more concerned with issues of dominance to maintain group functioning, so verbal exchanges serve largely to establish hierarchies and to protect an individual's turf. For girls, the main concern tends to be maintaining intimacy; for boys, it tends to be maintaining independence (Tannen, 1990).

These gender differences are not absolute, but a matter of degree. For the most part, males are socialized into *doing* together, females into *being* together. Considerable evidence shows that the interactive patterns found in same-sex dyads or groups in adolescence and adulthood are very similar to those that prevailed in the gender-segregated groups of childhood (Maccoby, 1990). It is difficult to identify the point in the developmental cycle at which the interactional style of girls and boys begins to diverge, or to identify the forces that cause them to diverge. Of interest here is how such behaviors carry over into the workplace (Tannen, 1994).

Men and the Success Element

"Next to the negative injunction, 'don't be like a girl'"—which in itself has misogynist undertones—"no other element is as important and universal for defining a male's role as the one that positively charges him to be a SUCCESS" (Doyle, 1989, p. 167, capitals in original). The traditional role of the male being a good provider as the primary success element for men arises from socialization into a competitive worldview. From the time most men are small boys, they are encouraged to be the best at something (e.g., the most talented academically, the most gifted athletically, the most accomplished aesthetically). A boy who is the best class clown receives at least a grudging measure of respect from his classmates, despite his disruptive behavior. Being a winner is very masculine. To be winners, most men have been socialized into the belief that they must compete.

The Competitive Worldview

Competition occurs when two or more people seek a reward that can only be achieved by one (Doyle, 1989). Young boys learn that competition is an important feature of life. Beating out the other guy becomes vital, especially because losers are not loved. A major problem with the emphasis on competition arises when men begin to see everything in their world solely in terms of competition. For many men, this mind-set is part of what they were socialized into from an early age, what Peacock (1998) calls the **Boy Code**. The Boy Code dictates that boys hide the vulnerable, caring, gentle parts of themselves, and that shaming a boy—repeatedly—will toughen him up and make him manly.

This distorted worldview has at least three assumptions about what the world is really like. First, an impaired competitive spirit forces men to think that everything of worth or value in the world is limited or comes in fixed quantities. Thus, a man's masculinity can be measured as if it were a quantifiable element. In the workplace, many men translate their sense of masculinity into how much money they earn, the size and decor of their office, their job title, the number of workers they manage, and the cost and model of their car.

Second, if valued things are limited, then there are just so many of them to go around. This often creates a problem in male-male relationships, where every other man becomes a potential rival for the limited and available proofs of success. Many men quickly learn ways to make their own track record look better than other's.

Third, most men assume that competition is always good, never bad or neutral. Whether on the playground or in the classroom, the good thing is to be a competitor who wins. This distorted competitive spirit becomes even more warped when men believe that competitiveness and winning are exclusively male characteristics.

Many men make the mistake of believing that women do not have the same drive or ambition to succeed that men supposedly have (Doyle, 1989; Krebs, 1993). In the minds of these men, action and achievement are more likely to be synonymous with masculinity. The belief that men are competitive and that women, therefore, are co-operative, produces another problem: many men may feel that their own cooperative attempts will be perceived by others as unmanly, whereas many women may think that their own competitiveness will diminish their femininity in others' eyes. Some men, motivated by the fear of losing their male co-workers' respect, denigrate co-operation as a viable way of solving problems or gaining valued goals.

The Male Provider Role

Given most men's belief about being a good provider, pressures can build, particularly if that man bases his masculinity on how successfully he contributes to his family's material well-being. Throughout most of prerecorded history, men and women apparently shared provider responsibilities, and there is some evidence that, at times, women's contribution was more important than men's (Doyle, 1989). For countless centuries there was little distinction between producers and consumers of goods. Men and women lived and worked in close proximity in open fields, cottages, and small shops. Work environments were similar. However, with the advent of the Industrial Revolution, they became more divided in their lifestyles. Specialization became commonplace. The distinction between producers and consumers became more pronounced. The factory and its centralized location forced most men to leave their homes and journey some distance to work. New gender role definitions evolved as a result of separate work environments for men and women.

The **male provider role** dates from this period. Being a good provider became a prominent standard among men for achieving success. Many men began to equate

Practical Applications

Assessing the connected voice and separate voice orientations of women and men and the interaction of such orientations with vocational difficulties allows practitioners to conceptualize career issues in a new framework (Forrest & Mikolaitis, 1986). Any models of career development that fail to address how women and men blend career and relationship domains in their lives do not accurately represent people's realities (Cook, 1993). Practitioners need to

1. be aware of how varied people can be, including marital status, sexual orientation, and parenthood status.
2. avoid steering clients toward one voice or the other.
3. recognize and value clients' need for connection.
4. remember that career decisions can be affected when clients' care of others results in a lack of care for themselves (Hotelling & Forrest, 1986).
5. consider the gendered context of the work environment more seriously in preparing clients for career transitions.
6. examine how their own gender lens may distort the possibilities open to others (Cook, 1993).

We propose contextualizing these two voices with multicultural clientele; for us, the separate voice sometimes appears to characterize much of the English-speaking, U.S. mainstream experience, regardless of gender. In contrast, the connected voice sometimes appears to characterize much of the ethnic, racial, and linguistic minority experience (see also, Mikulas, 2002). A willingness to relocate for career progress, for example, may be more readily evident in a client with dominant cultural values than for a client from a minority background who may be rooted to family and a culturally hospitable community.

Vocational practitioners need to ask themselves and their clients some hard questions about our society's work values, especially about the myth of rugged individualism (Cook, 1993). The men who explored and settled the wild American frontier could never have done so without the women who journeyed beside them, the other men who agreed to join them, and the indigenous peoples they encountered along the way. Along with Cook, we question the psychological health implications of perpetuating the rugged individualist myth.

Vocational practitioners must be open to exploring the dynamics of dominant-subordinate relationships between men and women in clients' workplaces. Many avenues merit examination, such as how both genders benefit from workplaces that reinforce traditional gender roles, or how clients often have contradictory expectations of how the genders should behave on the job. Practitioners' gender biases also need to be acknowledged and confronted on a regular basis.

their manhood with the amount of money they earned. The value placed on material goods received more emphasis. Many women were placed in a vulnerable position because their contributions to the family in either goods or services were not reimbursed. The male provider role was solidly embedded in the U.S. national psyche by the beginning of the twentieth century.

The Great Depression of the 1930s precipitated a form of psychological emasculation for millions of men whose loss of a job equaled a loss of self-respect and a loss of the primary means for validating their masculinity. Although World War II returned a sense of masculinity to countless men, the women who substituted as laborers in jobs vacated by men at war illustrated their innate competencies and capacities. Though women returned to the home during the baby boom years, there was a realization that they were valuable workforce members whose skills could qualify them for previously unavailable employment opportunities. Women's entry into the workforce has been unprecedented over the last fifty years. Changes in societal values have since reduced support for the male provider role. For men who wholeheartedly embraced the male provider role as the image of masculine success, questions have arisen about the value of success at all costs and about alternative bases for self-respect.

Women's Vocational Development

Women are a growing number of the people working and the people maintaining job tenure (Herman et al. 2003). Traditionally, twenty-five- to forty-four-year-old women have made up about half of the women who work in the United States. Although the proportion of women in the total workforce is growing, the actual number of women entering the job market in recent years has declined. The U.S. Department of Labor expects the number of women job seekers to increase slowly. More older women are expected to enter the workforce. Increases are projected at 6 percent labor participation for women ages 40–50, 8 percent for women ages 55–64.

New explanatory concepts account for women's vocational behavior (Betz & Fitzgerald, 1987; Krebs, 1993; Laird, 1994; Morrison, White, & Van Velsor, 1987; Nichols, 1994; Silver, 1994; Walsh & Osipow, 1994). Forrest and Mikolaitis (1986) review three trends in the development of theories explaining and predicting women's vocational development. Initially, evidence about women's career development that contradicted prevailing theories was either ignored or not explored further; the trend was to apply to women the well-established vocational theories developed for men without recognizing the limitations of such a strategy. A second trend assumed that theories developed for men could not be applied to women and that new theories were needed to explain women's career development. A third trend has been the attempt to incorporate concepts that explain career development for both women and men. Forrest and Mikolaitis (1986) write that one concept that provides useful direction for this third trend is self-in-relation theory (e.g., Chodorow, 1978; Gilligan, 1982).

The tendency has been for women to be socialized into defining themselves, in large part, through their connection with and responsiveness to others. This tendency refers to the *connected voice* orientation. In contrast, the tendency has been for men to be socialized into defining themselves, in large part, through their differentiation from others in terms of abilities and attributes. This tendency refers to the *separate voice* orientation.

Building on these two orientations, Cook (1993) makes two major points. First, through the socialization process, women and men tend to develop different orientations with respect to occupational achievement and interpersonal relationships. These differences interact with broader sociocultural norms for the sexes' behavior that produce disparate lifestyle opportunities and demands, especially where home and career intersect. Second, work environments are gendered, embodying accepted sociocultural assumptions and expectations for the sexes. This gendered work context markedly influences the daily choices and expectations that the sexes face, including day-care policies, persistent inequality in pay, promotion, and perquisites (Fitzgerald & Harmon, 2001), and sexual harassment.

Sexual Harassment

In the workplace, sexual harassment is both an issue and a stress factor that affects women more than men (Barnett & Rivers, 1996; Gutek, 1985; J. Solomon, 1998; Webb, 1991). As many as 88 percent of working women and 15 percent of working men have experienced some form of sexual harassment (Webb, 1991). The problem occurs in all jobs, at all salary levels, in all age and racial groups, and in both the private and public sectors. More than 95 percent of all sexual harassment cases involve men as the offenders. Working women who are married or widowed seem to be less likely to be harassed than working women who are divorced, separated, or never married (Gutek, 1985). Male harassers are usually older, predominantly married, and less physically attractive than other male co-workers. The male initiator tends to behave the same way toward younger and older female co-workers.

Since the issue of sexual harassment burst upon the U.S. public's awareness in 1991 with Anita Hill's challenges at Clarence Thomas's confirmation hearings for the Supreme Court, complaints to the Equal Employment Opportunity Commission (EEOC) have more than doubled—to 15,549—while monetary awards have more than tripled (Yang, 1996). However, the underfunded EEOC is struggling to stay on top of a heavy caseload, with a backlog of 97,000 cases. Sexual harassment cases often boil down to a matter of credibility, pitting the accuser against the accused. Vindication through the two best avenues available for help—law enforcement agencies and the courts—entails many delays. Maremont and Sassen (1996) write that few women have the fortitude or finances to blow the proverbial whistle.

Behavioral Definition of Sexual Harassment The behavioral definition of sexual harassment is "deliberate and/or repeated sexual or sex-based behavior that is not welcome, not asked for, and not returned" (Equal Employment Opportunity Commission, *Guidelines on Discrimination Because of Sex,* 1980, cited in Webb, 1991, pp. 25–26). Three key elements of the definition are that it is

1. Sexual in nature or sex-based
2. Deliberate and/or repeated
3. Not welcome, not asked for, and not returned (Webb, 1991)

There are also two qualifiers of the definition of sexual harassing behavior:

1. The more severe the behavior is, the fewer times it needs to be repeated before reasonable people define it as harassment; the less severe it is, the more times it needs to be repeated.
2. The less severe the behavior is, the more responsibility the receiver has to speak up (because some people like this kind of behavior); the more severe it is, the less responsibility the receiver has to speak up because the initiator of the behavior should be sensitive enough in the first place to know that it is inappropriate (Webb, 1991).

Sexual harassment may be verbal, nonverbal, or physical. Verbal harassment includes jokes, wisecracks, comments, and remarks; these behaviors constitute most of the complaints and investigations. Nonverbal harassment includes whistles, innuendoes, and staring (Gutek, 1985), certain kinds of looks, gestures, leering, ogling, photographs, or cartoons (Webb, 1991). Physical harassment includes touching, pinching, rubbing, or "accidentally" rubbing against someone's breasts or buttocks; these behaviors are the most severe form of harassment and can involve criminal charges.

Legal Definition of Sexual Harassment The legal definition of sexual harassment requires that it

1. Occurs because of the person's sex
2. Is unwelcome, not returned, not mutual
3. Affects the terms or conditions of employment, including the work environment itself

Finally, sexual harassment is a power trip. The harasser either thinks or knows, consciously or unconsciously, that he or she has more power in the workplace than the harassee. Otherwise, there would be no harassment because the harasee could turn to the harasser and demand that it stop and there would be no issue (Webb, 1991).

Or, as Florence (2001) puts it on the basis of recent Supreme Court rulings:

> It is sufficient that an employee merely overhear offending jokes or conversations and feel powerless to stop them or escape hearing them. It is sufficient that the employee sees what he or she considers to be harassing behavior between others, whether those directly involved feel harassed or not. It is sufficient that the employee sees offending photographs, cartoons, graffiti or written jokes somewhere in the workplace—and not necessarily in public or common areas of the workplace. The offending material may be in a coworker's private office where the employee would have to make a real effort to see it. Just knowing it is there can be sufficient to create sexual harassment (p. 49).

More than 50 percent of working women will experience sexual harassment on the job (Barnett & Rivers, 1996). In a poll of 1,300 members of the National Association for Female Executives, 53 percent said they were sexually harassed by people who had power over their careers. Of those, 64 percent did not report the harassment, and more than half of those who did report it say the problem was not resolved to their satisfaction (Webb, 1991). In the most extensive survey to date in the United States, involving 23,000 federal employees, 42 percent of women describe experiencing some form of sexual harassment. A United Nations survey reveals that as many as one in twelve women in the industrialized world are forced out of jobs by sexual harassment (*Boston Globe,* December 1, 1992). In Japan, a survey by the Santama Group to Consider Sexual Discrimination at Work disclosed that 70 percent of Japanese women say they have experienced some type of sexual harassment on the job, and 90 percent said they were sexually harassed while commuting to and from work (Webb, 1991).

Such harassment is not confined to females in the workplace. When young women in high school were targets of sexual harassment from members of a young men's athletic team, coaches and administrators were slow to respond (Ratcliffe, 1996). The anti-woman atmosphere that pervaded the annual Tailhook Association Conventions of the U.S. Navy—an enormous corporation with assets equal to those of the first seven Fortune 500 corporations—created a climate where sexual assaults on women occurred at several of the yearly meetings, with subsequent attempts to cover up the incidents (Vistica, 1995). In both the high school and the U.S. Navy instances, the women who blew the whistle on the abuse experienced reprisals and repercussions, including attempts to discredit them. More recently, when female cadets at the Air Force Academy reported acts of sexual harassment, in some instances the rape victims were punished while their abusers or attackers went unpunished. In these instances, media publicity forced those in authority to respond by confronting the harassers and dealing with them in an appropriate manner.

CASE EXAMPLES

Protecting the Rapists

The rape scandals at the United States Air Force Academy (U.S.A.F.A.) are certainly one of the most reprehensible instances of sexual harassment in recent times. The Air Force Academy Honor Code is, "We will not lie, steal, or cheat, nor tolerate among us anyone who does" (U.S.A.F.A., Center for Character Development, 2003). Perhaps rape should have been explicitly added to the "we will nots." Females were first admitted to the Air Force Academy in 1976 (Edmonson, 2003). However, a climate of fear and mistrust prevailed at the U.S.A.F.A. in the ten years preceding the change of command there in 2003 (Gehrke, 2003). Of 142 alleged sexual attacks reported by women cadets since 1993, adequate evidence existed in only 61 cases. Not one cadet has ever been court-martialed for sexually assaulting another cadet (Ferrugia, 2003). Female cadets who reported being raped by male cadets found themselves punished instead: ostracized by their peers, permanently expelled from the academy by administrators. A culture developed where:

- A male cadet was permanently expelled for lying but received only a minor reprimand for date rape
- Women cadets found their days numbered at the academy if they reported a rape by another cadet
- Women cadets who were raped got a reprimand for having sexual activity in the academy dorms and another reprimand for fraternization with an upperclassman, both of which are still reasons for permanent expulsion

Essentially, a woman cadet who reported a rape was victimized again by the investigation that followed.

In the spring of 2003, an *Agenda for Change* was announced (U.S.A.F.A., Policy Directives and Initiatives, March 26, 2003). This agenda was committed to rededicating the Air Force Academy to its core values of "integrity, service, and excellence" (p. 1). The agenda's purpose was to "establish and nurture policies that emphasize the character expected from commissioned Air Force officers . . . [of] the greatest air and space force on the planet" (p.1). The statement makes clear that loyalty to any individual at the Academy should not be confused with covering up a fellow cadet's criminal activity, which is not loyalty to a comrade. As part of the Academy leadership's seriousness to its commitment to timely justice, several changes were enacted, including:

1. Orientation during Basic Training on sexual assault prevention
2. Separate billeting in the dormitories for male and female cadets
3. Amnesty from Academy discipline for cadets involved in cases of sexual assault, with the exception of the alleged assailant and any cadet involved in covering up such an incident or hindering its investigation

Alleged rape victims say intended reforms will do little good if those commanders who ignored rape reports aren't punished, too (Weller, 2003). The academy's top four commanders were replaced by the end of the 2002–2003 academic

Continued

Continued

year ("Our Turn," 2003), but an entrenched culture remains of disrespect for and violence against women. It "will take time to transform" such an entrenched culture (Kohler, 2003, no page number provided). No sooner was the Agenda for Change instituted than did the U.S.A.F.A. become embroiled in an underage drinking scandal (Goldenberg, 2003). Seven 20- and 21-year-old male cadets were caught in an off-campus hotel with two young women, ages 16 and 18 ("Air force to warn cadets after drinking incident," 2003). Any cadet who provided alcohol to a minor would likely face expulsion under the new zero-tolerance policy that is part of the Agenda for Change.

In the autumn of 2003, the *Report of the Panel to Review Sexual Misconduct Allegations at the U.S. Air Force Academy* was submitted to Secretary of Defense Donald Rumsfeld. The panel's single priority was to address the safety and well-being of the women cadets at the Academy. The report is damning. It speaks of "a chasm in leadership" (p. 1) that helped create a culture where sexual assault was part of life at the Academy, where 81 percent of the female cadets who were sexually assaulted didn't report it. Names are named. And the Panel calls for accountability for leadership failures both at the Academy and at Air Force headquarters at the Pentagon in Washington, D.C.

The report also says the Agenda for Change does "not go far enough to institute enduring changes in the institutional culture and gender climate at the Academy" (p. 3), and eliminates the Academy's policy of confidentiality for reporting sexual assault, which may have the unintended result of reducing sexual assault reporting. Earlier warnings of serious sexual misconduct at the Academy went unheeded. And previous changes in sexual assault reporting procedures went unmonitored. The fact that one out of five male cadets believe female cadets have no business at the Academy is also indicative of the hostile climate against women. The panel found "an atmosphere that helped foster a breakdown in values which led to the pervasiveness of sexual assaults and is perhaps the most difficult element of the problem to solve" (p. 6).

The inability of the Air Force to adequately police and investigate itself contributes to such a problem, as well as the lack of a sufficient number of highly-qualified male and female role models to provide cadets with guidance. Consistent adherence to the Academy Honor Code and persistent oversight from both internal and external bodies, plus the establishment of a response team to allegations of sexual assault, should help to create long-term change. It remains to be seen how and if reforms of the institutional culture at the Air Force Academy can occur, or if it is all lip service and window dressing.

Protecting the Harasser

A young woman came to the office of one of the authors of this text, having been sent by her lawyer for assessment and evaluation. She was a receptionist for a company, and she reported that the CEO of the company had sexually harassed her for many weeks. It escalated so she then reported it to the appropriate personnel. Nothing changed so she decided to pursue it legally. She ended up going to court and facing her boss. She was a young, attractive Hispanic woman, and he was a middle-aged white male. She had no money so she had to hire a lawyer who was willing to take the case for the sake of justice. The CEO, however, hired the most aggressive legal team in the city. Needless to say, she lost her case and her job and felt further humiliated. She eventually left town.

Ageism

Another form of discrimination is ageism. Older workers sometimes feel inadequate in the job market. Discrimination is a common experience for people over forty. Ageism affects both men and women, blue-collar worker and executive alike, and shows little regard for educational level (Jordan, 1997). Because the number of senior level jobs is smaller than the number of midlevel managers, a move up the career ladder is difficult. And even though older workers may have more job experience, the skills they possess may no longer be in demand. Failure to maintain a skill level that is vital to an employer's needs will cause the impact of ageism to become more pronounced in the future.

Technological advances, and the speed at which job demands can change in this era of intellectual capital, will only accelerate the problem of matching skills to jobs and increase the need for workers to upgrade their skills continually if they are to remain viable and employed, much less advance their careers. These advances can only result in more dramatic instances of ageism. The rapid updating of skills, in an era of ever greater demand for new skills, requires workers to be responsible for their own continued relevance if they are to stand any chance against the advance of ageism.

Vital Aging Network (VAN), a Web site for older people (http://www.van. umn.edu) that is a significant resource for older adults interested in options and finding personal directions, shares the following values regarding ageism and older workers:

- Self-determination is central for the realization of civil and human rights.
- Everyone should be encouraged and supported in being as self-sufficient as possible.
- The vital involvement and integration of older adults in communities is necessary for individual and community health.
- Older adults are a community resource. Their productivity and contributions must be recognized, encouraged, and supported.
- Communities should recognize and support the mutuality of interests across generations.
- Ageism is a pervasive form of bigotry that must be challenged.

Under the Age Discrimination in Employment Act (ADEA), an employer may not discharge, refuse to hire, or otherwise discriminate on the basis of age. This law is a worker's primary defense against age discrimination. Visit the EEOC Web site (http://www.eeoc.gov) for more information. In the future, this defense gets stronger. Burd and Davies (2003) point out that after October 2006, employers will be able to bring age-biased claims before the courts with prospects of unlimited compensation. Age limits for jobs will be unlawful and terminating older workers will be problematic. For more information e-mail: employment@lewissilkin.com.

> ## CASE EXAMPLE
> ### Subtle Ageism
>
> Genevay (2000), a geriatric social worker, discussed the impact of ageism in employment as being subtle and insidious. Joan was a sixty-one-year old bookkeeper who had worked in an agency for fifteen years. She was well liked and was an excellent bookkeeper. A new executive, hired to cut costs, decided to terminate Joan because her salary and benefits were more costly to the agency than a new and less experienced employee's would be. Joan had arthritis and occasionally complained about her fingers. The executive never used written or verbal language that could contribute to an age discrimination suit, but he frequently commiserated with Joan about how hard it must be to "keep up with her work" with arthritic fingers.
>
> He kept his voice empathetic and his words benign, but Joan was fearful. And he was able to force her out through subtle intimidation. Joan lost social security benefits and other retirement benefits. She eventually found another job with a lower salary and fewer benefits, but she had to work many more years in order to be able to afford retirement (Peterson & González, 2000).

Many young workers face a different problem. They lack sufficient experience with little opportunity to obtain the needed skills that experience teaches. Regardless of the reasons, it is illegal to discriminate against someone on the basis of age.

The American Association of Retired People (AARP) conducted several studies of perceptions of employers toward older employees. Sicker (1997) reported two sets of stereotypes that evolved: one states that older workers are stable, reliable, responsible, trustworthy, in possession of a strong work ethic, and serious about work commitment; the other stereotype is that older workers are inflexible, noninnovative, technologically inferior, and unable to work in teams (p. 1). The results of these stereotypes suggest that the positive attributes are excellent for low-pay, low-skill jobs, whereas the negative perceptions inhibit employers from hiring or retraining older workers who are in higher paying jobs. In either instance, the older worker is relegated to a less important place in the workforce, which the author suggests needs to be confronted.

Because half of the workforce is now forty or older, employers need to rethink their strategies by contracting for a settlement with an acceptable severance package, working with supervisors to rank which jobs should be cut, and averaging the age of the layoffs so that no one group is disproportionately cut (Armour, 1997). As most of us have experienced, not all employers are at this level of thinking.

Practical Applications

Vocational practitioners need be aware of discrimination laws and practices to help older workers market themselves. Practitioners can establish communication with employers to challenge the myths and stereotypes connected with older workers. Jordan (1997) suggests that in assisting older workers to combat ageism in the workforce, it is necessary to

- commit to a strong work ethic.
- be able to work with teams as well as individually.
- practice excellent interpersonal skills.
- be able to adapt to change in the workplace, including a willingness to

learn new technology and to continue education and training experiences.
- improve written and oral communication skills.
- avoid talk of retirement plans.
- maintain excellent health and wellness.

Although these issues in the workplace are real, concerns about change and transitions are common whether inside the company or outside the corporate setting. These issues involve values, attitudes, and coping abilities. Intergenerational differences in value systems form the next part of the chapter.

Policies and practices that an organization can incorporate to combat ageism include recognition, gradual and incrementally based changes, appropriate rewards, specific feedback on expectations, short-term and long-term goals, job rehearsal, and accepting a culture of change.

According to the U.S. Department of Labor, Bureau of Labor Statistics (2004), the percentage of workers between ages 25–39 and 40–65 were equal in 1992. By 2002, the number of workers ages 40–65 had increased to 50 percent of workers while those 25–39 had decreased to 35 percent; by 2012 the projection is 53 percent ages 40–65 and only 32 percent ages 25–39. Furthermore, by 2012, it is projected that more than 3 percent of the labor force will be 65 or older, a growth of one percent. These statistics indicate the need to find effective ways to intervene with older workers.

Intergenerational Differences in Values

Adults, Ages 18 to 25 Zemke, Raines, and Filipczak (2001), in the book *Generations at Work*, described the various age groups by date of birth: The Veterans, 1922–1943; The Baby Boomers, 1943–1960; Generation Xers, 1960–1980; and Generation Nexters, 1980–2000. According to Morrow (2002), this youngest generation, the Generation Nexters, are the coddled and confident offspring of the most age-diverse

---

Practical Applications

Due to the worldviews, beliefs, and realities of the Generation Xers and Nexters, vocational practitioners must be able to accommodate this new work ethic. Practitioners need to be aware of their own biases and work values that may conflict with those of clients from different generations, thus interfering with the counseling process. This is also important for supervisors and managers to understand in their work with personnel.

---

group of parents ever. They are the digital generation with a complete grasp of technology. They are both optimistic about the future and realistic about the present.

Adults, Ages 25 to 45 This group has been labeled the *Babybusters* or *Generation Xers*. According to Morrow (2002), Generation Xers don't expect lifelong employment with any one company. They expect they will have several careers in their lifetime. They are very much at home with the technology of today and look down on the other generations who aren't. Extremely casual in both dress and communication style, they are drawn to workplaces that provide a casual atmosphere.

CASE EXAMPLE

Passed Over

A single woman in her mid-twenties had worked for a company for seven years, starting in high school. She continued to work full time and attend classes to complete both a Bachelors and Masters degree. As she was completing her Masters, an opportunity for a promotion in the company appeared, and she applied for it because she met all the qualifications in the job description. She also had received consistent excellent evaluations and always completed her work in a timely manner. A co-worker filled the position. She talked with her supervisor to obtain feedback on the decision and was informed that the job had been given to her male co-worker because he was married and had children and "needed the money." He also had been more willing to work long hours. What are the issues in this case? What would you suggest to be the best course of action for her?

Adults, Ages 45 to 65 This group has been labeled the *baby boomers*. According to Morrow (2002), the boomers tend to be optimistic and think of themselves as the star of the show. They have pursued their own gratification, uncompromisingly, and often at a high price to themselves and others. Many of them are now worried about having enough money for retirement. Boomers need to know that their experience will be valued and want public recognition and perks. Many of them are now just hitting their stride at work and are not thinking of retirement.

Adults 65 and Older This group has been labeled the *Veterans*. According to Morrow (2002), the Veterans have a strong work ethic and are generally loyal to their employer. They are confused, however, by the recent lack of loyalty from the company to the employee. They tend to use the old style command-and-control leadership they learned in World War II and Korea. They are dependable and tend to value obedience over individualism on the job.

Adults in Transition

The world of work is a world of starts and stops, of accelerations and waiting periods. . . . Thinking about adult career development as a *transition process* of moving in, through and out of the workforce helps explain what is, in essence, a highly fluid process. The length of time someone stays in each phase depends on the person, and his or her . . . career plan, and available and perceived options. Each individual's needs, along with appropriate interventions, will differ depending on where the person is in the system (Schlossberg, 1996, p. 93, italics in original).

Job Change One of the most significant times in a person's life can involve job change. Super (1990) discusses these transitions at length, but he acknowledges that not all changes are planned transitions. Some job changes are sudden—personal problems or corporate changes can result in a lost job, lost sense of security, and profound upheaval, both physically and emotionally. Other job changes are more planned and can result in a change of title or moving up a career ladder. This time of transition is often when a practitioner is contacted to help intervene. Much of the information in earlier chapters regarding models, assessment, computer systems, and life planning is applicable to this group of people.

There are several theories available to counselors to broaden the perspective for this particular population: a values-based approach to dealing with career change (Brown, 1996, as in Chapter 2); an integrated life planning model (Hansen, 1997, as in Chapter 7); a community career center (Loeb, 1994), effectiveness of career services for the *educationally disadvantaged* (Champagne, 1987, as in Chapter 10); a model for effective continuous adult learning (MacKinnon-Slaney, 1994, later in this chapter);

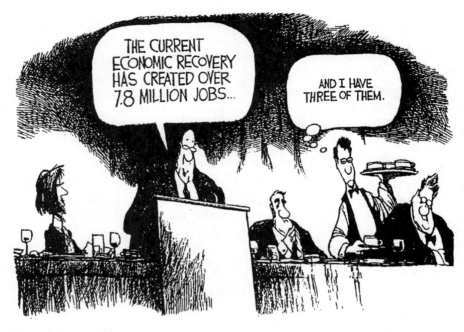

The truth about new jobs

© 1995 MacNelly—Chicago Tribune. Reprinted with permission.

the role of leisure (McDaniels, 1996, as in Chapter 2); and the use of self-efficacy instruments such as the CSI (as described in Chapter 6).

A promising assessment instrument for adults in transition is the Career Transition Inventory (CTI), developed by Heppner, Multon, and Johnston (1991). It was designed specifically to "assess and understand internal, dynamic psychological processes that may get in the way of the career transition process" (p. 220). Five basic factors that the instrument attempts to assess are: readiness, confidence, perceived support, control, and decision independence. The CTI is available from Mary Heppner, Ph.D., 305 Noyes Hall, University of Missouri, Columbia, MO, 65211.

Goodman (1994) proposes a Dental Model in which clients plan to have *regular checkups* and accomplish more *routine maintenance* to learn adaptability. Because most adults will report career/life transitions several times in their lives, learning the process and learning to be adaptable are keys to continued employment. She urges practitioners to understand the process of transition, saying "they need to be able to determine which adults need information, which need motivation, and which perhaps need adaptability training. They then need to know how to deliver that training" (p. 83).

Quitting Jobs People often leave jobs on their own volition. Herman et al. (2003) have worked to understand this process. The five major reasons found for people leaving jobs are:

1. "It doesn't feel good around here." The sense the employee has usually has to do with the organization—its apparent instability, poor reputation, issues of safety, comfort, or lack of a sense of direction.

2. "They wouldn't miss me if I were gone." A man in a job that was part of a large group of workers died unexpectedly at work. Within an hour of his chair being empty, a new employee was working. The lack of acknowledgment from supervisors, the sense of being unimportant, and feeling of being expendable will drive an employee to go where she or he might be appreciated.

3. "I don't get the support I need to get my job done." Oftentimes responsible employees are given tasks but little support to help complete the task. A feeling of being used and unappreciated or of having too many rules or too much red tape can lead to disillusionment. Poor and incapable supervisors also give the employee a sense of hopelessness.

4. "There's no opportunity for advancement." Herman points out that the issue is not about promotion as much as it is about having appropriate challenges and being able to learn. When employees find a job is at a dead end with no possibility of learning new skills and using new information, they will become disenchanted.

5. "Compensation is the last reason most people leave." Obviously, employees want to be fairly compensated for their job, but many are willing to work for less when the job is interesting, the company is potentially strong and well-managed, and the satisfaction of their work is based on meaning and being appreciated (Herman et al., 2003, pp. 315–316).

Unemployment/Underemployment Davey and Leonhardt (2003) of the *New York Times* report that our nation is in difficult economic times. Many of the unemployed have dropped out of the labor force, causing them to be invisible and not counted in the unemployment rate. They suggest that some of these unemployed have gone back to school or have gotten new job training, whereas others have chosen to stay home with young children or aging parents or rely on their spouses' incomes. The remainder are waiting and living on government benefits and hoping that the economy will get better. In 2002 and 2003, the number of Americans in the labor force fell 0.9 percentage points to 66.2 percent, the largest drop in almost 40 years.

Watts (1997, cited in Patton, 2002) identifies three main ways in which career practitioners operate with unemployed people:

1. Increase individuals' employability to help them secure what jobs are available.

2. Focus on coping with the experience, including focusing on mental health and financial concerns.

3. Focus on opportunity creation, in the form of self-employment or cooperatives.

Campbell (2000), when discussing unemployment issues and outplacement interventions, describes the philosophy that personal happiness derives from a balance in life of having

1. Meaningful work—something to do that you love
2. Meaningful relationships—someone to love
3. A spiritual base—something to believe in

This encompasses the interconnectedness of vocational, relational, and spiritual needs (Peterson & González, 2000, *Career Counseling Models for Diverse Populations*, pp. 247–248). Campbell further explains that more than in any other field of counseling, the career counselor must be prepared to assist clients who are unemployed in multiple ways, that is, personal issues counseling, marital family counseling, career assessment, mental health assessment, depression, anxiety, financial and credit counseling.

Male unemployment can increase the danger to women in abusive relationships. An article by Pisano (2003) discusses male unemployment as a predictor of women's slayings. A nationwide study led by Jacquelyn Campbell, a professor at John Hopkins University School of Nursing, reports that unemployment is one of the biggest predictors of the killing of women in abusive relationships. Unemployment was the strongest social factor found in homicide of women and can increase their risk by four times. "Researchers say its an issue health care providers, battered women's shelter workers, and police officers need to be aware of if such deaths are to be prevented" (p. 1K).

Losing one's job is a devastating experience. Psychological ramifications of unemployment include high stress levels that can lead to poor health and major depression. When an individual returns to the workforce, his or her mental as well as physical health improves dramatically (Aubrey, Tefft, & Kingsbury, 1990; Peregoy & Schliebner, 1990; Wanberg, 1995; Wanberg, Watt, & Rumsey, 1996). Adams, Hayes, and Hopson (1977) developed an effective model to describe the mood across time for a person who loses a job (see Figure 11.1).

Even though this model was developed many years ago, it is still useful for adults who are fired, forced to resign, downsized, or laid off due to a company closure. The seven-phase model identifies the initial shock and elation and minimalization, where a person denies the change is happening. Then self-doubt sets in regarding one's ability to provide for self and others. Once the person starts to let go of the anger, frustration, resentment, and fear, energy builds to start the process of searching for meaning. Internalization occurs when the person has changed values and lifestyle and developed new coping skills.

If a person is in career transition due to job change, loss of job or career, or change in health or abilities, then career centers at universities or Workforce Development Centers can be a resource for those seeking employment. Careful determination of the reason for the change is part of an interview process. If the change is due to fac-

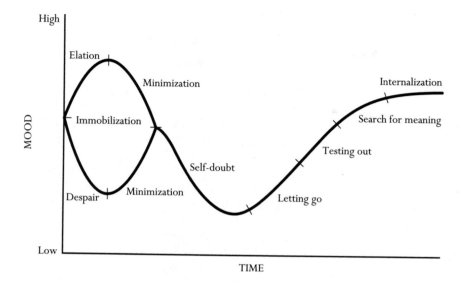

FIGURE 11.1 A Seven-Phase Model of Stages Accompanying a Transition

SOURCE: *J. Adams, J. Hayes, and B Hopson,* Understanding and Managing Personal Change. *Copyright 1977 by Sage Publications, Inc., p. 38.*

tors outside the individual's control, then job placement may be the major consideration. However, if there are other factors involved, then more involved assessment procedures may be necessary. Super's Salience Inventory, Values Scale, and Adult Career Concerns Inventory each may be helpful with this population, as will Holland's Self-Directed Search and/or the Strong Interest Inventory. If a change of career is desired or necessary, then computer assisted career guidance programs (CAGC) may be helpful. More specific information can be located in Chapter 10.

Creating a résumé/portfolio is primary, and using networking skills, interviewing skills, job information interviews, and job databases will also be important. If the need for further training becomes obvious, then a different approach will be needed.

A job club can meet weekly or biweekly to share the information each member has found to keep current on job listings and experiences in job seeking. Offering mutual support is a strong component of this group. Equipment should be available to develop cover letters/résumés/portfolios. Videotaping practice interviews can be helpful. These activities can also be effective with people who have been injured and are seeking to return to the workforce. Work hardening and rehabilitative services can be part of the function of a job club. For more information on these services, see Chapters 10, 14–16, and 19 in Peterson and González (2002), *Career Counseling Models for Diverse Populations.*

Practical Applications

Job search groups and job clubs can be effective interventions for the unemployed. Benefits can be:

- mutual support and encouragement.
- job search strategies.
- instruction in resumes and correspondence.
- a positive outlook.
- interview practice and preparation.
- telephone technique.
- belonging.

Stidham and Remley (1992) developed a job club methodology based on the U.S. Department of Health and Human Services *Guide for Group Job Seeking Programs.* The program was designed specifically for welfare recipients in order to help them experience a feeling of success by developing a more positive self esteem, readiness for training, and employability. "Job Club methodology ensures that clients understand the expectations of them through instruction, behavioral rehearsal and practice. The problems of fear, guilt and lack of motivation are addressed by positive reinforcement and support within the group" (p. 74). The job club technique could prove itself useful to state agencies as they attempt to help people move from welfare to work.

Vocational practitioners will have to use a variety of skills when working with the unemployed, especially those who are not voluntarily out of work. The possible emotional effects are complex and need to be addressed by the practitioner.

Peregoy and Schliebner (1990) have developed a Personal Employment Identity Model (PEIM) to assist practitioners in selecting appropriate interventions based on four types of vocational ego identity problems that unemployed people exhibit.

1. The person whose identity was tied to the job and who now has lost a sense of self. These people are likely to be strongly affected by loss of income and loss of emotional involvement.

2. The person whose identity was tied to the challenge of the job. These people usually have a strong sense of failure and loss of status, experiencing self-rejection, dissatisfaction, and helplessness.

3. The person who has lost identity due to the strain of being unemployed. These people often experience sadness, frustration, and apathy.

4. The person who had little investment in her or his last job. These people express concern with their economic situation and their lack of hope in finding a new job, and often personalize their job rejections, lack information about alternatives, have confusion about their skills, and demonstrate symptoms of hopelessness by exhibiting poor motivation or burnout in the process of job seeking.

Identifying which type of vocational ego-identity problems the client presents can assist practitioners in asking appropriate questions and getting the necessary information from past employment to work effectively toward reemployment.

To move from unemployment to reemployment, Eby and Buch (1995) propose that job loss can result in career growth. Their study of the victims of downsizing resulted in several practical suggestions:

1. Provide psychological counseling to deal with the negative effects of job loss and to build optimism and self-efficacy.

2. Help clients use support mechanisms around them and maintain an active daily schedule with various helpful routines.

3. For women, it appears that a flexible, adaptive family is important, and encouraging communication with family members is likely to be helpful.

4. For men, problem-focused and emotion-focused interventions are important.

A recent development is a nonprofit organization called the Talent Alliance, an agency organized by several of the largest companies in the United States to help with the ebb and flow of available jobs in the large companies. Spearheaded by AT&T, the Alliance is composed of such companies as GTE, Lucent Technologies, NCR, TRW, Union Pacific Resources Group, Unisys, and UPS. Services include things such as job postings between companies, a Futures Forum to explore new ways of thinking and doing that is based on research findings, training and education services, and career growth centers. The Talent Alliance is headquartered in Morristown, NJ.

Career Development in Organizations Hall (1996) offers a relational approach to career development in organizations. "Models based on notions of organizations as pyramids and careers as regular progressions through ladder-like job sequences seem as outdated as the organizational forms on which they were based" (p. 1). Rather than focusing on moving up in a career, Hall suggests focusing on the importance of relationships to one's career growth. "The object of growth in the relational model is not individual mastery but rather interdependence" (p. 2). Hall believes that although resources are declining in the work world, relations between workers are at their best.

People are looking for meaning in their lives, and hence, in their work. Because the workplace is constantly reinventing itself, a person must be able to adapt to the changing environment, which means that they must be able to adjust their skills and learn new ones to fit into the new situations. "This sense of meaning and purpose, along with good opportunities for continuous learning and development, has become the new corporate contribution to the contract, replacing job security" (Hall, 1996, p. 5). Continuous learning and the ability to change and "to redirect one's life and career" are essential, and the energy to produce becomes the primary motivation in the workplace today. "Fewer people are pursuing the external 'carrot' (be it power, money, or security) because in today's flatter organization and lower-paying wage structure, it simply doesn't exist" (p. 6).

With this new perspective on careers in the corporate workplace, a holistic approach that includes personal identity and work identity is necessary. "Viewing the career as a personal quest also implies finding influences on development that are uniquely equipped to promote personal development" (Hall, 1996, p. 7). Rethinking the meaning of career and how it functions with personal life, reframing employer/ employee relationships and understanding, using flexibility at work, and adjusting the work environment to reduce stress and promote a sense of security are all part of the holistic approach to intervention. While all of this is the ultimate, the reality is that not all employees are capable of learning new skills and adapting to the changing work environment, and not all employers provide the time and money to assist in these changes.

Davenport's (1999) human capital theory describes the "worker as investor" (p. 22). A model of human capital based on this context is shown in Figure 11.2.

This model could be useful for employees and employers. If an employer realizes what each employee contributes in those five areas, it could be a useful career development model to see if the employee meets the criteria for the position she or he holds and, if not, to see what is needed for the employee to determine if there are areas where the organization is not making the best use of the individual's human capital. In order to improve one's human capital, there must be lifelong dreaming and

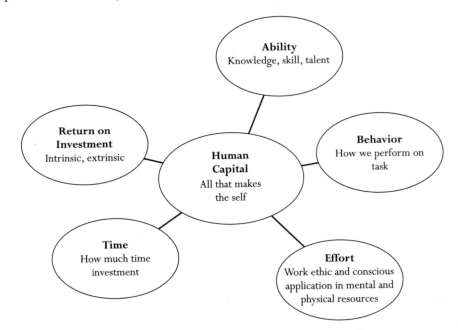

FIGURE 11.2   Total Human Capital Investment = [Ability + Behavior] × Effort × Time

personal flexibility. Some organizations do provide career development services for their employees. These services can include upgrading current skills and competencies, providing opportunities for advancement, or assistance in helping an employee with resume and interviewing skills training.

Career Plateau/Career Resiliency/Career Renewal With the ongoing threat of corporate downsizing, career plateauing has become a concern for managers and other employees. "The pyramidal shape of most organizations dictates that virtually all careers will level out before an employee reaches the top of the institution, agency, or corporation" (Tan & Salomone, 1994, p. 291). Career plateauing means that an employee has advanced to the point where there will be no further promotions. In other words, the business world regards career plateauing as meaning no chance for movement. Organizations can help with career plateauing by "(a) education and candor [about the realities of the situation], . . . (b) alternative work forms and reward systems, . . . (c) second career expectations, . . . and (d) encouraging further education (Tan & Salomone, 1994, pp. 298, 299). Interventions that practitioners may make on an individual level concern the areas of "career goal reassessment, . . . refocused learning goals, . . . and loss and transition" (pp. 299, 300).

One way to survive the changing workplace is to develop career self-reliance (Collard, Epperheimer, & Saigon, 1996) or **career resiliency** (Waterman, Waterman, & Collard, 1994). Career resilience characterizes a person who is (1) self-aware, (2) values-driven, (3) dedicated to continuous learning, (4) future-focused, (5) connected, and (6) flexible (Collard et al., 1996).

Basic assumptions of career development have been transformed. In traditional patterns, there were stable economic patterns; in career resilience, there is no economic stability. Hierarchy was basic to traditional thinking, but flattened organizations are the new reality. Some jobs have become contract/outsourcing or temporary situations with few distinct roles and no use of teams.

Rather than thinking of careers as job matching, upward movement, linear in direction, and management directed, career resiliency is a lifelong process that is proactive, based on values and their effect on work, self-direction with horizontal moves as important as upward mobility.

Career renewal is "a transitional stage that takes place for people generally at the end of the establishment stage and the beginning of the maintenance stage of a job or career" (Beijan & Salomone, 1995, p. 52). It is often related to what is commonly known as midlife transitions and was not included in Super's lifespan events. This process usually includes rethinking (1) career goals, (2) commitment, (3) self and work, (4) potential changes or adjustments that reflect one's current situation, (5) values, and (6) changes in the work environment. Leisure counseling is included in the process to encourage individuals to find sources other than work to fulfill needs and meet personal goals.

Another aspect to career renewal is that it can be considered a regeneration. Land and Jarman (1992) observed that in order to survive or grow, any entity needs to initiate a change in its status or a state of eventual decline will occur. If left unchanged, this will lead to its demise. This concept can be applied to workers and their jobs as well. The challenge that comes with this concept is that in order for it to work, the initiation of the change must occur while the individual or entity is still on an apparent path of success or increasing performance. They refer to these points of change as *breakpoints*. They contend that these breakpoints must, and do, occur throughout a successful continued existence.

As Engels (1995) states,

> the information age and the pending communication age call for career development that emphasizes life-long career resilience and renewal predicated on self understanding, learning to learn, self respect, respect for others, lifelong learning and other knowledge skills highlighted in the competencies designated by the Secretary's Commission on Achieving Necessary Skills (SCANS, 1992), as being essential for success in a global economy (p. 83).

Hudson (1991) describes commitments in life as cyclical. They encompass traits developed in the twenties and thirties: (1) personal identity, (2) intimacy, (3) achievement at work, (4) play and creativity, (5) search for meaning, and (6) compassion and contribution. In midlife, these commitments need to be examined and rethought. The primary cycles that affect adult life are the change cycle and the lifecycle. The cycle of change "requires living creatively with the flow of internal and external change" (p. 48). In a person's lifecycle, the "sense of purpose shifts with the changes of aging, social forces and self-development" (p. 48). Hudson's model of self/career renewal is seen in Figure 11.3.

Vocational practitioners need to be aware of these life structures and transitions in adult development to effectively assist these clients in times of reevaluation. We have explored how career specialists can assist adults while in the job. Our concerns now go to those services available for employees who are being displaced, replaced, or terminated.

Outplacement As companies have downsized, reorganized, or closed, many have provided job search services for employees affected by the changes. Companies can hire a team to provide services to employees and encourage employees to participate by reimbursing them for the time spent in the program or by giving them time from work.

The job of the outplacement counselor was considered to be one of the hot jobs in the 1990s by *Newsweek* magazine. "Outplacement services differ widely. They range from providing laid-off workers job search, access to company telephones, computers, and secretarial help to comprehensive relocations packages that cover all moving expenses" (Kirk, 1994, p. 10). Career planning and the ancillary help of resume writ-

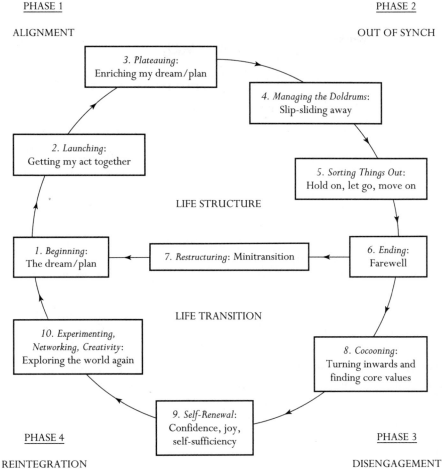

FIGURE 11.3 The Cycle of Change: Ten Personal Skills That Empower Adults Through Life Structures and Transitions

SOURCE: *F. M. Hudson,* The Adult Years: Mastering the Art of Self-Renewal, *1991, p. 53. Copyright by Jossey-Bass Inc.*

ing and portfolio preparation often are provided as well as preretirement planning—investigating possible businesses and alternative careers.

There are many reasons why companies provide these services, including

- Maintaining a positive public image
- Helping the morale of those remaining
- Lessening the potential for legal actions

While there are national organizations that provide this type of counseling service, the authors believe Kirk's model can make effective use of local resources and practitioners. Kirk's model is seen in Figure 11.4.

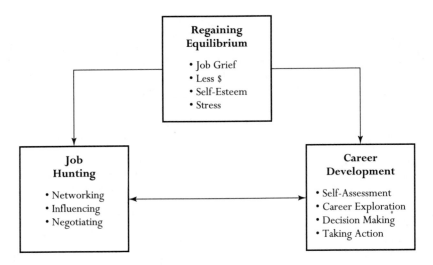

FIGURE 11.4 Holistic Outplacement Model

SOURCE: Reprinted from Kirk, "Putting Outplacement in Its Place," Journal of Employment Counseling, 31, p. 11. © ACA. Reprinted with permission. No further reproduction authorized without the written permission of the American Counseling Association.

Kirk's (1994) Holistic Outplacement Model consists of three functional elements. The first is called regaining equilibrium and deals with job grief, loss of income, the affect on self esteem, and stress. This leads to a future orientation that can go two directions and can move laterally between these elements. One concerns career development, including self-assessment, career exploration, decision-making and taking action, whereas the other focuses on job hunting, which involves networking, influencing, and negotiating. In recent conversations with two outplacement counselors from national firms, fewer corporations are providing less, if any, outplacement services to their employees (Nadene Peterson, 2004, conversations with Steve Wright of Right Associates and Rebecca Fulton, formerly of Drake, Beam and Morin).

Mentor Relationships In ancient Greece, when Odysseus went off to fight in the Trojan War, he left his son Telemachus in the care of Mentor, a wise and trusted friend. Later, after Telemachus grew to young manhood, the goddess Athena assumed Mentor's identity when Telemachus departed in search of his father. Thus, mentoring originally had both a Western and masculine tradition. Nowadays, one definition of a **mentor** is "an experienced, productive . . . [senior worker] who relates well to a less experienced employee and facilitates his or her personal development" (Karsten, 1994, p. 117). Both men and women can benefit from understanding what an appropriate mentor-protégé relationship is and is not (Edwards, 1991). Murphy and Ensher (1997) provide a cross-cultural perspective to mentoring.

Because today's professional milieu is so complex and ever-changing, few adults can effectively mentor adult workers/professionals. One of the authors of this text is mindful that "mentoring moments" can occur when more experienced professionals are consulted informally, without the tensions and competitiveness that a more for-

---

Practical Applications

To deal with the rage, anger, and depression that many laid-off and fired workers experience, vocational practitioners can provide support groups and job clubs to give these people a place to deal with these feelings without letting them affect their job interviewing or job search skills.

Outplacement career counseling is about helping people who have lost their jobs due to mergers and downsizing. People need to be able to make well-informed and positively motivated decisions about how they will continue their career after a layoff or a firing. This involves encouraging individuals to perceive that

- it is their decision to make the most of it.
- they have strengths and weaknesses to acknowledge.
- they have transferable skills.
- there will be opportunities open to them of which they are not aware.

To make the most of these opportunities, certain skills, such as research and self-marketing skills, may need to be developed.

Individuals need guidance to make the right choices with regard to education and employment. Oftentimes, they do not know how to make a positive match between their personal traits and the job environment. The mismatching of employee and employment leads to greater stress. There is a definite link between mental and physical stress and unemployment, with increased rates of murder, suicide, cirrhosis of the liver, and heart disease occurring among the unemployed population.

Counseling can help people to face unemployment more positively and/or choose a more appropriate career path to follow. People are then better able to accept advice and endure less anxiety about making decisions. (See the Yellow Pages for outplacement services in your local area.)

---

mal mentor-protégé relationship often contains (Levinson, 1978). Hudson (1991) suggests a model to train professional adult mentors with an understanding of (1) the change cycle or life cycle of adults, (2) life/career planning, (3) coaching, (4) leadership training, and (5) networking and referrals. The mentor would not function as a clinician but more as a role model, resource, and coach. Adult mentors need to be aware of adult developmental psychology, human systems management, career, leisure, and work-family issues. They also need to know what educational resources for training are available in the geographic area and need to have some knowledge of financial and retirement planning.

Another resource for adult mentoring information is Cohen (1995). He describes core mentor behavioral functions such as relationship, information, facilitation, confrontation, motivation, and encouragement. The Principles of the Adult Mentoring Scale (PAMS) is discussed as well.

Personality Disorders in Employment Meinz (2001) states that one in fifteen people in the general population have a personality disturbance and that about five in ten clients who seek counseling have personality disorders. Because many career counselors work with people with a wide range of disabilities, it seemed appropriate to include a section about this in this chapter. The more a client can talk about the part of his/her personality that seems to be causing conflict in the workplace, the easier it is for the counselor to make appropriate recommendations to a career path that doesn't reinforce that part. Meinz (2001) explains schizoid, avoidant, histrionic, dependent, obsessive-compulsive, antisocial, narcissistic, passive-aggressive, paranoid, schizotypal, and borderline personality disorders. With each one, he describes employment strengths, counseling tips, and specific job areas that would be appropriate.

An example would be a client with a dependent personality disorder. This type of client tends to cling to others. They are seen as stronger and more competent than they really are and often lack self confidence to make decisions on their own. At a mild level of severity, this client can function fairly well in the workplace in routine, unpressured jobs. However, if the dependency becomes moderate to severe, then that can put an inordinate amount of stress on the employee's supervisor. An employee with a dependent personality disorder will prefer work where he is told what to do, will rarely be insubordinate, and will want to do good work. Specific job areas suggested are clerical pool, nurses aide, court reporter, data entry, medical transcription, laundry worker, production worker, and bookkeeper. If career/vocational practitioners have clients with specific personality disorders, Meinz's book can be very helpful in developing appropriate interventions.

A study by Bernes (2002) describes three cases using the DSM IV multi-axial assessment as a basis for understanding the issues of psychopathology as it may affect the careers of individuals. For a further example, refer to Peterson & González (2000), Chapter 17, Chronic Mental Illness and Work.

Assessments for Adults

1. Adult Basic Learning Examination (ABLE)
2. Adult Career Concerns (ACC)
3. Adult Measure of Essential Skills (AMES)
4. Ball Aptitude Battery (BAB)
5. Campbell Interest & Skills Survey (CISS)
6. Career Values Card Sort (CVCS)
7. Career Attitude Strategies Inventory: An inventory for understanding adult concerns (CASI)
8. Myers-Briggs Type Indicator (MBTI Combined with SII)
9. 16 PF-Career Personal Development Profile (CPDP)
10. Strong Interest Inventory (SII)
11. Tests of Adult Basic Education (TABS)

STRESS AT WORK

Two common workplace occurrences that can be personally experienced but socially negated are stress and **burnout.** One's work ethic and balance between work and leisure can unexpectedly go haywire. Stress at work and career burnout can then happen. The ever-increasing baseline tempo of life in the United States has been called "a harried, Lucy Ricardo-in-the candy-factory level of frenetic activity that's impossible for anyone to sustain except in a state of mental and physical overload" (Sharp, 1996, p. 1). Stress can be both good and bad—depending on its nature, duration, and resources available to respond to it. The term *stress* connotes feelings of anxiety, a sense of powerlessness, and sometimes alienation and burnout. Most individuals in all occupations will experience job-related stress to some extent. Stress is a part of life and work. When stress changes from a positive motivator into negative feelings about work or abilities or to feelings of depression and burnout, it becomes a serious problem.

Shore (1992) classifies stress at work into three categories: biochemical, physical, and psychosocial. Biochemical stress refers to the exposure to chemical and biological substances that interfere with normal body functioning. The mysterious illnesses that afflict thousands of Desert Storm veterans may be due to exposure to chemical agents in the Persian Gulf (Gannett News Service, 1996). Physical stress includes noise, ventilation, heat, pace of production, and time of shift (Shore, 1992). Nurses who work on rotating shifts increase their risk of heart disease, and those who work them for more than six years are as much as 50 percent to 70 percent more likely to have serious cardiac problems, including heart attacks (Schieszer, 1996). Psychosocial stress occurs as a result of a potential or actual conflict between a worker and some aspect of the worker's company. This includes conflicting job demands, negative patterns of supervision and communication, lack of respect and recognition, racism, and sexism.

Barnett and Rivers (1996) summarize previous research and identify seven factors related to work stress.

1. Skill discretion—job complexity and challenge, extent to which a worker can control use of his or her own skills.

2. Decision authority—the extent to which a worker can control authority or use of resources to get her or his job done.

3. Schedule control—the extent to which a worker has control over hours worked.

4. Job demands—the number of tasks to perform, time allowed, and number of conflicting demands placed on one's time.

5. Pay adequacy—how much one earns compared to others doing similar work.

6. Job security—one's perception of the likelihood of being fired, laid off, or downsized.

7. Relations with supervisor—how well one gets along with one's boss.

Issues related to skill discretion and job demands have a significant negative impact on mental health for both men and women (Barnett & Rivers, 1996). The most

CASE EXAMPLES
Work Stress

Police Work

Police officers have received a bad rap in the last several years due to many incidents that have received high-profile media attention. Symptomatic drinking by police officers is most directly effected by level of stress (Violante, Marshall, & Howe, 1985). The indirect effect of job demands (e.g., emotional dissonance) mediated by stress and coping (e.g., cynicism) is approximately four times greater than its direct effect. Stress, job demands, and coping all have a meaningful effect on police officer alcohol abuse. Killing someone in the line of duty and experiencing a fellow officer being killed are the top two of 60 ranked stressors for police officers (Violanti & Aron, 1994). Seven organizational/administrative stressors rank among the top 20: shift work, inadequate department support, incompatible partner, insufficient personnel, excessive discipline, inadequate support by supervisors, and inadequate equipment. Racial conflicts rank last among police stressors. Organizational stressors mediated by job satisfaction and organizational orientation are a source of stress for police officers approximately 6.3 times greater than the inherent stressors related to the dangers of police work (Violanti & Aron, 1993). Officers dealing with organizational stress have lower job satisfaction. Ambiguous, conflicting organizational goals also decrease job satisfaction. These organizational stressors remain largely unknown to the general public and those considering police work. Entrenched attitudes and practices in the upper ranks are hidden stressors that contribute to the job stress experienced by police officers, and these have a cumulative effect greater than the inherent dangers of the job.

Full-Time Female Homemakers

Barnett and Rivers (1996) summarize why full-time female homemakers score higher on stress indexes than women who work outside the home:

- Long hours of monotonous, boring, repetitive housework
- Being on call twenty-four hours a day
- The isolation and loss of freedom when home alone with young children
- The myth that housework is not really work
- The low status of housework ("just a housewife")

This reality contributes to high rates of depression and other symptoms of psychological distress. Permanently dropping out of the workforce after the birth of a child can be more harmful to a woman's health than being employed full time. Women who lose earned income can also lose a sense of entitlement (see also, McKenna, 1997) that decreases mental and physical health. Involvement in activities that give a homemaker a sense of independence, autonomy, and respect from others diminishes the tedious nature of housework and boosts her self-regard.

unhealthy combination is a tedious job—that is, a lack of variety and challenge—with heavy demands. Employees who experience threats to their reputations with their supervisors or managers are likely to experience emotional distress that goes home with them from work (Doby & Caplan, 1995). That is when work stress can also impinge on the family function.

Eustress is the exhilarating feeling of accomplishment that results from effectively coping with stress. **Distress** occurs when a person experiences too many stressors or when they continue for too long. Work conditions may cause the body's immune system to be compromised. When this happens, employees are left vulnerable to infection, physical illness, and disease. According to Sharp (1996), stress-related illness costs the United States $300 billion a year in medical costs and lost productivity.

Workaholism has many definitions:

- An addiction to work
- An escape from the unpleasantries of life
- Competitiveness caused by a craving for constant stimulation and an over-abundance of energy
- The result of compensating for a self-image damaged in childhood
- Behavior learned from parents and other role models

Workaholism can harm one's health, personal life, and work environment. "Workaholics surely need the assistance of career and mental health counselors to achieve [the] balance [between meaningful productive work and recreative leisure activities for life satisfaction and mental health]" (Seybold & Salomone, 1994, p. 8).

Warning Signs and Sources of Job Stress

Some workers experience stress to a slight degree; others may be incapacitated. Warning signs include intestinal distress; frequent illness; insomnia; persistent fatigue; irritability; nail biting; lack of concentration; increased use of drugs and alcohol; and a hunger for sweets. Other signs are resistance to going to work everyday; lackluster job performance; procrastination on minor tasks; avoiding discussion of work with co-workers; preoccupation with petty aspects of the job; feelings of guilt and inadequacy; working late; and frequent physical illness or accidents. When one's identity is largely based upon work, losing a job through downsizing leads many people to stress-induced illnesses (Uchitelle & Kleinfield, 1996).

John Schaubroeck et al. (2001) cited in Hewlett (2001) looked at job demands, control, and individual differences to find out if there is an effect on upper-respiratory disease. The findings revealed that workers who prefer not to have control tend to consistently view negative work outcomes as being their fault and consequently exacerbated the unhealthy effects of stress. Schaubroeck and his colleagues found that efficacy—how employees feel about their abilities to do their work—is an important determinate on how one uses control at work. A further point is that the attributional styles—the way people assign blame or credit to themselves—of people who are error prone tend to have low self-esteem. The researchers suggested that organizations train their employees in terms of attribution style as a prevention to stress and health related issues (p. 58).

Sometimes stress can have a positive effect on an employee group, especially if it is a cohesive group, and can lead to a higher overall performance and meeting quotas and deadlines. Other times the strain caused by the stress can lead to

1. psychological reactions (job dissatisfaction, depression, burnout, anxiety).

2. physiological reactions (high blood pressure, exhaustion, headaches).

3. behavioral reactions (smoking, drug and alcohol abuse).

Affected individuals are less capable of responding to work demands. Job strain reduces motivation and the work performance. Individuals try to escape from the situation through tardiness and absenteeism (Drummond & Ryan, 1995).

Sources of career stress in organizations take many forms: role conflict, task overload, role ambiguity, discrimination and stereotyping, marriage/work conflicts, interpersonal stress, feelings of inadequacy, discordant values, and lack of progress toward career goals (Hirschorn, 1988). Another stressor is sexual harassment (Barnett & Rivers, 1996). Sexual harassment places an unendurable burden, particularly on working women, and has been associated with anxiety, depression, headaches, sleep disturbance, gastrointestinal disorders, weight loss or gain, nausea, and sexual dysfunction. It costs a typical Fortune 500 company nearly $7 million per year (Barnett & Rivers, 1996).

Anxiety becomes a precursor of a more serious problem as it progresses or persists (Herr & Cramer, 1996). Feelings of anxiety are the fundamental roots of distorted or alienated relationships at work. A work group manages its anxiety by developing and deploying a set of social defenses by which people can

- retreat from role, task, and organizational boundaries.

- manage their anxiety by projection of blame.

- bureaucratize their work.

- resort to excessive paperwork to reduce face-to-face communications.

- engage in excessive checking and monitoring of their work to reduce the anxiety of making difficult decisions.

One obvious distortion of meaning is that millions in the U.S. workforce feel that because of corporate cost-cutting, they can no longer take time off when they are sick. Not all employees are afraid of losing their jobs, and some say loyalty is the main reason they work when they are sick. However, an increasing number of workers feel that, with so many co-workers lost to cutbacks, there are no extra bodies to fill in if they take a sick day.

Practical Applications

Vocational practitioners can help workers understand how work stress affects them by

- getting them to analyze and identify the parts of their job that are sources of stress.
- helping them learn their own stress reactions.
- helping them determine what they can do about job stress (Shore, 1992).

Long-range strategies for dealing with stress need to be developed as workers and the work environment change. Stress can be reduced when the organization

- defines the work roles and responsibilities more clearly.
- provides career development and counseling services.
- provides social support systems.
- encourages meaningful stimulation.
- redesigns jobs to allow workers to use their skills.
- reduces work loads.
- rethinks work schedules.
- involves workers in decision making (Drummond & Ryan, 1995).

The Occupational Stress Inventory (OSI-R) measures domains of occupational adjustment that include: occupational stress; the ability to cope effectively with stressors in the workplace; and coping resources available to the individual to combat the effects of stressors. This could be a valuable tool for practitioners to help understand the individual's capacity for managing stress.

Most companies, big or small, are working with fewer staff. Over the last decade, the nation's largest companies eliminated 4.7 million positions, or one-quarter of their workforce. The perception is that managers, increasingly looking at the bottom line, prefer to have people in the office even if they are sick. Worries about job security have brought employees into work during blizzards, even after employers have told them to stay home (Wilde, 1996).

Conscientiousness can become overcompensation for lack of satisfaction in other areas of life (Cobble, 1996). An employee spending too much time on the job may show disinterest in family, friends, and leisure time. Lunch frequently is skipped, and only a small amount is eaten at one's desk to maintain a consistent level of frenzied activity. These employees may perceive their work environment to be so competitive they feel they have to outperform each other and work twice as long to keep up, sacrificing their health.

Tension between work and family life is a major source of stress for many workers. Productivity drops when employees have difficulty with dependent care. Bank Street College found that problems with child care caused absenteeism and unproductive time (Solomon, 1991). In a study conducted by the Families and Work Institute in New York City, employees who have latchkey children missed 13 days of work per year as compared to an average of 7 to 9 days for the other workers. Another survey conducted found that more than half of men and women report being interrupted at work because of elder care responsibilities (Solomon, 1991).

Career Burnout

If stressors continue in the workplace with no hope of change, burnout can eventually occur. A person may no longer care about work performance outcome. Burnout is not a single event but a process of gradual change in behavior, eventually reaching intense reactions and often leading to a crisis, if left unresolved. Burnout has been associated with (1) role conflict, (2) work overload, (3) repetitious work tasks, (4) boredom, (5) ambiguity, (6) lack of advancement opportunities, and (7) shortage of time.

Cherniss (1995) studied 26 human services professionals (7 high school teachers, 6 public health nurses, 7 mental health practitioners, and 6 lawyers) at two points in time. Initially, stressors faced by these new professionals and their coping efforts were examined as they ended their first year on the job. Unstructured interviews obtained the most penetrating information on the work experiences of research participants. Unstructured, follow-up interviews were conducted twelve years later on all the original participants. The following discussion is based on the findings by Cherniss. After completing their educational preparation, several sources of stress characterized the first-year professionals' work.

1. New professionals often experienced crises of confidence and feelings of inadequacy.
2. Independence and autonomy attracted many to human service professions, but work sites limited these motivations.
3. Difficult clients tested these new professionals' sense of competence. Dishonest, manipulative clients were the worst.
4. Boredom and routine occurred more than hoped-for meaningful and interesting work.
5. A lack of collegiality left many new professionals feeling alone and vulnerable at their work sites.

At the twelve-year follow-up of this study, only 10 of the 26 original research participants remained in the helping professions 1 was permanently disabled, 2 were caring for young children at home full time, 13 had left public service). Those who left public service did so to

- achieve greater financial rewards.
- obtain more intellectually stimulating work or higher-status employment.

- become self-employed.
- work with less difficult clients.

Those who remained in public service did so because of family obligations, economic considerations, or because a career change was too stressful to contemplate.

Krumboltz (1993), cited in Miller (2002), listed questions that help counselors explore career problem areas. For example, questions pertaining to job burnout include:

How do you feel about your job at this point?

What is most stressful for you?

What is most motivating for you?

What is your image of an ideal job for yourself at this point in your life?

How can other life roles provide the meaning for you that may be missing in your job?

What immediate actions can you take to provide support for yourself?

How can you move closer to the your current ideal career goal? (p. 278)

Practical Applications

Training programs (e.g., teacher education, the mental health professions, nursing, law) that adopt a tone of moral communities, not just service delivery systems, can also help to prevent burnout. "Helping professionals are less likely to burn out when they are committed to a transcendent set of moral beliefs, and when they work in a community based on those beliefs" (Cherniss, 1995, p. 186). A singular, unique feature of burnout is that most workers do not realize until too late that they have passed the threshold of their capacities and tolerance. Burnout prevention in the workplace needs greater emphasis. To prevent burnout, a client must be able to recognize what in their work environment causes stress. The client can act to either change the situation within the organiza-

tion so that the stressors are less acute or consider a job change. Feelings of helplessness emerge when a client perceives no options, leading to depression and burnout. Often when clients become aware of the problem, they will take action. To facilitate this action, Pines and Aronson (1988) have a four-step plan for dealing with career burnout:

1. Recognize the symptoms
2. Activate a plan for solving the causes
3. Distinguish between what can be changed and what cannot be changed
4. Develop new coping skills and refine old ones

Anticipating stressful times of the year can help workers in certain occupations to reduce the risk of burnout.

Continued

Continued

Examples of these acute times of inevitable stress are:

1. for accountants, certified public accountants, and tax lawyers—tax season
2. for retailers and choir directors at schools and churches—holiday season
3. for florists—Mother's Day and Valentine's Day
4. for students, teachers, and professors at colleges and universities—final exam week.

Knowing the busiest times of the year can help employees mentally prepare for unavoidable onslaughts.

Cherniss (1995) suggests several antidotes for burnout:

1. A combination of autonomy and support from bosses.
2. Professionals with a history of individual coping effectiveness during their early adult years are less likely to suffer burnout. Those who do not directly enter graduate or professional school after their undergraduate years are less likely to experience burnout.
3. Early development of career insight, such as (a) self-knowledge of strengths, weaknesses, and preferences; and (b) a clear and accurate idea of what one likes to do best and what one can do best; with (c) periodic testing of other possibilities.
4. Improving organizational negotiation skills, such as (a) avoiding or resolving stressful interpersonal conflicts, (b) overcoming bureaucracy, and (c) obtaining support for meaningful and innovative projects helps professionals regain commitment to and satisfaction with their work.
5. Maintaining a balance between one's work life, personal life, and leisure. When family life and relaxation are just as important as work, recovery from burnout becomes easier.
6. *Doing* less and *being* more enhances more realistic goals about what can be accomplished at work. Burnout can be avoided and recovery improved when the need to achieve is moderated by other goals.

CASE EXAMPLE

Total Burnout

A professional friend of one of the authors, who worked for a social service agency, unexpectedly resigned from his job and literally left town in order to find perspective again. He realizes now that he was experiencing total burnout and was not paying attention to his own emotional cues as to how much he was losing his motivation. Had a burnout prevention program been in place at this agency and had personnel been paying more attention to the well-being of their employees, this situation could probably have been avoided. The agency lost a very competent professional, and he lost his sense of professional worth.

Violence in the Workplace

Daw (2001) indicates that work stress is leading more people to engage in counterproductive workplace behaviors. A recent phone survey of 1,305 American employees conducted by Integra Realty Resources shows that stress leads to physical violence in one in 10 work environments. Almost half of those surveyed said yelling and verbal abuse where frequent in their workplace. *Desk rage,* as explained by the popular media, includes acts of aggression, hostility, rudeness, and physical violence. Nearly a quarter of the people surveyed reported being driven to tears by workplace stress and half said they skip lunch routinely to get their work done (Daw, 2001).

Violence in the workplace is increasing and is becoming a greater source of stress than ever before. In *The Gift of Fear: Survival Signs that Protect Us from Violence* (1997), Gavin de Becker describes **pre-incident indicators**, with increasing levels of seriousness, that can be detected before violence in the workplace occurs.

> Stepping on the first rung of a ladder is a significant pre-incident indicator to reaching the top; stepping on the sixth [rung] even more so. Because everything a person does is created twice—once in the mind and once in its execution—ideas and impulses are pre-incident indicators for action (p. 18).

Pre-incident indicators are part of systematized intuition that de Becker's company uses to advise workplaces about managing employees who are likely to act out violently. A unique stressor about workplace violence is that the work site is the main place where most people have to interact with others whom they may not otherwise have chosen to include in their everyday life. Violence in the workplace can be predicted (de Becker, 1997), but too often, warning signs are ignored and tragedy occurs. Ironically, many people usually are in a position to notice such warning signs. A clear sign of trouble in any context, workplace or not, is the refusal to take *no* for an answer, and eleven elements of prediction can be measured (de Becker, 1997, Appendix 6, pp. 315–319).

Daw (2001) reports that Eric Shaw, PhD, a former psychologist with the U.S. Central Intelligence Agency, is developing interesting new software that can detect anger and mood changes in employees by detecting negativity in sets of phrases and words in the employees' e-mails. This software would be used to provide a red flag and could be a useful way in identifying changes in emotional state that signal at-risk individuals (p. 54).

Employee emotion is a force to be reckoned with in the age of takeovers, mergers, and downsizing. Problems begin when a job applicant is hired without an extensive check of references and work background. Many employees are managed in ways that bring out the worst in them (de Becker, 1997). Often, managers and bosses receive no training in leadership and decision-making skills and can show an appalling lack of character and ethics themselves. Job loss can be as painful as the death of a loved one, and support is rarely forthcoming.

The effects of domestic violence also are spreading into the job site (Burney, 1995). Domestic violence is not supposed to be a workplace problem, yet violence at home is costing businesses between \$3 billion and \$5 billion a year in lowered employee productivity, increased absenteeism, and higher employee turnover. People are reluctant to tell their employer when they are victims of domestic violence, partly from years of conditioning by employers that they should keep their personal problems outside the workplace and partly from a realistic fear of being fired because their employer does not want the hassle of dealing with the problem.

According to Linda Osmundson, executive director of CASA, a Pinellas County, Florida, woman's shelter, employers can help fight domestic violence in at least five ways (cited in Burney, 1995).

1. Make employees aware that employers know domestic violence is a problem; make brochures from local spouse–abuse shelters available to employees; and publicly support domestic abuse shelters.

2. Make it an explicit policy not to fire victims of domestic abuse.

3. Review and consider the increase in security at the business and in its parking lot.

4. If the employer suspects that an employee is being abused, ask her or him if there is something in their personal life that the employer should know about. The "her or him" is crucial here; victims of domestic abuse range from top executive women down to male assembly line workers. Employers are encouraged not to *accuse* the employee of being abused; it's the employee's choice to make that revelation.

5. Offer support for employees who say they are being abused—this can be as simple as walking them to their car or giving a picture of the abuser to security guards. While workplace politics can definitely hinder employee self-disclosures of domestic abuse, management that is genuinely respectful and responsive to an abused employee will find that others will feel safe enough to come forward with the same issue.

CASE EXAMPLE

Missing the Signs

An employee at a nationally-known real estate company went into work as usual at about 2 P.M. He (unbeknownst to the office personnel) had three guns in his office. He took out one of the guns and killed two office co-workers and seriously injured another. He drove away in his car, and when a police chase ensued, he veered off the road and killed himself with a gun. As in most cases, there were some signs, but his demeanor of friendliness and apparent enthusiasm for his work did not make the other signs appear significant. Looking for signs from both office personnel and family members may have helped detect what was about to happen.

OLDER WORKERS

We is faced with insurmountable opportunities.

—Pogo
(Walt Kelly)

Doris Fisher thought that by now, at age 77, she'd be living out her golden years in a house by the sea. She worked hard, "all my life," she says. She saved money and thought she'd retire. The problem is she can't afford to. After decades as an independent small business owner, the stock market decline and a divorce depleted her financial resources. As for Fisher, she's just hopeful she'll find work. "I think I'll be fine," she says. "Like I said, I'm a positive thinker or a dreamer. I don't know which." She'll take whichever pays the bills, reports CBS News correspondent Bobbi Harley. (Excerpt taken from CBSNEWS.com article, Seniors Scan 'Help Wanted' Ads.)

Older adults in the workplace are becoming "situated in a dynamic pattern of active employment, temporary disengagement from the workplace, and reentry into the same or new career" (Stein & Rocco, 2001, p. 1). The authors suggest that there is a third stage of working life—including older workers as active agents within the workplace. Older workers desire opportunities for career development, but are still neglected by most workplaces because of the misconceptions about older workers. Stein and Rocco discuss the myths of the older adult work force. These include

1. *The age myth*—there is an age when one becomes an older worker.
2. *The retirement myth*—retirement is the final stage of working life.
3. *The declining productivity myth*—Older workers are liabilities.
4. *The career development myth*—Older workers do not need lifelong development.

The realities of the adult workers are that they are assets and a significant component of the population in work. They are viewed as workers who can be recruited, retrained, and retained in the work force. "Rather than being seen as a liability, the older worker is becoming an investment in continuing productivity" (Stein & Rocco, 2001, p. 1).

Governments in many developed countries are searching for ways to decrease the drain of aging populations on future national resources. According to United Nations data, life expectancy in developed countries is expected to increase from 75.8 years currently to 81.6 by 2050. This increase in life expectancy increases the median age by 2050 to well over 50 for Japan and Sweden, 47 for the United Kingdom, and 40 for the United States. This projected increase in median age forecasts the coming jobs crisis. There may not be enough workers to fill needed jobs. This will create a demand to keep older workers in the workforce. Businesses may need to develop more incentives for keeping older workers on the payrolls longer. In the United States, the percentage of money going into social security has increased steadily, and less money is available for meeting other national priorities.

CASE EXAMPLES

Boomer Work Life

Unemployment as a Blessing

Unemployment taught 50-year-old Joan Allen of Baltimore a valuable lesson, and being an unemployed boomer was a blessing rather than a crisis. She worked as a marketing director. She never married and had no children. She was laid off eleven years ago and decided to seek out a series of projects. She worked as a freelancer, did a documentary on teenage depression, wrote a book for single boomers, and turned a family recipe into a brownie making business (p. 1D).

A Third Career

Norman (2003) described Ron Saienni, a 56-year-old who is in what he calls a third career. He lists his careers as first childhood, then rigorous vocation-building, and now a comfortable work life. By his third career, he had to decide what he wanted to do with the rest of his life. He wanted to be able to please himself and make the world a better place. He used skills that he learned from being the president of Biltmore Communities, Inc., and contacts he developed over thirty years in real estate to develop a business that pleases him. Saienni's third career was to build the country's largest independent equity broker for real estate projects. He "believes that any baby boomer can replicate his creation of a personalized company that uses past skills yet delivers greater happiness" (p. 2G).

Policies such as completely privatizing social security may be developed (Wagner, 2003). Japan, Sweden, and the United Kingdom have already initiated reforms in their retirement policies. Japan has enacted benefit cuts to its national pension system, causing some workers to work to later ages. "Sweden changed the entire structure of its social security system from 'pay-as-you-go' to a defined benefit plan (where the pensions that retirees receive depend on what they put into the system)" (Wagner, 2003). The United Kingdom has a phased higher pension eligibility age for women, and the new system will reward people for staying longer on the jobs with higher pensions. In order to keep older workers in the workforce, societies may need to require new education and training programs and change attitudes that undervalue older workers.

An occupational area that seems a natural transition for older workers is caregiving, that is, nurses, home health aides, nursing home administrators, therapists, dietitians, and janitors and cleaners for assisted living facilities. "By 2015, just under 20 percent of the labor force—or one out of every five participants may be 55 or older up from about one in eight in 1999" (Rix, 2001). This increase in the elderly population will cause a far larger demand for such caregivers, creating an opportunity for older workers. Rix indicates that employers will have little choice but to dip into

---

Practical Applications

Brewington and Nassar-McMillan (2000) suggest that counselors need to be well informed about issues pertaining to older workers and be equipped to help these clients in a number of ways.

1. Encourage clients to anticipate and prepare for change.
2. Process emotions associated with job loss, unemployment, and transitions, including grief over job loss, fear of financial insecurity, and worries about retraining.

3. Help older clients select occupations that are congruent with their interests and abilities.
4. Facilitate recycling through the career stages their transitions necessitate.
5. Encourage clients to participate in lifelong learning in a world of rapidly changing technology.
6. Counselors must be receptive to change and keep themselves well informed if they expect to help clients do the same.

---

the older labor force because that is where the workers will be. Older workers are desirable to employers in the caring professions because of their attributes, including experience, maturity, loyalty, good judgment, dependability, and reliability. Employers will be faced with implementing policies and programs to meet the needs of the older population to encourage postponing retirement, mid-life career changes, and retirees returning to the workforce. Employers may be able to take advantage of the experience of women who leave the labor force to care for an older relative and later return to work. These women may be receptive to formal training for jobs in caregiving. Employers in the future can expect to pay more for caregivers than today and will need to design work options and work incentives that look beyond the pool of traditional caregivers for help. Age should not discourage employers from hiring this older population of workers in caregiving work (Rix, 2001).

Bergstein (2003) reports that many baby boomers are now feeling the pinch and are finding themselves competing in an abbreviated job market. Many baby boomers are hunting for work for the first time in decades, but are limited by their inability to move and pressure to provide for their children or elderly parents. According to the U.S. Bureau of Labor Statistics, the unemployment rate for 45–54 year olds is 4.1 percent, up from 2.4 percent three years ago.

As we progress through the new century, our attitudes toward older workers will be altered. Instead of older workers no longer being useful, they will be considered to have valuable experience, be able to learn new skills, and have the ability to be flexible. Older workers cannot be stereotyped. They come from highly diverse backgrounds (e.g., life experience, education level, cultural identity). When counseling older workers, the practitioner must be aware of characteristics that can be generalized to fit the needs of older workers. For purposes of definition, Lefkovich (1992) cites Kelly's (1990) five subgroups that categorize workers by age.

1. *Midlife career changers.* These are younger-older workers ages 50–62. They have most likely changed jobs due to a midlife transition and are interested in reaping the benefits of experience, such as pay raises, job advancement, and health care and retirement benefits.

2. *Displaced workers aged 62 and younger.* These people have most likely lost jobs due to the changes in corporate structure (downsizing, mergers, acquisitions). They may not have any income or may be living on a limited severance pay. This group is looking for work that has health and retirement benefits. If they go very long without being hired, they begin to believe their job skills no longer have value and can easily develop a strong sense of hopelessness and helplessness.

3. *Retirees aged 62 and younger.* These people are receiving some health coverage and benefits as a result of accepting an early retirement package. They often find themselves with too much leisure and not enough income.

4. *Retirees aged 62 to 69 who are receiving social security.* Even though this group receives social security benefits, they often are not ready to quit working, either for financial or sense-of-meaning issues. Most, however, will not want to work full time and are somewhat insecure about their health and ability. They also worry about how potential employers will see them and their ability. Flexible work hours are important to this group.

5. *Retirees aged 70 or older who are on social security.* While often less able to work, these people may be similar to the group above, with more emphasis on part-time work.

Lefkovich (1992) suggests that the following are incentives for people to work: "(a) age, (b) career status, (c) economics, (d) health, (e) family responsibilities, (f) education, (g) the need for health and medical coverage, (h) future family and retirement planning, (i) social interests, (j) the need for personal interactions, or (k) for the intellectual stimulation and challenge" (Lefkovich, 1992, p. 64).

While corporate managers are usually somewhat older people themselves, it has been the practice of companies to enact policies that urge older people to leave their job, often to be replaced by a younger person. While this may appear to be the natural order of things, changing demographics may slow this process.

Group Counseling for Older Workers

Many studies address the effectiveness of group counseling in conducting a job search with older adults (Amundeson & Borgen, 1988; Rife & Belcher, 1993; Stidham & Remley, 1992). Zimpfer and Carr (1989) suggest some reasons for using groups.

Practical Applications

Jensen-Scott (1993) cites several barriers when counseling older adults.

First, although a number of older adults apparently feel highly dissatisfied with their current situation, the counselor may have difficulty reaching those persons most in need of intervention. . . . A second barrier is the potential difficulty in establishing a counseling relationship. . . . A third barrier concerns the tendency for assessment to be difficult with this population. . . . A final barrier concerns possible lack of job and volunteer opportunities available for older adults (pp. 264–65).

Vocational practitioners need to understand some key elements when working with adults: a perspective on aging, a transitional life-events framework for counseling, and teaching coping skills (Schlossberg, 1996). Aging is a time when significant losses take place, and has positive and negative transitions and experiences. One's choices depend on the knowledge and values one holds. Practitioners need to observe when an older adult is experiencing (1) transitions, (2) life events, (3) stresses, and (4) pleasures, as well as (5) biological, (6) personal, (7) physical, (8) psychological, and (9) social changes. Ask how any change affects the client's self-perception. "The more the event or nonevent alters an [older] adult's roles, routines, assumptions, and relationships, the more the person will be

affected by the transition and have to cope with it" (Schlossberg, 1990, p. 9). She further suggests that mastering change can be broken down into three major steps.

1. Approaching change—teach adults to look at the changes in their lives and determine how extensive they are.
2. Taking stock of one's resources—teach adults to identify their potential and decide what needs strengthening.
3. Taking charge—teach adults ways to turn a low resource into a high resource (Schlossberg, 1990).

Washington (1993) observed specific differences that practitioners need to be concerned with when working with the more experienced client.

1. Older clients know more what they *don't* want.
2. Older clients have more work experience so have developed more work content skills.
3. Older individuals need to identify job families and all the individual occupations connected to that particular family of occupations.
4. Older clients do not want to take major pay cuts.
5. Older clients need to develop a results-oriented portfolio and during interviews learn to tell stories that make a convincing case for their job skills.

Groups (1) are efficient, (2) provide social context, (3) have potential for reality test-ing, and (4) have demonstrated effectiveness. The authors offer some recommenda-tions for consideration for groups for adult workers. These include:

1. Assessment instruments that are more sensitive to the changes in self concept that take place with adults

2. The importance of follow-up interventions

3. Test outcomes that involve generalizable skills versus specific job-finding skills need to be developed

PRE-RETIREMENT AND RETIREMENT

Miller (2002) indicates that the definition of retirement is changing. Increasingly, re-tirement is seen as a process rather than a single event. "Older workers who choose not to retire cite reasons such as not planning wisely for retirement, need to contrib-ute, appreciation from others, and the desire to create something" (p. 268). Miller re-ports that in an AARP (2002) study, eight in ten baby boomers say they plan to work at least part-time during their retirement years. He further cites Curnow and Fox (1994) who refer to retirement or the "Third Age," a period beyond the career/job and parenting that can last up to 30 years.

In a speech given in 2002, William Novelli, Executive Director and CEO of American Association of Retired Persons (AARP) reported that an AARP survey in-dicated that older employees possess all but one of the top seven general qualities that companies see as being most desirable. These include: commitment to doing quality work, getting along with co-workers, solid performance records, basic skills, someone you can count on in a crisis, and loyalty (Novelli, 2002). The only quality on which the older employees rated low was the willingness to be flexible about doing differ-ent tasks.

> The survey indicated that about 50 percent of human resource staff recognized the value of strategies for more fully utilizing older employees, but a much lower percentage have implemented approaches such as special benefit pack-ages, part-time arrangements, educating managers about older employees, and skill training for older workers" (Miller, 2002, p. 269).

Trends that need to be considered by counselors when working with older adult populations are:

- Many mature workers have experienced involuntary job loss and change, whereas others are redefining their career goals and directions to respond proactively to these changes.

- An important population of adults have employment that is not protected by adequate retirement benefits, including mature adults who have health prob-lems and who are working in physically demanding jobs.

- Retirement is being viewed as a process rather than a single event. Most baby boomers intend to continue some type of employment after leaving their "career job."

- Although employers are experiencing a serious shortage of available workers, few have implemented benefit plans and flexible work arrangements that support employment of older workers (Miller, p.278).

Miller also cites Krumboltz's (1993) list of questions that help counselors explore career problem areas. For example, for questions to help clients explore issues related to retirement planning, counselors can ask:

- When you think about retiring, how do you feel? What does retirement mean to you?

- Are you aware that many people are looking at retirement in new ways (as a process rather than an event)?

- Are you experiencing physical health or working conditions that make it hard for you to continue in your current job?

- Have you discussed possible work adaptations with your employer?

- Have you reviewed your retirement benefits and return-to-work policies?

- Have you received other benefits for which you are eligible?

- Why would it be important or not important for you to engage in some paid work in the future?

- When you review your career plan at this point in your life, what goals do you have?

- How can you fulfill these in other paid work situations?

Genevay (2000) suggests recreating oneself in old age, by building on all the work and life experience that has gone before and by maintaining throughout life a strong identity, self-esteem, and constructive life-coping skills. The care and maintenance of personal and work identity involves an evaluation process and an action process and rests on the core identity of the person—mind, body, emotions, and spirit—regardless of age (Peterson & Gonzalez, 2000, *Career Counseling Models for Diverse Populations*, p. 262). The Shamrock Model shown in Figure 11.5 illustrates graphically the utilization of the older person's resources.

Kadlec (2002) described staged or gradual retirement as a model that was originally designed to cover those who worked because of financial necessity. It consists of three parts:

1. Downsize your career. As you approach retirement age, consider your financial situation, including housing, bills, and the like, and begin to think about working fewer hours.

2. Let your savings grow. Through investments, savings accounts, and continued income, plan to not use any invested or saved money for as long as possible.

Utilizing All of the Older Person's Resources

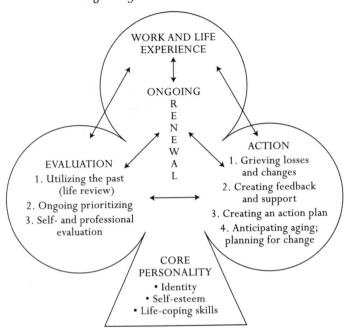

FIGURE 11.5   The Shamrock Model

SOURCE: *N. Peterson & R. C. González*, Career Counseling Models for Diverse Populations, *Brooks/Cole, 2000*.

3. Quit for good. If there is enough now that you can continue your basic lifestyle and can do the things you want without earning income through working, stop working and plan for how you will live your life.

Schlossberg (2004) in her book, *Retire Smart Retire Happy*, describes lessons for retirement. They are as follows:

1. Prepare for Adventure and Surprise.

2. Learn Optimism.

3. Get Involved, Stay Involved.

4. Keep Dreaming of "My Time."

5. Balance Your Psychological Portfolio.

6. Seize Opportunities.

7. Acknowledge Your Emotions.

8. Go With the Flow, Don't Fight the Undertow.

9. Plan A—Always Have a Plan B.

10. A Plan for Everyone.

Retirement is one of the transitions that occur at this stage and, due to the societal importance of occupation/career, retirement can become a period of upheaval and stress in a person's life. However, because people react very differently to the issue of retirement, career counseling must take on a more individualized approach that meets the needs of each individual rather than retirees as a whole. With structured counseling, retirement can become a positive transition in a person's life.

Krain (1995) recognizes the loss of boundaries when looking at the transition from work to retirement. He suggests that education needs to continue as well as some involvement in work and leisure activities. He gives the following social policy objectives to facilitate changes and alleviate problems for older people:

1. Distribute the available work to as many as possible

2. Extend income to those out of work

3. Extend work life of older workers

4. Redesign education to be directed as much to adults and the elderly as to youth and children

5. Base retirement decisions on the assessment of worker fitness

6. Reform the private pension system

7. Popularize appropriate models of successful integration of education, work, and leisure.

In an annual review of vocational behavior research, Brown, Fukunaga, Umemoto, and Wicker (1996) looked at issues of social class and retirement. Individuals with higher income and education tend to engage in activities that involve travel and reading, whereas those of lower income and education tend to be involved more in arts and crafts hobbies and watching television. Lower-income people tend to live in mobile homes, higher-income people in planned communities with more elaborate homes and social and sports amenities. Adjustment to retirement appears to be affected by previous occupational status, education, and income. Lower-income people tend to retire earlier and for different reasons than those of higher-income people. Carter and Cook (1995) studied the influence of social and work roles on retirement adjustment. They developed a model to demonstrate their results, as seen in Figure 11.6.

Those individuals who do not derive their major source of identity from the work role have "low work role attachment" (p. 72). For many retirees, nonwork roles become more important than work roles. If one has a strong work ethic and her/his personal identity and worth has been attached to a job, then leaving a job may bring feelings of deprivation that can lead to dissatisfaction in retirement. "Leaving the workforce may involve role redefinition or expansion. The success of role redefinition may be determined by one's social roles, work roles, and the internal resources needed to negotiate role changes" (p. 79). Jensen-Scott (1993) developed a list of tasks for dissatisfied retirees and offered suggestions for interventions to aid them. These are given in Table 11.1.

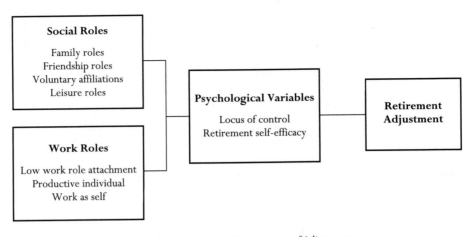

FIGURE 11.6 Roles and Psychological Resources as Determinants of Adjustment

SOURCE: *Carter & Cook (1995), p. 73.*

TABLE 11.1 Possible Tasks of Dissatisfied Retirees and Suggested Interventions

CLIENT'S DISSATISFACTION	TASK	INTERVENTION
Difficulty with change	Adjustment to change	Exploring feelings about retirement, meaning of job and retirement, function of job, and perspectives on aging Provide information
Job is low in hierarchy	Provision of information	Provide information
Job is moderately high or low in hierarchy	Reorder the hierarchy	Values clarification Self-esteem building Decision-making skills Considerations of lifestyle options Communication skills building Provide information
Job is high in hierarchy and job-related goals are met	Reorder the hierarchy	See previous suggestions
Job is high in hierarchy and job-related goals are not met	Acquisition of job or substitute	Explore interests, abilities Research job market Consider volunteer opportunities Provide information
Job is high in hierarchy and goals are not met and unable to obtain job	Reorder the hierarchy	See previous suggestion

SOURCE: Jensen-Scott, (1993), p. 262.

Practical Applications

Jensen-Scott (1993) cautions vocational practitioners to be aware of the specific needs of retirees. First, they are difficult to reach, and the counselor needs to go where they are because most mental health services are underused by older adults. Second, they are more hesitant to develop a counseling relationship for any problem. Third, there are few assessment instruments developed for older adults seeking vocational counseling. Fourth, there is a lack of job and volunteer opportunities for retirees.

For many individuals, part-time employment is a positive option if they find retirement activities to be unsatisfying. Simon and Osipow (1996) offer a description of a counseling technique for older workers as they approach retirement. Using vocational scripts and life reviews, they propose that the process uses three distinct tasks to develop a way to prepare for meaningful retirement. "The first entails helping people define the connections among their various life events and personality changes" (p. 159). A second task "encourages people to define their work experiences as a career" (p. 159), devel-

oping themes, areas of expertise and preferred activities, rewards, both inner and outer, and responses to these ideas. The third task focuses on the future, with emphasis on "perseverance and developing autonomy within roles and relationships" (p. 160). Vocational practitioners can be involved as "good coaches, explaining modeling, encouraging, and reinforcing development of the career definition into a vocational script" (p. 160).

Finding the balance between work and leisure and how to live productive retirement years is a further area for research. The life planning/career path throughout adulthood rarely follows a straight path. There are many turns in the road, adaptations that need to be made, and flexibility, which is the hallmark of resiliency. With the technological advances that have been made, information about jobs and careers is readily accessible. Vocational practitioners who provide comprehensive services to help older clients to read the road maps that unfold will play an increasingly important role in their lives.

Resources

The American Association for Retired Persons (AARP) provides information about employment topics for older adults. One such item is a list of the top 50 companies in the U.S. for older adults to find work. Information can be obtained through http://www.research.aarp.org. Additional information on working with older adults on employment issues (AARP, 2003) includes:

LaBauve, B. J. & Robinson, C. R. (1999). Breaking the Stereotypes of Older Adults Online. *The Older Wiser Wired*. Available at http://www.org/olderwiserwired/Articles/a2003-02-20-oww-barriers.html.

Land, D. (2003). Adjusting to Retirement: Considerations for Counselors. *ADULTSPAN Journal*, 1, 2–12.

McKeon, M. C. (2002). *Career Targeting and Transition*. Media, PA: Delaware County Community College. Available at http://www.boomercareer.com.

The Older Worker. Myths and Realities, No. 18. Ohio State University Center on Education and Training for Employment. Available at http://ericacve.org/fulltext.asp; http://www.fiveoclockclub.com/about_frame.html; http://www.2young2retire.com/default.html.

Parker, D. (2003). *The Aging Work-Force,* Parts 1–3. UI News Wisconsin: Heartland Cobalt Corporation. Available at http://www.heartland.cobaltcorporation.com/pdf/2001-4%20.pdf; http://www.heartland.cobaltcorporation.com/pdf/2002-1.pdf; http://www.heartland.cobaltcorporation.com/pdf/2002-q2.pdf.

Pouncey, M. (2003). *Age Discrimination is Killing High Tech. Seniors Aging Well, Wisely and Successful*. Available at: http://www.go60.com/age-discrimination-high-tech.html.

Stein, D. & Rocco, T. S. (2003). The best companies for older workers. *AARP The magazine Online*. Available: http://aarpmagazine.org.

These are some recommended Web sites for further exploration.

2 Young 2 Retire	http://www.2young2retire.com
AARP	http://www.aarp.org
Administration on Aging	http://www.aoa.dhhs.gov
EDD Senior Worker Advocate Office	http://www.edd.cahwnet.gov/swaoind.htm
Experience Works	http://www.experienceworks.org
Healing Place	http://www.ahealingplace.org/spirit_work
Maturity Works (Nat'l Council or Aging)	http://www.maturityworks.org
My Generation	http://www.mygeneration.org
SeniorNet	http://www.seniornet.org
SPRY Foundation	http://www.spry.org
Third Age	http://www.thirdage.com

McDaniels Combines Work and Leisure After thirty years of studying the work/leisure relationship, McDaniels has devised the concept that Career = Work + Leisure for the following reasons:

1. Combining Work and Leisure is More Holistic.
2. Combining Work and Leisure is Life Span Oriented.
3. Combining Work and Leisure is Future Oriented.
4. Combining Work and Leisure is Ever Present. (McDaniels, 1996, pp. 53–54).

This completes our survey of career development counseling, models, programs, assessments, and resources across the lifespan. Ideally, the vocational practitioner should be able to focus on the unique differences between age groups, and make appropriate interventions and vocational strategies for each. The complexity of these developmental needs require that the practitioner be able to meet the challenges and changes as the world evolves.

We now turn to look at the potential for the future.

Epilogue

❖

Pulling It All Together
for the Future

"MAMAS, DON'T LET YOUR BABIES GROW UP TO BE CPA'S"
Job growth and job skills are increasing concerns of our . . .political and business
leaders. Herewith some food for thought. The arts, humanities and allied fields
will be the brightest sectors of the next century's economy, and the only fields to
see sustainable job growth. Here's why: As technology has improved productivity,
fewer and fewer people have been needed for the routine labor of assembling and
distributing industrial products, food, clothing and shelter. That trend will
continue. . . . We're accustomed to regarding progress as synonymous with
increasingly rational ways of making, distributing, organizing and knowing.
But we are entering an era in which progress will be gauged by derationalization,
a time in which peculiarly human, imaginative, ruminative, unstandardizable
pursuits and products weigh ever heavier in the economy, because those things are
what people want. I mean that both labor and leisure, for so long confined in the
starched uniform of rationalization, will increasingly depend on the creative
abilities of more and more people, and less on by-the-book skills or drudge labor.
Creative work will be more widely dispersed through the workforce. We will
require imaginative labor from architects, from line technicians, as well as the
director of product development. But the future of the economy will see the
biggest growth in demand for artists, designers, musicians and dancers, for
philosophers and historians and poets. Our physical needs can be met by fewer
and fewer people. But the mind has an infinite thirst for wonder and delight, for
beauty and provocation, for questioning and stimulation, Wow! and Aha!
—Greenberg, 1997

As Greenberg says, creative activities and technology will be hallmarks of the twenty-first century. How these help us meet our intellectual, spiritual, and esthetic needs—whether through labor or leisure—is vital to how we will live in this changing world. We begin this chapter with an overview of the influences shaping the twenty-first century, especially as it relates to the role of work in people's lives. Second, we address cultural diversity and postmodernism in vocational psychology. Third, we argue for a rethinking of the role of work in people's lives to include a balance of training, work, and leisure. Fourth, we cite the changing role of the vocational practitioner and the applied skills that will be required.

Finally, we dare to project what occupational guidance will be like in the year 2015.

INFLUENCES SHAPING THE TWENTY-FIRST CENTURY

Future Influential Trends

Herman, Olivo, and Gioia (2003) observe the following influencing trends for the world of work.

1. *Job Movement Condoned* Job tenure has plummeted from 4.6 years in 1990, to 3.5 years in 2000, as it is acceptable to shop around for better jobs.

2. *Change in Employer-Employee Relationship* The employee now has influence over his or her job due to the growing options of employment.

3. *Employee Attitudes* Many employees today do not feel that they can trust management or supervisors.

4. *Manager Attitudes* Many managers cling to the old notion that employees work *for you* and not *with you*. As the work environment changes, managers are forced increasingly to work with employees.

5. *Mercenary Darwinism* Many employers believe that they can solve vacancy problems by increasing new employee bonuses, which can result in employees that only care for the salary and have little loyalty to the company.

6. *Employee Value Shifts* For many employees, especially Generation X, questions arise: Is it worth it? They want more time with their families, control over their career path, and life-work balance.

7. *Increase in Telecommuting/Self-Management* Known as *infotechies*, these remote workers can be located anywhere in the world.

8. *Importance of Human Resources* This part of the company will be vital to offset turnovers and vacancies in the future employee shortage.

9. *Personnel Strength* Employers will need to retain the most productive and skilled employees and let go of the dead wood.

10. *Globalization* As companies go global, expect more outsourcing as the global labor pool expands.

11. *Age Factors* As younger people enter the workforce, older employees will need to adjust to different generational values.

12. *Older Workers Not Retiring* Older workers are remaining in the workforce longer because of personal values and the need to be productive. Their own need to generate sufficient income to live into older age will drive them to work longer.

13. *A Faster World* "Information overload increases the difficulty in separating the important from the urgent" (p. 79).

14. *Technology* With increased technology, many jobs that can be done more efficiently by machine will disappear, requiring workers to adapt by increasing technical skills.

15. *Rise of Women* Women are assuming stronger roles in business in large part because of their special ability to be nurturing and to provide supportive leadership.

16. *Children: Parents' Greatest Challenge* Need for adequate child care and family structural strength will be of increasing importance and concern for employers, especially for dual-income families.

17. *Inadequacy of Education* Increasingly, colleges and universities are not preparing students with all the skills needed for the workforce. Closer relationships between schools, the community, corporations, and corporate leaders will need to be established.

18. *Immigration* Applications for U.S. citizenship increased by 121 percent from May 2001 to May 2002. This picture, however, may be not hold because of more restrictive immigration rules, concern about safety in the United States, and better living conditions in the country of origin (Herman, Olivo, & Gioia, 2003, pp. 57–89).

The scope of the various influences as presented above is potentially staggering in its implications. There will be few areas in our lives that will be untouched by these changes.

There are also two other major forces affecting our work and how we do it. The first is that one important outcome of the global economy will be increased outsourcing and immigration to fill the need for skilled labor and meet cost demands. White collar, skilled jobs will migrate overseas as companies search for cheaper labor. Already this is being seen in the tech industry as white collar jobs such as programmers and tech support are moved to India. Forrester Research expects 3.3 million service jobs to move off shore within 15 years (Stone, 2003).

The second is that rapid advances in microelectronic technology have put information service into products and distribution, such as e-commerce and e-business.

> ## CASE EXAMPLE
> ### The Case of the "Missing" Computers
>
> In an urban high school in a low-income district, a newly hired career technology teacher asked school administrators about the availability of computers for use in his classes. He was told there was a large room filled with computers no one had used. It turned out that most of the teachers did not know these were available, and no one had been trained to teach the faculty how to use them. How could their disadvantaged students have much opportunity to become competent for the world they are going to face later?

Laptops, fax machines, cellular phones, networks, e-mail, and voice mail are making **telecommuting** a way of doing business that satisfies the strategic goals of spending more time with customers and using commute time better. One example is the expected rise in the numbers of those with disabilities using telecommuting. Douglas Kruse, professor of human resource management at Rutgers University, estimates that in 1997 4.1 percent of employed people with disabilities worked twenty hours or more a week from home, 7 percent do currently, and in ten years at least 10 percent will (Tahmincioglu, 2003).

Our major concern about these fast-paced technology advances is with schools and families that do not have access to the tools of technology. Even though there have been impressive attempts to remedy this problem in schools, our observations and experience suggest that career counselors will need to be aware of training programs that can remedy persistent gaps in opportunity.

RETHINKING JOBS AND WORK

Unwanted and unexpected change can be a debilitating experience for many people. When a person loses a job, he or she is forced into a situation in which they must find something new. It may not seem like it at the time, but job loss can bring about positive changes because it forces a person into a new and possibly more fulfilling situation. Many people who have gone through losing their jobs have discovered that there is "life after work." The greater the repertoire of work-related skills a person has, the greater the likelihood of rejuvenating a career in the marketplace.

As the necessary skills change for most jobs, there will be people left unemployed and/or underemployed. The global changes that are now impacting the workforce increase the need for vocational practitioners who are knowledgeable about the different types of unemployed and the emotional effects of unemployment on the individual and the family unit. The skills to deal with both personal and career issues are needed by career counselors.

Warren Bennis, a professor at USC, claims that an employee will be forced to keep learning in order to remain competitive. "The half life of any particular skill set is, at most, five years. And that's on the long side. What will keep you alive? Be curious, be willing to learn, have a moral compass and know what gives your life meaning" (*Newsweek Online Forum*, 2003, April).

"The civilian labor force is projected to increase by 17 million over the 2000–2010 period, reaching 158 million in 2010." In 2010, it is estimated that there will be a skilled labor shortage of approximately 10 million (Bureau of Labor Statistics, 2001). This labor shortage will be caused by a competency deficit, baby boomers retiring, and rapidly evolving technology (Herman et al., 2003).

Another concern we have deals with employee benefits. Medical plans in which individuals can participate when working as an independent contractor are a crucial issue that needs to be addressed. Vocational psychology will also need to learn how to assist individuals in pre-retirement and retirement planning as aging baby boomers create more elderly people than ever before.

Technology and Its Impact on Job Security

The workplace of today requires one to be literate in technology in order to remain employed. Brainpower is replacing manual labor as technical advancements change the nature of jobs in the United States. Future workers must continually educate themselves and increase their skills in order to maintain their value in the workplace.

Workforce Training in the Twenty-First Century

E-learning means "diverse learning strategies and technologies from CD-ROMs and computer-based instruction to video conferencing, satellite delivered learning and virtual education networks" (Pantazis, 2002, p.22). When done well, e-learning can provide an economical way to provide training for employees before and while on the job. Various companies provide this type of training. An example is General Motors University Online, where "employees can create individual development plans, track their individual training histories, and Web-based tools to align their training with development plans in 16 functional areas of the company" (p. 24). The money purportedly saved or earned by the company is impressive.

Pantazis (2002) refers to a collaboration between the U.S. Department of Defense's Advanced Distribute Learning Initiative and other government, academic, and private sector groups on working toward the development of an online learning basic archi-

---

CASE EXAMPLE

Keeping a Job in a Downsizing World

A friend called to say her employer, a major insurance company, had just experienced its third downsizing in three years. Before, there had been a warning. This time, her unit of thirty employees was summoned to a meeting and informed that they needed to eliminate half of the staff. Those eliminated would be given the option of providing the work they had been doing on an outsource basis. She was one of the people who stayed on the job, but she was given the responsibility for managing these outsourcing operations. She had no experience with outsourcing, but because she had kept her skills updated, had been able to adapt them to new situations, and had taken a leadership role at critical times, she was chosen for the job. Her experience highlights the need for flexibility and leadership on the part of those who want to remain valued employees.

---

tecture. To guarantee success, organizations must maintain some flexibility to learn new skills and find ways to manage knowledge and information. It can further aid in lessening "skills and income gaps by expanding just-in-time access to high-quality training opportunities" (p. 22).

James Canton (1999), president of the Institute for Global Futures, identifies the top ten business technology trends for the twenty-first century.

1. Managing the convergence of twenty-first century power tools, such as computers, networks, biotech, and nanotech.

2. Shaping customer relationships and enhancing customer satisfaction through the use of technology innovation will be critical for every business enterprise.

3. Every business that wants to survive in the future must learn to evolve into an e-business.

4. The convergence of television, computer, Net, and telephone will result in new business models, markets, and electronic channels that will revolutionize business.

5. The social impact of leading edge technology on a longer-living, digitally savvy, globally connected marketplace will provide many new opportunities.

6. Real-time agility—how fast an enterprise can embrace leading edge technology—will determine the efficiency, speed, and cost-effectiveness of its operations.

7. High-performance education about leading edge technological solutions will become a central strategy for all companies.

8. Managing rapidly emerging technological change within an organization will be one of the central capabilities for everyone across the enterprise.

9. Technology-enabled products and services that incorporate deep customer contact, on demand choices, and intuitive interactions will drive business success.

10. Learning to celebrate technology innovation, risk taking, and out-of-the-box thinking will be critical for the twenty-first century business enterprise (pp. 17–18).

The emphasis by the various experts cited clearly points out the necessity of participating in the world of technology as a major tool in the practice of education, business and commerce, and communication. The need to develop full competency can be seen in the job outlook for the future.

JOB OUTLOOK IN THE TWENTY-FIRST CENTURY

Statistical Projections

According to the Bureau of Labor Statistics (2004), professional and related occupations are projected to add over 6.5 million jobs, or 23 percent more, while service occupations are expected to add 5.3 million jobs, or 20 percent more. Within these groups computer and mathematical operations and healthcare support services are each projected to have an impressive 34 percent increase in jobs. On the other hand, production operations and office and administrative support occupations are expected to add only three percent more jobs.

IT and Technology

The projected job growth reflects the development of technology and its impact on occupations. The pervasive use of computer and mathematical operations across the spectrum of work, whether business, manufacturing, sales, education, government, office and administrative areas, or management emphasizes the need for competent people for positions in these areas. E-learning, e-commerce, robotic procedures, and medical advances involve IT.

However, even the field of information technology is not immune to the effects of globalization. The Information Technology Association of America (ITAA) predicted that the hiring of IT workers would lessen in 2004 and later because of cheaper labor overseas (ITAA, 2003).

The globalization of work, the change in practice of producing goods only as quickly as are needed by retail outlets, and technical advances in production have all worked to reduce the growth of jobs in manufacturing. This leads to increased imports and fewer new jobs, as well as the loss of established jobs. E-commerce—"the business of buying, selling, or conducting other transactions via the Internet" (Future-work, 2000, p. 33)—has a profound impact on retail businesses, and its effects can already be seen in the travel industry.

Technology to diagnose and understand physical ills, the ability to cure or repair medical problems—thereby extending life—and the aging of the population are major reasons for the projected addition of health care workers. Advances help "people recover completely from ailments and injuries that decades ago would have been fatal or permanently disabling" (p. 31).

Many families now have two working adults, and with the changes in welfare laws, more single parents are working. This level of work is both possible and necessary because of the technological advances in managing houses. A consequence of this change is an increase in child care workers as well.

According to Friedman (1996), the economic world is changing rapidly into three distinct economies:

1. The *Networked*—"consists of densely packed concentrations of entrepreneurs and companies in urbanized areas that generate virtually all the nation's globally competitive, high-wage industries" (p. 52).

2. The *Kluge*—consists of "the concentration of public-sector bureaucracies, universities, and closely aligned private companies in government related industries like utilities or defense—exists virtually side by side with the networked economy" (p. 52).

3. The *Provincial*—"self-consciously styles itself as a more moral, less 'Klugey' alternative for Networked businesses and is driven by the deployment of less competitive business and offers America a 19th century answer for twenty-first century competition" (p. 54).

Kluge is a slang term used by computer programmers to describe a "code that is an ill-assorted collection of poorly matching parts, forming a distressing whole" (p. 52). The Kluge is the least productive of the three economies. The combination of the Kluge and Networked economies account for 50 million jobs, "of which 15% to 18% are directly accounted for by the government" (pp. 52–53).

With this type of global thinking as a background, we want to provide the culmination of the perspective we have attempted to build in this book. This final chapter deals with the convergence of thinking that appears to be shaping the events of the next few years. We began our text with a call for a transformation of vocational psychology to keep pace with the often painful and always profound shifts in the role of work in people's lives. Part of this transformation concerns future trends. Until now, the relevance of vocational psychology for women, racial and ethnic groups, people with disabilities, gay/lesbian/bisexual people, lower-income groups, the permanent underclass, and international populations has been limited at best. In the twenty-first century, primary attention needs to be given to diversity issues.

CULTURAL DIVERSITY AND POSTMODERNISM

Cultural Diversity

In the United States, it behooves us to take advantage of the diversity of our population to remain competitive in the global marketplace, for economic motives if not for moral reasons. Sometimes the urgency of this issue appears to escape people in a position to make a difference. White males are making up less of the increase in the workforce. While still dominant in the workplace, they are now a statistical minority —in 1990, racial and ethnic minorities, women, and immigrants were already more than 50 percent of the workforce. The challenge for the future will be to maximize the potential of women, minorities, and immigrants, which will require an increase in supervisors' abilities to manage diversity so that all kinds of people—including White males—can contribute to workplace productivity.

In a workplace where competence will matter more than ever before, Thomas (1990) suggests ten ways in which individual differences should be not merely tolerated, but celebrated:

1. *Clarifying motivations.* Legal compliance, community relations, fulfilling social and moral responsibilities, placating an internal group, or pacifying an outside organization are usually good reasons for learning to manage diversity. From a strictly business perspective, the long-term motivation will be sustained only if learning to manage diversity makes a workplace more competitive. And most workplaces are already diverse or soon will be.

2. *Clarifying vision.* If management conveys the attitude that the human resource potential of every member of the workplace is going to be tapped, the White male culture is more likely to give way to respecting differences and individuality and less likely to cling to a vision—consciously or unconsciously —that leaves them in the driver's seat.

3. *Expanding focus.* With an overall objective of creating a dominant heterogeneous culture, this minimizes the traditional affirmative action pattern that required the structural assimilation of women, minorities, and immigrants into a dominant White-male culture workplace.

4. *Auditing workplace culture.* This is often impossible to do without outside help because of hidden rules, unspoken assumptions, unexamined values, and unfounded mythologies that will have created a workplace culture in the first place. Likening workplace culture to a kind of tree, where roots are assumptions about both the workplace and the world, and where branches, leaves, and seeds are behavior, the leaves will not be changed without changing the roots. Nor will peaches grow on an oak tree. Thus, if one wants to grow peaches, then the tree's roots have to be peach-friendly. (Gibson and Billings [2003] provide a useful, engaging narrative on how their consultative guidance helped change the workplace culture at Best Buy.)

5. *Modifying assumptions.* The work culture tree has root guards that turn out in full force whenever a basic assumption is threatened. The challenge is to define belonging "in terms of a set of values and a sense of purpose that transcend the interests, desires, and preferences of any one group" (Thomas, 1990, p. 116).

6. *Modifying systems.* Performance appraisals, promotions, and mentoring are among such systems. For example, the unexamined practices and patterns of performance appraisal have had pernicious effects on women and minorities in the past. Accurate performance feedback often came through the grapevine and differed substantially from official performance appraisals, which made it difficult for women and minorities to correct or defend their alleged shortcomings. In many work sites, obtaining promotion has often required a personal advocate, yet mentors have historically been unwilling to sponsor people too much unlike themselves.

7. *Modifying models.* Most often, this means allowing employees to do the job they have been hired to do, with supervisors supporting and empowering their subordinates.

8. *Helping employees pioneer.* With no one tried-and-true solution to diversity management, this means there are also multiple barriers that face any workplace and that supervisors and employees who travel uncharted territory will be judged as pioneers and will make mistakes.

9. *Applying the special consideration test.* This can be answered by one question: "Does this program, policy, or principle give special consideration to one group?" (Thomas, 1990, p. 117). If the answer is yes, a given workplace is not on the road to managing diversity.

10. *Continuing affirmative action.* Affirmative action is vital for creating and maintaining a diverse workplace. Yet, affirmative action does not address root causes such as prejudice and inequality and does little to maximize the potential contributions of each woman and man in the workplace. Therefore, the goal of diversity management is to increase the capacity to accept, incorporate, develop, and empower the multiple human talents that make the United States the most diverse nation on the earth.

Thomas (1990) concluded his analysis by pointing out that diversity is our reality, and it needs to become our strength. What Thomas wrote a good 15-plus years ago *still* holds true today. This means that vocational psychology will have to admit just how much it is a sociopolitical activity, with interfaces "between personal and societal needs, between individual aspirations and opportunity structures, between private and public identities" (Watts, 1996, p. 229).

We appreciate Thomas's (1990) conciliatory and practical tone. But affirming diversity threatens the vested interests of many White males. For years—if not generations—entrenched White males have occupied positions of authority without possessing the requisite talents and abilities to exercise the power their jobs allow. The future vocational counseling needs of those who are not White males cannot be swept under the carpet. We limit our discussion here to three diverse populations: women and children; gays, lesbians, and bisexuals; and people with disabilities.

Women and Children The late Bella Abzug, former member of Congress and founder of the Women's Environment and Development Organization, summarized the plight of women worldwide as the twentieth century came to a close:

> [By 2005] more than half the world's population will live in cities, including millions who will swell "megacities," those with populations of more than 10 million. Those cities and megacities create problems, and those problems will hurt women more than others, because 70 percent of the world's 1.3 billion poorest people are female.
>
> [As of 1996,] women account for only 10 percent of legislators worldwide, a pittance of mayors and only 1 percent of executives in corporate and financial board rooms. . . . According to a [United Nations] estimate, women perform about 60 percent of the world's work but earn just 1 percent of the world's income.
>
> Women and girls migrating to the cities are particularly vulnerable to economic exploitation and hazardous working conditions. Some of the worst offenders are multinational firms whose overseas operations don't comply with U.S. laws (Abzug, 1996, p. 8A).

Abzug added, "Women need political power to fight poverty and inequality" (p. 8A).

It remains to be seen if vocational psychology can articulate a global perspective on the role of work in women's lives. Certainly, the universality of knowledge claims about occupational development derived from scientific objectivity have yet to be extensively confirmed in international research populations, be they women or men. New paradigms and a multidisciplinary approach could enact a metamorphosis in the way women's work lives are understood.

The question is whether scholars and researchers can rise to the occasion and provide practical applications for intervening in women's and girls' occupational development on an international scale (see also Mays, Rubin, Sabourin, & Walker, 1996). A reconceptualization of the discipline of vocational psychology will have to occur before global relevance can happen. Until such time, only a minuscule portion of women's—much less men's—occupational development will be explained through the persistent use of largely American research participants, which we believe is an unbecoming, insular worldview. While we do not believe that a White upper-class, intellectualized brand of feminism is appropriate for conceptualizing the occupational development of all women, we do believe in giving full "value [to] the female voice" (Myss, 1996, p. 108).

Consequently, vocational psychology will have to continue to become less androcentric in the twenty-first century before discussions of theoretical convergence can

FIGURE E.1 Photograph of Angie Elizabeth Hernández at Age 6,
Child Laborer (Street Juggler/Clown) in Mexico City

be anything more than an academic exercise. Likewise, classism in vocational psychology will be reduced when greater attention is given to populations who have no choice but to work from an early age. Figure E.1 is a photograph of six-year-old Angie Elizabeth Hernández, a little girl in present-day Mexico City. She is the member of a family where everyone works to earn a living. Her weekend job is to be dressed as a clown who entertains motorists at a stoplight with a juggling act. "Out of half-opened windows hands offer small coins before the traffic starts up. An average day brings about ten dollars" (Parfit, 1996, p. 43). In the background are Angie Elizabeth's mother Gabriela, baby sister Sara Nayeli, and uncle José. "'Necessity taught us how to entertain people this way,'" explains Gabriela (p. 43).

Girls as child laborers are nothing new. However, vocational psychology has virtually ignored this phenomenon. For example, the sexploitation of girls as young as eight is an international industry that generates $5 billion a year internationally (Abzug, 1996) and has been called "the underside of the global economy that is rarely seen" (New York Times News Service, 1996, p. 12A).

More recently, Cockburn (2003) reports that nearly 27 million people worldwide live in slavery, having been bought and sold, held captive and brutalized, and exploited for profit. Nearly two-thirds of the world's captive laborers—15 to 20 million people—are debt slaves in India, Pakistan, Bangladesh, and Nepal. Most of these slaves accrued their impossible-to-repay debts to pay for medical care or funerals. Slave labor contributes an estimated $13 billion annually to the global economy.

Perhaps vocational theorists in the twenty-first century will deem it worthwhile to examine of the influence of post-colonialism (which we discussed in Chapter 5) and its by-products, including debt slavery, on the global economy. Research methods that would further clarify the role of work in women and children's lives are discussed below in the section on postmodernism.

Gays, Lesbians, and Bisexual People   Gays/lesbians have had increasing acceptance and gay/lesbian issues have had increasing public attention in this new millennium. In 2000, 56 percent of Americans reported having a gay friend or acquaintance (Gigloff, 2003). Then gays and lesbians took the spotlight in June 2003 when the Supreme Court overturned a Texas antisodomy law and "effectively legalized homosexuality." Shortly thereafter, gay/lesbian issues again were in the media forefront as the Episcopal Church elected its first openly gay bishop.

Fassinger (1995) feels the need for more adequate, less pathologizing models of sexual identity development. He writes

> none of the existing [sexual] identity development models sufficiently take
> environmental context into account. Perhaps because lesbian and gay identity
> theories are built (implicitly or explicitly) on early work in the development of
> Black racial and political consciousness, the models tend to imply that fully
> integrated and mature identity necessitates full public disclosure and political
> activism. Such a stance ignores the cultural location, life choices, and environ-
> mental constraints of lesbians and gay men diverse in age, historical context,
> geographic location, race and ethnicity, class, religion, and other forms of de-
> mographic diversity that exert a profound impact on the identity development
> process. Resultant models are thus subtly homophobic in their common view
> of nonpublic, nonpoliticized behavior as developmental arrest, in that they
> blame the victim for her or his own inability to come to terms with an op-
> pressed identity (p. 152).

In addition, Fassinger notes "relatively little empirical research [on] actual counseling interventions . . . related to vocational concerns . . . [of lesbians and gays]" (p. 164). Sexual identity concerns are inextricably bound with occupational development, and traditional vocational assessment may be of little value.

Broadly speaking, Prince (1995) notes that "current theories of men's career development ignore altogether the impact of sexual-identity formation as a moderating variable and offer little guidance for understanding such influences" (p. 170). In reference to gay men, "career development theory is equally lacking in its attention to [both the early career development and] the later career development stages of gay men" (p. 172). Other unanswered research questions include how stages of relationship development influence gay men's career development and overall psychological adjustment on career choice.

Empirical research on the career decision-making of gay, lesbian, and bisexual people is still lacking (Chung, 1995). Nor have adherence to traditional work values "(e.g., achievement, status, stability)" (p. 182) or the relation between sex role socialization and the development of vocational skills been explored.

"There is not a body of empirical research of sufficient breadth and depth to identify which practices are most important and effective [with gay and lesbian clients]" (Pope, 1995, p. 191). A review of fifteen articles published between 1940 and 1994 on recommended career counseling interventions for gays and lesbians revealed the following three themes. First, counselors were encouraged to focus on themselves. Included here were counselors' learning about sexual identity development, examining their own biases, using special assessment procedures, and affirming the gay/lesbian/bisexual lifestyle. Second, specific counseling activities were mentioned. These included "openly discussing coming out in the workplace, openly discussing employment discrimination, working with both individuals in the couple on dual-career couple issues, and helping clients overcome internalized negative stereotypes" (Pope, 1995, p. 201). Third, interventions were directed at social-community action. Included here were practitioners "supporting and encouraging gay and lesbian professionals as role models" (p. 201). The author of the article concludes by stating, "Much research remains to be done on the types of special career counseling interventions that are empirically justified for lesbian and gay populations" (p. 202). As we stated in Chapter 5, queer theory has yet to be incorporated into conceptualizations of career development.

People with Disabilities Like women and children and like gay, lesbian, and bisexual people, those with disabilities do not fit traditional, androcentric models of career development. Stodden (1998) suggests five ways that people with disabilities can be better served in their occupational development needs. There is a need to

1. ...[coordinate] education and work preparation programs and services implemented under a unified vision and purpose.... Currently, policy, legislation, and funding streams for special programs within education, transition, work preparation, rehabilitation, and special education are separate and autonomous, and often have conflicting purposes and overlapping initiatives.

2. ...build consensus concerning use of the term 'all' when referring to the participation of children and youth with special needs in education and training programs.

3. ...refocus resources and program agendas from an arena of dependency (i.e., welfare, social work, social services) to the arena of independence ... (i.e., improved education and training programs) ...

4. . . . focus on student results from, and satisfaction with, participation in education and training programs.

5. . . . capture excellent practices and supports that have been generated through . . . separate needs programs and the transition initiative to ensure that such practices . . . improve general education curriculum sequences and generic work preparation programs (pp. 74–75).

People with disabilities, like women and children and like gay, lesbian, and bisexual people, can benefit immensely by increased attention from vocational psychology. Postmodern approaches to work are one means of attending to these populations.

Postmodernism and the Technologies of Social Saturation

Neimeyer (1995) upholds the narrative viability of multiple perspectives espoused by postmodernism:

> nearly any model of psychotherapy can be a legitimate resource for the post-modern practitioner, as long as it is interpreted as a historically and culturally bounded set of provisional metaphors and guidelines rather than as an applied science that compels only a certain conceptualization of the problem and only a single approved form of intervention (p. 16).

Postmodern approaches to work offer some exciting and innovative ways for clinical practitioners to consult with clients regarding work-related issues in clinical practice—provided such approaches are used in a scrupulous manner and not as a cover for deceit and dishonesty. Experience has taught us that social constructionism is hardly immune to misrepresentations of reality and halftruths.

It will be recalled that modernism's lineage is based on logical positivism, a twentieth-century philosophical movement that asserts that all knowledge can be discovered through use of the scientific method. The use of observation and experiment (i.e., empiricism) are respected as the only valid means for adding to the knowledge base. Reality is held to be objective in nature and awaiting to be discovered, hence the use of the term scientific objectivity. Furthermore, objective reality is presumed to exist independently of a person and must be detected by the person in order to be known (Burr, 1995). In other words, rules or structures are presumed to already exist and merely await detection. From a modernist perspective, these *hidden structures* can be discovered through the use of reason and rationality.

Postmodernism's rejection of the tradition that the real world has underlying rules and hidden structures is also known as **poststructuralism** (Burr, 1995). Thus, postmodern architecture can seem to disregard all the conventional wisdom that make for a good building design. Postmodern art repudiates the idea that pop art is any less equal to the works of the great masters. In the field of literary criticism, the postmodern perspective is reflected in the assertion that there cannot be a *true* reading of a novel or poem, that each reader's interpretation of a piece of literature was equally valid, and that the original author's intended meaning cannot be discerned. From a cultural standpoint, postmodernism becomes evident in the rise of multiculturalism and diversity (González, 1994, 1997, 1998).

Limitations and Strengths of Postmodernism in Vocational Practice

The shortcomings and promises of postmodernism in vocational practice cannot be examined without first addressing postmodernism in the social sciences. Postmodernism in the social sciences can take on either an extreme or moderate tone (Rosenau, 1992).

To us, extreme postmodernism appears like preposterous nihilism lacking any sort of coherence that fails to offer any useful alternatives to that which it deconstructs. Extreme postmodernists strain their credibility, undermine their integrity, and can end up resembling members of a lunatic fringe with their self-contradictory claims that all perspectives are valid. In our view, moderate postmodernism resists "throwing the baby out with the bath water," but allows the baby to have several different bubble baths from which to choose. Moderate postmodernism is more likely to include modernism as one broadly agreed upon view while also allowing for originality and creativity in devising solutions to problems.

For postmodernism to remain viable in the social sciences, extreme postmodernists will have to be vigilant about positioning themselves into ideological apartheid. Extreme postmodernists can become too hobbled by their own language to be able to exercise the spirit of reconceptualizations about how we explain and experience the world around us (Minuchin, 1991). Rosenau (1992) states that part of the problem is that some postmodernists "do not extend themselves to use words precisely" (p. 178). She points out seven contradictions within postmodernism.

Some postmodern deconstructions of modern science appear unsubstantiated. Science never presumed to include mystical, spiritual, and metaphysical dimensions of human existence, yet is deconstructed in part for not having done so. When modern science is deconstructed in part for not providing adequate guidance for the purposes to which scientific knowledge should be put, the existence and purpose of bioethics is ignored. When science is deconstructed in part for posing as the only legitimate truth, there is a disregard for modern scientists who staunchly adhere to "the *probability* of verifying, not so much as discovering, knowledge or truth" (Earl Jennings, personal communication, February 28, 1995, italics added).

Verification instead of discovery via quantitative methods has a moderate postmodern spirit. *Both* quantitative *and* qualitative approaches may benefit the social sciences (see Light & Pillemer, 1982; Polkinghorne, 1984, 1991; Reichardt & Cook, 1979, for discussions on moving beyond the either/or dichotomy).

The complete exclusion of one research method in favor of the other is inconsistent with postmodernists' claims to respecting multiple views. Nevertheless, extremists who use postmodernism as a cover for antimodernism risk deconstructing themselves and/or dismissal by others.

The contradictions of postmodern approaches to clinical practice have been soundly criticized. Minuchin (1991) challenges postmodern therapists who deny the legitimacy of their own clinical expertise to avoid the appearance of control, thereby anointing themselves as the new crew of experts. He warns that postmodern therapists risk clinical irrelevance by getting too wrapped up in abstractions about the subjectivity of all truths. Furthermore, he points out the ethical issue of impairment among postmodern therapists, "wounded healers" who, like some of their modernist practitioner counterparts, often are reluctant to seek help for themselves and their relationships. Efran and his colleagues (1988) caution against using postmodernism as a means of trifling with established words and meanings: "those who make their living being experts on the implications of language ought to think twice before taking too many liberties with it" (p. 34).

Efran and Clarfield (1992) contend that the postmodern idea that hierarchy can be eliminated in therapy is absurd and counterproductive. "To act as if all views are equal and that we—as therapists—have no favorites among them undercuts the very sort of frank exchange we want and expect to have with our clients" (p. 208). González (1997) notes that postmodernists can resemble some of their modernist counterparts in their lack of basic *people skills* and a failure to practice what they preach, the latter of which does not prevent the disparagement of those not of their ideological clique. Another concern González (1998) raises is whether postmodern paradigms are foisted onto unsuspecting clients without their informed consent. Practitioners can easily "manipulate naive clients' realities under the guise of co-construction" (p. 369). Without a system of checks and balances, so-called conversational artistry can readily degenerate into "con artistry" (Efran & Fauber, 1995). Postmodernists are challenged to squarely and courageously face this underside of themselves or risk a rigid paradigmatic stratification, or segregation, that is the antithesis of postmodernism.

Postmodern advocacy without honoring diverse viewpoints can appear as ludicrous posturing. An indispensable point is made by Anderson and Goolishian (1991): "Keep in mind that negative connotation, or the invalidation, of any major participant (including one's colleagues) is destructive to the process of opening space for conversation" (p. 7). The perpetual challenge is for postmodernists of any ilk to contain the tendency to assume a totalizing view within themselves. Totalizing is the assumption of "a totality, a total view. By extension this rejects other perspectives. Postmodernists criticize totalizing theories" (Rosenau, 1992, p. xiv). Credibility is enhanced when advocates of emerging postmodern paradigms strive to espouse the tenets of these paradigms interpersonally, professionally, and organizationally. Such striving will be a lifelong effort.

Postmodernism challenges vocational psychology to examine how its theories are historically, socially, and culturally bound. The modernist approaches we presented in

Chapters 4 through 8 are going to be hard-pressed to move from abstract —and some would add, inert —theorizing to a demonstration of the real-life consequences of their interventions (see also, Greenfield, 1998). Doubtless, many modernist-trained vocational psychology scholars and career counseling practitioners are disconcerted by postmodernism.

But modernism has had its chance at articulating the occupational development of people, and the caliber of scientific objectivity used has left much to be desired. For example, a methodological critique of eight years of research articles on multicultural career development published in three leading career journals was conducted by Koegel, Donin, Ponterotto, and Spitz (1995). Some of the results are as follows:

- Number of articles published in the *Journal of Employment Counseling, Journal of Vocational Behavior,* and *The Career Development Quarterly,* from 1985 to 1992: $n = 884$

- Number and percentage of articles that emphasized multicultural concerns: $n = 116$ (14%)

- Number and percentage of multicultural concerns that were (1) quantitative, empirically based studies: $n = 68$ (59%); (2) conceptual, nondata-based reports: $n = 45$ (39%); (3) quantitative empirical investigations: $n = 3$ (2.5%)

- Most commonly used sample populations: high school students $n = 14$; college undergraduates and graduates $n = 19$; professionals and semi professionals $n = 5$; veterans $n = 2$; others $n = 28$

In evaluating these results, Koegel et al. (1995) write that the over-reliance on student samples is troubling in two respects. First, questions can be raised about how representative student populations are of the community at large.

Second, questions can also be raised about the appropriateness of using a population whose dominant environment is academe to investigate career- or work-related behaviors. Thus, the results of nearly one-half of the reviewed multicultural career articles may have limited generalizability to the larger population (pp. 59–60). Reid (1993) refers to student samples as populations of convenience.

An over-reliance on such research participants, whether in vocational psychology generally or in multicultural vocational concerns specifically, has provided postmodernists with the premise they need to question the reliability and validity of the modernist enterprise in vocational psychology. Journal editors and their review boards must bear some of the responsibility for allowing a proliferation of research publications comprised of social science with extremely limited generalizabily. We propose broadening the research base in vocational psychology research so that populations of convenience, especially college student samples, are used less and nonprofessional adult workers, students at technical and vocational schools, and noncollege-bound populations are used more.

We are not, however, calling for the elimination of quantitative research in vocational psychology, only for more sophisticated research designs and sampling techniques. Sociologist William Julius Wilson (1996), for instance, uses a stratified probability sample ($n = 2{,}490$) of African American, non-Hispanic White, Mexican, and Puerto Rican parents ages 18 to 44 to produce *When Work Disappears: The World of the New Urban Poor.* His findings on the attitudes toward work and welfare among Chicago poverty-tract parents by race or ethnic/immigrant status (see Wilson, 1996, Table 4, p. 251) provide a deeper level of understanding of within-group differences than any population of convenience could ever provide. We respect his efforts to discern work attitudes among less privileged populations.

Logical positivism has yet to convincingly verify through observation and experiment—empiricism—the universal truths about the role of work in people's lives. The scientific method has been misapplied in much of the vocational psychology research. Knowledge claims about occupational development have inaccurately and incompletely reflected the experience of multicultural and diverse populations (Gelberg & Chojnacki, 1996; Leong, 1995). The overuse of modernist objectivity has yet to successfully discover the universal meaning presumed to underlie the occupational development of people not of the dominant culture in the United States, much less elsewhere.

Postmodern contextual interpretativism merits consideration as a valid alternative in vocational psychology, especially in view of the unprecedented impact of the global economy and the social saturation of the self wrought by technology (Gergen, 1991). In many respects, the meaning of work is socially legitimated in particular communities through localized or situated knowledge. We see no contradiction in the duality of existence of *both* logical positivism *and* contextual interpretivism in vocational psychology. *Both* universality *and* particularity are relevant to the role of work in people's lives.

The "technologies of social saturation" of which Gergen (1991) writes are another persuasive argument for integrating more of a postmodern perspective into vocational psychology. A business-as-usual approach will simply not work anymore. Theories of occupational development are not keeping pace with advances in telecommunication that impact the role of work in a global economy. Rather than taking an either/or position, we espouse *both* modernism *and* postmodernism in the research and practice of vocational psychology. In a modification of Savickas (1993), reality is *both* objective *and* subjective. Language *both* reflects *and* produces reality. Meaning is *both* discovered *and* invented. Moreover, meaning resides *both* in the world *and* in the word. As much as possible, clients receive a combination of *both* predefined services *and* are active and independent agents in interpreting and shaping their own lives.

For the field of vocational psychology to be relevant for the twenty-first century, we agree with Richardson (1993) that career counseling should become a subspecialty within vocational psychology. We also suggest that future research

1. gives more attention to both the conceptual and technical aspects of instrument development.

2. studies the occupational behavior of multicultural and diverse populations in a more coherent fashion than has happened up to now.

3. studies people other than those facing occupational decisions during the entry and early years of work life.

4. evaluates the effectiveness and utility of vocational interventions (for generic examples of postmodern program evaluation, see Mabry & Stake, 1997).

The Role of Work and the Psychology of Work The vigor that is currently present in the field of vocational psychology is exciting and indicates a bright and important future to help all of us cope with the impending changes. The reaching out to studies of minority groups, the adaptation to current thinking regarding assessment standards that allows for more effective understanding of clients, and the concerns about working on the convergence of theories while developing new, more appropriate ideas are all major steps for vocational psychology to claim its place in the spectrum of psychology. There are challenges for this lively field as well.

Betz's (2001) survey of the development of vocational psychology demonstrates the advances made in calls for more research into "the needs of poor and working-class youths and adults" . . . [and] "those historically 'left out' of middle-class American prosperity" (p. 277). Blustein (2001) also calls for more understanding of those individuals who are outside the realm of opportunity as opposed to those who have been the source of our major concerns. We hope the issues we have raised will be addressed as challenges for further understanding.

More information on the relationship of children to a developmental concept of the importance of the role of work in our lives will help prepare them better for the world of work. The ability to integrate this into curricula in schools and training institutions must be pursued as well.

Blustein (2001) eloquently suggests that vocational psychology "extends [its] reach . . . by charting the course for an integrative and inclusive psychology of work" (p. 171). This has been a major thrust of our book, as indicated in the title, and we appreciate his clear call.

The global relevance of vocational psychology has become more pressing than ever before. We believe that, rather than fear the global market as a threat to the U.S. economy, we should embrace the possibilities for increased opportunities. Thus, we believe that the current English-only and the antibilingual education sentiments in the United States are particularly ill-timed. As with any change, there are both positives *and* negatives. Those who pursue the positive will be ahead of the crowd, and those who fight change will be among those who will be left behind. We hope vocational psychology and career counseling more explicitly emphasize sociopolitical factors in the twenty-first century.

THE CHANGING ROLE OF
THE VOCATIONAL PRACTITIONER

In a time of change, theorists are rethinking, restating, or expanding current practices and ideas that are shaping our lives. Some of these are considered below to indicate future trends in the how we work as career specialists. Ironically, the thing that people crave most—meaning—is the one thing that science hasn't been able to give them.

—Eleanor Arroway (*Contact*)

Based on our survey of the field of vocational psychology, and using Hansen's (1993) conclusions as a basic guide, we believe the following need to be considered.

1. The changes in the workplace are permanent. Therefore, vocational practitioners need to be able to assist individuals in the change process.

2. The vocational counseling process must be revised and reinvented to meet the changes in the workplace, in values, and in the actualities of the shift in the age of major population groups.

3. Occupational development programs need to be integrated continuously into the regular curriculum and classroom. School counselors, parents, and teachers need to be involved in helping students develop both short- and long-term plans.

4. More specific strategies are needed to deal with the "underserved, underrepresented, deprived populations" (Hansen, 1993, p. 20), using such techniques as mentoring, shadowing, work cooperatives, and on-the-job training.

5. Vocational practitioners will need to be aware of the technological tools available as aids and know how to use and process the information obtained with students/clients.

6. Occupational decision making needs to include logical, rational, intuitive, personal, family, and spiritual processes in order to integrate life/work planning.

7. Developmental-contextual and integrative vocational approaches will become more appropriate modalities. Working people in general will be forced to rethink the role of work in their lives.

8. It is the duty of policymakers, economists, business leaders, educators, and occupational development professionals to work together to be proactive in planning for this century, and these plans must be incorporated into services for youth and adults.

9. Occupational development specialists will need to have training in the psychology of work, family roles and work, career/life planning, theoretical advances and applications, educational/information systems, and vocational/educational assessment.

10. Vocational psychology scholars and researchers will need to interface more with other academic disciplines, including but not limited to: (1) international business, (2) management, (3) political science, (4) sociology, (5) women's studies, (6) gay and lesbian studies, (7) social psychology, (8) developmental psychology, (9) gerontology, and (10) anthropology. Ethnographic and other constructivist research methods will also need more incorporation into vocational psychology as never before.

11. The role of work in people's lives needs to be emphasized more in the fields of teacher education (including special education and bilingual education), educational leadership, social work, clinical psychology, rehabilitation counseling, marriage and family therapy, and pastoral counseling.

Counselor education, in particular, needs to be expanded to include training on all levels. Certification of vocational practitioners needs to be rethought with emphasis on the knowledge base that is needed to make effective interventions. It is not enough to deal solely with career and job issues, when that is often just the tip of the iceberg. Being prepared for the gamut of problems that arise and knowing when to refer a client to another therapist are part of the necessary training of occupational counselors. A model for training programs is described in Osborne and Usher (1994) with a description of programs that include undergraduate, graduate, and doctoral students.

OCCUPATIONAL GUIDANCE SERVICES 2010

As we have attempted to distill all the information we have gathered and looked at the predictions, the directions, and the hopes for the future, we would like to formulate a view of the workforce of the future and propose some specific occupational guidance services.

The Workforce

The changes in the workforce and attitudes toward education, work, and leisure are likely to undergo substantive changes. The great increase in workers who are aging and dealing with retirement combined with fewer available workers in this new generation to fill the needs of the job market will make an older workforce inevitable. Added to this mixture is a change in the values of commitment to the job in terms of time and loyalty on the part of the new generation of workers. Bolles's (1981) vision of the future still holds, with the "three boxes of life—education, work and leisure," less associated with a specific time of life, but rather seen as activities that are undertaken throughout the life span. Retirement will be redefined and rethought. How that will develop is not clear—what is clear is that retirement will not be what it was for the boomer's parents.

K–12

The American people will be made aware of the directions of employment opportunities through media campaigns and other guidance, which will shift the emphasis from college-bound postsecondary education to more technical preparation in order to meet the projected needs in the world of work. In addition, the need for flexibility and the use of technological aids to work in various environments will be considered basic tools for work success.

Educational associations, starting at the state level and moving down through independent school district boards, will be more informed about current employment information, will work to mandate changes in educational requirements, and will motivate schools to develop programs that will reflect the realities of the workforce.

Administrators and teachers will be fully aware of the relationship of work and the curriculum and will provide programs that motivate students as much as possible in the academic pursuits as well as help them envision themselves as productive workers in occupations. Especially challenging will be dealing with involuntary minorities (Ogbu, 1992) who view educational attainment as trying to be too much like White people. Teacher education in a global society (Gutek, 1993) is inextricably related to occupational education in the schools.

School counselors will be able to provide a comprehensive career guidance program for students from K–12 to become familiar with the world of work, see the possibilities for themselves, and use various assessments in order to focus planning and training. In addition, counselors will be able to provide basic job seeking skills at the level needed by each individual student.

Post-High School Adults

Those who go on to higher education will primarily receive two types of training: specialized skills training and professional training. The individuals who get two-year, vo-tech, specialized skill training will be filling approximately 60 percent of the jobs (Handy, 1996). Even for those who earn a Bachelors degree, Schaffer (1999) suggests that high-tech careers will attract people with little technical expertise (low-tech ability and training) because of the need for writers, thinkers, and creative people. The creation of these training programs is paramount, and many community colleges, four-year colleges, and universities will find themselves cooperating with local industries to provide education and training for the personnel the industries expect to need. There will be a great emphasis on these types of programs.

The second group will be the traditional professional training of four-year and graduate school studies. The predictions indicate that there will be less need for highly trained professionals than currently, which will result in downsizing or consolidating programs, higher entrance standards, higher performance requirements, and extended training. The best schools will be at the forefront of these changes.

Adults in transition will need a variety of services. Among them will be job clubs, career development services in industry, and programs for special populations. In addition, good entrepreneurs will develop one-stop centers that serve people in easily accessible places, providing basic services apart from highly specialized offices. These career centers will be located in shopping malls and other places where people gather. The centers will have computer programs, access to the government Internet services such as the O★Net, state and local statistical information regarding work, and contacts with the business community. They will need *trained personnel* who are certified occupational counselors and specialists. The services provided will include more than simply matching people and jobs; they will involve life and work planning and individual counseling services for situations that relate to obtaining, maintaining, and increasing job productivity. These centers will also provide services for those of retirement age who want to remain involved with a productive life.

Feller (1991) concludes that the next twenty-five years will demand that vocational practitioners "integrate new rules, consider new foundations, and constantly assess the gaps between what is needed and what is available. Only then will a client's employment and career development be better served in a world of change" (p. 19).

IS THIS IN OUR FUTURE?

Convergence of Eastern and Western Traditions

Mikulas (2002) proposes the concept of **Conjunctive Psychology** "that seeks the gradual development of an integrated, multilevel psychology of behavior change and personal growth that draws from all the world's major psychologies" (p. 21). Based on a practical and heuristic value, which should serve to encourage research, Conjunctive Psychology recognizes that people exist at four interrelated levels: biological, behavioral, personal, and transpersonal.

The biological level works with the body, and a therapist may work with "nutrition, exercise, breathing, environmental pollution, bodywork, or drugs" (p. 22). The behavioral level, which is a specialty of Western psychology, "refers to what the person does, including overt behavior, emotional responses, and thoughts and images" (p. 22). The behavioral level exists to help the body meet its needs and to help the personal level attain its wants and goals. A therapist may work with learning new behaviors and thought patterns or extinguishing undesired behaviors and patterns of thinking. The personal level, another specialty of Western psychology, "includes the individual's conscious experiential sense of self, will, and personal reality" (p. 22). A therapist may work with structure of the self, including self concept, self esteem, understanding of traits or states, perceived abilities, will, and training in understanding how to discriminate. Myths and stories are important for a culture to shape personal realities of people in the culture. Mikulas suggests "the self is the central star in the great melodrama of the personal reality" (p. 128).

The final level of being is the transpersonal. Beyond the personal is the literal meaning of the word. This "level includes those forces, processes and domains of being that are superordinate to and prior to the personal . . ." (p. 22). It includes how one is part of family, community and culture. In addition, it operates to provide us awareness of the contents of the mind.

What can the body and the transpersonal, which our psychology has studied less, add to the construct of career, decision making, satisfaction, and meaning?

Quantum Theory and Career Development

The development of quantum theory and its application to the social sciences and to psychology, and vocational psychology in particular, is a new field. **Chaos theory**, an outgrowth of quantum physics, suggests that structures as we have described them may not be based on patterns and foundations as we thought. Rather, they may be discovered or created even as we live, because everything in the universe is related to everything else. If this is so, then the result is to recognize that what we have built and perceived as observable cannot explain the randomness of behavior. In psychology, we are confronted with behaviors that we cannot explain. In career development, we can plan and decide while an unknown reality takes us in another direction. Krumboltz's (1998) *planned happenstance* (see Chapter 6) is a likely result of this realization.

Stephen Wolinsky (1993; 1994) has proposed a Quantum Psychology based on quantum physics. He discusses

> [a] theory of human behavior which describes the creation of personality. More simply put, an *organizing principle* that can explain the way personality is created, developed, and maintained—with the context not only being the individual, but including the entire universe. With this understanding in mind, Quantum Physics has demonstrated that everything is connected to everything else. In this way, behind all appearances of differences there exists a unified field of interconnected wholeness (pp. 1–2).

One's consciousness is not only observed by one, but that the person is actually the creator of the consciousness.

The New (Quantum) Careering Model

Anna Miller-Tiedeman (1999) has expanded her life career model to include ideas of quantum thinking. She suggests in her book, *Learning, Practicing, and Living the New Careering,* that life changes by the minute in a manner that is changeable ad infinitum. In the context of these changes, one lives a Life-As-Career. The role of the counselor is to become a New Career Developer, who does little interpretation, but aids clients in the creation and living of their own Life-As-Career existence.

More work will be done in this area and new paradigms for the understanding of career development will emerge.

Appendix 1

❖❖

Code of Fair Testing Practices
in Education

The Code of Fair Testing Practices in Education states the major obligations to test takers of professionals who develop or use educational tests. The Code is meant to apply broadly to the use of tests in education (admissions, educational assessment, educational diagnosis, and student placement). The Code is not designed to cover employment testing, licensure or certification testing, or other types of testing. Although the Code has relevance to many types of educational tests, it is directed primarily at professionally developed tests such as those sold by commercial test publishers or used in formally administered testing programs. The Code is not intended to cover tests made by individual teachers for use in their own classrooms.

The Code addresses the roles of test developers and test users separately. Test users are people who select tests, commission test development services, or make decisions on the basis of test scores. Test developers are people who actually construct tests as well as those who set policies for particular testing programs. The roles may, of course, overlap as when a state education agency commissions test development services, sets policies that control the test development process, and makes decisions on the basis of the test scores.

The Code presents standards for educational test developers and users in four areas:

A. Developing/Selecting Tests

B. Interpreting Scores

C. Striving for Fairness

D. Informing Test Takers

The Code has been developed by the Joint Committee on Testing Practices, a cooperative effort of several professional organizations, that has as its aim the advancement, in the public interest, of the quality of testing practices. The Joint Committee was initiated by the American Educational Research Association, the American Psychological Association, and the National Council on Measurement in Education. In addition to these three groups, the American Association for Counseling and Development/Association for Measurement and Evaluation in Counseling and Development, and the American Speech-Language-Hearing Association are now also sponsors of the Joint Committee.

This is not copyrighted material. Reproduction and dissemination are encouraged. Please cite this document as follows:

Code of Fair Testing Practices in Education. (1988) Washington, DC. Joint Committee on Testing Practices. (Mailing Address: Joint Committee on Testing Practices, American Psychological Association, 1200 17th Street, NW, Washington, DC 20036.)

Organizations, institutions, and individual professionals who endorse the Code commit themselves to safeguarding the rights of test takers by following the principles listed. The Code is intended to be consistent with the relevant parts of the *Standards for Educational and Psychological Testing* (AERA, APA, NCME, 1985). However, the Code differs from the Standards in both audience and purpose. The Code is meant to be understood by the general public, it is limited to educational tests, and the primary focus is on those issues that affect the proper use of tests. The Code is not meant to add new principles over and above those in the Standards or to change the meaning of the Standards. The goal is rather to represent the spirit of a selected portion of the Standards in a way that is meaningful to test takers and/or their parents or guardians. It is the hope of the Joint Committee that the Code will also be judged to be consistent with existing codes of conduct and standards of other professional groups who use educational tests.

DEVELOPING/SELECTING APPROPRIATE TESTS*

Test developers should provide the information that test users need to select appropriate tests.

Test users should select tests that meet the purpose for which they are to be used and that are appropriate for the intended test-taking populations.

Test Developers Should:

1. Define what each test measures and what the test should be used for. Describe the populations for which the test is appropriate.

2. Accurately represent the characteristics, usefulness, and limitations of tests for their intended purposes.

3. Explain relevant measurement concepts as necessary for clarity at the level of detail that is appropriate for the intended audiences.

4. Describe the process of test development. Explain how the content and skills to be tested were selected.

5. Provide evidence that the test meets its intended purpose(s).

Test Users Should:

1. First define the purpose for testing and the population to be tested. Then, select a test for that purpose and that population based on a thorough review of the available information.

2. Investigate potentially useful sources of information, in addition to test scores, to corroborate the information provided by tests.

3. Read the materials provided by test developers and avoid using tests for which unclear or incomplete information is provided.

4. Become familiar with how and when the test was developed and tried out.

5. Read independent evaluations of a test and of possible alternative measures. Look for evidence required to support the claims of test developers.

---

*Many of the statements in the Code refer to the selection of existing tests. However, in customized testing programs test, developers are engaged to construct new tests. In those situations, the test development process should be designed to help ensure that the completed tests will be in compliance with the Code.

6. Provide either representative samples or complete copies of test questions, directions, answer sheets, manuals, and score reports to qualified users.

7. Indicate the nature of the evidence obtained concerning the appropriateness of each test for groups of different racial, ethnic, or linguistic backgrounds who are likely to be tested.

8. Identify and publish any specialized skills needed to administer each test and to interpret scores correctly.

6. Examine specimen sets, disclosed tests or samples of questions, directions, answer sheets, manuals, and score reports before selecting a test.

7. Ascertain whether the test content and norms group(s) or comparison group(s) are appropriate for the intended test takers.

8. Select and use only those tests for which the skills needed to administer the test and interpret scores correctly are available.

INTERPRETING SCORES

Test developers should help users interpret scores correctly.

Test users should interpret scores correctly.

Test Developers Should:

9. Provide timely and easily understood score reports that describe test performance clearly and accurately. Also explain the meaning and limitations of reported scores.

10. Describe the population(s) represented by any norms or comparison group(s), the dates the data were gathered, and the process used to select the samples of test takers.

11. Warn users to avoid specific, reasonably anticipated misuses of test scores.

12. Provide information that will help users follow reasonable procedures for setting passing scores when it is appropriate to use such scores with the test.

13. Provide information that will help users gather evidence to show that the test is meeting its intended purpose(s).

Test Users Should:

9. Obtain information about the scale used for reporting scores, the characteristics of any norms or comparison group(s), and the limitations of the scores.

10. Interpret scores taking into account any major differences between the norms or comparison groups and the actual test takers. Also take into account any differences in test administration practices or familiarity with the specific questions in the test.

11. Avoid using tests for purposes not specifically recommended by the test developer unless evidence is obtained to support the intended use.

12. Explain how any passing scores were set and gather evidence to support the appropriateness of the scores.

13. Obtain evidence to help show that the test is meeting its intended purpose(s).

STRIVING FOR FAIRNESS

Test developers should strive to make tests that are as fair as possible for test takers of different races, gender, ethnic backgrounds, or handicapping conditions.

Test users should select tests that have been developed in ways that attempt to make them as fair as possible for test takers of different races, gender, ethnic backgrounds, or handicapping conditions.

Test Developers Should:

14. Review and revise test questions and related materials to avoid potentially insensitive content or language.

15. Investigate the performance of test takers of different races, gender, and ethnic backgrounds when samples of sufficient size are available. Enact procedures that help to ensure that differences in performance are related primarily to the skills under assessment rather than to irrelevant factors.

16. When feasible, make appropriately modified forms of tests or administration procedures available for test takers with handicapping conditions. Warn test users of potential problems in using standard norms with modified tests or administration procedures that result in noncomparable scores.

Test Users Should:

14. Evaluate the procedures used by test developers to avoid potentially insensitive content or language.

15. Review the performance of test takers of different races, gender, and ethnic backgrounds when samples of sufficient size are available. Evaluate the extent to which performance differences may have been caused by inappropriate characteristics of the test.

16. When necessary and feasible, use appropriately modified forms of tests or administration procedures for test takers with handicapping conditions. Interpret standard norms with care in the light of the modifications that were made.

INFORMING TEST TAKERS

Under some circumstances developers have direct communication with test takers. Under other circumstances, test users communicate directly with test takers. Whichever group communicates directly with test takers should provide the information described below.

Under some circumstances, test developers have direct control of tests and test scores. Under other circumstances, test users have such control. Whichever group has direct control of tests and test scores should take the steps described below.

Test Developers or Test Users Should:

17. When a test is optional, provide test takers or their parents/guardians with information to help them judge whether the test should be taken, or if an available alternative to the test should be used.

Test Developers or Test Users Should:

19. Provide test takers or their parents/guardians with information about rights test takers may have to obtain copies of tests and completed answer sheets, retake tests, have tests rescored, or cancel scores.

18. Provide test takers the information they need to be familiar with the coverage of the test, the types of question formats, the directions, and appropriate test-taking strategies. Strive to make such information equally available to all test takers.

20. Tell test takers or their parents/guardians how long scores will be kept on file and indicate to whom and under what circumstances test scores will or will not be released.

21. Describe the procedures that test takers or their parents/guardians may use to register complaints and have problems resolved.

Note: The membership of the Working Group that developed the Code of Fair Testing Practices in Education and of the Joint Committee on Testing Practices that guided the Working Group was as follows:

Theodore P. Bartell
John R. Bergan
Esther E. Diamond
Richard P. Duran
Lorraine D. Eyde
Raymond D. Fowler
John J. Fremer
    (Co-chair, JCTP and Chair, Code Working Group)

Edmund W. Gordon
Jo-Ida C. Hansen
James B. Lingwall
George F. Madaus
    (Co-chair, JCTP)
Kevin L. Moreland
Jo-Ellen V. Perez
Robert J. Solomon
John T. Stewart

Carol Kehr Tittle
    (Co-chair, JCTP)
Nicholas A. Vacc
Michael J. Zieky
Debra Boltas and Wayne Camara of the American Psychological Association served as staff liaisons

Appendix 2

❖

National Career Development Association Ethical Standards (Revised 1991)

These Ethical Standards were developed by the National Board for Certified Counselors (NBCC), an independent, voluntary, not-for-profit organization incorporated in 1982. Titled "Code of Ethics" by NBCC and last amended in February 1987, the Ethical Standards were adopted by the National Career Development Association (NCDA) Board of Directors in 1987 and revised in 1991, with minor changes in wording (e.g., the addition of specific references to NCDA members).

PREAMBLE

NCDA is an educational, scientific, and professional organization dedicated to the enhancement of the worth, dignity, potential, and uniqueness of each individual and, thus, to the service of society. This code of ethics enables the NCDA to clarify the nature of ethical responsibilities for present and future professional career counselors.

SECTION A: GENERAL

1. NCDA members influence the development of the profession by continuous efforts to improve professional practices, services, and research. Professional growth is continuous through the career counselor's career and is exemplified by the development of a philosophy that explains why and how a career counselor functions in the helping relationship. Career counselors must gather data on their effectiveness and be guided by their findings.

2. NCDA members have a responsibility to the clients they are serving and to the institutions within which the services are being performed. Career counselors also strive to assist the respective agency, organization, or institution in providing the highest caliber of professional services. The acceptance of employment in an institution implies that the career counselor is in agreement with the general policies and principles of the institution. Therefore, the professional activities of the career counselor are in accord with the objectives of the institution. If, despite concerted efforts, the career counselor cannot reach agreement with the employer as to acceptable standards of conduct that allow for changes in institutional policy that are con-

ducive to the positive growth and development of clients, then terminating the affiliation should be seriously considered.

3. Ethical behavior among professional associates (e.g., career counselors) must be expected at all times. When accessible information raises doubt as to the ethical behavior of professional colleagues, the NCDA member must make action to attempt to rectify this condition. Such action uses the respective institution's channels first and then uses procedures established by the American Counseling Association, of which NCDA is a division.

4. NCDA members neither claim nor imply professional qualifications which exceed those possessed, and are responsible for correcting any misrepresentations of these qualifications by others.

5. NCDA members must refuse a private fee or other remuneration for consultation or counseling with persons who are entitled to their services through the career counselor's employing institution or agency. The policies of some agencies may make explicit provisions for staff members to engage in private practice with agency clients. However, should agency clients desire private counseling or consulting services, they must be apprised of other options available to them. Career counselors must not divert to their private practices, legitimate clients in their primary agencies or of the institutions with which they are affiliated.

6. In establishing fees for professional counseling services, NCDA members must consider the financial status of clients and the respective locality. In the event that the established fee status is inappropriate for the client, assistance must be provided in finding comparable services of acceptable cost.

7. NCDA members seek only those positions in the delivery of professional services for which they are professionally qualified.

8. NCDA members recognize their limitations and provide services or only use techniques for which they are qualified by training and/or experience. Career counselors recognize the need, and seek continuing education, to assure competent services.

9. NCDA members are aware of the intimacy in the counseling relationship, maintain respect for the client, and avoid engaging in activities that seek to meet their personal needs at the expense of the client.

10. NCDA members do not condone or engage in sexual harassment which is defined as deliberate or repeated comments, gestures, or physical contacts of a sexual nature.

11. NCDA members avoid bringing their personal or professional issues into the counseling relationship. Through an awareness of the impact of stereotyping and discrimination (e.g., biases based on age, disability, ethnicity, gender, race, religion, or sexual preference), career counselors guard the individual rights and personal dignity of the client in the counseling relationship.

12. NCDA members are accountable at all times for their behavior. They must be aware that all actions and behaviors of a counselor reflect on professional integrity and, when inappropriate, can damage the public trust in the counseling profession. To protect public confidence in the counseling profession, career counselors avoid public behavior that is clearly in violation of accepted moral and legal standards.

13. NCDA members have a social responsibility because their recommendations and professional actions may alter the lives of others. Career counselors remain fully cognizant of their impact and are alert to personal, social, organizational, financial, or political situations or pressures which might lead to misuse of their influence.

14. Products or services provided by NCDA members by means of classroom instruction, public lectures, demonstrations, written articles, radio or television programs, or other types of media must meet the criteria cited in Sections A through F of these Ethical Standards.

SECTION B: COUNSELING RELATIONSHIP

1. The primary obligation of NCDA members is to respect the integrity and promote the welfare of the client, regardless of whether the client is assisted individually or in a group relationship. In a group setting, the career counselor is also responsible for taking reasonable precautions to protect individuals from physical and/or psychological trauma resulting from interaction within the group.

2. The counseling relationship and information resulting from it remains confidential, consistent with the legal obligations of the NCDA member. In a group counseling setting, the career counselor sets a norm of confidentiality regarding all group participants' disclosures.

3. NCDA members know and take into account the traditions and practices of other professional groups with whom they work, and they cooperate fully with such groups. If a person is receiving similar services from another professional, career counselors do not offer their own services directly to such a person. If a career counselor is contacted by a person who is already receiving similar services from another professional, the career counselor carefully considers that professional relationship and proceeds with caution and sensitivity to the therapeutic issues as well as the client's welfare. Career counselors discuss these issues with clients so as to minimize the risk of confusion and conflict.

4. When a client's condition indicates that there is a clear and imminent danger to the client or others, the NCDA member must take reasonable personal action or inform responsible authorities. Consultation with other professionals must be used where possible. The assumption of responsibility for the client's behavior must be taken only after careful deliberation, and the client must be involved in the resumption of responsibility as quickly as possible.

5. Records of the counseling relationship, including interview notes, test data, correspondence, audio or visual tape recordings, electronic data storage, and other documents are to be considered professional information for use in counseling. They should not be considered a part of the records of the institution or agency in which the NCDA member is employed unless specified by state statute or regulation. Revelation to others of counseling material must occur only upon the expressed consent of the client; career counselors must make provisions for maintaining confidentiality in the storage and disposal of records. Career counselors providing information to the public or to subordinates, peers, or supervisors have a responsibility to ensure that the content is general; unidentified client information should be accurate and unbiased, and should consist of objective, factual data.

6. NCDA members must ensure that data maintained in electronic storage are secure. The data must be limited to information that is appropriate and necessary for the services being provided and accessible only to appropriate staff members involved in the provision of services by using the best computer security methods available. Career counselors must also ensure that electronically stored data are destroyed when the information is no longer of value in providing services.

7. Data derived from a counseling relationship for use in counselor training or research shall be confined to content that can be disguised to ensure full protection of the identity of the subject/client and shall be obtained with informed consent.

8. NCDA members must inform clients, before or at the time the counseling relationship commences, of the purposes, goals, techniques, rules and procedures, and limitations that may affect the relationship.

9. All methods of treatment by NCDA members must be clearly indicated to prospective recipients and safety precautions must be taken in their use.

10. NCDA members who have an administrative, supervisory, and/or evaluative relationship with individuals seeking counseling services must not serve as the counselor and should refer the individuals to other professionals. Exceptions are made only in instances where an individual's situation warrants counseling intervention and another alternative is unavailable. Dual relationships with clients that might impair the career counselor's objectivity and professional judgment must be avoided and/or the counseling relationship terminated through referral to another competent professional.

11. When NCDA members determine an inability to be of professional assistance to a potential or existing client, they must, respectively, not initiate the counseling relationship or immediately terminate the relationship. In either event, the career counselor must suggest appropriate alternatives. Career counselors must be knowledgeable about referral resources so that a satisfactory referral can be initiated. In the event that the client declines a suggested referral, the career counselor is not obligated to continue the relationship.

12. NCDA members may choose to consult with any other professionally competent person about a client and must notify clients of this right. Career counselors must avoid placing a consultant in a conflict-of-interest situation that would preclude the consultant's being a proper party to the career counselor's efforts to help the client.

13. NCDA members who counsel clients from cultures different from their own must gain knowledge, personal awareness, and sensitivity pertinent to the client populations served and must incorporate culturally relevant techniques into their practice.

14. When NCDA members engage in intensive counseling with a client, the client's counseling needs should be assessed. When needs exist outside the counselor's expertise, appropriate referrals should be made.

15. NCDA members must screen prospective group counseling participants, especially when the emphasis is on self-understanding and growth through self-disclosure. Career counselors must maintain an awareness of each group participant's welfare throughout the group process.

16. When electronic data and systems are used as a component of counseling services, NCDA members must ensure that the computer application, and any information it contains, is appropriate for the respective needs of clients and is nondiscriminatory. Career counselors must ensure that they themselves have acquired a facilitation level of knowledge with any system they use including hands-on application, search experience, and understanding of the uses of all aspects of the computer-based system. In selecting and/or maintaining computer-based systems that contain career information, career counselors must ensure that the systems provide current, accurate, and locally relevant information. Career counselors must also ensure that clients are intellectually, emotionally, and physically compatible with the use of the computer application and understand its purpose and operation. Client use of a computer application must be evaluated to correct possible problems and assess subsequent needs.

17. NCDA members who develop self-help, stand-alone computer software for use by the general public, must first ensure that it is initially designed to function in a stand-alone manner, as opposed to modifying software that was originally designed to require support from a counselor. Secondly, the software must include program statements that provide the user with

intended outcomes, suggestions for using the software, descriptions of inappropriately used applications, and descriptions of when and how counseling services might be beneficial. Finally, the manual must include the qualifications of the developer, the development process, validation data, and operating procedures.

SECTION C: MEASUREMENT AND EVALUATION

1. NCDA members must provide specific orientation or information to an examinee prior to and following the administration of assessment instruments or techniques so that the results may be placed in proper perspective with other relevant factors. The purpose of testing and the explicit use of the results must be made known to an examinee prior to testing.

2. In selecting assessment instruments or techniques for use in a given situation or with a particular client, NCDA members must evaluate carefully the instrument's specific theoretical bases and characteristics, validity, reliability, and appropriateness. Career counselors are professionally responsible for using unvalidated information with special care.

3. When making statements to the public about assessment instruments or techniques, NCDA members must provide accurate information and avoid false claims or misconceptions concerning the meaning of psychometric terms. Special efforts are often required to avoid unwarranted connotations of terms such as IQ and grade-equivalent scores.

4. Because many types of assessment techniques exist, NCDA members must recognize the limits of their competence and perform only those functions for which they have received appropriate training.

5. NCDA members must note when tests are not administered under standard conditions or when unusual behavior or irregularities occur during a testing session and the results must be designated as invalid or of questionable validity. Unsupervised or inadequately supervised assessments, such as mail-in tests, are considered unethical. However, the use of standardized instruments that are designed to be self-administered and self-scored, such as interest inventories, is appropriate.

6. Because prior coaching or dissemination of test materials can invalidate test results, NCDA members are professionally obligated to maintain test security. In addition, conditions that produce most favorable test results must be made known to an examinee (e.g., penalty for guessing).

7. NCDA members must consider psychometric limitations when selecting and using an instrument, and must be cognizant of the limitations when interpreting the results. When tests are used to classify clients, career counselors must ensure that periodic review and/or retesting are conducted to prevent client stereotyping.

8. An examinee's welfare, explicit prior understanding, and agreement are the factors used when determining who receives the test results. NCDA members must see that appropriate interpretation accompanies any release of individual or group test data (e.g., limitations of instrument and norms).

9. NCDA members must ensure that computer-generated assessment administration and scoring programs function properly, thereby providing clients with accurate assessment results.

10. NCDA members who are responsible for making decisions based on assessment results, must have appropriate training and skills in educational and psychological measurement—including validation criteria, test research, and guidelines for test development and use.

11. NCDA members must be cautious when interpreting the results of instruments that possess insufficient technical data, and must explicitly state to examinees the specific purposes for the use of such instruments.

12. NCDA members must proceed with caution when attempting to evaluate and interpret performances of minority group members or other persons who are not represented in the norm group on which the instrument was standardized.

13. NCDA members who develop computer-based interpretations to support the assessment process must ensure that the validity of the interpretations is established prior to the commercial distribution of the computer application.

14. NCDA members recognize that test results may become obsolete, and avoid the misuse of obsolete data.

15. NCDA members must avoid the appropriation, reproduction, or modification of published tests or parts thereof without acknowledgment and permission from the publisher.

SECTION D: RESEARCH AND PUBLICATION

1. NCDA members will adhere to relevant guidelines on research with human subjects. These include:
   a. *Code of Federal Regulations*, Title 45, Subtitle A, Part 46, as currently issued.
   b. American Psychological Association. (1982). *Ethical principles in the conduct of research with human participants.* Washington, DC: Author.
   c. American Psychological Association. (1981). Research with human participants. *American Psychologist, 36,* 633–638.
   d. Family Educational Rights and Privacy Act. (Buckley Amendment to P. L. 93–380 of the Laws of 1974)
   e. Current federal regulations and various state privacy acts.

2. In planning research activities involving human subjects, NCDA members must be aware of and responsive to all pertinent ethical principles and ensure that the research problem, design, and execution are in full compliance with the principles.

3. The ultimate responsibility for ethical research lies with the principal researcher, although others involved in research activities are ethically obligated and responsible for their own actions.

4. NCDA members who conduct research with human subjects are responsible for the subjects' welfare throughout the experiment and must take all reasonable precautions to avoid causing injurious psychological, physical, or social effects on their subjects.

5. NCDA members who conduct research must abide by the following basic elements of informed consent:
   a. a fair explanation of the procedures to be followed, including an identification of those which are experimental.
   b. a description of the attendant discomforts and risks.
   c. a description of the benefits to be expected.
   d. a disclosure of appropriate alternative procedures that would be advantageous for subjects.
   e. an offer to answer any inquiries concerning the procedures.
   f. an instruction that subjects are free to withdraw their consent and to discontinue participation in the project or activity at any time.

6. When reporting research results, explicit mention must be made of all the variables and conditions known to the NCDA member that may have affected the outcome of the study or the interpretation of the data.

7. NCDA members who conduct and report research investigations must do so in a manner that minimizes the possibility that the results will be misleading.

8. NCDA members are obligated to make available sufficient original research data to qualified others who may wish to replicate the study.

9. NCDA members who supply data, aid in the research of another person, report research results, or make original data available, must take due care to disguise the identity of respective subjects in the absence of specific authorization from the subject to do otherwise.

10. When conducting and reporting research, NCDA members must be familiar with, and give recognition to, previous work on the topic, must observe all copyright laws, and must follow the principles of giving full credit to those to whom credit is due.

11. NCDA members must give due credit through joint authorship, acknowledgment, footnote statements, or other appropriate means to those who have contributed significantly to the research and/or publication, in accordance with such contributions.

12. NCDA members should communicate to others the results of any research judged to be of professional value. Results that reflect unfavorably on institutions, programs, services, or vested interests must not be withheld.

13. NCDA members who agree to cooperate with another individual in research and/or publication incur an obligation to cooperate as promised in terms of punctuality of performance and with full regard to the completeness and accuracy of the information required.

14. NCDA members must not submit the same manuscript, or one essentially similar in content, for simultaneous publication consideration by two or more journals. In addition, manuscripts that are published in whole or substantial part in another journal or published work should not be submitted for publication without acknowledgment and permission from the previous publication.

SECTION E: CONSULTING

Consultation refers to a voluntary relationship between a professional helper and help-needing individual, group, or social unit in which the consultant is providing help to the client(s) in defining and solving a work-related problem or potential work-related problem with a client or client system.

1. NCDA members acting as consultants must have a high degree of self-awareness of their own values, knowledge, skills, limitations, and needs in entering a helping relationship that involves human and/or organizational change. The focus of the consulting relationship must be on the issues to be resolved and not on the person(s) presenting the problem.

2. In the consulting relationship, the NCDA member and client must understand and agree upon the problem definition, subsequent goals, and predicted consequences of interventions selected.

3. NCDA members must be reasonably certain that they, or the organization represented, have the necessary competencies and resources for giving the kind of help that is needed or that may develop later, and that appropriate referral resources are available to the consultant.

4. NCDA members in a consulting relationship must encourage and cultivate client adaptability and growth toward self-direction. NCDA members must maintain this role consistently and not become a decision maker for clients or create a future dependency on the consultant.

5. NCDA members conscientiously adhere to the NCDA Ethical Standards when announcing consultant availability for services.

SECTION F: PRIVATE PRACTICE

1. NCDA members should assist the profession by facilitating the availability of counseling services in private as well as public settings.

2. In advertising services as private practitioners, NCDA members must advertise in a manner that accurately informs the public of the professional services, expertise, and counseling techniques available.

3. NCDA members who assume an executive leadership role in a private practice organization do not permit their names to be used in professional notices during periods of time when they are not actively engaged in the private practice of counseling.

4. NCDA members may list their highest relevant degree, type, and level of certification and/or license, address, telephone number, office hours, type and/or description of services, and other relevant information. Listed information must not contain false, inaccurate misleading, partial, out-of-context, or otherwise deceptive material or statements.

5. NCDA members who are involved in partnership or corporation with other professionals must, in compliance with the regulations of the locality, clearly specify the separate specialties of each member of the partnership or corporation.

6. NCDA members have an obligation to withdraw from a private-practice counseling relationship if it violates the NCDA Ethical Standards; if the mental or physical condition of the NCDA member renders it difficult to carry out an effective professional relationship; or if the counseling relationship is no longer productive for the client.

PROCEDURES FOR PROCESSING ETHICAL COMPLAINTS

As a division of the American Counseling Association (ACA) the National Career Development Association (NCDA) adheres to the guidelines and procedures for processing ethical complaints and the disciplinary sanctions adopted by ACA. A complaint against an NCDA member may be filed by any individual or group of individuals ("complainant"), whether or not the complainant is a member of NCDA. Action will not be taken on anonymous complaints.

For specifics on how to file ethical complaints and a description of the guidelines and procedures for processing complaints, contact:

ACA Ethics Committee
c/o Executive Director
American Counseling Association
5999 Stevenson Avenue
Alexandria, VA 22304
(800)347-6647

Appendix 3

❖

Tests and Publishers

MAJOR PUBLISHERS

American College Testing
2201 N. Dodge Street
PO Box 168
Iowa City, IA 52243
(800) 498-6065 CFKR

Career Materials, Inc.
PO Box 439
Meadow Vista, CA 95722
(800) 525-5626

Consulting Psychologists Press (CPP)
3803 E. Bayshore Road
PO Box 10096
Palo Alto, CA 94303
(800) 624-1765

CTB McGraw-Hill
20 Ryan Ranch Road
Monterey, CA 93940
(708) 392-3380

Educational and Industrial Testing Services (EdITS)
PO Box 7234
San Diego, CA 92107
(619) 222-1666

Institute for Personality and Ability Testing (IPAT)
1801 Woodfield Drive
Savoy, IL 61874
(217) 352-4739

NCS Assessments (NCS)
PO Box 1416
Minneapolis, MN 55440
(612) 939-5000

Psychological Assessment Resources, Inc. (PAR)
PO Box 998
Odessa, FL 33556
(800) 331-8378

The Psychological Corporation (PSYCORP)
555 Academic Court
San Antonio, TX 78204-2498
(800) 228-0752

Research Psychologists Press, Inc. (SIGMA)
PO Box 610984
Port Huron, MI 48061-0984
(800) 265-1285

Vocational Psychology Research
University of Minnesota
Elliot Hall N620
75 E. River Road
Minneapolis, MN 55455-0344
(612) 625-1367

Western Psychological Services (WPS)
12031 Wilshire Boulevard
Los Angeles, CA 90025-1251
(310) 478-2061

ABILITY TESTS	**PUBLISHER**
American College Testing (ACT)	American College Testing
Armed Services Vocational Aptitude Battery (ASVAB)	Department of Defense Defense Manpower Data Center Personnel Testing Division 99 Pacific Street, Suite 155A Monterey, CA 93940 (408) 583-2400
APTICOM	Vocational Research Institute 1528 Walnut Street #1502 Philadelphia, PA 19102 (215) 875-7387
Differential Aptitude Test (DAT)	PsyCorp
General Aptitude Test Battery (GATB)	Western Assessment Research and Devel. Ctr. 140 East Third Street Salt Lake City, UT 84111

INTEREST TESTS	PUBLISHER
Campbell Interest and Skills Survey (CISS)	NCS
Career Assessment Inventory (CAI)	NCS
Copsystem Interest Inventory (COPS)	EdITS
Explore the World of Work (EWOW)	CFKR Career Materials, Inc.
Ideas, Determination, and Assessment System (IDEAS)	NCS
Jackson Vocational Interest Inventory (JVII)	SIGMA
Kuder Occupational Interest Survey (KOIS)	CTB McGraw-Hill (All Kuder Instruments)
Minnesota Satisfaction Questionnaire (MSQ)	Vocational Psych. Research
My Vocational Situation (MVS)	CPP
Rockwell Occupational Approval Grid (ROAG)	Taylor Rockwell, Brownlee Dolan Stein Associates, Inc. 90 John Street New York, NY 10038
Self-Directed Search (SDS)	PAR
Strong Interest Inventory (SII)	CPP
Vocational Interest Inventory (VII)	WPS
Vocational Preference Inventory (VPI)	WPS
Wide Range Interest, Opinion Test (WRIOT)	Riverside Publishing Co. 425 Spring Lake Drive Itasca, IL 60143-2070
World of Work (WOW)	World of Work, Inc. 2923 North 67th Place Scottsdale, AZ 85251 (602) 946-1884
Work Attitudes Questionnaire (WAQ)	Marathon Consult. and Press P.O. Box 09189 Columbus, OH 43209-0189 (614) 235-5509

PERSONALITY TESTS	**PUBLISHER**
Adjective Checklist (AC)	CPP
California Psychological Inventory (CPI)	CPP
Edward's Personal Preference Schedule (EPPS)	PsyCorp
Eysenck Personality Inventory (EIP)	EdITS
Millon Clinical Multiaxial Inventory (MCMI)	NCS
Minnesota Multiphasic Personality Inventory (MMPI)	NCS
Myers-Briggs Type Indicator (MBTI)	CPP
Neuroticism, Extroversion, and Openness Personality Inventory—Revised (NEO-PI-R)	PAR
Sixteen PF Personal Career Development Profile (16F)	IPAT

VALUES TESTS	**PUBLISHER**
Family Environment Scale (FES)	CPP
Minnesota Importance Questionnaire (MIQ)	Vocational Psych. Research
Rokeach Value Survey (RVS)	CPP
Salience Inventory (SI)	CPP
Values Scale (VS)	CPP
Work Values Inventory (WVI)	Houghton Mifflin Company 1 Beach Street Boston, MA 02107

CAREER DEVELOPMENT INVENTORIES TESTS	**PUBLISHER**
Adult Career Concerns Inventory (ACCI)	CPP
Assessment of Career Decision Making (ACDM)	WPS
Career Adjustment and Development Inventory (CADI)	Dr. J. W. Pickering Old Dominion University Norfolk, VA 23529

Career Attitudes and Strategies Inventory (CASI)	PAR
Career Beliefs Inventory (CBI)	CPP
Career Confidence Scale (CCS)	CPP
Career Decision Profile (CDP)	Lawrence K. Jones North Carolina State Univ. Box 7801 Raleigh, NC 27695 (919) 515-6359
Career Decision Scale (CDS)	PAR
Career Development Inventory (CDI)	CPP
Career Maturity Inventory (CMI)	Crites Career Consultants 5460 White Place Boulder, CO 80303 (303) 447-1639
Career Thoughts Inventory	PAR
Geriatric Depression Scale (GDS)	T.L. Brink 1103 Church Street Redlands, CA 92374 (909) 793-8288
Harrington O'Shea Career Decision Making System Revised (CDMS-R)	American Guidance Service 4201 Woodland Road Circle Pines, MN 55014 (800) 328-2560
Occupational Stress Inventory (OSI)	PAR
Work Environment Scale (WES)	CPP

Appendix 4

❖

Sources of Occupational Information

BASIC LIBRARY RESOURCES

- *Occupational Outlook Handbook*
- *Dictionary of Occupational Titles*
- *Enhanced Guide for Occupational Exploration*
- *Dictionary of Holland's Occupational Codes*
- *Peterson's Guides and Directories*
- *Careers in the Non-Profit Sector*
- *The Complete Guide to Public Employment*
- *National Trade and Professional Associations*
- *Global Employment Guide*
- *Directory of Special Programs for Minority Group Members*
- *Directory of Special Opportunities for Women*

BASIC SOURCES OF INFORMATION

O★NET
U.S. Department of Labor Office of Policy and Research/ETA/O★NET
200 Constitution Avenue NW
Mail Stop N5637
Washington, DC 20210
Telephone: (202) 219-7161
Fax: (202) 219-9186
For information on the O★NET replacement of the *Dictionary of Occupational Titles,* the O★NET's
Web site is http://www.doleta.gov/programs/onet. The Web page has the latest developments of
the O★NET and the timetable for availability of its components.

Other Department of Labor information can be accessed through http://www.dol.gov. The
Bureau of Labor Statistics has a Web page for information about employment projections that is
related to the *Occupational Outlook Handbook.* The URL is http://stats.bls.gov/emphome.htm.

U.S. Government Printing Office
710 N. Capitol Street, NW
Washington, DC 20401
Telephone: (202 512-1800
Fax: (202 512-1355
U.S. Government Bookstores (24) have the latest government information. These are located in
Atlanta, GA; Birmingham, AL; Boston, MA; Chicago, IL; Cleveland, OH; Columbus, OH; Dallas,
TX; Denver, CO, Detroit, MI; Houston, TX; Jacksonville, FL; Kansas City, MO; Laurel, MD;
Los Angeles, CA; Milwaukee, WI; New York, NY; Philadelphia, PA; Pittsburgh, PA; Portland, OR;
Pueblo, CO; San Francisco, CA; Seattle, WA; Washington, DC.

Periodical Subscriptions

- *Occupational Outlook Quarterly*
- *Career Opportunities News*
- *Federal Jobs Digest*

Because books and sources of information are regularly updated, we have chosen to list
some basic sources. No list can be exhaustive, and new ones come into being on a regular basis.

GOVERNMENTAL AND BASIC ORGANIZATIONS

National Career Development Association
10820 E. 45th Street
Tulsa, OK 74176
(918) 663-7060
Web site: http://www.ncda.org
It is possible to download the NCDA Guidelines for the Use of the Internet for Provision of
Career Information and Planning Services.

The Center for Education and Work
University of Wisconsin
964 Educational Sciences Building
1025 W. Johnson Street
Madison, WI 53706-1796
(800) 446-0399 for U.S. & Canada
95.800.446.0339 for Mexico
Fax: (608) 262-9197
E-mail: cewmail@soemadison.wisc.edu
Web site: http://www.cew.wisc.edu

The Center for Technology in Counseling and Career Development
Florida State University College of Education
Department of Human Services and Studies
Tallahassee, FL 32301
(904) 644-6431

The Missouri Career Center
110 Noyes Hall
Columbia, MO 65211
(573) 882-6801
Fax: (573) 882-5440
Web site: http://www.missouri.edu/~cppcwww/main.html
The University of Missouri–Columbia maintains an extensive database of information about work, careers, and jobs, as well as helpful guides for job-seeking activities.

Academic Innovations (school)
3463 State Street, Suite 219A
Santa Barbara, CA 93105
(805) 967-8015
Fax: (805) 967-4357

AGS (American Guidance Service) (school)
4201 Woodland Road
PO Box 99
Circle Pines, MN 55014-1796
(800) 328-2560
Fax: (612) 786-0907
E-mail: ags@skypoint.com
Web site: http://www.agsnet.com

Cambridge Career Products
PO Box 2153
Dept. CC18
Charleston, WV 25328-2153
(800) 468-4227

RESOURCES FOR ALL-LEVEL CAREER COUNSELING

Career Development Systems
5225 Verona Road, Building #3
Madison, WI 53711-4495
(888) 237-9297
Web site: http://www.cdsways.com

Career Planning & Adult Development NETWORK
PO Box 611930
San Jose, CA
(800) 888-4945; Fax: (408) 441-9101

Career Research & Testing
PO Box 611930
San Jose, CA 95161
(800) 888-4945
Jump Start Your Job Skills—creates a personal data base of skills, résumés
Achieving Your Career—an interactive approach to define the job-search process
Building Your Job Search Foundation—key questions that strengthens job search
Computerized DOT, Résumé Maker

Career Track (for all ages)
MS20-13
PO Box 18778
Boulder, CO 80308-1778
(800) 334-1018
Fax: (800) 622-6211
Web site: http://www.careertrack.com

Careerware: STM Systems Corporation
955 Green Valley Crescent
Ottawa, ON K2C 3V4 CANADA
(800) 267-7095

Chronicle Guidance Publications, Inc. (CGP) (for all ages)
PO Box 1190
Moravia, NY 13118-1190
(800) 622-7284
Fax: 315/497-3359
E-mail: 101565.1244@CompuServe.com

CFKR Career Materials (school)
11860 Kemper Road, Unit 7
Auburn, CA 95603
(800) 525-5626
Fax: (800) 770-0433

The Cress Company (school)
10 W. Elm Street
Chicago, IL 60610
(800) 637-2449
E-mail: eric@cressco.com
Interactive CD-ROMs for students

Consulting Psychologists Press, Inc.
3803 E. Bayshore Road
PO Box 10096
Palo Alto, CA 94303
(800) 624-1765
(415) 969-8901
Web site: http://www.cpp-db.com

Curriculum Innovations Group (school)
Weekly Reader Corp.
3001 Cindel Drive
Delran, NJ 08370
(800) 446-3355

EdITS (for K–12)
PO Box 7234
San Diego, CA 92167
(619) 222-1666
Fax: (619) 226-1666
Provides a variety of assessment instruments, including Career Occupational Preference System (COPS)

Ferguson Publishing Company (school)
200 W. Madison Street, Suite 300
Chicago, IL 60606
(800) 306-9941

International Quality & Productivity Center (IQPC)
150 Clove Road
PO Box 401
Little Falls, NJ 07424-0401
(800) 882-8684
(973) 256-0211
Fax: (973) 256-0205
E-mail: info@iqpc.com
Web site: http://www.iqpc.com

BUSINESS AND ORGANIZATIONAL INFORMATION AND WORKSHOPS

JIST (school and college)
720 N. Park Avenue
Indianapolis, IN 46202
(800) 648-JIST
Fax: (800) JIST-Fax
Sound & color descriptions of jobs in *Occupational Outlook Handbook*

Kidsway Entrepreneur Club Product Catalog
Kidsway, Inc.
5585 Peachtree Road
Chamblee, GA 30341
(888) KIDSWAY

Live Wire Media (school)
3450 Sacramento Street
San Francisco, CA 94118
(800) 359-KIDS

MAR-CO Products, Inc. (school)
Dept. 596 1443
Old York Road
Warminster, PA 18974
(800) 448-2197

Meridian Education Group (school)
Dept. CG-97
Bloomington, IL 61701
(800) 727-5507

The National Center for School to Work Training (NIMCO, Inc.)
PO Box 9
102 Highway 81 North
Calhoun, KY 42327-0009
(800) 952-6662
Web site: http://www.nimcoinc.com
Provides information on school-to-work programs, training, funding, and resources.

National Employer Leadership Council
1001 Connecticut Ave. NW, Suite 3109
Washington, DC 20036
(800) 360-NEIC
Web site: http://www.nelc.org

National TeleLearning Network, Inc.
5801 River Road
New Orleans, LA 70123-5106
(800) 432-3286

The New Careers Center, Inc. (school)
1515 23rd Street
PO Box 339-SK
Boulder, CO 80306
(800) 634-9024
Fax: (303) 447-8684

New Concepts Corp. (school)
Career Development Programs
2341 S. Friebus Avenue
Tucson, AZ 85713
(520) 323-6645
(800) 828-7876
Fax: (520) 325-5277

ORYX (school)
4041 N Central Avenue, Suite 700
Phoenix, AZ 85012-3397
(800) 279-6799
Pearson NCS Assessments
5605 Green Circle Drive
Minnetonka, MN 55343
(800) 627-7271
Fax: (612) 939-5199
Web site: http://www.ncs.com
Assessments for all age groups.

Psychological Assessment Resources, Inc. (PAR)
PO Box 998
Odessa, FL 33556
(800) 331-TEST
Fax: (800) 727-9329
Web site: http://www.parinc.com
Assessment instruments for children and adults.

Rosen Publishing Company (school)
29 E. 21st Street
New York, NY 10010
(800) 237-9932
Hardcover books written for teens. Excellent for school libraries.

Sigma Assessment Systems, Inc.
PO Box 610984
Port Huron, MI 48061-0984
(800) 265-1285
Fax: (800) 361-9411
E-mail: sigma@mgl.ca
Web site: http://www.mgl.ca/-sigma
Computer assisted guidance programs.

Southern School Media
415 Park Row, Dept. S
Bowling Green, KY 42101-2242
(800) 736-0288
Films, videos, and resources.

Sunburst Communications (school)
101 Castleton Street
Pleasantville, NY 10570
(914) 769-2109
Films, videos, and other materials.

The Education ConneXtion
12118 Elysian Court
Dallas, TX 75230
(972) 991-5252
(800) 991-2460
Fax: (972) 991-5261
A thorough collection of all types of materials for all school ages.

VGM Career Books (for all ages)
4255 W. Touhy Avenue
Lincolnwood, IL 60646-1975
(800) 323-4900
(847) 679-5500
Fax: (847) 679-2494

Wintergreen/Orchard House Career Services (school)
PO Box 15899
New Orleans, LA 70175-5899
(800) 321-9479

Chuck Eby's Counseling Resources is an example of a self-maintained site.
Web site: http://www.cybercom.net/~chuck/guide.html

Gail Hackett at Arizona State University also maintains a list of helpful sites.
Web site: http://www.seamonkey.ed.asu.edu/~gail/career.htm.

Appendix 5

❖❖❖

Useful Circular
and Reflexive Questions
for Work-Related Issues

In order to create a constructivist dialogue, circular and reflexive questions can be used. Rather than emphasizing facts, they are designed to develop a narrative with the client in order to understand meaning to the client rather than knowing all the details of interactions.

CIRCULAR QUESTIONS

These questions attempt to assess the varied influences that contribute to the client's work-related issues. They are circular in that the feedback clients give provides information to solicit further information about relationships.

Category Difference Questions

between persons:

"At your work site, who is more homophobic, Carlos or Wesley?"

between interpersonal relationships:

"Whose advice is your boss most likely to take, yours or hers?"

between perceptions, ideas, or beliefs:

"Is the high turnover rate in your workplace because people get fed up and leave, or is it because they find better paying jobs?"

"Who thinks selling your business is a good idea? Who thinks this second most strongly? Third most strongly?"

"Who at work believes most strongly in affirmative action? Who believes this second most strongly? Third most strongly?"

between actions and events:

"When a customer gets annoyed, who at work tries hardest to smooth things over? Who tries second most hardest?"

Categorical Context Questions

the relationship between meaning and action:

"When you think your co-worker is trying to manipulate you, what does your co-worker do?"

the relationship between action and meaning:

"When your manager keeps on working at her computer keyboard when you try to discuss matters with her, what do you take that to mean?"

Temporal Difference Questions

between past and past:

"Was optimism higher when you first opened the business eight years ago, or when you merged with the other company three years ago?"

between past and present:

"Was your boss more receptive to your advice when she believed you thought the same as she did, or is she more receptive now?"

between past and future:

"If you don't allow your youngest daughter to get a part-time job when she gets to high school, like you did your oldest son, what do you think will happen?"

between present and future:

"If you keep going over your boss's head to his supervisor, what kind of working relationship will you have with your boss a year from now?"

between future and future:

[As a follow-up to the question immediately above.] "If next month, the supervisor suddenly felt your boss really did have the company's best interests at heart, would the supervisor be more receptive to your views or less?"

REFLEXIVE QUESTIONS

An extension of circular questions are reflexive questions. These go beyond circular in that they extend the examination of constructs to create an understanding of levels of meaning. The idea is that reflexive questions approach symptoms as communication acts embedded in interaction patterns of repetitive sequences between persons. They too work from different perspectives.

Future-Oriented Questions

for personal goals:

"What are your occupational plans?"

"Have you considered anything else?"

"What kind of education or training would you need for that occupation?"

"How will you get that education or training?"

for collective goals for self and others:

> "What occupational goals do you have in mind for yourself? For your child? For your spouse?"

to operationalize vague goals:

> "How will you know when you/your child/your spouse has successfully reached those goals?"
>
> "What exact behaviors would show you that you/your child/your spouse has successfully reached those goals?"

to explore anticipated outcomes:

> "How much progress will you/your child/your spouse make toward those goals in the next month? In the next six months? In the next year?"

to highlight potential consequences:

> "Who will be most surprised if you/your child/your spouse meets those goals?"
>
> "Now that your boss has found a new job, who among your co-workers is most likely to become your new boss?"

to explore catastrophic expectations:

> "Who will be most disappointed if you/your child/your spouse fails to meet those goals?"
>
> "Suppose your boss denied your request for a raise? A transfer? A reference? Then, what?"

Observer-Perspective Questions

to enhance self-awareness:

> "How did you react when that happened at work?"
>
> "What did you make of what happened that led you to feel that way?" "Now how do you feel about the way you reacted to what happened at work?"
>
> "If you had the chance to react all over again, would you act differently to anything?"

to encourage "other" awareness:

> "What do you suppose your boss thought about that? Your co-workers? Your spouse?"
>
> "What do you suppose your boss goes through when that happens? Your co-workers? Your spouse?"
>
> "When your boss does that, what do you suppose your boss is feeling? Your co-workers? Your spouse?"

to explore interpersonal perception:

> "What do you suppose is going on with your co-worker when he/she threatens to quit?"
>
> "What do you suppose is going on with your boss when he threatens to quit?"

to explore interpersonal reaction:

> "What do you do when your boss gets stressed out? Your co-worker?"
>
> "What does your boss/co-worker do when you get stressed out?"
>
> "What does your co-worker do when your boss praises you? Reprimands you?"
>
> "What do you suppose your boss/co-worker feels when you do outstanding work? Lousy work?"

Unexpected Context Change Questions

to explore opposite content:

"Since you were fired, what do you find enjoyable about that?"

"Since your contract was not renewed, for what are you most grateful?"

to explore opposite context:

"With all the turmoil you describe at work, who among your co-workers enjoys it the most?"

"Who among your co-workers would feel the greatest loss if all the turmoil would stop?"

"With all the long hours you have to put in at work, who in your family do you suppose misses you the least?"

"Who among your family would feel the most disappointed if you did *not* have to work so many hours and were at home more?"

to explore a need to preserve the status quo:

"Why would the turmoil you describe at work need to continue?"

"How come you need to keep putting in long hours at work?"

"What other more serious problems at home may this work turmoil/working of long hours be solving? Preventing?"

"Who in your family is going to be least thrilled about you getting your GED? Going back to work? Going back to school?"

Distinction-Clarifying Questions

to clarify causal attributions:

"Do you think your son's/brother's not following in his father's footsteps means more that your son/brother will never amount to anything, more that your son/brother will never fulfill his potential, or more that he'll never make his father proud?"

"Do you think your college educated daughter's/sister's marrying a man with no education means more that she's marrying beneath her, more that he'll never be able to take care of her, or more that there will always be a gap between them?"

to clarify categories:

"When your wife/mother says she wants to go back to school, is it because she's thinking only of herself, thinking that the kids are older now and don't need her as much, or thinking it'll make her a more interesting person?"

"Do you think your husband/father has difficulty telling the difference between someone thinking only of herself or thinking her growth will benefit everyone?"

to clarify dilemmas:

"Which is more important to you, this job promotion and working longer hours for more money, or seeing your children more often and being a part of their lives?"

Normative-Comparison Questions

to draw a contrast with a social norm:

"Do you think you are more upset than other people who get laid off in December?"

"Do you think you are more nervous than other people who've had four job interviews and haven't heard any news yet?"

to raise a contrast with a developmental norm:

"Do most members of your family prefer to stay in the area and live and work, or do most of them relocate for school or a job?"

social normalization:

"Lots of students who transfer to another school are concerned about making new friends. When did you first realize you were concerned?"

developmental normalization:

"Lots of parents hate leaving their children off at day care for the first time. Who else do you know who would understand how you feel?"

cultural normalization:

"If your parents found out that most American parents disliked it when their grown children with grandchildren relocated across the country, would your parents be surprised?"

inclusive normalization:

"Do you imagine any other co-workers would feel disconnected when returning to work after two months away because of major surgery?"

Written by Roberto Cortéz González, Ph.D.

Adapted from Tomm, K. (1987). Inventive interviewing: Part II. Reflexive questioning as a means to enable self-healing. *Family Process, 26,* 167–183.

Glossary

A

ability—the inherent skills one possesses.

ability tests—"measure skills in terms of speed, accuracy, or both" (Kaplan & Saccuzzo, 1997, p. 11).

acculturation—the process of accepting both one's original group values and the values of at least one other group (Olmedo, 1979); and the accumulation and incorporation of the beliefs and customs of at least one alternative culture (Mendoza & Martínez, 1981).

achievement tests—measure previous learning.

active agents—individuals responsible for one's own career planning.

adaptive skills—a set of skills needed to survive in the world of work, including the following: skills of problem recognition and definition, handling evidence, analytical skills, skills of implementation, human relations, [and] learning skills (The U.S. Congress Office of Technology Assessment, pp. 131, 132).

AFDC (Aid to Families with Dependent Children)—see **House Rule (HR) 3734,** the Personal Responsibility and Work Opportunity Reconciliation Act.

affirmative action—the "planning and acting to end the absence of certain kinds of people—those who belong to groups that have been subordinated or left out—from certain jobs and schools" (Bergman, 1996, p. 7).

African Americans—descriptive term used by the U.S. Bureau of the Census to refer to people of African ancestry or origin now living in the United States.

Afrocentrism—the idea that behaviors based on an African cultural heritage account for differences between Black and White student behaviors.

agentic behavior—interpreting and shaping one's own life through action and independence.

ally—heterosexuals who are professionally and personally affirmative to gay, lesbian, and bisexual people.

androcentric—the focus on White male standards to define normality.

Anglo—a misnomer used to refer to White people of various ethnic ancestries that presumes English cultural uniformity.

anti-Semitism—anti-Jewish **prejudice** and **discrimination.**

anxiety—one of several factors that can be part of career indecision. These factors are: (1) anxiety, (2) external locus of control, (3) problems in self-perception, (4) interpersonal difficulties and dependency, (5) interests, (6) ability levels, and (7) cognitive styles (Newman, Fuqua, & Seaworth, 1989).

aptitude tests—the potential for acquiring a specific skill.

Archway Model—Super's (1990) graphic representation of the synthesis of theories and models of life-span, life-space approach to career counseling.

artistic type—this development of an artistic pattern of activities, competencies, and interests creates a person who is predisposed to exhibit the following behavior:

1. Prefers artistic occupations or situations in which one can engage in preferred activities and competencies and avoid the activities demanded by conventional occupations or situations.
2. Uses artistic competencies to solve problems at work and in other settings.
3. Perceives self as expressive, original, intuitive, nonconforming, introspective, independent, disorderly, having artistic and musical ability, and ability in acting, writing, and speaking.
4. Values aesthetic qualities (Holland, 1992, p. 20).

These demands, opportunities, and artistic people create a characteristic atmosphere that operates to produce the following outcomes:

1. It stimulates people to engage in artistic activities.

2. It fosters artistic competencies and achievements.

3. It encourages people to see themselves as expressive, original, intuitive, nonconforming, independent, and as having artistic abilities (acting, writing. and speaking).

4. It encourages people to see the world in complex, independent, unconventional, and flexible ways.

The artistic person is apt to be: complicated, imaginative, intuitive, disorderly, impractical, nonconforming, emotional, impulsive, original, expressive, independent, sensitive, idealistic, introspective, open (Holland, 1992, p. 21)

Asian American/Pacific Islander—descriptive term used by the U.S. Bureau of the Census to refer to people of Asian ancestry or origin now living in the United States.

assessment—a procedure used to evaluate an individual in terms of current and future functioning (Kaplan & Saccuzzo, 1997).

assessment tool—another name for **test**.

assimilation—the merging of cultural traits from previously distinct cultural groups (*Random House Dictionary*, 1979).

associative learning experiences—occur when an individual pairs a situation that has been previously neutral with one that is positive or negative. Two types of associative learning experience are observation, and classical conditioning. This is an extension of the classical conditioning paradigm.

avocational activities—activities pursued systematically and consecutively for their own sake; the objective is for other than monetary gain, which may incidentally occur (Super, 1976).

avocational pursuits—hobbies.

B

baby boomers—those born between 1946 and 1964, the big postwar population boom.

babybusters—people who are in their twenties and are making an impact on the world of work.

basic academic skills—the ability to read, follow directions, and use mathematics.

basic skills—reading, writing, arithmetic, and mathematics, speaking, and listening (U.S. Department of Labor, Special Commission on Achieving Necessary Skills, 1991).

behavior—overt actions such as driving a car or playing a guitar (Van Hoose & Paradise, 1979).

behavior-based conflict—see **work-family conflict.**

belief in a just world—the tendency for laypeople to view victims as the cause of their own misfortune.

between-group differences—differences that occur between two or more racial or ethnic groups; cross-cultural comparisons.

birth order—the order of a child's birth, which is thought to affect the child's place in her/his family and on a larger scale, the child's future placement in society.

Black Cultural Learning Style (BLS)—an example of attempts to use cultural values as a primary explanation for behaviors that benefit or impede educational attainment and its related occupational development for African Americans.

blaming the victim—an ideological process that stigmatizes the victim by accounting for their victimization by locating the malignant nature of poverty, injustice, slum life, and racial difficulties as located within the victim (Ryan, 1971).

Buddhism—cultural value where self-improvement can be found through doing good work and study and through the control of undesirable emotions; optimism, calmness, and harmony are valued (Axelson, 1993, p. 438).

burnout—a process of gradual change in behavior, eventually reaching intense reactions and often leading to a crisis, if left unresolved.

C

calculus—the relationship within and between types or environments that can be ordered according to the hexagonal model for defining Holland's typology. Types adjacent to each other on the hexagonal model are presumed to be most similar. Types opposite each other are presumed to be most dissimilar.

Calvinism—ideas put forth by Protestant reformer John Calvin (e.g., the fulfillment of duties through work is the highest form of moral activity an individual can assume).

career—the "sequence of occupations in which one engages" (Tolbert, 1980, p. 31).

career adaptability—a construct that Super and Knasel (1979) proposed to describe the balance an individual attempts to maintain between the work world and personal environment.

career counseling—"planning and making decisions about occupations and education" (Tolbert, 1980, p. 32). The term has evolved into being most applicable to those of the professional class.

career death—job loss that may force a person into a situation in which they must find some new work.

career decision-making self-efficacy—beliefs about one's ability to decide on an appropriate career choice.

Career Decisions Software Solutions (CDSS)—a computer program that assists a person in making career decisions by providing accurate career information from an office or a computer. It provides a list of occupations that matches the person's characteristics or the characteristics of the desired vocation.

career development—"the lifelong process of developing work values, crystallizing a vocational identity, learning about opportunities, and trying out plans in part-time, recreational, and full-time work situations" (Tolbert, 1980, p. 31); used interchangeably with **occupational development** and **vocational development**.

career first, then family—observations that Richter, Morrison, and Salinas (1991) make about ways to deal with the issue of dual careerism in which the couple must deal with the issues of (1) the biological time clock for women, (2) men's physical degeneration and lowering of stamina, (3) age differences in child raising, and (4) ambivalence/reality testing.

career indecision—the "state of being undecided about a career" (Newman, Fuqua, & Seaworth, 1989).

career maturity—a hypothetical construct of a constellation of physical, psychological, and social characteristics; psychologically, it is both cognitive and affective. It includes the degree of success in coping with the demands of earlier stages and substages of career development and especially with the most recent.

career myths—"irrational attitudes about the career development process. These irrational attitudes most often are generated from historical, familial patterns of career ignorance and negative career development experiences" (Herring, 1990, p. 13).

Career Navigator—a Computer Assisted Career Guidance System that places more emphasis on job search assistance than on self-exploration.

career plateauing—"the point in a career when the likelihood of additional hierarchical promotion is very low" (Ferrence, Stoner, & Warren, 1977).

career renewal—a transitional stage that takes place for people generally at the end of the establishment stage and at the beginning of the maintenance stage of a job or career (Beijan & Salomone, 1995, p. 52).

career resiliency—one who is: (1) self-aware; (2) values driven; (3) dedicated to continuous learning; (4) future-focused; (5) connected; and (6) flexible (Collard, Epperheimer, & Saign, 1996).

career search self-efficacy—the "individual's degree of confidence that they can successfully perform a variety of career exploration activities, including their judgments about their ability to successfully explore personal values and interests, effectively network with professionals in a field of interest, [and] successfully interview for a job" (Solberg, Good, Fischer, Brown, & Nord, 1995, p. 448).

Career Transition Inventory—an assessment instrument for adults in transition. It was designed specifically to "assess and understand internal, dynamic psychological processes that may get in the way of the career transition process" (p. 220). Five basic factors the instrument attempts to assess are (1) readiness; (2) confidence; (3) perceived support; (4) control; and (5) decision independence (Heppner, 1991).

casual register—language that is (1) used between friends, (2) with a general, nonspecific word choice, (3) dependent upon nonverbals for assistance in conveying meaning, and (4) that often uses incomplete syntax.

CASVE Cycle—a cycle of generic career problem-solving and decision-making skills that includes:

1. communication—understanding the external demands and internal states that signal the need to begin problem solving
2. analysis—clarifying or obtaining knowledge about self, occupations, decision making, or metacognitions
3. synthesis—elaborating and synthesizing alternatives
4. valuing—prioritizing alternatives and making tentative primary and secondary choices
5. execution—formulating a plan for implementing a tentative choice that includes a preparation program, reality testing, and employment seeking.

"The cycle is a recursive process, in which individuals move backward and forward through the cycle in response to their emerging decision needs and the availability of information resources" (Sampson et al., 1992 p. 68).

caves and commons—environments arranged by grouping private work areas around larger communal team space.

chance processes—capitalizing on chance and unforeseen events.

character—that within an individual that makes wise and kind (i.e., moral) choices (Pipher, 1996).

child care options—observations Richter, Morrison, and Salinas (1991) make about ways to deal with the issue of dual careerism, in which the couple must deal with the options of (1) parental care—staggered hours, (2) care by extended family member, (3) family day care, (4) group care, (5) full-time babysitter/housekeeper/nanny, (6) two parents who can dovetail their work schedules, (7) taking a child to work, (8) parent cooperative, (9) children in charge of themselves, (10) drop-in centers, (11) working from home, and (12) a combination of the above.

child time—a pace that is flexible and mainly slow. It entails patiently making allowances for "oversee[ing] the laborious task of tying a [child's] shoelace, [tolerating] a [child's] prolonged sit on the potty, [and listening] to the scrambled telling of a tall tale" (Hochschild, 1997, p. 5).

CHOICES—a Computer Assisted Career Guidance System intended for high school students to assist them in making informed and educated decisions about their future, whether it be to attend a university or begin a career.

classism—the pathological labeling of behavior patterns that differ from middle- and upper-class norms. Often, such alternative behavior patterns may be functional in a lower socioeconomic class person's community (Payne, 1995).

Code of Fair Testing Practices in Education—a valuable resource for comprehending the uses and abuses of assessment procedures written for the general public, especially test takers and/or their parents or guardians.

cognitive career/vocational counseling—an approach that helps clients challenge their irrational vocational beliefs so that they can attain their career and personal goals.

Cognitive Information Processing (CIP)—perspective used by Sampson, Peterson, Lenz, and Reardon (1992) to describe the career development of individuals.

collectivism—"in-group norms and role relations provide both the motivating force that drives the individual and the compass from which the individual takes direction" (Ross & Nisbett, 1991, p. 181).

collectivistic orientation—an inclination toward the collective rather than the individual. Greatly influenced by culture.

coming out of the closet—an ongoing process in which lesbians and gays reveal their sexual orientation to the world in which they live. Also known as *coming out*.

commitments—an individual's ability to act on one's values when it is neither convenient nor easy (Pipher, 1996).

competence assumption—a political view of human nature, as described by Lawrence W. Mead in *The New Politics of Poverty* (1992), shared by both conservative and liberal political thinkers when discussing poverty in America. The competence assumption takes for granted "that the individual is willing and able to advance his or her own economic interests. . . . Americans are in motion toward economic goals" (p. 19).

Conduct—when a person voluntarily chooses between alternative courses of action.

Confucian work ethic—teaches children that they are required to do well because they owe it to their parents (Butterfield, 1990).

Confucianism—cultural value where patriarchal ideas are embraced and a formal relationship system emphasizes humility, politeness, and respect (Axelson, 1993, p. 438).

congruence—the process of an environment fit to the person; different personality types requiring different model work environments.

connected voice—describes women's orientation with respect to occupational achievement and interpersonal relationships, due to being socialized into defining themselves through their connection with and responsiveness to others.

consciousness—the moment when a person's mind awakens and learns "to perceive social, political, and economic contradictions, and to take action against the oppressive elements of reality" (Freire, 1970/1993, p. 17).

consequentiality—an act cannot be labeled occupationist unless it is potentially harmful or helpful to a person's interests, which is termed consequentiality. "The effects of occupationist acts may be either harmful or beneficial to an individual's interests, depending on the circumstances" (Carson, 1992, p. 492).

consistency—the degree of relatedness between personality types or between model work environments.

consolidation—a period of establishment in a career by advancement, status, and seniority (Zunker, 1994).

constructive developmental theory—an individual's meaning-making framework, for career transitions.

constructive developmentalism—an approach to career counseling where life is viewed as a learning process and, from experience, one constructs one's own reality and meaning. The approach promotes the development of self-awareness, meaning-making, and choices, helping people lead more "self-directed, decision-guided" lives.

constructivism—a theory of clinical practice in which individuals actively construct their personal realities and create their own representational models of the world (Meichenbaum & Fong, 1993).

constructivist epistemologies—the conceptualization of human beings as "active agents who, individually or collectively, co-constitute the meaning of their experiential world" (R. A. Neimeyer, 1993a, p. 222).

content bias—occurs when test items are more familiar to one racial or ethnic group than another. (One of the text author's experience as a multicultural fairness reviewer of tests has shown that content bias also includes familiarity with objects and terms based upon one's geographical region.)

contextual interpretation—the understanding of people's behavior as embedded in the context of their lives (Savikas & Walsh, 1996, pg. 352). Meaning is invented with the goal of attaining that which is socially useful, relevant, and viable.

conventional type—this development of a conventional pattern of activities, competencies, and interests creates a person who is predisposed to exhibit the following behavior:

1. Prefers conventional occupations or situations in which one can engage in preferred activities and avoid the activities demanded by artistic occupations or situations
2. Uses conventional competencies to solve problems at work and in other situation
3. Perceives self as conforming, orderly, and as having clerical and numerical ability
4. Values business and economic achievement (Holland, 1992, p. 22)

These demands, opportunities, and conventional people create an atmosphere that produces the following goals and outcomes:

1. It stimulates people to engage in conventional activities, such as recording and organizing data and records.
2. It fosters conventional activities and competencies.
3. It encourages people to see themselves as conforming, orderly, nonartistic, and as having clerical competencies; it encourages them to see the world in conventional, stereotyped, constricted, simple, dependent ways.
4. It rewards people for the display of conventional values: money, dependability, and conformity (p. 40).

The conventional person is apt to be: careful, inflexible, persistent, conforming, inhibited, practical, conscientious, methodical, prudish, defensive, obedient, thrifty, efficient, orderly, unimaginative (p. 23).

corporate anorexia—a term that describes the massive downsizing occurring in the workforce.

correspondence—when the individual and the environment are attuned and when work meets the needs of the individual and the individual meets the demands of the work environment. Correspondence is an everchanging process because both the needs of the individual and the demands of the job change. However, if the correspondence continues, job tenure is extended.

countertransference—when a boss or coworker reacts toward a person in a manner similar to a significant person in the boss's or coworker's past or present life.

criterion-referenced test—describes the specific types of skills, tasks, or knowledge of an individual relative to a well-defined mastery criterion.

crystallization—a cognitive process period of formulating a general vocational goal through awareness of resources, contingencies, interests, values, and planning for the preferred occupation (Zunker, 1994).

cultural inversion—a process whereby certain behaviors, events, symbols, and meanings that involuntary minorities are apt to consider as inappropriate for themselves because these characterize White Americans.

cultural racism—societal "beliefs and customs that promote the assumption that the products of the dominant culture (e.g., language, traditions, appearance) are superior to other cultures" (J. Jones, 1972, cited in Atkinson, Morten, & Sue, 1993, p. 11).

culturally deprived—see **culturally disadvantaged.**

culturally disadvantaged—the term *culturally deprived* suggests an absence of culture, while *culturally disadvantaged* refers to a person who lacks the cultural background formed by the dominant social and political structure (Atkinson, Morten, & Sue, 1993, chapter 1).

culturally learned expectations and values—these make behavior meaningful from a multicultural perspective and promote a tolerance for a varied and complex **worldview.**

D

decided-decisive client—clients classified thus could be treated through support because this is not a diagnosable problem.

decided-indecisive client—clients in this state are in self-conflict. They have formed a temporary decision, but are unable to make an actual choice. They are in conflict because they want to pursue one career, but have interest in a dissimilar career (adapted from Miller, 1993).

decided-undecided state—temporary indecision that accompanies many decision-making tasks.

decision-making skills—understanding and mastering the decision-making process.

decisive-indecisive trait—a more permanent trait that is part of decision-making tasks.

deconstruction—"a postmodern method of analysis. Its goal is to undo all constructions. Deconstruction tears a text apart, reveals its contradictions and assumptions" (Rosenau, 1992, p. xi).

defense mechanisms—coping strategies to fend off unpleasant ideations and/or feelings.

developmental perspectives—presumes that how people see themselves changes over time as a consequence of age and life experience.

developmental tasks—a new accomplishment or responsibility to be faced at a certain point in an individual's life, the successful achievement of which leads to happiness and success.

dialogic community—where language is the primary vehicle for creating meaning in the workplace.

differential validity—the extent to which a test has different meanings for different groups of people, such as a test that may be a valid predictor of college success for White students but not Black students.

differentiation—the degree to which a person or an environment is well-defined.

discourse—"a system of statements, practices, and institutional structures that share common values" (Hare-Mustin, 1994, p. 19).

DISCOVER—a Computer Assisted Career Guidance System released in a multimedia version in 1997, which is available in English and French and adapted for use in Canada and Australia, using occupational information relevant to those countries.

discriminability—occurs when people make judgments based on the relative position of a person's occupation within "an almost universally agreed upon" occupational "prestige hierarchy" (Krumboltz, 1991b, p. 310).

discrimination—"treatment or consideration of or making a distinction in favor of or against a person or thing based on the group, class, or category to which that person or thing belongs rather than on individual merit" (*Random House Dictionary,* 1979).

discursive practices—"*rules by which discourses are formed, rules that govern what can be said and what must remain unsaid, and who can speak with authority and who must listen*" (McLaren, 1994, p. 188, italics in the original).

disparate impact—"discrimination caused by the consequences of a particular practice used by the employer" (Hagan & Hagan, 1995, p. 5).

disparate treatment—instances in which an employee is subject to adverse treatment because of the employee's race, color, religion, sex, or national origin.

dispositionism—the belief "that individual differences or traits can be used to predict how people will behave in new situations" (Ross & Nisbett, 1991, p. 3).

distress—when there are too many stressors or when they continue for too long.

diversity—a broad term that considers gender, age, culture, ethnicity, disabilities, sexual orientation, etc.

dominance—when one option is better than another in at least one aspect and is at least as good as the other for each of the other relevant aspects (Gati, 1990).

downsizing—job losses incurred by higher-paid, white collar workers.

dual-career couple—a relationship in which both partners are employed, usually in different occupations.

dual-career families—a major factor altering the family for years to come; see also **dual-career couple.**

dynamics of dominant-subordinate relationships—the development of a cultural identity that determines clinician and client attitudes toward (1) self, (2) others of the same group, (3) others of a different group, and (4) the White, dominant cultural group.

E

early recollections—one's childhood memories, usually those from before the age of eight, which coincide with the individual's pattern of lifestyle and the manner in which they are retained is purposeful and deliberate. Early recollections are an integral part of a lifestyle's maintenance.

Echo boom generation—born between 1977–1997), enters the workforce as the largest generation ever at 80 million, will easily displace the baby boomers. This group is well versed in computers and new electronic media and exhibits several differences from the previous two generations:

educational attainment—the highest level of formal schooling one has obtained.

emic—a perspective that is culture-specific and examines behavior using criteria related to the internal characteristics of the culture, presumably from a position within that culture (Dana, 1993).

emotional resources—the ability to exercise self control and stamina to weather negative situations and feelings and, most importantly, to move up from one class to the other.

empiricism—the belief that observation and experiment are the only valid means for adding to the knowledge base.

enterprising type—this development of an Enterprising pattern of activities, competencies, and interests creates a person who is predisposed to exhibit the following behavior:

1. Prefers enterprising occupations or situations in which one can engage in preferred activities and avoid the activities demanded by investigative occupations and situations.
2. Uses enterprising competencies to solve problems at work and in other situations.
3. Perceives self as aggressive, popular, self-confident, sociable, possessing leadership and speaking abilities, and lacking scientific ability.
4. Values political and economic achievement (Holland, 1992, p. 22).

These demands, opportunities, and enterprising people create a characteristic atmosphere that operates to produce the following goals and outcomes:

1. It stimulates people to engage in enterprising activities such as selling, or leading others.
2. It fosters enterprising competencies and achievements.
3. It encourages people to see themselves as aggressive, popular, self-confident, sociable, and as possessing leadership and speaking ability. It encourages people to see the world in terms of power, status, responsibility, and in stereotyped, constricted, dependent, and simple terms (p. 39).

The enterprising person is apt to be: acquisitive, energetic, flirtatious, adventurous, exhibitionistic optimistic, agreeable, excited, self-confident, ambitious, seeking, sociable domineering, extroverted, talkative (p. 21).

entrepreneurial skills—job skills needed to operate a full- or part-time business out of the home as an alternative to the corporate world.

environmental conditions—refers to (1) the number and nature of job opportunities; (2) the number and nature of training opportunities; (3) social policies and procedures for selecting trainees and workers; (4) rate of return for various occupations; (5) labor laws and union rules; (6) physical events such as earthquakes, droughts, floods, and hurricanes; (7) availability and demand for natural resources; (8) technological developments; (9) changes in social organization; (10) family training, experiences, and resources; (11) educational systems; (12) neighborhood and community influences, and other social, cultural, political, and economic considerations.

environmental constructs—the physical nature of the workplace (e.g., architectural design, job accommodation).

epistemology—the origin, structure, and methods of knowing, and the standards of judging and validating knowledge about the world (Dervin, 1994; Peterson, 1970).

equal access to occupational opportunities—determined by external, structural factors.

equity theory—job satisfaction based on what is obtained, such as justice, equity, personal fairness, versus what is desired, such as pay and working conditions.

ethics—represent an objective inquiry about behavior.

ethnic identity development—"one's sense of belonging to an ethnic group and the part of one's thinking, perceptions, feelings, and behavior that is due to ethnic group membership" (Rotheram & Phinney, 1987, p. 13).

ethnicity—an imprecise concept that relies on various criteria for definition, including race, language, and region (Petersen, 1980).

ethnocentrism—where one culture's values matter more than those of another culture (Atkinson et al., 1993).

etic—a perspective that emphasizes universal behaviors of human beings where many cultures are examined and compared, presumably from a position outside those cultures (Dana, 1993).

Eurocentrism—". . . the conviction that Europe is an inevitable and necessary global reference point as it is the cultural, political, and economic centre [*sic*] of the world" (Harrison, 2003, p. 107). One finds Eurocentrism in ". . . all societies into which the imperial force of Europe has intruded" (Ashcroft, Griffiths, & Tiffin, 1995, p. 2).

eustress—the exhilarating feeling of accomplishment that results from effectively coping with stress.

existential approach—existentialism is rooted in the philosophy that humans control their destiny. When applied to career counseling, the client's growth is based upon his or her chosen philosophy, which can be altered. Each person has a unique view of life through which he or she tries to understand the world through an interpretation of his or her experiences.

exploitation—when "the energies of the have-nots are continuously expended to maintain and augment the power, status, and wealth of the haves" (Young, 1992, p. 183).

external locus of control—the sense that events are outside one's control.

extraversion (5)—in the extraverted attitude (5) of the **MBTI**, attention seems to flow out, or to be drawn out to the objects and people of the environment. . . . [The following are] characteristics associated with extraversion: awareness and reliance on the environment for stimulation and guidance; an action-oriented, sometimes impulsive way of meeting life; frankness; ease of communication; or sociability.

extreme postmodernism—"is revolutionary; it goes to the very core of what constitutes social science and radically dismisses it" (Rosenau, 1992, p. 4).

F

face validity—the extent to which items on a test appear to be meaningful and relevant. Face validity is actually not a form of validity, because it is not a basis for inference (Kaplan & Saccuzzo, 1997).

face visibility—judging workers on their actual amount of time present in the workplace, regardless of **productivity.**

familism—the inclusion of biological and nonbiological members into a family.

family first, then career—observations Richter, Morrison, and Salinas (1991) make about ways to deal with the issue of dual careerism is which the couple must deal with the issues of (1) less affluence, (2) less money, (3) fewer options for having material things, (4) shorter or lessened career opportunities, (5) fewer guilt feelings for neglect of family-oriented values, (6) more marital satisfaction if the person is oriented to family values, and (7) one staying at home for a few years while the other works, then then trading off.

family-in-relation—a contextual understanding of the family used by **MCT.**

family systems—an analysis of roles, boundaries, values, traditions, and messages, within a family.

family systems approaches—an approach to clinical practice that focuses on the interactions between individuals within a family.

fantasy—stage of career development of childhood (before age 11) characterized by purely play orientation in the initial stage; near the end to this stage, play becomes work oriented.

feeling (6)—one of four basic mental functions or processes. "Feeling is the function by which one comes to decisions by weighing the relative values and merits of the issues. Feelings rely on an understanding of personal and groups values; thus, it is more subjective than thinking. . . . [P]ersons making judgments with the feeling function are more likely to be attuned to the values of others . . . [have] a concern with the human as opposed to the technical aspects of problems, a need for affiliation, a capacity for warmth, a desire for harmony, and a time orientation that includes preservation of the values of the past (Myers & McCaulley, 1985, p. 12).

filial piety—a child's sense of allegiance and obligation to parents. Especially associated with Asian religions.

financial resources—having money and purchasing power.

first-order change—"any change in a system that does not produce a change in the structure of the system" (Lyddon, 1990, p. 122).

flex-time—an opportunity for a worker to adjust the hours on the job to a schedule that is suitable for other concerns, such as family responsibilities.

floating family—a blurring of boundaries with traditional family units related by blood, common residence, and shared surnames (Gergen, 1991a), and resulting in a family that consists of relationships that can be in a more continuous state of flux than with one's family of origin. Floating family networks are based on affectional ties of choice rather than blood ties of chance, and often occur when traditional family members withdraw from the family's orbit through connections established by the technologies of social saturation.

folkways—"the normative structure of values, customs and meanings that exist in any culture" (Fischer, 1989).

formal register—language which is used (1) in work and school, (2) with a specific word choice, and (3) with complete sentences and standard syntax.

formative evaluation—program-evaluation activities that are conducted during the course of a program. Formative evaluation is somewhat more flexible in that adjustments and corrections can be made to evaluation procedures during their ongoing activities.

formed family—evolves for those people who do not have access to a supportive biological family or for those who prefer a community of friends to the families into which they were born. The staying power of a formed family is contingent upon whether its members stay together despite disagreements, lend each other money when one member loses a job, or visit one another in a convalescent center after one has been paralyzed in a car crash (Pipher, 1996).

free agent—describes employees who have decided to manage their own careers.

fundamental attribution error—the failure to recognize the power of the situation.

G

Gelatt decision-making model—a type of decision-making model that provides: (1) a framework from which methods and techniques can be derived and used as guidelines in career-counseling programs; (2) a system to determine values as a significant part of the decision-making process; and (3) a concept of a series of decisions—immediate, intermediate, and future—pointing out that decision making is a continuous process.

gender exploitation—when the labor and energy expenditure of women benefits men, be it a homemaker who performs domestic tasks for a husband on whom she's economically dependent or women wage-earners whose energies are expended in the workplace—often unnoticed, unacknowledged, and under compensated—to "enhance the status of, please, or comfort others, usually men" (Young, 1992, p. 184).

gender role analysis—assesses the potential costs and benefits for women and men in terms of adopting traditional and nontraditional gender role behavior.

gender stratification—"the hierarchical distribution by gender of economic and social resources in a society" (Andersen, 1983, p. 77).

Generation Nexters—the youngest age group, born 1980–2000.

Generation X—those born between 1965–1976

generational poverty—families who have lived in poverty for two or more generations.

genetic endowment—the innate aspects rather than those that are learned. These include: (1) physical appearance, (2) race, (3) sex, (4) physical appearance, (5) intelligence, (6) musical ability, (7) artistic ability, (8) muscular coordination, and (9) predisposition to certain physical illnesses.

genogram—a format for drawing a family tree that records information about family members and their relationships over at least three generations. Genograms display family information graphically in a way that provides a quick gestalt of complex family patterns and a rich source of hypotheses about how a clinical problem may be connected to the family context and the evolution of both problem and context over time (McGoldrick & Gerson, 1985, p. 1).

"gettin' ghetto"—reverting back to behaviors one exhibited when living earlier in poverty or in the working-class, which can remain useful in specific times and places.

global competition—see **global economy.**

global economy—the increasing interdependence of trade and commerce that links economics across the globe.

Grand Narrative—a legacy of the Puritan work ethic, where one's work and career is central. The grand narrative of the twentieth century emphasizes new advances in human productive capacities founded upon reason and freedom.

group tests—tests given to more than one person at a time (Kaplan & Saccuzzo, 1997).

H

hand-me-down dreams—the goals, interests, and behaviors that families both encourage and discourage, ignore, and punish; the values about work, money, success, and happiness that families convey; and the roles and rules applied to different family members.

healthy paranoia—can characterize any individual or subgroup that has experienced extreme oppression.

hermeneutic activity—career counseling principal where the interpretation of the meaning of a client's story becomes primary.

heteronormativity—presumes that heterosexuality is a normal and natural fact, a simple extension of a biological process, and that other forms of sexual behavior are deviations from this norm.

heterosexism—the culturally conditioned bias that heterosexuality is intrinsically superior to homosexuality (Rochlin, 1985).

heterosexual privilege—the rights and freedoms taken for granted by many heterosexuals, which include: (1) heterosexual partners can publicly display affection without fear of comment or attack by others, (2) inheritance rights, (3) access to a partner in a hospital, (4) the legal right to marry, and (5) the ability to adopt children.

hidden rules—see **knowledge of hidden rules.**

hidden transcripts—"take place 'offstage,' beyond the observation direct observation of power holders" (Scott, 1990, p. 4).

Hispanic—descriptive term used by the U.S. Bureau of the Census to refer to people of at least partial Spanish ancestry or origin now living in the United States.

historical context—past events with enduring effects in the present.

Hmong—an ethnic group originally from the mountains of southwest China, where many remain. They migrated to Southeast Asia, in the northern parts of Laos, Vietnam, and Thailand, with small groups in Burma (Tapp, 1993).

homophobia—irrational dread and loathing of homosexuality and homosexual people.

hoteling—an alternative for management of office space. Space would be available for office meetings, team meetings, and in-services, but at other times the individual would be operating primarily from her/his car or home.

House Rule (HR) 3734, the Personal Responsibility and Work Opportunity Reconciliation Act—so-called welfare reform actually refers to House Rule (HR) 3734, the Personal Responsibility and Work Opportunity Reconciliation Act, passed by both Houses of Congress in August 1996. HR 3734 replaced (1) AFDC—Aid to Families with Dependent Children which expired in October 1996, (2) JOBS—the Job Opportunities and Basic Skills training program, (3) Emergency Assistance programs, and (4) ended entitlements to cash assistance (Hard & Schoenmakers, 1997). TANF—Temporary Assistance for Needy Families was created in October 1996 and replaced the AFDC and JOBS programs. Block grants are provided to each state in the form of cash assistance and employment services for TANF.

human ability tests—an assessment of achievement, aptitude, and intelligence (Kaplan & Saccuzzo).

I

identification—relating to another person or idea by taking on aspects of the object to which one is relating.

identification with the oppressor—when an individual obtains a position of power and authority, that person becomes an oppressor who do exactly to others what was done to them.

identity—an estimate of the clarity and stability of a person's identity or a model work environment's identity.

Ikhwàn al-Safá—a group of five to ten Muslim reformers thought to have lived in the Basra region of what is now southern Iraq, who collectively called themselves Ikhwàn al-Safá to hide their individual identities for fear of reprisal by Islamic fundamentalists. They wrote the text, Rasa'il Ikhwàn al-Safá wa-Khulln al-Wafa (commonly translated as **Treatises of the Brothers of Purity**, also known as the TBP).

implementation—completing training for vocational preference and entering employment (Zunker, 1994).

index person—the individual who is the primary focus of a **genogram.**

individual psychology (IP)—conveys an awareness of the human being as indivisibly embedded in the social world. IP regards the person's movement in response to the challenges of the life tasks to be self-determined and purposeful in every expression of thought, feeling, and action. IP considers each individual's lifestyle as based on convictions and attitudes initially assumed in childhood and rehearsed and refined thereafter in an unself-conscious manner.

individual tests—can be given to only one person at a time by a test administrator; group tests can be given to more than one person at a time (Kaplan & Saccuzzo, 1997).

individualism—"an emphasis on personal goals, interests, and preferences. Social relationships are dictated by commonality of interests and aspirations and are therefore subject to change as those interests and aspirations shift over time" (Ross & Nisbett, 1991, p. 181).

individualistic orientation—an inclination toward individual rather than collectivism. Greatly influenced by culture.

industrialism—the rise of industries that manufactured products, particularly by the assembly line method.

inequality—see **inequity**.

inequity—unequal treatment in hiring, education, job pay and promotion; often occurs on the basis of gender or racial/ethnic origin.

inference—logical deductions made from evidence about something that one cannot observe directly.

information and planning—a competence dimension concerning specificity of information individuals have concerning future career decisions and past planning accomplished.

information competencies—includes acquiring and evaluating data, organizing and maintaining files, interpreting and communicating, and using computers to process information (U.S. Department of Labor, Special Commission on Achieving Necessary Skills, 1991).

infostructure—information-based infrastructure.

institutional racism—"social policies, laws, and regulations whose purpose it is to maintain the economic and social advantage of the racial/ethnic group in power" (J. Jones, 1972, cited in Atkinson, Morten, & Sue, 1993, p. 11).

instrumental learning experiences—occur when the individual acts upon the environment in such a way as to produce desirable consequences. An instrumental learning experience has three components: antecedents, behavior, and consequences.

intelligence tests—tests measure the potential to solve problems, adapt to changing circumstances, and profit from experiences (Kaplan & Saccuzzo, 1997).

Interactive Life Planning (ILP)—a model of career planning based on a holistic view of adult life with career and work as part of a life plan, combining aspects of traditional career planning with a more philosophical approach and focusing on the person as a whole (Hansen, 1997).

interest inventories—usually result in a profile in which clients' responses to questions about interests in activities, competencies, and occupations are matched with interests of people already working in various occupations who self-report that they enjoy the work they do. Interest inventories do not tell clients what to do for a living.

internal structure bias—pertains to the relationship among items of a test and the manner in which test takers perceive the items.

interpersonal skills competencies—working on teams, teaching others, serving customers, leading, negotiating, and working well with people from culturally diverse backgrounds (U.S. Department of Labor, Special Commission on Achieving Necessary Skills, 1991).

in the closet—concealing their sexuality from others by gays and lesbians.

intrinsic interests—show themselves in a person's "enduring interest in activities that engage their feelings of personal efficacy and satisfaction" (Lent, Larkin, & Brown, 1989, p. 280).

introversion (I)—in the introverted attitude (I), energy is drawn from the environment, and consolidated within one's position. The main interests of the introvert are in the inner world of concepts and ideas. . . . [Introverts have the following] characteristics associated with introversion: interest in the clarity of concepts and ideas; reliance on enduring concepts more than on transitory external events; a thoughtful, contemplative detachment; and enjoyment of solitude and privacy (Myers & McCaulley, 1985, p. 13).

intuitive (N)—one of four basic mental functions or processes as measured by the **Myers-Briggs Type Indicator.** "Intuition (N) refers to perception of possibilities, meanings, and relationships by way of insight. . . . Intuition permits perception beyond what is visible to the senses, including possible future events. Thus, people oriented toward intuitive perception may become so intent on pursuing possibilities that they may overlook actualities. They may develop the characteristics than can follow from emphasis on intuition and become imaginative, theoretical, abstract, future oriented, or creative.

investigative type—this development of an investigative pattern of activities, competencies, and interests creates a person who is predisposed to exhibit the following behavior:

1. Prefers occupations or situations in which one can engage in preferred activities and competencies and avoid activities demanded by enterprising occupations and situations.
2. Uses investigative competencies to solve problems at work and in other settings.
3. Perceives self as scholarly, intellectual, having mathematical and scientific ability, and lacking in leadership ability.
4. Values science (Holland, 1992, p. 20).

These demands, opportunities, and investigative people create a characteristic atmosphere that operates to produce the following outcomes:

1. It stimulates people to perform investigative activities.
2. It encourages scientific competencies and achievements.
3. It encourages people to see themselves as scholarly, as having mathematical and scientific ability, and as lacking leadership ability; it encourages them to see the world in complex, abstract, independent, and original ways.
4. It rewards people for the display of scientific values (p. 37).

The investigative person is apt to be: analytical, helpful, responsible, cooperative, idealistic, sociable, patient, empathetic, tactful, friendly, kind, understanding, generous, persuasive, warm (p. 20).

invisible daddy track—means that while men are not vocal about child-care concerns, the public is quite unaware of the strain placed on fathers (Hall, 1989).

involuntary minorities—immigrants to a country through enforced slavery, political expulsion from their homelands, or other economic or military developments beyond their control (Triandis, 1993) and are inclined to secondary cultural differences.

irrational beliefs—errors in thinking (e.g., dichotomous thinking, overgeneralization, personalization, magnification) that Albert Ellis's RET calls irrational beliefs and that Aaron T. Beck's cognitive therapy calls cognitive distortions.

J

jingoism—a pronounced chauvinism and nationalism marked by a belligerent foreign policy.

job—"a group of similar positions in a business, industry, or other place of employment" (Tolbert, 1980, p. 31).

JOBS (the Job Opportunities and Basic Skills training program)—see **House Rule (HR) 3734**, Personal Responsibility and Work Opportunity Reconciliation Act.

job satisfaction—the result of an appropriate match of personality traits, interests, and work environment.

job sharing—two people accomplishing one job by dividing the hours required by the job.

job shock—changes caused by downsizing, layoffs, and restructuring of corporations, forcing many well-paid, highly skilled, white-collar workers into unemployment (Dent, 1995).

job stress—anxiety caused by a mismatch of job, skills, interests, and work environment, or a work overload.

judging (J)—in the judging attitude (J), a person is concerned with making decisions, seeking closure, planning operations, or organizing activities. For thinking-judging (TJ) types the decisions and plans are more likely to be based on logical analysis; for feeling-judging (FJ) types the decisions and plans are more likely to be based on human factors. But for all people who characteristically live in the judging (J) attitude, perception tends to be shut off as soon as they have observed enough to make a decision. . . . Persons who prefer J often seem in their outer behavior to be organized, purposeful, and decisive. . . . It is important to make sure it is understood that judgment refers to decision making, the exercise of judgment, and is a valuable and indispensable tool (Myers & McCaulley, 1985, p. 14).

K

Kluge—a distinct economy that consists of the concentration of public-sector bureaucracies, universities, and closely aligned private companies in government-related industries, and that exists virtually side by side with the networked economy.

knowledge of hidden rules—having an awareness of the unspoken understandings and cues that allow an individual to fit into a certain group—which is essential if one wishes to survive in a particular socioeconomic class.

L

labor force representation—refers to those who are eligible or actively seeking jobs.

Latino disconnect—a lack of awareness of one's roots and history, a result of post-colonialism, that impedes Latino success in business and in life in the United States.

learning experiences—"One's career preferences are a result of her or his prior learning experiences. An individual may have millions of prior learning experiences that will eventually influence his or her career decision" (Sharf, 1997, p. 328).

leisure—activities intended as a relaxation from work demands; leisure time is often stolen by habitual television viewing and happy hour activities.

Life-Career Rainbow—a model used by Super (1990) to describe the various roles one plays during his/her life.

life space—the major roles in an individual's life.

life span—the course of an individual's life.

lifestyle—a coherent, consistent and unitary perceptual adaptational set, which serves as a stable frame of reference for the individual, providing a method for both organizing and interpreting internal and external events (Watkins, 1984, p. 29).

life theme—Csikszentmihalyi and Beattie (1979) define life theme as "an affective and cognitive representation of existential problems which a person wishes to resolve. It becomes the basis for an individual's fundamental interpretation of reality and a way of coping with that reality" (p. 45).

localized knowledge—awareness about how the world of work is differentially manifested in various communities.

location of study—or **situated knowledge**, is "a point of view, a perspective of the knower in relation to what is known" (Richardson, 1993, p. 427).

logical positivism—a twentieth-century philosophical movement that contends that all genuine knowledge can be discovered through the use of the scientific method.

loss of face—humiliation of one who is already socialized to behave with humility; pertains to **Asian Americans.**

M

maintaining face—inhibited expression of undesirable emotions; pertains to Asian Americans.

male provider role—for many men the male provider roles means his sense of self-worth is derived from occupational status and income.

marginality—life on the periphery of both the native and colonial cultures, or of both the dominant and minority cultures.

marginalization—when labor markets systematically cannot or will not employ people, creating a permanent underclass that does not participate in socially productive activity. Also a political practice that overtly and covertly prevents the full participation in life-enhancing opportunities of individuals from social categories that have been labeled as inferior or deviant.

McDonaldization—*"the process by which the principles of the fast-food restaurant are coming to dominate more and more sectors of American society as well as the rest of the world"* (Ritzer, 2000, p. 1, italics in the original).

MCT—see **multicultural counseling and therapy**.

mean—the arithmetic average of a set of scores on a variable (from Kaplan & Sacuzzo, 2001).

mechanistic models—aim to discover scientifically the processes that can describe the true mechanisms that explain a given phenomena (Flew, 1984).

median age—the age where half of a population are below and half are above a given age.

median income—the income level where half earn below and half earn above a given amount.

mental resources—having the abilities and skills (e.g., reading, writing, computing) to process information and use it to negotiate daily life—is an advantage that lends itself to self-sufficiency.

mentor—a senior employee who helps younger employees in his or her development.

metacognitions—self-talk, self-awareness, and the monitoring of cognitions.

metatheory—a "theory of theories" (Sue, Ivey & Pedersen, 1996, p. 12).

Mirror of Human Life—one of the earliest comprehensive compilations of occupational descriptions, *Speculum Vitae Humanae* (*Mirror of Human Life*), published by Bishop Rodrigo Sánchez de Arévalo in 1468, the late Spanish medieval period that immediately preceded the joint reigns of King Fernando of Aragón (reigned 1479–1516) and Queen Isabel of Castile (reigned 1474–1504).

mission—according to the *Random House Dictionary*, is "an assigned or self-imposed duty or task." Synonyms are *calling* and *vocation*.

model minority—an inaccurate **stereotype** of Asian Americans.

moderate postmodernism—encourages substantive redefinition and innovation in the social and behavioral sciences (Rosenau, 1992).

modernism—see **logical positivism.**

morality—concerns itself with action that is purposeful and for the good of all. The goodness or badness of a behavior is the provenance of morality; choosing wisely and decently how one will be in the universe (Pipher, 1996) broadly defines morality.

multicultural counseling—a specialized aspect, or subfield, of clinical practice.

multicultural counseling and therapy (MCT)—is a **metatheory** that forms a means of understanding the numerous helping approaches developed by humankind by considering the totality and interrelationships of experiences (individual, group, and universal) and contexts, such as, individual, family, and cultural milieu (Sue, Ivey, & Pedersen, 1996).

multicultural perspective—a philosophical orientation that encompasses the entire field of multicultural clinical practice beyond all previously used terms (e.g., minority group counseling, pluralistic counseling, cross-cultural counseling).

multiculturation—the accumulation and incorporation of the belief and customs of one's own racial or ethnic group and the elements of several other groups.

multiculturalism—(1) Pedersen's multicultural perspective in clinical practice that includes demographic, ethnographic, status, and affiliation variables; (2) Sue, Ivey, and Pedersen's multicultural counseling and therapy metatheory.

multiple helping roles—the one-to-one encounter approach used by **MCT** aims at remediation in the individual, larger social units, systems intervention, and prevention—developed by many culturally different groups and societies.

multiple role realism—may be defined as "the recognition that multiple role involvement is a complex and potentially stressful lifestyle, paired with awareness of the need for careful planning and consideration of the interface between work and family roles (Weitzman, 1994, p. 16).

multipotentiality—"the ability to select and develop any number of career options because of a wide variety of interests, aptitudes, and abilities. The broad range of opportunities available tends to increase the complexity of decision making and goal setting, and it may actually delay career selection" (Kerr, 1990).

Myers-Briggs Type Indicator (MBTI)—based on a theory of personality devised by Swiss psychologist and psychiatrist Carl Gustav Jung [1875–1961]. For career purposes, the instrument is used primarily with interests and aptitude assessments. The MBTI manual (Myers & McCaulley, 1985) lists work environments in which various types of people labor, suggesting that the MBTI can apply to career adjustment as well.

myth of rugged individualism—the legacy of the Backcountry people that pervades the work ethic in the United States today.

N

narcissism—self-absorption and self-preoccupation (Pipher, 1996).

narrative approaches—an approach to clinical practice that focuses on the stories clients tell about themselves and others in attempts to make sense out of the world around them (Penn, 1991; Sarbin, 1986).

narrative approaches to career counseling—an approach that focuses on the stories clients tell about themselves and others as a way of making meaning of the world, which can also help clients address the subjective experience of their careers (Savickas, 1992).

narrative viability—means the newly emergent story (**personal narrative**) has to cohere into the larger system of personally and socially constructed realities into which it is incorporated (Granvold, 1996).

National Career Development Association (NCDA)—sets standards and goals for career counseling.

National Career Development Guidelines—a handbook of information for anyone responsible for career development in any setting for any age group. The purpose of the handbook is "to strengthen and improve comprehensive, competency-based career counseling, guidance and education programs" (p. i).

National Certified Career Counselors—have passed NCOA exam on standards and goals for career counseling.

negotiation—an important *art* in the dual-career marriage.

Net generation—see echo-boom generation.

networked—densely packed concentrations of entrepreneurs and companies in urbanized areas that generate virtually all the nation's globally competitive, high-wage industries.

New Economy—Roger Alcaly's (2003) term for the technological revolution that has occurred since the 1980s, which will continue to impact and focus the economy for many years to come. "[T]he last few decades of the [20th] century marked the beginning of great innovation and revitalization whose impact is likely to be felt for at least another generation. . ." (p. 4).

normative sample—see **standardization sample.**

norm-referenced test—a test that evaluates each individual relative to a normative group (from Kaplan & Sacuzzo, 2001).

norms—a summary of the performance of a group of individuals on which a test was standardized. The norms usually include the mean and the standard deviation for the reference group and information on how to translate a raw score into a percentile rank (from Kaplan & Sacuzzo, 2001).

O

objective personality tests—see **structured personality tests.**

occupation—"a definable work activity that occurs in many different settings" (Tolbert, 1980, p. 31).

occupational development—see **career development.**

occupational knowledge—information about individual occupations and a schema for organizing occupations.

occupational segregation—an overrepresentation of specific population groups in some occupations while being underrepresented in others (Leong & Serafica, 1995).

occupationism—discrimination against individuals based solely on their occupation.

oppressed groups—groups of people who are deprived of some human right or dignity where such people are (or perceive that they are) powerless to do anything about it (Goldenberg, 1978).

oppression—"Any situation in which 'A' objectively exploits 'B' or hinders his or her pursuit of self-affirmation as a responsible person is one of oppression" (Freire, 1970/1993, p. 37).

organization-in-relation—a contextual understanding of the organization used by **MCT.**

organizational transference—where a boss or co-worker reminds an employee of an important family member (Weinberg & Mauksch, 1991).

orientation to vocational choice—an attitudinal dimension determining if the individual is concerned with the eventual vocational choice to be made.

outcome constructs—job satisfaction, work adjustment, job stress, discrimination, and prejudice.

P

paradigm—"a central overall way of regarding phenomena . . . [and] may dictate what kind of explanation will be found acceptable" (Flew, 1984, p. 261).

parental intentions—Young and Friesen (1992) describe ten categories of parental intentions: (1) skill acquisition; (2) acquisition of specific values and beliefs; (3) protection from unwanted experience; (4) increase independent thinking or action; (5) decrease sex role stereotyping; (6) moderation of parent–child relationships; (7) facilitation of human relationships; (8) enhancement of character development; (9) development of personal responsibility;

and (10) achievement of parent's personal goals. The parent's side of the parent–child interaction sequence is particularly appropriate to the study of parental influence in the career development of their children. It was the parent who interacted with the child or intervened on the child's behalf and whose action had intention.

parenting issues—observations Richter, Morrison, and Salinas (1991) make about ways to deal with the issue of dual careerism in which the couple must deal with the need to decide (1) how it will be done, (2) who is going to do it, (3) who is going to be responsible for discipline, and (4) what are the shared responsibilities—quality time with children, physical needs, security, recreation/leisure time, allowing autonomy for children, delegation of household chores.

percentile ranks—the proportion of scores that fall below a particular score.

perceptive (P)—in the perceptive attitude (P) of the **MBTI**, a person is attuned to incoming information. For sensing-percepting (SP) types, the information is more likely to be the immediate realities. For intuitive-perceptive (NP) types, the information is more likely to be new possibilities. But for both SP and NP types, the perceptive attitude is open, curious, and interested. People who characteristically live in the perceptive attitude seem in their outer behavior to be spontaneous, curious, and adaptable, open to new events and changes, and aiming to miss nothing.

Personal Employment Identity Model (PEIM)—a career/job decision model developed by Peregoy and Schliebner (1990) to assist practitioners in selecting appropriate interventions based on four types of vocational ego-identity problems unemployed people exhibit.

personal qualities skills—individual responsibility, self-esteem, sociability, self-management and integrity (U.S. Department of Labor, Special Commission on Achieving Necessary Skills, 1991).

Personality test—measure overt and covert traits, temperaments, and dispositions (Kaplan & Sacuzzo, 2001).

Person by Environment (PxE) Fit—trait-factor theory **personality tests**; measure overt and covert traits, temperaments, and dispositions (Kaplan & Saccuzzo, 1997).

person-centered approaches—in person-centered approaches to career counseling and vocational guidance, the practitioner does not assume responsibility from the client nor lead or direct the client to make a choice the practitioner may believe is best for the client. The client is the center of the process, and the determiner of the content of the process and its outcome.

phenomenological perspective—a clinical counseling perspective that "seeks to comprehend the meaning of clients' interests and abilities as part of a life pattern" (Savickas, 1992, p. 337).

phenotype—an individual's physical appearance, especially their complexion.

physical resources—being able-bodied and mobile—like mental resources—is another advantage that lends itself to self-sufficiency.

population of convenience—student samples used in research.

position—a "group of activities, tasks, or duties performed by one person" (Tolbert, 1980, p. 32).

Positive Uncertainty—A "whole-brained approach to planning your future" (p. vi). "Uncertainty describes the condition of today's river of life. The successful decision maker navigating the river needs to be understanding, accepting, even positive about that uncertainty" (Gelatt, 1991, p. 1).

post-colonial theory—the very first moment of contact between the colonizer and the colonized (Ashcroft, Griffiths, & Tiffin, 1995). *Post-colonial* does *not* mean *after-colonial* or *after independence*. Post-colonialism concerns itself with the imperial process of **Eurocentrism**. The term *post-colonial* also refers to an individual identity as much as a group process. Some post-colonized individuals have internalized the image and guidelines of the oppressor (Freire, 1970/1993), which produces **identification with the oppressor**.

postmodernism—the belief that there are many beliefs, multiple realities, and a profusion of worldviews.

poststructuralism—postmodernism's rejection of the tradition that the real world has underlying rules and hidden structure.

potential biases in career assessment instruments—can lead to the dissemination of misleading information to minority clients at best or potentially damaging information at worst.

poverty rate—the number of people living below an income level set by the government.

power—"the capacity to influence for one's own benefit the forces that affect one's life space and/or as the capacity to produce desired effects on others" (Pinderhughes, 1995, p. 133).

predictive validity—the extent to which a test forecasts scores on the criterion at some future time.

pre-incident indicators—part of systematized intuition that de Becker's company uses to advise workplaces about managing employees who are likely to act out violently.

prejudice—"the emotional aspect of racism" (Axelson, 1993, p. 168).

a presumption against my competence—occurs when White men in the world of work question a Black man's ability to perform well in something other than athletics or the entertainment field.

Primary cultural differences—"existed before two groups came in contact, such as before immigrant minorities came to the United States" (Ogbu, 1992, p. 8). Voluntary immigrants are inclined to have them.

privileged complacency—a lack or awareness and respect for **oppression. discrimination, racism, sexism, classism,** and **ageism.**

productivity—judging workers on the excellence of their job performance.

Professional class—people whose occupations require specialized knowledge and often long and intensive academic preparation (for example, medicine, law, banking, accountancy, education, journalism).

projective personality tests—a personality test that provides ambiguous test stimuli where response requirements are less clear. "Rather than being asked to choose among alternative responses, as in structured personality tests, the individual is asked to provide a spontaneous response" (Kaplan & Saccuzzo, pp. 10–11).

protected careers—occupations where other members of the African American community tend to congregate, such as, education, social work, and the social sciences—where less racial discrimination is perceived to occur (Murry & Mosidi, 1993).

Protestant Reformation—religious movement begun by Martin Luther in Germany in 1517 that inadvertently resulted in a split from the Catholic Church and gave rise to the Protestant churches.

Protestant work ethic—teaches that work should be the main, if not defining, focus of one's life, and presumes that everyone has equal access to occupational opportunities.

provincial—an economy that self-consciously styles itself as a moral alternative for networked businesses, is driven by the deployment of less competitive business, and offers America a nineteenth-century answer for twenty-first-century competition.

psychoanalysis—"(1) a theory of personality and psychopathology, (2) a method of investigating the mind, and (3) a theory of [clinical] treatment" (Wolitzky, 1995, p. 12).

Psycho-Clarity Process—the goal of self-understanding is reached through engaging clients in the Psycho-Clarity Process (Powers & Griffith, 1987, cited in Powers & Griffith, 1993). The purpose of the Psycho-Clarity Process is to assist clients in understanding (1) what they are doing; (2) what their purpose is in doing these things; (3) what costs are involved in doing as they do; and (4) what else is open to them to do in whatever situations they find themselves.

psychodynamic approaches—traditional psychoanalysis and its variants.

public transcripts—subordinate discourse in the presence of the powerful; impression management in power-laden situations is one of the survival skills of subordinate groups.

Puritan work ethic—the belief that work is virtuous, that poverty is the result of one's lack of moral centeredness, and that people lacking virtue require charity (e.g., welfare) (Whitmore, 1971).

Q

quality time—the attempt to improve the time spent with one's family to compensate for work's encroachment into the familial domain. It presumes that the time workers devote to family relationships can be separated from ordinary time, with the hopes that scheduling intense periods of family togetherness will compensate for the lost time devoted to work, in the belief that parent–child relationships will suffer no loss of quality.

Queer theory—contends that the conventional, binary categories of gender identification like male/female and sexual identifications like heterosexual/homosexual, gay/straight, in the closet/out of the closet are social, cultural, and political constructions that have no basis in nature, but rather are created by discursive practices (Jagose, 1996; Spargo, 1999).

Quick Job Hunting Map—an assessment tool developed by Richard Bolles that is used to evaluate skills.

R

race-holding—"any self-description that serves to justify or camouflage a person's fears, weaknesses, and inadequacies" (Steele, 1990, p. 26).

race norming—"adjusting the scores or using different cut-offs based on the race of the person who takes the test" (Hagan & Hagan, 1995, p. 6).

racial and ethnic role models—provide influential motivational information crucial for the career decision making of racial and ethnic minorities.

racially and ethnically specific exploitation—when "a segmented labor market . . . tends to reserve skilled, high-paying, unionized jobs for whites" (Young, 1992, p. 185).

racism—"the belief that some races are *inherently* superior to others" (Axelson, 1993, p. 168, italics in original).

Rational-Emotive Therapy (RET)—RET posits an A-B-C model where emotional, behavioral, and physiological disturbances are most likely the results of beliefs about the activating event.

realistic—stage of career development of middle adolescence (seventeen to young adulthood) marked by an integration of capacities and interests: further development of values; specification of occupational choice; crystallization of occupational patterns; as proposed by theorists Ginzberg, Ginsburg, Axelrad, and Herma (1951).

realistic type
1. Prefers realistic occupations or situations—electrician—in which one can engage in preferred activities and avoid activities demanded by social occupations or situations.
2. Uses realistic competencies to solve problems at work and in other settings.
3. Perceives self as having mechanical and athletic ability and lacking ability in human relations.
4. Values concrete things or tangible personal characteristics—money, power, and status (Holland, 1992, p. 19).

The demands, opportunities, and people of the realistic type, create a characteristic atmosphere that operates in the following way:
1. It stimulates people to perform realistic activities such as using machines and tools.
2. It fosters technical competencies and achievements.
3. It encourages people to see themselves as having mechanical ability and lacking ability in human relations; it encourages them to see the world in simple, tangible, and traditional terms.
4. It rewards people for the display of conventional values and goods, money, power, and possessions (pp. 36–37).

The realistic person is apt to be: asocial, materialistic, self-effacing, conforming, natural, inflexible, frank, normal, thrifty, genuine, persistent, uninsightful, hard-headed, practical, uninvolved (p. 19).

reality of rugged collectivism—the collective, community-based values that contributed to the settling of the frontier.

reasonable accommodation—any modification or adjustment to a job or the work environment that will enable a qualified applicant or employee with a disability to participate in the application process or perform essential job functions. Reasonable ac-commodation also includes adjustments to assume that a qualified individual with a disability has rights and privileges in employment equal to those of employees without disabilities (U.S. Equal Employment Opportunity Commission, 1992).

recursive process—a cycle in which individuals move backward and forward through the process in response to their emerging decision needs and the availability of information resources (Sampson et al., 1992).

reliability—"the accuracy, dependability, consistency, or repeatability of test results. In more technical terms, reliability refers to the degree to which test scores are free of measurement error" (Kaplan & Saccuzzo, 1997, p. 12).

responsible stewardship—an opportunity and a challenge to make use of the God-given resources, both in oneself and in the environment (see **work**).

Roe's eight occupational groups—
1. Service: occupations concerned with catering to and serving the personal tastes, needs, and welfare of other people. Occupations include social worker, guidance/career counselor, domestic and protective services (e.g., house manager, executive housekeeper, waiter, waitress.)
2. Business Contact: occupations concerned with sale of commodities, investments, real estate, and services with persuasion as a basic task.
3. Organization: occupations concerned with organization and efficient functioning of commercial enterprises and governmental agencies, such as administrative and management positions.
4. Technology: occupations concerned with production, maintenance, and transportation of commodities and utilities, including engineering, crafts, machine and tool operators, transportation, and communication.
5. Outdoor: occupations concerned with cultivation, preservation, and gathering of items that grow in the earth's environment for food and use in other products. These include farmers, fishermen, foresters, and harvesters of all kinds.
6. Science: occupations concerned with scientific theory and its application. These include natural scientists, social scientists, physical scientists, physicians, psychologists, chemists, and physicists.
7. General Culture: occupations concerned with preservation and transmission of cultural heritage, with interest in human activities rather than individuals. These include educators, journalists, law specialists, religious functionar-

ies, linguists, and people who function in the humanities.

8. Arts and Entertainment: occupations concerned with the use of special skills in the creative arts and entertainment. These include painters, writers, musicians, dancers, poets, and entertainers (Roe & Lunneborg, 1990, adapted from Roe & Klos, 1972).

Rokeach Values Survey—an assessment tool used to evaluate values.

role flexibility—the inconstant in who is the head of the family or parental figure.

role models—knowing and having access to adults who are nurturing and appropriate in their behavior toward children and who do not demonstrate habitually self-destructive behavior are particularly helpful in teaching one how to emotionally live one's life.

S

salience—the importance of a role in a person's life.

SDS-Computerized Version—a computer program adaptation of Holland's (1985) paper-and-pencil assessment, the Self-Directed Search.

secondary cultural differences—"arose after two populations came into contact or after members of a given population began to participate in an institution controlled by the dominant group, such as the schools controlled by the dominant group" (Ogbu, 1992, p. 8).

second-order change—"a type of change whose occurrence alters the fundamental structure of a system" (Lyddon, 1990, p. 122); change that occurs "when the generations can shift their status relations and reconnect in a new way [so that] the family can move on developmentally" (Carter & McGoldrick, 1989, p. 14).

selection bias—occurs when a test's predictive validity is differential across groups.

self-concept—self-definition.

Self-Directed Search—an assessment tool used to evaluate interests.

self-efficacy—perceived judgments of one's capacity to successfully perform a given task or behavior (Bandura, 1977, 1984, 1986).

self-esteem—the value one places upon oneself.

self-in-relation—a contextual understanding of the individual used by **MCT**.

self-knowledge—knowledge of one's own values, interests, and skills.

self-regard—When one behaves according to one's own value system, she or he shows character through self-regard. Self-regard implies hard-won self-knowledge (Pipher, 1996).

self-serving bias—whereby laypeople invoke situational causes to justify their own conduct, especially in circumstances viewed negatively by others, with a minimization of traits and dispositional causes.

sensing (S)—one of four basic mental functions or processes of the **MBTI**. Sensing (S) refers to perceptions observable by way of the senses. Sensing establishes what exists. Because the senses can bring to awareness only what is occurring in the present moment, people oriented toward sensing perception tend to focus on the immediate experience and often develop characteristics associated with this awareness, such as enjoying the present moment, realism, acute powers of observation, memory for details, and practicality.

separate voice—describes men's orientation, with respect to occupational achievement and interpersonal relationships, with emphasis on differentiation from others.

sequential elimination approach—Gati's decision making model that used the idea that each occupational alternative has a series of aspects and that at each stage of the selection process, the importance of the aspect becomes the criterion for keeping or eliminating the alternative. It is considered to be a rational manner to approach career decision making, especially when many alternatives are present.

sexism—prejudice based on gender, typically relates to women.

sexual orientation—sexual behavior, including sexual attractions, emotional preferences, social preferences, sexual fantasies, lifestyle choices, and sense of identity (Klein, Sepekoff, & Wolfe, 1985).

share career and family together—observations Richter, Morrison, and Salinas (1991) make about ways to deal with the issue of dual careerism in which the couple must deal with the issues of both sharing the problem of task overload and emotional overload and both sharing in the best of both worlds.

SIGI—a Computer Assisted Career Guidance System designed to assist college students to clarify values, identify occupational options, and develop rational **career decision-making (CDM) skills**.

SIGI PLUS—an expansion of **SIGI** developed to include adults and organization needs.

situated knowledge—see **localized knowledge**.

situationalism—the belief that the ability to predict how people will react in certain situations is actually quite limited (Ross & Nisbett, 1991).

situational poverty—families who have lived in poverty for a shorter time, often due to circumstances such as death, illness, or divorce.

social constructionism—"maintains that individuals' sense of what is real—including their sense of the nature of their problems, competencies, and possible solutions—is constructed in interaction with others as they go through life" (De Jong & Berg, 1998, p. 226); a clinical practice that views meanings and understandings of the world as developed through social interaction (Gergen, 1985).

social saturation—an accelerating social connectedness marked by the technological advances of the late twentieth century—computers, electronic mail, satellites, faxes—that is leading to a state of multiphrenia, where the individual is split into a multiplicity of self-investments (Kenneth J. Gergen, 1991b).

social type—this development of a social pattern of activities, competencies, and interests creates a person who is predisposed to exhibit the following behavior:

1. Prefers social occupations and situations in which one can engage in preferred activities and competencies and avoid the activities demanded by realistic occupations and situations.
2. Uses social competencies to solve problems at work and in other settings.
3. Perceives self as liking to help others, understanding others, having teaching ability, and lacking mechanical and scientific ability.
4. Values social and ethical activities and problems (Holland, 1992, p. 21).

These demands, opportunities, and social people create a characteristic atmosphere that operates to produce the following goals and outcomes:

1. It stimulates people to engage in social activities.
2. It fosters social competencies.
3. It encourages people to see themselves as liking to help others, understanding of others, cooperative, and sociable; it encourages them to see the world in flexible ways.
4. It rewards people for the display of social values (p. 38).

The social person is apt to be: ascendant, helpful, responsible, cooperative, idealistic, sociable, patient, empathetic, tactful, friendly, kind, understanding, generous, persuasive, warm (p. 21).

specification—a period of moving from tentative vocational choices toward a specific vocational preference (Zunker, 1994).

Spirit—"*the activating force or essential principle that helps to give life to physical organisms*" (Savickas, cited in Bloch and Richmond, 1997, p. 4, italics in the original).

spiritual resources—believing in a higher power that provides guidance and understanding for life's purpose, which helps see oneself not as hopeless but as capable, worthy, and valuable.

spontaneity—elements of self-expression and self-realization in our responses to situations. Spontaneity is a major key to differentiating work from play.

stabilization—a period of confirming a preferred career by actual work experience and use of talents to demonstrate career choice as an appropriate one (Zunker, 1994).

standard deviation—the square root of the average squared deviation around the mean (or the variance). It is used as a measure of variability in a distribution of scores (from Kaplan & Sacuzzo, 2001).

standard error of measurement—tells how much a score varies on the average, from a true score. The standard deviation of an observed score and the reliability of the test are used to compute estimates of the standard error of measurement.

standardization sample—a comparison group consisting of individuals who have been administered a test under standard conditions; the instructions, format, and general procedures are usually outlined in the test manual for the standardized administration of a test (Kaplan & Saccuzzo, 1997). Also known as a normative sample.

standardized administration—see **standardization sample.**

Standards for Educational and Psychological Testing—a discussion of the ethical issues involved in educational and psychological testing by the joint committee of the American Education Research Association, the American Psychological Association, and the National Council on Measurement in Education.

strain-based conflict—see **work-family conflict.**

stress experience—a process that occurs when a person is confronted by a demand that is perceived to exceed the emotional or physical resources available to effectively respond to it (Zacarro & Riley, 1987).

structured personality tests—personality tests based on self-report statements where the test taker answers *true* or *false* or *yes* or *no.*

sublimation—substituting hostile, aggressive, or sexual impulses into a more socially accepted form.

summative evaluation—program evaluation activities that are conducted at the end of a program.

support systems—having friends and family who have valuable knowledge to share and who will back up a person in times of need.

Survey of Career Development (SCD)—a computerized system that can be used with **DISCOVER**. Recently, this program has been used to measure the effectiveness of career planning and computerized guidance systems.

systems competencies—understanding social, organizational, and technological systems, monitoring and correcting performance, and designing or improving systems (U.S. Department of Labor, Special Commission on Achieving Necessary Skills, 1991).

T

TANF (Temporary Assistance for Needy Families)—TANF aims to provide in-home care for children of needy families; end government dependency by promoting job preparation, work, and marriage; prevent out of wedlock pregnancies; and encourage two-parent families (Hard & Schoenmakers, 1997).

Taoism—cultural value where ancestor worship provides guidance and advice for present living. Traditionally, Taoists are attached to burial sites (location) of ancestors where they can go to pray, meditate, and pay respect before the graves of their ancestors (Axelson, 1993, p. 438).

task approach skills—understanding how an individual approaches a task is one of the most important parts of career decision making. Task approach skills include: (1) goals setting, (2) value clarification, (3) generating alternatives, and (4) obtaining career information. Interactions among genetic endowment, environmental conditions, and learning experiences lead to skills in doing a variety of tasks (Sharf, 1997).

Task interest—gives a person more motivation to interact with the task, which in turn offers more of a chance for "personal and vicarious success experiences, and further self-efficacy enhancement" (Lent et al., p. 287).

technology competencies—selecting equipment and tools, applying technology to specific tasks, and maintaining and troubleshooting technologies (United States Department of Labor, Special Commission on Achieving Necessary Skills, 1991).

telecommuting—a way of doing business using laptops, fax machines, cellular phones, networked computers, e-mail, and voicemail that satisfies a goal of spending more time with customers and using commute time more efficiently.

tentative—the stage of adolescent career development (ages 11–17) marked by gradual recognition of work requirements and recognition of interests, abilities, work reward, values, and time perspec-

tives, as proposed by theorists Ginzberg, Ginsburg, Axelrad, and Herma (1951).

test administration—the act of giving a test and the procedures surrounding the giving of a test.

test battery—a collection of tests whose scores are used together to appraise an individual.

test bias—see **content bias**, **internal structure bias**, and **selection bias**.

tests—measurement instruments that quantify behavior.

Theory of Work Adjustment (TWA)—the theory is that work adjustment is a "continuous and dynamic process by which a worker seeks to achieve and maintain a correspondence with a work environment" (Dawis & Lofquist, 1984, p. 237).

thinking skills—thinking creatively, making decisions, solving problems, imagining, and knowing how to learn and reasoning (U.S. Department of Labor, Special Commission on Achieving Necessary Skills, 1991).

time-based conflict—see **work-family conflict.**

time ways—"attitudes toward the use of time, customary methods of time keeping, and the conventional rhythms of life" (Fischer, 1989, p. 9).

trait-factor theory—the matching approach to vocational psychology using assessment to match the individual to training programs or occupations.

traits—learned interests, special aptitudes, and scholastic aptitudes.

transference—a client reacting toward a boss or coworker in a manner similar to a significant person in the client's past or present.

Treatises of the Brothers of Purity—the text, Rasa'il Ikhwàn al-Safá wa-Khulln al-Wafa (also known as the TBP), written around 955 A.D. by what is believed to be a group of five to ten Muslim reformers who lived in the Basra region of what is now southern Iraq. The initial goal of the authors of the TSB was to compile all the known sciences into one work, regardless of the cultural origins of such knowledge.

two-by-four process—a decision-making process offered by Gelatt (1991) that includes two attitudes and four factors. The attitudes are (1) accept the past, present, and future as uncertain and (2) be positive about uncertainty. The four factors to consider are (1) what you want; (2) what you know; (3) what you believe; and (4) what you do (Gelatt, 1991, p. 6).

Type A behavior—Type A behavior consists of five components. First, it is above all a continuous struggle, an unremitting attempt to accomplish or achieve more and more things or participate in more and more events in less and less time, frequently in the face of opposition—real or imagined—from other people. Second, the Type A personality is dominated by covert insecurity of status, or hyperaggressiveness, or both. Third, struggle eventually fosters a sense of time urgency. Fourth, as the struggle continues, the hyper-aggressiveness (and also perhaps the status insecurity) usually shows itself in the easily aroused anger termed free-floating hostility. Fifth and finally, if the struggle becomes severe enough and persists long enough, it may lead to a tendency toward self-destruction. Type B behavior refers to an absence of these five components.

Type B behavior—see **Type A behavior.**

U

unconscious motivation—the mechanism that determined human behavior as posited by Freud. Unconscious motivation presumably occurs out of one's awareness but is revealed clinically through free association and in daily life through behaviors such as slips of the tongue and the jokes one finds funny.

undecided-decisive client—clients in this state merely need more information and would most benefit from assessment and/or career counseling.

undecided-indecisive client—clients in this state are experiencing choice anxiety. These clients suffer from anxiety, low self-concept, immaturity, and other negative personality traits that impair career counseling. Personal and career counseling are recommended.

undue hardship—an "action requiring significant difficulty or expense" when considered in light of a number of factors . . . [including] . . . the size, resources, nature, and structure of the employer's operation." Undue hardship is determined on a case-by-case basis.

unjustifiability—occurs when "a property of occupationism is related to the degree of knowledge an individual has of the quality of work performed by another" (Carson, 1992, p. 492).

unspoken cues—see **knowledge of hidden cues.**

V

validity—"the meaning and usefulness of test results . . . [and] the degree to which a certain inference or interpretation based on a test is appropriate" (Kaplan & Saccuzzo, 1997, p. 12).

value-indicator—denotes a value in the process of *becoming.*

values—(1) worth in terms of usefulness (a principle), (2) that which is of importance to the possessor (a standard), and (3) utility or merit (a quality). As a verb, value means to regard highly, to esteem, or to prize.

Values-based model—a career/job decision process developed by Duane Brown (1996) for dealing with people in transition, whether the change was planned or unplanned.

values clarification activities—help clients prioritize what is important for them, usually based on the seven standards for constructing a value (Raths, Harmin, & Simon, 1966).

variance—the average squared deviation around the mean, the standard deviation squared (from Kaplan & Sacuzzo, 2001).

vocational development—see **career development.**

vocational irrational beliefs—see **irrational beliefs.**

vocational practitioner—our term for the career counselor who works with a broader spectrum of the population seeking job/occupational or career counseling.

vocational psychology—a social and behavioral science that attempts to explain, predict, and control how people choose their initial occupations and pursue their ongoing careers.

voluntary minorities—immigrants who go to a country voluntarily to improve their economic situation (Traindis, 1993) and are inclined to primary cultural differences.

W

wavering—entails movement toward meaning and a life-shaping decision that can alter the course of a person's life.

weekend warriors—individuals (more often men than women) who engage in athletic activities for which they are not in shape and risk physical injury.

White people skills—knowledge of how to interact with Whites—and the ability to distinguish which Whites are willing to be open.

will—an individual's ability to act on one's values (Pipher, 1996).

within-group differences—differences that occur within one racial or ethnic group; intercultural comparisons.

Women of Color—racial and ethnic minority adult females.

work—"purposeful mental, physical, or combined mental-physical activity that produces something of economic value . . . [and] may produce a service to others as well as a material product" (Tolbert, 1980, p. 32).

work adjustment—see **Theory of Work Adjustment.**

workaholism—a cluster of behaviors which may include: (1) an addiction to work, (2) an escape from the unpleasantries of life, (3) competitiveness caused by a craving for constant stimulation and an overabundance of energy, (4) the result of compensating for a self-image damaged in childhood, and (5) behavior learned from parents and other role models.

work ethic—the principles of conduct that govern a person's work-related behaviors.

workers' productive use of resources competencies—allocating time, money, materials, space, and staff (U.S. Department of Labor, Special Commission on Achieving Necessary Skills, 1991).

work–family conflict—(1) time-based conflict—time can only be spent on one role, which neglects the other roles; (2) strain-based conflict—stress from one role effects all areas of performance; and (3) behavior-based conflict—behavioral styles are not compatible throughout all roles (Greenhaus & Beutell, 1985).

workforce—a person is said to be in the workforce when that person is either employed or unemployed but has sought a **position** within the past six months (Asante & Mattson, 1992).

workplace culture—as derived on McLaren (1994), *". . . the particular ways in which a* [work] *group lives out and makes sense of its 'given' circumstances and* [work] *conditions"* [and] *". . . a set of practices, ideologies, and values from which different groups draw to make sense of the* [workplace] *. . ."* (p. 180, italics in the original).

work ways—"work ethics and work experiences; attitudes toward work and the nature of work" (Fischer, 1989, p. 9).

worldview—"the frame of reference through which one experiences life. It is the foundation for values, beliefs, attitudes, [and] relations" (Fouad & Bingham, 1995, p. 335).

Z

zone of applicability—Pipher's (1996) term for the limits of time, place, occupation, gender, and income that constrict any clinical approach.

References

Chapter 1

Abramson, H. J. (1980). Assimilation and pluralism. In S. Thernstrom (Ed.), *The Harvard encyclopedia of American ethnic groups* (pp. 150–160). Cambridge, MA: Belknap Press.

Ajgaonkar, S. M. T. (Ed.). (n.d.). *Mahatma: A golden treasury of wisdom—thoughts and glimpses of life.* Mumbai [formerly Bombay], INDIA: India Printing Works.

Alcacly, R. (2003). *The new economy: What it is, how it happened, and why it is likely to last.* New York: Farrar, Straus & Giroux.

Alch, M. L. (2000, July). Get ready for the net generation. *USA Today*, pp. 26–27.

Allan, P. (2002, June 1). The contingent workforce: Challenges and new directions. *American Business Review.* Retrieved 05/03/2003 from http://elibrary.bigchalk.com/libweb/elib/do/document?set=search&groupid=1&requestid=li...

Arbona, C. (1995). Theory and research on racial and ethnic minorities: Hispanic Americans. In F. T. L. Leong (Ed.), *Career development and vocational behavior of racial and ethnic minorities* (pp. 37–66). Mahwah, NJ: Erlbaum.

Armendariz, Y. (1997, April 11). Today women's pay catches up to men's. *El Paso Times*, p. C1.

Asante, M. K., & Mattson, M. T. (1992). *Historical and cultural atlas of African Americans.* New York: Macmillan.

Axelson, J. A. (1993). *Counseling and development in a multicultural society* (2nd ed.). Pacific Grove, CA: Brooks/Cole.

Bacon, J. (1998, January 30). Texaco diversity. *USA Today*, p. 10A.

Bandura, A. (2002). Social cognitive theory in cultural context. *Applied Psychology: An International Review, 51* (2), 269–290.

Baruth, L. G., & Manning, M. L. (1991). *Multicultural counseling and psychotherapy: A lifespan perspective.* New York: Macmillan.

Baruth, L. G., & Manning, M. L. (2003). *Mutlicultural counseling and psychotherapy: A lifespan perspective* (3rd ed.). Upper Saddle River, NJ. Merrill Prentice Hall.

Be yourself: Questions and answers for Gay, Lesbian, and Bisexual youth. (1994). Washington, DC: Parents and Friends of Lesbians and Gays [booklet].

Becker, G. S. (2003, April 21). When globalization suffers, the poor take the heat. *Busniess Week*, p. 28.

Bellah, R. N., Madsen, R., Sullivan, W. M., Swidler, A., & Tipton, S. M. (1992). *The good society.* New York: Vintage.

Bennett, A. (1990). *The death of the organizational man.* New York: William Morrow.

Berg, I. K., & De Jong, P. (1996). Solution-building conversations: Co-constructing a sense of competence with clients. *Families in Society: The Journal of Contemporary Human Sciences, 77* (6), 376–391.

Bergmann, B. R. (1996). *In defense of affirmative action.* New York: Basic Books.

Berner, R., & Zellner, W. (2003, April 28). Driving the SUV to the food pantry. *Business Week*, p. 68.

Betz, N. E. (2001). Perspectives on the future directions in vocational psychology. *Journal of Vocational Behavior, 59* (2), 275–283.

Boroughs, D. L., Guttman, M., Mallory, M., McMurray, S., & Fischer, D. (1996, January 22). Winter of discontent: With wages frozen, American workers find themselves out in the cold. *U.S. News & World Report*, pp. 47–52, 54.

Bowman, S. L. (1995). Career intervention strategies and assessment issues for African Americans. In F. T. L. Leong (Ed.), *Career development and vocational behavior of racial and ethnic minorities* (pp. 137–164). Mahwah, NJ: Erlbaum.

Boyle, J. S. (1999). Culture, family, and community. In M. M. Andrews & J. S. Boyle *Transcultural concepts in nursing care* (3rd ed.) (pp. 308–337). Philadelphia: Lippincott.

Bragg, R. (1996a, March 5). More than money, they miss the pride a good job brought. *New York Times*, p. A17–A18.

Bragg, R. (1996b, March 5). Big holes where the dignity used to be. *New York Times*, pp. A1, A16, A18.

Bridges, W. (1994). *Job shift: How to prosper in a workplace without jobs.* Reading, MA: Addison-Wesley.

Brown, L. (2001, November). The special breed: You eat

together, you sleep together and you die together. *Men's Journal, 10* (10), 84.

Brown, L., Flaven, C., & Postel, S. (1992, May–June). A planet in jeopardy. *The Futurist, 10.*

Brown, M. T. (1995). The career development of African Americans: Theoretical and empirical issues. In F. T. L. Leong (Ed.), *Career development of and vocational behavior of racial and ethnic behaviors* (pp. 7–36). Mahwah, NJ: Erlbaum.

Carter, S. G. (1996, March 14). Should downsizing lead to a new system? Blacks and insecurity. *New York Times,* p. 22A.

Carter, S. L. (1991). *Reflections of an affirmative action baby.* New York: Basic Books.

Cauchon, D. (2003, June 23). Special report: Bad moves, not economy, behind busted state budgets. *USA Today,* p. A1–A2.

Cauchon, D., & Moore, M. T. (2002, September 6–8). Miracles emerge from debris. *USA Today,* pp. 1A, 4A–5A.

Columbia Accident Investigation Board. (2003, August). *Report,* Vol. I. Washington, DC: U.S. Government Printing Office.

Court, B., Dean, J., Flynn, S., Foster, T., Friedman, D., Markels, A. et al. (2001, November). The fire-fighters. *Men's Journal, 10* (10), 66–74, 78, 80, 82–83, 87–88, 90.

Dawis, R. V. (1992). The individual differences tradition in counseling psychology. *Journal of Counseling Psychology, 39* (1), 7–19.

De Jong, P., & Berg, I. K. (1998). *Interviewing for solutions.* Pacific Grove, CA: Brooks/Cole.

Dent, H. (1995). *Job shock.* New York: St. Martin's Press.

Dervin, B. (1994). Information–Democracy. An examination of underlying assumptions. *Journal of the American Society for Information Science, 45* (6), 369–85.

Downsizing and its discontents. (1996, March 10). *The Sunday New York Times,* Section 3, p. 14.

Drummond, R., & Ryan, C. (1995). *Career counseling: A developmental approach.* Englewood Cliffs, NJ: Merrill.

Eastland, T. (1997). *Ending affirmative action: The case for colorblind justice.* New York: Basic Books.

Ehrenreich, B. (2001). *Nickel and dimed: On (not) getting by in America.* New York: Henry Holt.

Evans, K., & Herr, E. L. (1991). The influence of racism and sexism in the career development of African-American women. *Journal of multicultural counseling development, 19* (3), 130–135.

Feller, R. (1996). Redefining "career" during the work revolution. In R. Feller & G. Walz (Eds.), *Career transitions in turbulent times: Exploring work, learning, and careers* (pp. 143–161). Greensboro, NC: ERIC Counseling and Student Services Clearinghouse.

Fouad, N. A. (1995). Career behavior of Hispanics: Assessment and career intervention. In F. T. L. Leong (Ed.), *Career development and vocational behavior of racial and ethnic minorities* (pp. 165–191). Mahwah, NJ: Erlbaum.

Frank, R., & Cook, P. (1995). *Winner take all society: How more and more Americans compete for ever fewer and bigger prizes, encouraging economic waste, income inequality, and an impoverished cultural life.* New York: Martin Kessler/Free Press.

Freire, P. (1993). *Pedagogy of the oppressed.* (Rev. ed.) (M. B. Ramos, Trans.) New York: Continuum. (Original work published 1970).

Friedman, D. (2001, November). The fire fighters. *Men's Journal, 10* (10), 67–68, 70.

Gaskell, J., & Willinsky, J. (Eds.). (1995). *Gender in/forms curriculum: From enrichment to transformation.* New York: Columbia University Teachers College Press.

Gibbs, N. (2003, August 25). Lights out. *Time, 162* (8), 30–39.

Gilligan, C., & Noel, N. (1995, April). *Cartography of a lost time: Women, girls, and relationships.* Workshop sponsored by the Austin Women's Psychotherapy Project, Austin, TX.

Gollnick, J. M., & Chinn, P. C. (1998). *Multicultural education in a pluralistic society* (5th ed.). Upper Saddle River, NJ: Merrill Prentice Hall.

González, R. C. (1997). Postmodern supervision: A multicultural perspective. In D. B. Pope-Davis & H. L. K. Coleman (Eds.), *Multicultural counseling competencies: Assessment, education and training, and supervision* (pp. 350–386). Thousand Oaks, CA: Sage.

González, R. C. (1998). A technically eclectic blend of paradigms and epistemologies for multicultural clinical relevance. In C. Franklin & P. S. Nurius (Eds.), *Constructivism in practice: Methods and challenges* (pp. 349–735). Milwaukee, WI: Families International.

Gonzalez, R. C. (2002a, November). *International perspectives on work in people's lives: Mexico.* Presented at the International Career Development Conference, 19th Annual California Career Development Conference, Irvine, CA.

Gonzalez, R. C. (2002b, August). Unpaved roads to the academy. In M. Englar-Carson, Chair, *Class jumping into academia—from dirt roads to ivory towers.* Symposium presented at the 110th Annual Convention of the American Psychological Association, Chicago, IL.

González, R. C., & Peterson, N. (2001, June). *Contemporary family issues in career counseling and their effect on career choice.* Professional Development Institute presented at the National Career Development Association 10th Global Career Development Conference, Tucson, AZ.

González, R. C., & Peterson, N. (2001, June). A five-generation work-related genogram. *Journal of Career Planning and Adult Development; Special Issue: Family Influences on Career Choice and Success,* 17 (2), 115–127.

Gordon, M. M. (1964). *Assimilation in American life.* New York: Oxford University Press.

Gorman, B. (2002). Employee engagement after two decades of change. *SCM,* 7 (1), 12–15.

Grieco, E. M., & Cassidy, R. C. (2001, March). U. S. Census Bureau, *Overview of Race and Hispanic Origin, 2000.* Washington, DC: U. S. Government Printing Office.

Hagan, J. W., & Hagan, W. W., II. (1995). What employment counselors need to know about employment discrimination and the Civil Rights Act of 1991. *Journal of Employment Counseling, 32,* 2–10.

Halberstam, D. (2002). *Firehouse.* New York: Hyperion.

Hall, D. T., & Associates. (1997). *The career is dead—long live the career.* San Francisco: Jossey-Bass.

Hare-Mustin, R. T. (1994). Discourses in the mirrored room: A postmodern analysis of therapy. *Family Process, 33,* 19–35.

Helms, J. E., & Richardson, T. Q. (1997). How "multiculturalism" obscures race and culture as differential aspects of counseling competency. In D. B. Pope-Davis & H. L. K. Coleman (Eds.), *Multicultural counseling competencies: Assessment, education and training, and supervision* (pp. 60–79). Thousand Oaks, CA: Sage.

Herman, R., Olivo, T., & Gioia, J. (2003). *Impending crisis: Too many jobs, too few people.* Winchester, VA: Oakhill Press.

Hernandez, R. (1998, August 21). Poverty opens computer gap. *El Paso Times,* p. 11A.

Herr, E. L., Cramer, S. H., & Niles, S. G. (2004). *Career guidance and counseling throughout the lifespan* (6th ed.). Boston: Pearson, Allyn and Bacon.

Higher Education and National Affairs. (2003, June). U. S. Supreme Court upholds affirmative action in University of Michigan admissions Cases. Retrieved September 25, 2003, from www.acenet. edu/washington/presidents/2003/pres._06_23_SPECIAL.cfm.

Hollinger, R. (1994). *Postmodernism and the social sciences: A thematic approach.* Thousand Oaks, CA: Sage.

Holmes, S. A. (1996, June 20). Income disparity between poorest and richest rises. *New York Times,* pp. A1, A18.Institute of Management & Administration. (2002, January). *Is your corporate climate breeding future thieves?* Security Director's Report. Retrieved 12/21/2003 from http://ollusa.edu.2066/serlet/BCRC?vrsn=2.0&locID=txshracd2535&srchtp=glb&c . . . Author.

Johnson, K. (1996, March 7). In the class of '70, wounded winners. *New York Times,* pp. A1, A20–A22.

Kadlec, D., & Baumohl, B. (1997, April 28). How CEO pay got away. *Time,* 59–60.

King, M. A. (2001, May/June). Skilling up the workforce for new technologies. *Facilities Manager,* pp. 27–31.

Kleinfield, N. R. (1996, March 4). The downsizing of America: In the workplace musical chairs; the company as family, no more. *New York Times,* pp. A1, A12–A14.

Koss-Chioino, J. D., & Vargas, L. A. (1992). Through the cultural looking glass: A model for understanding culturally responsive psychotherapies. In L. A. Vargas & J. D. Koss-Chioino (Eds.), *Working with culture: Psychotherapeutic interventions with ethnic minority children and adolescents* (pp. 1–22). San Francisco: Jossey-Bass.

Kramer, M. (1997, January 20). Job training has to be reworked. *Time,* 62.

Landrine, H., & Klonoff, E. A. (1996). *African American acculturation: Deconstructing race and reviving culture.* Thousand Oaks, CA: Sage.

Langewiesche. W. (2002). *American ground: Unbuilding the World Trade Center.* New York: North Point Press.

Lee, C. C. (1997). Cultural dynamics: Their importance in culturally responsive counseling. In C. C. Lee (Ed.), *Multicultural issues in counseling: New approaches to diversity* (2nd ed.) (pp. 15–30). Alexandria, VA: American Counseling Association.

Leong, F. T. L., & Gim-Chung, R. H. (1995). Career assessment and intervention with Asian Americans. In F. T. L. Leong (Ed.), *Career development and vocational behavior of racial and ethnic minorities* (pp. 193–226). Mahwah, NJ: Erlbaum.

Leong, F. T. L., & Serafica, F. C. (1995). Career development of Asian Americans: A research area in need of a good theory. In F. T. L. Leong (Ed.), *Career development and vocational behavior of racial and ethnic minorities* (pp. 67–102). Mahwah, NJ: Erlbaum.

Loesch, L. C. (1995). Preparation for helping professionals working with diverse populations. In N. A. Vance, S. B. DeVaney, & J. Wittmer (Eds.), *Experiencing and counseling multicultural and diverse populations* (3rd ed.) (pp. 339–61). Bristol, PA: Accelerated Development.

Madrick, J. (1996). *The end of affluence: The causes and consequences of America's economic dilemma.* New York: Random House.

Marín, G., Sabogal, F., Marín, B. V., Otero-Sabogal, R., & Pérez-Stable, E. J. (1987). Development of a short acculturation scale for Hispanics. *Hispanic Journal of Behavioral Sciences, 9,* 183–205.

Martin, W. E., Jr. (1991). Career development and American Indian living on reservations: Cross-cultural factors to consider. *Career Development Quarterly, 39,* 273–78.

McCain, T., & Jukes, I. (2001). *Windows on the future: Education in the age of technology.* Thousand Oaks, CA: Corwin Press.

McGoldrick, M. (1982). Ethnicity and family therapy: An overview. In McGoldrick, M., Pearce, J. K., & Giordano, J. (Eds.), *Ethnicity and family therapy* (pp. 3–30). New York: Guilford Press.

McLaren, P. (1994). *Life in schools: An introduction to critical pedagogy in the foundations of education* (2nd ed.). White Plains, NJ: Longman.

McWhorter, J. (2003). *Authentically Black: Essays for the Black silent majority.* New York: Gotham Books.

Mendoza, R. H., & Martínez, J. L. (1981). The measurement of acculturation. In A. Barón, Jr. (Ed.), *Explorations in Chicano psychology* (pp. 71–82). New York: Praeger.

Mercer, M. (1992 December/1993 January). On "savage inequalities": A conversation with Jonathan Kozol. *Educational Leadership,* 4–9.

Michelozzi, B. (1996). *Coming alive from 9 to 5* (5th ed.). Mountain View, CA: Mayfield.

Morris, B. (2001). White collar blues. Free agency is over. Layoffs are back. Many of the people losing their jobs are white collar and well educated. You could be next. *Fortune, 144* (2), p. 98.

Morrison, P. (1990, March–April). Applied demography. *Futurist,* 9–15.

Nelson, M. L. (2002, August). Imposter in academia: Confessions from the wrong side of town. In M. Englar-Carson, Chair, *Class jumping into academia—from dirt roads to ivory towers.* Symposium presented at the 110th Annual Convention of the American Psychological Association, Chicago, IL.

Newman, K. (1988). *Falling from grace: The experience of downward mobility in the American middle class.* New York: Free Press.

New York Times News Service. (1996, December 29). Study says minority progress in classroom shows reversal. *San Antonio Express-News,* p. 16A.

New York Times News Service. (1997, January 27). College moves further from reach of poor. *El Paso Herald-Post,* p. A1.

Occupational Outlook Quarterly. (Summer, 2000). Futurework: Trends and challenges for work in the 21st century, p. 32.

Okun, B. F., Fried, J., & Okun, M. L. (1999). *Understanding diversity: A learning-as-practice primer.* Pacific Grove, CA: Brooks/Cole.

Olmedo, E. L. (1979). Acculturation: A psychometric perspective. *American Psychologist, 34,* 1061–1070.

Orenstein, P. (1994). *School girls: Young women, self-esteem, and the confidence gap.* New York: Anchor.

Osipow, S. H., & Fitzgerald, L. F. (1996). *Theories of career development* (4th ed.). Boston: Allyn & Bacon.

O'Toole, P. (1993, November). Redefining success. *Working Woman,* 49–55, 96–97.

Pantazis, C. (2002). Maximizing e-learning to train the 21st century workforce. *Pbulic Personnel Management, 31* (1), 21–26.

Park, E. R. (1950). *Race and culture.* Glencoe, IL: Free Press.

Pedersen, P. (1990). The multicultural perspective as a fourth force in counseling. *Journal of Mental Health Counseling, 12* (1), 93–95.

Perryman, M. R. (1996, March 21). Number of working moms expected to rise. *El Paso Herald-Post,* p. C5.

Peterson, J. A. (1970). *Counseling and values: A philosophical examination.* Scranton, PA: International Textbook.

Peterson, N., & Peterson, R. (2002, November). *International perspectives on work in people's lives: India.* Presented at the International Career Development Conference, 19th Annual California Career Development Conference, Irvine, CA.

Peterson, W. (1980). Concepts of ethnicity. In S. Thernstrom (Ed.). *The Harvard encyclopedia of American ethnic groups* (pp. 234–242). Cambridge, MA: Belknap Press.

Pethokoukis, J. (2003, April). From workforce to armed forces and back. *HR Magazine,* pp. 55–59.

Pipher, M. (1994). *Reviving Ophelia: Saving the selves of adolescent girls.* New York: G. P. Putnam's.

Pipher, M. (1996). *The shelter of each other: Rebuilding our families.* New York: Ballantine.

Poole, G. A. (1996, March 7). Revolution of computers in schools has two faces: Students in private schools have advantages over kids in public schools when it comes to technology. *El Paso-Herald Post,* pp. C5, C6.

Population profile of the United States: 2000. Washington, DC: U.S. Government Printing Office, 12-2, 3.

Prospect Centre. (1991). *Growing an innovative workforce.* Kingston upon Thames: Prospect Centre.

Purnell, L. D., & Paulanka, B. J. (1998). *Transcultural healt care: A culturally competent approach.* Philadelphia: F. A. Davis.

Reingold, J. (1997, April 21). Executive pay. *Business Week,* 58, 60, 62, 64, 66.

Richardson, G. D. (1997, November 14). Reality is, whites are already preferred. *USA Today,* p. 15A.

Richardson, M. S. (1993). Work in people's lives: A location for counseling psychologists. *Journal of Counseling Psychology, 40,* 425–33.

Richie, B. S. (1992). Coping with work: Interventions with African-American women. *Women and Therapy, 12* (1–2), 7–111. In *Finding voice: Writing by new authors.*

Richmond, L. J. (1999). Transcultural counseling European Americans. In J. McFaddene (Ed.), *Transcultural counseling* (2nd ed.)(pp. 297–315). Alexandria, VA: American Counseling Association.

Rifkin, J. (1987). The clocks that make us run. *East-West Journal, 44.*

Rimer, S. (1996, March 6). A hometown feels less like home. *New York Times,* pp. A1ff.

Roberts, B.-E. (1998). *Roberts vs. Texaco: The true story of race and corporate America.* New York: Avon Books.

Roberts, S. V., Friedman, D., Sieder, J. J., Schwartz, D. A., & Sapers, J. (1996, January 22). Workers take it on the chin. *U.S. News & World Report,* 44–46.

Roberts, S. V., Thornton, J., Gest, T., Cooper, M., Bennefield, R. M., Hetter, K., Seter, J., Minerbrook, S., & Tharp, M. (1995, February 13). Affirmative action on the edge. *U.S. News & World Report,* 32ff.

Robinson, T. L., & Howard-Hamilton, M. F. (2000). *The convergence of race, ethnicity, and gender: Multiple identities in counseling.* Upper Saddle River, NJ: Prentice-Hall.

Rochlin, M. (1985). Sexual orientation of the therapist and therapeutic effectiveness with gay clients. In J. C. Gonsiorek (Ed.), *A guide to psychotherapy with gay and lesbian clients* (pp. 21– 29). New York: Harrington Park Press.

Rodriguez, M. A. (1994). Preparing an effective occupational information brochure for ethnic minorities. *Career Development Quarterly, 43,* 178–84.

Rodriguez, R. (1982). *Hunger of Memory.* New York: Bantam Books.

Roland, A. (1994). Identity, self, and individualism in a multicultural perspective. In E. P. Salett & D. R. Koslow (Eds.), *Race, ethnicity, and self: Identity in a multicultural perspective* (pp. 11–23). Washington, DC: National MultiCultural Institute.

Rosenau, P. M. (1992). *Post-modernism and the social sciences: Insights, inroads, and intrusions.* Princeton, NJ: Princeton University Press.

Ross, L., & Nisbett, R. E. (1991). *The person and the situation: Perspectives of social psychology.* New York: McGraw-Hill.

Rotheram, M. J., & Phinney, J. S. (1987). Introduction: Definitions and perspectives in the study of children's ethnic socialization. In J. S. Phinney & M. J. Rotheram (Eds.), *Children's ethnic socialization: Pluralism and development* (pp. 10–31). Newbury Park, CA: Sage.

Roysircar, G. (2003). Understanding immigrants: Acculturation theory and research. In F. D. Harper & J. McFadden (Eds.), *Culture and counseling: New approaches* (pp. 164–185). Boston: Allyn and Bacon.

Sadker, M., & Sadker, D. (1995). *Failing at fairness: How our schools cheat girls.* New York: Touchstone.

Sanger, D. E., & Lohr, S. (1996, March 9). A search for answers to avoid the layoffs. *New York Times,* Section 1, pp. 1ff.

Savickas, M. L. (1994). Vocational psychology in the postmodern era: Comment on Richardson (1993). *Journal of Counseling Psychology, 41,* 105–7.

Savickas, M. L. (1995). Current theoretical issues in vocational psychology: Convergence, divergence, and schism. In W. B. Walsh & S. H. Osipow (Eds.), *Handbook of vocational psychology* (2nd ed.) (pp. 1–34). Mahwah, NJ: Erlbaum.

Schwartzbeck, C. (1997, January 20). Foreign ways: Cultural family differences require counseling changes. *El Paso Herald-Post,* p. D2.

Scott, J. C. (1990). *Domination and the arts of resistance: Hidden transcripts.* New Haven and London: Yale University Press.

Solomon, C. (1991, August). 24-hour Employees. *Personnel Journal,* 56–63.

Steele, S. (1990). *The content of our character: A new vision of race in America.* New York: HarperPerennial.

Stein, H. (1989, June). Problems and nonproblems in American economy. *AEI Economist,* 56–70.

Stiglitz, J. (2003). *Globalization and its discontents.* New York: Norton.

Storke, W. F., & Kelman, A. R. (Producers), Donner, C. (Director). (1984). *A Christmas Carol.* [Motion picture]. Hollywood, CA: 20th Century Fox.

Sue, D. (1992). The challenge of multiculturalism: The road less traveled. *American Counselor, 1,* 6ff.

Sue, D. W., Ivey, A. E., & Pedersen, P. B. (1996). *A theory of multicultural counseling and therapy.* Pacific Grove, CA: Brooks/Cole.

Sue, D. W., & Sue, D. (1990). *Counseling the culturally different: Theory and practice* (2nd ed.). New York: John Wiley.

Sue, D., & Sue, D. W. (1993). Ethnic identity: Cultural factors in the psychological development of Asians in America. In D. R. Atkinson, G. Morten, & D. W. Sue, (Eds.), *Counseling American minorities: A cross-cultural perspective* (4th ed.) (pp. 199–210). Madison, WI: Brown & Benchmark.

Super, D. E., & Hall, D. T. (1978). Career development: Exploitation and planning. *Annual Review of Psychology, 29,* 333–72.

Symonds, W. C. (2003, April 28). Crisis: As costs spin out of control, funding is in retreat. Bottom line: Some fundamental changes lie ahead. *Business Week,* pp. 73–78.

Tagliabue, J. (1996, June 20). In Europe, a wave of lay-offs stuns white-collar workers. *New York Times,* pp. A1ff.

Tatum, B. D. (1997). *"Why are all the Black kids sitting together in the cafeteria?" and other conversations about race.* New York: BasicBooks.

Taylor, J. M., Gilligan, C., & Sullivan, A. M. (1995). *Between voice and silence: Women and girls, race and relationships.* Cambridge, MA: Harvard University Press.

Tinsley, H. E. A. (1994). Construct your reality and show us its benefits: Comment on Richardson (1993). *Journal of Counseling Psychology, 41,* 108–11.

Tolbert, E. L. (1980). *Counseling for career development* (2nd ed.). Boston: Houghton Mifflin.

Tolchin, S. (1996). *The angry American: How voter rage is changing the nation.* Boulder, CO: Westview Press.

Uchitelle, L. (2003, August 10). The perils of cutbacks in higher education. *New York Times.* Retrieved 2003, August 10 from http://www.nytimes.com/2003,08/10/business/yourmoney/10VIEW.html?ei=5059&en=el . . .

Uchitelle, L., & Kleinfield, N. R. (1996, March 3). On the battlefield of business, millions of casualties. *New York Times,* Section 1, pp. 1ff.

United Way Strategic Institute. (1990, July–August). Nine forces reshaping America. *Futurist,* 9–16.

USA Today. (2003, June 23). How the 50 states rank in taxing and spending wisely, p. A2.

Valdez, D. W. (1995, December 22). Companies don't save bad news for new year. *El Paso Times,* pp. 8E, 5E.

Vidueira, J. R. (1996, August). Loss of language? What does the lack of Spanish fluency among young Hispanic Americans mean for their future—and the future of America? *Vista, 11*(12), 16.

Vondracek, F. (2001). The development of perspective in vocational psychology. *Journal of Vocational Psychology, 59* (2) 252–261.

Vontress, C. E., Johnson, J. A., & Epp, L. R. (1999). *Cross-cultural counseling: A casebook.* Alexandria, VA: American Counseling Association.

Wahlgren, E. (2002, August 21). CEO Pay Tomorrow: Same as Today. *Business Week.*

Walberg, M. (1996, March 4). Workplace security can start at home. *El Paso Herald-Post,* p. B4.

Wehrly, B. (1995). *Pathways to multicultural counseling competence: A developmental journey.* Pacific Grove, CA: Brooks/Cole.

Weinberg, R. B., & Mauksch, L. B. (1991). Examining family-of-origin influences in life at work. *Journal of Marital and Family Therapy, 17,* 233–242.

Welch, D. (2002, August). Challenges of a poor boy in academia. In M. Englar-Carlson, Chair, *Class jump-*
ing into academia—from dirt roads to ivory towers. Symposium presented at the 110th Annual Convention of the American Psychological Convention, Chicago, IL.

Wilde, A. D. (1996, January 14). Earning it; Who's really essential? In a blizzard, it's a blur. *New York Times,* Section 3, p. 10.

Woods, J. D. (1994). *The corporate closet: The professional lives of gay men in America.* New York: The Free Press.

Yanico, B. J. (2002, August). Stranger in a strangle land: Academia from a less than privileged background. In M. Englar-Carlson, Chair, *Class jumping into academia—from dirt roads to ivory towers.* Symposium presented at the 110th Annual Convention of the American Psychological Convention, Chicago, IL.

Yates, R. (1995, October 29). Workers' anger grows as layoffs continue to rise. *San Antonio Express News,* p. 6J.

Young, C. (1989). Psychodynamics of coping and survival of the African-American female in a changing world. *Journal of Black Studies, 20,* 208–23.

Young, I. M. (1992). Five faces of oppression. In T. E. Wartenberg (Ed.), *Rethinking power* (pp. 174–195). Albany, NY: State University of New York Press.

Chapter 2

Accounting in crisis. Reform is urgent. Here's what needs to be done. (2002, January 28). *Business Week Online.* Retrieved August 27, 2003 from http://www.businessweek.com/@@aUps6ocQ26ZFXhIA/magazine/content/02_04/b37677.

Allport, G. W., Vernon, P., & Lindzey (1970). *Study of Values* (3rd ed., rev.). Chicago: Riverside.

Andersen, M. L. (1983). *Thinking about women: Sociological and feminist perspectives.* New York: Macmillan.

Anderson, H. D., & Goolishian, H. A. (1991, January). *New directions in systemic therapy: A language systems approach.* Symposium presented at the Texas Association of Marriage and Family Therapy, Dallas, TX.

Anderson, P. (2002, October 24). Job satisfaction: Oxymoron? *CNN, Career Trends.* http://www.cnn.com.

Andreski, S. (1983). Introduction. In S. Andreski (Ed.), *Max Weber on capitalism, bureaucracy, and religion: A selection of texts* (Trans. by S. Andreski) (pp. 1–12). London: Allen & Unwin.

Ashley, M. (1980). *The house of Stuart.* London: J. M. Dent.

Associated Press. (1997, February 19). Clinton hears from critics of welfare reform. *El Paso Times,* p. 5A.

Atkinson, D. R., & Hackett, G. (Eds.) (1993). *Counseling diverse populations.* Madison, WI: Brown & Benchmark.

Atkinson, D. R., Morten, G., & Sue, D. W. (1993). *Counseling American minorities: A cross-cultural perspective* (4th ed.). Madison, WI: Brown & Benchmark.

Axelson, J. A. (1993). *Counseling and development in a multicultural society* (2nd ed.). Pacific Grove, CA: Brooks/Cole.

Barnett, R. C., & Rivers, C. (1996). *She works, he works: How two-income families are happier, healthier, and better off.* Harper San Francisco.

Baxandall, R., & Gordon, L. (1995). *America's working women: A documentary history, 1600 to the present* (revised and updated). New York: W. W. Norton .

Becvar, D. S., & Becvar, R. (1996). *Family therapy: A systemic integration* (3rd ed.). Boston: Allyn and Bacon.

Berger, P. (1990). *The human shape of work.* New York: Macmillan.

Bloch, D. P. (1997). Spirituality, intentionality, and career success: The quest for meaning. In D. P. Bloch & L. J. Richmond (Eds.), *Connections between spirit and work in career development: New approaches and practical perspectives* (pp. 185–208). Palo Alto, CA: Davies-Black.

Bloch, D. P., & Richmond, L. J. (1997). *Connections between spirit and work in career development: New approaches and practical perspectives.* Palo Alto, CA: Davies-Black.

Borow, H. (1973). Shifting postures toward work: A tracing. *American Vocational Journal, 48,* 28–29, 108.

Bowman, S. L. (1995). Career intervention strategies and assessment issues for African Americans. In F. T. L. Leong (Ed.), *Career development and vocational behavior of racial and ethnic minorities* (pp. 137–164). Mahwah, NJ: Erlbaum.

Bragg, R. (1996a, March 5). More than money, they miss the pride a good job brought. *New York Times,* p. A17–A18.

Bragg, R. (1996b, March 5). Big holes where the dignity used to be. *New York Times,* pp. A1, A16, A18.

Briskin, A. (1996). *The stirring of soul in the workplace.* San Francisco: Jossey-Bass.

Brown, D. (2002). The role of work values and cultural values in occupational choice, satisfaction and success: A theoretical statement. In Brown, D. & Associates (Eds.), *Career choice and development* (4th ed.) (pp. 465–509). San Francisco: Jossey-Bass.

Buenning, M., & Tollefson, N. (1987). The cultural gap hypothesis as an explanation for the achievement patterns of Mexican-American students. *Psychology in the Schools, 24,* 264–272.

Burr, V. (1995). *An introduction to social constructionism.* London, England: Routledge.

Butterfield, F. (1990, January 21). Why they excel. *Parade,* 4–6.

Carter, R. T. (1991). Cultural values: A review of empirical research and implications for counseling. *Journal of Counseling and Development, 70,* 164–173.

Corey, G. (1996). *Theory and practice of counseling and psychotherapy* (5th ed.). Pacific Grove, CA: Brooks/Cole.

Corey, G., & Corey, M. S. (1997). *I never knew I had a choice* (6th ed.). Pacific Grove, CA: Brooks/Cole.

Corey, G., Corey, M. S., & Callanan, P. (1993). *Issues and ethics in the helping professions* (4th ed.). Pacific Grove, CA: Brooks/Cole.

Cose, E. (1996, September 9). No work, no workfare. *Newsweek,* 46–47.

Crace, R. K., & Brown, D. (1996). *Life Values Inventory.* Chapel Hill, NC: Life Values Resources.

Dawis, R. (1984). Job satisfaction: Workers aspirations, attitudes, and behavior. In N. C. Gysbers (Ed.), *Designing careers, counseling to enhance education, work, and leisure* (pp. 65–90). San Francisco: Jossey-Bass.

Dawis, R. V. (1992). The individual differences tradition in counseling psychology. *Journal of Counseling Psychology, 39* (1), 7–19.

Dervin, B. (1994). Information-Democracy. An examination of underlying assumptions. *Journal of the American Society for Information Science, 45* (6), 369–385.

Doherty, W. J. (1991, September/October). Family therapy goes postmodern. *Family Therapy Networker, 15* (5), 37–42.

Dosick, W. (1995). *Golden rules: The ten ethical values parents need to teach their children.* HarperSanFrancisco.

Eichenwald, K. (2002a, February 3). Enron's many strands: The overview; Enron panel finds inflated profits and self-dealing. Retrieved August 27, 2003 from http://query.nytimes.com/search/restricted/article?res=F60B10F839590C708CDDAB0894.

Eichenwald, K. (2002b, June 17). Enron's many strands: The overview; Andersen trial yields evidence in Enron's fall. Retrieved August 27, 2003 from http://query.nytimes.com/search/restricted/article?res=F20713FC35580C748DDDAF0894.

Eichenwald, K. (2003, February 9). Company man to the end, after all. Retrieved August 27, 2003 from http://query.nytimes.com/search/restricted/article?res= F60C12FE395F0C7A8CDDAB089.

Feiler, B. (2002). *Abraham: A journey to the heart of three faiths.* New York: HarperCollins.

Feixas, G. (1990). Approaching the individual, approaching the system: A constructivist model for integrative psychotherapy. *Journal of Family Psychology, 4* (1), 4–35.

Festinger, L. (1957). *A theory of cognitive dissonance.* Stanford, CA: Stanford University Press.

Festinger, L., Schacter, S., & Back, K. (1950). The spatial ecology of group formation. In L. Festinger, S. Schacter, & K. Back (Eds.), *Social pressure in informal groups* (pp. 33–59). New York: Harper.

Fischer, D. H. (1989). *Albion's seed: Four British folkways in America.* New York: Oxford University Press.

Fitzgerald, L. F., & Nutt, R. (1985). The Division 17 principle concerning the counseling/ psychotherapy of women: Rationale and implementation. *The Counseling Psychologist, 14,* 180–216.

Flew, A. (1984). *A dictionary of philosophy* (2nd ed., rev.). New York: St. Martin's Press.

Fouad, N. A., & Bingham, R. P. (1995). Career counseling with racial & ethnic minorities. In W. B. Walsh & S. H. Osipow (Eds.), *Handbook of vocational psychology: Theory, research, and practice* (2nd ed.) (pp. 331–365). Mahwah, NJ: Erlbaum.

Foucault, M. (1970). *The order of things.* New York: Random House.

Frisby, C. L. (1993). One giant step backward: Myths of Black cultural learning styles. *School Psychology Review, 22* (3), 535–557.

Frymier, J., Cunningham, L., Duckett, W., Gansneder, B., Link, F., Rimmer, J., & Scholz, J. (1995, September). *Values on which we agree.* Bloomington, IN: Phi Delta Kappa International.

Frymier, J., Cunningham, L., Duckett, W., Gansneder, B., Link, F., Rimmer, J., et al. (1996, September). Values and the schools: Sixty years ago and now. *Research Bulletin; Phi Delta Kappa; Center for Evaluation, Development, and Research, 17,* 1–4.

Fuentes, C. (1992). *The buried mirror: Reflections on Spain and the New World.* Boston: Houghton Mifflin.

Gelatt, H. B. (2002). *The process of illumination: Looking at your worldview.* NATCON Papers, 2002 Les actes du CONAT.

Gergen K. J. (1985). The social constructionist movement in modern psychology. *American Psychologist, 40,* 266–275.

Gergen, K. J. (1994). *Realities and relationships: Soundings in social construction.* Cambridge, MA: Harvard University Press.

Gilbert, D. T., & Jones, E. E. (1986). Perceiver-induced constraints: Interpretation of self generated reality. *Journal of Personality and Social Psychology, 50,* 269–280.

Glancy, M. (1986). Participant observation in the recreation setting. *Journal of Leisure Research, 18,* (2) 59–80.

Goren, A. A. (1980). Jews. In S. Thernstrom (Ed.), *The Harvard encyclopedia of American ethnic groups* (pp. 571–598). Cambridge, MA: Belknap Press.

Granvold, D. K. (1996). Constructivist psychotherapy. *Families in Society: The Journal of Contemporary Human Services, 77,* 345–57.

Hacker, A. (1992). *Two nations: Black and White, separate, hostile, and unequal.* New York: Charles Scribner's.

Hackman, J., & Oldham, G. (1981). Work redesigned: People and their work. In J. O'Toole, J. Sheiber, & L. Wood (Eds.), *Working changes and choices* (pp. 173–182). Sacramento, CA: The Regents of the University of California.

Hare-Mustin, R. T. (1994). Discourses in the mirrored room: A postmodern analysis of therapy. *Family Process, 33,* 19–35.

Herman, R., Olivio, T., & Gioia, J. (2003). *Impending crisis: Too many jobs, too few people.* Winchester, VA: Oakhill Press.

Herr, E. L., & Cramer, S. H. (1996). *Career guidance and counseling through the lifespan* (5th ed.). New York: HarperCollins.

Herr, E. L., Cramer, S. H., & Niles, S. G. (2004). *Career guidance and counseling throughout the lifespan* (6th ed.). Boston: Pearson, Allyn and Bacon.

Herz, F. M., & Rosen, E. J. (1982). Jewish families. In M. McGoldrick, J. K. Pearce, & J. Giordano (Eds.), *Ethnicity and family therapy* (pp. 364–392). New York: The Guilford Press.

Herzberg, F. (1966). *Work and nature of man.* New York: World.

Herzberg, F., Mausner, B., & Snyderman, B. (1959). *The motivation to work.* New York: John Wiley.

Hochschild, A. R. (1997). *The time bind: When work becomes home and home becomes work.* New York: Henry Holt.

Holstein, W. J. (2003, February 23). Book value; A culture turned against itself at Andersen. Retrieved August 27, 2003 from http://query.nytimes.com/search/restricted/article?res=FB0E1EFA38590C708EDDAB089.

Holland, J. L., Gottfredson, G. G., and Nafziger, D. H. (1973). *A diagnostic scheme for specifying vocational assistance.* Baltimore: Johns Hopkins University Center for Social Organization of Schools. (Report No. 164).

Hsia, J., and Hirano-Nakanishi, M. (1989, November/December). The demographics of diversity: Asian Americans and higher education. *Change,* 20–27.

Ibrahim, F. A. (1991). Contribution of a cultural worldview to generic counseling and development. *Journal of Counseling and Development, 20,* 13–19.

Imel, S. (2002). Career Development for Meaningful Life Work. ERIC Clearinghouse on Adult, Career and Vocational Education (ERIC/ACVE). Retrieved November 11, 2003 from http://icdl.uncg.edu/ft/071701-01.html.

Jones, E. E. (1979). The rocky road from acts to dispositions. *American Psychologist, 34,* 107–117.

Kadlec, D., with Baughn, A. J., Fonda, D., & Parker, C. (2002, July 8). WorldCom nailed for the biggest bookkeeping deception in history, a fallen telecom giant gives investors one more reason to doubt corporate integrity. Retrieved May 3, 2003 from http://elibrary.bigchalk.com/libweb/elib/do/document?set=search&groupid=1&requestid=li.

Kadlec, D., & Baumohl, B. (1997, April 28). How CEO pay got away. *Time,* 59–60.

Kahn, J. (2003a, December 7). An Ohio town is hard hit as leading industry moves to China. *New York Times,* p. 8.

Kahn, J. (2003b, December 7). Ruse in Toyland: China workers' hidden woe. *New York Times,* pp. 1, 8.

Keller, E. (2003). *Transformational ethics: The right side of the Bell Curve.* Unpublished Manuscript.

Koh, H. H. (1994, Fall). Bitter fruit of the Asian immigration cases. *Constitution,* 68–77.

Kopelman, R. E., Rovenport, J. L., & Allport, R. B. (2002). *Study of Values* (4th ed.). Available at richard_kopelman@baruch.cuny.edu.

Kopelman, R. E., Rovenport, J. L., & Guan, M. (2003). *The Study of Values:* Construction of the fourth ed. *Journal of Vocational Behavior, 62,* 203–230.

Leong, F. T. I., & Serafica, F. C. (1995). Career assessment and interventions with Asian Americans. In F. T. E. Leong, (Ed.), *Career development and vocational behavior of racial and ethnic minorities* (pp. 67–102). Mahwah, NJ: Erlbaum.

Lessnoff, M. H. (1994). *The spirit of capitalism and the Protestant ethic: An enquiry into the Weber thesis.* Brookfield, VT: Edward Elgar.

Leuthy, H. (1970). Once again: Calvinism and capitalism. In D. Wrong (Ed.), *Makers of modern social science: Max Weber* (pp. 123–134). Englewood Cliffs, NJ: Prentice Hall.

Licht, W. (1988, February). How the workplace has changed in 75 years. *The Monthly Labor Review,* 19–24.

Lipset, S. (1990, Winter). The work ethic: Then and now. *Public Interest,* 61–69.

Lyddon, W. J. (1995). Forms and facets of constructivist psychology. In R. A. Neimeyer & M. J. Mahoney (Eds.), *Constructivism in psychotherapy* (pp. 69–92). Washington, DC: American Psychological Association.

Macaulay, D. (2001). *Mill times* [Motion picture]. United States: PBS Home Video.

Macoby, M., & Terzi, K. (1981). What happened to the work ethic? In J. O'Toole, J. Scheiber, & L. Wood (Eds.), *Working changes and choices* (pp.162–171). Sacramento, CA: The Regents of the University of California.

Maylunas, A., & Mironenko, S. (1997). *A lifelong passion: Nicholas and Alexandra, their own story* (D. Galy, Trans.). New York: Doubleday.

McAuliffe, G. J. (1993). Constructive development and career transition: Implications for counseling. *Journal of Counseling and Development, 72,* 23–28.

McGeeney, P. (1987). *The limitations of contemporary work in providing meaning.* (Unpublished manuscript).

McKenna, E. P. (1997). *When work doesn't work anymore: Women, work, and identity.* New York: Delacorte Press.

Meichenbaum, D., & Fong, G. T. (1993). How individuals control their own minds: A constructive narrative approach. In D. W. Wegner & J. W. Pennebaker (Eds.), *Handbook of mental control* (pp. 473–490). Englewood Cliffs, NJ: Prentice Hall.

Michelozzi, B. (1996). *Coming alive from nine to five: The career search handbook* (5th ed.). Mountain View, CA: Mayfield.

Miller, K. L. (2002, July 8). The giants stumble. *Newsweek International.* Retrieved May 3, 2003 from http://elibrary.bigchalk.com/libweb/elib/do/document?set=search&groupid=1&requested=li.

Miller, S. M. (1971). Introduction. In S. M. Miller (Ed.), *Max Weber* (pp. 1–17). New York: Thomas Y. Crowell.

Morrow, L. (1981, May 11). *Time,* p. 94.

Murry, E., & Mosidi, R. (1993). Career development counseling for African Americans: An appraisal of the obstacles and intervention strategies. *Journal of Negro Education, 62,* 441– 47.

Naisbitt, J., Naisbitt, N., & Phillips, D. (1999). *High tech, high touch: Technology and our accelerated search for meaning.* London: Nicholas Beasley.

Neimeyer, R. A. (1995a). Client-generated narratives in psychotherapy. In R. A. Neimeyer & M. J. Mahoney (Eds.), *Constructivism in psychotherapy* (pp. 231–246). Washington, DC: American Psychological Association.

Nisbett, R. E., & Ross, L. (1980). *Human inference: Strategies and shortcomings of social judgment.* Engelwood Cliffs, NJ: Prentice Hall.

Norris, F. (2003, January 16). Accounting rules changed to bar tactics used by Enron. Retrieved August 27, 2003 from http://query.nytimes.com/search/restricted/article?res=FB091EFA3A550C758DDDA8089.

Nussbaum, B. (2002, January 28). Can you trust anybody anymore? The scope of the Enron debacle undermines the credibility of modern business culture. Let's get back to basics. Retrieved August 27, 2002 from http://www.businessweek.com:/print/magazine/content/02_04/b3767701.htm?mz.

Oppel, Jr., R. A., & Glater, J. D. (2001, December 5). Enron's collapse: The overview; Congress is zeroing in on the complex deals at Enron. Retrieved August 27, 2003, from http://query.nytimes.com/search/restricted/article?res=FB0911FD3C580C768CDDAB099.

Osipow, S. H., & Fitzgerald, L. F. (1996). *Theories of career development* (4th ed.). Boston: Allyn and Bacon.

O'Toole, P. (1993, November). Redefining success. *Working Woman, 49*–50, 52–53, 96–97.

Packer, J. I. (1990). *A quest for Godliness: The Puritan vision of the Christian life.* Downers Grove, IL: Crossway.

Payne, R. K. (1995). *A framework for understanding and working with students and adults from poverty.* Baytown, TX: RFT.

Pedersen, P. (1990). The multicultural perspective as a fourth force in counseling. *Journal of Mental Health Counseling, 12* (1), 93–95.

Penn, P. (1991). Letters to ourselves. *Family Therapy Networker, 15* (5), 43–45.

Perugia, L. (Producer), and Zeffirelli, F. (Director) (1972). *Brother sun sister moon* [Motion picture]. Rome: Euro International Films, and London: Vic Film (Productions).

Peterson, J. A. (1970). *Counseling and values: A philosophical examination.* Scranton, PA: International Textbook.

Pipher, M. (1996). *The shelter of each other: Rebuilding our families.* New York: Ballantine Books.

Pipher, M. (1997, August 14). *Homes without walls.* Luncheon presentation sponsored by Loretto Academy, El Paso, TX.

Pritchard, R. (1969). Equity theory: A review and critique. *Organizational Behavior and Human Performance, 4,* 176–211.

Raths, L. E., Harmin, M., & Simon, S. B. (1966). *Values and teaching: Working with values in the classroom.* Columbus, OH: Charles E. Merrill.

Ray, P. H., & Anderson, S. R. (2000). *The cultural creatives: How 50 million people are changing the world.* New York: Three Rivers Press.

Reich, R. (1997, June 13–15). Being a dad: Rewarding labor. *USA Weekend,* 10–11.

Reingold, J. (1997, April 21). Executive pay. *Business Week,* pp. 58, 60, 62, 64, 66.

Reuters. (2003). Tyco takes charge of $1.1 billion on more accounting woes. Retrieved April 20, 2003 from http://www.nytimes.com/reuters/business/business- manufacturing-tyco-accounting.html.

Richardson, M. S. (1993). Work in people's lives: A location for counseling psychologists. *Journal of Counseling Psychology, 40,* 425–33.

Richardson, T. Q. (1993). Black cultural learning styles: Is it really a myth? *School Psychology, 22* (3), 562–567.

Ritzer, G. (2000). *The McDonaldization of society* (new century ed.). Thousand Oaks, CA: Pine Forge Press.

Rokeach, M. (1973). *The nature of human values.* New York: Free Press.

Ross, L., & Nisbett, R. E. (1991). *The person and the situation: Perspectives of social psychology.* New York: McGraw Hill.

Ryan, W. (1971). *Blaming the victim.* New York: Random House.

Saracho, O. N. (1989). Cultural differences in the cognitive style of Mexican-American students. In B. J. Robinson Shade (Ed.), *Culture, style, and the educative process* (pp. 129–136). Springfield, IL: Charles C. Thomas.

Sarbin, T. R. (Ed.). (1986). *Narrative psychology: The storied nature of human conduct.* New York: Praeger.

Savickas, M. L. (1993). Career counseling in the postmodern era. *Journal of Cognitive Psychotherapy: An International Quarterly, 7* (3), 205–215.

Savickas, M. L. (1995). Current theoretical issues in vocational psychology: Convergence, divergence, and schism. In W. B. Walsh & S. H. Osipow (Eds.), *Handbook of vocational psychology* (2nd ed.) (pp. 1–34). Mahwah, N.J.: Erlbaum.

Savickas, M. L. (1997). The spirit in counseling: Fostering self-completion through work. In D. P. Bloch, & L. H. Richmond, *Connections between spirit and work in career development: New approaches and practical perspectives* (pp. 3—25). San Francisco: Davies-Black.

Schultz, W. (2001). *A man's garden.* New York: Houghton Mifflin.

Semple, K. (2003). Oklahoma files criminal charges against WorldCom. Retrieved August 27, 2003 from http://www.nytimes.com/2003/08/27/business/27CND-PHONE.html?hp.

Severy, M. (1983, October). The world of Luther. *National Geographic,* 418–463.

Simon, S. B., Howe, L. W., & Kirschenbaum, H. (1995). *Values clarification.* New York: Warner Books.

Smith, L. B. (1971). *This realm of England: 1399–1688* (2nd ed.). Lexington, MA: D. C. Heath.

Sorkin, A. R., and Berenson, A. (2002, December 31). Corporate conduct: The overview; Tyco admits using accounting tricks to inflate earnings. Retrieved August 27, 2003 from http://query.nytimes.com/search/restricted/article?res=F30A11F93E5B0C728FDDAB0994.

Stone, E., & Taylor, P. (1991, November–December). The overworked American. *New Age Journal,* pp. 34–43, 101–104.

Strong, R. (1992). *Royal gardens.* New York: Pocket Books.

Sue, D. (1992). The challenge of multiculturalism: The road less traveled. *American Counselor, 1,* 6ff.

Sue, D. W., & Sue, D. (1990). *Counseling the culturally different: Theory and practice* (2nd ed.). NY: John Wiley.

Super, D. (1976). *Career education and the meaning of work*. Monographs on Career Education. Washington, DC: The Office of Career Education, U.S. Office of Education.

Suzuki, H. (1989, November/December). Asian Americans as the "Model Minority": Outdoing Whites? Or media hype? *Change*, 13–19.

Tawney, R. H. (1958). Forward. In M. Weber, *The Protestant ethic and the spirit of capitalism* (T. Parsons, Trans.) (pp. 1–11). New York: Charles Scribner's.

Texas Education Agency. (1996). *Building good citizens for Texas. Character education resource guide*. Austin, TX: Author.

The backlash against business; Corporate scandals and politics. (2002, July 6). *The Economist*. Retrieved May 3, 2003 from http://elibrary.bigchalk.com/libweb/elib/do/document?set=search&groupid=1&requestid=li.

Van Hoose, W. H., & Paradise, L. V. (1979). *Ethics in counseling and psychotherapy*. Cranston, RI: The Carroll Press.

Vecchio, R. (1980). The function and meaning of work and the job. Morse and Weiss (1955) revisited. *Academy of Management Journal, 23,* 361–367.

Weber, M. (1958). *The Protestant ethic and the spirit of capitalism* (T. Parsons, Trans.). New York: Charles Scribner's Sons. (Original work published in 1904–05)

Weber, M. (1976). *The agrarian society of ancient civilizations* (R. I. Frank, Trans.) (pp. 37–67). London: New Left Books. Reprinted in S. Andreski (Ed.) (1983). *Max Weber on capitalism, bureaucracy, and religion* (pp. 30–58). London: Allen & Unwin. (Original work published in 1891.)

Whitmore, H. (1971). Horrible conspiracies. In R. Graham (Director and Producer), *Elizabeth R* [*Masterpiece Theater* dramatic series]. London: British Broadcasting Corporation.

Will, G. (1997, February 20). Enjoyable film showed Jefferson's good, bad sides. *El Paso Times*, p. 6A.

Wilson, W. J. (1996). *When work disappears: The world of the new urban poor*. New York: Alfred A. Knopf.

Wrong, D. (1970). Introduction: Max Weber. In D. Wrong (Ed.), *Makers of modern social science: Max Weber* (pp. 1–76). Englewood Cliffs, NJ: Prentice Hall.

Yang. J. (1991). Career counseling of Chinese American students. In C. C. Lee (Ed.), *Counseling for diversity: A guide for school counselors and related professionals* (pp. 61–83). Boston: Allyn and Bacon.

Zeffirelli, F. (Director), & Perugia, L. (Producer). (1972). *Brother Sun, Sister Moon* [Motion picture]. Rome: Euro International Films, and London: Vic Film (Productions), Ltd.

Zucchino, D. (1997). *Myth of the welfare queen*. New York: Scribner.

Chapter 3

American Education Research Association, American Psychological Association, and National Council on Measurement in Education. (1985). *Standards for educational and psychological testing*. Washington, DC: American Psychological Association.

American School Counselors Association. (1997). *Sharing the vision- The national standards for school counseling programs*. Alexandria, VA: Author.

Associated Press. (1996a, December 27). Jackson reconsiders Ebonics plan. *El Paso Herald-Post,* p. A7.

Associated Press. (1996b, December 25). Recognizing Black English troubles U.S. education chief. *El Paso Times,* p. 9A.

Association for Counselor Education and Supervision (ACES) and the National Career Development Association. (2000). *Preparing counselors for career development in the new millennium* (Working Paper, 4th draft).

Bemak, F., & Hanna, F. J. (September 1998). The twenty-first century counsellor: An emerging role in changing times. *International Journal for the Advancement of Counselling, 20,* 209–218.

Bench, M. (2001). "Career coaching: The new methodology for maximizing personal fulfillment and human capital." In G. Walz, R. Knowdell, & C. Kirkman (Eds.), *Staying innovative and change-focused in the new economy*. ERIC/CASS.

Betz, N. E. (2000). Contemporary issues in testing use. In C. E. Watkins, Jr., & V. L. Campbell (Eds.), *Testing and assessment in counseling practice* (2nd ed.) (pp. 481–516). Mahwah, NJ: Erlbaum.

'Black English' is stumbling block for black children. (1996, December 27). *El Paso Herald- Post,* p. A4.

Bloch, D. (1992). The application of group interviews to the planning and evaluation of career development programs. *Career Development Quarterly, 40,* 340–350.

Boer, P. M. (2001). *Career counseling over the Internet: An emerging model for trusting and responding to online clients*. Mahwah, NJ: Erlbaum.

Bowman, S. L. (1995). Career intervention strategies and assessment issues for African Americans. In F. T. L. Leong (Ed.), *Career development and vocational behavior of racial and ethnic minorities* (pp. 137–164). Mahwah, NJ: Erlbaum.

Busacca, L. A. (2002). Career problem assessment: A conceptual schema for counselor training. *Journal of Career Development, 29* (2), 129–146.

Butcher, J., Dahlstrom, W., et al. (1989). *Manual for the restandardized MMPI/MMPI 2: An administrative and interpretive guide*. Minneapolis, MN: University of Minnesota Press.

Campbell, D., Strong, E. K., & Hansen, J.–I. C. (1985). *Strong Interest Inventory.* Palo Alto, CA: Consulting Psychologists Press.

Carson, A. D., & Altai, N. M. (1994). 1000 years before Parsons: Vocational psychology in classical Islam. *Career Development Quarterly, 43,* 197–206.

Cattell, R. (1949). *Sixteen Personality Factor Questionnaire: Manual for forms A and B.* Champaign, IL: Institute for Personality and Ability Testing.

Cervantes, R. C., & Acosta, F. X. (1992). Psychological testing for Hispanic Americans. *Applied & Preventive Psychology, 1,* 209–19.

Chabassus, H., & Zytoski, D. G. (1987). Occupational outlook in the fifteenth century: Sanchez de Arevalo's *Mirror of human life. Journal of Counseling and Development, 66,* 168–170.

Chartrand, J. M., and Walsh, W. B. (2001). Career assessment: Changes and trends. In F. T. L. Leong and A. Barak (Eds.), *Contemporary models in vocational psychology: A volume in honor of Samuel H. Osipow* (pp. 231–255).

Clark, G. M., & Kolstoe, O. P. (1995). *Career development and transition education for adolescents with disabilities* (2nd ed.). Boston: Allyn and Bacon.

Code of Fair Testing Practices in Education. (1988). Washington, DC: Joint Committee on Testing Practices.

Conger, D., Hiebert, B., & Hong-Farrell, E. (1993). *Career and employment counseling in Canada.* Ottawa, Ontario, Canada: Canadian Labor Force Development Board.

Crites, J. (1981). *Career counseling: Models, methods, and materials.* New York: McGraw-Hill.

Curnow, T. C. (1989). Vocational development of persons with disability. *Career Development Quarterly, 37,* 269–278.

Dana, R. H. (1993). *Multicultural assessment perspectives for professional psychology.* Boston: Allyn and Bacon.

Dumont, F., & Carson, A. D. (1995). Precursors of vocational psychology in ancient civilizations. *Journal of Counseling and Development, 73,* 371–378.

Engels, D. (Ed.). (1994). *The professional practice of career counseling and consultation: A resource document* (2nd ed.). Alexandria, VA: National Career Development Association.

Fassinger, R.E. (1998, August). Gender as a factor in career services delivery. A modest proposal. Paper presented at the annual convention of the American Psychological Association, San Francisco, CA.

Flynn, R. (1994). Evaluating the effectiveness of career counselling: Recent evidence and recommended strategies. *Canadian Journal of Counselling, 28,* 77–90.

Fouad, N. A. (1993). Cross-cultural vocational assessment. *Career Development Quarterly, 42,* 4–13.

Fouad, N. A. (1995). Career behavior of Hispanics: Assessment and career intervention. In F. T. L. Leong (Ed.), *Career development and vocational behavior of racial and ethnic minorities* (pp.165–191). Mahwah, NJ: Erlbaum.

Fretz, B. R. (1981). Evaluating the effectiveness of career interventions [monograph]. *Journal of Counseling Psychology, 28,* 77–90.

Gelberg, S., & Chojnacki, J. T. (1996). *Career and life planning with gay, lesbian, and bisexual persons.* Alexandria, VA: American Counseling Association.

González, R. C., and Peterson, N. (2001, June). *Contemporary family issues in career counseling and their effect on career choice.* Professional Development Institute presented at the National Career Development Association 10th Global Career Development Conference, Tucson, AZ.

Gough, H. (1957). *California Psychological inventory manual.* Palo Alto, CA: Consulting Psychologists Press.

Gough, H. (1990). The California Psychological Inventory. In C. Watkins, Jr., & V. Campbell (Eds.), *Testing in counseling practice* (pp. 37–62). Hillsdale, NJ: Erlbaum.

Grieger, I., & Ponterotto, J. G. (1995). A framework for assessment in multicultural counseling. In J. G. Ponterotto, J. M. Casas, L. A. Suzuki, & C. M. Alexander (Eds.), *Handbook of multicultural counseling* (pp. 357–374). Thousand Oaks, CA: Sage.

Gysbers, N. C., & Henderson, P. (1997). *Developing and managing your school guidance program.* Alexandria, VA: American Counseling Association.

Gysbers, N. C., & Henderson, P. (2000). *Developing and managing your school guidance program,* 3rd ed. Alexandria, VA: American Counseling Association.

Gysbers, N., Hughey, K., Starr, M., & Lapan, R. (1992). Improving school guidance programs: A framework for program, personnel, and results evaluation. *Journal of Counseling and Development, 70,* 565–570.

Hackett, G., & Lonborg, S. D. (1993). Career assessment for women: Trends and issues. *Journal of Career Assessment, 1* (3), 197–216.

Harris-Bowlsbey, J. H., Dikel, M. R., & Sampson, Jr., J. P. (2002). *The Internet: A tool for career planning: A guide to using the Internet in career planning* (2nd ed.). Tulsa, OK: National Career Development Association.

Hathaway, S. and McKinley, J. (1943). *Minnesota Multiphasic Personality Inventory.* Minneapolis, MN: National Computer Scoring Systems.

Heppner, M., O'Brien, K., Hinkelman, J., & Flores, L. (1996). Training counseling psychologists in career development: Are we our own worst enemies? *The Counseling Psychologist, 24* (1), 105–125.

Herr, E. L., & Cramer, S. H. (1996). *Career guidance and counseling throughout the lifespan* (5th ed.). New York: Harper Collins.

Hiebert, B. (1994). A framework for quality control, accountability, and evaluation: Being clear about the legitimate outcomes of career counselling. *Canadian Journal of Counselling, 28,* 344–345.

Holland, J. L. (1997). *Making vocational choices: A theory of vocational personalities and work environments* (3rd ed.). Lutz, FL: Psychological Assessment Resources.

Horan, K., & Cady, D. C. (1990). The psychological evaluation of American Indians. *Arizona Counseling Journal, 15,* 6–12.

Hutchinson, N. (1995). Using performance assessments to evaluate career development programs. *Guidance and Counselling, 11* (3), 3–7.

Ivey, A. E., & Gluckstern, N. B. (1984). *Basic influencing skills.* North Amherst, MA: Microtraining Associates.

Ivey, A. E., Gluckstern, N. B., & Ivey, M. B. (1982). *Basic attending skills.* North Amherst, MA: Microtraining Associates.

Johansson, C. (1982). *Manual for the Career Assessment Inventory* (2nd ed.). Minneapolis, MN: National Computer Systems Interpretive Scoring System.

Kapes, J., Mastie, M., & Whitfield, E. (2002). *A counselor's guide to career assessment Instruments* (4th ed.). Alexandria, VA: National Career Development Association.

Kaplan, R., & Saccuzzo, D. (2001). *Psychological testing: Principles, applications, and issues* (5th ed.). Pacific Grove, CA: Brooks/Cole.

Kellett, R. (1994). The evaluation of career and employment counseling: A new direction. *Canadian Journal of Counselling/Revue canadienne de counseling, 28* (4), 346–352.

Kileen, J., & Kidd, J. (1991). *Learning outcomes of guidance: A review of recent research* (Research paper No. 85). London, England: National Institute for Careers Education and Counseling.

Kileen, J., White, M., & Watts, A. (1993). *The economic value of careers guidance.* London, England: Policy Studies Institute.

Kirschner, T., Hoffman, M., & Hill, C. (1994). Case study of the process and outcome of career counseling. *Journal of Counseling Psychology, 41,* 216–226.

Krug, S. (1991). The Adult Personality Inventory. *Journal of Counseling and Development, 69,* 266–274.

Krumboltz, J. D., and Vidalakis, N. K. (2000). Expanding learning opportunities using career assessments. *Journal of Career Assessment, 8* (4), 315–327.

Kuder, F. (1991). *Kuder Occupational Interest Inventory.* Monterey, CA: CTB McGraw-Hill.

Ladero Quesada, M. A. (2003). Isabel and the Moors. In D. A. Boruchoff (Ed.), *Isabel la Católica, Queen of Castile: Critical Essays.* New York: Palgrave MacMillan.

Leong, F. T. L., & Gim-Chung, R. H. (1995). Career assessment and intervention with Asian Americans. In F. T. L. Leong (Ed.), *Career development and vocational behavior of racial and ethnic minorities* (pp. 193–226). Mahwah, NJ: Erlbaum.

Levinson, E. M., Peterson, M., & Elston, R. (1994). Vocational counseling with persons with mental retardation. In D. C. Strohmer & H. L. Prout (Eds.), *Counseling and psychotherapy with persons with mental retardation and borderline intelligence* (pp. 257–304). Brandon, VT: Clinical Psychology Publishing.

Martin, W. E., Jr. (1995). Career development assessment and intervention strategies with American Indians. In F. T. L. Leong (Ed.), *Career development and vocational behavior of racial and ethnic minorities* (pp. 227–248). Mahwah, NJ: Erlbaum.

Montross, D., Kane T, & Ginn, R. (1997). *Career coaching for kids.* Palo Alto, CA: Davies-Black.

Multon, K., & Lapan, R. (1995). Developing scales to evaluate career and personal guidance curricula in a high school setting. *Journal of Career Development, 21,* 293–305.

Murry, E., & Mosidi, R. (1993). Career development counseling for African Americans: An appraisal of the obstacles and intervention strategies. *Journal of Negro Education, 62,* 441– 47.

Myers, I., & McCauley, M. (1985). *Manual: A guide for the Myers-Briggs Type Indicator.* Palo Alto, CA: Consulting Psychologists Press.

Nadeau, K. G. (1995). ADD in the workplace: Career consultation and counseling for the adult with ADD. In K. G. Nadeau (Ed.), *A comprehensive guide to attention deficit disorder in adults* (pp. 308–334). New York: Bruner/Mazel.

Nevo, O. (1990). Career counseling from the counselee perspective: Analysis of feedback questionnaires. *Career Development Quarterly, 38,* 314–24.

Orenstein, P. (1994). *School girls: Young women, self-esteem, and the confidence gap.* New York: Anchor Books.

Paniagua, F. A. (1994). *Assessing and treating culturally diverse clients: A practical guide.* Thousand Oaks, CA: Sage.

Parsons, F. (1909). *Choosing a vocation.* Boston: Houghton Mifflin.

Pérez, J. (2003). Isabel la Católica and the Jews. In D. A. Boruchoff (Ed.), *Isabel la Católica, Queen of Castile: Critical essays.* New York: Palgrave MacMillan.

Pope, M., & Minor, C. W. (Eds.) (2000). *Experiential activities for teaching career counseling classes and for facilitating career groups,* 1st ed. Columbus, OH: National Career Development Association.

Raths, L. E., Harmin, M., & Simon, S. B. (1966). *Values and teaching: Working with values in the classroom.* Columbus, OH: Charles E. Merrill.

Robitschek, C., & DeBell, C. (2002). The reintegration of vocational psychology and counseling psychology: Training issues for a paradigm shift. *The Counseling Psychologist, 30* (6), 801–814.

Rochlin, M. (1985). Sexual orientation of the therapist and therapeutic effectiveness with gay clients. In J. C. Gonsiorek (Ed.), *A guide to psychotherapy with Lesbian and Gay clients* (pp. 21–29). New York: Harrington Park Press.

Sattler, J. M. (1988). *Assessment of children* (3rd ed.). San Diego, CA: Author.

Savickas, M. L. (1992). New directions in career assessment. In D. H. Montross & C. J. Shinkman (Ed.), *Career development: Theory and practice* (pp. 336–352). Springfield, IL: Charles C. Thomas.

Splete, H., & Hopping, J. (2000). The emergence of career development facilitators. *Journal of Employment Counseling, 37,* 107–161.

Spokane, A. (1991). *Evaluating career intervention.* Englewood Cliffs, NJ: Prentice Hall.

Stewart, D. (1979). *The Alhambra.* New York: Newsweek.

Stratford, D. (2001). Executive Coaching. david.stratford @right.com.

Sue, D. W., & Sue, D. (1990). *Counseling the culturally different: Theory and practice* (2nd ed.). New York: John Wiley.

Suzuki, L. A., & Kugler, J. F. (1995). Intelligence and personality assessment: Multicultural perspectives. In J. G. Ponterotto, J. M. Casas, L. A. Suzuki, & C. M. Alexander (Eds.), *Handbook of multicultural counseling* (pp. 493–515). Thousand Oaks, CA: Sage.

Swanson, J. L. (2002). Understanding the complexity of clients' lives: Infusing a truly integrative career-personal perspective into graduate training. *The Counseling Psychologist, 30* (6), 815–832.

Texas evaluation model for professional school counselors (TEMPSC). (1991). Austin, TX: Texas Counseling Association.

The Holy Qur'an. Text, translation, and commentary. (1934/2001). (A. Y. Ali, Trans.). Elmhurst, NY: Tahrike Tarsile Qur'an.

Tinsley, H. E. A. (1994). Construct your own reality and show us its benefits: Comment on Richardson (1993). *Journal of Counseling Psychology, 41,* 108–111.

Walsh, W. B., & Betz, N. (1990). *Tests and assessments* (2nd ed.). New York: Prentice Hall.

Ward, C. M., and Bingham, R. P. (2001). Career assessment for African Americans. In W. B. Walsh, R. P. Bingham, M. T. Brown, & C. M. Ward (Eds.), *Career Counseling for African Americans* (pp. 27–48). Mahwah, NJ: Erlbaum.

Warnke, M., Kim, J., Koetzlow-Milster, D., Terrell, S., Dauser, P., Dial, S., et al. (1993). Career counseling practicum: Transformations in conceptualizing career issues. *Career Development Quarterly, 42,* 180–85.

Watkins, E. (1992). Historical influences on the use of assessment methods in counseling psychology. *Counseling Psychology Quarterly, 5,* 177–88.

Woods, J. D. (1994). *The corporate closet: The professional lives of gay men in America.* New York: The Free Press.

Zytowski, D. (1985). 1984 Division 17 presidential address: Frank, Frank, where are you now that we need you? *The Counseling Psychologist, 13,* 129–35.

Chapter 4

American College Testing. (1988). *ACT assessment program: Technical manual.* Iowa City, IA: Author.

Arbona, C. (1995). Theory and research on racial and ethnic minorities: Hispanic Americans. In F. T. L. Leong (Ed.), *Career development and vocational behavior of racial and ethnic minorities* (pp. 37–66). Mahwah, NJ: Erlbaum.

Bennett, G. K., Seashore, H. G., & Wesman, A. G. (1991). *Differential Aptitude Test with the Career Interest Inventory Counselor's manual.* San Antonio, TX: The Psychological Corporation.

Betz, N. E. (1994). Basic issues and concepts in career counseling for women. In W. B. Walsh & S. H. Osipow (Eds.), *Career counseling for women* (pp. 1–41). Hillsdale, NJ: Erlbaum.

Betz, N. E., & Fitzgerald, L. F. (1987). *The career psychology of women.* Orlando, FL: Academic Press.

Bohart, A. C. (1995). The person-centered psychotherapies. In A. S. Gurman & S. B. Messer (Eds.). *Essential psychotherapies: Theory and practice* (pp. 85–127). New York: Guilford.

Bordin, E. (1946). Diagnosis in counseling and psychotherapy. *Educational Psychology Measurement, 68,* 169–184.

Boy, A. V., and Pine, G. J. (1990). *A person-centered foundation for counseling and psychotherapy.* Springfield, IL: Thomas.

Bozarth, J. D., and Fisher, R. (1990). Person-centered career counseling. In W. B. Walsh & S. H. Osipow (Eds.), *Career counseling: Contemporary topics in vocational psychology* (pp. 45–78). Hillsdale, NJ: Erlbaum.

Brown, D., & Associates. (2002). *Career Choice and Development* (4th ed.). San Francisco: Jossey-Bass.

Brown, M. T. (1995). The career development of African Americans: Theoretical and empirical issues. In F. T. L. Leong (Ed.), *Career development of and vocational behavior of racial and ethnic behaviors* (pp. 7–36). Mahwah, NJ: Erlbaum.

Buhrke, R. A., and Douce, L. A. (1991). Training issues for counseling psychologists in working with lesbian women and gay men. *Counseling Psychologist 19* (2), 216–234.

Butcher, J., Dahlstrom, W., et al. (1989). *Manual for the restandardized MMPI: MMPI-2: An administrative and interpretive guide.* Minneapolis: University of Minnesota Press.

Campbell, D. P. (1992). *Campbell Interest and Skill Survey manual.* Minneapolis: NCS Assessments.

Campbell, D. P., Strong, E. K., & Hansen, J.–I. C. (1985). *Strong Interest Inventory Manual.* Palo Alto, CA: Consulting Psychologists Press.

Carson, A. D., & Mowsesian, R. (1991). Moderators of the prediction of job satisfaction from congruence: A test of Holland's theory. *Journal of Career Assessment, 1,* 130–44.

Cattell, R. B., Eber, H. W., & Tatsuoka, M. M. (1970). *Handbook for the Sixteen Personality Factor Questionnaire (16PF).* Champaign, IL: Institute for Personality and Ability Testing.

Chartrand, J. M. (1991). The evolution of trait-factor career counseling: A person and environment fit approach. *Journal of Counseling and Development, 69,* 518–24.

Chartrand, J. M., & Bertok R. L. (1993). Current trait-factor career assessment: A cognitive interactional perspective. *The Journal of Career Assessment, 1* (4), 323–40.

Cohen, B. N. (2003). Applying existential theory and intervention to career decision-making. *Journal of Career Development, 29* (3), 195–208.

Corey, G. (1996). *Theory and practice of counseling and psychotherapy* (5th ed.). Pacific Grove, CA: Brooks/Cole.

Costa, P. T., Jr., & McCrae, R. R. (1985). *The NEO Personality Inventory.* New York: Psychological Assessment Resources.

Dawis, R. V. (1994). The theory of work adjustment as convergent theory. In M. L. Savickas & R. W. Lent (Eds.), *Convergence in Career Development Theories: Implications for Science and Practice.* Palo Alto, CA: CPP Books.

Dawis, R. V., England, G. W., & Lofquist, L. H. (1964). A theory of work adjustment. *Minnesota Studies in Vocational Rehabilitation, 15.*

Dawis, R. V., & Lofquist, L. H. (1984). *A psychological theory of work adjustment.* Minneapolis: University of Minnesota Press.

Dawis, R. V., Lofquist, L. H., & Weiss, D. J. (1968). A theory of work adjustment (a revision). *Minnesota Studies in Vocational Rehabilitation, 23.*

Dillon, M., & Weissman, S. (1987). Relationship between personality types on the SCII and MBTI. *Measurement and Evaluation in Counseling and Development, 120,* 68–79.

Dorn, F. (1992). Occupational wellness: The integration of career identity and personal identity. *Journal of Counseling and Development, 71,* 176–178.

Educational Testing Service. (1992). *ETS Test collection catalogue* (Vol. 6). Phoenix, AZ: Oryx Press.

Edwards, A. L. (1959). *Edwards Personal Preference Schedule manual.* The Psychological Corporation.

Flew, A. (1984). *A dictionary of philosophy* (2nd ed., rev.). New York: Random House.

Fouad, N. (1993). Cross-cultural vocational assessment. *Career Development Quarterly, 42,* 4–13.

Fouad, N. A. (1995). Career behavior of Hispanics: Assessment and career intervention. In F. T. L. Leong (Ed.), *Career development and vocational behavior of racial and ethnic minorities* (pp. 165–191). Mahwah, NJ: Erlbaum.

Freeman, S. C. (1990). C. H. Patterson on client-centered career counseling: An interview. *Career Development Quarterly, 38,* 291–301.

Gelberg, S., & Chonjakci, J. T. (1995). Developmental transitions of gay/lesbian/bisexual-affirmative, heterosexual career counselors. *Career Development Quarterly, 43,* 267–273.

Gelberg, S., & Chojnacki, J. T. (1996). *Career and life planning with gay, lesbian, and bisexual persons.* Alexandria, VA: American Counseling Association.

Goodyear, R., Roffey, A., & Jack, L. (1994). Edward Bordin: Fusing work and play. *Journal of Counseling and Development, 72,* 563–572.

Gottfredson, G. D., & Holland, J. L. (1990). A longitudinal test of the influence of congruence: Job satisfaction, competency utilization, and counterproductive behavior. *Journal of Counseling Psychology, 37,* 389–98.

Gough, H. (1957). *California Psychological Inventory manual.* Palo Alto, CA: Consulting Psychologists Press.

Grevious, C. (1985). A comparison of occupational aspirations of urban Black college students. *Journal of Negro Education, 54,* 35–42.

Hackett, G., & Lonborg, S. D. (1993). Career assessment for women: Trends and issues. *Journal of Career Assessment, 1* (3), 197–216.

Hammer, A. L. (1993). *Introduction to type and careers.* Palo Alto, CA: Consulting Psychologists Press.

Hammer, A. L., & Kummerow, J. M. (1993). *Strong-MBTI career development workbook.* Odessa, FL: Psychological Assessment Resources.

Harrington, T., & O'Shea, A. (1993). *Harrington-O'Shea Career Decision-Making System—Revised (CDM-R) manual.* Circle Pines, MN: American Guidance Service.

Harris, J. A., & Dansky, H. (1992). *APTICOM.* Philadelphia: Vocational Research Institute.

Helms, S. T. (1996). Some experimental tests of Holland's congruency hypothesis: The reactions of high school students to occupational simulations. *Journal of Career Assessment, 4* (3), 253–68.

Helms, S. T., & Williams, G. D. (1973). *An experimental study of the reactions of high school students to simulated jobs.* (Research Report No. 161). Baltimore: Center for Social Organization of Schools, Johns Hopkins University. (ERIC Document Reproduction Service No. ED 087 882.)

Hershonson, D. B. (1996). Work adjustment: A neglected area in career counseling. *Journal of Counseling and Development, 74,* 442–446.

Hesketh, B. (1993). Toward a better adjusted theory of work adjustment. *Journal of Vocational Behavior, 43,* 75–83.

Hogan, R., DeSoto, C., & Solano, C. (1977). Traits, tests, and personality research. *American Psychologist, 32,* 255–64.

Holland, J. L. (1973). *Making vocational choices: A theory of careers.* Englewood Cliffs, NJ: Prentice Hall.

Holland, J. L. (1985/1992). *Making vocational choices: A theory of vocational personalities and work environments* (2nd ed.). Englewood Cliffs, NJ: Prentice Hall.

Holland, J. L. (1994). *The Self-Directed Search: Professional manual.* Odessa, FL: Psychological Assessment Resources.

Holland, J. L. (1997). *Making vocational choices: A theory of vocational personalities and work environments* (3rd ed.). Lutz, FL: Psychological Assessment Resources.

Holland, J. L., Daiger, D. C., & Power, P. G. (1980). Some diagnostic scales for research in decision-making and personality: Identity, information and barriers. *Journal of Personality and Social Psychology, 39,* 1191–1200.

Horvath, A. O., & Greenberg, L. S. (1989). Development and validation of the Working Alliance Inventory. *Journal of Counseling Psychology, 36* (2), 223–233.

Horvath, A. O., & Greenberg, L. S. (1994). *The working alliance: Theory, research and practice.* New York: Wiley.

Horvath, A. O., & Symonds, B. D. (1991). Relation between working alliance and outcome in psychotherapy: A meta-analysis. *Journal of Counseling Psychology, 38* (2), 139–149.

Jackson, D. (1977). *Manual for the Jackson Vocational Interest Survey.* Port Huron, MI: Research Psychologists Press.

Johansson, C. B. (1986). *Manual for the Career Assessment Inventory.* Minneapolis: NCS Assessments.

Johansson, C. B. (1990). *Ideas, Determination and Assessment System (IDEAS) manual.* Minneapolis: NCS Assessment.

Johnson, M. J., Swartz, J. L., & Martin, W. E., Jr. (1995). Applications of psychological theories for career development with Native Americans. In F. T. L. Leong (Ed.), *Career development and vocational behav-ior of racial and ethnic minorities* (pp. 103–33). Mahwah, NJ: Erlbaum.

Klein, K., & Weiner, Y. (1977). Interest congruency as a moderation of the relationship between job tenure and job satisfaction and mental health. *Journal of Vocational Behavior, 10,* 91–98.

Knapp, R. R., & Knapp, L. (1990). *Career Occupational Preference System Interest Inventory (COPS) manual.* San Diego: EDITS.

Kuder, F. (1991). *Kuder Occupational Interest Survey, Form DD (KOIS): General manual.* Monterey, CA: CTB McGraw-Hill.

Lent, E. B. ((2001). Welfare-to-work services: A person-centered perspective. *Career Development Quarterly, 50,* 22–32.

Leong, F. T. L., & Gim-Chung, R. H. (1995). Career assessment and intervention with Asian Americans. In F. T. L. Leong (Ed.), *Career development and vocational behavior of racial and ethnic minorities* (pp. 193–226). Mahwah, NJ: Erlbaum.

Leong, F. T. L., & Serafica, F. C. (1995). Career development of Asian Americans: A research area in need of a good theory. In F. T. L. Leong (Ed.), *Career development and vocational behavior of racial and ethnic minorities* (pp. 67–102). Mahwah, NJ: Erlbaum.

Levinson, E. M., Peterson, M., & Elston, R. (1994). Vocational counseling with persons with mental retardation. In D. C. Strohmer & H. L. Prout (Eds.), *Counseling and psychotherapy with persons with mental retardation and borderline intelligence* (pp. 257–304). Brandon, VT: Clinical Psychology Publishing.

Lofquist, L. H., & Dawis, R. (1969). *Adjustment to work, a psychological view of man's problems in a work-oriented society.* New York: Appleton-Century Crofts.

Martin, W. E., Jr. (1995). Career development assessment and intervention strategies with American Indians. In F. T. L. Leong (Ed.), *Career development and vocational behavior of racial and ethnic minorities* (pp. 227–248). Mahwah, NJ: Erlbaum.

Matre, G., & Cooper, S. (1984). Concurrent evaluations of career indecision and indecisiveness. *Personnel and Guidance Journal, 62,* 637–639.

Meara, N. M., & Patton, J. P. (1994). Contributions of the working alliances in the practice of career counseling. *Career Development Quarterly, 43,* 161–167.

Meir, E. (1989). Integrative elaboration of the congruence theory. *Journal of Vocational Behavior, 35,* 219–30.

Miller, M. (1988). Integrating Holland's typology with the Myers-Briggs Type Indicator: Implications for career counselors. *Journal of Human Behavior, 5,* 25–28.

Miller, M. (1992). Synthesizing results from an interest and a personality inventory to improve career decision making. *Journal of Employment Counseling, 29,* 50–59.

Miller, M. (1993). A career counseling diagnostic model: How to assess and counsel career-concerned clients. *Journal of Employment Counseling, 30,* 35–43.

Murray, H. (1938). *Explorations in personality.* New York: Oxford University Press.

Nevill, D. D., & Super, D. E. (1989). *The Values Scale (VS) manual.* Palo Alto, CA: Consulting Psychologists Press.

Osipow, S. (1983). *Theories of career development.* Englewood Cliffs, NJ: Prentice Hall.

Osipow, S. H., Carney, C. G., Winer, J., Yanico, B., & Koschier, M. (1987). *Career Decision Scale (CDS) manual.* Odessa, FL: Psychological Assessment Resources.

Parsons, F. (1909). *Choosing a vocation.* Boston: Houghton Mifflin.

Patterson, C. H. (with C. F. Watkins, Jr.). (1982). Some essentials of a client-centered approach to assessment. *Measurement and Evaluation in Guidance, 15,* 103–106.

Payne, R. K. (1995). *A framework for understanding and working with students and adults from poverty.* Baytown, TX: RFT.

Pietrzak, D. R., and Page, B. J. (2001). An investigation of Holland types and the Sixteen Personality Factor Questionnaire-Fifth Edition. *Career Development Quarterly, 50,* 179–188.

Pines, A. M., and Yanai, O. Y. (2001). Unconscious determinants of career choice and burnout: Theoretical model and counseling strategy. *Journal of Employment Counseling, 38,* 170–184.

Pittenger, D. J. (1993). The utility of the Myers-Briggs Type Indicator. *Review of Educational Research, 63,* 467–88.

Prince, J. P., Uemura, A. K., Chao, G. S., & Gonzales, G. M. (1991, Spring). Using career interest inventories with multicultural clients. *Career Planning and Adults Development Journal,* 45–50.

Raskin, N. J., and Rogers, C. R. (1989). Person-centered therapy. In R. J. Corsini & D. Wedding, (Eds.), *Current Psychotherapies* (pp.155–194). Itasca, IL: Peacock.

Richardson, M. S. (1993). Work in people's lives: A location for counseling psychologists. *Journal of Counseling Psychology, 40,* 425–433.

Rogers, C. R. (1979). *Client-centered therapy.* Boston: Houghton Mifflin.

Rounds, J., & Tracey, T. (1990). From trait-factor to person-environment fit counseling: Theory and process. In W. B. Walsh & S. H. Osipow (Eds.), *Career counseling: Contemporary topics in vocational psychology* (pp. 1–44). Hillsdale, NJ: Erlbaum.

Rounds, J. B., Jr., Henly, G. A., Dawis, R. V., & Lofquist, L. H. (1981). *Manual for the Minnesota Importance Questionnaire: A measure of needs and values.* Minneapolis: Vocational Psychology Research, University of Minnesota.

Salamone, P. (1982). Difficult cases in career counseling, II: The indecisive client. *Personnel and Guidance Journal, 60,* 496–500.

Schwartz, R. (1992). Is Holland's theory worthy of so much attention, or should vocational psychology move on? *Journal of Vocational Behavior, 40,* 170–87.

Segal, S. (1961). A psychoanalytic analysis of personality factors in vocational choice. *Journal of Counseling Psychology, 8,* 202–210.

Sharf, R. (2002). *Applying career development theory to counseling.* Pacific Grove, CA: Brooks/Cole.

Simpson, S. (writer, director, and producer). (1987, September 1). *NOVA: Freud under analysis.* Boston: WGBH.

Super, D. E. (1970). *Work Values Inventory: Manual.* Boston: Houghton Mifflin.

Tinsley, D. J. (1993). Extensions, elaborations, and construct validity of the theory of work adjustment. *Journal of Vocational Behavior, 43,* 67–74.

Tuel, N. D., and Betz, N. E. (1998). Relationships of career self-efficacy expectations to the Myers-Briggs Type Indicator and the Personal Styles Scales. *Measurement & Evaluation in Counseling & Development, 31* (3), 150–164.

U.S. Department of Defense. (1992). *Armed services vocational aptitude battery forms 18/19.* Monterrey, CA: Defense Manpower Data Center.

Walsh, W. B., & Betz, N. E. (1990). *Tests and assessment* (2nd ed.). Englewood Cliffs, NJ: Prentice Hall.

Weiss, D. J., Dawis, R. V., England, G. W., & Lofquist, L. H. (1967). *Minnesota Satisfaction Questionnaire manual.* Minneapolis: Vocational Psychology Research, University of Minnesota.

Williamson, E. G. (1939). *How to counsel students: A manual of techniques for clinical counselors.* New York: McGraw-Hill.

Williamson, E. G. (1965). *Vocational counseling: Some historical, philosophical, and theoretical perspectives.* New York: McGraw-Hill.

Wolitzky, D. L. (1995). The theory and practice of traditional psychoanalytic psychotherapy. In A. S. Gurman & S. B. Messer (Eds.) *Essential psychotherapies: Theory and practice* (pp. 12–54). New York: Guilford.

Chapter 5

About Our Children (1995, Rev. ed.). Los Angeles, CA: Parents and Friends of Lesbians and Gays. [Booklet].

Arbona, C. (1990). Career counseling research and Hispanics: A review of the literature. *The Counseling Psychologist, 18,* 300–23.

Arbona, C. (1995). Theory and research on racial and ethnic minorities: Hispanic Americans. In F. T. L. Leong (Ed.). *Career development and vocational behavior of racial and ethnic minorities* (pp. 37–66). Mahwah, NJ: Erlbaum.

Archer, S., & Waterman A. (1983). Identity in early adolescence: A developmental perspective. *Journal of Early Adolescence, 3,* 203–14.

Ashcroft, B., Griffiths, G., and Tiffin, H. (Eds.). (1995). *The post-colonial studies reader.* London and New York: Routledge.

Atkinson, D. R., & Hackett, G. (1998). *Counseling diverse populations* (2nd ed.). Boston: McGraw Hill.

Atkinson, D. R., Morten, G., & Sue D. W. (1989). *Counseling American minorities* (3rd ed.). Dubuque, IA: William C. Brown.

Baker, C. (2002, April). The ADA in the marketplace. *Dermatology Nursing, 14* (2), 103–104.

Baltes, P. B., Lindenberger, U., & Staudinger, U. M. (1998). Life-span theory and developmental psychology. In R. M. Lerner (Ed.). *Theoretical models of human development* (5th ed.). Vol. 1, pp. 1029–1143. New York: Wiley.

Be yourself: Questions and answers for Gay, Lesbian, and Bisexual youth. (1994). Washington, DC: Parents and Friends of Lesbians and Gays. [booklet].

Bhabha, H. K. (1994). *The location of culture.* London and New York: Routledge.

Bhabha, H. K. (1995). Signs taken for wonders. In B. Ashcroft, G. Griffiths, and H. Tiffin (Eds.), *The post-colonial studies reader* (pp. 29–35). London and New York: Routledge.

Blanchard, C. A., & Lichtenberg, T. (2003). Compromise in career decision making: A test of Gottfredson's theory. *Journal of Vocational Behavior, 62,* 250–271.

Bolles, R. N. (1991). *Job-hunting tips for the so-called handicapped or people who have disabilities.* Berkeley, CA: Ten Speed Press.

Borgen, F. H. (1991). Megatrends and milestones in vocational behavior: A twenty-year counseling psychology perspective. *Journal of Vocational Behavior, 39,* 263–290.

Brodwin, M., Parker, R. M., & DeLaGarza, D. (1996). Disability and accommodation. In E. M. Szymanski & R. M. Parker (Eds.), *Work and disability: Issues and strategies in career development and job placement* (pp. 165–207). Austin, TX: PRO-ED.

Brown, D., Brooks, L., & Associates. (1991). *Career choice and development* (2nd ed.). San Francisco: Jossey Bass.

Brown, D., Brooks, L., & Associates. (1996). *Career choice and development* (3rd ed.). San Francisco: Jossey Bass.

Bruyere, S. M., Erickson, W. A., and Ferrentino, J. T. (2003, February). Identity and disability in the workplace. *William and Mary Law Review.* Retrieved June 6, 2003 from http://web.lexis-nexis.com/universe/document?_m=2d937fbfb01704bbe57fl4dd8dde25ad&_docnum=2&wc . . .

Burr, V. (1995). *An introduction to social constructionism.* London, England: Routledge.

Cass, V. C. (1979). Homosexual identity formation: A theoretical model. *Journal of Homosexuality, 4* (3), 219–235.

Christie, S. (1997, July/August). Beyond gym teacher: Dyke jobs today. *Girlfriends.* 24–27.

Curnow, T. C. (1989). Vocational development of persons with disability. *Career Development Quarterly, 37* (3), 269–278.

Curry, H., Clifford, D., & Leonard, R. (1996). *A legal guide for lesbian and gay couples* (9th national ed.). Berkeley, CA: Nolo Press.

Dalgin, R. S., and Gilbride, D. (2003, Winter). Perspectives on people with psychiatric disabilities on employment disclosure. *Psychiatric Rehabilitation Journal, 26* (3), 306–310.

Delsen, L. (1989). Improving the employability of the disabled: A practical approach. *International Journal for the Advancement of Counselling, 12,* 125–35.

During, S. (1995). Postmodernism or post-colonialism today. In B. Ashcroft, G. Griffiths, and H. Tiffin (Eds.), *The post-colonial studies reader* (pp. 125–129). London and New York: Routledge.

Enright, M. S., Conyers, L. M., & Szymanski, E. M. (1996). Career and career-related educational concerns of college students with disabilities. *Journal of Counseling and Development, 75,* 103–14.

Erikson, E. (1950). *Childhood and society.* New York: Norton.

Erikson, E. (1959). Identity and the life cycle. *Psychological Issues, 1,* 18–164.

Erikson, E. (1963). *Childhood and society* (2nd ed.). New York: Norton.

Erikson, E. (1968). *Identity: Youth in crisis.* New York: Norton.

Everyone can work. (1995). Attainment Films.

Farmer, H. S. (1997). Women's motivation related to mastery, career salience, and career aspiration: A multivariate model focusing on the effects of sex role socialization. *Journal of Career Assessment, 5* (4) 355–381.

Fassinger, R. E. (1996). Notes from the margins: Integrating lesbian experience into the vocational psychology of women. *Journal of Vocational Behavior, 48,* 160–75.

Fouad, N. A., & Arbona, C. (1994). Careers in a contextual context. *Career Development Quarterly, 43,* 96–104.

Freire, P. (1993). *Pedagogy of the oppressed.* (Rev. ed.) (M. B. Ramos, Trans.) New York: Continuum. (Original work published 1970).

Friskopp, A., & Silverstein, S. (1995). *Straight jobs, gay lives: Gay and lesbian professionals, the Harvard Business School, and the American workplace.* New York: Touchstone.

Gelberg, S., & Chojnacki, J. T. (1995). Developmental transitions of gay/lesbian/bisexualaffirmative, heterosexual career counselors. *Career Development Quarterly, 43,* 267–73.

Gelberg, S., & Chojnacki, J. T. (1996). *Career and life planning with gay, lesbian, and bisexual persons.* Alexandria, VA: American Counseling Association.

Gelberg, S., & Chojnacki, J. T. (1996). *Career and life planning with gay, lesbian, and bisexual persons.* Alexandria, VA: American Counseling Association.

Ginzberg, E. (1971). *Career guidance: Who needs it, who provides it, who can improve it?* New York: Columbia University Press.

Ginzberg, E. (1984). Career development. In D. Brown, L. Brooks, & Associates. *Career choice and development* (pp. 169–191). San Francisco: Jossey-Bass.

Ginzberg, E., Ginsburg, S., Axelrad, S., & Herma, J. (1951). *Occupational choice: An approach to a general theory.* New York: Columbia University Press.

Goodman, J. (1994). Career adaptability in adults: A construct whose time has come. *Career Development Quarterly, 43,* 74–84.

Goodyear, R., Roffey, A., & Jack, L. (1994). Edward Bordin: Fusing work and play. *Journal of Counseling and Development, 72,* 563–72.

Gottfredson, L. S. (1996). Gottfredson's theory of circumscription and compromise. In D. Brown, L. Brooks, & Associates, *Career choice and development* (3rd ed.). San Francisco: Jossey-Bass.

Greenson, R. R. (1967). *The technique and practice of psychoanalysis.* New York: International Universities Press.

Grevious, C. (1985). A comparison of occupational aspirations of urban Black college students. *Journal of Negro Education. 54,* 35–42.

Hagner, D., Fesko, S. L., Cadigan, M., Kiernan W., & Butterworth, J. (1996). Securing employment: Job search and employer negotiation strategies in rehabilitation. In E. M. Szymanski & R. M. Parker, (Ed.). *Work and disability: Issues and strategies in career development and job placement* (pp. 309–340), Austin, TX: PRO-ED.

Han, S.-K., & Moen, P. (1999). Work and family over time: A life course approach. *Annals of the American Academy of Political and Social Sciences, 562,* 98–110.

Harrison, G. (2003). Eurocentrism. In G. Bolaffi, R. Bracalenti, P. Braham, and S. Gindro (Eds.), *Dictionary of race, ethnicity, & culture* (pp. 107–109). London: Sage.

Herr, E. L. (1997). Super's life-span, life-space approach and its outlook for refinement. *Career Development Quarterly, 45,* 238–246.

Herr, E. L., Cramer, S. H., & Niles, S. G. (2004). *Career guidance and counseling through the lifespan.* Boston: Allyn and Bacon.

Hetherington, C., & Orzek, A. (1989). Career counseling and life planning with lesbian women. *Journal of Counseling and Development, 68,* 52–57.

Jagose, A. (1996). *Queer theory: An introduction.* New York: New York University Press.

Jepsen, D. A., & Dickson, G. L. (2003). Continuity in life-span career development: career exploration as a precursor to career establishment. *Career Development Quarterly, 51,* 217–233.

Johnson, M. J., Swartz, J. L., & Martin, W. E., Jr. (1995). Applications of psychological theories for career development with Native Americans. In F. T. L. Leong (Ed.), *Career development and vocational behavior of racial and ethnic minorities* (pp. 103–33). Mahwah, NJ: Erlbaum.

Journal of Vocational Behavior. (2002). 61. [Special issue].

Leong, F. T. L. (1991). Career development attributes and occupational values of Asian American and White American college students. *Career Development Quarterly, 39,* 221–30.

Leong, F. T. L., & Serafica, F. C. (1995). Career development of Asian Americans: A research area in need of a good theory. In F. T. L. Leong (Ed.), *Career development and vocational behavior of racial and ethnic minorities* (pp. 67–102). Mahwah, NJ: Erlbaum.

Levinson, E. M., Peterson, M., & Elston, R. (1994). Vocational counseling with persons with mental retardation. In D. C. Strohmer & H. L. Prout (Eds.), *Counseling and psychotherapy with persons with mental retardation and borderline intelligence* (pp. 257–304). Brandon, VT: Clinical Psychology Publishing.

Luzzo, D. A., James, T., & Luna, M. (1996). Effects of attributional retraining on the career beliefs and career exploration behavior of college students. *Journal of Counseling Psychology, 43,* 415–422.

MacDonald-Wilson, K. L., Rogers, E. S., and Massaro, J. (2003). Identifying relationships between functional limitations, job accommodations, and demographic characteristics of persons with psychiatric disabilities. *Journal of Vocational Rehabilitation, 18,* 15–24.

Madill, H. M., Montgomerie, T. C., Stewin, L. L., Fitzsimmons, G. W., Tovell, D. R., Armour, M. A., et al. (2000). Young women's work values and role salience in grade 11: Are there changes three years later? *Career Development Quarterly, 49,* 16–28.

Magiera-Planey, R. (1990). Special populaitons. In C. Schiro-Geist (Ed.), *Vocational counseling for special populations* (pp. 45–63). Springfield, IL: Charles C. Thomas.

Martin, W. E., Jr. (1995). Career development assessment and intervention strategies with American Indians. In F. T. L. Leong (Ed.), *Career development and vocational behavior of racial and ethnic minorities* (pp. 227–48). Mahwah, NJ: Erlbaum.

McNeil, J. (2001, March 1). Americans with disabilities: 1997. Retrieved June 10, 2004, from http://www.census.gov/hhes/www/disable/sipp/disab97/asc97.html.

Mohr, R. D. (1988). Gay basics: Some questions, facts, and values. In C. Pierce & D. Van DeVeer, (Eds.), *AIDS: Ethics and public policy* (pp. 193–205). Belmont, CA: Wadsworth.

Nadeau, K. G. (1995). ADD in the workplace: Career consultation and counseling for the adult with ADD. In K. G. Nadeau (Ed.), *A comprehensive guide to attention deficit disorder in adults* (pp. 308–334). New York: Bruner/Mazel.

Niles, S. G. (2001). Using Super's Career Development Assessment and Counselling (C-DAC) model to link theory and practice. *International Journal for Educational and Vocational Guidance, 1* 131–139.

Osborne, W. L., Brown, S., Niles, S., & Miner, C. U. (1997). *Career development assessment and counseling: Applications of the Donald E. Super C-DAC approach.* Alexandria, VA: American Counseling Association.

Osipow, S. H., & Littlejohn, E. M. (1995). Toward a multicultural theory of career development: Prospects and dilemmas. In F. T. L. Leong (Ed.), *Career development and vocational behavior of racial and ethnic minorities* (pp. 251–61). Mahwah, NJ: Erlbaum.

Our Daughters and Sons: Questions and answers for parents of gay, lesbian, and *bisexual people.* (1995). Washington, DC: Parents and Friends of Lesbians and Gays.

Pipher, M. (1996). *The shelter of each other: Rebuilding our families.* New York: Ballantine Books.

Powell, D. F., & Luzzo, D. A. (1998). Evaluating factors associated with the career maturity of high school students. *Career Development Quarterly, 47,* 145–158.

Power, S. J., & Rothausen, T. J. (2003). The work-oriented midcareer development model: An extension of Super's maintenance stage. *The Counseling Psychologist, 31,* 157–197.

Powers B., & Ellis, A. (1996). *A family and friends' guide to sexual orientation.* New York: Routledge.

Price, L. A., and Gerber, P. J. (2001, May/June). At second glance: Employers and employees with learning disabilities in the Americans with Disabilities Act era. *Journal of Learning Disabilities, 34* (8). Retrieved June 6, 2003 from http://web12.epnet.com/delivery.asp?tb=1&_ua=shn+36+9D99&_ug=dbs+0+ln+en-us+sid+ . . .

Richardson, M. S. (1993). Work in people's lives: A location for counseling psychologists. *Journal of Counseling Psychology, 40,* 425–33.

Richardson, M. S. (2002). A metaperspective for counseling practice: A response to the challenge of contextualism. *Journal of Vocational Behavior, 61,* 405–423.

Roessler, R. T., & Rumrill, P. D., Jr. (1995). Promoting reasonable accommodations: An essential post-employment service. *Journal of Applied Rehabilitation Counseling, 26* (4), 3–7.

Rowse, A. L. (1977). *Homosexuals in history: A study of ambivalence in society, literature, and the arts* (2nd ed.). New York: MacMillan.

Sauerman, T. H. (1996). *Read this before coming out to your parents.* Los Angeles: Parents and Friends of Lesbians, Gays. [booklet].

Savickas, M. (1997). Career adaptability: An integrative construct for life-span, life-space theory. *Career Development Quarterly, 45,* 247–59.

Savickas, M. L. (2001a). A developmental perspective on vocational behaviour: Career patterns, salience and themes. *International Journal for Educational and Vocational Guidance: 1,* 49–57.

Savickas, M. L. (2001b). The next decade in vocational psychology: Mission and objectives. *Journal of Vocational Psychology, 59,* 284–290.

Savickas, M. L., Briddick, W. C., & Watkins Jr., C. E. (2002). The relation of career maturity to personality type and social adjustment. *Journal of Career Assessment, 10* (1) 24–41.

Seligman, L. (1994). *Developmental career counseling and assessment.* Thousand Oaks, CA: Sage.

Smith, M. D., Belcher, R. G., & Juhrs, P. D. (1995). *A guide to successful employment for individuals with autism.* Baltimore: Paul H. Brookes.

Smith, S. L. (1991). *Succeeding against the odds: How the learning disabled can realize their promise.* New York: G. P. Putnam's.

Sophie, J. (1985/86). A critical examination of stage theories of lesbian identity development. *Journal of Homosexuality, 12,* 39–51.

Spargo, T. (1999). *Foucault and queer theory.* Cambridge, England, UK: Icon Books.

Starnes, S. (1999, Winter). Psychiatric disabilities & the ADA: An analysis of conventional defenses and the EEOC. *Review of Litigation, 18* (1). Retrieved June 6, 2003, from http://web21.epnet.com/delivery.asp?tb=1&_ug=dbs+0+ln+en-us+sid+C8619EB7-5A1F-43...

Super, D. E. (1974). *Measuring vocational maturity for counseling and evaluation.* Washington, DC: National Vocational Guidance Association.

Super, D. E. (1980). A lifespan-lifespace approach to career development. *Journal of Vocational Behavior, 16,* 282–98.

Super, D. E. (1990). A lifespan/lifespace approach to career development. In D. Brown, L. Brooks, & Associates (Eds.), *Career choice and development: Applying contemporary theories to practice* (2nd ed.) (pp. 197–261). San Francisco: Jossey-Bass.

Super, D. E., Osborne, W. L., Walsh, D. J., Brown, S. D, & Niles, S. G. (1992). Developmental career assessment and counseling: The C-DAC model. *Journal of Counseling and Development, 71,* 74–83.

Super, D. E., Savickas, M., & Super, C. N. (1996). The life-span, life-space approach to careers. In D. Brown, L. Brooks, & Associates (Eds.) *Career choice and development* (3rd ed.) (pp. 121–78). San Francisco: Jossey-Bass.

Super, D. E., Sverko, B, & Super, C. N. (Eds.) (1995). *Life roles, values, and careers: International findings of the work importance study.* San Francisco: Jossey-Bass.

Switzer, J. V. (2001). The Americans with Disabilities Act: Ten years later. *Policy Studies Journal, 29* (4), 629–632.

Szymanski, E. M., Hershenson, D. B., Enright, M. S., & Ettinger, J. M. (1996). Career development theories, constructs, and research: Implications for people with disabilities. In E. M. Szymanski & R. M. Parker (Eds.), *Work and disability: Issues and strategies in career development and job placement* (pp. 79–126). Austin, TX: PRO-ED.

Szymanski, E. M., Hershenson, D. B., Ettinger, J. M., & Enright, M. S. (1996). Career development interventions for people with disabilities. In E. M. Szymanski & R. M. Parker (Eds.), *Work and disability: Issues and strategies in career development and job placement* (pp. 255–276). Austin, TX: PRO-ED.

Tahvonen, H. M. (2003, February). Disability-based harassment: Standing and standards for a "new" cause of action. *William and Mary Law Review.* Retrieved June 6, 2003 from http://web.lexisnexis.com/universe/document?_m=5ac63d75526 afd9daa28065bbf6a108&_docnum=2&wc . . .

Tiedeman, D., & O'Hara, R. (1963). *Career development: Choice and adjustment.* Princeton, NJ: College Entrance Examination Board.

Thompson, A. R., & Hutto, M. D. (1992). An employment counseling model for college graduates with severe disabilities: A timely intervention. *Journal of Applied Rehabilitation Counseling, 23* (3), 15–17.

Thompson, M. (Ed.). (1994). *Long road to freedom: The Advocate history of the gay and lesbian movement.* New York: St. Martin's Press.

U.S. Equal Employment Opportunity Commission. (1991a). *La ley para personas con impedimentos: Los derechos laborales de las personas con impedimentos (EEOC-BK-21).* Washington, DC: U.S. Government Printing Office.

U.S. Equal Employment Opportunity Commission. (1991b). *La ley para personas con impedimentos, preguntas y respuestas (EEOC-BK-22).* Washington, DC: U.S. Government Printing Office.

U.S. Equal Employment Opportunity Commission. (1991c). *Sus responsabilidades cómo empleador (EEOC-BK-20).* Washington, DC: U.S. Government Printing Office.

U.S. Equal Employment Opportunity Commission. (1991d). *The ADA, Your employment rights as an individual with a disability (EEOC-BK-18).* Washington, DC: U.S. Government Printing Office.

U.S. Equal Employment Opportunity Commission. (1991e). *The ADA, Your employment rights as an employer (EEOC-BK-17).* Washington, DC: U.S. Government Printing Office.

U.S. Equal Employment Opportunity Commission. (1992, September). *The Americans with Disabilities Act, Questions and Answers (EEOC-BK-15).* Washington, DC: U.S. Government Printing Office.

Vondracek, F. (1992). The construct of identity and its use in career research. *Career Development Quarterly, 41,* 130–43.

Vondracek, F. W., & Hartung, P. J. (2002). Introduction: Innovating career development using advances in life course and life-span theory. *Journal of Vocational Behavior, 61,* 375–380.

Wagner, J. (1994). *Edith Ann: My life, so far.* New York: Hyperion.

Winner, B. J. (2000). Disability and the ADA: Learning impairment as a disability. *The Journal of Law, Medicine, & Ethics, 28* (4), 410–411.

Woods, J. D. (1994). *The corporate closet: The professional lives of gay men in America.* New York: The Free Press.

Zunker, V. G. (2002). *Career counseling: Applied concepts* (5th ed.). Pacific Grove, CA: Brooks/Cole.

Chapter 6

Arbona, C. (1990). Career counseling research and Hispanics: A review of the literature. *The Counseling Psychologist, 18,* 300–23.

Arbona, C. (1995). Theory and research on racial and ethnic minorities: Hispanic Americans. In F. T. L. Leong (Ed.). *Career development and vocational behavior of racial and ethnic minorities* (pp. 37–66). Mahwah, NJ: Erlbaum.

Bandura, A. (1977). Self-efficacy: Toward a unifying theory of behavior change. *Psychology Review, 84,* 191–215.

Bandura, A. (1984). Recycling misconceptions of perceived self-efficacy. *Cognitive Therapy and Research, 8,* 231–55.

Bandura, A. (1986). *Social foundations of thought and action: A social cognitive theory.* Englewood Cliffs, NJ: Prentice Hall.

Bandura, A. (1997). *Self-efficacy: The exercise of control.* New York: W. H. Freeman.

Bandura, A., Barbaranelli, C., Caprara, G.V., Pastorelli, C. (2001). Self-efficacy beliefs as shapers of children's aspirations and career trajectories. *Child Development, 72* (1) 187–206.

Betz, N. E. (1992). Counseling uses of career self-efficacy theory. *Career Development Quarterly, 41,* 22–26.

Betz, N. E. (1994). Career counseling for women in the sciences and engineering. In W. B. Walsh & S. H. Osipow (Eds.), *Career counseling for women* (pp. 237–61). Hillsdale, NJ: Erlbaum.

Betz, N. E. (2000). Self-efficacy theory as a basis for career assessment. *Journal of Career Assessment, 8* (3) 205–222.

Betz, N. E., Borgen, F. H., Rottinghaus, P., Paulsen, A., Halper, C. R., & Harmon, L. W. (2002). The Expanded Skills Confidence Inventory: Measuring basic dimensions of vocational activity. *Journal of Vocational Behavior, 62,* 76–100.

Betz, N. E., & Fitzgerald, L. F. (1987). *The career psychology of women.* Orlando, FL: Academic Press.

Betz, N. E., & Gwilliam, L. R. (2002). The utility of measures of self-efficacy for the Holland themes in African American and European college students. *Journal of Career Assessment, 10* (1) 283–300.

Betz, N. E., & Hackett, G. (1981). The relationship of career-related self-efficacy expectations to perceived career options in college women and men. *Journal of Counseling Psychology, 28,* 399–410.

Betz, N. E., & Hackett, G. (1983). The relationship of mathematics self-efficacy expectations to the selection of science-based college majors. *Journal of Vocational Behavior, 23,* 329–345.

Betz, N. E., Harmon, L. W., & Borgen, F. H. (1996). The relationships of self-efficacy for the Holland themes to gender, occupational group membership, and vocational interests. *Journal of Counseling Development, 43* (1) 90–98.

Bingham, M., & Stryker, S. (1995). *Things will be different for my daughter: A practical guide to building her self-esteem and self-reliance.* New York: Penguin Books.

Blustein, D. L., & Phillips, S. D. (1990). Relation between ego identity statuses and decisionmaking styles. *Journal of Counseling Psychology, 37,* 160–68.

Brown, M. T. (1995). The career development of African Americans: Theoretical and empirical issues. In F. T. L. Leong (Ed.), *Career development of and vocational behavior of racial and ethnic behaviors* (pp. 7–36). Mahwah, NJ: Erlbaum.

Brown, S. D., Lent, R. W., & Gore, P. A., Jr. (2000). Self-rated abilities and self-efficacy beliefs: Are they empirically distinct? *Journal of Career Assessment, 8* (3) 223–235.

Byrnes, J. P. (1996). *Cognitive development and learning in instructional contexts.* Boston: Allyn and Bacon.

Candrl, K. I., & Heinzen, C. J. (1994). Career Quest: An innovative student organization designed to meet the needs of "deciding" students. *Journal of Career Development, 21,* 141–48.

Chartrand, J. M., Borgen, F. H., Betz, N. E., & Donnay, D. (2002). Using the Strong Interest Inventory and the Skills Confidence Inventory to explain career goals. *Journal of Career Assessment, 10* (2) 169–189.

Church, A. T., Teresa, J. S., Rosebrook, R., & Szendre, D. (1992). Self-efficacy for careers and occupational consideration in minority high school equivalency students. *Journal of Counseling Psychology, 39,* 498–508.

Cohen, C. R., Chartrand, J. M., & Jowdy, D. P. (1995). Relationships between career indecision subtypes and ego identity development. *Journal of Counseling Psychology, 42,* 440–47.

Czerlinsky, T., & Chandler, S. L. (1993). *Vocational Decision-Making Interview-Revised, Administration manual.* Dallas, TX: ProPublishing.

del Pinal, J. (1995). The Hispanic population. In U.S. Bureau of the Census, Current Population Reports, Series P23-189, *Population profile of the United States: 1995* (pp. 46–47). Washington, DC: U.S. Government Printing Office.

Eastman, C., & Marzillier, J. S. (1984). Theoretical and methodological difficulties in Bandura's self-efficacy theory. *Cognitive Therapy and Research, 8,* 213–29.

Elium, J., & Elium, D. (1994). *Raising a daughter: Parents and the awakening of a healthy woman.* Berkeley: Celestial Arts.

Fouad, N. A. (1993). Cross-cultural vocational assessment. *Career Development Quarterly, 42,* 4–13.

Fouad, N. A. (1995). Career behavior of Hispanics: Assessment and career intervention. In F. T. L. Leong (Ed.), *Career development and vocational behavior of racial and ethnic minorities* (pp.165–191). Mahwah, NJ: Erlbaum.

Gati, I. (1986). Making career decisions: A sequential elimination approach. *Journal of Counseling Psychology, 33,* 408–417.

Gati, I. (1990). Why, when, and how to take into account the uncertainty involved in career decisions. *Journal of Counseling Psychology, 37,* 277–80.

Gati, I., Fassa, N., & Houminer, D. (1996). Applied sequential elimination approach. *Career Development Quarterly, 43,* 211–221.

Gelatt, H. (1989). Positive uncertainty: A new decision making framework for counseling. *Journal of Counseling Psychology, 36,* 252–56.

Gelatt, H. (1991). *Creative decision-making: Using positive uncertainty.* San Jose, CA: Crisp.

Gelberg, S., & Chojnacki, J. T. (1996). *Career and life planning with gay, lesbian, and bisexual persons.* Alexandria, VA: American Counseling Association.

Germeijs, V., & De Boeck, P. (2003). Career indecision: Three factors from decision theory. *Journal of Vocational Behavior, 62,* 11–25.

González, R. C. (1990). *Cognitive assessment in computerized nicotine fading.* Unpublished doctoral dissertation, Stanford University.

Griffith, A. R. (1980). Justification for a Black career development. *Counselor Education and Supervision, 19,* 301–10.

Hackett, G., & Betz, N. E. (1981). Self-efficacy approach to the career development of women. *Journal of Vocational Behavior, 18,* 326–39.

Hall, A. S. (2003). Expanding academic and career self-efficacy: A family systems framework. *Journal of Counseling and Development, 81,* 33–39.

Harrington, T. F. (1991). The cross-cultural applicability of the career decision-making system. *Career Development Quarterly, 39,* 209–20.

Heppner, M. J., & Heindricks, F. (1995). A process and outcome study examining career indecision and indecisiveness. *Journal of Counseling and Development, 73,* 426–37.

Johnson, M. J., Swartz, J. L., & Martin, W. E., Jr. (1995). Applications of psychological theories for career development with Native Americans. In F. T. L. Leong (Ed.), *Career development and vocational behavior of racial and ethnic minorities* (pp. 103–33). Mahwah, NJ: Erlbaum.

Jurgens, M. (2000). The undecided student: Effects of combining levels of treatment parameters on career certainty, career indecision, and client satisfaction. *Career Development Quarterly, 48* (3), 237–250.

Kozol, J. (1991). *Savage inequalities: Children in American schools.* HarperPerennial.

Krumboltz, J. (1998). Serendipity is not serendipitous. *Journal of Counseling Psychology, 45* (4) 390–392.

Krumboltz, J. D. (1981). A social learning theory or career decision making. In D. H. Montrose & C. J. Shinkman (Eds.). *Career development in the 1980's: Theory and practice* (pp. 43–66). Springfield, IL: Charles C. Thomas.

Krumboltz, J. D. (1991). *Career Beliefs Inventory.* Palo Alto, CA: Consulting Psychologist Press.

Krumboltz, J. D. (1992). The wisdom of indecision. *Journal of Vocational Behavior, 41,* 239–244.

Krumboltz, J., & Hamel, D. (1977). *Guide to career decision making skills.* New York: Educational Testing Services.

LaFromboise, T. D., Trimble, J. E., & Mohatt, G. V. (1990). Counseling intervention and American Indian tradition: An integrative approach. *The Counseling Psychologist, 18,* 628– 54.

Lent, R. W., & Hackett, G. (1987). Career self-efficacy: Empirical status and future directions. *Journal of Vocational Behavior, 30,* 342–82.

Lent, R. W., Larkin, K. C., & Brown, S. D., (1989). Relation of self-efficacy to inventoried vocational interests. *Journal of Vocational Behavior, 34,* 279–88.

Leong, F. T. L., & Serafica, F. C. (1995). Career development of Asian Americans: A research area in need of a good theory. In F. T. L. Leong (Ed.), *Career development and vocational behavior of racial and ethnic minorities* (pp. 67–102). Mahwah, NJ: Erlbaum.

Levinson, E. M., Peterson, M., & Elston, R. (1994). Vocational counseling with persons with mental retardation. In D. C. Strohmer & H. L. Prout (Eds.), *Counseling and psychotherapy with persons with mental retardation and borderline intelligence* (pp. 257–304). Brandon, VT: Clinical Psychology Publishing.

Maddux, J., Stanley, M., & Manning, M. (1987). Self-efficacy theory and research: Applications in clinical and counseling psychology. In J. Maddux, C. Stoltenberg, & R. Rosenwein (Eds.), *Social processes in clinical and counseling psychology* (pp. 39–55). New York: Springer-Verlag.

Marone, N. (1988). *How to father a successful daughter.* New York: Fawcett Crest.

Martin, W. E., Jr. (1995). Career development assessment and intervention strategies with American Indians. In F. T. L. Leong (Ed.), *Career development and vocational behavior of racial and ethnic minorities* (pp. 227–48). Mahwah, NJ: Erlbaum.

Marzillier, J. S., & Eastman, C. (1984). Continuing problems with self-efficacy theory: A reply to Bandura. *Cognitive Therapy and Research, 8,* 257–62.

McAuliffe, G. (1992). Assessing and changing career decision-making self-efficacy expectations. *Journal of Career Development, 19,* 25–36.

McDaniels, R. M., Carter, J. K., Heinzen, C. J., Candrl, K. I., & Weinberg, A. M. (1994). Undecided/undeclared: Working with "deciding" students. *Journal of Career Development, 21,* 135–39.

Mitchell, L., & Krumboltz, J. (1984). Research of human decision making: Implications for career decision makers and counselors. In D. Brown & R. Lent (Eds.), *Handbook of counseling psychology* (pp. 238–80). New York: Wiley.

Mitchell, L. K., & Krumboltz, J. D. (1990). Social learning approach to career decision-making: Krumboltz's theory. In D. Brown, L. Brooks, & Associates. *Career choice and development: Applying contemporary theories to practice* (2nd ed.) (pp.197–261). San Francisco: Jossey-Bass.

Newman, J., Fuqua, D., & Seaworth, T. (1989). The role of anxiety in career indecision: Implications for treatment. *Career Development Quarterly, 37,* 221–37.

O'Brien, K. M., Heppner, M. J., Flores, L. Y., & Bikos, L. H. (1997). Career Counseling Self-Efficacy Scale: Instrument development and training applications. *Journal of Counseling Psychology, 44,* 20–31.

Ogbu, J. U. (1992). Understanding cultural diversity and learning. *Educational Researcher, 21,* 5–14.

Orenstein, P. (1994). *School girls: Young women, self-esteem, and the confidence gap.* New York: Anchor Books.

Paa, H. K., & McWhirter, E. H. (2000). Perceived influences on high school students' current career expectations. *Career Development Quarterly, 49,* 29–44.

Perrone, K. M., Perrone, P. A., Chan, F., & Thomas, K. R. (2000). Assessing efficacy and importance of career counseling competencies. *Career Development Quarterly, 48,* 212–225.

Perrone, K. M., Zandardelli, G., Worthington, E. L., Jr., & Chartrand, J. M. (2002). Role model influence of the career decidedness of college students. *College Student Journal, 36* (1) 109–113. Retrieved September 9, 2003 from Academic Search Premier.

Pipher, M. (1994). *Reviving Ophelia: Saving the selves of adolescent girls.* New York: G. P. Putnam.

Polkinghorne, D. E. (1984). Further extensions of methodological diversity for counseling psychology. *Journal of Counseling Psychology, 31,* 416–29.

Polkinghorne, D. E. (1991). Two conflicting calls for methodological reform. *The Counseling Psychologist, 19,* 103–14.

Reid, P. T. (1993). Poor women in psychological research: Shut up and shut out. *Psychology of Women Quarterly, 17,* 133–50.

Rottinghaus, P. J., Larson, L. M., & Borgen, F. H. (2003). The relation of self-efficacy and interests: A meta-analysis of 60 samples. *Journal of Vocational Behavior, 62,* 221–236.

Sadker, M., & Sadker, D. (1994). *Failing at fairness: How our schools cheat girls.* New York: Touchstone.

Savickas, M. (1990). Annual review: Practice and research in career counseling and development, 1988. *Career Development Quarterly, 41,* 100–34.

Sharf, R. (1997). *Applying career development theory to counseling* (2nd ed.). Pacific Grove, CA: Brooks/Cole.

Smith, H. M., & Betz, N. E. (2002). Development and validation of a Scale of Percieved Social Self-Efficacy. *Journal of Career Assessment, 8* (3) 283–301.

Solberg, V. S., Good, G. E., Fischer, A. R., Brown, S. D., & Nord, D. (1995). Career decision making and career search activities: Relative effects of career search self-efficacy and human agency. *Journal of Counseling Psychology, 42,* 448–55.

Solberg, V. S., O'Brien, K., Villarreal, P., Kennel, R., & Davis, B. (1993). Self-efficacy and Hispanic college students: Validation of the College Self-Efficacy Instrument. *Hispanic Journal of Behavioral Sciences, 15,* 80–95.

Taylor, K. M., & Betz, N. (1983). Applications of self-efficacy theory to the understanding and treatment of career indecision. *Journal of Vocational Development, 22,* 63–81.

Temple, R. D., & Osipow, S. H. (1994). The relationship between task-specific self-efficacy egalitarianism and career indecision for females. *Journal of Career Assessment, 2,* 82–90.

Triandis, H. C. (1993). Comments on "multicultural career counseling." *Career Development Quarterly, 42,* 50–52.

Tversky, A. (1972). Elimination by aspects: A theory of choice. *Psychology Review, 79,* 281–90.

Wilson, W. J. (1996). *When work disappears: The world of the new urban poor.* New York: Knopf.

Zunker, V. (1990). *Career counseling: Applied concepts of life planning* (3rd ed.). Pacific Grove, CA: Brooks/Cole.

Zunker, V. G. (2002). *Career counseling: Applied concepts* (5th ed.). Pacific Grove, CA: Brooks/Cole.

Chapter 7

Anderson, H., & Goolishian, H. A. (1998). Human systems as linguistic systems: Preliminary and evolving ideas about the implications for clinical theory. *Family Process, 27,* 371–393.

Axelson, J. A. (1993). *Counseling and development is a multicultural society* (2nd ed.). Pacific Grove, CA: Brooks/Cole

Bauman, Z (1993). *Postmodern ethics.* Cambridge, MA: Blackwell Publishers.

Becvar, D. S., & Becvar, R., (1996). *Family therapy: A systemic integration* (3rd ed.). Boston: Allyn & Bacon.

Benhabib, S. (1992). *Situating the self: Gender, community and postmodernism in contemporary ethics.* New York: Routledge.

Berger, P. L., & Luckmann, T. (1996). *The social construction of reality.* New York: Doubleday.

Bergmann, B. R. (1996). *In defense of affirmative action.* New York: Basic Books.

Best, S., & Kellner, D. (1991). *Postmodern theory: Critical integrations.* New York: Guilford.

Brooks, L., & Forrest, L. (1994). Feminism and career counseling. In W. B. Walsh & S. H. Osipow (Eds.). *Career counseling for women* (pp.87–134). Hillsdale, NJ: Erlbaum.

Brown, D., & Associates. (2002). *Career choice and development* (4th ed.). San Francisco: Jossey-Bass.

Burr, V. (1995). *An introduction to social constructionism.* London, England: Routledge.

Capper, C. A. (1995, October). *Discourses of dysfunction: Being silenced and silencing.* Paper presented at the University Council for Educational Administration Annual Convention, Salt Lake City, UT.

Carter, R. T. (1991). Cultural values: A review of empirical research and implications for counseling. *Journal of Counseling and Development, 70,* 164–173.

Coale, H. W. (1992). The constructivist emphasis on language: A critical conversation. *Journal of Strategic and Systemic Therapies, 11,* 12–26.

Cochran, L. (1991). *Life-shaping decisions.* New York: Peter Lang.

Czikszentmihalyi, M., & Beattie, O. V. (1979). Life themes: A theoretical and empirical exploration of their origins and effects. *Journal of Humanistic Psychology, 19* (1), 45–63.

Doherty, W. J. (1991, September/October). Family therapy goes postmodern. *Family Therapy Networker, 15,* (5), 37–42.

Draper, R. (1995, December). Carrillo's crossing. *Texas Monthly,* 118–121, 139–142, 143–144.

Eastland, T. (1997). *Ending affirmative action: The case for colorblind justice.* New York: Basic Books.

Erikson, E. (1963). *Childhood and society* (2nd ed). New York: Norton.

Feixas, G. (1990). Personal construct theory and systemic therapies: Parallel or convergent trends? *Journal of Marital and Family Therapy, 16* (1), 1–20.

Feixas, G. (1995). Personal constructs in systemic practice. In R. A. Neimeyer & M. J. Mahoney (Eds.), *Constructionism in psychotherapy* (pp. 305–337). Washington, DC: American Psychological Association.

Fisher, H. (1995). Whose right is it to define the self? *Theory and Psychology, 5,* 323–352.

Flew, A. (1984). *A dictionary of philosophy* (2nd ed., rev.). New York: St. Martin's Press.

Forster, J. R. (1982). *The Job Attribute Clarifier.*

Forster, J. R. (1986). *The Goals Review and Organizing Workbook.*

Forster, J. R. (1992). Eliciting personal constructs and articulating goals. *Journal of Career Development, 18* (5), 175–185.

Fouad, N. A., Smith, P. L., & Zao, K. E. (2002). Across academic domains: Extensions of the social-cognitive career model. *Journal of Counseling Psychology, 49* (2) 164–171.

Freire, P. (1993). *Pedagogy of the oppressed.* (Rev. ed.) (M. B. Ramos, Trans.) New York: Continuum. (Original work published in 1970.)

Gergen, K. J. (1985). The social constructivist movement in modern psychology. *American Psychologist, 40,* 266–275.

Gergen, K. J. (1991). *The saturated self: Dilemmas of identity in contemporary life.* New York: Basic Books.

Gergen, K. J. (1994). Exploring the postmodern. Perils or potentials? *American Psychologist, 49,* 412–416.

Gonçalves, Ó. F. (1995). Cognitive narrative psychotherapy: The hermeneutic construction of alternative meanings. In M. J. Mahoney (Ed.), *Cognitive and constructive psychotherapies: Theory, research, and practice* (pp.139–162). New York: Springer.

González, R. C. (1997). Postmodern supervision: a multicultural perspective. In D. B. Pope-Davis & H. L. K. Coleman (Eds.), *Multicultural counseling competencies: Assessment, education and training, and supervision* (pp. 350–386). Thousand Oaks, CA: Sage.

González, R. C. (1998). A technically eclectic blend of paradigms and epsitemologies for multicultural clinical relevance. In C. Franklin & P. S. Nurius (Eds.). *Constructivism in practice: Methods and challenges.* Milwaukee, WI: Families International.

Granvold, D. K., (1996). Constructivist psychotherapy. *Families in society: The Journal of Contemporary Human Services, 77,* 345–357.

Guidano, V. F. (1995). Constructivist psychotherapy: A theoretical framework. In R. A. Neimeyer & M. J. Mahoney (Eds.), *Constructivism in pyshotherapy* (pp. 93–108). Washington, DC: American Psychological Association.

Hackett, G., & Betz, N. E. (1981). A selfi-efficacy approach to career development of women. *Journal of Vocational Behavior, 18,* 326–336.

Haldane, B., & Forster, J. R. (1988). The Dependable Strengths Articulation Process Short Form.

Hansen, L. S. (2001). *Integrative life planning: Critical tasks for career development and changing life patterns.* San Francisco: Jossey-Bass.

Harding, S. (1993). Rethinking standpoint epistemology: What is "strong objectivity"? In L. Alcoff & E. Potter (Eds.). *Feminist epistemologies* (pp. 49–82). New York: Routledge.

Hare-Mustin, R. T. (1994). Discourses in the mirrored room: a postmodern analysis of therapy. *Family Processes, 33,* 19–35.

Hartung, P. J. (1992). Balancing work and love: The case of Rosie. *Career Development Quarterly, 42,* 56–60.

Heppner, M. J., Fitzgerald, K., and Jones, C. A. (1989). Examining counselors' creative processes in cousneling. In J. A. Glover & R. R. Ronning (Eds.). *Handbook of creativity* (pp. 271–280). New York: Plenum Press.

Heppner, M., O'Brien, K., and Hinkleman, J. (1994). Shifting the paradigm: The use of creativity in career counseling. *Journal of Career Development, 21* (2) 77–86.

Hoffmann, L. (1991). A reflexive stance for family therapy. *Journal of Strategic and Systemic Therapies, 10,* 4–17.

Hollinger, R. (1994). *Postmodernism and the social sciences: a thematic approach.* Thousand Oaks, CA: Sage.

Imbimbo, P. V. (1994). Integrating personal and career counseling: A challenge for counselors. *Journal of Employment Counseling, 31,* 50–59.

Kirschner, T., Hoffman, M. A., & Hill, C. E. (1994). Case study of the process and outcome of career counseling. *Journal of Counseling Psychology, 41* (2) 216–226.

Krumboltz, J. D., Blando, J. A., & Kim, H. (1994). Embedding work values in stories. *Journal of Counseling Development, 73* (1) 57–62.

Lent, R. W., & Brown, S. D. (1996). Social cognitive approach to career development: An overview. *Career Development Quarterly, 44,* 310–321.

Lent, R. W., Brown, S. D., & Hackett, G. (1996). Career development from a social cognitive perspective. In D. Brown, L. Brooks, & Associates, *Career choice and development* (3rd ed.) (pp. 373–421). San Francisco: Jossey-Bass.

Leong, F. T. L. (1995). *Career development and vocational behavior of racial and ethnic minorities.* Mahwah, NJ: Erlbaum.

Leong, F. T. L., Hartung, P. J., Goh, D., & Gaylor, M. (2001). Appraising birth order in career assessment: Linkages to Holland's and Super's models. *Journal of Career Assessment, 9* (1) 25–39.

Lyddon, W. J. (1990). First- and second-order change: Implications for rationalist and constructivist cognitive therapies. *Journal of Counseling and Development, 69,* 122–127.

McAuliffe, G. (1993). Constructive development and career transition: Implications for counseling. *Journal of Counseling and Development, 72,* 23–28.

McKenna, E. P. (1997). *When work doesn't work anymore: Women, work, and identity.* New York: Delacorte Press.

Michelozzi, B. (1992). *Coming alive from nine to five* (2nd ed.). Mountain View, CA: Mayfield.

Miller-Tiedeman, A. (1999). The new (quantum) careering model. In A. Miller-Tiedeman, *Living, learning and living the new careering* (pp. 48–??). Philadelphia: Accelerated Development.

Neimeyer, R. A. (1995). Constructivist psychotherapies: Features, foundations, and future directions. In R. A. Neimeyer & M. J. Mahoney (Eds.). *Constructivism in psychotherapy* (pp. 11–38). Washington, DC: American Psychological Association.

Ogbu, J. U. (1992). Understanding cultural diversity and learning. *Educational Researcher, 21,* 5–14.

O'Hara, M., & Anderson, W. T. (1991). Welcome to the postmodern world. *Family Therapy Networker, 15* (5), 19–25.

Osbeck, L. M. (1991, August). *Social constructionism and the pragmatic standard.* Paper presented at the 99th Meeting of the American Psychological Convention, San Francisco, CA:

Pedersen, P. (1990). The multicultural perspective as a fourth force in counseling. *Journal of Mental Health Counseling, 12* (1), 93–95.

Peterson, G. W., Sampson, J. P., Jr., and Reardon, R. C. (1991). *Career development and services: A cognitive approach.* Pacific Grove, CA: Brooks/Cole.

Peterson, G. W., Sampson, J. P., Jr., Reardon, R. C., & Lenz, J. G. (1996). Becoming career problem solvers and decision makers: A cognitive information processing approach. In D. Brown & L. Brooks (Eds.), *Career choice and development* (3rd ed.) (pp. 423–475). San Francisco: Jossey-Bass.

Peterson, G. W., Sampson, J. P., Jr., Reardon, R. C., & Lenz, J. G. (2003). *Core concepts of a cognitive approach to career development and services.* Retrieved June 23, 2003 from http://www.career.fsu.edu/do.../ Core%20Concepts%20of% 20a%20Cognitive%20 Approach.ht.

Powers, R., & Griffith, J. (1993). The case of Rosie: An Adlerian response. *Career Development Journal, 42,* 69–75.

Pipher, M. (1996). *The shelter of each other: Rebuilding our families.* New York: Putnam.

Rabinow, P. (Ed.). (1984). *The Foucault reader.* New York: Bantam Books.

Richardson, M. S. (1993). Work in people's lives: A location for counseling psychologists. *Journal of Counseling Psychology, 40,* 425–433.

Rockwell, T. (1987, Fall). The social construction of careers: Career development and career counseling viewed from a sociometric perspective. *JGPPS,* 93–107.

Rosenau, P. M. (1992). *Post-modernism and the social sciences: Insights, inroads, and intrusions.* Princeton, NJ: Princeton University Press.

Russell, R. L., & Gaubatz, M. D. (1994). Contested affinities: Reaction to Gergen's (1994) and Smith's (1994) postmodernism. *American Psychologist, 50,* 389–390.

Sampson, J. P., Jr., Peterson, G. W., Lenz, J. G., & Reardon, R. C. (1992). A cognitive approach to career services: Translating concepts into practice. *Career Development Quarterly, 41,* 67–74.

Sampson, J. P., Jr., Peterson, G. W., Lenz, J. G., & Reardon, R. C. (1996). *Career Thoughts Inventory.* Odessa, FL: Psychological Assessment Resources.

Sampson, J. P., Jr., Peterson, G. W., Reardon, R. C., & Lenz, J. G. (2003a). *Designing career services to cost-effectively meet individual needs.* Center for the Study of Technology in Counseling and Career Development, University Center, Suite A4100, Florida State University, Tallahassee, FL 32306-2490.

Sampson, J. P., Jr., Peterson, G. W., Reardon, R. C., & Lenz, J. G. (2003b). Key elements of the CIP approach to designing career services. Retrieved June 6, 2003 from http://www.career.fsu.edu/documents/cognitive%20information%20pro.../Key%20Elements.ht.

Sampson, J. P., Jr., Reardon, R. C., Peterson, G. W., and Lenz, J. G. (2004). *Career counseling and services: A cognitive information processing approach.* Pacific Grove, CA: Brooks/Cole.

Santrock, J. (2003). *Psychology 7* (7th ed). New York: McGraw Hill.

Savickas, M. L. (1989). Career-style assessment and counseling. In T. Sweeney (Ed.), *Adlerian counseling: A practical approach for a new decade* (3rd ed.). Muncie, IN: Accelerated Development.

Savickas, M. L. (1993). Career counseling in the postmodern era. *Journal of Cognitive Psychology, 7* (3), 205–215.

Savickas, M. L. (1995b). Constructivist counseling for career indecision. *Career Development Quarterly, 43,* 363–373.

Savickas, M. L. (1995b). Current theoretical issues in vocational psychology: Convergence, divergence, and schism. In W. B. Walsh & S. H. Osipow (Eds), *Handbook of vocational psychology* (2nd ed.) (pp. 1–34). Mahwah, NJ: Erlbaum.

Savickas, M. L. (2003). Toward a taxonomy of human strengths: Career counseling's contribution to positive psychology. In B. W. Walsh (Ed.), *Counseling psychology and optimal human functioning.* Malwah, NJ. Erlbaum.

Savickas, M. L., & Lent, R. W. (1994). *Convergence in career development theories.* Palo Alto. CA: CPP Books.

Simpson, S. (Writer, Director, and Producer). (1987, September 1). *NOVA: Freud under analysis.* Boston: WGBH.

Skovholt, T. M., Morgan, J. I., Negron-Cunningham, H. (1989). *Journal of Counseling and Development, 67* (5) 287–292.

Smith, H. (1989). *Beyond the post-modern mind.* Wheaton, IL: Theosophical Publishing House.

Srivastra, S., Fry, R. E., & Cooperrider, D. L. (1990). Introduction: The call for executive appreciation. In S. Srivastra, D. L. Cooperrider, & Associates (Eds.), *Appreciative management and leadership: The power of positive thought and action in organizations* (pp. 1–33). San Francisco: Jossey-Bass.

Sue, D. (1992). The challenge of multiculturalism. The road less traveled. *American Counselor, 1,* 6ff.

Sue, D. W., & Sue, D. (1990). *Counseling the culturally different: Theory and practice* (2nd ed.). New York: Wiley.

Terkel, S. (1975). *Working.* New York: Avon Books.

Tolbert, E. L. (1980). *Counseling for career development* (2nd ed.). Boston: Houghton Mifflin.

Vygoysky, L. (1978). *Mind in society: The development of higher psychological processes.* Cambridge, MA: Harvard University Press.

Watkins, C. E. (1984). The individual psychology of Alfred Adler: Toward an Adlerian vocational theory. *Journal of Vocational Behavior, 24,* 28–47.

Watts, R., & Engels, D. (1995). The life task of vocation: A review of Adlerian research literature. *Texas Counseling Association Journal,* 9–19.

Watzlawick, P., Weakland, J., & Frisch, R. (1974). *Change: Principles of problem formation and problem resolution.* New York: Norton.

Wolinsky, S. (1993). *Quantum consciousness: The guide to experiencing quantum psychology.* Connecticut: Bramble Books.

Chapter 8

Arbona, C. (1990). Career counseling research and Hispanics: A review of the literature. *Counseling Psychologist, 18,* 300–23.

Arbona, C., & Novy, D. M. (1991). Career aspirations and expectations of Black, Mexican American, and White students. *Career Development Quarterly, 39,* 231–39.

Associated Press. (1996a, February 28). Immigration reform worries companies. *El Paso Herald-Post,* p. A2.

Associated Press. (1996b, September 17). Anglos receive most welfare, study says. *El Paso Times,* p. 4A.

Associated Press. (1996c, September 11). Fewer workers have health insurance. *El Paso Herald- Post,* p. A2.

Associated Press. (1997a, September 16). Keep families in mind, CEO tells colleagues. *El Paso Times,* p. 5D.

Associated Press. (1997b, December 26). Off welfare and into the work force. *El Paso Times,* p. 4B.

Associated Press. (1997c, June 30). Welfare's old ways at an end. *El Paso Herald-Post,* p. A2.

Associated Press. (1998, August 10). Statistics paint complex picture of U.S. poverty. *El Paso Times,* p. 7A.

Atkinson, , D. R., Morten, G., & Sue, D. W. (Eds.). (1998). *Counseling American minorities: A cross-cultural perspective* (5th ed.). Boston: McGraw Hill.

Axelson, J. A. (1993). *Counseling and development in a multicultural society* (2nd ed.). Pacific Grove, CA: Brooks/Cole.

Baber, K., & Monaghan, P. (1988). College women's career and motherhood expectations: New options, old dilemmas. *Sex Roles, 19,* 189–203.

Barnes, J. S., & Bennett, C. E. (2002). The Asian population: 2000. U.S. Bureau of the Census, *Current*

Population Reports, C2KBR/01-16. Washington, DC: U.S. Government Printing Office.

Barnett, R. C., & Rivers, C. (1996). *She works, he works: How two-income families are happier, healthier, and better off.* San Francisco: Harper.

Baruth, L. G., & Manning, M. L. (1991). *Multicultural counseling and psychotherapy: A lifespan perspective.* New York: Macmillan.

Becvar, D. S., & Becvar, R. (1996). *Family therapy: A systemic integration* (3rd ed.). Boston: Allyn & Bacon.

Betz, N. E. (1994). Basic issues and concepts in career counseling for women. In W. B. Walsh & S. H. Osipow (Eds.), *Career counseling for women* (pp. 1–41). Hillsdale, NJ: Erlbaum.

Bingham, R. P., & Ward, C. M. (2001). Career counseling with African American males and females. In W. B. Walsh, R. P. Bingham, M. T. Brown, & C. M. Ward (Eds.), *Career counseling for African Americans* (pp. 49–75). Mahwah, NJ: Erlbaum.

Bradley, R. (1982). Using birth order and sibling dynamics in career counseling. *The Personnel and Guidance Journal, 31,* 25–31.

Bragg, R. (1996, March 5). Big holes where the dignity used to be. *New York Times,* pp. A1, A16, A18.

Brown, M. T., & Pinterits, E. J. (2001). Basic issues in the career counseling of African Americans. In W. B. Walsh, R. P. Bingham, M. T. Brown, & C. M. Ward (Eds.), *Career counseling for African Americans* (pp. 1–25). Mahwah, NJ: Erlbaum.

Butterfield, F. (1990, January 21). Why they excel. *Parade Magazine,* 4–6.

Carter, B., & McGoldrick, M. (1989). Overview: The changing family life cycle—A framework for family therapy. In B. Carter & M. McGoldrick (Eds.), *The changing family life cycle: A framework for family therapy* (2nd ed.) (pp. 3–28). Boston: Allyn & Bacon.

Center for Public Policy Priorities. (1997, March 14). *Policy Page, 44,* 1–5.

Chen, S., & Leong, F. T. L. (1997). Case study: The case of Jessica Chang. *Career Development Quarterly, 46,* 142–47.

Clark, R. M. (1983). *Family life and school achievement: Why poor Black children succeed or fail.* Chicago: University of Chicago Press.

Cook, E. P. (1997). Gender discrimination in Jessica's career. *Career Development Quarterly, 46,* 148–54.

Cose, E. (1996, September 9). No work, no welfare. *Newsweek,* 46–47.

Davies, M., & Kandel, D. (1981). Parental and peer influences on adolescents educational plans: Some further evidence. *American Journal of Sociology, 87,* 363–87.

Day, J. C. (1996). Projections of the number of households and families in the United States: 1995 to 2010. U.S. Bureau of the Census, *Current Population Reports,* P25-1129. Washington, DC: U.S. Government Printing Office.

Dell'Angela, T. (2004, January 4). On an education mission. Powerful lawyer fights to keep Latinos from skipping college. *San Antonio Express-News,* pp. 1K, 3K.

Derr, C. (1986). *Managing the new careerists: The diverse career success orientations of today's workers.* San Francisco: Jossey-Bass.

Edwards, A., & Polite, C. K. (1992). *Children of the dream: The psychology of Black success.* New York: Doubleday.

ERIC Digest, No. 75, (1988).

Fassinger, R. E. (1996). Notes from the margins: Integrating lesbian experience into the vocational psychology of women. *Journal of Vocational Behavior, 48,* 160–75.

Fields, J. (2003, June). Children's living arrangements and characteristics: March 2002. U.S. Bureau of the Census, *Current Population Reports,* P20-547. Washington, DC: U.S. Government Printing Office.

Fields, J., & Casper, L. M. (2001, June). America's family and living arrangements. U.S. Bureau of the Census, *Current Population Reports,* P20-537. Washington, DC: U.S. Government Printing Office.

Fischer, D. H. (1989). *Albion's seed: Four British folkways in America.* New York: Oxford University Press.

Fouad, N. A., & Tang, M. (1997). Caught in two worlds: Jessica Chang from a cross-cultural perspective. *Career Development Quarterly, 46,* 155–60.

Friesen, J. (1986). The role of family in vocational development. *International Journal for the Advancement of Counseling, 9,* 87–96.

Fulmer, R. H. (1989). Lower-income and professional families: A comparison of structure and life cycle process. In B. Carter & M. McGoldrick (Eds.), *The changing family life cycle: A framework for family therapy* (2nd ed.) (pp. 545–78). Boston: Allyn & Bacon.

Gelardin, S. (2001). (Ed.). Special issue: Family influences on career choice and success. *Career Planning and Adult Development Journal, 17* (2).

Gergen, K. J. (1991a). The saturated family. *Family Therapy Networker, 15* (5), 27–35.

Gilbert, L. A., & Bingham, R. P. (2001). Career counseling with dual-career heterosexual African American couples. In W. B. Walsh, R. P. Bingham, M. T. Brown, & C. M. Ward (Eds.), *Career counseling for African Americans* (pp. 77–98). Mahwah, NJ: Erlbaum.

Gilligan, C. & Noel, N. (1995, April). *Cartography of lost time: Women, girls, and relationships.* Workshop sponsored by the Austin Women's Psychotherapy Project, Austin, TX.

Goldenberg, I., & Goldenberg, H. (1985). *Family therapy: An overview* (2nd ed.). Pacific Grove, CA: Brooks/Cole.

Gysbers, N. C., & Moore, E. J. (1987). *Career counseling: Skills and techniques for practitioners.* Boston: Allyn and Bacon.

Hall, D. (1989). Promoting work/family balance: An organization-change approach. *Organizational Dynamics,* 5–18.

Hard, N. L., & Schoenmakers, C. (1997, May). *Common terms and acronyms—care and education of young children.* [hand-out]

Hardy, K.V. (1993). Live supervision in the postmodern era of family therapy: Issues, reflections, and questions. *Contemporary Family Therapy, 15,* 9–20.

Harmon, L. (1989). Longitudinal changes in women's career aspirations: Developmental or historical? *Journal of Vocational Behavior, 35,* 46–63.

Harrar, S., & Dollemore, D. (2002). The work/home split. *Prevention, 55* (11). Retrieved from www.prevention.com/cda/feature2002/0,2479,s1-6113,00.html.

Hartung, P. (1992). Balancing work and love: The case of Rosie. *The Career Development Quarterly, 42,* 56–60.

Hawkins, D. (1996, September 23). The most dangerous jobs. *U.S. News & World Report,* 40– 41.

Hedges, S. J., Hawkins, D., & Loeb, P. (1996, September 23). The new jungle. *U.S. News & World Report,* 34–45.

Herring, R. D. (1990). Attacking career myths among Native Americans: Implications for counseling. *School Counselor, 38,* 13–18.

Hsia, J., & Hirano-Nakanishi, M. (1989, November/December). The demographics of diversity: Asian Americans and higher education. *Change,* 20–27.

Ivey, A. E. (1988). *Intentional interviewing and counseling* (2nd ed.). Pacific Grove, CA: Brooks/Cole.

Jacobsen, M. H. (1999). *Hand-me-down dreams: How families influence our career paths and how we can reclaim them.* New York: Three Rivers Press.

Jamieson, A., Curry, A., & Martinez, G. (2001, March). School enrollment in the United States—Social and economic characteristics of students. U.S. Bureau of the Census, *Current Population Reports,* P20-533. Washington, DC: U.S. Government Printing Office.

Jones, D., & Belton, B. (1997, September 30). Median income up $410. *USA Today,* p. 3B.

Kaplan, P. (1993). *The human odyssey: Life-span development.* Minneapolis/St. Paul: West.

Keller, L. (2000, November 13). Dual earners: Double trouble. *CNN.com.* Retrieved November 26, 2003 from http://www.cnn.com/2000/CAREER/trends/11/13/dual.earners/.

Kuehr, W. (1997). *Processes and outcomes of mentoring relationships in selected at-risk elementary students.* Unpublished doctoral dissertation, Our Lady of the Lake University.

LaFromboise, T. D., Trimble, J. E., & Mohatt, G. V. (1990). Counseling intervention and American Indian tradition: An integrative approach. *The Counseling Psychologist, 18,* 628– 54.

Langewiesche, W. (1998, February 23 and March 2). A reporter at large: Invisible men. *New Yorker,* 138ff.

Leong, F. T. L. (1993). The career counseling process with racial-ethnic minorities: The case of Asian Americans. *Career Development Quarterly, 42,* 26–40.

Leong, F. T. L., & Gim-Chung, R. H. (1995). Career assessment and intervention with Asian Americans. In F. T. L. Leong (Ed.), *Career development and vocational behavior of racial and ethnic minorities* (pp. 193–226). Mahwah, NJ: Erlbaum.

Leong, F. T. L., & Serafica, F. C. (1995). Career development of Asian Americans: A research area in need of a good theory. In F. T. L. Leong (Ed.), *Career development and vocational behavior of racial and ethnic minorities* (pp. 67–102). Mahwah, NJ: Erlbaum.

Leong, F. T. L., & Tata, S. P. (1990). Sex and acculturation differences in occupational values among Chinese American children. *Journal of Counseling Psychology, 37,* 208–12.

Loerch, K. J., Russell, J. E. A., & Rush, M. C. (1989). The relationships among family domain variables and work—family conflict for men and women. *Journal of Vocational Behavior, 35,* 288–308.

Los Angeles Times. (1997, October 14). Advocates urge disability cutoff appeals. *El Paso Times,* p. 4A.

MacGregor, A, & Cochran, L. (1988). Work as enactment of family drama. *Career Development Quarterly, 37,* (2) 138–48.

Marquez, M. (1996, January 7). Immigrant bashers won't face facts. *El Paso Times,* p. 6A.

Martin, W. E., Jr. (1991). Career development and American Indian living on reservations: Cross-cultural factors to consider. *Career Development Quarterly, 39,* 273–78.

Maslow, A. M. (1954). *Motivation and personality.* New York: Harper & Row.

McDaniels, C., & Gysbers, N. (1992). *Counseling for career development.* San Francisco: Jossey-Bass.

McGoldrick, M. (1989a). Ethnicity and the family life cycle. In B. Carter & M. McGoldrick (Eds.), *The changing family life cycle: A framework for family therapy* (2nd ed.) (pp. 69–90). Boston: Allyn & Bacon.

McGoldrick, M. (1989b). The joining of families through marriage: The new couple. In B. Carter & M. McGoldrick (Eds.), *The changing family life cycle:*

A framework for family therapy (2nd ed.) (pp. 209–233). Boston: Allyn & Bacon.

McGoldrick, M. (1989c). Women and the family life cycle. In B. Carter & M. McGoldrick (Eds.), *The changing family life cycle: A framework for family therapy* (2nd ed.) (pp. 29–68). Boston: Allyn & Bacon.

McGoldrick, M., & Gerson, R. (1985). *Genograms in family assessment.* New York: W. W. Norton.

Mead, L. M. (1992). *The new politics of poverty: The nonworking poor in America.* New York: Basic Books.

Meeks, S., Arnkoff, D., & Glass, C. (1986). Wives' employment status, hassles, communication and relational efficacy: Intra- and extra-relationship factors and marital adjustment. *Family Relations Journal of Applied Family and Child Studies, 35,* (2) 249–55.

Minuchin, S. (1974). *Families and family therapy.* Cambridge, MA: Harvard University Press.

Mitchell, L., & Krumboltz, J. (1984). Research of human decision making: Implications for career decision makers and counselors. In D. Brown & R. Lent (Eds.), *Handbook of counseling psychology* (pp. 238–280). New York: Wiley.

Mizokawa, D. T., & Ryckman, D. B. (1990). Attributions of academic success and failure: A comparison of six Asian-American ethnic groups. *Journal of Cross-Cultural Psychology, 21,* 434–51.

Moon, S., Coleman, V., McCollum, E., Nelson, T., & Jensen-Scott, R. (1993). Using the genogram to facilitate career decisions: A case study. *Journal of Family Psychotherapy, 4,* (1), 45–56.

Muwakkil, S. (1988, June 22–July 5). Getting black males off the endangered species list. *In These Times,* p. 7.

New York Times News Service. (1996, March 4). Keeping José out could cost billions. *El Paso Herald-Post,* pp. A1ff.

New York Times News Service. (1997, May 5). Aid for immigrants back in budget. *El Paso Herald-Post,* p. A2.

O'Hara, M., & Anderson, W. T. (1991). Welcome to the postmodern world. *Family Therapy Networker, 15* (5), 19–25.

Okiishi, R. (1987). The genogram as a tool in career counseling. *Journal of Counseling and Development, 66,* 139–43.

Orentstein, P. (1994). *School girls: Young women, self-esteem, and the confidence gap.* New York: Anchor Books.

Owens, T. (1992). The effect of post-high school social context on self-esteem. *Sociological Quarterly, 33* (4), 553–77.

Parham, T. A., & McDavis, R. J. (1987). Black men, an endangered species? Who's really pulling the trigger? *Journal of Counseling and Development, 66,* 24–27.

Payne, R. K. (1995). *A framework for understanding and working with students and adults from poverty.* Baytown, TX: RFT.

Pedigo, J. (1983, January). Finding the "meaning" of Native American substance abuse: Implications for community prevention. *The Personnel and Guidance Journal,* 273–77.

Penick, N. (1990). *An exploratory investigation of the relationship between measures of family functioning and adolescent career development.* Unpublished doctoral dissertation, University of Iowa.

Pinderhughes, E. (1995, March). Empowering diverse populations: Family practice in the 21st century. *Families in Society: The Journal of Contemporary Human Services,* 131–40.

Pipher, M. (1994). *Reviving Ophelia: Saving the selves of adolescent girls.* New York: Putnam's.

Powers, R., & Griffith, J. (1993). The case of Rosie: An Adlerian response. *Career Development Quarterly, 42,* 69–75.

Procter, B. D., & Dalaker, J. (2003, September). Poverty in the United States: 2002. U.S. Bureau of the Census, *Current Population Reports,* P60-222. Washington, DC: U.S. Government Printing Office.

Rabinow, P. (Ed.). (1984). *The Foucault reader.* New York: Pantheon Books.

Rachlin, V, & Hansen, J. (1985). The impact of equity or egalitarianism on dual-career couples. *Family Therapy, 12* (2), 151–64.

Rawlings, S. W. (1995). Households and families. In U.S. Bureau of the Census, *Current Population Reports,* Series P23–189, Population Profile of the United States, 1995 (pp. 22–23). Washington, DC: U.S. Government Printing Office.

Richardson, M. S. (1993). Work in people' lives: A location for counseling psychologists. *Journal of Counseling Psychology, 40,* 425–433.

Richter, C., Morrison, D. L., & Salinas, A. (1991). *The dual-career family and implications for the career counselor.* Unpublished paper.

Roe, A. (1957). Early determinants of vocational choice. *Journal of Counseling Psychology, 4,* 212–17.

Roe, A., & Lunneborg, P. (1990). Personality development and career choice. In D. Brown, L. Brooks, and Associates (Eds.). *Career choice and development: Applying contemporary theories to practice.* (2nd ed.) (pp. 68–102). San Francisco: Jossey-Bass.

Sadker, M., & Sadker, D. (1995). *Failing at fairness: How our school cheat girls.* New York: Touchstone.

Savickas, M. L. (1989). Career-style assessment and counseling. In T. Sweeney (Ed.), *Adlerian counseling: A practical approach for a new decade* (3rd ed.). Muncie, IN: Accelerated Development.

Shahnasarian, M. (1997). The case of Jessica Chang: A business and industry perspective. *Career Development Quarterly, 46,* 155–160.

Single Parent Central: The Online Resource for Single Parent Families. (2004a). Quick facts about child care and after school care. Retrieved January 3, 2004 from http://www.singleparentcentral.com/factstat5.htm.

Single Parent Central: The Online Resource for Single Parent Families. (2004b). Quick facts about child support. Retrieved January 3, 2004 from http://www.singleparentcentral.com/factstat4.htm.

Single Parent Central: The Online Resource for Single Parent Families. (2004c). Quick facts about divorce. Retrieved January 3, 2004 from http://www.singleparentcentral.com/factstat3.htm.

Single Parent Central: The Online Resource for Single Parent Families. (2004d). Quick facts about single parenting. Retrieved January 3, 2004 from http://www.singleparentcentral.com/factstat2.htm.

Single parents: Career-related issues and needs. (1988). ERIC Digest No. 75. Columbus, OH: Clearinghouse on Adult, Career and Vocational Education.

Sodowsky, G. R., Kwan, K.-L. K., & Pannu, R. (1995). Ethnic identity of Asians in the United States. In J. G. Ponterotto, J. M. Casas, L. A. Suzuki, & C. M. Alexander (Eds.), *Handbook of multicultural counseling* (pp. 123–54). Thousand Oaks, CA: Sage.

Sosa, L. (1998, January/February). The *Americano* dream: How Latinos can achieve success in business and in life. *Hispanic, 88*, 90, 92, 94.

Sowell, T. (1994). *Race and culture: A world view* (chapter 2, pp. 32–60). New York: Basic Books.

Spencer, K. I., & Featherman, D. L. (1978). Achievement ambitions. *Annual Review of Sociology, 4*, 373–420.

Srivastva, S., Fry, R. E., & Cooperrider, D. L. (1990). Introduction: The call for executive appreciation. In S. Srivastva, D. L. Cooperrider, & Associates (Eds.), *Appreciative management and leadership: The power of positive thought and action in organizations* (pp. 1–33). San Francisco: Jossey-Bass.

Steele, S. (1990). *The content of our character: A new vision of race in America*. New York: Harper Perennial.

Sue, D., & Sue, D. W. (1993). Ethnic identity: Cultural factors in the psychological development of Asians in America. In D. R. Atkinson, G. Morten, & D. W. Sue, (Eds.), *Counseling American minorities: A cross-cultural perspective* (4th ed.) (pp. 199–210). Madison, WI: Brown & Benchmark.

Sue, D. W., & Sue, D. (1990). *Counseling the culturally different: Theory and practice* (2nd ed). New York: John Wiley.

Sullivan, S. (1992). Is there a time for everything? Attitudes related to women's sequencing of career and family. *Career Development Quarterly, 40*, 234–42.

Taylor, J. M., Gilligan, C., & Sullivan, A. M. (1995). *Between voice and silence: Women and girls, race and relationships*. Cambridge, MA: Harvard University Press.

Thomas, R. R., Jr. (1990, March–April). From affirmative action to affirming diversity. *Harvard Business Review*, 107–17.

Urrea, L. A. (2004). *The devil's highway*. New York: Little, Brown, & Company.

von Bertalanffy, L. (1968). *General systems theory: Foundation, development, application*. New York: George Braziller.

Voydanoff, P. (1988). Work and family: A review and expanded conceptualization. *Journal of Social Behavior and Personality, 3* (4), 1–22.

Walsh, F. (1989). The family in later life. In B. Carter & M. McGoldrick (Eds.), *The changing family life cycle: A framework for family therapy* (2nd ed.) (pp. 311–34). Boston: Allyn & Bacon.

Washington Post. (1996, September 24). 1st conditions of welfare law take effect amid confusion. *El Paso Times*, p. 4A.

Watkins, C. E. (1984). The individual psychology of Alfred Adler: Toward an Adlerian vocational theory. *Journal of Vocational Behavior, 24*, 28–47.

Watkins, C. E., & Savickas, M. L. (1990). Psychodynamic career counseling. In W. B. Walsh & S. H. Osipow (Eds.), *Career counseling: Contemporary topics in vocational psychology* (pp. 79–116). Hillsdale, NJ: Erlbaum.

Watts, R., & Engels, D. (1995). The life task of vocation: A review of Adlerian research literature. *Texas Counseling Association Journal*, 9–19.

Weiberg, R. B., & Mauksch, L. B. (1991). Examining family-of-origin influences in life at work. *Journal of Marital and Family Therapy, 17*, 233–42.

Weitzman, L. (1994). Multiple role realism: A theoretical framework for the process of planning to combine career and family roles. *Applied and Preventive Psychology, 3*, 15–25.

Yagi, D. T., & Oh, M. Y. (1995). Counseling Asian-American students. In C. C. Lee (Ed.), *Counseling for diversity: A guide for school counselors and related professionals* (pp. 61–83). Boston: Allyn & Bacon.

Yang, J. (1991). Career counseling of Chinese American women: Are they in limbo? *Career Development Quarterly, 39*, 350–359.

Young, R., & Friesen, J. (1992). The intentions of parents in influencing the career development of their children. *Career Development Quarterly, 40*, 198–205.

Young, R., Friesen, J., & Dillabough, R. (1991). Personal constructions of parental influence related to career development. *Canadian Journal of Counselling, 25*, 183–90.

Zucchino, D. (1997). *Myth of the Welfare Queen*. New York: Scribner's.

Chapter 9

Adderholdt-Elliott, M. (1987). *Perfectionism—what's bad about being too good?* Minneapolis, MN: Free Spirit.

Allen, J. M. (1994). School counselors collaborating for student success. *ERIC Digest,* Report No. EDO-CG-94-27. Greensboro, NC: Clearinghouse on Counseling and Student Services.

American Association of University Women. (1991, January). *Shortchanging girls, shortchanging America: Executive summary.* Washington, DC: Author.

American School Counselor Association. (1997). Alexandria, VA: American Counseling Association.

Amundson, N. E., & Penner, K. (1998). Parent involved career exploration. *Career Development Quarterly, 47,* 135–144.

Belvis, R., Rodriguez, R., & Fellan, E. (1996). Integrating career exploration in the middle school curriculum. Unpublished paper.

Berenstain, S., & Berenstain, J. (1974). *The Berenstain bears' new baby.* New York: Random House.

Berman, J., & Cosca, T. (1992). The 1990–2005 job outlook in brief. *Occupational Outlook Handbook, 36,* 6–41.

Bingham, M., Edmonson, J., & Stryker, S. (1984). *Choices: A teen women's journal for self-awareness and planning.* Santa Barbara, CA: Advocacy Press.

Bingham, M., & Stryker, S. (1995). *Things will be different for my daughter: A practical guide to building her self-esteem and self-reliance.* New York: Penguin Books.

Bireley, M. (1991). Learning styles: One way to help gifted adolescents understand and choose lifestyles. In M. Bireley & J. Genshaft. *Understanding the gifted adolescent: Educational, developmental, and multicultural issues.* New York: Teachers College Press.

Bireley, M., & Genshaft, J. (1991). *Understanding the gifted adolescent: Educational, developmental, and multicultural issues.* New York: Teachers College Press.

Boyd, G., Hemmings, B., & Braggett, E. (2003). The development of a career education program for gifted high school students. Retrieved September 30, 2003 from http://aare.edu.au/00pap/hem00464.htm.

Brown, D., Minor, C., & Jepsen, D. (1992). Public support for career development activities America's schools: Report of the 1989 NCDA survey. *The School Counselor, 39,* 257–62.

Brzowsky, S. (1998, February 8). Are girls being shortchanged? *Parade Magazine,* 10.

Burress, J., & Kaenzig, L. (2003. Introversion: The often forgotten factor impacting the gifted. The College of William & Mary Center for Gifted Education. http://cfge.wm.edu/Publications/Introversion.html.

Byrnes, J. P. (1996). *Cognitive development and learning in instructional contexts.* Boston: Allyn & Bacon.

Campbell, C. A., & Dahir, C. A. (Eds.). (1997). *The National Standards for School Counseling Programs.* Alexandria, VA: American School Counselor Association.

Canfield, J., & Wells, H. C. (1994). *100 ways to enhance self-concept in the classroom.* Boston: Allyn & Bacon.

Catherine, L. (1997). *Career education guide: Comprehensive, PK-adult.* San Antonio, TX: East Central Independent School District.

Catlett, J. (1992). The dignity of work: School children look at employment. *Career Development Quarterly, 27,* 150–54.

Cobb, R. B., & Neubert, D. A. (1998). Vocational education: Emerging vocationalism. In F. R. Rusch & J. G. Chadsey (Eds.), *Beyond high school: Transition from school to work* (pp. 101–26). Belmont, CA: Wadsworth.

Cohen, J. L. (1992). *Tu puedes ser una ingeniera* (J. M. Yáñez, Trans. from English). Culver City, CA: Cascade Pass.

Cohen, J. L. (1995). *You can be a woman engineer.* Culver City, CA: Cascade Pass.

Colangelo, N. (2003, Fall). Counseling gifted and talented student. National Research Center on the Gifted and Talented Newsletter. Retrieved on October 10, 2003 from http://www.sp.uconn.edu/~nrcgt/news/fall02/fallo22.html.

Covey, S. (1990). *Seven Habits of Highly Effective People.* New York: Simon & Schuster.

Dabrowsky, K. (1993). The overexcitiabilities in counseling the gifted and talented. In L. Silverman (Ed.). *Counseling the gifted and talented.* Denver, CO: Love (pp. 13–22).

Elium, J., & Elium, D. (1994). *Raising a daughter: Parents and the awakening of a healthy woman.* Berkeley, CA: Celestial Arts.

Ettinger, J. (2001). *A Guide to Planning and Implementing K–12 Career Development Programs,* Center on Education and Work, School of Education, University of Wisconsin-Madison, Madison, Wisconsin.

Flouri, E., & Buchanan, A. (2002). The role of work-related skills and career role models in adolescent career maturity. *Career Development Quarterly, 51,* 36–43.

Freeman, B. (1996). The use and perceived effectiveness of career assessment tools: A survey of high school counselors. *Journal of Career Development, 22,* 185–96.

The Futurist. (2002, January–February). Success without college, p. 8.

Gabriel, D. L., & Cohen, J. L. (1993a). *Tu puedes ser paleontóloga* (J. M. Yáñez, Trans. from English). Culver City, CA: Cascade Pass.

Gabriel, D. L., & Cohen, J. L. (1993b). *You can be a woman palentologist.* Culver City, CA: Cascade Press.

Ghez, A. M., & Cohen, J. L. (1995). *You can be a woman astronomer.* Culver City, CA: Cascade Press.

Grant, D. (1997). *Report card paycheck program.* San Antonio, TX: Northside Independent School District.

Gray, K. C., & Herr, E. L. (2000). *Other ways to win: Creating alternatives for high school graduates* (2nd ed). Thousand Oaks, CA: Corwin Press.

Gysbers, Norman C. (2001). *School Guidance and Counseling in the 21st Century: Remember the Past Into the Future.* Retrieved August 6, 2003 from: http://web16.epnet.ocm/citation.asp?tb=0&_ug=In+en%2Dus+sid+E8FBF93%2D994E%2.

Gysbers, Norman C. (2002). *Comprehensive School Guidance Programs in the Future: Staying the Course.* Retrieved August 6, 2003 from http://new.firstsearch.oclc.org/WebZ/FSFETCH?fetchtype=fullrecord:sessionid=sp05sw01-.

Gysbers, N. C., & Henderson, P. (2000). *Developing and Managing Your School Guidance Program* (3rd ed.), Alexandria, VA: American Counseling Association.

Hall, A., Kelly, K., & VanBuren, J. (1995). Effects of grade level, community of residence, and sex on adolescent career interests in the zone of acceptable alternatives. *Journal of Career Development, 21,* 223–31.

Hanley-Maxwell, C., Pogoloff, S. M., & Whitney-Thomas, J. (1998). Families: The heart of transition. In F. R. Rusch & J. G. Chadsey (Eds.), *Beyond high school: Transition from school to work* (pp. 234–64). Belmont, CA: Wadsworth.

Harris-Bowlsbey, J. H., Dikel, M. R., & Sampson, Jr., J. P. (2002). *The Internet: A tool for career planning: A guide to using the Internet in career planning.* (2nd ed) Tulsa, OK: National Career Development Association.

Henderson, P. (1996). *Facilitating students' career development through comprehensive guidance programs: Delivery systems activities.* San Antonio, TX: Northside Independent School District.

Herr, E. L., Cramer, S. H., & Niles, S. G. (2004). *Career guidance and counseling through the lifespan.* Boston: Allyn & Bacon.

Hill, R. B., & Rojewsky, J. W. (1999). Double jeopardy: Work ethnic differences in youth at risk of school failure. *Career Development Quarterly, 47,* 267–279.

Hollinger, C. (1991). Career choices for gifted adolescents: Overcoming stereotypes. In M. Bireley & J. Genshaft (Eds.). *Understanding the gifted adolescent: Educational, developmental, and multicultural issues.* New York: Teachers College Press. (pp. 49–61).

Hourcade, J. (2002). Mental retardation: Update 2002. ERIC EC Digest #E637. Retrieved October 16, 2003 from http://ericec.org.digests/e637.html.

Hoyt, K. B. (1989). *Counselors and career development—A topic in educational reform proposals: A selected review of national education reform documents.* Columbus, OH: Center on Education and Training for Employment, Ohio State University.

Hoyt, K. B. (1994). Youth apprenticeship: American style and career development. *Career Development Quarterly, 42,* 216–23.

Hoyt, K. B. (2001). *Career Education and Education Reform: Time for a Rebirth,* Retrieved May 12, 2003 from: http://web13.epnet.com/citation.asp?tb=0&ug-In+en%2Dus+sid+FB2A685D%2D1AA5.

Hoyt, K. B., Hughey, J. K., & Hughey, K. F. (1995). An introduction to the "Counseling for High Skills: Vo-Tech Career Options" project. *School Counselor, 43,* 10–18.

Hoyt, K. B. & Wickwire, P. N. (2001, March). *Knowledge-Information-Service Era Changes in Work and Education and the Changing Role of the School Counselor in Career Education, Career Development Quarterly, 49,* 238–249.

Johnson, L. S. (2000). The relevance of school to careers: A study in student awareness. *Journal of Career Development, 26* (4), 263–276.

Keown, R. (2003). Extract from an unpublished study for the University of Waikato. http://www.reap.org.nz/~ftritt/robin.html.

Kerr, B. (1985). *Smart Girls, Gifted Women.* Dayton: Ohio Psychology Press.

Kerr, B. (1991). *Handbook for counseling the gifted and talented.* Alexandria, VA: American Counseling Association.

Kuczynski, L. B. (1997). *Life planning and career assessment: Eighth grade at-risk students model.* Unpublished paper.

Kush, K., & Cochran, L. (1993). Enhancing a sense of agency through career planning. *Journal of Counseling Psychology, 40,* 434–39.

Kyle, M. T., & Hennis, M. (2000). Experiential model for career guidance in early childhood education. In Peterson, N. & González, R. C. (Eds.). *Career counseling models for diverse populations: Hands-on applications for practitioners.* Belmont, CA: Wadsworth/Brooks/Cole.

Laney, M. (2002). *The introvert advantage: How to thrive in an extrovert world.* New York: Workman.

Lapan, R. T., Osana, H. P., Tucker, B., & Kosciulek, J. F. (2002). Challenges for creating community career partnerships: perspectives from practitioners. *Career Development Quarterly, 51,* 172–190.

Lichtenstein, S. (1998). Characteristics of youth and young adults. In F. R. Rusch & J. G. Chadsey (Eds.), *Beyond high school: Transition from school to work* (pp. 3–35). Belmont, CA: Wadsworth.

Lingg, M. A. (1996). Training for job-skills confidence. *Journal of Career Development, 22*, 261– 71.

Mahoney, A. (1998). The gifted identity formation model. *Roeper Review, 20* (3) 222–226.

Marcos, K. (2003). Gearing-up for career awareness: profile of a middle school career program. *ERIC Digest*. Retrieved November 17, 2003 from http://icdl.undg.edu/ft/060403-02.html.

Marone, N. (1988). *How to father a successful daughter.* New York: Fawcett Crest.

Marshall, A., Shepard, B., & Batten, S. (2002). First nations and rural youths: Career exploration narratives.

Mau, W.-C. (1995). Educational planning and academic achievement of middle school students: A racial and cultural comparison. *Journal of Counseling and Development, 73,* 518–26.

National Association for Gifted Children. (2003). Recent Research on Guidance, Counseling and Therapy for the Gifted. *Literature reviews: As part of the Counseling & Guidance Division's Affective Issues and the Gifted Series.* http://www.nagc.org/CounGuide/guide.html

National Occupational Information Coordinating Committee (NOICC). (1996). *The National Career Development Guidelines.* Washington, DC: NOICC.

Nelson, D. E., & Gardner, J. L. (1998). *An evaluation of the comprehensive guidance. program in Utah public schools.* Salt Lake City: Utah State Office of Education.

Orenstein, P. (1994). *School girls: Young women, self-esteem, and the confidence gap.* New York: Anchor Books.

Paige, J. (2003). *Career counseling for the gifted: From "At-Risk" to "At-Promise."* Unpublished paper.

Peterson, N., & González, R. (Eds.). (2000). *Career counseling models for diverse populations: Hands-on applications for practitioners.* Belmont, CA: Wadsworth/Brooks/Cole.

Post, P., Williams, M., & Brubaker, L. (1996). Career and lifestyle expectations of rural eighth grade students: A second look. *Career Development Quarterly, 44,* 250– 57.

Pyne, D., Bernes, K., Magnusson, K., & Poulsen, J. (2002). A description of junior high and senior high school students' perceptions of career and occupation. *Guidance and Counseling, 17*(3), 67–72.

Rea-Poteat, M., & Martin, P. (1991). Taking your place: A summer program to encourage non-traditional career choices for adolescent girls. *Career Development Quarterly, 40,* 182–88.

Redborg, R., & Cohen, J. L. (1996). *You can be a woman cardiologist.* Culver City, CA: Cascade Press.

Reis, S. (1998). *Work left undone: Choices and compromises of talented females.* Bridgeport, CN: Creative Learning Press.

Robinson, N. (2002, Fall). Assessing and advocating for gifted students: Perspectives for school and clinical psychologists. *National Research Center on the Gifted & Talented Newsletter.* http://www.sp.uconn.edu/~nrcgt/news/fall02/fall024.html

Robinson, N. (2003, September). Assessing and advocating for gifted students: Perspectives for school and clinical psychologists. National Research Center on the Gifted and Talented.

Roeper, A. (1995). *Annemarie Roeper: Selected writings and speeches.* Minneapolis: Free Spirit.

Rusch, F. R., & Millar, D. M. (1998). Emerging transition best practices. In F. R. Rusch & J. G. Chadsey (Eds.), *Beyond high school: Transition from school to work* (pp. 36–59). Belmont, CA: Wadsworth.

Sadker, M., & Sadker, D. (1995). *Failing at fairness: How our schools cheat girls.* New York: Touchstone.

Saskatchewan Department of Education. (1995). *The middle level guidance curriculum.* www.sasked.gov.sk.ca/docs/midcareer/usi.html

Schmidli, K. W. (2001). Infusing the career development facilitator curriculum into career and technical teacher education: A model for fundamental change to improve outcomes for all students. *Journal of Industrial Teacher Education, 38* (4), 62–83.

Siegel, M., & Cohen, J. L. (1992a). *Tu puedes ser una arquitecta* (J. M. Yáñez, Trans. from English). Culver City, CA: Cascade Press.

Siegel, M., & Cohen, J. L. (1992b). *You can be a woman architect.* Culver City, CA: Cascade Press.

Siegel, S. (1998). Foundations for a school-to-work system that serves all students. In F. R. Rusch & J. G. Chadsey (Eds.), *Beyond high school: Transition from school to work* (pp. 146– 78). Belmont, CA: Wadsworth.

Silverman, L. K. (Ed.). (1991). *Counseling the gifted and talented.* Denver, CO: Love.

Silverman, L. K. (2003). *Testing on the SBL-M? Better hurry!* Gifted Development Center. http://www.gifteddevelopment.com/SBLM%20Media/testing_on_the_sblm.htm

Solberg, V. S., Howard, K.A., Blustein, D. L., & Close, W. (2002). Career development in the schools: Connecting school-to-work-to-life. *Counseling Psychologist, 30* (5), 705–725.

Stasz, C., & Stern, D. (1999). Work-based learning for students in high schools and community colleges. *NSEE Quarterly, 24* (2), 8–14.

Szymanski, E. M. (1998). Career development, school-to-work transition, and diversity: An ecological approach. In F. R. Rusch & J. G. Chadsey (Eds.), *Beyond high school: Transition from school to work* (pp. 127–45). Belmont, CA: Wadsworth.

Taylor, J. M., Gilligan, C., & Sullivan, A. M. (1995). *Between voice and silence: Women and girls, race and relationship.* Cambridge, MA: Harvard University Press.

Thompson, V., & Cohen, J. L. (1992). *You can be a woman zoologist.* Culver City, CA: Cascade Press.

Thompson, V., & Cohen, J. L. (1993). *Tu puedes ser una zoóloga* (J. M. Yáñez, Trans. from English). Culver City, CA: Cascade Press.

Thurlow, M., & Elliott, J. (1998). Student assessment and evaluation. In F. R. Rusch & J. G. Chadsey (Eds.), *Beyond high school: Transition from school to work* (pp. 265–296). Belmont, CA: Wadsworth.

Turner, S., & Lapan, R. T. (2002). Career self-efficacy and perceptions of parent support in adolescent career development. *Career Development Quarterly, 51* (1), 44–55.

Tye, K., & Bireley, M. (1991). Moral and spiritual development of the gifted adolescent. In M. Bireley, & J. Genshaft. *Understanding the gifted adolescent: Educational, developmental, and multicultural issues.* New York: Teachers College Press, New York.

United States Department of Labor, Special Commission on Achieving Necessary Skills. (1991). *What work requires of schools: A SCANS report for America 2000.* Washington, DC: United States Department of Labor.

Wagner, J. (1994). *Edith Ann: My life, so far.* New York: Hyperion.

Willars, T. (2003). *Counselors in a Christian school setting.* Unpublished paper.

William T. Grant Foundation Commission on Work, Family, and Citizenship. (1988, February). The forgotten half: Non-college bound youth in America. *Phi Delta Kappan,* 409– 414.

Wood, S. (1990). Initiating career plans with freshmen. *School Counselor, 37,* 233–37.

Chapter 10

Accreditation Council of Continuing Education and Training (ACCET) Report. (1991). U.S. Department of Education.

Agency Group 09. (2002a/2/26). Executive Summary. *FDCH Regulatory Intelligence Database.* Retrieved June 12, 2003 from http://search.epnet.com/direct.asp?an=32W1449323021&db=buh&tg=AN.

Agency Group 09. (2002b/2/26). Reform Food Stamps to Promote *Work* Overview. *FDCH Regulatory Intelligence Database.* Retrieved June 12, 2003 from http://search.epnet.com/direct.asp?an=32W317894876&db=buh&tg=AN.

Agency Group 09. (2003/1/14). President Calls For Action on *Welfare* Reform. *FDCH Regulatory Intelligence Database.* Retrieved June 12, 2003 from

http://search.epnet.com/direct.asp?an=32W1914459965&db=buh&tg=AN.

American Association of Community Colleges. (1996) *Developing the world's best workforce: An agenda for America's community colleges—Executive summary.* Washington, DC: Author.

Bell, S. H., & Orr, L. L. (2002). Screening (and creaming?) applicants to job training programs: the AFDC homemaker-home health aid demonstrations. *Labour Economics, 9,* 279–301.

Bingham, R., & Ward, C. (1994). Career counseling with ethnic minority women. In W. B. Walsh & S. H. Osipow (Eds.). *Career counseling for women.* Hillsdale, NJ: Erlbaum.

Bireley, M. (1991). Learning styles: One way to help gifted adolescents understand and choose lifestyles. In M. Bireley & J. Genshaft. *Understanding the gifted adolescent: Educational, developmental, and multicultural issues.* New York: Teachers College Press.

Bireley, M., & Genshaft, J. (1991). *Understanding the gifted adolescent: Educational, developmental, and multicultural issues.* New York: Teachers College Press.

Bloom, J. W., &and Walz, G. R. (Eds.). (2000). *Cybercounseling and cyberlearning: Strategies and resources for the millennium.* Alexandria, VA: American Counseling Association.

Boyd, G., Hemmings, B., & Braggett, E. "The Development of a career education program for Gifted high school students." *Understanding the Gifted Adolescent: Educational, Developmental, and Multicultural Issues.* September, 2003. http://www.aare.edu.au/00pap/hem00464.htm

Bradley, R. W., & Mims, G. A. (1992). Using family systems and birth order dynamics as the basis for a college career decision-making course. *Journal of Counseling & Development, 70,* 445–48.

Burress, J., & Kaenzig, L. *Introversion: The often forgotten factor impacting the gifted.* The College of William & Mary Center for Gifted Education. Retrieved, September, 2003, http://cfge.wm.edu/Publications/Introversion.html

Career Navigator Series. (2002). Career Development Center, University of Cincinnati. (See Jurgens, J. C. [2002].)

Casto, M. (2003). Retrieved March 30, 2003 from getsmartseries@yahoogroups.com.

Center for Public Policy Priorities. (1997, March 14). *Policy Page, 44,* 1–5.

Colangelo, Nicholas. (2002, Fall). Counseling Gifted and Talented Students. *National Research Center on the Gifted & Talented* [Newsletter]. Retrieved September 2003, http://www.sp.uconn.edu/~nrcgt/news/fall02/fall022.html.

Crosby, O. (2002–03, Winter). Associate degree: Two years to a career or a jump start to a bachelor's degree. *Occupational Outlook Quarterly, 46* (4), 2–13. Washington, DC: U.S. Department of Labor.

Crozier, S. (1991). Empowering the liberal arts student with personal flexibility for the world of work. *Canadian Journal of Counselling and Development, 25,* 97–109.

Danziger, S., Heflin, C. M., Corcoran, M. E., Oltmans, E., & Wang, H.-C. (2002). Does it pay to move from welfare to work? *Journal of Policy Analysis and Management, 21* (4), 671–692.

Elwood, J. A. (1992). The pyramid model: A useful tool in career counseling with university students. *Career Development Quarterly, 41,* 51–54.

Ettinger, J. (2001). *A Guide to Planning and Implementing K–12 Career Development Programs,* Center on Education and Work, School of Education, University of Wisconsin-Madison, Madison, Wisconsin.

Gati, I. (1994). Computer-assisted counseling: Dilemmas, problems and possible solutions. *Journal of Counseling and Development, 73,* 51–57.

Gysbers, N. C., & Moore, E. J. (1987). *Career counseling: Skills and techniques for practitioners.* Boston: Allyn & Bacon.

Halasz, T. J., & Kempton, C. B. (2000). Career Planning Workshops and Courses. In D. A. Luzzo, (Ed.). *Career counseling of college students.* Washington, DC: American Psychological Association.

Hall, C., Hayes, R., Morris, S., Rendón, I, & Zepeda, F. (1993). *Vocational Schools.* Unpublished manuscript.

Hard, N. L., & Schoenmakers, C. (1997, May). Promoting work/family balance: An organization-change approach. *Organizational Dynamics,* 5–18.

Harris-Bowlsbey, J. H., Dikel, M. R., & Sampson, Jr., J. P. (2002). *The Internet: A tool for career planning: A guide to using the Internet in career planning* (2nd ed.). Tulsa, OK: National Career Development Association.

Healy, C., and Mourton, D. (1987). Career exploration, college jobs, and GPA. *Journal of College Student Personnel, 28,* 27–34.

Heppner, M., & Duan, C. (1995). From a narrow to expansive world view: Making career centers a place for diverse students. *Journal of Career Development, 22,* 87–100.

Heppner, M., & Johnston, J. (1993). Career counseling: A call to action. In J. Rayman (Ed.), *Contemporary career services.* San Francisco: Jossey-Bass.

Isaacson, L., and Brown, D. (1993). *Career information, career counseling, and career development* (5th ed.). Needham Heights, MA: Allyn & Bacon.

Jurgens, J. C. (2000). The undecided student: Effects of combining levels of treatment parameters on career certainty, career indecision, and client satisfaction. *Career Development Quarterly, 48,* 237–250.

Jurgens, J. C. (2002). The Career Navigator sails. *Journal of College Student Development, 43* (1), 137–142.

Katz, M. J. (1993). *Computer-assisted career decision making: The guide in the machine.* Hillsdale, NJ: Erlbaum.

Kerr, B. (1985). *Smart Girls, Gifted Women.* Dayton, OH: Psychology Press, 1985.

Kerr, B. (1991). *Handbook for counseling the Gifted & Talented.* Alexandria, VA: American Counseling Association.

Kerr, Barbara. (1990). Career planning for gifted and talented youth. *ERIC EC Digest* #E492, ED 321 497, 1990. http://www.kidsource.com/kidsource/content/career_planning.html.

Kivlighan, D. M., Jr., Johnston, J. A., Hogan, R. S., & Mauer, E. (1994). Who benefits from computerized career counseling? *Journal of Counseling and Development, 72,* 289–282.

Koonce, R. (1997). Using the Internet as a career planning tool. *Training and development, 51,* 15–16.

Luzzo, D. (1996). Exploring the relationship between the perception of occupational barriers and career development. *Journal of Career Development, 22,* 239–48.

McCarthy, C. J., Moller, N., & Beard, L. M. (2003). Suggestions for training students in using the Internet for career counseling. *Career Development Quarterly, 51,* 368–382.

McDonald, D. L. (2002). Career counseling strategies to facilitate welfare-to-work transition: The case of Jeanetta. *Career Development Quarterly, 50,* 326–330.

McWhirter, E. (1994, August). *Perceived barriers to education and career: Ethnic and gender differences.* Paper presented at the Annual Convention of the American Psychological Association, Los Angeles.

Montoya, I. D., Bell, D. C., Atkinson, J. S., Nagy, C. W., & Whitsett, D. D. (2002). Mental health, drug use, and the transition from welfare to work. *Journal of Behavioral Health Services & Research, 29* (2), 144–156.

National Occupational Information Coordinating Committee (NOICC). (1996). *The National Career Development Guidelines.* Washington, DC: Author.

Nyre, G., and Reilly, K. (1987). *A study of career/vocational counseling in California community colleges.* Santa Clara, CA: C/VEG Publications.

Olson, T., & Matkin, R. (1992). Student and counselor perceptions of career counselor work activities in a community college. *Career Development Quarterly, 40,* 324–333.

Paige, J. (2003). *Career counseling for the gifted: From "At-Risk" to "At-Promise."* Unpublished paper.

Peterson, N., & González, R. C. (Eds.). (2000). *Career counseling models for diverse populations: Hands-on applications for practitioners.* Belmont, CA: Wadsworth/Brooks/Cole.

Pharr, M., & Glover, J. (1995). Training and outcomes for federal college work-study. *Journal of Student Employment, 6,* 6–17.

Pipher, M. (1996). The shelter of each other: Rebuilding our families. New York: Ballantine Books.

Pyle, K. R. (1985). "Hi tech-hi touch": A synergy applicable to career development using the computer in group counseling. *Journal of Career Development, 10,* 333–341.

Robinson, C. R. (1996). *Increasing the value of career courses.* Paper presented at the Texas Vocational Guidance Association/Texas Career Guidance Association Mid-Winter Conference, Austin, TX.

Routh, L., Chretien, C., & Rakes, T. (1995). Career centers and work-study employment. *Journal of Career Development, 22,* 125–133.

Sampson, J. P., Jr. (1994). Factors influencing the effective use of computer-assisted guidance services: The North American experience. *British Journal of Guidance and Counselling, 22,* 91–106.

Sampson, J. P., Jr. (1997, January). Ethical delivery of computer-assisted guidance services: Supported vs. stand-alone system use. In R. C. Reardon (Chair), *Ethical issues in using computers to deliver career services: counseling intervention, equality of access, and the Internet.* Symposium conducted at the National Career Development Association Conference, Daytona Beach, FL.

Sampson, J. P., Jr., Kolodinsky, R. W., & Greeno, B. P. (1997). Counseling on the information highway: Future possibilities and potential problems. *Journal of Counseling and Development, 75,* 203–212.

Silverman, Linda K. "Testing on the SBL-M? Better Hurry!" *Gifted Development Center.* 2003. http://www.gifteddevelopment.com/SBLM%20Media/testing_on_the_sblm.htm.

Smith, G. E. (1987). *A study of the career development characteristics of first-year community college business majors with implications for additional research and a suggested advisement model.* Paper presented at the American Vocational Association Convention, Las Vegas, NM. ERIC ED 290032.

Sue, D. W., & Sue, D. (1990). *Counseling the culturally different: Theory and practice* (2nd ed). New York: John Wiley.

Swanson, J. L. & Tokar, D. M. (1991). Development and initial validation of barriers to career development. *Journal of Vocational Behavior, 39,* 92–106.

Tye, K., & Bireley, M. (1991). Moral and Spiritual Development of the Gifted Adolescent. In M. Bireley, & J. Genshaft, (eds). *Understanding the Gifted Adolescent: Educational, Developmental, and Multicultural Issues.* New York: Teachers College Press.

Yaegel, J. (1978). Certainty of vocational choice and the persistence and achievements of liberal arts community college freshman. *Dissertation Abstracts International, 38,* 118A.

Zagora, M., & Cramer, S. (1994). The effects of vocational identity status on outcomes of a career decision making intervention for community college students. *Journal of College Student Development, 35,* 239–47.

Zunker, V. (1994). *Career counseling: Applied concepts of life planning* (4th ed.). Pacific Grove, CA: Brooks/Cole.

Chapter 11

Adams, J., Hayes, J., & Hopson, B. (1977). *Transition: Understanding and managing personal change.* Oxford, England: Allanheld & Osmun.

"Air force to warn cadets after drinking incident." (2003, August 27). *Washington Post,* p. A06. Retrieved September 6, 2003, from http://www.washingtonpost.com/wp-dyn/articles/A50868-2003Aug26.html.

Amundson, N. E., & Borgen, W. A. (1988). Factors that help and hinder group employment counseling. *Journal of Employment Counseling, 25,* 104–14.

Armour, S. (1997, October 24). Age-bias case sounds warning. *USA Today,* p. B1.

Aubrey, T., Tefft, B., & Kingsbury, N. (1990). Behavioral and psychological consequences of unemployment in blue-collar workers. *Journal of Community Psychology, 18,* 99–109.

Barefoot, J. C., Larsen, S., von der Leith, L., & Schroll, M. (1995). Hostility, incidence of acute myocardial infarction, and mortality in a sample of older Danish men and women. *American Journal of Epidemiology, 142,* 477–84.

Barnett, R. C., & Rivers, C. (1996). *She works/he works: How two-income families are happy, healthier, and better.* San Francisco: Harper.

Beijan, D., & Salomone, P. R. (1995). Understanding midlife career renewal: implications for counseling. *Career Development Quarterly, 44,* 52–64.

Bergstein, B. (2003, June 23). Baby boomers feeling the pinch. *San Antonio Express News,* p. D1.

Bernes, K. (2002). *Are they nuts? When psychopathology interferes with career issues.* NATCON Papers 2002 Les actes du CONAT.

Betz, N. E., & Fitzgerald, L. H. (1987). *The career psychology of women.* San Diego, CA: Academic Press.

Brewington, J. O., & Nassar-McMillan. (2000). Older adults: Work-related issues and implications for counseling. *Career Development Quarterly, 49,* 2–15.

Brown, D. (1996). Brown's values-based holistic model of career and life-role choices and satisfaction. In

D. Brown, L. Brooks, & Associates (Eds.), *Career Choice and Development,* (3rd ed.) (pp. 337–72). San Francisco: Jossey-Bass.

Brown, M., Fukunaga, C., Umemoto, D., & Wicker, L. (1996). Annual review, 1990–1996: Social class, work and retirement behavior. *Journal of Vocational Behavior, 49,* 159–89.

Bullfinch's Mythology. (1978). New York: Avenel Books.

Burd, M., & Davies, J. (2003, September). Workplace rights: Age shall not wither them. *Management Today,* p. 25.

Bureau of Labor Statistics. (2004). Distribution of the population and labor force by age and sex. Retrieved April 18, 2004 from http://www.bls.gov/emp/emplab2002-08.htm.

Burg, M. M. (1995). Anger, hostility, and coronary heart disease: A review. *Mind/Body Medicine, 1,* 159–72.

Burney, T. (1995, December 11). It's not supposed to be a workplace issue: But the effects of domestic violence are spreading into the workplace. *El Paso Herald-Post,* p. B5.

Campbell, C. (2000). Unemployment issues and outplacement interventions. In N. Peterson, & R. C. González (eds). *Career counseling models for diverse populations: Hands-on applications by practitioners.* Belmont, CA: Wadsworth/Brooks/Cole.

Carter, M., & Cook, K. (1995). Adaptation to retirement: role changes and psychological resources. *Career Development Quarterly, 44,* 67–83.

CBSNEWS.com (2003, July 16). *Seniors Scan 'Help Wanted' Ads.* Retrieved September 5, 2003 from http://www.CBSNEWS.com.

Champagne, D. (1987). Disadvantaged adult learners: can career counseling enhance adult education program effectiveness? *Adult Education Quarterly, 37,* 63–77.

Cherniss, C. (1995). *Beyond burnout: Helping teachers, nurses, therapists, and lawyers recover from stress and disillusion.* New York: Routledge.

Chodorow, N. (1978). *The reproduction of mothering.* Berkeley: University of California Press.

Cobble, D. (1996, February 29). Be wary of employees who overwork. *El Paso Herald-Post,* p. A10.

Cohen, N. (1995). *Mentoring adult learners: A guide for educators and trainers.* Melbourne, FL: Krieger.

Collard, B., Epperheimer, J. S., & Saigon, D. (1996). *Career resilience in a changing workplace.* Adapted from ERIC Information Series No. 366.

Cook, E. P. (1993). The gendered context of life: Implications for women's and men's careerlife plans. *Career Development Quarterly, 41,* 227–37.

Curnow, B., & Fox, J. M. (1994). *Third age careers.* Brookfield, VT: Gower.

Davenport, T. O. (1999). *Human Capital.* San Francisco, CA: Jossey-Bass.

Davey, M., & Leonhardt, D. (2003). Jobless and hopeless, many quit the labor force. *The New York Times.* Retrieved April 27, 2003 from http://www.nytimes.com/2003/04/27/national/27JOBS.html.

Daw, J. (2001). Road rage, air rage, and now 'desk rage'. *Monitor on Psychology,* July/August.

Deary, I. J., Fowkes, F. G. R., Donnan, P. T., & Housley, E. (1994). Hostile personality and risks of peripheral arterial disease in the general population. *Psychosomatic Medicine, 56,* 197–202.

de Becker, G. (1997). *The gift of fear: Survival signals that protect us from violence. Boston:* Little.

Deutschman, A. (1990, August 27). "What twenty-five year olds want." *Fortune,* 42–48.

Doby, V. J., & Caplan, R. D. (1995). Organizational stress as threat to reputation: Effects on anxiety at work and at home. *Academy of Management Journal, 38* (4), 1105–1123.

Doyle, J. A. (1989). *The male experience* (2nd ed.). Dubuque, IA: Wm. C. Brown.

Drummond, R., & Ryan, C. (1995). *Career counseling: A developmental approach.* Englewood Cliffs, NJ: Prentice Hall.

Eby, L. T., & Buch, K. (1995). Job loss as career growth: Responses to involuntary career transitions. *Career Development Quarterly, 44,* 26–43.

Edmonson, G. (2003, August 30). Poll: 1 in 5 female cadets assaulted; most Air Force Academy cases not reported. *The Atlanta Journal Constitution,* p. 3C. Retrieved September 19, 2003, from http://proxy.lib.iastate.edu:2053/universe/printdoc..

Edwards, O. (1991). *Upward nobility: How to succeed in business without losing your soul.* New York: Crown.

Emener, W., & Rubin, S. (1980). Rehabilitation counselor roles and functions and sources of role strain. *Journal of Applied Rehabilitation Counseling, 11* (2), 57–69.

Engels, D. (1995). Common themes in midlife career transitions. *Career Development Quarterly, 44,* 83–89.

Farber, B., & Heifetz, L. (1981). The satisfaction and stresses of psychotherapeutic work: A factor analytic study. *Professional Psychology, 12* (5), 621–30.

Ferrugia, J. (2003, February 12). 7NEWS investigates: Honor, code, betrayal at Air Force Academy (Television broadcast). Denver, CO: TheDenver Channel.com. Retrieved September 20, 2003, from http://www.thedenverchannel.com/print/1974754/detail.html?use=print.

Filipczak, B. (1994, April). It's just a job: Generation X at work. *Training,* 21–27.

Fitzgerald, L. F., & Harmon, L. W. (2001). Women's career development: A postmodern update. In F. T. L. Leong & A. Barak (Eds.), *Contemporary models in vocational psychology: A volume in honor of Samuel H. Osipow* (pp. 207–230). Mahwah, NJ: Erlbaum.

Florence, M. (2001). *Sex at work: Attraction, orientation, harassment, flirtation, and discrimination.* Los Angeles: Silver Lake.

Forrest, L., & Mikolaitis, N. (1986). The relational component of identity: An expansion of career development theory. *Career Development Quarterly, 35,* 76–88.

Friedman, M., & Rosenman, R. H. (1975). *Type A behavior and your heart.* New York: Knopf.

Gannett News Service. (1996, March 28). Immune system behind gulf illness, expert says. *El Paso Times,* pp. 1A, 6A.

Gati. (1994). Computer-assisted career counseling: Dilemmas, problems, and possible solutions. *Journal of Counseling and Development, 73* (1), 51–56.

Gehrke, R. (2003, September 5). Confidentiality, climate among issues facing congressional panel. *The Associated Press State & Local Wire* [no page number provided]. Retrieved September 19, 2003, from http://proxy.lib.iastate.edu:2053/universe/printdoc.

Geller, A. (2003). Survival jobs keep displaced white collars barely afloat. *Pittsburgh Tribune-Review.* Retrieved August 19, 2003 from http://www.pittsburghlive.com.

Genasci, L. (1995, December 20). Take two aspirin and get back to work. *El Paso Herald-Post,* pp. B5, B6.

Genevay, B. (2000). There is life after work: Re-creating oneself in the later years. In Peterson, N., & Gonzalez, R.C. (Eds), *Career Counseling Models: For Diverse Populations* (pp. 258–269). Belmont, CA: Wadsworth/Brooks Cole.

Gilligan, C. (1982). *In a different voice.* Cambridge, MA: Harvard University Press

Gilster, P. (1997). *The Web Navigator.* New York: Wiley.

Goodman, J. (1994). Career adaptability in adults: A construct whose time has come. *The Career Development Quarterly, 43,* 74–84.

Gray, K. C., & Herr, E. L. (1995). *Other ways to win: Creating alternatives for high school graduates.* Thousand Oaks, CA: Corwin Press.

Gross, D. M., & Scott, S. (1990, July 16). Proceeding with caution. *Time,* 56–62.

Gutek, B. A. (1985). *Sex and the workplace: The impact of sexual behavior and harassment on women, men, and organizations.* San Francisco: Jossey-Bass.

Guzman, R. A. (2003, July, 18). Overeducated and underemployed: Meet the new professional. *San Antonio Express News,* pp. 1F, 6–7F.

Hall, D. T., & Associates. (1996). *The career is dead long live the career: A relational approach to careers.* San Francisco: Jossey-Bass.

Hansen, L. S. (1997). *Integrative life planning: Critical tasks for career development and changing life patterns.* San Francisco: Jossey-Bass.

Heppner, J. J., Multon, K. C., & Johnston, J. A. (1991). Assessing psychological resources during career change: Development of the Career Transitions Inventory. *Journal of Vocational Behavior, 44,* 55–74.

Herman, R., Olivo, T., & Gioia, J. (2003). *Impending crisis: Too many jobs too few people.* Winchester, VA: Oakhill Press.

Herr, E. L. (1997). Super's life-span, life-space approach and its outlook for refinement. *Career Development Quarterly, 45,* 238–246.

Herr, E. L., & Cramer, S. H. (1996). *Career guidance and counseling through the lifespan: Systematic approaches.* Boston: Allyn & Bacon.

Hewlett, K. (2001, July/August). Can low self-esteem and self-blame on the job make you sick? *Monitor on Psychology, 32* (7), 58.

Hirschhorn, L. (1988). *The workplace within: Psychodynamics of organizational life.* Cambridge, MA: MIT Press.

Hotelling, K., & Forrest, L. (1985). Gilligan's theory of sex-role development: A perspective for counseling. *Journal of Counseling and Development, 64,* 183–86.

Hudson, F. (1991). *The adult years: Mastering the art of self-renewal* (1st ed.). San Francisco: Jossey-Bass.

Jensen-Scott, R. L. (1993). Counseling to promote retirement adjustment. *Career Development Quarterly, 41,* 257–67.

Jordan, K. (1997, September 11). Ageism in the workplace: Fact or fiction [8 paragraphs]. *Online Solutions* [On-line serial].

Kadlec, D. (2002, July 29). The new "staged" retirement. *Time Magazine on the Web.* Retrieved September 21, 2003, from http://weblinks1.epnet.com

Karsten, M. F. (1994). *Management and gender.* Westport, CT: Quorum Books.

Kelly, J. L. (1990, January). What went wrong? *Personnel Journal,* 43–55.

Kirk, J. J. (1994). Putting outplacement in its place. *Journal of Employment Counseling, 31,* 10–18.

Klarreich, S. H. (1988). *The stress solution: A rational approach to increasing corporate and personal effectiveness.* Toronto: Key Porter Books.

Kohler, J. (2003, September 3). Senator: Pentagon report will offer broad data on Air Force Academy. *The Associated Press State and Local Wire* [no page number given]. Retrieved September 19, 2003, from http://proxy.lib.iastate.edu:2053/universe/printdoc.

Krain, M. A. (1995). Policy implications for a society aging well. *American Behavioral Scientist, 39,* (2), 131–51.

Krebs, N. B. (1993). *Changing woman, changing work.* Aspen, CO: MacMurray & Beck.

Krumboltz, J. D. (1993). Integrating career and personal counseling. *Career Development Quarterly, 42,* 143–153.

LaBauve, B. J. & Robinson, C. R. (1999). Breaking the Stereotypes of Older Adults Online. *The Older Wiser Wired.* Available at http://www.org/olderwiserwired/Articles/a2003-02-20-oww-barriers.html

Laird, J. (1994). Changing women's narratives: Taking back the discourse. In L.V. Davis (Ed.), *Building on women's strengths: A social work agenda for the twenty-first century* (pp. 179–210). New York: The Haworth Press.

Land, D. (2003). Adjusting to Retirement: Considerations for Counselors. *ADULTSPAN Journal, 1,* 2–12.

Land, G., & Jarman, B. (1992). *Breakpoint and beyond: Mastering the future.* New York: HarperPerennial.

Lefkovich, J. (1992). Older workers: Why and how to capitalize on their powers. *Employment Relations Today,* 63–79.

Levinson, D. (1978). *The seasons of a man's life.* New York: Knopf.

Loeb, L. (1994). Community career services: The past, present, and future. *Journal of Career Development, 21,* 167–69.

Maccoby, E. E. (1990). Gender and relationships: A developmental account. *American Psychologist, 45,* 513–20.

MacKinnon-Slaney, F. (1994). The adult persistence in learning model: A road map to counseling services for adult learners. *Journal of Counseling and Development, 72,* 268–75.

Mallinckrodt, B., & Fretz, B. R. (1988). Social support and the impact of job loss on older professionals. *Journal of Counseling Psychology, 35,* 281–86.

Maremont, M., & Sassen, J. A. (1996, May 13). Abuse of power: The astonishing tale of sexual harassment at Astra U.S.A. *Business Week,* 86ff.

McDaniels, C. (1996). Career + Work + Leisure (C = W + L): A developmental/trait factor approach to career development. In R. Feller & G. Walz (Eds.) *Career Transitions in Turbulent Times* (pp. 45–55). Greensboro, NC: ERIC/CASS.

McKenna, E. P. (1997). *When work doesn't work anymore: Women, work, and identity.* New York: Delacorte Press.

McKeon, M. C. (2002). *Career Targeting and Transition.* Media, PA: Delaware County Community College. Available at http://www.boomercareer.com.

Meinz, R. I. (2001). *Employment counseling with personality disorders: An accommodation model.* Edmonds, Washington: Rodger I. Meinz.

Mikulas, W. L. (2002). *The integrative helper: Convergence of Eastern and Western traditions.* Pacific Grove, CA: Brooks/Cole.

Miller, J.V. (2002). Career counseling for mature workers. In Niles, S. G. (Ed.), *Adult Career Development: Concepts, Issues, and Practices* (3rd ed.) (pp. 267–283). Tulsa, OK: National Career Development Association.

Morrison, A. M., White, R. P., & Van Velsor, E. (1987). *Breaking the glass ceiling.* Reading, MA: Addison-Wesley.

Morrow, P. (2002). Managing the generations. Retrieved January 5, 2004 from http://www.frogpond.com/printversion.cfm?atricleid=pmorrow/08.

Murphy, S. E., & Ensher, E. A. (1997). The effects of culture on mentoring relationships. In C. S. Granrose & S. Oskamp (Eds.), *Cross-cultural work groups* (pp. 212–33). Thousand Oaks, CA: Sage.

Murray, P. (1993). Outplacement and careers: Giving your client a feel for work. *Employee Counseling Today, 5* (2), 14–17.

Nichols, N. A. (Ed.). (1994). *Reach for the top.* Cambridge, MA: Harvard Business Review.

Norman, J. (2003, February 9). Job satisfaction: Boomer builds his third and most rewarding career. *San Antonio Express News,* p. 2G.

Novelli, W. (2002). How aging boomer will impact American business. http://www.aarp.org/leadership-ceo/Articles/a2003-01-03-agingboomer.html

The Older Worker. Myths and Realities, No. 18. Ohio State University Center on Education and Training for Employment. Available at http://ericacve.org/fulltext.asp; http://www.fiveoclockclub.com/about_frame.html; http://www.2young2retire.com/default.html.

"Our Turn; Reforms at academy rank a high priority; a new survey of Air Force Academy women shows the extent to which they have not been protected." (2003, September 8). *San Antonio Express-News,* p. 6B. Retrieved September 19, 2003, from http://proxy.lib.iastate.edu:2053/universe/printdoc.

Parker, D. (2003). *The Aging Work-Force,* Parts 1–3. UI News Wisconsin: Heartland Cobalt Corporation. Available at http://www.heartland.cobaltcorporation.com/pdf/2001-4%20.pdf; http://www.heartland.cobaltcorporation.com/pdf/2002-1.pdf; http://www.heartland.cobaltcorporation.com/pdf/2002-q2.pdf.

Patton, W. (2002). Career guidance and counselling in changing economic times: Working with people who are unemployed. Retrieved from http://www.careers-journal.com/old/079905s.htm

Pavot, W., Diener, E., Colvin, C., & Sandvik, E. (1991). Further validation of the Satisfaction with Life Scale: Evidence for the cross-method convergence of well-being measures. *Journal of Personality Assessment, 57,* 149–61.

Pedersen, P., Goldberg, A., & Papalia, T. (1991). A model for planning career continuation and change through increased awareness, knowledge and skill. *Journal of Employment Counseling, 28,* 74–79.

Pedrotti. A. (1990, August 24). Change is part of today's job market. *Today's Catholic,* 19.

Peregoy, J. J., & Schliebner, C. T. (1990). Long term unemployment: Effects and counseling interventions. *International Journal for the Advancement of Counselling, 13,* 193–204.

Peterson, N., & González, R. C. (Eds.). (2000). *Career counseling models for diverse populations: Hands-on applications for practitioners.* Belmont: CA: Wadsworth/Brooks/Cole.

Pines, A., & Aronson, E. (1988). *Career burnout: Causes and cures.* New York: Free Press.

Pisano, M. (2003). Job status linked to femicide. (2003, July 13). *San Antonio Express News,* p. K1.

Pollack, W. (1998). *Real boys: Rescuing our sons from the myths of boyhood.* New York: Henry Holt.

Polonsky, W. (1997, October 6). *Personality, motivation, and health: A seminar for health professionals.* Workshop presented by Mind Matters Seminars, El Paso, TX.

Pouncey, M (2003a). *Age Discrimination is Killing High Tech. Seniors Aging Well, Wisely and Successful.* Available at: http://www.go60.com/age-discrimination-high-tech.html.

Pouncey, M. (2003b). The best companies for older workers. *AARP The Magazine Online.* Retrieved July 6, 2003 from http://www.aarpmagazine.org/tools/Articles/a2003-01-23-bc .

Ratcliffe, K. (1996, July). Five girls fight back. *Seventeen,* 110ff.

Rife, J., & Belcher, J. (1993). Social support and job search intensity among older unemployed workers: Implications for employment counselors. *Journal of Employment Counseling, 30,* 98–107.

Rix, S. E. (2001). The role of older workers in caring for older people in the future. *Generations, 25,* 29–35. Retrieved May 3, 2003, from http://elibrary.bigchalk.com

Schatz, R. D. (1997). The aging of the workforce. *Working Woman, 22* (5), 64–66.

Schieszer, J. (1996, January 16). Shifts that'll make your stomach turn. *El Paso Herald-Post,* pp. B3, B4.

Schlossberg, N. K. (1996). A model of worklife transitions. In R. Feller and G. Walz (Ed.), *Career transitions in turbulent times* (pp. 93–104). Greensboro, NC: ERIC/CASS.

Schlossberg, N. K. (2004). *Retire smart, retire happy: Finding your true path in life.* Washington, DC: American Psychological Association.

Secretary's Commission on Achieving New Skills (SCANS). (1992). *Learning a living.* Washington, DC: U.S. Department of Labor.

Seybold, K. C., & Salomone, P. R. (1994). Understanding workaholism: A review of causes and counseling approaches. *Journal of Counseling and Career Development, 73,* 4–9.

Sharp, D. (1996, March 15–17). So many lists, so little time. *USA Weekend,* 1, 4–6.

Shore, L. (1992). Stress. In L. Jones, (Ed.), *The encyclopedia of career change and work issues* (pp.138–51). Phoenix, AZ: Onyx Press.

Sicker, M. (1997, March). Age discrimination in employment [8 paragraphs]. *Modern Maturity, 40* (2), 77, 79 [On-line serial]. Hostname: http://db.texshare.edu/utexas.

Silver, A. D. (1994). *Enterprising women: Lessons from 100 of the greatest entrepreneurs of our day.* New York: American Management Association.

Simon, J., & Osipow, S. H. (1996). Continuity of career: The vocational script in counseling older workers. *Career Development Quarterly, 45,* 154–62.

Smith, T. (1992). Hostility and health: Current status of a psychosomatic hypothesis. *Health Psychology, 11,* 139–50.

Solomon, C. (1991, August). 24-hour Employees. *Personnel Journal,* 56–63.

Solomon, J. (1998, March 16). An insurance policy with sex appeal. *Newsweek,* 44.

Stein, D., & Rocco, T. S. (2001). The older worker. *Myths and Realities, No. 18* Ohio State University: Center on Education and Training for Employment. Retrieved from http://ericacve.org/fulltext.asp.

Stein, D. & Rocco, T. S. (2003). The best companies for older workers. *AARP The magazine Online.* Available: http://aarpmagazine.org.

Stidham, H. H., & Remley, T. P., Jr. (1992). Job club methodology applied to a workfare setting. *Journal of Employment Counseling, 29,* 69–76.

Super, D. (1990). A life-span, life-space approach to career development. In D. Brown, L. Brooks, & Associates (Ed.), *Career choice and development* (2nd ed.) (pp. 197–261). San Francisco: Jossey-Bass.

Tan, C., & Salomone, P. (1994). Understanding career plateauing: Implications for counseling. *Career Development Quarterly, 42,* 291–301.

Tannen, D. (1990). *You just don't understand.* New York: Ballantine.

Tannen, D. (1994). *Talking from 9 to 5.* New York: William Morrow.

Tichy, N. M., & Sherman, S. (1993, June). Walking the talk at GE. *Training and Development.* 27–35.

Uchitelle, L., and Kleinfield, N. R. (1996, March 3). On the battlefield of business, millions of casualties. *New York Times,* Section 1, pp.1ff.

U.S.A.F.A., Center for Character Development. *Air Force Academy Honor Code.* Retrieved September

20, 2003, from http://www.usafa.af.mil/34cwc/cwch/cwchmb.htm.

U.S.A.F.A., Policy Directives and Initiatives. (March 26, 2003). *Agenda for Change.* Retrieved September 20, 2003 from http://www.usafa.afa.mil/agenda.cfm.

Violante, J. M., & Aron, F. (1993). Sources of police stressors, job attitudes, and psychological distress. *Psychological Reports, 72,* 899–904.

Violante, J., M., & Aron, F. (1994). Ranking police stressors. *Psychological Reports, 75,* 824–26.

Violante, J. M., Marshall, J. R., & Howe, B. (1985). Stress, coping, and alcohol use: The police connection. *Journal of Police Science & Administration, 13,* 106–10.

Vistica, G. L. (1995). *Fall from glory: The men who sank the U.S. Navy.* New York: Simon & Schuster.

Wagner, C. (2003). Keeping older workers on the job. *The Futurist, 37*(4). Retrieved from http://www.wfs.org.

Walsh, W. B., & Osipow, S. H. (Eds.). (1994). *Career counseling for women.* Hillsdale, NJ: Erlbaum.

Wanberg, C. R. (1995). A longitudinal study of the effects of unemployment and quality of reemployment. *Journal of Vocational Behavior, 46,* 40–54.

Wanberg, C. R, Watt, J. D., & Rumsey, D. J. (1996). Individuals without jobs: An empirical study of job-seeking behavior and reemployment. *Journal of Applied Psychology, 81,* No. 1, 76–87.

Washington, T. (1993, Winter). Career counseling the experienced client. *Journal of Career Planning and Employment, 53,* 37ff.

Waterman, R. H., Jr., Waterman, J. A., & Collard, B. A. (1994, July–August). Toward a career resilient workforce. *Harvard Business Review,* 87–95.

Watts, A. G. (1997). Socio-political ideologies and career guidance. *Educational and vocational guidance in the European community.* Luxembourg: Office for Official Publications of the European Communities.

Webb, S. L. (1991). *Step forward: Sexual harassment in the workplace.* New York: Master Media.

Weller, R (2003, September 15). Air Force Academy cadets who reported sex assaults skeptical about reforms. *The Associated Press* [no page number provided]. Retrieved September 20, 2003, from http://proxy.lib.iastate.edu:2053/universe/printdoc.

Wilde, A. D. (1996, January 14). Earning it; Who's really essential? In a blizzard, it's a blur. *The New York Times,* Section 3, p. 10.

Yang, C. (1996, May 13). Getting justice is no easy task. *Business Week,* 98.

Zacarro, S., & Riley, A. (1987). Stress, coping and organization effectiveness. In A. Riley & S. Zacarro (Eds.), *Occupational stress and organizational effectiveness* (pp. 3–47). New York: Praeger.

Zemke, R., Raines, C., & Filipczak, B. (2001). Generations at work: Managing the clash of veterans, boomers, xers, and nexters in your workplace. AMACOM.

Zimpfer, D., & Carr, J. (1989). Groups for midlife career change: A review. *Journal for Specialists in Group Work, 14,* 243–50.

Zunker, V. (1995) *Career counseling: Applied concepts of life planning* (4th ed.). Pacific Grove, CA: Brooks/Cole.

Epilogue

Abzug. (1996). p. 8A.

Anderson, H., & Goolishian, H. A. (1988). Human systems as linguistic systems: Preliminary and evolving ideas about the implications for clinical theory. *Family Process, 27,* 371–93.

Betz, N. E. (2001). Perspectives on future directions in vocational psychology. *Journal of Vocational Psychology, 59,* 275–283.

Blustein, D. L. (2001). Extending the reach of vocational psychology: Toward an inclusive and integrative psychology of working. *Journal of Vocational Behavior, 59,* 171–182.

Bolles, R. (1981). *Three boxes of life.* Berkeley, CA: Ten Speed Press.

Bureau of Labor Statistics. (2001, May 2). *More temporary workers expected in certain blue-collar operations.* Retrieved May 19, 2003 from http://www.bls.gov/opub/ted/2001/ apr/wk5/art03.htm.

Bureau of Labor Statistics (2004). *Table 2. Employment by major occupational group, 2002 and projected 2012.* Retrieved 04/17/2004 from http://www.bls.gov/news.release/ecopro.t.02.htm

Burr, V. (1995). *An introduction to social constructionism.* London: Routledge.

Canton, J. (1999). *Technofuture: How leading edge technology will transform business in the 21st century.* Carlsbad, CA: Hays House.

Chung, Y. B. (1995). Career decision making of lesbian, gay, and bisexual individuals. *Career Development Quarterly, 44,* 178–190.

Cockburn, A. (2003, September). 21st century slaves. *National Geographic, 204* (3), 2–25.

Efran, J. S., & Clarfield, L. E. (1992). Constructionist therapy: Sense and nonsense. In S. McNamee & K. J. Gergen (Eds.), *Therapy as social construction* (pp. 200–217). London: Sage.

Efran, J. S., & Fauber, R. L. (1995). Radical constructivism: Questions and answers. In R. A. Neimeyer & M. J. Mahoney (Eds.), *Constructivism in psycho-*

therapy (pp. 275–304). Washington, DC: American Psychological Association.

Efran, J. S., Lukens, R. J., & Lukens, M. D. (1988). Constructivism: What's in it for you? *Family Therapy Networker, 12* (5), 27–35.

Fassinger, R. E. (1995). From invisibility to integration: Lesbian identity in the workplace. *Career Development Quarterly, 44,* 148–167.

Feller, R. (1991). Employment and career development in a world of change: What is ahead for the next twenty-five years? *Journal of Employment Counseling, 28,* 13–20.

Friedman, D. (1996). Are you ready for a networked economy? *Inc., 18,* 62–65.

Futurework: Trends and challenges for work in the 21st century. (2000, Summer). *Occupational Outlook Quarterly,* 31–36.

Gelberg, S., & Chojnacki, J. T. (1996). *Career and life planning with gay, lesbian, and bisexual persons.* Alexandria, VA: American Counseling Association.

Gergen, K. J. (1991). *The saturated self: Dilemmas of identity in contemporary life.* New York: Basic Books.

Gibson, E., & Billings, A. (2003). *Big change at Best Buy: Working through hypergrowth to sustain excellence.* Palo Alto, CA: Davies-Black.

Gigloff, D. (2003, August). Gays force the issue. *U.S. News and World Report.* Retrieved from http://www.usnews.com/usnews/issue/030818/usnews/18gays.htm.

González, R. C. (1994, August). Multiculturalism and social constructionism: An overview. In J. M. Georgoulakis (Chair), *Multiculturalism in therapy: Social constructionist applications.* Symposium presented at the American Psychological Association Annual Convention, Los Angeles, CA.

González, R. C. (1997). Postmodern supervision: A multicultural perspective. In D. B. Pope- Davis & H. L. K. Coleman (Eds.), *Multicultural counseling competencies: Assessment, education and training, and supervision* (pp. 350–386). Thousand Oaks, CA: Sage.

González, R. C. (1998). A technically eclectic blend of paradigms and epistemologies for multicultural clinical relevance. In C. Franklin & P. S. Nurius (Eds.), *Constructivism in practice: Methods and challenges* (pp. 349–735). Milwaukee, WI: Families International.

Greenberg, M. (1997, November 2). Mamas, don't let your babies become CPAs. *San Antonio Express News.* p. OH.

Greenfield, M. (1998, April 20). "Paperizing" policy. *Newsweek,* p. 74.

Gutek, G. L. (1993). *American education in a global society.* New York: Longman.

Handy, C. (1996). *Beyond certainty: The changing world of organizations.* Boston: Harvard Business School Press.

Hansen, L. S. (1993). Career development trends and issues in the United States. *Journal of Career Development, 20,* 7–24.

Herman, R., Olivo, T., & Gioia, J. (2003). *Impending crisis: Too many jobs, too many people.* Winchester, VA: Oakhill Press.

Information Technology Association of America (ITAA). (2003). *2003 Workforce Survey.* Retrieved from http://www.itaa.org.workforce/studies/03execsumm.pdf.

Jennings, Earl. (1995, February 28). *Personal communication.*

Koegel, H. M., Donin, I., Ponterotto, J. G., & Spitz, S. (1995). Multicultural career development: A methodological critique of 8 years of research in three leading career journals. *Journal of Employment Counseling, 32,* 50–63.

Krumboltz, J. D. (1998). Serendipity is not serendipitous. *Journal of Counseling Psychology, 45,* 390–92.

Leong, F. T. L. (Ed.). (1995). *Career development and vocational behavior of racial and ethnic minorities.* Mahwah, NJ: Erlbaum.

Light, R. J., & Pillemer, D. B. (1982). Numbers and narrative: Combining their strengths in research reviews. *Harvard Educational Review, 52,* 1–26.

Mabry, L., & Stake, R. E. (Eds.). (1997). *Evaluation in the post-modern dilemma.* Greenwich, CT: Jai Press.

Mays, V. M., Rubin, J., Sabourin, M., & Walker, L. (1996). Moving toward a global psychology: Changing theories and practice to meet the needs of a changing world. *American Psychologist, 51,* 485–87.

Mikulas, W. L. (2002). *The integrative helper: Convergence of Eastern and Western traditions.* Pacific Grove, CA: Brooks/Cole.

Miller-Tiedeman, A. (1999). *Learning, practicing, and living the New Careering.* Philadelphia: Accelerated Development.

Minuchin, S. (1991). The seductions of constructivism. *Family Therapy Networker, 15* (5), 47– 50.

Myss, C. (1996). *Anatomy of the spirit: The seven stages of power and healing.* New York: Three Rivers Press.

Neimeyer, R. A. (1995). Constructivist psychotherapies: Features, foundations, and future directions. In R. A. Neimeyer & M. J. Mahoney (Eds.), *Constructivism in psychotherapy* (pp. 1–38). Washington, DC: American Psychological Association.

New York Times News Service. (1996, August 9). Grim look offered at world of child porn. *San Antonio Express-News,* p. 12A.

Newsweek Online Forum (2003, April 28). No job is safe. Never will be. Retrieved 06/23/2003 from http://www.msnbc.com/news/902506.asp?0cb=-71c151428.

No job is safe. Never will be. (2003, April28). Newsweek Online Forum. http://www.msnbc.com/news/902506.asp?0cb-71c151428.

Ogbu, J. U. (1992). Understanding cultural diversity and learning. *Educational Researcher, 21*, 5–14.

Osborne, W. L., & Usher, C. H. (1994). A Super approach: Training career educators, career counselors and researchers. *Journal of Career Development, 20*, pp. 219–225.

Pantazis, C. (2002, Spring). Maximizing e-learning to train the 21st century workforce. *Public Personnel Management, 31* (1), 21–26.

Parfit, M. (1996, August). Mexico City: Pushing the limits. *National Geographic, 190* (2), 24–43.

Polkinghorne, D. E. (1984). Further extensions of methodological diversity for counseling psychology. *Journal of Counseling Psychology, 31*, 416–29.

Polkinghorne, D. E. (1991). Two conflicting calls for methodological reform. *The Counseling Psychologist, 19*, 103–14.

Pope, M. (1995). Career interventions for gay and lesbian clients: A synopsis of practice knowledge and research needs. *Career Development Quarterly, 44*, 191–203.

Prince, J. P. (1995). Influences on the career development of gay men. *Career Development Quarterly, 44*, 168–77.

Reichardt, C. S., & Cook, T. D. (1979). Beyond quantitative versus qualitative methods. In T. D. Cook & C. S. Reichardt (Eds.), *Qualitative and quantitative methods in evaluation research* (pp. 7–32). Beverly Hills, CA: Sage.

Reid, P. T. (1993). Poor women in psychological research. *Psychology of Women Quarterly, 17*, 133–50.

Richardson, M. S. (1993). Work in people's lives: A location for counseling psychologists. *Journal of Counseling Psychology, 40*, 425–33.

Rosenau, P. M. (1992). *Post-modernism and the social sciences: Insights, inroads, and Intrusions.* Princeton, NJ: McGraw-Hill.

Savickas, M. L. (1993). Career counseling in the postmodern era. *Journal of Cognitive Psychology: An International Quarterly, 7* (3), 205–215.

Schaffer, W. A. (1999). *High-tech careers for low-tech people.* (2nd ed.) Berkeley, CA: Ten Speed Press.

Schwarzbaum, L. (1997, December 26/1998, January 2). Ellen DeGeneres: Entertainer of the year. *Entertainment Weekly, 411/412*, 16–18.

Stodden, R. A. (1998). School-to-work transition: Overview of disability legislation. In F. R. Rusch & J. G. Chadsey (Eds.), *Beyond high school: Transition from school to work.* Belmont, CA: Wadsworth.

Stone, B. (2003, August 11). Men at overwork. *Newsweek.* Retrieved August 20, 2003 from http://www.msnbc.com/news/946725.asp

Tahmincioglu, E. (2003, July 20). By telecommuting the disabled get a key to the office and a job. *New York Times*, H20.

Thomas, R. R., Jr. (1990, March–April). From affirmative action to affirming diversity. *Harvard Business Review*, 107–17.

Watts, A. G. (1996). The changing concept of career: Implications for career counseling. In R. Feller & G. Walz (Eds.), *Career transitions in turbulent times: Exploring work, learning, and careers* (pp. 229–35). Greensboro, N.C.: ERIC Counseling and Student Services Clearinghouse.

Wilson, W. J. (1996). *When work disappears: The world of the new urban poor.* New York: Alfred A. Knopf.

Wolinsky, S. (1993). *Quantum consciousness: The guide to experiencing quantum psychology.* Las Vegas, NM: Bramble Books.

Wolinsky, S. (1994). *The Tao of chaos: Essence and the Enneagram.* Las Vegas, NM: Bramble Books.

Index

Abilities, 154
Ability tests, 99
Absenteeism, child care and, 459
Academic development, national
   standards for, 335
Academic performance, gender differ-
   ences and, 364
Academic skills, 26
Acculturation, 11–12
   Asian Americans and, 328–329
   assessment procedure and, 105
   Hispanics and, 323
   practical applications, 12
Achievement tests, 99, 111
Achieving Success Identity Pathways
   (ASIP), 372
ACT, Inc., 368
Active agents, 402
Adaptive skills, 26
Adelphia scandal, 35
Adjective Checklist (ACL), 167, 410
Adjective Self-Description (ASD), 167,
   410
Adlerian vocational counseling, 236–
   239
   assessment steps for, 238–239
   multicultural applications of, 237–
   238
   Savickas's adaptation of, 238
Adolescents
   counseling, 348
   female
      math and science ability and, 364
      multicultural, 380
   Myers Briggs Type Inventory for,
      357
   transformation of family system and,
      297
Adult Basic Learning Examination
   (ABLE), 454
Adult Career Concerns (ACC), 454
Adult Career Concerns Inventory
   (ACCI), 183, 184, 445
Adult Measure of Essential Skills
   (AMES), 454
Adult mentors, 453
Adult Personality Inventory, 114–115
Adults
   with ADD, 205
   career counseling for, 426–502
   National Career Development
      Competencies for, 389
   occupational guidance services for,
      500–501
   personal skills that empower, 451
Adults in transition
   career development in organizations
      and, 447–449
   career plateau and, 449
   career renewal and, 449
   career resiliency and, 449
   job change and, 441–442
   mentor relationships, 452

occupational guidance services for,
   501
outplacement, 450–452
personality disorders and, 454
quitting jobs, 442
unemployment/underemployment,
   443–447
Affirmative action, 15–19, 285, 487
African American males
   hoop dreams of young, 50
   power of, 322
African Americans
   acculturation and, 12
   affirmative action and, 18
   career assessment and, 105–107
   decline in earnings of, 38
   definition in Census 2000 of, 24
   downsizing and, 37
   gifted education and, 409
   Holland's typology and, 144
   learning styles of, 49
   legacy of slavery, 64
   percentage of U.S. population, 23
   Protestant work ethic and, 60
   racism and, 322
   reported median income of, 29
   science/technology explosion and,
      29
   self-efficacy theory and, 215
   single-parent families and, 320–322
   social learning theory and, 223
   Super's theory and, 185
   trait-factor theory and, 131
African American students
   academic performance and, 364
   high school guidance counselors
      and, 379
African American women
   expectation to work, 322
   Holland codes for, 404
   racism, sexism and, 5
Afrocentrism, 49–50
Age
   meaning in work and leisure and,
      78
   values and, 480
Age Discrimination in Employment
   Act (ADEA), 437
Ageism
   subtle, 438
   workplace environment and, 437
Agentic behavior, 69
Aid to Families with Dependent
   Children (AFDC), 395
Alaska Native, definition in Census
   2000, 24
Alienation, feeling of, gifted students
   and, 360
Allocation, 381–382
Ally, 157
American Association of Community
   Colleges (AACC), 392
American Association for Counseling
   and Development, 503

American Association of Retired
   People (AARP), 438, 470, 475
American Association of University
   Women, 364
American College Testing (ACT), 129
American Education Research Asso-
   ciation, 101, 503
American Indian
   definition in Census 2000 of, 24
   See also Native American
American Management Association
   (AMA), 27, 63
American Psychological Association
   (APA), 6, 98, 101, 503
American School Counselor Associa-
   tion (ASCA), 85, 343, 345
   national standards, 335
   portfolio system, 96
American Speech-Language-Hearing
   Association, 503
American workers, increase in work
   time for, 48, 71
Americanization, 14
Americans with Disabilities Act
   (ADA), 199–200
Androcentrism, 116
Anglo, use of term, 65
Anti-Semitism, 60
Apprenticeship programs, 373
APTICOM, 129
Aptitude tests, 99, 111, 129
Archway Model, 176–177, 185, 187
Armed Services Vocational Aptitude
   Battery (ASVAB), 129, 184
Art media, 271
Artistic type, 133, 135, 137–138
Asian, definition in Census 2000, 24
Asian Americans, 185–186
   acculturation and, 328–329
   career assessment and, 107–108
   collective self-efficacy and, 216
   Confucian work ethic, 60–61
   families, 326–329
   Holland's typology and, 144–145
   racism and, 5
   social learning theory and, 223
   trait-factor theory, 131
Asian Americans/Pacific Islanders,
   acculturation and, 12
Assembly line, 67
Assessment, 97–117
   Adlerian vocational counseling and,
      238–239
   adults, 454
   cognitive information processing
      and, 243–244
   defined, 97
   elementary school students, 346
   gifted students, 362–363, 365
   high school students, 375–376
   middle school students, 357
   multicultural and diverse popula-
      tions, 102–113
   personal construct psychology, 258